BRIGHT
DARK SH

THE REAL STORY OF ABBA

BRIGHT LIGHTS DARK SHADOWS

THE REAL STORY OF ABBA

CARL MAGNUS PALM

OMNIBUS PRESS

London/New York/Sydney/Paris/Copenhagen/Madrid/Tokyo

Cover designed by Chloë Alexander
Picture research by Carl Magnus Palm & Nikki Lloyd

ISBN: 0.7119.9194.4
Order No: OP48796

Exclusive Distributors:
Music Sales Limited,
8/9 Frith Street,
London W1D 3JB, UK.

Music Sales Corporation,
257 Park Avenue South,
New York, NY 10010, USA.

Macmillan Distribution Services,
53 Park West Drive,
Derrimut,
Victoria 3030, Australia.

To the Music Trade only:
Music Sales Limited,
8/9 Frith Street,
London W1D 3JB, UK.

Printed in Great Britain by Cox & Wyman Ltd, Reading, Berkshire.
Typeset by Galleon Typesetting, Ipswich.

A catalogue record for this book is available from the British Library.

www.omnibuspress.com

Contents

Introduction

The story of Abba is the story of how four musicians from a remote country in northern Europe and their industrious, headstrong manager took on the world and won. It is a personal story and a public story, with all the sweeping torrents of a great Nordic saga, encompassing triumph and tragedy, poverty and wealth, and romance and heartbreak, all accompanied by a soundtrack of brilliant pop music that is loved across the globe.

Of the two instrumentalists in Abba, one was a self-taught musician with a streak of determination that carried him and the group all the way, the other a gifted songwriter whose talent was inherited from his grandfather. Of the two singers, one was a reluctant sex-symbol for whom fame became a poisoned chalice, the other an orphan who carried on reinventing herself until she became, quite literally, a princess. His diligence in making them what they were, equally literally, had fatal consequences for their manager.

At the very highest levels of pop The Beatles are generally credited with having sold most records worldwide, with Elvis Presley at number two. Thanks to an ongoing revival that shows no signs of diminishing, Abba remain as one of the few contenders to third place. Two decades after they last performed together, they have one of the strongest back catalogues in the history of popular music. As a group, they were active between 1972 and 1982 and broke sales records during that period. The compilation CD *ABBA Gold*, released in 1992, has become their biggest selling album ever with worldwide sales of over 20 million. In 1999 alone, 6.5 million Abba albums were sold worldwide. Their total sales are now said to exceed 300 million.

Abba remain huge in virtually every corner of the world, not least in countries where most other western rock and pop music has failed to penetrate. In the United States, which was considered Abba's weakest territory during their active days, they are today more popular than ever before, with the *ABBA Gold* album having now sold far more than any of their previous albums. In Australia their popularity matches even that of The Beatles. In the UK, and elsewhere, the current Abba musical *Mamma Mia!* is sold out months in advance.

Time has proven that Abba's popularity is not dependent on fluke "revivals", but is constant at any given time. They are a consistently strong presence in the world's gay communities. In the ongoing and almost certainly permanent absence of the real thing, Abba "tribute" bands are multiplying across the globe. New generations are constantly discovering Abba's music, and almost all of today's European hit factories cite Abba as their main inspiration.

In today's parlance, Abba are, indeed, mega.

Surprising as it may seem in light of this phenomenal global popularity, this book is the first major biography about Abba. There have been chronological, diary-format accounts of their career, photo-based narratives, and one or two trashy, hastily compiled and often inaccurate books that are dependent purely on hearsay and press cuttings. But for some reason, up until now, no one has attempted an objective, in-depth account of their story.

In Abba's native Sweden there's no tradition of rock book writing, and established music journalists – as in Great Britain and America – are generally more interested in the lives and work of Anglo/Saxon and African-American artists. Abba, with their middle-class suburban image and perceived cabaret cheesiness, just aren't your average rock writer's first choice of subject material.

However, Abba's story is as fascinating as any, a story begging to be told which is long overdue. It offers several captivating plot elements: a fight to overcome abject poverty in rural, depression-era Sweden, a child born out of wedlock in the shadow of the Second World War, fatal illness, suicide, teenage parenthood, record-breaking record sales, fan hysteria, disastrous business deals – and all this before Abba even existed. When the world at large became aware of the group after they won the Eurovision Song Contest with 'Waterloo' in 1974, all four members had been recording artists for the best part of ten years; some reaching extraordinary domestic fame, others with almost no commercial success at all.

There's also the crucially important historical and cultural context from which they sprang and within which they worked. If Abba were a product of the optimism and progress that swept across the Western World in the decades following the Second World War, their saga was also a particularly Swedish version of this development, running parallel with the nation's rise from poverty and economic stagnation into a highly developed post-industrial society.

Then there's the geography. Sweden is cold and dark for the better part of the year, so it's not surprising that an air of bleakness characterises its people. They're hard-working and pragmatic, a bit reserved and introspective, often keen not to be seen to rise above their station. It is all the more unusual, then, that this nation has given the world some of its best-loved pop music.

But although Abba's songs were often delivered with beaming smiles and a glossy sheen of euphoria, there was always a contrast between the affirmative delivery and the tone of sadness and regret that coloured even the jolliest of tunes. That strand of melancholy is also a prominent trait of Sweden's national character, which in itself springs from the country's geographical circumstances.

Located on the Scandinavian Peninsula in northern Europe, the chilly climate and limited daylight hours in the autumn and winter have given birth to a Nordic version of the blues. The wistful whisper through the fir trees in the wide open forests can be felt in most of Sweden's folk music, extending its legacy to all forms of musical expression in the nation, not least the pop music that has managed to reach an international audience.

The spiritual roots of the Abba story are deeply imbedded in Sweden's geographic and historical heritage. It is a country that has been at peace for the best part of two centuries: the doctrine of "nonalignment in peace aiming at neutrality in war" is a prominent feature in the nation's foreign policy. Sweden's role in the international political landscape has been to provide a fulcrum among the world's conflicting ideological and political systems. This seems entirely logical for a nation whose social structure is to a large extent based on the concept of homogeneity and mutual agreement.

The framework that gave rise to Abba contained crucial elements that aligned themselves with that philosophy: it was a democratic, practical organisation where each vote counted – "the Swedish way", as Björn Ulvaeus once so aptly put it. Abba's story is certainly not that of an overnight sensation: a violent explosion on the world's pop music scene. They may have sung about meeting their Waterloo as they achieved their international breakthrough, but it was hardly an intense, bloody battle that brought them to that point.

Abba managed to realise their potential by embracing the beneficial aspects of Swedish culture and ignoring the restrictive tendencies that could have taken the wind out of their spirit. An unwavering commitment to reaching outside the nation's borders with their music was probably the most crucial factor in achieving worldwide fame.

According to Swedish lore, the nation's famed work ethic and pragmatism are especially prominent features in the southern province of Småland. It makes sense that one half of Abba – Björn Ulvaeus and Agnetha Fältskog – hail from Småland. Even more relevant, perhaps, is the fact that the group's manager, Stig Anderson, was born and raised in the neighbouring county of Västergötland, where much of this same spirit prevails.

One could be forgiven for thinking that it was a conscious decision on the part of the Abba members to spend ten years practising at being stars in Sweden before stepping out on the international market, just to be on the safe side. When they finally developed into a group, they stumbled upon that magic constellation where each member brings something vital to the equation – the prerequisite for all musical entities that aspire to an impact at the highest level.

Björn Ulvaeus became the backbone of the group, its unofficial leader, evaluator, public face and, eventually, its astute lyricist. Benny Andersson was its musical motor, an intuitive tunesmith, the easygoing bloke in the midst of an eternal flow of melodies. Anni-Frid "Frida" Lyngstad was the dark beauty with the wondrous voice, a mixture of fortitude and vulnerability born of a rags-to-riches life that defies belief. Agnetha Fältskog was the blonde, homely girl who became a reluctant superstar, the purveyor of heartbreak, the group's sex symbol.

In Abba's endeavours to reach the world with their music, manager Stig Anderson's role was almost as a fifth member of the group. Stig was a volatile mix of determination, a desperate need to prove himself and a genuine love of show business. Because of the structure of the group and the way it developed, his persistence and belief in their work made his position more crucial than that of most other managers in the history of pop music.

Most great pop bands pay their dues by playing the club circuit before being discovered by an impresario, who then struggles to land them a record contract. Abba were different, evolving from within Stig Anderson's music company. It was almost an accident, certainly an experiment, that his Polar Music record label began releasing records by them. In the early days he was even a co-writer of their material, and a few years into Abba's career they had all become intrinsically linked to each other through a complex structure of interrelated business interests. That it all fell apart in acrimony after the group's demise, with vast fortunes slipping through their fingers, carries an eerie echo of the same fate that befell so many of Abba's peers elsewhere in the world.

Beyond the marriages, divorces, and incredible record sales that have hitherto made up the essence of Abba's predominant public image, lie other truths. Their professional showbiz façade has been unusually successful in serving to hide the true nature of the people that made this phenomenon happen, and the reality of the lives they have lead. In many cases, it's not even Abba themselves who have kept up the front: curiously, the international media have seemed quite eager to do that for them, often ignoring the members' occasional attempts to offer a glimpse into their real, untold story.

Perhaps that story was waiting for another pragmatic Swede, just like Abba themselves, to come along and present it in all its multi-faceted, unshapely glory. At least, that's what I have attempted to do. I hope that I have succeeded.

Carl Magnus Palm
Stockholm, May 2001

PART I

The Days Before

Chapter 1

The town of Västervik lies in the southern Swedish province of Småland, its population numbering around 20,000 with not much more than twice that figure in the surrounding area. Nevertheless, this small town by the Baltic sea has produced more than its share of world-famous citizens. Jazz and *schlager* singer Alice Babs enjoyed a fruitful collaboration with Duke Ellington in the Sixties and Seventies. Stefan Edberg became the world's number one tennis player for two years in the early Nineties. But there is another whose fame outshines even that of Babs and Edberg who spent his formative years in Västervik.

The son of Gunnar and Aina Ulvaeus, Björn Kristian Ulvaeus was born on April 25, 1945 on the island of Hisingen. The island is situated outside Gothenburg on Sweden's west coast, the country's second largest city. Famous as the home of the world-renowned Volvo car, for its shipyard industry and its position as the leading port in Scandinavia, this is where Björn took his first breath in the last trembling days of the Second World War.

Gunnar Ulvaeus and his two brothers Esbjörn and Lennart had been born with the unusually widespread Swedish surname of Andersson. The three brothers had all decided that they would make their different mark in the world and chose new surnames when they became adults and left home: while Esbjörn went for Ulfsäter, Gunnar and Lennart chose Ulvaeus.

Gregarious, with a subtle sense of humour and a keen interest in literature, Gunnar was especially fond of classic Swedish poets and was rarely seen without a volume of poetry in his hand. He was also an avid fan of American western novels, which he liked to read in their original language, often devouring a complete novel in a single sitting.

During the war years, while he was a lieutenant in the infantry, Gunnar met the gentle and friendly Aina Bengtsson. At the time, Aina was working as a shop assistant in a store that sold chemicals. They were married the year before Björn was born and after the war ended, in 1946, the little family moved to Hunnebostrand, a small fishing village north of Gothenburg, where the enterprising Gunnar started a shipyard for small boats. With a small child to take care of, Aina quit her job and settled comfortably into the role of housewife. In March 1948 the family became four when their daughter Eva was born.

Björn suffered serious bouts of croup as a small child, but was otherwise a healthy, lively boy. He loved hanging around his father's shipyard, helping out whenever he could. Björn would join in painting the red lead on the boats, more often than not making a mess of himself, much to his mother's exasperation.

On one occasion, when his sister was still very small, Björn showed early signs of the head for business for which he was to become renowned as an adult. Becoming tired of Eva hanging around wherever he went, he managed to "sell" her to one of the men working at the shipyard. The sale was cancelled when Björn suddenly felt a pang of regret. It seems this was as bad a case of sibling rivalry as ever occurred between Björn and Eva.

When Björn was around the age of five, a brief recession hit Sweden and his father's shipyard took a downturn as demand declined. Gunnar struggled to save the business, but it eventually went bankrupt. He lost a good deal of money, and was obliged to take work in a shop for industry glass in Gothenburg to provide for his wife and children. It was a blow to his confidence and dreams, a humiliating setback that little Björn found difficult to comprehend.

Before long help arrived in the shape of Gunnar's brother Esbjörn. Four years Gunnar's senior, Esbjörn Ulfsäter had worked as a salesman for various companies before taking up employment at the paper mill in Västervik in the mid-Thirties. Over the years he'd worked his way up the company ladder until he was in a position to buy out the firm and become its sole owner. By the end of the Forties he was a very wealthy man. With his brother in financial straits, Esbjörn offered him a managerial job at the paper mill. Gunnar accepted gratefully and, in 1951, moved to Västervik with his wife and children. After a few years at different addresses in the town, the Ulvaeus family settled in an apartment on the centrally located street Norrtullsgatan, not far from the seafront.

They were not alone in moving to Västervik during these first post-war decades. Thanks to the flourishing industries in the area, the town was to almost double its population between 1940 and 1970. The picturesque location by the sea with its attendant boat-life was an added attraction. The preponderance of small-scale wooden houses, and a Town Hall dating from 1795, completed the impression of a picturesque idyll.

After their early, slightly turbulent years in the Gothenburg area, Björn and his sister were now able to enjoy a secure, middle-class upbringing that thrived amid the general boom in the nation. While the rest of the countries in Europe were recovering from the horrors of the Second World War and the damage inflicted on their economies, Sweden, which had remained neutral, prospered and was able to take advantage of the relative lack of export competition from other countries.

Considering how severely the nation had suffered during the years of the Great Depression, this was a remarkable development. The turning point came in the mid-Thirties, when the Social Democrats embarked on what turned out to be an unbroken 40-year rule over the nation. The decades that followed saw Sweden develop into a well-organised state, based on what became known internationally as "the Swedish model". The model referred primarily to the country's mixed economy system, and a labour market characterised by mutual agreements between employers and unions. Crowned by a well-developed welfare system, the spirit of the programme is best summed up by the Swedish term *folkhemmet* – society viewed as a "home" for the people, taking care of their needs in unemployment, sickness, and old age.

Future generations were expected to make full use of the opportunities bestowed on them, not least in the Ulvaeus household where the pressure was on young Björn to make good. The failure of Gunnar Ulvaeus' own business dream was an additional motivation. Esbjörn Ulfsäter was the owner of a paper mill, while Lennart Ulvaeus had become the head of a paper agency in Germany. Gunnar himself had to settle for a less prestigious life as an employee in Esbjörn's company.

"As I myself had lost a fortune in shipbuilding I had decided that my son should be a world-famous shipbuilder with the highest possible degrees," he later recalled. Aina Ulvaeus confirmed: "I remember when Björn got home with a paper and had got the second highest grade on it. His father said, 'Only the second highest when you could have had the highest?'"

The pre-teen Björn was a fairly average student. Like most of his school friends he was a happy-go-lucky kid, more interested in playing football and ice-hockey with the other boys than concentrating on boring school work. His favourite subjects were physics, Swedish and English, and as part of his interest in languages he began writing poetry at an early age. This was due mainly to his teacher at the time, an eccentric old lady who insisted that each Saturday the whole class should devote themselves to artistic endeavours. "The inspiration was flowing," recalled Björn. "All the while our teacher would be sitting at her desk, cleaning fish!"

Music played only a minor role in the life of the Ulvaeus household. Gunnar played the mandolin but, recalled Björn, "to be quite honest it didn't sound very good". The family didn't have a record player at home, so their main source of popular music came through the radio, which by today's standards broadcast a very limited output of what could be described as light entertainment.

Buried among the long-winded lectures on farming was the Sunday morning show *En glad ton på grammofon* (*A Cheerful Tune On The Gramophone*), a 30-minute programme on which hits of the day were played alongside popular folk music. The show commenced airing in the late Forties and became something of a soundtrack for the generation growing up in the Fifties, the only chance that kids like Björn had to hear what passed for "pop" music.

Popular music in Sweden at the time was synonymous with so-called *schlager* music, which featured prominently on *En glad ton*. The word *schlager*, which translates as "hit" or "pop song", is of German origin and came into use in Sweden in the Twenties. Bereft of any inflections whatsoever from American jazz or rhythm & blues, typical *schlager* music has its roots in genres as diverse as German military marches, Austrian operettas, Italian and Eastern European folk music, and the French *chanson*. For Swedes, the genre has also been coloured by their own traditional folk music.

Sweden in the early Fifties was still very much a rural society, at least in spirit, and a widespread longing for "simpler times" was reflected in its popular culture. This was the cultural climate that became the backdrop for the young Björn Ulvaeus' earliest musical memories. One especially strong emotional experience came from Thory Bernhards, a highly successful singer in those days. The sentimental waltz ballad 'Vildandens sång' ('The Song Of The Wild Duck') was a traditional song made popular by Bernhards in 1952. A harrowing tale of a pair of wild ducks in which the male half gets shot by a hunter, the song was delivered with maximum pathos, accompanied by accordion, tinkling piano and a single violin that underscored the melody.

"It was a hit one summer when I visited my cousins on the west coast," Björn recalled. "I heard it on the radio and I thought it was so unbearably sad. It was the first hit that really got to me." Björn also remembered being captivated by Alice Babs' Swedish versions of the equally sentimental 'Mockin' Bird Hill' (Les Paul & Mary Ford; Patti Page) and 'A Dear John Letter' (Jean Shepard), both of which were hits around the same time. The combination of gentle melodies and plaintive lyrics made an indelible impression on the young boy.

Less stimulating were the recorder classes Björn joined with some reluctance in the mid-Fifties. Recorder lessons, taken by Swedish children outside normal school hours since the Forties, are meant as a stepping-stone to studying a proper instrument, like the violin or the piano. Like many other children over the decades, Björn found it all dreadfully boring and started cutting classes, preferring instead to be outside playing with his friends. "It didn't amount to anything," he remembered.

Instead, Björn's path to the world of music came by way of the skiffle craze that started in Great Britain in the mid-Fifties and then spread to other European countries. "My cousin Joen was one year older than me and was very musical. He had started playing instruments like trumpet and piano long before that. He used to perform when the families got together and I was intrigued. He got into skiffle and bought a lot of records by some of the more obscure acts, like The Vipers, rather than those made by really popular artists such as Lonnie Donegan."

Skiffle made its first impact in Sweden in 1957. On Christmas Day of that year Björn had a touching experience, sitting with Joen at the grand piano in the Ulfsäter family home, playing duets. "I felt that music was something fantastic. When I went home that night with my mum and dad, I started nagging at them: 'Please, you've got to give me something that I can play on.'" So it was that the following spring, on his 13th birthday, Björn got his first acoustic guitar, at the time a fairly unusual gift. Björn still recalls it as being one of the happiest moments of his life.

Just like the embryonic Beatles and other British bands that became popular in the Sixties, Björn and Joen formed a skiffle band, featuring the classic line-up of guitars, tea chest bass and washboard. "I was attracted both to the playing music part of it and the performing side of it," remembered Björn.

Through playing with the band Björn got to know bass player Tony Rooth. Tony went to the same class as Joen Ulfsäter, and would soon become Björn's best friend. "Joen's dad was very rich and they had a big house," he recalls. "In the house there was a basement where we could play music and be as noisy as we wanted to." Support also came from Björn's father, who arranged for Tony's bass to be assembled out at the paper mill.

The band's repertoire was culled mainly from Joen's skiffle albums. "But they didn't print the lyrics on the album sleeves in those days," Björn remembered. "Our English wasn't good enough to understand exactly what they were singing, so we ended up with some kind of phonetic gibberish."

To some extent, the same approach characterised the work of many of the immensely popular early Swedish rock artists in the late Fifties. Swedish cover versions of hits by the likes of Elvis Presley, Buddy Holly and Gene Vincent often featured more than a few slurred words that probably wouldn't be found in any English language dictionaries. "That shows you how little it meant," noted Björn. "The lyrics had no relevance whatsoever beyond the sound of them, and that was the climate I grew up in."

In the safe, idyllic, prosperous Sweden of the late Fifties, rock's often defiant lyrics were mostly lost on record buyers. Its roots as "race music" and its function as a means for teenage rebellion had even less meaning. In youth magazines, rock'n'roll was first mentioned during the latter half of 1956, and then only as a novelty offshoot of jazz: a new American dance craze. Rock'n'roll as a distinct music genre didn't gain a stronghold on the Swedish music scene until late 1957, and the attitude of Swedish radio at the time didn't exactly help. The first radio show to be specifically tailored to a teenage audience began broadcasting earlier that year, but the hosts openly declared that although the intention was to provide entertainment for everyone, "the only point we are firm about is that we hate rock'n' roll". Jazz was deemed far more suitable for listeners, at least according to the hosts of this show.

For Björn, the conflict between jazz and rock'n'roll was neither here nor there. All he knew was that he was smitten by music and wanted to play guitar in his cousin's skiffle group. It took a while to master his instrument, though. "I bought one of those books where they print the chords with dots so that you know exactly which strings to press down. At first, I didn't really know how to do that, so I had to rationalise a bit and ignore the hardest bits. I ended up with some funny chords."

Björn's mother Aina often found it difficult to tolerate her son's amateurish guitar struggles. "I would put on my coat and get out of the house, just to avoid having to listen to it," she recalled. As Björn later acknowledged, it was a testament to his parents' encouragement of his interests that they let him carry on playing at home.

In August 1956, Björn started junior secondary school and his grades gradually improved over the next few years. Although he wasn't exactly a well-behaved student all the time he was certainly no juvenile delinquent either. Björn was just a friendly, middle-class boy who didn't make waves, although it was clear even at this age that he had a sharp intellect.

Tony Rooth recalls: "When I think of the young Björn, the first thing that strikes me is how intelligent he was. His grades were excellent and I never noticed that he studied more than anyone else. Languages came very easily to him. Our English teacher, who had been in the profession around 40 years at the time, told me in confidence that she had never had a pupil who was as good at English as he was."

When Joen Ulfsäter decided that his band should abandon skiffle and take up trad jazz, or Dixieland, Björn acquired a taste for this music as well, switching from guitar to banjo. It was a development that was fairly common among Swedish skiffle fans. As the term suggests, trad jazz was in itself a revival of the original early 20th century New Orleans jazz, and teenagers practising this kind of music were assured of an approving pat on the back from older generations.

Although hindsight tells us that the youth of the Western world took rock'n'roll music to its heart in the mid to late Fifties, it is well worth remembering that Björn and his friends were well brought up middle-class boys. In that environment, in Sweden and elsewhere, the official word on rock music was that it was "simplistic" music for the working classes, not quite immoral but certainly low culture.

The rock'n'roll that slowly made an impact in Sweden was almost exclusively performed by white acts like Elvis Presley, while the pioneering black artists were virtually unknown to most rock fans. Björn, who continued being a closet rock fan, later confirmed: "I liked Elvis, of course, but not someone like Chuck Berry. His music wasn't played in my circles, I didn't even know he existed. In the high schools in Swedish small towns at that time you didn't really listen to rock music. It was only folk music, Dixieland and skiffle."

With the notable exception of Little Richard, who had two hits around this time, the statistics confirm Björn's recollections. Elvis' first hit in Sweden was 'Hound Dog' in January 1957 – Chuck Berry was nowhere to be seen on the charts until 'Memphis Tennessee' in May 1963.

By the late Fifties, Björn had become proficient enough on guitar to strum and sing his way through the hits of the day. He'd bring along his guitar wherever he went. "I played and sang for whoever wanted to listen, at school or wherever," he remembered. When his family enjoyed the traditional Swedish midsummer celebrations in the country, Björn used to perform songs like 'Teddy Bear' and 'You Are My Sunshine'. Like guitar pickers the world over, he also discovered that playing and singing was a great way to attract girls. With his sunny demeanour and charming ways Björn was becoming a popular boy in school, losing his virginity while still in his early teens.

In the summer of 1959, the 14-year-old Björn was sent to London on his own to work at a paper mill for three weeks, a job obtained through his uncle's connections. Although trips abroad had become more common during the previous ten years, it was still fairly unusual for a boy of his age to travel such a distance all alone. On the boat over to England, Björn entertained his fellow passengers by performing his renditions of recent hits like Paul Anka's 'Diana'. It was obvious his confidence in his own ability as a performer had grown.

Being on his own in the English capital city was one big adventure for Björn, but also very useful for his personal growth. "At first I was a little shy and miserable, living alone at a small hotel off Sloane Square. But it was a good way to become self-sufficient, because I had no one to turn to."

In London, Björn took the opportunity to cultivate his interest in trad jazz. He visited jazz clubs in Oxford Street and attended concerts by the likes of Acker Bilk, Chris Barber and other famous names of the day. It was an exciting experience, as he recalled. "London was an altogether different place at that time. If I had been out somewhere, I could walk home for hours all by myself without feeling scared." Björn had acquired an extra layer of confidence as he returned home to Sweden and went back to school.

The Swedish economy continued its upward curve, and the paper mill in Västervik became one of the larger industries in the area. Under the leadership of Björn's uncle Esbjörn it was quickly developing into the leading force in Swedish paper recycling, providing Gunnar Ulvaeus with a safe position at his brother's company. When Björn and his sister Eva were old enough to take care of themselves, Aina started working part-time at a shoe shop.

With Swedish industry prospering, Björn's parents envisioned a safe career for him as a civil engineer in shipbuilding. He knew their thinking was right, but something else was stirring inside. Although he applied himself to his studies, music and the arts in general were fast becoming far more attractive. As Björn entered senior high school in August 1960, his love of music was joined by a reawakened interest in poetry. "At that time you still read a lot of poetry in school," he remembered. "A few decades earlier the poets used to be like idols in Sweden, and some of that feeling was still around during my school years."

Björn was even elected secretary of the mysterious and secret Delta-Sigma society at his high school. Girls were not allowed in the society and instead were treated as objects of romantic devotion. Björn would write love poems in rhyme and give them to those girls that interested him. "The language would be a bit flowery," he later said of these teenage efforts. Every Delta-Sigma member was expected to bring along a poem to each of their weekly meetings, and Björn found that he really enjoyed the challenge. "There were quite a few people who wrote poetry in high school during those days. I realise now that doing it on a regular basis and getting familiar with concepts like structure and metre must have been a help for me in my work later on. I'm sure it did mean quite a lot."

Parallel with studies and poetry writing, he kept on playing with the trad jazz band. The members had bought into the whole package and would dress in the typical Dixieland fashion of duffle coats and rubber soled shoes. The band obtained regular bookings at local jazz clubs, but were also required to provide dance music from time to time with Björn playing the electric guitar. They would also play at private parties, as Tony Rooth recalls. "Since Joen's dad owned the paper mill, he associated with a lot of the other bigwigs in Västervik. So we'd sometimes be performing at some managing director's fancy residence. They would sit there with their cigars and brandies or champagne, and gave us a little money or food and soft drinks for our efforts."

One of the groups competing for the attention of the Västervik youth was a skiffle band called Mackie's Skiffle Group. By the early Sixties, the group had already evolved into a folk music band. Leader Hansi Schwarz and fellow members Johan Karlberg and Håkan Hven were motivated by the emerging American folk music movement. Their main inspiration were groups like The Kingston Trio, who broke through with their chart-topping rendition of 'Tom Dooley', and The Brothers Four. Folk music was gradually replacing jazz as the acceptable form of musicianship for Swedish middle-class youth.

In 1961, when Björn was 16, his cousin Joen left Västervik to study in another town, leading to the dissolution of their trad jazz band. Meanwhile, Mackie's Skiffle Group had changed its name to The Partners. Their weakest link was an unaccomplished bass player, who was unable to learn even rudimentary bass playing skills. "Hansi had found out that our band was collapsing from within and wanted to recruit Tony to play bass in his band instead," recalled Björn. "But Tony said, 'Okay, I'll join you, but only if my pal Björn can come along as well.' I don't think Hansi was too happy about that, because they already had three guitar players and it wasn't like they really needed a fourth one."

It's tempting to speculate what would have happened if Tony hadn't been so loyal to his friend. Would Björn had given up music altogether and concentrated on his studies and, eventually, a safe career as a civil engineer, as his parents had planned? Björn himself believes he would have continued with the music. "Perhaps I would have joined a pop group instead a few years later, or started one myself. When The Beatles broke through I realised that I would have preferred to be doing something like that."

But back in 1961 Tony persisted – "Björn and I had become best friends," he says – and Hansi begrudgingly relented. The new line-up of The Partners consisted of Hansi Schwarz, Johan Karlberg, Håkan Hven and Björn alternating on guitars or banjos, and Tony Rooth on bass.

Hansi, who was born in Germany, came to Sweden in 1958. Compared to his Swedish friends he had a head start on American music through listening to the radio station American Forces Network which offered homegrown musical entertainment for the occupying American forces. German youths, eager to leave the old, nationalistic Germany behind them and embrace the exciting American teenage culture, also tuned in. Hansi was a keen record collector and bought every folk music album he could lay his hands on, with The Kingston Trio his particular favourite. The American group was the role model when he started his first group in the late Fifties and that's how it continued.

Hansi was sharing a run-down two-room apartment with Håkan Hven that was just a minute's walk from the high school. The band would get together there and listen to records. "The apartment had a stove, a sink and cold water, that was all," says Hansi. "But we could rehearse our act there, we didn't have to go looking for any other rehearsal facilities. We were at it almost daily. I used to say, 'No one comes here before eight – I have to do my homework – but then we can play.'"

The Partners showed no interest in traditional Swedish folk music which they considered passé. Their act consisted almost entirely of American folk standards like 'Where Have All The Flowers Gone', 'Sloop John B' and 'Good News'. "The old Swedish songs were something you had in your repertoire just in case old ladies wanted to make a request," Björn recalled.

Joining The Partners was a turning point for Björn, who suddenly acquired a sense of purpose for his intelligence. Now he could apply it to something more constructive and exciting than simply sailing through school with a minimum of effort. Although he was the youngest member of the band, his leadership qualities quickly emerged as he started making decisions about musical arrangements. He remembered: "When we were rehearsing I gradually became the one who decided how the songs should be performed, how to structure them, what the harmony parts should be and things like that. It was just a natural development."

The new five-man line-up of The Partners would perform at different school functions and dances arranged by the local youth centre. Playing together on a regular basis, and with the less committed and less accomplished members from their previous groups now gone, they developed into a tight little band. To their Kingston Trio influences were added The Everly Brothers whose soaring harmonies and choppy rhythm guitars became a genuine source of inspiration, just as they had for The Beatles. "We used to perform during the breaks at school dances and started noticing that we got a great deal of encouragement and appreciation from the audience," confirms Tony Rooth.

But encouragement was one thing, actually getting anywhere another. Hansi Schwarz had ambitions for the group and recalls an increasing frustration as they failed to achieve a break. "As the band leader I would see to it that we entered different talent contests. But it was really stupid, because they weren't pure music contests. We'd be up against some cute six-year-old who did a little dance, and acts like that would invariably win while we ended up second or third."

No sooner had the group become a local attraction than they discovered that another group, who were already famous on a national level, were also using the name The Partners. This prompted a change of name to the West Bay Singers, "West Bay" being a literal translation of Västervik.

In the summer of 1963 The Beatles began to make waves in Sweden, but the contrast between the folk music scene and British pop was just as polarised as the earlier clash between trad jazz and American rock. Björn noted this new, brasher pop music with interest, but there was no talk about the folk-purist West Bay Singers taking their music in that direction.

When Håkan Hven graduated from senior high school in the early summer of 1963, one year before the rest of the band, he left the group to do his compulsory military service. Said Björn: "He was a very talented student. There was never any talk of him remaining in the group."

Down to their core foursome, in July 1963 the group crammed themselves into an old Volvo and embarked on a six-week holiday trip and "tour" of Europe. Not only had they turned into a strong musical unit over the past two years, but they had also become very close friends, sharing their most intimate thoughts with each other. "The four of us got along really well," says Tony Rooth. "A few years later, when we would be out on long tours and had to stay together at hotels all the time, we still continued going on holidays together."

In preparation for their trip the boys had taken summer jobs. Björn, Hansi and Tony were working at the paper mill while Johan Karlberg spent a few weeks at his dad's car firm. By the time they embarked on their journey, the four friends had each scraped together 1,000 (£70)* kronor as pocket money, but their room and board were mainly paid for by whatever concert opportunities turned up along the way.

The trip became a true summer adventure for the young foursome. Hansi was the eldest at 21; 18-year-old Björn was the junior member of the gang. Tony Rooth recalls the sense of freedom on his first ever trip abroad. "All of a sudden you were away from your parents and could have

---

* The different values of the krona mentioned throughout this book reflect its approximate relation to the British pound at specific points in time.

a glass of wine without anyone saying anything about that. There was a lot of drinking and partying going on during that holiday." The four friends kept a diary of their adventures, taking turns to chronicle the day's events. Tony Rooth still has the diary. "We were four young guys out on a trip like this," he recalls. "Our hormones were raging and we were looking for girls in every corner."

A few days after arriving in Sitges, an idyllic place near Barcelona in Spain, Björn writes in the diary: "We went to Pepe's Club filled with a burning desire, mixed with gentle adoration, for four Spanish girls. With the help of a lousy microphone we performed a few songs from our extensive repertoire. As far as women were concerned, once again our hopes were shattered." And in this respect, nothing much changed during the course of the trip, as Tony confirms: "We never managed to pull anything off."

While seducing olive-skinned continental girls proved a bridge too far for these small-town Swedish boys, they had better luck with their musical performances. The trip further boosted their confidence as in their diary they noted the positive reaction from the local audiences.

In the autumn of 1963 the four West Bay Singers entered their final year at high school, a crucial time if they were to graduate successfully the following spring. With all the fun that music had to offer as a distraction, the past 12 months hadn't exactly been marked by serious application to their studies. But at the same time, there was never any serious talk of making music a full-time occupation. The course had been set: high-school graduation with good grades, followed by university studies. "We decided that we should put the group on the back burner this last period up until our graduation so that we would get at least reasonable grades," says Tony Rooth.

Also, encouraging as the Europe trip had been, the boys were frustrated at never really getting anywhere with their music. Says Hansi Schwarz: "We never knew if we had missed the boat completely or if we simply were too early. It turned out that we'd been too early; people didn't understand what we were trying to do."

Then, just as it seemed as if the group was destined to go the way of so many teenage bands, fate intervened in the shape of Björn's mother. Aina Ulvaeus no longer left the house when her son played his guitar, and had become increasingly impressed with the prowess of the West Bay Singers. She remembered that day in the late summer of 1963: "I was at home, listening to the radio, when I heard that they were announcing a talent contest. When Björn came home I said, 'You sound so good now that you should try to enter that contest.'"

Björn, who secretly wanted to devote his time to music rather than studies, followed his mother's advice and sent in an application. The talent contest, called *Plats på scen* ("On Stage"), had been hastily concocted because professional Swedish artists were presently on strike, and their music was no longer heard on the airwaves. The only way to supply musical entertainment on the radio was by engaging amateurs in the guise of a contest.

On September 13, 1963, the West Bay Singers duly travelled to a radio studio in the town of Norrköping. Together with numerous other contestants they waited for their chance to perform before the selection jury at these try-out heats. Their rival competitors were an eclectic bunch. "Even though it was for the radio, some people came there and performed magic tricks and stuff like that," recalls Tony Rooth.

Among the other hopefuls was a 17-year-old singer called Anni-Frid Lyngstad. Today, none of the former West Bay Singers has any recollection of her presence there; with a total of 153 contestants parading before the jury it is more than likely that they didn't even meet that day.

The West Bay Singers were supposed to perform their act in the early evening, but the proceedings were running late and by 9 p.m. the group was still waiting. Hansi Schwarz recalls: "We said, 'What's the point in hanging around? They've been watching and listening to all those acts the whole day. They will be bored by anything now.' We were almost about to go home."

But the group decided to hang around after all. When they were asked to do another song besides the one they had already performed, they realised they were in with a chance. Both the West Bay Singers and Anni-Frid Lyngstad were among the six participants considered talented enough to continue to the first proper stage of the contest, which was to be broadcast on the radio a little over two weeks later.

The day after this first heat, a small article about the contest was printed in the Swedish newspaper *Expressen*. It caught the attention of Bengt Bernhag, producer at a brand new record company in Stockholm called Polar Music. During the past decade, Bengt had become almost legendary in the Swedish music business for his uncanny ability to see the hit potential in a song or an act.

Now he had got it into his head that when everybody else was looking for rebellious Beatle-type bands singing in English, he would go in the opposite direction. Polar needed something that didn't exist on the record market, he felt: a well-mannered folk music act singing in Swedish, a sort of domestic version of The Kingston Trio.

Singled out as "a top act" in the article about the talent contest was a "boy quartet from Västervik fronted by Björn Ulvaeus", calling them-selves the West Bay Singers. The name alone suggested they could be exactly the kind of folk music act Bengt was looking for. His interest was piqued.

Bengt contacted the band and asked them to send a tape to Polar. He liked what he heard, and the group was informed that his partner in the record company was coming to see them. Before long the boys and their parents found themselves staring into the animated features of Stig Anderson.

Chapter 2

"The circumstances of my adolescence came to play a major part in my life," Stig Anderson would say, reflecting on the strange driving force that pushed him ever onwards to new challenges through the years. "You don't have to psychoanalyse it, romanticise it or in any other way try to rationalise what happened to me when I was growing up. The reality is potent enough, the framework was important: an unmarried woman in the Sweden of the Thirties, 'father unknown'. It went beyond moral condemnation – women like my mother almost didn't exist."

Stig Erik Leopold Andersson (originally with double "s") was born on January 25, 1931 at the Mariestad maternity hospital. He was raised in a small town called Hova, 18 miles outside Mariestad between lakes Vänern and Vättern in the southern county of Västergötland. The son of unmarried Ester Andersson and a father he never knew, Stig and his mother were on the bottom rung of the ladder, very much a part of the impoverished society of early Thirties Sweden. Living in a small town with only a few thousand inhabitants meant that everybody knew everything about everybody else – and everybody knew about Stig and his mother.

The modern Swedish welfare system was little more than an idea at the time, and Ester Andersson had no choice but to work herself to the bone to take care of her son as best she could. The child's illegitimacy was talked about behind her back but Ester made no demands on the community at large, and people had enough problems of their own to care too much about her misfortune.

Stig would later point out that in those days poverty in itself was no shame, it was just troublesome for those who found themselves in that predicament. "You had to try to find ways to work your way out of it," he said. "In this part of the world, most people virtually had nothing, a few had next to nothing, and rich people were something you didn't even think about."

Ester Andersson and her son lived in a small, shed-like cottage. Stig later described it as "four walls, a leaky roof and a cold-water tap that froze during the winter". But Ester was a traditional Västergötland woman, entrepreneurial, resourceful and hardworking, qualities that her young son would inherit in abundance. Ester took in laundry and ironing, and worked as a hairdresser. Although her skills in this area were fairly basic, she was so successful in her trade that she even had clients from a nearby village. It wasn't as if the money rolled in, but Ester was somehow able to make ends meet for herself and her young son.

During the worst years of the Great Depression most people in Hova could ill afford to have someone else clean their shirts, which could have been disastrous had Ester not acquired an additional source of income through opening a small confectionery kiosk twelve miles away. She hired someone else to run the business while she spent the day doing laundry and cutting hair. After a hard day's work, she would cycle to the kiosk to check up on the day's business. Stig vividly remembered sitting on the back of his mother's bicycle on long journeys through the dark woods. The small boy was scared to death by the darkness and the sounds of the forest. "I'd look straight up at the sky, towards a brighter band that ran across the blackness of the forest," he recalled.

But the kiosk business was badly run by those whom Ester had entrusted with its maintenance and it turned out to be a fairly disastrous enterprise. If nothing else, the incident taught Stig a lesson he would never forget, and for the rest of his life he detested and harangued those who failed to do their very best when trusted with a responsibility. The loss of the kiosk was alleviated somewhat when Ester married the local tailor, Paul Gustafsson, and her financial situation became more secure as a result.

Stig was quick to pick up his mother's ingenuity and head for small business. Watching her efforts to make ends meet, making the best use of whatever talents she had, was undoubtedly inspirational for the young Stig. "I started working in my spare time, even during my school days," he recalled. "There was plenty of work to be had for anyone who wanted it. There were mainly two kinds of jobs: the ones you were paid for and the ones you did as part of club activities. You just had to organise it all so that there were no conflicts between your assignments." Stig did everything and anything he could. For the princely sum of five kronor (25 pence) per term he would rise at dawn to start the fire in the school's furnace. He would also personally deliver the electricity bills in Hova, about 600 in number.

After six years of elementary school, Stig quit because his mother was unable to afford to keep him there, and at 13 he began work as a delivery boy for the local grocery store. The wages were far too small to count as any real income, so Stig had to find other ways to boost his finances.

Local sports were very popular, but relied on voluntary work. Supporters were obliged to contribute to the community spirit of their own free will, without payment. The resourceful Stig found a way around this by becoming the store manager for the Hova Sports Club. He offered to take care of the gear for the entire football team, clean the changing room, chalk the football field, arrange the water supply, and perform any other necessary tasks. In exchange he was allowed sole rights to the kiosk at the Club and any money he could make from the selling of candy and soft drinks. On a good Sunday, when the A-team was playing, Stig would make a huge profit.

Although Stig had grown up in a very deprived household, when he was about five years old his mother had somehow managed to buy an old gramophone and six 78 rpm records. Stig felt an immediate connection to music, singing along to the hits of the day and the records his mother chose. It wasn't long before he discovered that he also enjoyed singing in front of people.

"I grabbed every chance I got to sing before an audience, especially in school," he recalled. "I noticed that singing had an effect on people. You became the centre of attention, people would notice someone who made a noise. The conclusion was that music was something you should go for. I wanted to be liked by people."

In those pre-television days, especially in rural environments, entertainment was provided largely by the people themselves. It was up to the local community to arrange club activities, or just get together and sing at informal gatherings. The radio offered only a scant few hours of light entertainment each week, so the only other source of music was gramophone records. The young Stig now had a regular position in the local store and was becoming a keen music customer.

Playing records was one thing but performing could turn you into a local star. The chance to mix entertainment with making money was not lost on the teenage Stig, nor was Ester willing to let any opportunity to boost the family income go by. She spent 15 kronor (£1) on a guitar for her son, even sewing a cover to go with it. Stig practised hard and started performing in local revues, where musical performances were mixed with comical skits and monologues.

The staging of a revue was something that engaged the whole community. For Stig, it was a perfect outlet for his restless teenage energy and industrious nature. He thoroughly enjoyed being a part of making things happen, often putting forward suggestions on how to improve the shows. On stage Stig would perform the current *schlagers*, but he also began writing songs of his own that became part of his act. Rejection from a girl he fancied set the ball rolling. "I went home and wrote a satirical ballad about her. Then I performed it during a meeting with the local temperance society and got a great response. That's when I realised that it's fun to write songs."

He was only 16 when he wrote 'Tivedshambo' ('Hambo From Tived'), which in time became the first of his songs to be recorded. A folksy number, its colourful depiction of a particularly wild traditional Swedish dance festivity in the woods proved that Stig was already able to tap into the public consciousness. The song was to become one of his most well known, as well as a Swedish accordion classic.

With the end of the Second World War, a new optimism swept across Sweden. Its borders were again opened to outside cultural influences, and from the United States came jazz which reached even as far as isolated rural societies like Hova. Stig became an ardent be-bop fan and played guitar with a couple of local jazz bands.

Around this time the local newspaper ran a letter to the editor from a mother protesting about the unnatural excitement this type of music brought about in the town's innocent youth. Young Stig Andersson submitted an angry reply, maintaining that jazz music was very important for the local youth. "You must be a highly sexually charged sort of person if you feel that jazz music does nothing but arouse people!" he fired off. It was an early glimpse of the hot-tempered, highly opinionated character who would cause such outrage in the Swedish media in years to come.

With only a few songs under his belt, Stig started dreaming about national success as a songwriter. In 1947, aged 16, he sent a couple of his songs to music business figures whom he thought might help him get ahead. One reply came from the popular composer Ulf Peder Olrog, one of Stig's musical heroes. Olrog's mix of catchy melodies and subtly satirical, tongue-in-cheek lyrics appealed to a large slice of the population.

To some extent, these ingredients would colour many of Stig's own efforts as a songwriter, and the shadow of Olrog hovers over many of his best lyrics. But where Olrog, who was a university graduate, often tended to be slightly more subtle and academic in his work, Stig seldom strayed too far from subject matter and catchphrases that could strike a chord with every facet of the population.

In his fairly long letter back to Stig, Olrog noted that Mr Andersson was very talented but that he needed to develop his prowess, especially in terms of lyric writing. Stig was advised to study poetry in order to become a better lyricist, and the letter closed with the words: "Keep on writing and get back to me in a couple of years." Stig never forgot the encouraging letter – later in life he kept it framed, hanging on a wall in his office. "It gives me food for thought when I pass judgement on the efforts of others," he reflected.

In July 1948 Ulf Peder Olrog was performing in the town of Örebro, a relatively short distance from Hova. Stig and a friend took the train to meet up with the composer. Confronted with the aspiring young songwriter and his friend, the surprised artist bought them strawberries and cream. During their talk Olrog told Stig that he should study music at the Ingesund folk high school. Stig returned to Hova with this important piece of advice ringing in his ears, but of even greater magnitude was the realisation that it was possible to actually make a living from music. He concluded that it wouldn't hurt to further himself a little; that studying at the folk high school might provide him with a secure future, and at the same time develop his love for music.

Eighteen was the minimum age for students at Ingesund folk high school. Stig, only 17, moved to the town of Arvika near Ingesund and worked in a food store. All the while he kept up his interest in performing and songwriting and it wasn't long before he'd connected with people who put on local revues. Among the more important new acquaintances he made in the Arvika revue crowd was a student called Bengt Bernhag. They soon realised they shared an ambition and a will to make things happen, be it through hard work or shameless hype – or both. While Stig was a loud, in-your-face extrovert who wore his self-confidence on his sleeve, Bengt was discreet and unassuming and tended to achieve his results on the quiet. As their friendship and working relationship developed, this would turn out to be an especially winning combination.

In the autumn of 1949, Stig began his studies at the folk high school. Among the other pupils studying there was an attractive, soft-spoken girl called Gudrun Rystedt, the daughter of farmer Karl Rystedt and his wife Astrid. Farming within the peasant society, an important part of the Swedish economy as late as the Thirties, was now on its way out. Gudrun's parents could see it coming. It was clear their six children would need something beside the farm to rely on for their futures, and they were all sent away to educate themselves. Gudrun ended up at Ingesund, where she studied weaving, cooking, housekeeping and English.

She vividly recalled her first impression of the 18-year-old Stig. "At first I thought he seemed almost insane. He was on the go all the time, there was never any time when he took it easy. He questioned everything: 'Why must it be done that way? Why can't we do it this way instead?' "

Over the years, Stig had found that being a singer and guitarist was a great way to make an impression on girls. He had even written a few love songs that were dedicated exclusively to his current love interest, and when his eyes fell on Gudrun he tried to woo her the same way, to little avail. After he was through with his seductive performance he was curtly informed that, in fact, she wasn't terribly interested in music. Stig liked girls who talked back and decided it was Gudrun he wanted. It didn't take long before he had won her over and they became an item at the school. In 1951 the pair became engaged.

Parallel with their studies, Stig, Bengt Bernhag and a friend called Börje Crona put together a stage act based on Stig's songs, interspersed with bad jokes and silly gags. The trio would perform locally with varying degrees of success. "You could say that we were before our time," Stig recalled with a heavy dose of irony. "We . . . tried to establish the current 'crazy' vogue in the deep forests."

After staging yet another revue at the Ingesund folk high school in March 1950 – and encouraged by the few truly positive words in the reviews – Stig, Bengt and Börje sent a letter to the radio show *Frukostklubben (The Breakfast Club)*, a popular variety show broadcast each Saturday morning. Up-and-coming artists making a good appearance on *Frukostklubben* were often signed to a record contract.

After securing a publishing deal for the Andersson composition 'Grädde på moset' ('The Icing On The Cake'), Stig and his friends were invited to appear on *Frukostklubben*. Their successful performance of the song led to a recording by Harry Brandelius, one of the most popular singers in Sweden at that time. 'Grädde på moset' was released in the autumn of 1950.

This was the first appearance on record of a Stig Andersson composition but it was a huge disappointment for the budding songwriter. From the moment he first heard Brandelius' less than energetic interpretation, his heart sank. Despite the immense popularity of the singer, he knew instinctively that the record was not going to be a hit. The lesson learned was that you could have the right song and the right singer, but if the performance in itself wasn't right, the result would not make an impression with the general public.

Still, the recording led to an interview with Stig in a popular weekly, and his very earliest composition, 'Tivedshambo', was recorded by comedian Rolf Bengtson in February 1951. The B-side was also an Andersson effort. 'Tivedshambo' didn't exactly rock the foundations of the music industry, but the spirited performance was a step in the right direction. Stig, now 20, took it as an encouraging sign but at the same time he realised that a career as an entertainer and songwriter was unlikely to offer much security. After graduating from the folk high school in the spring of 1951, he decided he needed to get an "honest" profession. There were three realistic ways to go: he could become a journalist, a teacher or a policeman. The latter appealed to him because it had the bonus of a free uniform, but in the end he chose teaching. In order to train as a teacher, he had to take a preparatory course of study in the town of Karlstad but his studies were temporarily broken off when he was required to do his mandatory Swedish military service in Skövde.

Always on the go, Stig didn't let this period of involuntary absence from civil life go entirely to waste. While standing guard he would compose songs, and he also kept an eye on developments in show business. Gudrun, who had moved with him to Skövde, lived in a rented room, working as a maid.

Stig came close to hitting the big time in January 1952, when a singing sports star known as Snoddas made his début on the popular radio show *Karusellen* (*The Merry-Go-Round*). Snoddas' repertoire consisted mainly of songs recorded by Harry Brandelius, and as he auditioned for the show, he chose to perform Stig's 'Grädde på moset'. But show host Lennart Hyland, a powerful and intimidating figure in Swedish show business, didn't like the song and requested an alternative. Snoddas submitted another title, which met with Hyland's approval.

After his performance on *Karusellen*, the country was hit by Snoddas fever, and he quickly became one of the most popular artists in Sweden. Similarly, when the song Hyland had chosen was released on record, it became the nation's biggest seller up to that point. With 250,000 copies sold, no other 78 rpm record would ever match its sales figures.

Stig recalled: "It would have been natural to use 'Grädde på moset' on the flip side of the record Snoddas was to make. But unfortunately, Snoddas was on the same label as Brandelius and since he had already recorded it, they selected another song. This angered me for a long time. [The record] sold in incredible numbers and I could really have used the money."

Better situated to keep track of things was Stig's friend Bengt Bernhag, who by now was living in Stockholm. Bengt had been pestering the newly established record company Philips to give him and his friends a chance to make a record. His stubbornness got results, and in the late summer of 1952 Stig was given temporary leave from his military duties to travel to Stockholm to make his very first recording. The chance to work professionally in the music business filled him with euphoria. "I've seldom been overcome with such a dizziness from freedom as when I took the train from Skövde station," he remembered.

Both sides of Stig's début record were written by the young composer. The A-side was 'Dom finns på landet' ('You'll Find Them In The Country', referring to "the girls who know how to do it"), a song he had written while marking time in the military service. "An awful piece of music and a terrible record," he later admitted.

History may not have been kind to the song as such, but the recording session turned out to be important for the future of Stig and Bengt Bernhag in other respects. The Philips house producer was impressed by Bengt's unobtrusive remarks during the session, and offered him the position as assistant producer on the spot. Bengt eagerly accepted.

As the Fifties progressed, Sweden, as elsewhere, slowly cast off the final remnants of the restrictive Forties and the rationing years. Hope was in the air as the nation grew increasingly prosperous. The recording industry was expanding along with the rest of society, with the old 10″ 78 rpm records being replaced by 7″ singles, EPs and albums. Radio had a restrictive policy on recorded music entertainment, however, which meant limited opportunities for record promotion.

When his military service finished in 1953, Stig decided to continue his teacher studies in Stockholm. The idea of succeeding in music and show business was still at the back of his mind, and he continued to write songs, trying to push them towards publishers and record companies. In 1954, he had yet another hit with 'Det blir inget bröllop på lördag' ('There Won't Be Any Wedding On Saturday'). The song was recorded by no less than seven artists, but the accumulated royalties were far from enough to support Stig and Gudrun.

Stig was fast coming to the conclusion that he wasn't much of a stage artist, and harboured similar doubts about his abilities as a composer. It was as if the melodies never really turned out better than average. One musician who played back-up on his records at that time was heard to remark sarcastically, "I hear that Stig has written 'Darktown Strutters' Ball' again," referring to the old jazz standard which seemed to inspire many of his melodies. "He was probably right," Stig later acknowledged. "I always felt like an amateur as a musician. Writing lyrics came easier, there was no resistance. Perhaps that was where my real talent lay?"

It was true that most of the praise he experienced as a songwriter was for his work as wordsmith. As early as his first copyright, 'Grädde på moset', the publisher had complained about the "monotonous" lyrics and asked Stig to change them. "The same afternoon I lay on the lawn outside the City Hall and rewrote the lyric. [The publisher] was very impressed that it had gone so fast and that I had understood what he had meant."

In August 1955, Stig and Gudrun finally got married and needed a place of their own in Stockholm. There was an acute housing shortage in Sweden's capital in the Fifties, so a few months later Stig and Gudrun had little choice but to negotiate an under-the-counter deal for the rental contract on a one-room apartment for 5,000 kronor (£350). At the time and under their circumstances, it was an enormous sum, and since it lacked heating, warm water and a toilet, the price seemed even steeper. The Anderssons' first child, a daughter they named Marie, was born in early 1957. That same year, Stig's teacher training was complete and he began work at the Aspudden Elementary School. The picture of a neat little family was further reinforced with the birth of a son called Lars in May 1958.

All the while Stig persevered as songwriter, recording artist and stage performer, touring the Swedish *folkparks* with different partners. Up until the Eighties, most artists would spend the summers on extensive nation-wide tours of these "people's parks" and it was an important way for them to build and sustain interest with their audience.

One of Stig's touring partners in the late Fifties and early Sixties was called Akke Carlsson. In order to establish a syntactic unity in the stage act, Stig gave himself the nickname Stikkan. In Sweden, but not elsewhere, he would become known by this name for the rest of his life. Around the same time he also lost one "s" in his surname, which now became Anderson. Curiously, the name change was never registered with the authorities: formally, Stig and his family all remained Anderssons. But despite the odd hit here and there, and regular stage engagements that would continue until the first few years of the Sixties, he continued working as a teacher to support his small family.

Sometimes it seemed a breakthrough in show business was waiting around the corner. Stig got his first sizeable hit in September 1958 when legendary Swedish football hero Nacka Skoglund recorded his compos-ition 'Vi hänger me' ('We're Still Here'). The record spent 20 weeks in the singles and EP chart, peaking at number six.

By then, the Andersons had abandoned their miserable one-room apart-ment in central Stockholm for the rented top floor of a villa in the suburbs. Now the revenues from 'Vi hänger me' were large enough to cover half the down-payment on a town house in Tullinge, south of Stockholm. For Gudrun, putting the key in the door of a home that was all her own was the happiest moment of her life.

Still, not even this songwriting success was enough for Stig to give up his day job, although he wouldn't give up on his dream of working full time in the music business. Recalled Gudrun Anderson: "I know that Stig was a good teacher. The kids often called him at home and wanted to talk to him. Sometimes he would play his new songs for the class. But I think that was more because he wanted to try out a new song than for any edu-cational purposes."

By this time, Stig had a fairly good grasp on how the publishing business worked, and he had established important contacts with several of the publishers in Stockholm. In late 1959, he wrote a song called 'Är du kär i mig ännu, Klas-Göran' ('Are You Still In Love With Me, Klas-Göran'). The artist he had in mind was the up-and-coming singer Lill-Babs, contracted to the record company Karusell. His old friend Bengt had recently left Philips and was now the staff producer at Karusell.

Over the past decade, Bengt Bernhag had fine-tuned his abilities as record producer and become one of the most respected figures in the Swedish music business. "He'd wear himself out completely during a recording session," said songwriter Peter Himmelstrand. "He paid attention to every single little detail. For several days before he was going to enter the studio he would fire himself up. He absorbed every single word in the lyrics and demanded that words that didn't feel right should be changed. After a few hours in the studio he would be completely exhausted for days."

Bengt was an intuitive producer who felt that making a record that struck a chord with the general public had more to do with gut feelings than technical accuracy. Despite a thorough education, he would act as if he didn't know a thing about musical terminology. Discussing something like a string run he'd simply ask the string section to "play that blurry stuff again". Stig rated Bengt as "the best record producer and 'hit picker' Sweden has ever known". The recording of 'Är du kär i mig ännu, Klas-Göran' was perhaps the first time he realised exactly how unique his talents were.

Stig had written the song as a romantic story of a girl pining for her lover. Bengt, however, had a hunch that it would be better to record the song as a comedy piece with Lill-Babs putting on a heavy, rural accent. He also thought she should be dressed in folk costume with braids when she performed the song on television. Lill-Babs eagerly seconded Bengt's opinion – she later recalled that the lyrics were "the most stupid I had ever seen".

Stig didn't agree at all, and they had a fierce argument about it. "I was so pissed off that I was thinking of financing a recording of my own . . . 'You have to realise that we're on to something big here,' replied Bengt . . . I thought it sounded awful and not at all serious." Bengt got his way, and Stig achieved his first truly major hit as a composer, with the song entering the charts at number one on January 1, 1960. "Bengt was always right in the end," he said later.

With this success, Stig began to question the wisdom of giving part of his songwriting royalties to an outside publisher. "I thought it was time to keep the whole cake for myself: retaining all rights and registering the song with my own publishing company. That's when I founded Sweden Music, giving the company a grand name from the start. It was time for thinking big."

Chapter 2

'Är du kär i mig ännu, Klas-Göran' became Stig's first self-published composition. He borrowed 500 kronor (£35) from a colleague at the school to pay for printing sheet music, initially letting another publishing company take care of distribution. The Sweden Music "offices" were located in the kitchen in the Tullinge town house.

Striking out on his own turned out to be the wisest decision Stig had made thus far. Local cover versions of 'Klas-Göran' became hits in Norway, Denmark, Finland and also earned him a gold record in The Netherlands. The Dutch version was published by a Belgian named Robert Bosmans who suggested that he and Stig should start a company together for the Scandinavian territory. The idea was that they would exchange publishing rights from each other's territories. In time, Bosmans suggested, the company could expand to make publishing deals all over Europe.

Stig was a little overwhelmed at first, but before long he and Bosmans had established a company called Bens Music. Stig set up a system where he acquired the rights to foreign hits and then stayed up nights at his kitchen table, writing the Swedish lyrics himself. He then made sure that the songs were recorded by the right artists. "I saw to it that no middlemen got any pieces of the pie. That way I could earn more money for the composer, for myself as lyricist, and for the foreign publisher. You could say that I applied my own basic business concept: to keep as much as possible under my own umbrella." Thus, a music business empire was founded.

On top of the success with 'Klas-Göran' and an expanding publishing business, Stig still kept his secure day job as a teacher. Urgent business matters occasionally resulted in the kids in his class being given irregular leave. Gudrun watched in silence as Stig wore himself out. Finally, she put her foot down. "I realised that the security didn't make Stig feel especially good. I told him that he should go for music one hundred per cent, quit teaching and spend the days instead of the nights at the kitchen table."

In late 1960, Stig took that final step out of the classroom and into full-time publishing. But with the royalties from successful songs such as 'Klas-Göran' trickling in very slowly, the first few years as music publishers turned out to be very lean for the Andersons. To make ends meet, Gudrun had to start working as a weaving teacher in the evenings. As Stig recalled, it was "a tough time. 1961 was a miserable year."

Sometimes the family didn't even have enough money to buy food, although something usually came up. "I remember one morning when we only had five kronor and didn't know if we should invest them in milk or black-pudding. But would you know: on that very day 150 kronor (£10) arrived in our mailbox as a prize in a crossword puzzle competition."

There was always a huckster side to Stig's personality, and never more so than during this first period when he was desperately trying to make his business work. Throughout his career he had a fondness for hype and bluffs: a necessary quality for most successful businessmen, and certainly in the music industry. But for the people who were at the receiving end of his schemes, the results sometimes left a particularly bitter taste in their mouths.

In the early Sixties, Stig was briefly involved in the career of Sweden's first successful music export, the pioneering instrumental guitar band The Spotnicks, best known for wearing space-suits on stage. The group garnered their first Top 30 hit on the UK charts in 1962, and global record sales since then have reached a total of around 20 million. The Spotnicks' recording career started in 1960, when lead guitarist Bo Winberg made quite professional-sounding recordings on fairly primitive equipment in a plastic factory in Gothenburg. A couple of these demos were released as the band's first single, 'The Old Spinning Wheel'/'Ghost Riders In The Sky', on Karusell Records in March 1961.

In later years Stig tried to claim a bigger role in The Spotnicks' success story than was actually the case. The episode highlighted an interesting duality in Stig's personality: although he couldn't resist trying to bask in the reflected glory, something seemed to stop him from going completely overboard with his claims.

In the authorised biography that was published by Sweden Music in 1983, it is suggested that Stig "travelled all over the world" to help break The Spotnicks on the foreign market. However, his exact involvement in such an extraordinary achievement is never made clear in the book. According to Bo Winberg, it was through Bengt Bernhag that Stig first got in touch with the group and offered to become their manager. The relationship got off on an encouraging note: it was at Stig's suggestion that the group recorded 'Orange Blossom Special' for their second single. It turned out to be their first international hit.

For the third single, Stig shrewdly submitted a Russian folk song, knowing that anyone who makes a new arrangement of a traditional song can claim full copyright as composer. Bo Winberg was no stranger to this practice, and much of The Spotnicks' success was down to his distinctive arrangement of older songs. "Stig sent me a tape with this song on it and I called him up and said, 'What do you want me to do with this? It's just the same melody over and over again'. He told me to just come up with something." Bo wrote a completely new bridge, and arranged the song for the group. But when the record was released under the title 'The Rocket Man', the sole composer credit was 'Trad. Arr. Stig Rossner', one of Stig's pseudonyms. "He didn't arrange or write one single note of that song. But I was young and naïve and didn't understand how the business worked."

All subsequent songwriting royalties for the recording, the accumulated sales of which should be several hundred thousand copies to date, went to Stig and Sweden Music. When the group re-recorded the song for an album in 1997, Bo Winberg changed the title to 'The Rocket Men', with an 'e' in 'Men', and claimed the arrangement credit for himself.

According to Winberg, Stig was at the bottom of a particularly sordid affair which cost The Spotnicks even more money. In 1961, Stig made a deal on the side with Philips Records in Finland for the group to release songs on their label. Since the group had a contract with Karusell Records in Sweden, the Philips singles billed the group as The Feenades to avoid detection. "There won't be any problems," Stig assured them.

Four songs were recorded for Philips, released exclusively in Finland without making many waves. A few years later, when Stig was no longer their manager, Bo Winberg remembered a song called 'Ajomies' from the Feenades sessions. Their new manager called Stig to ask for his permission to record a new version of the song. "By all means," said Stig. The song was re-recorded under the more palatable name 'Karelia'.

The Spotnicks had become very popular in Japan over the previous few years, and were signed to Polydor Records for that territory. In 1965, 'Karelia' was released as a single in Japan and became a huge hit. Around the same time a producer at Philips in Japan happened to hear the Feenades' version. Feeling that the melancholy melody could be a hit in his country, he decided to release the single. But when it was discovered that 'Ajomies' and 'Karelia' were in fact the same song recorded by the same group in virtually identical arrangements, all hell broke loose.

"Philips and Polydor started suing each other and Polydor threatened to sue me, although I had acted in good faith," says Bo Winberg. Stig Anderson and the record companies somehow managed to sort everything out between themselves, but someone had to shoulder the blame. The still fairly inexperienced Bo Winberg was sacrificed by the bigwigs. "'Karelia' ended up selling a million copies, but I got very little out of that recording."

In several interviews over the years, Stig also claimed that he was the one who came up with the name The Spotnicks. Bo Winberg denies it vehemently: "The hell he did. That name was invented by one of the engineers at the studio where they were cutting our first single. He thought our music sounded a bit spacey and got to think of the Sputnik satellite: 'The Spotnicks sounds good!' "

After a year as The Spotnicks' manager, Stig was fired: he had only got them one single gig during that period. Stig shrugged his shoulders and said that he was busy with other things anyway. The Spotnicks' international success came only after they had severed all ties with their former manager.

Stig was still juggling The Spotnicks' career when the breakthrough for Sweden Music as a publishing company finally arrived. In December 1961, he wrote the lyrics for 'Sånt är livet' ('That's Life'), the Swedish version of the Roy Hamilton hit 'You Can Have Her', recorded by singer Anita Lindblom. 'Sånt är livet' became a major success, reaching number one in January 1962 and spending five weeks at the top of the charts. Stig was smart enough to ensure that three of the four songs on the 'Sånt är livet' EP were titles published by Sweden Music. With this success the company was finally able to move to proper offices in central Stockholm.

Stig and Gudrun, who handled the finances, focused all of their energies on building up the business. Their children quickly learned that Sweden Music was a family company in every sense of the word. "We spent a lot of time there on the weekends," recalled their daughter Marie. "We'd come along when the two of them had to work."

The market for popular music in Sweden changed drastically in the early Sixties. The radio had previously been limited to two channels, P1 and P2, with only the occasional outlet for popular music. But in 1961 the pirate radio station Radio Nord became an unprecedented success as it churned out current hits mixed with commercials. As the British would do three years later, the Swedish population quickly developed an affection for maverick radio.

In an attempt to make Radio Nord redundant, Swedish Radio decided to start *Melodiradion* (*Melody Radio*) in May 1961. *Melodiradion* was broadcast for several hours every day, featuring an extensive playlist of current popular music. A year later a third radio channel, P3, opened which was exclusively geared towards light entertainment. Pirate radio was banned, and Radio Nord ceased broadcasting.

For a music businessman like Stig, *Melodiradion* was a dream come true. Not only did he and other music publishers have a much larger outlet for their music, thus increasing accumulated airplay royalty earnings, but sales of music on record were also stimulated, leading to further income from the songs.

Within a year, three major chart shows broadcast on P3 had been launched. *Tio i topp* (*The Top Ten*) was a chart based on votes that started on October 14, 1961. An immensely popular show broadcast on Saturday afternoons, the chart consisted primarily of English-language rock and pop music. Although success on *Tio i topp* didn't necessarily reflect actual record sales, it could help boost both positions in the sales chart as well as general popularity and opportunities for television appearances and gigs on the *folkpark* circuit.

On July 10, 1962, the combined singles and albums Top 20 sales chart *Kvällstoppen* (*The Evening Chart*) was started, airing on Tuesday evenings. The third chart, called *Svensktoppen* (*The Swedish Top Ten*), was introduced on October 13, 1962. The prerequisite for songs entering this chart was that they had to be sung in Swedish (or were instrumental). This was primarily a chart for *schlager/*easy listening acts, which aired on Sunday mornings.

The importance of these shows on the Sixties popular music scene cannot be overestimated. *Tio i topp* and *Svensktoppen*, which both had listening figures of several million, became extremely important for any artist who wanted to make an impact in Swedish show business. They also helped promote the music business and record sales in general.

By 1963, Stig had settled comfortably into his role as a successful publisher. Business was looking good, and his head was full of ideas that he wanted to develop. Among the most important was to start his own record company. Publishing was fine, but to make any real profits from it you had to own the rights to hundreds if not thousands of compositions. In addition, you had to make sure that as many of them as possible were recorded and performed. "I understood then that records were the future," Stig said later. "To work only as a publisher is extremely difficult. There isn't enough money."

And so Bengt Bernhag, with whom Stig had achieved some of his greatest hits over the years, left Karusell Records and, in the summer of 1963, joined Stig in launching a new record company they called Polar Music. They were a perfect match as business partners. Where Stig was brash, impulsive, impetuous and questioning, Bengt was calmly patient but stubborn, with an unrivalled feeling for hits. "It was like Stig and Bengt each had one half of the other guy's heart and brain," Björn Ulvaeus once noted.

The Polar record company founded, Bengt joined Stig and Gudrun at their Sweden Music offices. Now it was only a matter of finding the first act to sign to the new label. Bengt and Stig had a hunch that a folk music group could be worth banking their money on. True to form, they also decided that it would be even better if they could market them with the help of a gimmick. Bengt and Stig decided that connecting their act to the "hootenanny" concept, popularised by American folk singers like Pete Seeger, would conjure up the right connotations.

"Hootenanny was a growing movement in America, and the point was that the performers would be playing and singing for each other, with the audience participating," says Tony Rooth. "Stig and Bengt thought that if it's growing over there, then it will eventually come to Sweden as well." More importantly, at a time when industry wisdom dictated that popular music for young people should be performed in English, this group would be singing in Swedish.

Poring over the entertainment pages in the newspaper *Expressen* one day in September 1963, Bengt's eyes fell on a small news item about a talent contest arranged by Swedish radio. Among the contestants was a group called the West Bay Singers. They were contacted and asked to send a demo tape.

The excited West Bay Singers wasted no time in visiting the Swedish Broadcasting Corporation's Västervik studios to record their demo tape. All that anyone can remember today is that the very first track on the tape was a song called 'Ave Maria No Morro'. "I'm sure it sounded pretty convincing," said Björn. "Our playing and singing were enormously tight by that time." Stig confirmed his and Bengt's reactions on hearing the tape: "I will never forget how happy we were at Polar at the time. They were a find, no doubt about it!"

Bengt had done his part of the deal so far, which in this case meant sniffing out talent buried among newspaper print. It was time for Polar's persuasive and avuncular Managing Director, Stig Anderson, to take over. A phone call would not be enough to catch this potential golden egg, a trip to Västervik was what was needed. Stig saw no reason to waste time and drove down for a long evening meeting with the boys. "He came driving in a sports car, a white Volvo P1800, which really impressed us young students," remembers Hansi Schwarz.

The dynamic publisher and record company president sat with the boys in Björn's room for several hours – and talked and talked. "To be quite honest, my impression of him was that of a car salesman; he was very pushy and incredibly enthusiastic," says Hansi. "He had brought along his scrapbook to show us who he was, the artists he had worked with, that he had written 'Klas-Göran', how many copies it had sold, and so on."

Says Tony Rooth: "He told us all about showbiz: the pros and cons, what our chances were, and that it could all just as easily go to pieces. But he said that they really believed in us." When he'd finished delivering his sales pitch, Stig drove back to Stockholm, awaiting the boys' decision. Björn remembered: "We tried to be fairly sensible about this and said to ourselves, 'We can't just take the first offer we get. Is this a good contract? What if it's a bad deal?'"

The boys knew next to nothing about these things, and the only person they could think of that might give them some advice was a lady who worked in the music store in Västervik. "That shows you that we had absolutely no frame of reference whatsoever," said Björn. "Going to the lady in the music store was the nearest we could get to someone who had some kind of connection to the record business in Stockholm."

This music business oracle put the boys in touch with the more established record company RCA, whose curiosity was piqued when they found out that Polar were interested in the West Bay Singers. "But they offered the same low royalty as Polar and they couldn't even be bothered coming down to Västervik. We decided that Stig seemed more interested and on the go – which he was. The RCA people were unbelievably tired."

The lady in the music store and the man from RCA were less than complimentary about Stig, which made the band suspicious of their motives. It was almost as if they signed with Stig in protest against all the badmouthing. "We also chose him because he was smaller," concludes Tony Rooth. "We reasoned that the major record companies had all these other big acts, but he only had us."

The West Bay Singers never actually signed a record contract with Polar, instead making deals for each album to ensure that their rights would be protected. For the group, it was not an especially lucrative set-up: their royalty was a measly 2.45 per cent. "Stig was very fair in the sense that the contracts said more about our rights than our obligations, but in retrospect I believe we should have had a bigger slice of the pie," says Hansi Schwarz. "What we got wasn't much, but it was a standard deal for the times."

The next step was to mould the group into the hootenanny concept and to give them a Swedish repertoire. Stig and Bengt, who thought that West Bay Singers was "a silly name" anyway, dubbed them the Hootenanny Singers – a somewhat curious moniker that quickly became a millstone around the group's neck. "That was our only major negative reaction against Stig and Bengt," says Hansi Schwarz. "We didn't like that name because we knew what the word hootenanny meant. For us, as folk music fans, it was not in very good taste."

On September 30, the newly christened Hootenanny Singers took part in the first radio broadcast of the talent contest. Performing '500 Miles Away From Home', a traditional American folk ballad, they gave yet another convincing performance. The group were one of two out of six contestants who went on to the semi-finals.

Today Björn has only vague recollections of the other contestants. He certainly doesn't remember the ambitious 17-year-old singer who was entering talent contest after talent contest in the hope of achieving a breakthrough. At the end of the show, when prizes and flowers were distributed among the contestants, she even shared the stage with Björn, fate for one fleeting moment bringing together two teenagers who would one day unite in one of the best loved and most successful groups in the world.

The confident Björn and his friends would exit the stage and go on opening door after door, eventually becoming one of the most popular acts in Sweden. For Anni-Frid Lyngstad, however, the contest meant yet another setback in a life that so far had brought her more than her fair share of hard knocks.

Chapter 3

April 9, 1940 was for many the darkest day in the history of Norway. To a large extent it was the culmination of fatal decisions made a decade earlier, when the likelihood of invasion seemed too remote to contemplate. At that time Norway's relations with foreign powers were good and the risk of war was minimal, so an extensive arms limitation programme was implemented. It was a decision that would have disastrous consequences when the rumble of war advanced across Europe from Germany.

Sweden exported iron ore to Germany from its northern parts, the most convenient route for transportation being through Norway, which made the nation a key territory shortly after the Second World War broke out in September 1939. The Allies therefore became particularly eager to gain control over this part of Scandinavia. Well aware of their enemies' intentions, on April 9, 1940, the Germans instigated *Operation Weserübung*, the invasion of Denmark and Norway, thus securing control over the export passage.

The town of Narvik, a seaport in the northern part of Norway, was subject to a particularly dramatic chain of events during the German invasion. As the most important export harbour for iron ore from the Swedish towns of Kiruna and Gällivare, it was a key target for the Germans. For two months a bitter battle for Narvik and the iron ore raged between the invading German forces and the French, Polish and Norwegian troops on land, and the British Navy at sea.

On April 10, the British Navy managed to fight off the Germans and sink all ten destroyers deployed in the invasion. The battle continued on land and at sea, and on May 28, the Allied forces finally forced the Germans out of Narvik. But less than two weeks later the situation at the Western front suddenly required their immediate attention. With the Allies leaving Norway, the remaining Norwegian forces were unable to resist the German attacks, and on June 9, they capitulated. Norway was to remain occupied until May 1945, the very end of the war.

Two months of horror had virtually obliterated Narvik. As far as the Allies were concerned the iron ore shipping installations had to be destroyed at any cost. The bloody battles also affected the towns and communities along the coast, including Ballangen, some 20 miles south-west of Narvik. It was a small town with a population of less than 4,000, mostly either owners of small farms or employees of the Bjørkåsen Gruver mining company, the principal industry in the area.

In Ballangen's Bjørkåsen district there lived a family called Lyngstad. When war broke out, Arntine Kornelia Marie Lyngstad was a 41-year-old seamstress, her husband Simon a 59-year-old engineer at the power station of Bjørkåsen Gruver. Arntine had given birth to their first child, a daughter they named Aase, in September 1916, when she was just 18 years old. Since then the family had grown to include a son, Bonar, and a further four daughters: Maren, Inger, Olive and Synni. By the early Forties, most of Simon and Arntine's children were starting to raise families of their own. Arntine's youngest daughter, Synni, was born on June 19, 1926, and at the time of the German invasion, she was just two months short of her 14th birthday. Quiet and unassuming, Synni was a pretty girl who was well liked and loved music. It was said that she had a beautiful singing voice.

Its location by the coast meant that picturesque, peaceful Ballangen became drawn into the battle of Norway almost immediately during those anxious days in April 1940. Beneath the tall, snow-covered mountains that stretched down into the Ofot Fjord, two German destroyers were engaged in a battle with the British Navy. Three days later, one of the damaged German ships was sunk just outside Ballangen.

In the months and years that followed, the inhabitants of this quiet little village learned to cope with the dreadful realities of war. The German presence was reluctantly taken for granted, though never for a moment did they hide their contempt for the occupying forces, at least amongst themselves.

Simon Lyngstad, a commanding figure in the Bjørkåsen working-class community, sympathised strongly with the resistance movement. But in the summer of 1940, he fell sick and was diagnosed with cancer. In February 1941, at the age of 60, Simon Lyngstad lost his struggle against the illness that had ravaged his body. His grieving widow, Arntine – or Agny, as she was affectionately called – was left as the family matriarch. She was a proud and occasionally hot-tempered woman who would struggle fiercely to make ends meet after being left with the responsibility for raising her family on her own.

The terrible war continued and Simon had lain in his grave for two years when, in the late autumn of 1943, a 24-year-old German sergeant called Alfred Haase arrived in Ballangen. A handsome man with wavy hair and a well-trimmed moustache, he had been married to his wife Anna for one year. Their first child, a daughter, was born in 1943. Alfred's duties in Ballangen were to train young recruits and to oversee the building of fortifications and defences around the fjord.

To say that the Germans were despised by the local population would probably be an understatement. There was a clear division between the soldiers and the locals. Anyone seen speaking with a member of the occupying forces ran the risk of being branded a traitor. "None of us wanted anything to do with them," recalled one of the women who lived in Ballangen at the time. "To make their lives easier would have been to betray the resistance movement as well as our country."

In the shadow of the great battles and the deliberations of generals, the war begat many parallel developments. Circumstances brought together complete strangers, men and women from different countries, cultures and creeds were forced to find ways to live together in the same towns and streets. Men were separated from their wives, and wives from their husbands. Young men, boys not yet out of their teens, were sent away to war, leaving towns and villages bereft of partners for teenage girls. Stories of romantic liaisons between German soldiers and young women living in the occupied countries are many.

It's not hard to understand how it could happen. Lonely men arriving in a country where they would much rather not be; innocent, impressionable girls charmed by dashing men in uniform. Two souls searching for a tiny glimpse of light in the darkness, some warmth and comfort in the midst of horrifying events. In Norway, tens of thousands of local girls found themselves romantically involved with German soldiers.

By June 1944 Synni Lyngstad was no longer a child, but had grown into a truly beautiful 18-year-old woman. Every day during that summer, she attended to the flower beds and fruit trees in the orchard outside the house where she lived with her mother. The German soldiers passing on the road outside their house couldn't help being taken by her chestnut hair and slim figure.

Alfred Haase was one of many who gazed admiringly at Synni Lyngstad. The first time he laid eyes on her she was carrying a milk pail as she passed him on the road. The lonely Alfred was immediately captivated by Synni, and started dreaming about her at night. "Everybody in our platoon was fantasising about her," he recalled. "We were never able to get this close to any other women."

On their way to training, Alfred's platoon would walk past Synni's house every morning at seven o'clock. When Alfred had time off, he tried to make his way there on his own. He knew it would be difficult to find a way to talk to her, what with the local suspicion of the Germans. The ice was broken when he brought her a gift: a sack containing two kilos of potatoes; not very romantic, perhaps, but food was in short supply and the gift was most welcome.

Gradually, Synni's resistance was worn down. Her head might have told her that it was wrong to get involved with a German soldier, but her heart told a different story. Aside from the unusual circumstances of the occupation, life in Ballangen was fairly uneventful for a teenage girl like Synni. She was taken in, flattered even, by the courting of the handsome Alfred.

"We started going for long walks in the forest together," remembered Alfred. "We talked about what we were going to do after the war, about our dreams for the future, how it would feel to be allowed to visit foreign countries in a time of peace." They were growing closer, and soon the inevitable happened. One day by the water's edge they threw off their clothes and went swimming. Afterwards, they made love for the first time on the beach.

Soon after the consummation of their love affair, Alfred told Synni that he was married. Synni broke down in tears, but eventually she found a way to accept it. "I think she regarded our relationship as I did: the war meant that the conditions were different," Alfred recalled. "For many of us it was a matter of living for today – tomorrow we might be dead."

The romance blossomed in strict secrecy. Only Synni's family knew about it – and they didn't approve. "He will forget you as soon as he's back in Germany," they warned her, but she refused to listen. As the weeks went by, the relationship deepened. Synni would visit the little cabin where Alfred lived, bringing whale-meat for their secret romantic dinners.

The affair came to a sudden end in late October 1944, when Alfred was abruptly transferred to Bogenviken, 30 miles away. The transfer was a strategic move on the part of the German command, its purpose being to avoid exactly what had occurred between Alfred and Synni. The Germans, too, took pains to avoid friendly liaisons of any kind being established between soldiers and the local population.

For Alfred and Synni, this meant that all contact was broken. There was no way they could communicate through letters, and any visits were out of the question. Alfred recalled: "Before that I was on leave regularly, but now it got very hard to get any time off. The situation was becoming critical that autumn."

Germany's fortunes in the war were indeed worsening rapidly, not least in Norway. Their former allies in the Soviet Union had long since become their enemies, and on October 18, 1944, the Russian forces managed to cross the Norwegian border. Further south in Europe the Allies were closing in on Germany itself, and the German armies were needed for more urgent matters than as an occupying force in the northern territories. No one knew for certain what would happen, but by January 1945 it seemed likely that the Germans would not remain in Norway for much longer.

Synni and Alfred had met only occasionally since Alfred left Ballangen in October. At the end of January the troops were told to prepare for transport southwards. "On February 10 or 11 we were transferred to Narvik and told that we would be evacuated to Germany at seven the following morning," remembered Alfred. "I felt that I had to see Synni one more time before I left, so in the evening I borrowed a bicycle in Narvik and left in the dark. Ballangen was some way off and the snow was lying in drifts on the road. But I finally got there late in the evening."

Alfred knocked on the door, quietly so as not to disturb anyone else in the family. For the first and only time Alfred spent the night in Synni's room. "I had to leave at four in the morning if I was to get to the ship on time. It was dark and Synni stood by the gate. That's how I remember her still. She had wrapped herself in a thick woollen shawl. The tears were streaming down her cheeks. That was the last time I saw her."

Alfred promised to return after the war was over. Synni believed him, and the hope of seeing him again somehow kept her heart from breaking. Soon, however, she faced an even greater anguish than the loss of her lover: their lovemaking on that last night together had made her pregnant. For the Lyngstad family, it was a disaster but although Synni knew there would be trouble ahead, she refused to let the worries get to her. "She was so happy that she was going to have a baby," recalled her sister Olive.

There are conflicting versions of the events that followed. Alfred Haase has claimed that he never knew that Synni was pregnant, despite his efforts to get in touch with her. "I wrote to Synni several times after the war, but I never got a reply. Nor were my letters returned. I thought she had forgotten me." Olive, on the other hand, felt that Synni and Alfred must have had some sort of contact – after Synni realised her condition but before Alfred had arrived back in Germany. "He knew that Synni was pregnant and told her not to get an abortion. 'I will return,' he said."

Whatever the circumstances, Alfred and Synni never met again. Several years later the Lyngstad family tried to investigate the matter. Their conclusion was that the ship taking Alfred back to Germany must have been sunk by the Allies outside Denmark. As far as the Lyngstads were able to ascertain, Alfred Haase did not survive the war.

With the Germans surrendering in May 1945, and their troops leaving Norway for good, the situation for 19-year-old Synni became unbearable. Not only had she committed the unforgivable crime of becoming romantically involved with a German soldier, she was also carrying his child. Their passionate romance had turned into a tragedy.

Synni was not alone in her fate. No less than 10,000 children were born as a result of liaisons between Norwegian girls and German soldiers during the war. A girl who had been in a relationship with a German acquired the label "tyskertøs" ("a German's mistress"), her child was called a "tyskerunge" ("a German's child").

The hatred towards anything connected to the occupation was so deep that in 1945, official reports established that the offspring of German soldiers had the potential to grow up to become traitors because of their "nazi genes". Since the identity of her child's father was no secret in Ballangen, Synni was shunned by the community, and as the weeks turned into months and the fruits of her scandalous liaison with Alfred began to show, she was snubbed by the townspeople, insulted and made to feel truly wretched. Somehow, despite it all, she managed to ignore the slights, to carry on as best she could in an atmosphere of escalating malice.

On November 15, 1945, Synni gave birth to a baby girl. The local midwife was ill and her substitute didn't make it to Bjørkåsen in time, so Synni's mother and sisters had to help with the delivery themselves. The child was named Anni-Frid Synni Lyngstad.

Life became no easier for Synni after her child was born. The hatred hitherto reserved for Synni herself was now focused on her "tyskerunge" as well. The shame of a child born out of wedlock, and with a German soldier father to boot, meant that the Lyngstad family was now shunned by everyone. No one would speak to them or associate with them in any way.

Synni, bewildered and brokenhearted, was at a loss. Perhaps the situation would cool off if they just stuck it out? Her mother, intuitively wise to the ways of her neighbours, realised that this was unlikely to happen for a long time.* The best solution would be if the child was taken out of the country, she decided.

After much heart searching, it was agreed that Synni would stay behind to try to make a life of her own in Ballangen. Agny, meanwhile, packed a suitcase with a few belongings and took her granddaughter to Sweden. Her worries were many. Having worked hard all her life, and raised six children of her own, did she really have the strength to start taking care of

---

*Hindsight has proved her right, for most of the 10,000 Norwegian children fathered by German soldiers during the Second World War were stigmatised for several decades. A great number were left with a trauma that was to affect their entire lives. It is only in recent years that the air has been cleared.

a little baby at the age of 48? Would she be able to make ends meet working as a seamstress? And what about the language? Although Swedish and Norwegian sounded similar, the differences were sufficient to make life difficult for a middle-aged woman trying to start over in a new country. But such thoughts came a distant second: little Anni-Frid's safety was foremost in her mind.

Although there are no records to prove it, Agny and Anni-Frid probably arrived in Sweden in the spring of 1947, when Anni-Frid was around 18 months old. It is known that they spent some time in the province of Härjedalen in northern Sweden, close to the Norwegian border. Agny took whatever jobs she could find to make ends meet.

Meanwhile, back in Norway, the devastated Synni struggled on. Heartbroken and depressed at never hearing from Alfred, the mother of a child who was hated by everyone and whom she was unable to hold in her arms, her life was truly miserable. Before long she found that her maternal instincts were too strong: having lost Anni-Frid's father, she just couldn't give up her child as well. The longing overwhelmed her, and Synni decided to join her mother and daughter in Härjedalen.

It wasn't until the Lyngstads moved south in the late summer of 1947 that their presence in Sweden was entered in official records. Even then, it was only Agny and Synni who were registered, with no mention whatsoever of the little girl they had brought with them. It would take another eight months before Anni-Frid's immigrant status became official.

On August 18, 1947, Agny, Synni and Anni-Frid moved into an apartment in a small market town called Malmköping, 45 miles west of Stockholm. Synni found work at a café called Konditori Continental. The future was looking a little brighter: if Agny and Synni tried really hard, it was likely that they could all make a new start and build a new life of their own in Sweden.

But the glimmer of hope that things would work out all right in the end was soon extinguished. The events of the past few years had given Synni's love for life a hard beating and made her very frail. Shortly after starting work at the café, she began to complain of abdominal pains. Her local doctor concluded that there was a problem with her kidneys, but he was unable to give her any treatment that made any real difference. Synni's condition rapidly worsened.

On September 19, 1947, Synni collapsed in pain and fell unconscious. The doctor was called to her house, but there was nothing he could do. The girl needed specialist treatment, he decided, and Synni was rushed to a hospital in the neighbouring town of Flen, seven miles away. She was diagnosed as suffering from kidney failure and was given an immediate blood transfusion.

During her stay at the hospital, Synni's condition improved somewhat but it was a false dawn. In the late Forties it was still some 15 years before dialysis came into wide use in Sweden, and the doctors concluded there wasn't much that could be done. The increasingly weak Synni was coming to the realisation that her life was ebbing away. Lying in her hospital bed she begged her mother to take care of Anni-Frid for her. The devastated Agny promised that she would.

A little over a week after being hospitalised, Synni's condition again became critical. As well as the kidney problems, fluid had collected on her lungs. The doctors struggled desperately to save her life, but it was all too late. Just before noon on Sunday, September 28, 1947, Synni Lyngstad died. She had turned 21 only three months earlier; her daughter was not yet two years old.

Synni's body was brought to Narvik for the funeral and she was deeply mourned by her relatives in Norway. Two weeks after her death, a touching poem by one of her brothers-in-law was published in the local paper as a tribute to the memory of the youngest Lyngstad daughter. The family's pain and regret over the events of the past few years shone through in the last stanza: "We send you thanks from your near ones, for everything you gave them of tears and of smiles. We carry you with us in our thoughts, dear one, now that you have been laid to your final rest."

The funeral over and Synni laid to rest, there was no time for tears or smiles for Agny. The meagre income that she and her daughter had been able to scrape together was just enough to support two grown women and a little girl. Now she was faced with the reality of supporting herself and Anni-Frid as best she could. She took as many menial jobs as possible to make ends meet: sewing, cleaning, dishwashing – anything that came her way.

Agny and Anni-Frid remained in Malmköping until June 1949, at which point they moved to the town of Torshälla, where Anni-Frid would grow up. Torshälla is located just outside Eskilstuna, 45 miles west of Stockholm. Agny found work in the main industry of the town, at a metal refinery called Nyby Bruk. She and her granddaughter lived in the area surrounding the factory.

At the time Torshälla was an idyllic little town of around 5,000 inhabitants. On the west side of a small river that divided the community, the city layout dated from medieval times. This picturesque area was dominated by wooden houses, many of which were built in the 1800s. As in most small towns, life in Torshälla was fairly undramatic – in adulthood Anni-Frid would recall it as plain dull. "It was pretty uneventful," she admitted. "The town was small: you knew everybody who lived there, at least in the neighbourhoods surrounding your own."

Anni-Frid remembered her childhood as very lonely. She always had a great admiration for Agny, whom she came to call "mother", and the way she slaved to make sure her granddaughter had a secure upbringing. However, she also recalled that the age difference created a certain distance between them, that they shared little physical affection, and Anni-Frid never felt she could have a real heart-to-heart talk with her grandmother. "She had to work very hard to earn our living. We were very poor. I was a latch-key child and I really didn't have many friends either. I kept to myself most of the time."

It took many years for Agny to reconcile her concern about Anni-Frid's background and what might happen if they were ever to return to Norway. Anni-Frid's Aunt Olive recalled: "Mother and Anni-Frid came to visit me a while after Synni's death. I could sense a worry, a fear of the surroundings when they were out among strange people. Mother feared the future and wondered if she would be able to give the child the security that she needed."

The social authorities in Sweden were asking the same question. Although Agny had raised Anni-Frid and saw to it that she always had food, clothes and somewhere to live, she was not awarded full custody. Instead, a chief guardian was appointed to ensure Anni-Frid's welfare until she was old enough to take care of herself, a situation that almost certainly exacerbated the paucity of family feelings in the Lyngstad household.

Anni-Frid withdrew even further into herself, playing alone and creating her own world. "I would read a lot. I remember going to the library on Saturdays and borrowing a whole pile of books – it could be around 15 books – and then I just devoured them over the weekend."

Above all, Anni-Frid found comfort in music. She often spent her summers in Norway with her Aunt Olive and her family, who were very fond of singing and playing. "We would sing Norwegian songs together," Anni-Frid recalled. "I think this was where my interest in music started. And I'm sure I inherited my musicality and my voice from my mother."

Aunt Olive confirmed: "She would sing all the time and she was never off-key. The first time I played her a record by Alf Prøysen [a popular Norwegian singer and composer] she said, 'This music is so beautiful. When I grow up I'm always going to be singing and dancing!'" Soon music became the main source of comfort in Anni-Frid's life. At the age of seven she decided that she wanted to become a singer. "I never even considered doing anything else," she recalled.

Anni-Frid started school in August 1952. She applied herself to her studies, and was one of the best pupils in her class. She was a "nice girl", very well mannered and popular with her teacher, a bit unobtrusive. Fairly plain-looking, her hair was kept in a short, practical style that gave few hints of the beauty that would emerge later in life.

In school, Anni-Frid soon became known for her ability to sing well. "She was a clever girl who made everybody happy with her singing," remembered her teacher. "On Saturdays we always had an hour of fun and entertainment. Anni-Frid used to sing, and that was the best entertainment we ever had."

The encouragement of her aunt and schoolteacher were important for Anni-Frid. From an early age the hardships she'd encountered had created in her character a maturity beyond her years and also a certain distance: she knew all too well that there wasn't much love to be had in this world, and you couldn't trust anyone to be around for very long. She also knew that no one was going to give her anything for nothing – she had to arrange that for herself by getting good grades and winning awards. Anni-Frid thus developed into a competitive child who wanted to be the best at everything to which she applied herself.

When she was nine, Anni-Frid was elected Children's Day princess in Torshälla and rode in the procession through town. At the age of 10 she won a skating contest, and three years later she came out on top in the district finals of a slingball competition between local schools. "Later I realised that my grandmother really wanted the best for me, but was too worn out to have the energy to listen to me and my problems when she came home from work. But at that time it was very painful for me, because I felt like I had no one to talk to about my problems and my insecurities. I thought everything about me was wrong: my looks, that I had no talent – there was nothing about me that was worth loving."

Aunt Olive recalled that Anni-Frid was always seeking approval from grown-ups when she visited her family in the summers. "We did our best to make Anni-Frid feel that there were people who liked her, that she had her roots somewhere, that her mother and father had really cared for each other. She was always looking for contact, gentleness and warmth. When my husband came home she stood waiting for him and threw herself around his neck. I had a feeling that Anni-Frid was looking for a father in all the men that she ever encountered."

Although Anni-Frid was a quiet and sometimes lonely child, she didn't spend all her time alone in Torshälla. "I would go climbing mountains and trees and was up to a lot of mischief with the other children in the neighbourhood," she recalled. But at the same time there was an unusual quality about her that the other children could sense somehow. One of her childhood friends reflected: "We wanted her to get ahead in life, because we knew that she was living with her grandmother and had no mother or father. There was something romantic about her, almost like in the books we were reading at the time."

In February 1954, Agny and Anni-Frid moved to a two-room apartment at Thermaeniusgatan in Torshälla. Anni-Frid was eight years old, in her second year of school, and this was where she would live until she left home in the early Sixties. As if life wasn't hard enough for her, Agny took the job of caretaker of the two-storeyed building. "She was an unbelievably strong woman," Anni-Frid later acknowledged. "She would grow potatoes and vegetables, kept everything in perfect order and made all my clothes."

What Anni-Frid lacked in terms of physical affection and intimate conversations was offset by Agny's efforts in making sure that her granddaughter never wanted for the most basic needs in life. And her abilities as a seamstress were never in doubt. "We always thought that Anni-Frid wore such beautiful clothes," remembered her cousin Sølvi. "Anni-Frid looked like she'd stepped out of a fashion magazine. It made an impression on us here in Norway, where everyone was still really poor after the war."

Nevertheless Anni-Frid envied her friends' clothes during her teenage years. While they were scouring the shops for the latest fashions, Anni-Frid had to rely on the sewing-machine at Thermaeniusgatan. "I wanted one of those rib-knitted armless turtle neck sweaters," she recalled. "But buying something like that was out of the question as long as grandmother knew how to sew."

Agny also saw to it that Anni-Frid learned to sew herself and taught her many other useful skills. "A part of me will always be the same girl that lived with my grandmother, when she would drag me up and down the stairs to teach me everything you need to know when you're running a household." Agny was only too well aware of the importance of being self-sufficient.

Music remained Anni-Frid's main interest. Slowly but surely word started to spread that she could sing better than most girls her age. She started singing in the school choir, led by the local cantor. He noticed that Anni-Frid had special vocal talents and would often let her sing solo parts. It filled the young girl with pride.

Although she knew that she was good, her lack of self-belief meant it didn't take much to shake her confidence. "I remember the first time my voice was recorded on tape. I couldn't have been more than nine or ten, and we visited a family who had a tape recorder. I sang one of the current hits. But when I listened to the tape I thought it sounded so awful that I burst into a flood of tears."

Anni-Frid also started playing the piano around this time. Her grandmother could not afford such an expensive musical instrument, so other solutions had to be found. "I went around to the neighbours who owned pianos, knocked on their doors and asked them if they would allow me to play on them. Which they let me do most of the time." When Anni-Frid was 11, Agny rented a piano for her and she started taking formal lessons. She kept this up for a couple of years.

In the autumn of 1956, Anni-Frid started fifth grade. It was around this time, at the age of 11, that she made her stage début at a Red Cross charity event in Torshälla. Anni-Frid performed an a cappella rendition of the Swedish traditional song 'Fjorton år tror jag visst att jag var' ('I Was Fourteen Years Old, I Believe'). The song had recently been a hit for singer Ingeborg Nyberg, her idol at the time. "I was dressed in a Norwegian national costume that my aunt had made for me. I remember being terribly nervous."

Singing in front of a real audience for the first time was an encouraging experience for Anni-Frid. Her appetite for public appearances was whetted, and she started entering as many talent contests as she could in Torshälla and Eskilstuna – she found that she usually won them as well. Sometimes she would be out dancing with other kids her age, and occasionally she plucked up the courage to ask the band if they would let her sing with them. "I had a lot of determination. That was the only way I would be able to do what I really wanted to do. No one would have asked me if I hadn't shown an interest in it myself."

In June 1958, Anni-Frid graduated from elementary school in Torshälla with very good grades. After the summer holidays she started junior secondary school in Eskilstuna, joining the business education programme. She was almost 13 years old and had acquired the nickname Frida. This is the name by which friends and acquaintances have known her ever since, and in time it also became the name she used as an artist.

One Sunday afternoon in the autumn of 1958 Frida was at a dance at the Slagsta youth centre. The centre was located in a house on the road between Torshälla and Eskilstuna, and was formerly the childhood home of politician, ambassador and Nobel Peace Prize winner Alva Myrdal. Now converted into a meeting place for young people, the dining hall of this large house was the perfect size for dances.

A local orchestra called The Evald Ek Quintet, led by the 21-year-old hairdresser Evald Ek, used the house for rehearsals. "We didn't have any other place to rehearse, so we made a deal with the local authorities who owned the youth centre," he recalls. "In exchange for letting us rehearse there we agreed to play dance music for the youths for a couple of hours every Sunday afternoon."

On this particular Sunday, Frida approached Evald and asked if he would let her sing a couple of songs. "I said, 'Of course, but we're going to have a break now. Let's go upstairs and rehearse for a bit.' She told me what songs she would like to sing, and we decided on the right key. Then we went down again and she sang a few songs, and it sounded great. It's hard to believe that a young person like that can be such a good singer. I certainly couldn't believe that."

Evald Ek's band had been going since the mid-Fifties, and featured a fairly typical set-up for a medium-sized dance band of the day: accordion (played by the band-leader), vibraphone, clarinet or saxophone, bass and drums. Instrumentalists as well as vocalists had been coming and going at a fairly rapid pace over the years. When Frida approached the band they had no vocalist and Evald was anxious to hire one. In this young and eager girl he saw the perfect candidate. "I told her, 'We have a rehearsal booked for next Thursday. See to it that you are here then.' Which she was, and then she joined the band."

Frida was barely 13 years old when she started singing with Evald Ek. Legally, this meant she was not allowed to work, and Evald had to approach her chief guardian for special permission. Frida was soon a full-time member of the band, helping out with carrying heavy instruments and equipment to and from the Volkswagen bus they used for driving to engagements. "She didn't mind, she just thought everything was so much fun," recalls Evald.

The band would have up to three engagements a week, working between eight in the evening and one in the morning. For Frida, it was a dream come true: now she was a real singer with a real band. A new world of music opened up for her. Whereas her repertoire up to that point had consisted of folk songs and *schlagers* – the Swedish version of the 1956 Doris Day hit 'Whatever Will Be, Will Be (Que Sera, Sera)' was one of her favourites at the time – she now became acquainted with evergreens like 'All Of Me', as well as Cole Porter's 'Night And Day' and 'Begin The Beguine'.

"Frida wasn't at all familiar with the evergreens when she came to us, but 'Night And Day' was one of her real stand-out numbers during her time with my band," says Evald Ek. "She was so incredibly easy to rehearse with. She would hear a song for the very first time, study the lyrics and then she knew it. And she was never shy on stage or anything like that. The only thing I really taught her was to sing up. She had a tendency to hold back a little."

The band's repertoire consisted mainly of the old standards, *schlagers* of the day, tangos and slow waltzes. The dance band scene in the Eskilstuna area was thriving at the time. Although there were several bands competing for jobs – both big bands and smaller ensembles like Evald Ek's – there were lots of opportunities. Television, which wasn't officially launched in Sweden until 1956, hadn't really broken through on a large scale. At weekends, going out dancing was still the most popular form of entertainment for people of all ages.

The local papers would feature advertisements for "dance buses". Customers paid a few kronor and got on the bus which then took them to different dance halls in and around Eskilstuna. Sometimes the venues would be so crowded that the dance buses had to be turned away. "I remember one New Year's Eve when Frida was with us," says Evald Ek. "The place was so full of people that they couldn't move around enough to dance – we had to turn it into a concert instead."

Because the bands in Stockholm were more interested in playing Dixieland jazz, there was also a shortage of dance bands in the capital. That meant opportunities for even fairly modest ensembles like Evald Ek's, who'd be playing at fancy places like the Grand Hotel in Stockholm.

Up to this point Frida had always felt that music was a source of comfort for her, something to hold on to when life seemed tainted by insecurity and unfairness. Now, through being a member of a band, she also realised that music could serve as the basis for a new social environment. For the first time she got an inkling of what it could feel like to belong to a "family" with a true sense of community. It was a life-defining moment for her. "I turned away from my family, away from my entire life that more than anything felt like an enormous emptiness," she said. "As music came into my life my social relations changed completely, as did in fact my whole existence. I grew strong and dared to do things I had found insurmountable before."

Frida wanted to take every chance to move forward musically, to develop as a singer. Through her connection with Evald Ek, the teenage Frida got in touch with opera singer Folke Andersson. Something of a local celebrity after a career that had brought him national fame in the Thirties, Andersson would give Frida singing lessons for a couple of years.

Meanwhile, after a year in junior secondary school, Frida's motivation for studies had dropped dramatically. The money from the dance band work enabled her to finance her education, but it was clear that music had become her number one priority; everything else was simply a distraction. Her grandmother watched with puzzlement and concern as Frida's grades plummeted. "She wanted me to study and 'make something of myself', as she put it. I know that a lot of people thought I was really strange when I had no interest in studies. But I was able to disregard all that, for I knew what I wanted to do. Music was everything. It was sink or swim."

Agny remained quietly disapproving of Frida's devotion to the band. During the time with Evald Ek's, Agny never once came to watch her granddaughter perform. Nor were the band members ever invited to the Lyngstad home. "I only ever went in and said hi when I came to pick up Frida for that night's work," recalls Evald Ek.

Frida's background had made her an unusually independent child, and as a teenager she continued to seek out her own path. While other kids her age were being swept away by rock'n'roll and the emerging folk music scene, Frida was busy turning into a *chanteuse*, a traditional vocalist performing jazz standards that were usually delivered by singers at least twice her age.

In her teens Frida had become quite a beauty but she didn't have much time for boys. Although one or two might have taken her fancy, it seldom got beyond the flirting stage. Evald Ek recalls: "Sometimes when we were out working she would ask me if it was okay to go off stage for a while and dance, because it happened that boys came up and asked her to dance. 'Of course,' I said. But it was the actual dancing she was after, not the contact with the boys."

In June 1961 a couple of members in Evald Ek's band graduated from high school and left town to go on studying elsewhere. Evald, who was starting to feel that the band had run its course anyway, decided to call it a day. "There was too much travelling and I didn't feel up to rehearsing new members. I told them all, 'I've had enough, you will have to find another band.' That's what I said to Frida as well." Evald stowed his accordion in the closet and hasn't touched it since.

Frida was left without a regular band for a couple of months, but continued to do a few numbers here and there with other ensembles. In the autumn of 1961 she got an offer from Bengt Sandlund's big band, a local orchestra that had become quite popular over the past few years. One of the trombone players, a young man called Ragnar Fredriksson, was an admirer of Frida as a vocalist and recommended her to Bengt Sandlund. "The band had been going since the summer of 1959," says Sandlund's pianist Gunnar Sandevärn, a close friend of Frida's at the time. "Before that I had been playing for a year or so with Ragnar Fredriksson in his band, but the members of that ensemble were sort of incorporated into the big band. Bengt Sandlund's had previously had two different female vocalists, but they had both left, and now we were looking for a male and a female vocalist."

Frida got the job together with singer Lars Blomquist. Bengt Sandlund was a very energetic band-leader who saw to it that his orchestra got plenty of bookings all over the country. Sometimes he put together package deals where the band would provide dance music as well as put on regular shows. A curious mixture of cabaret and sideshow, this kind of entertainment was very popular in its day, as Sandevärn recalls. "If we were working in a *folkpark*, we would begin by playing dance music. Then, we would move to the stage and do our show. For instance, we had a trumpet player who would perform virtuoso musical pieces. His performance was followed by a couple of songs by the vocalists. Then we had a gymnastics troupe called the Tunafors girls who put on their show with the band providing musical back-up."

Frida started singing with Bengt Sandlund's big band on October 7, 1961. Becoming a part of this new musical family further broadened her musical spectrum, with jazz vocalists such as Ella Fitzgerald, Anita O'Day and Sarah Vaughan becoming her role models. She started listening to big bands like Glenn Miller, Count Basie, Duke Ellington and Woody Herman, from which much of Bengt Sandlund's repertoire was drawn. "It was a kick for me to get into songs like that," she said. "It was a completely new musical experience." Frida's repertoire in the band included songs such as 'Sweet Georgia Brown', 'Summertime' and 'Fly Me To The Moon'. With Lars Blomquist she would duet on numbers like Gershwin's 'Let's Call The Whole Thing Off'. Swedish and European *schlagers* of the day completed the mix.

Joining Bengt Sandlund's had a profound effect on Frida's life in ways outside of music. The trombonist who discovered her, 19-year-old Ragnar Fredriksson, was not only impressed by her singing. He couldn't help noticing that the voice that caught his attention belonged to a very attractive girl. Gunnar Sandevärn recalls: "Bengt Sandlund would rent a big bus, which we used for travelling to our various engagements. And there we were, crammed together in the bus: the 16 musicians in the band, two singers, plus the Tunafors girls. It's kind of obvious that people would take a fancy to each other here and there. It didn't take long before Frida and Ragnar found each other."

Ragnar was a somewhat plump young man with thick-rimmed glasses and a shy smile. When he was not playing with the band, he worked as a rug and carpet dealer in his parents' shop in central Eskilstuna. Four years Frida's senior, the quietly intelligent Ragnar became her first serious boyfriend, offering a kind of stability that balanced Frida's own restless personality, and therefore something of a father figure. "I think it was security I was looking for, above all," Frida later reflected. "My childhood wasn't especially secure, it lacked gentleness and love. When I met a man, it felt like I had found everything I was looking for. I built my whole life around him." She was now not only the vocalist in a popular big band but also the devoted girlfriend of a genuinely nice boy. Her low self-esteem was counterbalanced by the love and affection that came from Ragnar. For the first time since she was born life for Anni-Frid Lyngstad was looking pretty good.

Then, in the spring of 1962, around the time of her graduation from junior secondary school, something unexpected happened. Frida discovered she was pregnant. This wasn't at all what she had planned. She was still only a teenager and while she appreciated the stability Ragnar offered, her career as a singer remained her main priority in life. Now she was following in the footsteps of her mother and grandmother before her by becoming a teenage mother herself. It was a spanner in the works for her personal development, but she and Ragnar had no choice but to face up to the situation.

Frida's pregnancy meant that she had to leave Bengt Sandlund's band temporarily. But she was determined to go on singing, even if she couldn't handle any long coach journeys or weekend engagements. "She wasn't afraid to go onstage," confirms Gunnar Sandevärn. "I remember that we did a couple of local shows during that period, just me playing the piano and her singing."

On January 26, 1963, the 17-year-old Frida gave birth to a son she and Ragnar named Hans Ragnar. Despite the difficult circumstances, Hans was a welcome child and Frida did her best to adjust to life as a young mother. Nevertheless, it wasn't long before she was performing with Sandlund's again even though she was still living with her grandmother, who would act as babysitter.

During Frida's relatively short time away from the band the dance music scene had changed drastically. Over the past few years, rock and "twist" music had gradually taken over as the preferred dance music for young people. The Beatles' breakthrough in Sweden with 'Please Please Me' was just around the corner – Eskilstuna was one of the towns the group visited during their five-date tour of Sweden in October 1963. New pop bands were springing up all over the country. Some of the local, old-style dance bands even mutated into pop groups.

Bengt Sandlund was finding it increasingly difficult to get bookings for a fairly expensive big band like his. In the spring of 1963, he decided it was time to close down the orchestra. The band had its last engagement in April of that year.

Nevertheless, Frida refused to give up singing and become a full-time housewife. Ragnar had his job in the carpet store, but in terms of a career Frida had nothing beyond her ambition to make it as a singer. She kept the dream alive by performing in whatever circumstances she could, and entering as many talent contests as possible.

In the summer of 1963 Frida took part in a high-profile national talent contest, reaching the finals which were conveniently held in Eskilstuna that year. Performing the jazz standard 'Moonlight In Vermont', she won the approval of the local press, but disappointingly wasn't even placed among the top three contestants.

Although Frida and Ragnar remained unmarried, in August 1963 she and Hans finally moved into the apartment above the carpet store. Tied down by her life as a housewife and mother, and with her career development slowing down considerably, she felt like she was treading water.

In September, Frida learned about the Swedish radio talent contest called *Plats på scen* (*On Stage*). She went to Norrköping for the tryouts and, along with the West Bay Singers led by Björn Ulvaeus, was among the six acts selected to take part in the district finals.

A few weeks later, an excited Frida travelled to Stockholm to appear in the radio broadcast. A contest on national radio could turn out to be her first major break. It must have been a disappointing moment when she failed to progress to the next stage. There she was: standing on stage yet again, getting the same old "encouraging" bouquet of flowers, with the host patronisingly calling her "little Miss Lyngstad".

It was back to Eskilstuna again, back to Ragnar and Hans and her increasingly dull life as a young housewife. Ragnar was talking about starting a big band of his own, but nothing much came of these plans. She wasn't even 18 yet, and although she kept up a brave front, Frida felt she was caught in a trap.

While Frida languished in small-town obscurity, one of the two winners in this part of the contest, the four boys who now called themselves the Hootenanny Singers, were about to go from strength to strength.

Chapter 4

In October 1963, Stig Anderson and Bengt Bernhag had reason to feel satisfied with themselves. Their hunch about the Hootenanny Singers had proved right. The group had secured a place in the televised semi-finals of the *Plats på scen* talent contest, scheduled for broadcast in only a few weeks time. Swedish radio had already decided that there would be no actual winner, so the chance of coming out on top was not important. From Stig and Bengt's perspective it was the continued exposure to a national audience that mattered most.

It was time for stage two: deciding upon a suitable song for the group to record and perform. It would also be the release that launched the Polar record label, which made the choice even more crucial. Anderson and Bernhag knew that they needed to find a Swedish folk style song that would lend itself to gentle modernisation, in line with The Kingston Trio feel that was the Hootenanny Singers' trademark. "Bengt said to us, 'You have the music and the way to perform it, but you need the right song,'" remembers Hansi Schwarz. The choice ultimately fell upon 'Jag väntar vid min mila' ('I'm Waiting At The Stack'). Originally a poem by famous Swedish poet Dan Andersson, it had been set to music by composer Gunnar Turesson in the early Forties.

The group was invited to Stockholm and the Metronome recording studio. Under the auspices of Bernhag all four tracks for the first Hootenanny Singers single and EP were recorded in a few hours. "Those first recording sessions were just us four gathered around a microphone hanging down from the ceiling or put on a stand," recalls Tony Rooth.

Apart from 'Ave Maria No Morro', which had been included on the band's demo tape, the other tracks on the EP were Swedish songs selected by Bengt and Stig. At first, the group was reluctant to record in Swedish. They pictured themselves as the Swedish Kingston Trio, and had a strong preference for American folk songs, "They told us, 'You're going to sing in Swedish and you're going to sing 'Jag väntar vid min mila',"" recalled Björn. "'No, that's impossible,' we said. 'A corny thing like that!' But in the end we recorded it and it turned out really well." The resistance towards the Swedish material didn't last much longer than the end of this first recording session.

'Jag väntar vid min mila' was an excellent début record. The folk group sound – complete with a catchy acoustic guitar intro – coupled with a reassuringly familiar Swedish song, made for a winning combination. In the semi-finals of the talent contest, the Hootenanny Singers turned in a convincing performance and once again secured a place in the next stage.

The pre-taped semi-finals were broadcast on the same day as the Folkpark Forum in Malmö. This was where relatively unknown artists could perform in front of *folkpark* managers seeking artists for the following season. Stig Anderson had seen the opportunity for exposure, recognising the value of securing bookings on the lucrative park circuit. Hansi Schwarz remembers the excitement when the group managed to find a small TV with an antenna on the top and went outside the forum to watch their television début. The Hootenanny Singers ended up being one of the biggest attractions of the summer of 1964.

In January, a few weeks after the finals of the talent contest, the Hootenanny Singers garnered a Top Ten hit with 'Jag väntar vid min mila'. Although there was no official champion, there was little doubt who the true winners were in terms of career development.

The following month saw the release of the group's first album, titled simply *Hootenanny Singers*. It was a compromise between Stig's and Bengt's insistence that they should sing in Swedish, and the group's own love of American folk songs. The first side was all in their native tongue, ranging from translations of American folk songs to Swedish folk-style songs, while the second side was in English and Spanish (with one Swedish exception). Covering all bases on the business side, Stig and Bengt made sure that a considerable number of the songs were traditional or well past their copyright date, meaning that they would not have to pay a royalty to composers. They were more honourable in their dealings with the Hootenanny Singers than Stig had been to The Spotnicks, however, and many of the arrangements were credited to the group members.

Two of the songs on the album even featured a sole arranger's credit for the 18-year-old Björn, again putting the finger on his musical talent and ambition. "Björn had the best feeling for arrangements, that was obvious from the moment he joined the group," confirms Hansi Schwarz. "We were better for having him with us, no doubt about it."

Stig and Bengt had struck gold with Polar's very first single, EP and album releases, all of which were Hootenanny Singers titles. As they had predicted, with rock music sung in English becoming the dominant form of expression for young Swedish artists, there was a hole in the market for well-mannered youths singing a fairly modern kind of popular music in their native tongue.

But something inside Björn started nagging away even before the group had released their first record. On the same day that the Hootenanny Singers were making their début performance on Swedish television screens in late October 1963, The Beatles visited Sweden for the first time. It was their very first trip outside Great Britain after they achieved their breakthrough there. Beatlemania was on the boil, both in Britain and Sweden.

The Hootenanny Singers were already familiar with The Beatles, but opinions on their merits were divided within the group, as Hansi Schwarz recalls. "We heard The Beatles on our European trip in the summer of 1963, and Björn said, 'This is so great! I can't believe how good this is.' I didn't appreciate them at the time, I thought they were too noisy. Later on I also realised how good they were, but he liked them even back then."

When the full impact of The Beatles and all things British was felt on the Swedish music scene, Björn quickly realised that he would have preferred doing pop music instead of folk music. It was an embarrassment when reviewers started comparing the "loud, noisy and untalented" Beatles with the "nice and well-mannered" Hootenanny Singers. "I really hated that," he said. "I was held up as 'every mother-in-law's dream boy'. It was just awful."

To add insult to injury, contrary to Stig and Bengt's predictions, hootenanny turned out to be a particularly short-lived musical movement in America, and never took off at all in Sweden. In the first few months after their breakthrough, the Hootenanny Singers attempted to get the inhibited Swedish audiences to participate and sing along, hootenanny style, but with fairly miserable results.

The name change that had been so important lingered on as a somewhat inappropriate and embarrassing label with which to be lumbered. Björn laughed about it many years later: "The Hootenanny Singers is the worst name that any band has ever had. It's just so ugly – possibly only beaten by Abba." But he was still a teenager, and with everything else going really well he didn't complain but simply soldiered on.

After their definitive breakthrough in early 1964, the Hootenanny Singers quickly became one of the most successful groups in Sweden. The whole spring was lined up with concerts and appearances in radio and television. The summer saw them making their feature film début in a comedy called *Älskling på vift (Darling On The Loose)*, as well as embarking on a 150-date *folkpark* tour. Over the next few years the Hootenanny Singers would go on to notch up several big hits, placing them among the absolute cream of popular bands in Sixties Sweden.

Their success was a testament to the boys' talent and professionalism, but also to Stig Anderson's grand vision for his group and his own burgeoning music business empire. And his ambitions didn't stop at the Swedish borders either. Never one to apologise for being from a small country like Sweden, which in those days was considered fairly insignificant in international music business terms, he saw no reason why he should not be able to sell the Hootenanny Singers to other countries as well.

Over the past few years, Stig had built up a vast network of publishing and record company contacts in Europe and America, and he was determined to make the most use of them. He wasted no time in having 'Jag väntar vid min mila' released in Norway, Denmark and Finland. In the spring of 1964 the group's version of 'This Little Light Of Mine' was released in Belgium, The Netherlands and Luxembourg, while EPs of other songs from the group's first album were issued in Spain and France. None of these releases made many waves, however.

In the summer of 1964, the Hootenanny Singers recorded 'Gabrielle', a Swedish version of a Russian song written by one Arkady Ostrovsky. At the time, the Soviet Union had no deal for performance rights with the western world, which meant that the song was in the public domain. This fact again made it a favourable choice in the eyes of Bengt and Stig, who claimed credits for arrangement and Swedish lyrics.

'Gabrielle' became a big hit for the Hootenanny Singers during the autumn, reaching number five on the Swedish sales charts. Stig felt that this could be the song to really break the group abroad. In the course of late 1964 and the early part of the following year, the song was re-recorded in Finnish, German, Dutch, English and Italian. Polar even took out an ad in the American music trade paper *Cash Box*, boasting about the accomplishments of "The Hooten Singers", the somewhat ludicrous name they initially had to live with in North America.

Stig pulled every string at his disposal to make things happen. Through a connection with teen idol Paul Anka's father, Andrew Anka, who was appointed the group's American manager, he even secured the promise of an appearance on the coast-to-coast NBC television show *Hullabaloo*.

The group was to appear in a segment where Beatles manager Brian Epstein introduced acts from all over the world to American audiences. It would have been an excellent opportunity to ride on the coat-tails of a successful wave of acts that were currently crossing the Atlantic. Unfortunately, the featured artists were ultimately restricted to British acts, and the Hootenanny Singers were dropped from the *Hullabaloo* roster.

Despite regular television appearances in European countries such as West Germany, the Hootenanny Singers never had much success outside the Nordic countries. "The songs simply weren't good enough," Björn observed. "And the whole thing wasn't at all as focused as when we did it with Abba. We didn't have the same force behind it or the same self-confidence. We weren't even close to that. Deep inside we didn't believe at all that this was going to result in any major international career."

It's hard to fault Björn's line of reasoning, for many strange decisions were made on behalf of the group's international ventures. In 1967, an album entitled *Gabrielle* was released in the United States. Although the Hootenanny Singers had recorded enough English-language songs to fill the better part of an LP, the album didn't contain one single such track. American record buyers, assuming they were aware of it at all, were probably much bemused by an LP of music performed in the exotic Swedish language. Unsurprisingly, the *Gabrielle* album flopped completely.

For the group, the attempts to crack markets outside Scandinavia were more of an enjoyable adventure than anything else, and they paid little if any attention to the business aspects. "It was great to get out in the world and make records all over the place," says Hansi Schwarz. "At one point we did a live television broadcast together with The Everly Brothers in Italy, which I thought was just fabulous. I'm sure Björn felt the same way, because they were our heroes."

Perhaps the greatest significance in these optimistic overtures to achieve success abroad was Stig Anderson's growing belief that it actually could be done. There can be no doubt he gained much valuable experience from his attempts to break the Hootenanny Singers internationally and that the lessons he learned would come in handy a decade later. "The international break that he later achieved with Abba was a dream he had long before they came along," says Hansi Schwarz. "He felt we were the group that could do that for him, but I guess it was too early: he didn't know the European market well enough at the time."

November 1964 saw the release of the second Hootenanny Singers album – somewhat confusingly, it was eponymous just like the band's début. Only a year after signing the recording contract, the last traces of English-language folk music had been virtually erased. Every track on the album was performed in Swedish, and even the two token American folk music songs, 'Banks Of The Ohio' and 'All My Trials', had been translated. The Hootenanny Singers had now become a completely safe, easily accessible Swedish alternative to the rowdy pop acts singing in English.

Parallel with the group's growing popularity, the Swedish pop band wave exploded. In March 1965 a group called The Hep Stars achieved their breakthrough with 'Cadillac'. They went on to become the biggest band of the Sixties. Two of their major rivals on the pop scene, Tages and Shanes, had already had their first major hits at the end of 1964, and the third main contender, Ola & The Janglers, hit the charts soon after The Hep Stars.

Björn noted with interest what was going on and started buying fashionable clothes, as well as adopting a Mod-style haircut. His inclination to do pop music was growing stronger by the day. While perusing The Beatles' album sleeves and the labels on their singles he noted that John Lennon and Paul McCartney wrote their own songs. It was an inspirational realisation. "If they can write their own songs, then why can't we in our group try to do that as well?" he thought.

Tony Rooth remembers: "Björn called me up one day and said, 'Come on over and we'll try to write a song together!' We sat in his room and he was playing his guitar, but I didn't have much to contribute. I wasn't interested, I didn't believe it would amount to anything."

This was the crucial difference between Björn and his fellow band members: whereas they considered the Hootenanny Singers to be an adventure that would last a year or two before they went on to studies and regular careers, young Mr Ulvaeus envisaged a different turn of events. His secret ambition was to make a career in music.

With no help from his friends in the group, Björn decided to persevere as a songwriter on his own. Stig and Bengt certainly didn't try to stop him. They realised it was better to cover all bases with the folk music and *schlager* audience as well as the pop fans. And it could be an advantage if they were going to break the group abroad if they had English-language pop material to sell.

Meanwhile, on April 30, 1965, the Hootenanny Singers started their second summer tour of the *folkparks*, encompassing a staggering 165 concerts. The sheer number of gigs would have been enough to humble the most seasoned of artists. The often less than favourable circumstances surrounding the performances added further pressure on the group.

"Sometimes we wondered what kind of place we had come to," says Tony Rooth. "Many parks were really nice: they had proper dressing rooms and they'd offer us coffee and sandwiches when we got there. But other times we'd arrive in the middle of some forest where the stage was a lorry platform. We'd say, 'Where are we supposed to change into our stage costumes?' 'Oh, so you need to change?' Then we'd have to run as far away as we could into the forest, where no one would see us, and put on our costumes."

Even when the Hootenanny Singers had two or three gigs in one night the venues weren't necessarily very close to each other. Quite frequently, the group was booked so that it was virtually impossible to keep up with the schedule. "You can't be on stage at the second place at the same time as you're finishing at the first place," as Tony puts it.

The standard tour contracts contained a most unreasonable clause whereby if the group arrived 10 minutes late there would be a 10 per cent reduction on the fee, 20 minutes led to a 20 per cent reduction, and so on. If the delay was as much as an hour, the arranger could refuse to pay the fee altogether and even make a claim for damages. At times, the stress could become unbearable. "But there was almost never any arranger who evoked the reduction clause, it was just to make us drive as quickly as possible," said Tony. "We'd calculate: 'Will it be worth it if we get fined for speeding?' I can only recall one time when an arranger wanted to withhold our fee. The only reason we hadn't been able to start on time was because there were people queuing outside who hadn't got in yet. I remember how raving mad we were. I'm not even sure we ever got the money that was due to us."

Their conventional image might have affected the Hootenanny Singers' credibility as pop was dragged into the new age by The Beatles and their ilk, but this didn't stop them taking advantage of their status as young, cute pop stars. The boys were idols at their sexual peak, and the temptation to enjoy the girls who made themselves available during their tours was irresistible. "We took girls back to our hotels, of course we did," says Tony Rooth. "Personally, I had got engaged to my future wife, Christina, in 1963 and I wasn't that interested. Johan also had a girlfriend, so he took it easy. It was mostly Björn and Hansi who were quite eager. But all that had to be taken care of very discreetly."

Hansi acknowledges: "We had to party and have some fun to be able to go on working as hard as we did. But enjoying female company in hotel rooms was something everybody did." Sometimes the boys would be invited to private parties by girls, and Tony recalls ending up sitting close to some girl while Björn and Hansi were off with lady friends elsewhere. The situation could become fairly complicated for a boy who wanted to be faithful to his fiancée. "I would say, 'I already have a girl at home. Let's just sit here and talk until the others come out again.' And that's what we would do."

The parties may have been wild and loud, but for the most part they didn't really do much harm to anyone. Hansi Schwarz recalls the worst Hootenanny Singers tour incident: "We were at this Shell motel and some of the guys had bought air rifles. They were target shooting in the middle of the night and there was a lot of shattered glass and stuff. The motel manager was furious. He called Stig and said that we would be banned from every Shell motel in Sweden. But that was as bad as it got."

After the park tour, the group started work on their fourth album in September 1965. *International* had one side with recordings in Swedish, and one with songs in English, German, Italian and Spanish. It was also the first Hootenanny Singers LP to contain pop songs written by Björn. Those first attempts, 'No Time' and 'Time To Move Along', featured words by one-off collaborator Martin Dean. Appropriately for a group with roots in folk music, the songs were clearly adhering to the emerging folk rock genre.

In the hope of achieving an authentic British pop sound, the two songs had been recorded in London under the auspices of United Artists producer Martin Davis. As a song, 'No Time' was a reflection on how people devote their every waking hour to "making a dime". It aligned itself with the current light-protest, "what's to become of this world?" sentiments put forward in songs like Barry McGuire's 'Eve Of Destruction', a major hit during this period.

Considering they were Björn's début compositions, or at least the first to be made public, both 'No Time' and 'Time To Move Along' were more than credible attempts at folk rock. But there is no denying both songs were highly derivative, especially 'No Time', where Björn's lead vocal was heavily coloured by a Dylanesque nasal snarl. Some of his fellow band-members were less than impressed. "I've realised since that it wasn't so bad, but I didn't think it was particularly good at the time," says Tony Rooth.

Released as a single in the spring of 1966, 'No Time' became a Top 20 hit in Sweden, also featuring on the *Tio i topp* radio chart. It was released on the United Artists label in the UK and the US, where the group was now billed as The Northern Lights. The single was nowhere to be seen on the charts in those territories but made a surprising entry on the charts in South Africa. All in all, it was an encouraging sign for Björn that he had a talent for writing songs and that the group might have a future in pursuing a pop career.

The new pop leanings of the group were evident not only in some of the tracks on the *International* album but also on the cover, which featured the group – especially Björn – looking more like a moody, non-smiling pop band than a well-mannered, studenty folk music group. The liner notes even made a point of stressing that the band owned all the records released by The Beatles, and that "Hootenanny music is no longer their inspiration."

But the album also contained songs like 'Björkens visa' ('Song Of The

Birch'), yet another updated version of an old Swedish song. The recording kept the Hootenanny Singers firmly within the realm of "nice Swedish boys". 'No Time' may have gained some popularity, but 'Björkens visa' went on to become one of the group's biggest hits ever. Their attempts to keep one foot in Swedish folk music and the other in pop made for an uneasy career path over the next couple of years. Björn, who was emerging as the most popular member of the group, also remained most eager to keep up with the current fashions and attitudes.

He was thriving in his role as a teen idol and although he may have been painstaking in his work on musical arrangements for the group, he was quite carefree in other respects, far removed from his polite, rather studious image. "Back then, Björn was a bohemian and quite careless: difficult in many ways," recalled Stig Anderson. "He couldn't keep track of anything, least of all himself."

Just before starting their third *folkpark* tour in April 1966, the Hootenanny Singers began recording their fifth album. The title *Många ansikten/Many Faces* stressed the group's policy of recording one side in Swedish and the other in English. In terms of production values and quality pop songs, the group reached a definite peak on this album. It was clear that they had spent more time than ever in the recording studio.

Bengt Bernhag made an invaluable contribution as producer, proving that he had a good ear for modern sounds. He also made use of a trick he had picked up from the house producer at Philips in the Fifties. "Bengt taught us not to just listen to the big speakers in the studio, but to plug in a smaller speaker," says Tony Rooth. "He said, 'This is what it's going to sound like when people hear it on the radio.'" Bengt immersed himself completely in the recording process, seemingly never resting for one single moment. "He would often emerge from the toilet, having heard the song played through the door: 'Now I know what it really sounds like, you hear it best in the toilet!' Then he'd know exactly what changes we had to make."

The group listened and learned, not least Björn who was developing a keen interest in everything connected to the music business. The organiser/arranger side of him found that he really enjoyed spending time in the recording studio, slowly emerging as Bengt's unofficial co-producer. "He was my mentor, and very much so," Björn recalled. "He never said anything, but I'm sure I drove him crazy by calling him all the time, asking him which songs we should record, which television shows to appear in – everything. He was the one I was talking to, not Stig."

Hansi Schwarz makes a similar observation: "It was Bengt who really took care of us when we were recording in Stockholm. Stig was mainly the businessman. Bengt was a very warm and kind-hearted person who was like a fifth member, the person who knew how to achieve what we were aiming for. And if the group members were fighting about something in the studio, he was the one who would sort everything out between us."

Despite the fact that Bengt was in his late thirties, he wasn't opposed to moving with the times and trying to emulate the recording styles of current English and American artists. Said Björn: "That wasn't alien to him at all. He was the kind of producer who wanted to try new things. We would feel our way through: we had a song when we came to the studio, but we had no idea what would become of it."

To facilitate the attempts at breaking the UK and US markets, Stig had secured American and English expertise during sessions for the *Många ansikten/Many Faces* album. In the quest for an international sound, they brought in British singer and songwriter Mike D'Abo towards the end of the recording period. At this time D'Abo had just replaced Paul Jones as lead singer in the highly successful Manfred Mann and his vocals were to feature on hits such as 'Semi-Detached Suburban Mr. James', 'Ha Ha Said The Clown' and 'Mighty Quinn'. D'Abo's former group, A Band Of Angels, had recorded for the Hootenanny Singers' British record company, United Artists. In early October 1966 he flew to Stockholm to produce a version of his own composition 'Through Darkness Light'.

Mike D'Abo was joined on his visit by bassist Klaus Voorman, who was also a recent recruit to Manfred Mann. Moreover, Voorman was a close friend of The Beatles since their days in Hamburg in the early Sixties and had designed the sleeve for the recently released *Revolver* album. The Hootenanny Singers were excited at the prospect of working with two such prominent figures on the London pop music scene. Hansi Schwarz got on very well with the two pop stars, and on a later visit to London he even stayed at Klaus Voorman's house for a couple of days.

The American input on the album came from Sandy Alexander, a somewhat obscure arranger and producer who was said to have worked with Frank Sinatra. Alexander produced and provided lyrics for yet another of Björn's pop songs, 'Baby Those Are The Rules'.

Björn later stated that he felt this was the first of his songs that showed any promise. The melody as such was credible enough, but Alexander's lyrics were dreadful. Misogynist lines such as "never have other dates, even if I do/heaven help any guys that I catch with you", suggest that the most important aspect of the song was that it was a pop song in English. Björn's gleeful grinning delivery of the song on television shows implied that the message behind it had very little meaning for artist and audience alike.

Through its authentic British pop connection, Mike D'Abo's 'Through Darkness Light' was an obvious choice for release as a single A-side in Sweden, as well as the UK a while later. But the song failed to enter any charts. In Sweden, it was the B-side, 'Baby Those Are The Rules', that was the hit. "I remember that we played a couple of our current songs to some local kids," says Tony Rooth. "We wanted to find out which one would have the greatest hit potential, and they were supposed to vote for the song they liked best. I must admit I was very surprised when 'Baby Those Are The Rules' came out on top." The song became the Hootenanny Singers' biggest ever pop hit, reaching number two on the *Tio i topp* chart and 13 on the sales chart. It was an enormous boost for Björn's confidence.

The *Många ansikten/Many Faces* album, released in the autumn of 1966, contained another forgotten gem called 'In Thoughts Of You', featuring both words and music by Björn. Although vocally weak, as a pop song it wouldn't have been out of place on an album by any contemporary US or UK act. Songs like 'In Thoughts Of You' beg the question of what would have become of Björn as a composer if he had gone on writing songs by himself – certainly, his talent for coming up with a strong melody is much greater than he has been given credit for.

But all such musings will have to remain hypothetical, for within a couple of years Björn had written his very last solo composition, and had formed the songwriting partnership that has been the main thread of his career ever since. By the time 'In Thoughts Of You' was recorded, Björn had already met and written his first song with 19-year-old Benny Andersson.

Chapter 5

Few nations in the world have embraced social welfare programmes with the enthusiasm of Sweden. In the years following the Second World War its citizens benefited enormously from the country's emerging affluence, with top priority being given to increased security, equal opportunities and decent housing. Among the greatest symbols of this zeal for reform was the construction of the west Stockholm suburb of Vällingby.

Planned and built in the early Fifties, Vällingby was one of the first modern suburbs in Sweden. The planners' goal was that jobs, homes and a centre with shops and other necessary facilities should all be available in the same place. The area featured a mix of high-rise buildings, narrow blocks and town houses, and Vällingby residents were able to reach schools and shops on footpaths and cycleways, safely away from all motor traffic. The *tunnelbana* (the underground train system) was available for those who wanted to travel to the inner city.

Town planners, researchers and the curious from all over the world would visit Vällingby to marvel at this suburban wonder. At one point, there were so many visitors that special hostesses, known as Miss Vällingby, were hired to usher them around. For many years, Vällingby was even the home of Sweden's social democrat prime minister Olof Palme.

It is somehow fitting that the musical motor of one of the nation's greatest exports, a living symbol for the painstaking, goal-oriented Swedish work ethic, spent a large part of his adolescence in this suburb. After all, at least ostensibly, Vällingby was all about providing a platform for a happy and prosperous life.

Göran Bror Benny Andersson was born on December 16, 1946 in the district of Vasastan in central Stockholm. He was the son of 34-year-old construction engineer Gösta Andersson and his wife Laila, 26. Two years after Benny was born, in 1948, they had a daughter they named Eva-Lis.

For the first few years of Benny's life, the Anderssons moved around a lot. A period in the suburb of Djursholm was followed in the spring of 1949 by a move to Eskilstuna. Coincidentally, the family came to the new town just a month before Frida and her grandmother arrived in neighbouring Torshälla. For a number of years, the Anderssons' everyday existence was separated from the Lyngstads' by only a mile or two.

From his earliest days, Benny was immersed in music. His grandfather Efraim, a carpenter by trade, played traditional Swedish songs on his accordion, and even wrote some music of his own. "I think he'd rather have been a professional folk musician," Benny later reflected. Gösta Andersson shared his father's love for the accordion, glowing with pleasure as his fingers flew over the keyboards. The two men would often play together, especially during summers spent out on the island of Mjölkö in the Stockholm archipelago.

Around 200 families had been offered the opportunity to build their own cottages on the island, and Efraim didn't let the chance to own a summer house go by. This was where the young Benny would spend many childhood summers, enjoying an idyllic life filled with fun and games, as well as exciting boat excursions. It was also where important areas of Benny's musical tastes took root.

He recalled: "In the course of the day, my grandfather would always take the time to listen to the news on the radio, or shows like *En glad ton på grammofon* and *Musik under arbetet (Music While You Work)*." While Benny amused himself with his toys, the music his grandfather enjoyed would play constantly, a soundtrack to his childhood, melodies he would never forget. The radio shows featured a fairly eclectic mix of traditional songs, folk music and *schlagers,* some heartily affirmative, others shamelessly sentimental in style. Benny acquired a particular taste for the persistent and somewhat shrill sound of folk music played on fiddles, a prominent part of the Swedish musical tradition.

"Certain songs from that time still go straight into my heart, even though I've heard them a thousand times – especially if I'm caught off-guard," admitted Benny. "I believe it has to do with the things my parents and my grandfather used to listen to on the radio. And the music is so barren: it's one or two fiddles or sometimes a group of fiddlers, but it's actually not very much. It's not dressed up."

In the Andersson family the preferred instrument was the accordion, and it wasn't long before Benny wanted to follow in the family tradition and start playing himself. In December 1952, on his sixth birthday, he was given his first accordion. The instrument, inlaid with yellow mother-of-pearl, was small and easy to handle for a young boy.

Benny began practising with his father and grandfather, and the first song they taught him was the Swedish accordion classic 'Där näckrosen blommar' ('Where The Water-Lily Blooms'). "It was a pretty difficult song for a six-year-old to learn," he said. "I guess they thought it was easy because you could sort of play it slowly, one note at a time."

Benny learned to play the accordion with his grandfather during the summer months, on the porch at the house on Mjölkö. "Everyone should have someone who has the patience to play together with you even though you really can't play, and without *telling* you that you can't play. My grandfather was like that," he said.

For Benny, Efraim Andersson became a life-long inspiration, an ever-lasting symbol of his musical roots, the source of everything that came later. In the programme for the 1995 Andersson/Ulvaeus musical *Kristina från Duvemåla*, Benny's sole dedication was a photograph of his grandfather's accordion with the simple caption: "This accordion belonged to my grandfather Efraim Andersson. He used it when he taught me to play." Benny also posed with that same accordion on the cover of his first solo album in 1987, and later recorded a tune based on one of his grandfather's compositions.

Just a few years after Benny had started playing the accordion, the three generations of Andersson men were playing dance music on traditional open-air dance floors on Mjölkö. The trio would practice for an hour every day, eventually building up a repertoire of around 50 titles. "Dad liked *schlagers* of the day and grandfather liked more original folk music. That's what I preferred also."

With an affectionate wink towards their youngest member, Efraim and Gösta decided that they should call themselves Benny's Trio. It filled Benny with pride. His brimming confidence and sheer love for playing music became absolute when, at the end of a song, the dancing audience stood still for a moment and applauded. It wasn't long before he had a small repertoire of his own and took to entertaining the other kids in school with his music.

When Benny wasn't playing the accordion, he was a lively, active child, curious about his surroundings and inclined to try his hand at most anything. At home in Eskilstuna he was so fascinated by the street-sweepers that he would run out every morning to help them with their chores. To facilitate his work, his ever-supportive dad had to make a small broom for him.

There was also a mischievous side to Benny's activities, and he always seemed to be up to one prank or another. "He would exchange boiled eggs for raw when our dad was having breakfast, and put salt in the sugar bowl when mum was baking," recalled his sister Eva-Lis. "During the summers, he'd put grass snakes in the wheelbarrow he used for transporting his accordion to the dance floor. When he arrived, he would frighten old ladies with the snakes."

In May 1955, the Andersson family moved from Eskilstuna to an apartment in a high-rise building in Vällingby. They were far from alone in wanting to settle in the area. In line with its status as "the suburb of the future", the apartments in Vällingby were modern and spacious, and many young families with children living in overcrowded conditions in central Stockholm moved out to the attractive new estate. As a result, by the late Fifties, as much as a third of the around 11,000 inhabitants were under the age of 16.

The construction of Vällingby was still in full swing, and Gösta Andersson became a works manager at the housing firm Svenska Bostäder (Swedish Homes). The company, run by the city and still the largest single owner of buildings in Sweden, was also one of the suburb's major employers.

When the Anderssons arrived in Vällingby, Benny was just finishing his second year in school. He was a clever student who had learned to read and write before his teaching began. He remembered the first year as boring: while the other children were struggling with the alphabet, Benny would sit and read fairy tales. He didn't find the music classes very exciting either. "For me they were the classes where you could take it easy. I did pick up a thing or two, a little theory, but my main music education I got at home."

During his first few school years, much to the exasperation of his mother, Benny also developed a penchant for collecting all kinds of stuff: stamps, butterflies, birds, stones, fish. Benny was especially interested in birds, and after the collecting habit died down, birdwatching became his main hobby along with music. His interest in ornithology has remained with him in his adult years.

Benny's début as a stage performer came when he was eight, playing the accordion at a function in Stockholm's City Hall. At ten he was the main character in a local children's play called *Jocke och indianen* (*Jocke And The Indian*). Benny was "discovered" as a result of one of his pranks. He was caught stealing apples from a basement, but the owner was so impressed by his attempts to lie himself out of the situation that he decided to cast him in the play.

Whatever else took Benny's fleeting fancy, music overshadowed all his other interests and he worked hard at playing the accordion. His parents Gösta and Laila were struck by how dedicated their son was to his music. Gösta was especially pleased that the tradition of musicians in the family would continue, and both he and his wife did everything to encourage Benny.

The Anderssons were by no means rich, but sensible housekeeping meant that there was enough to put a little aside every now and then. In 1957, when Benny was ten, his parents surprised him with his first piano. "I got home from school one day, and there it was, in my room," Benny recalled. It was a dream come true. As he placed his hands on the keyboard for the first time, he was struck by a sensation that was both familiar and different. The black and white keys were the same as on the accordion but, as he soon discovered, playing the piano called for a very different approach.

Benny took formal piano lessons, but that didn't last long. The lessons were boring and seemed to counter everything that music meant to him. They were certainly no match for the stimulation of learning to play with a mentor like Efraim. His piano teacher's emphasis on formal teaching methods and learning to sight-read was in sharp contrast to his grandfather's encouraging smile and warm approach. In Benny's mind, an indestructible psychological bond had already been forged between the experience of playing music and its attendant feelings of companionship and delight. Indeed, the inclination to just play and play at every available opportunity gradually became a part of his being, as natural as eating and sleeping. By the time he was 12, he would be at the piano every day, sometimes for up to four hours at a time, his fingers dancing across the keys, playing whatever came into his head.

With the smorgasbord of different kinds of popular music that he heard on the radio, Benny would let every musical influence flow through him. The very first record he owned was 'Du bist Musik' ('You Are Music') by Italian *schlager* singer Caterina Valente. The languorous melody, lovingly delivered by Valente with a full string orchestra backing, struck a chord with the young boy. Typically European *schlagers* of this kind were highly prevalent in Fifties Sweden, and solidified Benny's taste for a pretty melody and sentimental emotions expressed in song.

The second record he bought, 'Jailhouse Rock' by Elvis Presley, couldn't have been more different. Elvis' direct attack, the fusion of guitars and drums, and the blues-based rhythmic structure was the antithesis of everything Benny had absorbed thus far, overturning all previous conceptions of what music was supposed to be like. "I thought it was fantastic, just because it was so far removed from folk music and *schlager*," he recalled.

The arrival of rock'n'roll brought a new prosperity to the Swedish recording industry in the late Fifties and early Sixties. In the general economic boom young people suddenly had money to spend and they could afford to buy their own record players. Modern living arrangements, in which teenagers often had their own rooms, tended to dilute the sense of community that led to shared musical experiences across the generations.

Benny remembered: "You'd buy these small, plastic record players that were relatively cheap. My parents and grandparents had wind-up gramophones and later on they bought radiograms. But as a kid, to have your own record player – that was the big thing. Hearing a song several times on the radio, it would gradually become a part of you. But now you could play your very own Elvis record a thousand times."

With so many young people living in Vällingby, it was natural that the local youth centre, Tegelhögen, became a focal point for teenage culture and music. In the greater Stockholm area, Tegelhögen became an important showcase for rock music in the late Fifties and early Sixties. Jerry Williams, one of Sweden's most popular singers in the later half of the 20th century, achieved his major breakthrough in a talent contest at Tegelhögen.

Like most other kids in Vällingby, Benny hung out at the youth centre. On Wednesdays and Saturdays, when there were concerts, he often jumped up on stage in the breaks and played a little boogie woogie piano. By 1961, 14-year-old Benny was proficient enough to get noticed by other teenagers with an interest in music.

The youth centre was the base for all sorts of activities, including rehearsals for a theatre group staging revues at different youth centres in the area. Among the girls working in the theatre group was a 17-year-old redhead called Christina Grönvall who befriended Benny when he applied for a part in one of the shows. Impressed by his piano-playing skills, she gave him the job.

Christina soon found herself charmed by Benny's obvious pleasure in playing his keyboards. She was the "grand prima donna" of the theatre group, and he added the role of singing cowboy to his piano-playing chores. They worked together closely in the theatre group, and it wasn't long before the two teenagers discovered a mutual attraction. Soon everybody realised that despite their age difference Benny and Christina were an item.

All the while, Benny continued playing whenever and with whomever he could. In June 1962, at the age of 15, he graduated from junior secondary school with excellent grades, and his teachers urged him to continue his studies, but Benny was restless and decided not to go on to high school. It was expected that he was going to follow in his father's footsteps and become a construction engineer.

After graduation he began an 18-month period as an apprentice engineer at a Svenska Bostäder building site, a job he later described as "pulling out nails and adjusting window-frames. I felt pretty worthless. I didn't know how to do anything." The tedium of construction work was relieved by evenings and weekends at the youth centre, playing with a band called The Gamblers and other musical groupings, or performing in the revues.

Christina Grönvall had been Benny's girlfriend for a year when, in the late autumn of 1962, just a few weeks before Benny's 16th birthday, she became pregnant. They got engaged immediately, and on August 20, 1963, Christina gave birth to a son they named Peter. For a boy of 16, it was impractical, not to mention untimely, to suddenly become a father. In accordance with the mores of the time, it was decided that Benny should leave most of the parenting to Christina. His son didn't even get Andersson for a surname, and was instead christened Hans Gösta Peter Grönvall. Benny's chances of becoming a responsible parent were dealt a further blow when, only a month after Peter's birth, the whole Andersson family moved from Vällingby to an apartment in central Stockholm. Around the same time, Benny quit his apprenticeship as a construction engineer and for some time remained unemployed.

In early 1964, Benny and Christina – still together and wanting to remain so – got in touch with a new band. Word of mouth about Benny's keyboard prowess and extensive repertoire of songs had spread to a group called Elverkets Spelmanslag (The Electricity Board Folk Music Group). Despite their name they were primarily a rock band, the "electricity" connection simply a punning reference to their electrical instruments. The pun was even extended to the lead singers' stage names: Christina called herself Volta Wattström and the male vocalist was billed as Björn Ampere.

The band played dances as well as regular concerts. Although they boasted two vocalists, their repertoire consisted mainly of instrumentals, and Benny would play keyboard-led numbers such as 'Baby Elephant Walk'. They also performed his very first attempts at songwriting: a few fairly undeveloped instrumentals now long since forgotten.

Typically, during Benny's time with Elverkets Spelmanslag they had more rehearsals than gigs. "It wasn't exactly the best band in the world," says guitarist Hans Englund, who joined them around the same time as Benny and Christina. The other members were amazed by Benny's love of playing, which transcended all practical purposes. "He wanted us to rehearse all the time even though we may not have a single gig in sight, just to get the opportunity to play together with the band."

When Benny and Christina joined the group their booking schedule was fairly regular, and sometimes they participated in local talent contests. At one point, in early 1964, Elverkets Spelmanslag was up against a band called The Hep Stars, who had existed for a year or so. The Hep Stars bass player and founding member, Lennart Hegland, couldn't help noticing the 17-year-old organist who seemed a true virtuoso on the keyboards. Hegland saw the band playing again at another venue, was again impressed by Benny's showmanship and made a mental note not to forget him.

At the time, The Hep Stars were working their way towards a permanent line-up. In March 1964, 19-year-old singer Svenne Hedlund joined the band, relieving guitarist Janne Frisk of his lead vocal duties. Svenne was formerly a singer with the group The Clifftones, and had performed occasional gigs with The Hep Stars before becoming a full-time member.

With organist Hasse Östlund and drummer and co-founder Christer Pettersson completing the line-up, The Hep Stars were becoming a popular band on the Stockholm club circuit. Lennart Hegland was the main driving force of the group, and he was adamant that they would go far if they were sufficiently determined. "Don't hesitate to do gigs almost for free," he often told the other members. "Learn to live on five kronor per week. The main thing is that we get as many jobs as possible so that people get to see us and learn who we are."

Through Lennart's persistence, The Hep Stars managed to acquire songwriter and publisher Åke Gerhard as their manager. Gerhard had made his fortune as the Swedish representative of Hill & Range, the American music publishers who controlled Elvis Presley's repertoire. He had also written no less than four Swedish entries in the Eurovision Song Contest. The money from the Presley songs enabled Åke Gerhard to start a record company called Olga. In July 1964 he released the first Hep Stars single, the novelty number 'Kana Kapila'. Initially it seemed that Gerhard's instincts had failed him – the record went virtually unnoticed in the record shops, selling only a few hundred copies.

To boost the meagre income from the struggling Hep Stars, Svenne Hedlund would drive other bands to gigs in his Volkswagen bus. In the summer of 1964 Elverkets Spelmanslag had a gig in the south of Sweden, but their own car had broken down. Svenne received a phone call from the band, asking if he could drive them. It was the first time he met Benny.

"It was a late night drive," Svenne remembered a few years later. "My girlfriend Stella came along and sat in the back with the boys and started talking to them. Benny was a little depressed for some reason. He showed her pictures of his son Peter, who was only one year old at the time, and talked about him all the time."

On stage at the venue, Benny's low spirits seemed to disappear completely. Under the lights he became a brilliant and charming performer. Today, Svenne recalls: "The one person in that band that made an impression on me was Benny. He seemed to have a lot of fun while he was playing. He had an impressive stage presence and was an excellent organist."

Elverkets Spelmanslag were desperate for gigs and would take every job they could get, no matter how odd. At one point they were hired as the backing for a band called Guy & The Turks, who'd released a few records. "The singer, Guy Bates, had already lost the original Turks when all of a sudden he got a short tour of five or six concerts," says Hans Englund. "We would start by playing some dance music, and then when he came on for the show we all had to dress up in fezzes and these puffy trousers."

Job opportunities for Elverkets Spelmanslag were few and far between, and Benny and Hans found they had a lot of free time on their hands. "I had graduated from high school and didn't really have a regular job at the time, so we would walk around the music shops and play every Hammond organ we could find. Benny was a very extroverted and happy guy, it was like he didn't have a care in the world. But he was still living at home, and although his parents were very supportive of his musical interests, they were pretty keen that he should get himself a proper job."

Later in the summer, when Elverkets Spelmanslag's gig sheet was a complete blank, Hans and Benny started looking for work as a duo. "The two of us went to a booking agency, playing guitar and keyboards in their offices. We got a job on the spot at this mountain hotel in a resort called Sälen."

It was a great adventure for the two young men. For Benny it was also something of a turning-point. "We were playing entertainment music for American tourists," he recalled. "Up to that point music had always been a hobby, but that was the first time I truly realised that you could actually make a living from it." When they weren't entertaining the American tourists, Benny and Hans sat outside amid the heather, gazing out over the mountains, dreaming about their glorious future as musicians.

Returning to Stockholm after their magnificent month in Sälen, the two musicians faced a harsh reality: Elverkets Spelmanslag had dissolved completely. Benny had little choice but to put the music dreams on hold for a while and get a proper job. "I was a door-to-door salesman, selling domestic appliances for a month without any success whatsoever. Except for the first door, where I sold a washing machine and earned 300 kronor (£20). But after that I didn't sell one single item."

Around the same time, The Hep Stars were experiencing problems with their own organist, Hasse Östlund. The latest in a succession of keyboard players, he was losing patience with the band and had very little faith in their future. It's not difficult to see why: the 'Kana Kapila' single was a very weak record, its failure well-deserved.

Chapter 5

Things came to a head in the autumn of 1964 at a gig at a youth centre when Hasse failed to show up for the first song after the break. It was the last straw: whether Hasse Östlund was fired or left of his own accord, the fact remained that he was no longer a member of The Hep Stars.

Lennart and Svenne well remembered the young organist who had made such an impression on them. One Saturday in October 1964 The Hep Stars were due to play at a school dance in the town of Avesta. Through a former member of Elverkets Spelmanslag, Lennart Hegland managed to locate Benny and ask him if he would play with them, just this once. A wildly enthusiastic Benny accepted the offer in an instant. He'd just started studying again, enrolling in a high school evening class, but he was no more enthusiastic about his classes than he was about construction engineering or selling domestic appliances. The phone call from Lennart Hegland came like a godsend.

Playing with Benny for the first time made The Hep Stars feel on top of the world. Svenne would never forget how Benny picked up on the wild energy of the band, taking off his tie after two songs and using it to fix the volume lever on his organ to the maximum position. "He was jumping and kicking so much that we realised that we had to have him."

That night a kind of magic aura seemed to spread throughout the entire room, as the singer recalled: "The audience was wonderful that night. Christer got all hot and threw his black turtleneck sweater into the audience. A new one was thrown up at once. I don't know, but for some reason that gave me a great feeling that we had made it. Or at least that we were about to make it – soon."

When Svenne asked Benny if he wanted to join The Hep Stars permanently, Benny agreed immediately. At first he tried to keep up his studies in parallel with his commitments to the band, but it was impossible when they had so many gigs. With one giant sigh of relief, Benny dropped out of high school.

Early publicity shots of The Hep Stars with Benny clearly reflect his status as a new arrival. He has a fairly well-groomed high school student look, his neatly combed hair considerably shorter than that of the other Hep Stars members. But the transformation to rock star was quick: only a few months later the length of Benny's locks surpassed The Beatles' famous mop-top look.

Svenne Hedlund describes Benny as he was during his first years with the band: "For us he was 'the little kid' – that was our affectionate term for him, because he was the youngest guy in the band. There were two sides to him: he was the one who always wanted to stop at the candy store and buy sweets when we were touring. He was forgetful and would constantly have to buy new clothes because he kept leaving his things behind at hotels. That was his childish side. But at the same time he could also be very grown-up and responsible for his age."

This duality in Benny also extended to his role as musician. One side of his personality was the introspective pianist who would sit and play by himself for hours, seemingly forgetful of time and space. But he also had a strong need to play together with other musicians, fully enjoying the companionship and opportunity to interact with a wide circle of friends.

It all added up to an unusually enigmatic personality, encompassing a range of seemingly conflicting character traits. Always eager to talk at length about subjects close to his heart, his integrity was nevertheless razor sharp when it came to discussing anything he felt was even remotely confidential, at least outside his closest circle of friends. Though Benny has evolved greatly as an artist through the decades, many of those who knew him in the mid-Sixties say that as a person he has remained just the same, "the same nice guy as he was back then".

Despite their lack of progress, Åke Gerhard hadn't given up on The Hep Stars just yet. In the spring of 1965 the group released no less than three singles simultaneously, hoping that at least one would become a hit and enter the *Tio i topp* chart. No one in the band saw himself as a songwriter, so they had to rely on cover versions. According to legend, the six single tracks were recorded within the space of 24 hours.

The choice of A-side material was relatively obscure. 'A Tribute To Buddy Holly' was a UK Top 30 hit for Mike Berry & The Outlaws in 1961. 'Farmer John' had hit the US Top 20 in a recording by The Premiers, and been recorded by The Searchers, although it reached The Hep Stars through a current Finnish cover version. The third A-side was a version of Eddie Cochran's more familiar 'Summertime Blues'.

"It must have been one of the cheapest sessions in the history of recorded music," said Benny. "We put two microphones on the stage of the assembly hall in a school and then we just played." According to Svenne Hedlund the songs were recorded on three-track tape, enabling them to put down the vocals separately.

Nothing much happened with the three singles and a short while later, The Hep Stars took a chance with yet another single. Svenne Hedlund was listening to the radio and happened to hear the song 'Cadillac', as recorded by a group called The Renegades. The song was a reworked interpretation of Vince Taylor's 1959 recording 'Brand New Cadillac'.★

Svenne realised the song's hit potential and rushed out to buy the single,

★ In 1979 it was covered by The Clash on their *London Calling* album.

but Åke Gerhard didn't share Svenne's enthusiasm for 'Cadillac'. "He thought it was a real piece of shit," Svenne remembered. The Hep Stars nevertheless decided to record the song themselves, on the sly. This time they went to a music shop in a southern Stockholm suburb which had a small recording studio on their premises. "We told Åke Gerhard, 'If you don't want it, perhaps some other label would be more willing.'" Gerhard was more or less forced to release the recording.

Issued shortly after the previous three singles, 'Cadillac' also failed to make any waves at first. But things turned around completely when The Hep Stars managed to secure an appearance on the popular television pop show *Drop In* on March 23, 1965. They only performed this one song, but that was enough for the sensation-hungry teenage audience. "We had something no other Swedish pop band had, which was a stage show," recalled Benny. "We were fun to watch as we jumped up on the speakers and shook our heads. Our show came across on television as well."

No visual trick went untried. The group would be running all over the stage, and Svenne Hedlund would duck while Lennart Hegland swung the neck of his bass across his head. Benny had his own stage antics, as Svenne remembers: "He had an organ with wheels on it so that he could run around. Now he was on my left side, now he was to the right. At other times he would tilt the organ and play it like it was an accordion."

The chart action following The Hep Stars' *Drop In* performance was mind-boggling. A few days after the broadcast 'A Tribute To Buddy Holly' entered the *Tio i topp* chart. On the sales chart, the band's first entry was the 'Cadillac' single on April 13, which reached number one on May 18. It was swiftly followed by the number five hit 'A Tribute To Buddy Holly'.

On May 25, 'Cadillac' was replaced on the number one spot by 'Farmer John', which remained on top for four weeks. Around the same time The Hep Stars occupied the number one, two and four positions on the *Tio i topp* chart. In just two months, the group had become the hottest pop band in Sweden, a position they were to retain for the remainder of the decade.

Bildjournalen, the leading youth magazine at the time, summed them up in their first major feature on the band: "Five rough, sloppy, loud, difficult guys who together constitute a group that in a shocking and groovy way makes the audience all ecstatic . . . A gang that surprises and entertains. Extremely musical and knowledgeable. Perhaps tomorrow's very biggest Swedish group."

Huge they certainly became and their stage act was definitely exciting, though musical precision was not their strongest point, at least not to begin with. Benny later admitted that they "weren't actually very much to listen to", singling out the wild stage show as their main point of attraction.

There can be no question that Benny was the most musically talented member of the group. A contemporary musician from a competing group put it more bluntly when he stated, "Benny was the only real musician in The Hep Stars", though as lead singer, Svenne Hedlund acquired a following all his own and contributed greatly to their popularity.

Another asset for the band was their decision to adopt a musical profile all of their own. During their first year of fame, at a time when Great Britain provided the main inspiration for most bands, The Hep Stars stuck to their late Fifties/early Sixties American rock'n'roll roots. Their début album *We And Our Cadillac*, released in October 1965, was loaded with covers like Little Richard's 'Send Me Some Lovin', Chuck Berry's 'Sweet Little Sixteen' and Elvis Presley songs such as 'That's When Your Heartaches Begin' and 'Young And Beautiful'. They also attempted The Ronettes' 'Be My Baby' and Neil Sedaka's 'Oh! Carol' with mixed results.

The Hep Stars were astute enough to realise that releasing covers as singles would only work if they found material that hadn't already been done to death. Among contemporary British beat groups, they admired more rocky exponents like The Kinks and unearthed two of their follow-up singles, 'Bald Headed Woman' and 'So Mystifying', on that band's début album.

Unusual covers aside, reviewers and competing bands were quick to criticise The Hep Stars for not recording original material. It was also becoming harder for them to find songs that had hit potential, yet hadn't been successful for other artists. At the same time, Benny was becoming increasingly inspired by The Beatles' prowess at writing their own songs. A few earlier attempts notwithstanding, in the late spring of 1965 Benny sat down to write the song that he now considers his first real composition. Learning by imitation was the name of the game.

"I wrote 'No Response' after having heard a song I liked – but I only liked parts of it," he recalled. "I thought, 'I guess I could change that one around a bit.'" The result was a somewhat quirky, two-part rocker with distinctly different moods in verse and chorus. "The song holds together pretty well, but the lyrics are just awful," was Benny's own retrospective verdict.

Svenne Hedlund recalls how Benny invited him up to his parent's apartment, where he was still living, to play the song for him the very first time. "I thought it was great to finally have a song that one of us had written, and especially since he had written a Fifties style rock song which still had a Sixties feel in the chorus. I liked the song immediately, and I felt that it could be a hit." The song was included in The Hep Stars' stage show in the summer of 1965 and became one of their more popular numbers. Released as a single in September, the group was rewarded with an encouraging number two hit on the sales chart. Benny was on his way as a songwriter.

Benny's emerging composer talent and Svenne Hedlund's status as Sweden's biggest teen idol were two important reasons for The Hep Stars' continued success. Almost as vital was the arrival in 1965 of a man called Lennart "Felle" Fernholm. He quickly became crucial to the band, and has in many ways remained the unsung hero of The Hep Stars' saga.

Formerly bass player with late Fifties rock king Little Gerhard, Felle worked as a road manager and also ran a car hire service. In May 1965, shortly after their national breakthrough, The Hep Stars' touring camper van broke down. Benny remembered Felle from when Guy & The Turks had rented a car from his company. He was contacted for help with new transportation, and ended up driving the band to their gig. Arriving at their destination, Felle, who'd picked up a few tricks from Little Gerhard's manager, realised that The Hep Stars needed help with their image.

"He told us to go into the dressing room and stay there," recalls Svenne Hedlund. "'But we have to bring in the equipment,' we said. 'No, that doesn't look right. I'll bring all that in, set it up and do a soundcheck.' He did all that and even tuned the instruments. We were quite impressed."

As The Hep Stars' personal manager, Felle quickly became an invaluable asset, brushing up their image as a touring band and injecting a much-needed element of professionalism into their lives. He made sure that when they arrived at a venue they were ushered in quickly, and that after the show they disappeared quickly, signing only a scant few autographs as they ran to their cars. In short, he taught The Hep Stars to act like stars, and made them seem as desirable, even remote, as was possible.

"He also handled the sound, sitting at the mixing desk beneath the stage. He'd do things like stereo effects and he'd raise the volume during guitar solos, which was very unusual at the time," says Svenne Hedlund. Recognising his value, the problem for The Hep Stars was that they didn't know how much to pay for his services.

The solution was as logical as it was unusual: in all future financial deals, Felle Fernholm would be regarded as a sixth member of the group. When The Hep Stars prospered, his bank account grew too, if they suffered setbacks, his piece of the cake would be as small as theirs.

Felle certainly earned his money, functioning as roadie, artistic adviser and even enhancing the musical precision on record by replacing Lennart Hegland in the studio. "He played the bass on several of our recordings, and he contributed quite a lot of backing vocals," confirms Svenne. "He had a very bright voice which often fitted perfectly."

Lennart Hegland's enthusiasm and essential qualities as a driving force weren't quite matched by his skills as a musician. At certain gigs, Felle would even be playing the bass behind the stage, while Lennart simply pretended to play in the front. Incredibly, as footage from the time reveals, sometimes Lennart's bass wasn't even plugged into the amplifier to maintain the illusion.

Felle's invaluable contributions notwithstanding, Benny remained The Hep Stars' main musical motor, rapidly developing as both an arranger and composer. If 'No Response' had showed a certain promise, Benny's next song, 'Sunny Girl', proved to be a major leap forward.

The Hep Stars' image as a Fifties retro-band was abandoned by the end of 1965, and the following year the group aligned themselves closer to the more up-to-date, British style of group, albeit tending more towards the melodic end of the pop spectrum. 'Sunny Girl', the group's first single of 1966, featured a baroque harpsichord accompaniment backing an unusually attractive melody.

It was the first time Benny had written a song with which he was truly pleased, although the words still left much to be desired. Benny's lyrical approach mirrored that of Björn Ulvaeus and other budding Swedish songwriters of the time. It was far more important for a song to have been written as "pop music in English" than to utilise correct grammar or any real sense of logic, commitment or significance. The crimes committed in the 'Sunny Girl' lyrics are many, one of the more obvious being the use of the word "property" in the line "she's domestic, she is property, she's slim like reed." The word was clearly supposed to be "proper" – the last syllable was only added to make the lyrics fit the melody.

" 'Sunny Girl' is a better song than 'No Response'," Benny determined many years later, "but the lyrics are embarrassingly lousy. The main thing was to have words to sing, and at the time my knowledge of English wasn't that great. It was straight out of the dictionary: I started with the rhymes and then I had to complete the lines from the end to the beginning so that I'd come up with the right number of syllables. It's just terrible."

Whatever its flaws, the success of 'Sunny Girl' proved to Benny that he had songwriting talent. The record was The Hep Stars' biggest hit up to that point, number one for six weeks on *Tio i topp*, and top of the sales chart for five weeks. Benny vividly remembers the feeling he got when he was told that his song was number one on *Tio i topp*. He was sitting in a dressing room before a concert when the news came through. "That made me very happy, because then I thought, 'perhaps I really know how to do this'."

The classical influences in 'Sunny Girl', added to the Swedish folk music, European *schlager* and American rock music already in Benny's musical bag, were introduced to him while on tour with The Hep Stars. "There was this man called Walter in the town of Falkenberg, and for some reason we stayed at his place. He was a classical music fan and would put on some records and say, 'Have you ever heard this? Do you know who Rossini is? Or Offenbach?' And of course I didn't have a clue." Walter even let Benny borrow the keys to a church outside Falkenberg so that he could sit there and play the church organ at nights.

Benny's third song, 'Wedding', released as a single in May 1966, featured an organ introduction that was clearly the work of someone who had heard a fugue or two. The song also represented a new stage in his songwriting, as it was a collaboration with Svenne Hedlund. "I'd sit down beside him while he was playing the piano and we'd exchange ideas," says Svenne. "I would hum a melody line which he would develop, or I'd suggest a chord or two, throwing it back and forth."

Benny would play this song on a church organ five years later at the wedding of Björn Ulvaeus and Agnetha Fältskog, but the lyrics are actually a fairly pessimistic meditation on the concept of marriage ("listen to the preacher praying/all the words he's saying/make me feel very cold inside").

Swedish audiences didn't pay very much attention to the words, but plans to release the song in Great Britain met with great resistance. "There was a hell of a fuss. 'You mustn't sing things like that about the holy matrimony!' " says Svenne Hedlund. "But we were stubborn and didn't want to change the lyrics. We were all young anyway and didn't have a thought of getting married."

There was more 'Wedding'-related trouble ahead. In circumstances that remain mysterious to this day, the maverick American producer and songwriter Kim Fowley had somehow come across a copy of the song. Fowley already had several major hits under his belt, including the US number one 'Alley Oop' by The Hollywood Argyles and the UK chart topper 'Nut Rocker' by B. Bumble & The Stingers, both acts being studio concepts rather than performing bands. Spending time in Great Britain in the mid-Sixties, Fowley began recording tracks under his own name, one of which was called 'Lights', released as a single on Luma Records in the autumn of 1966.

The Hep Stars were on their way to a Saturday night gig when they happened to hear 'Lights' on Radio Luxembourg. The song bore a strong resemblance to The Hep Stars' 'Wedding', especially the characteristic introduction. "We thought, 'How the hell did this happen?' " recalls

Svenne Hedlund. Benny and Svenne promptly flew over to London to sort things out.

"We met up with Kim Fowley, but he was very difficult to talk to," says Svenne. "I don't recall what his explanation was, but in the end the record company told us that they would pull back the record." The songwriting duo went back to Sweden, satisfied that the problem had been resolved. But as a coda to the story, Fowley simply took the recording of 'Lights' to EMI who released it on their Parlophone label. In the end it didn't matter, for the song never became a hit.

Perhaps the most significant point of the episode was that a fairly powerful, international producer like Kim Fowley had recognised the hit potential in 'Wedding'. Today, the song still stands up as one of The Hep Stars' finest recordings. Had it been recorded by a more hip British or American band at the time – and with a lyrical amendment or two – 'Wedding' would undoubtedly have become a sizeable international hit.

'Wedding' held further interest in that it seemed to sum up the life of 19-year-old Benny Andersson. The melody and arrangement embodied his joyful approach to music making and his sense of adventure in exploring new musical landscapes, while the lyrics almost certainly reflected his state of mind. He was still a teenager and wanted desperately to be free to enjoy life as a pop star, without being tied down by any family commitments whatsoever.

Not long after their breakthrough the members of The Hep Stars began to observe the first rule of popstardom. In a bid to remain as desirable as possible for the teenage girl audience, they decided to always keep their girlfriends secret, thus maintaining the illusion that one of their fans could become a girlfriend or perhaps even a wife. In an early interview, Benny had been asked what his dream girl looked like and had answered, "Like my fiancée." Another article had stated that he "sometimes spent time with a girl called Christina." That was the last the general public heard about Christina Grönvall for 18 months.

When The Hep Stars achieved national fame, Benny and Christina had been engaged for almost three years. Their son Peter was 18 months old, and Christina was already pregnant with a second child. A daughter they named Heléne was born on June 25, 1965. But Christina and the children didn't exist as far as The Hep Stars' fans were concerned. In the autumn of 1965, the whole group had gone on holiday to the island of Rhodes with their girlfriends. In the pictures that were released to the press the boys appeared to be holidaying alone.

"Benny was terrified that it would be known that he was engaged and the father of two children," Christina Grönvall later said. "His fans would be jealous, and that would be bad for his career. That's why the children and I have been kept secret."

As more and more of Benny's time was devoted to his life as a pop star, the relationship between him and Christina began to cool. With girls throwing themselves at his feet, it was hard for a young man to resist the temptation. Benny didn't even live with Christina and the kids, and when he was on tour in some godforsaken part of Sweden they seemed to be even farther away.

"My memories of those years are pretty vague," Benny later reflected. "I mainly remember that we ran around and were generally irresponsible, all of us. But perhaps you're allowed to behave like that when you're 19 years old?" Allowed or not, responsibilities were not the main concern in Benny Andersson's life in 1966. That summer he finally broke up with Christina. Peter and Heléne remained in her custody.

In hindsight, it seems obvious that a natural musical talent like Benny could not be contained or nurtured within the constraints of The Hep Stars. After all, the other band members were at best fairly adequate at their instruments, and had little musical vision beyond their enthusiasm for rock'n'roll and an appetite for fame.

But Benny probably didn't think much about the future at this stage. When 'Wedding' became The Hep Stars' fifth number one on the sales chart on May 31, 1966, he was still a teenager. Young Mr Andersson was living a 24-hour party: foot-loose and fancy free with money to throw around like there's no tomorrow.

Two of his first three proper songs had been number one hits, proving that he could write songs that struck a chord with a pop audience. The Hep Stars were out on a very successful *folkpark* tour with screaming fans everywhere, and the band was selling records like no other Swedish act had ever done: of the 4.5 million records that were sold in Sweden in 1966, a staggering 10 per cent were Hep Stars' releases.

Benny had little reason to question his position with The Hep Stars or start thinking of expanding his musical horizons with other collaborators. Still, as fate would have it, an all-important meeting that would change everything was just around the corner.

Chapter 6

The Hootenanny Singers had not expected it. What had started out as four friends playing folk music together for fun, hoping to attract some local attention, had turned into one of the biggest popular music acts in Sweden. But even when things got into full swing, they never forgot that the group was always meant to be temporary: fun while it lasted, but only a small adventure before they all went on to university and respectable careers.

As far as band member Johan Karlberg was concerned, it had been decided long ago that he and his brother should take over their father's car sales business. Björn Ulvaeus had known for several years that he was expected to become a civil engineer or something along those lines. "I thought this would only [last] for two years, if even that," he recalled.

But the success enjoyed by the Hootenanny Singers refused to fade away and the spring and early summer of 1966 saw them as busy as ever with recording sessions, the making of their own television special and a 90-date *folkpark* tour. In May they even managed to squeeze in their second film appearance: a musical interlude in the burlesque comedy *Åsa-Nisse i raketform* (*Åsa-Nisse In Rocket Shape*).

This summer would be somewhat different to the previous two for the Hootenanny Singers. Traditionally, after graduating from high school, Swedish men do their mandatory military service. The Hootenanny Singers had graduated in the spring of 1964, just after their breakthrough. Due to their extraordinary career, the authorities had let them off the hook two years in a row. But now there was no putting it off any longer – starting in June 1966 all group members, except German citizen Hansi Schwarz, would have to dress up in uniform for over a year.

For a born individualist like Björn, it was a nightmarish prospect. He had no interest in becoming part of a situation where somebody else made all the decisions, and certainly not for the purpose of learning how to kill. Hansi Schwarz recalls: "We'd become such a tight gang and I didn't want to lose that. I was toying with the idea to become a Swedish citizen and do the military service together with them. Björn nearly exploded when I told him. 'Are you out of your mind, you crazy bastard? Never! How can you even think of such a thing when you don't have to?' " Hansi decided to drop the idea.

The summer tour of 1966 started on April 30, which left the Hootenanny Singers a month to make as much as possible of the park season before the moment of truth arrived. For this year's *folkpark* trek they had acquired a brand new roadie, 19-year-old Hans "Berka" Bergkvist, who was a friend of Björn's sister Eva. He was keen on working in the music business and had been given the chance to help out on the tour.

On the day before they had to report to the military camp, the Hootenanny Singers were on their way to yet another of their many gigs that summer. They were one of the star attractions at a festival on the Ålleberg hill, three miles southeast of the town of Falköping. The hill flattens out to a plateau at the top, making it ideal for the glider school situated there. The location also lends itself to local festivities.

The date was Sunday, June 5, a particularly sunny afternoon. The Hootenanny Singers were due on at five o'clock on this third and final day of the festival. Before closing at nightfall, a total of 2,200 people would have attended the site. The entertainment on offer at the grounds included an amusement park, a car exhibition, a variety show featuring a magician and a sword-swallower, and the inevitable glider show. But the half-hour live concerts by some of Sweden's most popular acts were probably the main draw.

Driving along the gravel road towards the festival site in their Volvo, the Hootenanny Singers were confronted by a fleet of Ford Thunderbirds and Mustangs kicking up a dust cloud. Behind the wheels were the members of The Hep Stars, including the young Benny Andersson who didn't even have a driver's licence. The rock band had just finished their three o'clock show at the festival.

As two of the most popular acts in Sweden at the time, the groups were certainly aware of each other, but hadn't actually met before. "There were three groups that really had a lot of gigs on the park circuit at the time: The Hep Stars, Sven-Ingvars and us. So it would've been strange if we hadn't run into each other at some point," says Hansi Schwarz.

The width of the gravel road ensured that, even if they had wanted to, the two bands couldn't just drive past each other that Sunday afternoon. "The road was fairly narrow, so we had to meet slowly. We stopped the cars, wound down the windows and said hello," recalls Svenne Hedlund.

The Hootenanny Singers had already decided to have a send-off party at the Rally Hotel in the town of Linköping that night. Everything had been hastily arranged, "the more the merrier" being the only guideline, so The

Hep Stars were invited to come along after their last gig that day. The group, who never willingly missed out on a party, gladly accepted. The Thunder-bird/Mustang caravan continued on its way, while the Hootenanny Singers drove on up to the festival site and their performance.

Several hours later the Hootenanny lads were the focus of a wild party at the hotel in Linköping. There were quite a few other guests there as well, and the band had almost forgotten they'd invited The Hep Stars. "We never really expected them to come to the party, because Linköping would be quite a drive for them," Björn remembered.

But The Hep Stars had every intention of showing up, although a small misunderstanding almost overturned those plans. The band had misheard one of the letters in the name of the town and ended up in Lidköping (with a "d"), some 95 miles from Linköping. Undeterred, and no doubt charged with youthful enthusiasm, the group drove all the way to the other town on the chance that the party might still be going on when they arrived. "It turned out that driving 100 miles in the middle of the night was nothing for The Hep Stars, they wouldn't think twice about some-thing like that," explained Björn.

As luck would have it, the Hootenanny Singers were no strangers to partying all night long, and when The Hep Stars arrived at half past two in the morning, the shindig was still at its peak. But two noisy groups at the hotel was a bit too much for the other guests, and the complaints forced the two bands out to a nearby park.

The nine young musicians hit it off immediately. For The Hep Stars, being the number one pop band in the country, it was almost impossible to socialise with their main rivals. The Hootenanny Singers, whose success was based largely on a completely different kind of music and image, con-stituted no threat in that respect. The Hep Stars were also pleasantly sur-prised to discover that beneath the veneer of polite young men lurked a gang of party animals. The Hootenanny Singers was a group to their taste.

Similarly, the four folk singers felt an affinity with The Hep Stars, and especially with one of the members. "I felt from the beginning that Benny was the one who fitted best together with us, both socially and musically," says Hansi Schwarz. "You could tell that he was more of a kindred spirit than the others. He was the true connection between the two bands."

Most importantly, a special bond was forged between the two song-writers in the respective groups, even at that first meeting. Björn and Benny ended up with two guitars, sitting in the park playing Beatles and Kingston Trio songs in the warm summer dawn. Björn was well aware that Benny was the brains behind 'No Response', 'Sunny Girl', and the current 'Wedding'. And only the day before, Björn's 'No Time' had entered the *Tio i topp* chart, so Benny was familiar with Björn's song-writing aspirations as well.

Each recognised in the other the ambition not just to be part of a successful band, but to actually create music of their own, just like real songwriters, like John Lennon and Paul McCartney. "But all we said at the time was, 'Perhaps we could try to write something together at some point?'" remembered Benny.

The party didn't end until half past six on the Monday morning, and Björn, Tony and Johan didn't get much sleep before they had to report for their long and boring military duty. As it turned out, Hansi's fears that the group would drift apart were unfounded. His three friends were on leave a lot of the time, allowing the group to perform more concerts during the *folkpark* season than they had expected.

Tony Rooth recalls: "We had a great commanding officer who told the company that the powers that be were prepared to give us a little more leave than usual since we were in the middle of our career – but only if our comrades said yes. Which they did, and then it was just full speed ahead."

It was during one of those escapes from military life, less than three weeks after the get-together in Linköping, that Björn and Benny met for a second time. It was Thursday, June 23, the day before Midsummer's Eve, and The Hep Stars were invited to yet another party with the Hootenanny Singers. This time the location was a cottage in their native town of Västervik.

In between the drinks and the bawling Björn and Benny got into a deeper discussion about songwriting and their musical ambitions. Björn was growing increasingly frustrated with the musical limitations of the Hootenanny Singers and was upset that no one in the group had the slightest interest in writing songs with him. Benny's co-writing experience with Svenne had whetted his appetite for collaborative songwriting, and he felt an even stronger personal connection with Björn, who shared his love for contemporary British pop music.

On the spur of the moment, Björn and Benny decided that they would try to write a song together. They headed back to the apartment building where Björn's family were living and started setting up their equipment in the basement.

The noise they made resounded throughout the whole building, waking up an exasperated Gunnar Ulvaeus. He quickly ran down the stairs, telling them that they would wake up half the house. Where most parents would then have angrily slammed the door and gone back to bed, Gunnar again showed his supportive side at a crucial moment. His solution to the problem was to give Björn and Benny the keys to his office at the paper mill.

Hootenanny Singers roadie Berka had helped the eager songwriters get to the apartment building, and was now given new instructions. "I drove them out to the paper mill," he recalls. "My main memory is that it was a real pain to carry the organ and all the other equipment up this very long, narrow and unbelievably steep staircase."

Once settled in Gunnar's office with the amplifier plugged in, Benny put his fingers on the keyboards and Björn began strumming his guitar. They were both humming away, searching for a tune. After several hours, just as Västervik was waking up to a new day, the pair had completed the melody for a song they titled 'Isn't It Easy To Say'. Björn had an idea for lyrics, and Benny took it upon himself to finish them later. The first Andersson/Ulvaeus composition had been born.

Although it wasn't a bad attempt for a first collaboration, 'Isn't It Easy To Say' was a somewhat laboured piece of music. Parts of the melody sound a bit strained and painstakingly worked out – one can almost hear the two composers feeling each other out while they were writing the song. Both Björn and Benny had each written better and more solid stuff on their own before this first joint attempt.

Benny later admitted that 'Isn't It Easy To Say' "actually wasn't very good", but also recognised the significance of having a partner that was on the same wavelength. "There was a good connection between us immediately, because we liked the same kind of music and we both liked writing songs. And it was a bit boring to write on your own. You need someone to bounce your ideas off to enhance your capacity. It's hard to inspire yourself when you're working."

Later the same year, with Björn helping out on guitar, 'Isn't It Easy To Say' was recorded by Benny's band during sessions for their third album, *The Hep Stars*. There were tentative plans for the Hootenanny Singers to record a version of the song as well, but they never did.

During the months that elapsed between the writing and recording of 'Isn't It Easy To Say', the two groups had got together and had fun at every available opportunity. "If The Hep Stars found themselves close to Västervik, they would look us up and we'd have a party," confirms Hansi Schwarz. Socialising with the pop band also gave him an up-close view of what it was like to experience true idol hysteria.

"At one point the whole band managed to cram themselves into my miserable two-room apartment and slept there overnight. But the cars that were parked outside were clearly recognisable as theirs, and the next morning the whole yard outside was full of kids. I knew it wasn't for the Hootenanny Singers, because we didn't create hysteria on that level."

It was bad enough that it was virtually impossible for any Hep Star to get out of the house unscathed, but the situation was further complicated by the lack of hot water in Hansi's apartment. "Messrs Hedlund and Andersson both needed to wash their hair. They had a gig that day, and their hair had to be really fluffy and nice for that."

Hansi called the ladies' hairdresser, just a few yards away, and arranged for Benny and Svenne to come over and have their hair washed. Despite the short distance, it would have been impossible for them to just walk over. "They would have been ripped to pieces. So Felle Fernholm drove their car as close as possible up to the door and somehow managed to get them inside. Then, with a flying start, he just zoomed over to the hairdresser's. It was a pure miracle that none of the kids got hit."

Over the summer, the two bands got so close that magazines even speculated that they would soon turn into one nine-piece orchestra. This idea was obviously never seriously considered, but the friendship led to certain musical trades.

The Hep Stars included a recording of 'No Time' on their upcoming eponymous LP, while the Hootenanny Singers recorded a version of 'Sunny Girl' for the *Många ansikten/Many Faces* album. Benny also contributed organ to the track 'Blomman' ('The Flower') on that LP. Pre-dating Björn's guitar contribution to 'Isn't It Easy To Say', it marked the first time that two future Abba members appeared on the same record.

The friendship with Benny and The Hep Stars nurtured the pop music dream so close to Björn's heart. Through his friendship with the group he experienced one of the emotional highpoints of his music career at the end of the year.

The opportunity arrived when Hep Stars guitarist Janne Frisk got stuck at a restaurant he had opened in Spain, and was unable to make it home in time for a couple of concerts in the north of Sweden. The problem had to be solved quickly and Benny suggested that they should ask Björn. Benny could hardly have imagined how delighted Björn was when he was asked. Thus, on December 26, 1966, Björn joined The Hep Stars on stage for the first time. He took to the challenge with true gusto, relishing the chance to play the part of a fully fledged rock guitarist for one night, complete with all the right pop star moves.

That night in northern Sweden would remain one of his most treasured memories. "At Björn's 40th birthday party in 1985 I sat and talked with his mother Aina," recalls Svenne Hedlund. "She told me that Abba was nothing compared with the happiness Björn felt when he played with The Hep Stars. She had never seen such joy in him, before or since; he lived on that for a long while. 'Isn't that right, Björn?' she said. 'Oh yes, I still feel the same way.'"

The suggested merger with The Hep Stars may not have been on the cards for the Hootenanny Singers, but other significant changes were awaiting them just around the corner. As the last attempts to establish the group as a pop act and break them abroad came to another disappointing end, Bengt Bernhag and Stig Anderson decided it was time to take the boys' career in another direction.

Stig Anderson's publishing empire was growing as he brought home hit after hit from abroad, translating them for the Swedish market. But the successful versions were almost always on record labels other than Polar.

In late 1966 Stig secured the rights to Curly Putman's 'Green Green Grass Of Home', currently a hit for Tom Jones. Stig wrote Swedish lyrics, giving it the title 'En sång en gång för längesen' ('A Song Once Upon A Time, A Long Time Ago'). He and Bengt decided that it would be a perfect vehicle for the Hootenanny Singers.

The recording session for the track was held in December 1966. For the first time in the Hootenanny Singers career, Stig and Bengt decided that they should use an orchestral backing provided by session musicians: no member of the group played any instrument on the track.

Then, when the lead vocals were to be recorded, an attempt was made to record the song with all four members singing just like they used to. This didn't work – it was the kind of song that needed to be personalised and emanate from one single voice – and Björn was chosen as the sole lead vocalist on the song. In one instant, the spirit of unity that had marked the making of the *Många ansikten/Many Faces* album was thrown out of the window.

For Hansi Schwarz it was a painful experience to see the folk music group he had started suddenly become a *schlager* vehicle with Björn as lead singer. "The rest of us were relegated to the position of some kind of silly background choir. It wasn't the Hootenanny Singers anymore, it had become a product."

Tony Rooth, who was not opposed to moving the group into pop or middle of the road, still thought that the way 'En sång en gång' turned out was going too far. "Björn was the number one idol in the group, no question about that, but I don't think this recording turned out very well. His voice is not *that* good on its own."

It was a dividing line in terms of the group's future direction and Björn's ambitions to stay in the music business. "The others were annoyed that I got more and more of the solo parts. It used to be more democratic: we all had our lines or verses, no single member sang more than the others. But all feeling would've been erased with four guys singing together on a song like this."

From a commercial perspective, there was no denying that Stig and Bengt's instincts were absolutely right. When 'En sång en gång' was released as a single in January 1967 it became the group's biggest sales success ever, reaching number two on the chart.

Björn, who wanted to remain in the music business at any cost, was certainly more pragmatic about exploring new directions that could extend their career. "I recall in early 1967 when I was doing my military service and we were on some maneouvres in northern Sweden. I was listening to the radio and we were number two on *Tio i topp* with 'Baby Those Are The Rules', and number one on *Svensktoppen* with 'En sång en gång för längesen'. That was a kind of peak."

'En sång en gång för längesen' turned out to be yet another in a long line of Swedish versions of foreign hits acquired by publisher Stig Anderson and featuring new words by lyricist Stig Anderson. Not only did the song reach number two in the Hootenanny Singers' version, but it also peaked at the same position in a recording by actor and singer Jan Malmsjö. The combined sales of the two singles were 130,000 copies, an impressive figure for the times.

With his success as a songwriter, publisher and record company boss in the first few years of the Sixties, Stig Anderson's prominent position in the Swedish music business was absolute. At one point in 1967, he was the lyricist of no less than six of the ten entries on the *Svensktoppen* chart. One of the remaining four songs that week had been published by Sweden Music and was released as a Polar single.

When Stig emerged in the business, the older, more established publishing houses regarded him as a somewhat annoying maverick. One of his friends from the Ingesund folk high school, Boo Kinntorph, was now the Managing Director of the Philips record company. He recalled Stig's constant anger during those years.

"I think he felt humiliated. He was considered an outsider by some of the fancily dressed record company bosses and music publishers, who naturally felt threatened. Stig wasn't tactical, he had no patience, and he didn't feel any affinity with the holy traditions of the business. What he did was to run straight into the herd and tell them all how everything should be done."

Stig would question every single part of Swedish showbusiness and didn't hesitate to re-write the rules completely if it served his purposes. When the established publishers maintained that it was impossible for a Swedish company to handle copyrights for the rest of the Scandinavian countries, Stig's reply was a characteristic "Why is that?" Then he went out on extensive trips to the relevant countries, forging personal relations with everyone in the music business. That way he got all the important connections he needed to make inroads on the Scandinavian market.

Brows were also wrinkled when Stig started giving lyricists a larger cut of the royalty. Instead of the usual deal, fluctuating between 10 and 16⅔ per cent, Stig would pay out as much as a third of the publishing cut. It benefited him when he was the wordsmith, and was an encouragement for those he hired to write lyrics for Sweden Music copyrights. "It was purely for business reasons, and not because of any idealism on my part," he admitted.

Stig and others of his generation were on the whole more active players on the publishing scene, seeking out copyrights on long journeys to all corners of the world. And once those publishing rights had been acquired, Stig didn't just sit on them. For more than a decade he was a virtual word machine, at times churning out as many as three lyrics per day. "My main memory from childhood is that I had to be quiet after six o'clock, because that was when he was writing his lyrics," recalled his daughter Marie.

With the relatively small revenue to be earned for each title, Stig realised that only sheer volume would generate a substantial income. As a result, many of his lyrics during those years were workmanlike at best. But when inspiration hit, there were few in his genre who could touch his ability to combine singability, memorable catchphrases and clever lyrics – often in the shape of mini-stories – in neat little three-minute packages.

"It was hard work," he confirmed. "I had office work to take care of during the daytime, so I had to write the lyrics in the evenings. During the nighttime I would handle the correspondence with foreign publishers."

It was clear that Stig's workload hadn't diminished one bit since his days as a teacher – he was still caught up in the nightly work sessions that Gudrun had hoped would fade as he became a full-time publisher. Stretching his physical and mental resources to the limit, he would explode with anger when he felt that others didn't recognise the full value of his efforts.

Karl-Gerhard Lundkvist, formerly known as rock king Little Gerhard, became a record producer at the record company Cupol in the mid-Sixties. He remembers how Stig would be very cordial as long as things were done his way, but would fly into a rage when someone opposed him. "I'd tell him that I wanted a certain song, and he'd set to work on the Swedish lyrics. But sometimes my boss at the record company would unexpectedly say no. Stig would be absolutely furious: 'You said you wanted the song, and now all of a sudden you tell me you don't want it?!' Then you'd be out in the cold for a while, but the next time you used one of his songs everything was fine and dandy again."

Stig was eager to rid himself of whatever and whoever stood in the way of the further expansion of his empire. Sometimes he was helped along the way by deeply tragic occurrences. He always acknowledged a great debt to his Belgian partner, Robert Bosmans, who had been instrumental in teaching him the ropes. But by 1963 their partnership in Bens Music had become a hindrance and a complication in Stig's dealings on the international publishing scene.

"When I travelled around the world, buying music, I was often asked, 'Why don't you sign this to your own company, why do you have to take the detour through Brussels?' They wanted to deal directly with me. But I was stuck in an 'apprentice deal' with Robert Bosmans."

Meanwhile, in Belgium, Bosmans found himself overwhelmed by problems unrelated to his partnership with Stig. In 1964 he committed suicide by throwing himself off the roof of his office building. Stig mourned his friend, but the businessman in him also recognised that it solved a difficult problem that hindered his plans for the future expansion of Sweden Music. Straining his financial resources to the limit, he bought Bosmans' 50 per cent of Bens Music. A vital cornerstone of the empire had been brought into Stig's complete control.

In many ways it was a natural progression, for Stig had already shown on several occasions that the apprentice was rapidly becoming the master. When he recognised the potential in songs that Bosmans dismissed as rubbish, it sometimes led to particularly fortunate acquisitions.

As part of his work as publisher, Stig used to sit by his record player for hours on end, going through stacks of records in search of tunes that might be worth buying. One day in 1962 he found himself listening to a song called 'Surfin' Safari'. He fell for it immediately: it was exactly the kind of simple and direct song that he knew could be a hit. The fact that it was tied to a novelty craze like surfing didn't hurt either. But Robert Bosmans wasn't interested at all and said that Stig would have to go this one alone.

The group was called The Beach Boys and Stig secured the Scandinavian rights to the songs published by Sea of Tunes, the company that handled the songwriting of The Beach Boys' creative genius Brian Wilson. 'Surfin' Safari' spent four weeks at number one in Sweden.

The Sea of Tunes deal was clinched with Beach Boys manager Murry Wilson, father of the band's three Wilson brothers. Stig remembered Murry Wilson as "a wonderful madman": a somewhat generous appraisal – presumably made in all innocence – of a man who holds the title as one of the most violently abusive fathers in the history of rock music, leaving lifelong scars on the souls of his sons.

In November 1969, against the express wishes of Brian Wilson, Murry sold the entire Sea of Tunes catalogue to Almo/Irving, the publishing arm of A&M Records, for a reported $700,000. Murry Wilson was hoping to make a quick profit on a bunch of songs he thought would be all but forgotten only a few years later.

Stig had more foresight, and had inserted a clause in the original agreement, guaranteeing him the rights until 50 years after the songwriters' deaths. "Ever since [Almo/Irving] bought the catalogue, they have been chasing me to sell them back my Scandinavian rights. I always tell them to forget it!" a satisfied Stig said many years later.

Contrary to Murry Wilson's predictions, songs like 'I Get Around', 'California Girls', and 'Good Vibrations' rapidly achieved the status of timeless classics, and by the Nineties the estimated value of the catalogue was tens of millions of dollars. As a poignant coda to the story, both Sweden Music and Almo/Irving eventually ended up being owned by Universal Music Group: the worldwide rights were finally collected under one umbrella.

The Sea of Tunes deal was only one of many examples that proved Stig had become a true "music man" by the mid-Sixties. His hit-picking instincts and sixth sense for the long-term value of copyrights were invaluable assets as his company expanded. He was also becoming well known on the international music publishing scene, forging important alliances with heavyweights such as Brill Building mogul Don Kirshner.

Stig was also the first to acknowledge that there was often a bit of luck involved when business decisions were made – and fortune wasn't always on his side. In the early Sixties, Stig was friendly with a British publisher called Dick James. They were both up-and-coming in the business, and James was overjoyed when Stig managed to place one of his copyrights on a single B-side released by a major Swedish act.

But when it really mattered, Stig happened not to be in the right place at the right time. It was another hungry Swedish publisher with a newly founded publishing company who made the most fortuitous deal with Dick James. Stig never forgot how he missed out on the Scandinavian rights for Northern Songs, the publishing company set up to handle the work of two fresh-faced songwriters called John Lennon and Paul McCartney.

In July 1966 the last child in the Anderson family was born, a son named Anders. With Stig's fortunes escalating, the family left the town house in Tullinge and moved to a stately villa in the suburb of Nacka. The Sweden and Polar Music business continued as a small-scale operation, with Gudrun taking care of the finances as well as most of the other administrative work. Gudrun maintained her role as a quietly unifying presence in the Sweden Music group of companies for many years.

For all Stig's belief in records as the future of the music business, the Hootenanny Singers remained the only truly successful act on Polar Music up until the end of the Sixties. Out of the first 15 albums Polar released, eight were Hootenanny Singers titles. It was an odd contradiction: while Stig had several hits as publisher and lyricist for artists on other labels, he and Bengt seemed unable to apply the same magic formula to their own record company.

This was to remain the story of Polar Music until the company was sold in the late Eighties. At most, the label would have three or four successful acts signed at any one time. But the bulk of its releases failed to make an impression on record-buyers.

While the Hootenanny Singers were Stig's source of pride as recording artists, the group was starting to crumble from the inside. Ironically, the group was at the peak of its popularity when the members decided that it was time to cut down on their musical activities. No matter how many records they sold at the moment or how many gigs they still had, it couldn't last forever, they reasoned. University studies and "honest" jobs seemed the best bet for the future.

Björn half-heartedly agreed. After leaving military service in April 1967, he registered as a student at Stockholm University. In the autumn he began studying business economics and law.

Nevertheless, at the back of his mind he kept hoping for just one more hit to keep the group going, anything that would enable him to remain in the music business. The Hootenanny Singers' 1967 *folkpark* tour indicated that he didn't have to worry too much just yet. With an impressive catalogue of hits to their credit, the band performed a total of 150 gigs over the course of four months.

The final engagement of the tour took the shape of two concerts – one in the afternoon and one later at night – at the amusement park Gröna Lund in Stockholm on Sunday, September 3. Just a few hundred metres away from this venue lies the open-air museum and zoological park Skansen, a popular Swedish tourist attraction. The park has also hosted concert performances by innumerable Swedish and foreign acts over the years.

On this September night, while the Hootenanny Singers were idling away time between their two gigs, the lucky champion of a talent contest called *Nya ansikten* ("New Faces") was awarded her prize on the stage at Skansen. The winner, on the verge of her national breakthrough, was a 21-year-old housewife and mother of two: Anni-Frid Lyngstad.

Chapter 7

As an image of early Sixties marital bliss, the wedding photo was almost iconic in its depiction of a serious and paternal-looking groom and a happily smiling bride. Ever fashion-conscious, the 18-year-old bride had interpreted the chic Jackie Kennedy look to perfection, with a tulle-covered pillbox, Farah Diba hair-do and matching silk dress and coat. A lily-of-the-valley bouquet completed the picture. It was Friday, April 3, 1964, and in a simple ceremony at the Eskilstuna home of assistant vicar Marcus Winberg, Anni-Frid Lyngstad became Mrs Ragnar Fredriksson.

Seven months had elapsed since the pair started living together with their one-year-old baby boy Hans in Ragnar's Eskilstuna apartment. Ragnar was 22 and spent his days 17 miles away in the town of Köping, managing the local branch of the rug and carpet store owned by his parents. Frida and Ragnar's life mirrored that of any other small-town couple.

Yet the dream of becoming a successful singer remained Frida's number one goal in life. She also realised that she had to take care of her child, acknowledging Ragnar's role in providing her with security, both emotionally and on a practical level. With his help Frida had been able to shake off her identity as a poor little girl with an unusual family situation. Now she had everything most girls her age dreamed of: a child, a home and a loving man with a secure and respectable job.

But the price she paid had been high – to become a mother at 17 was not a part of the plan. In a way it was logical: circumstances had forced her to develop prematurely. The responsibilities and workload of an adult had been with her for years already. On the outside she may have looked like an average teenager, but inside she was much older. The insecurities and rootlessness of her background meant she was like a clean slate, ready to cast herself in the role that offered the best sense of comfort at any given moment. It was a tough challenge and it collided with her determination to succeed as a singer, but Frida resolved to become the perfect housewife.

The spring wedding was followed by a honeymoon trip to the Canary Islands. Before going away, Frida and Ragnar made plans for starting a trio together with pianist Gunnar Sandevärn. Still one of their closest friends, he had put together his own band after leaving Bengt Sandlund's. The well-known brand name, Gunnar Sandevärn's Orchestra, was now applied to this new constellation.

"Ragnar and Frida were gone on their honeymoon for a couple of weeks," recalls Sandevärn. "In the meantime I borrowed Ragnar's car and drove around to all the restaurants in the area and made a presentation of our little band. When they got back again I had secured engagements for six months – for a band that no one had heard. It was possible because by then all three of us had good reputations as music entertainers in previous bands."

Frida's status as "the songbird of Eskilstuna", as the local press had dubbed her, made her a special attraction: sometimes advertisements would bill them as "Sandevärn's with Anni-Frid Lyngstad". She was also very much a driving force within the band, her determination that the music should always come first shining through at every opportunity. "She was playing in another division than the vocalists I had been working with before," confirms Sandevärn. "She was very goal-oriented and always wanted us to work very hard. She didn't like it if you got slack or the breaks were too long, and she wanted us to rehearse constantly – all the things that mark out a real pro."

It was an odd little trio in which the smallness of scale was overcome by stretching their abilities to the limit, and sometimes beyond. "Ragnar was a trombonist, but he bought a drum set and learned how to play the drums. I was playing the piano and had to play the bass lines with my left hand, since we had no bass player. You had to play for all you were worth, otherwise it would have sounded a bit thin. And then Frida was singing: we almost didn't have any numbers without vocals. If she wasn't singing, she would be playing the tambourine or maracas."

Sensible economics were also applied to Frida's stage outfits. Ever since she started working as a vocalist, Frida had sewn her own dresses. This was something she continued doing well into the early Seventies. "I wouldn't dream of paying several hundred kronor for a garment that I might not even be alone in wearing," she remarked. Frida's hair was scooped up into an elaborate beehive which made her look considerably older than she really was.

On occasion Frida and Gunnar went out on duo jobs, and then the vocalist would sometimes help out with the instrumental backing in a most unexpected way. "Frida would say, 'Why don't you play a few jazz numbers while I play the drums?' 'Well, do you know how to?' 'Don't worry, it'll be fine'. And then she would be sitting there in her fancy dress, elegantly perched on the stool, and play the drums. She wasn't afraid to do things like that."

After a while, the band was asked by clients to bring in a fourth member to beef up the sound a little. Ragnar's brother Lennart had been playing the drums with various big bands, and now he joined the Sandevärn orchestra. Ragnar, meanwhile, had to learn yet another instrument. "He bought an electric bass and started practising in the rug and carpet shop, while he was waiting for the customers. In the end we had quite a good little band."

The repertoire of Gunnar Sandevärn's Orchestra rested on a base of well-known standards: numbers like 'All Of Me', 'Stars Fell On Alabama' and 'Misty', all of which were committed to an amateur tape recording around this time, with added Latin American rhythms in bossa nova titles like 'The Girl From Ipanema'. Swedish and European *schlagers* were also a strong presence in their act.

Frida was especially determined that the band should keep up to date with the latest hits. When she heard something she liked, she would immediately order the sheet music and have the band rehearse it. "I remember when she found 'Downtown'," says Gunnar Sandevärn. "I had never heard of it and just thought it sounded very strange at first. And she brought James Bond themes like 'Goldfinger' to us. She was really good at keeping her eye on these things."

When Frida wasn't busy with her duties as a housewife and mother, she devoted her energies almost exclusively to the band. She didn't think twice about helping out with the heavy equipment, just like she had always done. "I don't think she should have worked that hard. It couldn't have been very good for her when she had small children and everything. But that's how it was at the time: when you're only three or four people each person really has to give their all if you're going to get anywhere."

Sometimes Frida's determination and eagerness became a bit overbearing even for Ragnar and Gunnar, especially when she complained that they didn't focus enough on the band. "Ragnar stood in the shop selling rugs and carpets all day long, and I had started studying. I mean, you can't be on top form all the time. But she'd say, 'Are you musicians, or what? What are you doing all those things for?'"

Deep down inside Frida somehow knew she was destined for greater things than a local dance band. Those talent contests that seemed to be the only road to national discovery continued to haunt her. In September 1964, she reached the finals of a high profile national contest. Frida performed 'Besame Mucho', a song she heard for the first time on her honeymoon. This time her efforts paid off and she ended up the winner, leading to her first extensive coverage in the national press. The breakthrough seemed to be waiting around the corner: previous winners in the contest included singers that were now among the biggest stars in Sweden. "I'm sure something will happen," an expectant Frida told a local paper the day after the event.

But nothing did happen. No offers of record contracts were forthcoming, no chances to appear on radio or television – nothing. It seemed odd, but the explanation was probably to be found in her vocal style and general appearance. The amateur recordings with Gunnar Sandevärn's Orchestra present an expressive singer, firmly in control of her mezzo-soprano voice and hitting every note spot-on. But there was also a hint of vocal restraint in her interpretations. The Sixties Swedish public wanted either smiling perkiness or romantic wistfulness from their female singers: a knowing sophistication might impress, but it didn't win the hearts of the audience on a national level. Combined with her slightly distant onstage aura, she presented an image that would put a wedge between her and her audience for a long time to come.

The changes were few in Frida's life over the next few years. She was a housewife and mother during the daytime, a dance band vocalist at night. The quartet would have month-long engagements at the different restaurants, performing on Wednesdays, Fridays and Saturdays. They travelled to the performances in the car that belonged to Ragnar's rug and carpet shop.

In March 1965, Frida, Ragnar and Hans moved out of their apartment and into a Thirties villa in Eskilstuna. They'd socialise a lot with friends like the Sandevärns, throwing parties together and helping each other with babysitting. In the spring of 1966 Frida fell pregnant again, and on February 25, 1967, a daughter called Ann Lise-Lotte was born.

Paradoxically, the night-time cabaret environment seemed to offer Frida a stronger sense of belonging than her life in the villa. Later, Frida often recalled how it didn't matter that she had to work so hard when she loved singing so much. "I think she preferred spending time at these restaurants to the life as a housewife," Gunnar Sandevärn reflects. "She was very good at creating a familial atmosphere, to make friends with the staff and see to it that we felt at home there."

Frida was becoming firmly established as a local attraction in Eskilstuna and surrounding cities, but she also continued to enter talent contests. Her fellow band members feared that they would lose an excellent vocalist, but encouraged her attempts at breaking away from the restaurant circuit all the same. "As we sat in the car on our way to the gigs we often said to her, 'You're so damned good that you really shouldn't be wasting your time slogging away with us here,'" recalls Sandevärn.

In August 1966, Gunnar Sandevärn's Orchestra dissolved when the band-leader started playing in another dance band. Frida had to accept temporary work as vocalist with other orchestras to keep the music going. But by March 1967 the Fredrikssons had brought together a new group of musicians. With Frida's outstanding status as a public draw, it was perhaps inevitable that the band got the name Anni-Frid Four.

Only weeks after the birth of Lise-Lotte, the quartet could be found performing at the Hotel Rogge in the town of Strängnäs. The line-up consisted of Frida, Ragnar, drummer Conny Lindholm and organist-cum-trumpet player Agne Andersson. This multi-instrumentalist had a homemade contraption attached to his organ, enabling him to play the keyboard with the left hand and the trumpet with the right hand at the same time. Economy and efficiency, making the most of a small unit, was still the norm.

Although it was a kick to be fronting her very own band and being something of a local celebrity, Frida couldn't escape the feeling of being in a dull routine. "Being a dance band singer wasn't especially developing for me," she recalled. "Towards the end there was a feeling of stagnation, and I wanted to try something else, as a challenge for myself. I felt that I was pretty good and that I ought to take the chance to try something other than staying as a vocalist all my life."

It certainly wasn't in "off-Broadway" towns like Eskilstuna that the major record labels went looking for potential signings. Although it hadn't mattered if she won them or not so far, it still seemed that talent contests were the best bet for discovery.

In the summer of 1967, Frida noticed a newspaper ad for one of those competitions. *Nya ansikten* ("New Faces") was an annual event, arranged by the organisation Barnens dag ("Children's Day") in conjunction with the EMI record label. Frida saw a chance, and filled in the application form.

The prospect of breaking out on her own as a singer was tempting and frightening in equal measures. Fear took her in its grip, and for a while the old insecurities about her self-worth wrapped themselves around her shoulders like a black shawl. Frida carried the application form around in her handbag for several weeks before she finally found the courage to mail it. As ever, she was accepted into the contest and, as usual, she sailed through the first few stages with ease.

The semi-finals and the finals were to be held in Stockholm on the same day: Sunday, September 3, 1967. This also happened to be the day when Sweden changed from left-hand to right-hand traffic, with the new regulations coming into force at 5 a.m. on the Sunday morning. One hour later, Frida stepped out of the Eskilstuna villa and started her journey to

Stockholm. She remembered that late summer morning vividly.

"The roads were empty, it was just me and a girlfriend in an old Volvo. I was pretty nervous: it was a two-hour car drive to Stockholm, driving on the right side of the road for the first time, and then taking part in finals where I was supposed to sing well enough to win the contest."

Luckily, although the organisers had wanted a wide variety of contestants, they had all been divided into different categories. Frida was in the "pop singer" group: potential rivals, such as the 15-year-old pianist playing Chopin and the inevitable magician, wouldn't be standing in her way. Her win in the morning semi-finals secured, it was now only a matter of a nervous wait until the afternoon finals.

Her choice of song was titled 'En ledig dag' ('A Day Off', a cover of the fairly obscure song 'Weekend In Portofino'). It was a cool, uptempo bossa nova number, in line with her vocalist repertoire at the time. She had discovered the song a few months earlier when it was a minor radio hit.

The finals, starting at 1 p.m., took place on the Solliden stage at the Skansen park. Frida was nervous: her belief in herself, shaky at the best of times, was under severe strain in this high-profile situation. The compere, popular television personality Lasse Holmqvist, picked up on her nerves and tried to comfort her. "In the south of Sweden, where I come from, we don't have long-legged girls like you," he told Frida. This silly remark somehow gave her the extra boost of confidence she needed.

Frida went on stage in a dark, elegant two-piece outfit, her brown hair swept up according to the fashion of the day. She delivered a stellar performance of the song, complete with improvised virtuoso parts in her highest register. The jury was impressed, and before long the verdict was announced: Frida was the winner. "It must have been the tension of that whole day that made everything work out so well," she later reflected.

At 7 p.m. it was time for the awards ceremony. Standing on stage after receiving her prize – a transistor radio – she was happy but exhausted. Any reflections on what would happen now, except that there was a slight possibility of a record contract, had to wait until tomorrow. Holmqvist casually asked her, "So, what are you going to do tonight?" "I'm going home to Eskilstuna to get some sleep," she replied. Holmqvist smiled. "No, you're not. You're going to appear on television!"

In an attempt to keep people off the roads on the day the traffic changed from left to right, a special edition of the most popular television show in Sweden at the time, *Hylands Hörna* (*Hyland's Corner*, a Swedish mix of *The Tonight Show* and *The Ed Sullivan Show*) was aired. The tantalising title of this extra broadcast was *H-trafik rapport: Ikväll* (*R-traffic Report: Tonight*). In all secrecy, the arrangers of the talent contest had agreed with Swedish television that the winner would début live on the show that very same night.

A surprised Frida was whisked away to the studio by car. It was a dream come true: winning a talent contest was all well and good, but she knew that a television appearance was all-important if she was to get ahead in her career. Minutes later she was being interviewed by host Lennart Hyland in front of an audience of millions.

Hyland, who had stopped Stig Anderson's 'Grädde på moset' from being performed on his radio show 15 years earlier, was now a more powerful presence in show business than ever. At the time, Sweden still had only one television channel and Hyland's show used to have virtually the whole population seated in front of their sets.

The confrontation between the patronising, self-absorbed Hyland and the nervous and highly strung Frida didn't run smoothly. She conveyed a mix of shyness and distrust, and many of her replies to his questions were surprisingly ambiguous. Asked if she had hoped something would happen after her talent contest win in 1964, she said that she hadn't. She also claimed that she wasn't very experienced in terms of talent contests, when in fact she was doing them all the time. When Hyland, referring to her long career as a dance-band vocalist, remarked that she was "a professional young lady", only the physical pat on the head was missing. Frida rolled her eyes and didn't say anything.

And what did she do for a living, wondered Hyland. Her determination to succeed as a homemaker shone through in an answer that sounded almost pre-rehearsed: "I'm married with two children – that's my profession." It was a popular reply that was met with spontaneous applause. But when asked what she would do with her children if this contest win should lead to a greater career, she fell silent for a few seconds. The reply was almost whispered: "I can't answer that question." It was as if a conflict was raging within her at that very moment.

Frida's television début gave the impression of a determined woman with a mind of her own who wasn't going to let Hyland have his way with her. This might have been a good policy for her self-esteem, but it probably didn't help her much in winning the hearts of the audience. Nor was her performance of the winning song especially successful in that respect.

Although it was clear that she was firmly in charge of her voice, there was that knowing sophistication and tendency to hold back, which didn't do her any favours in communicating with the vast majority of viewers. But her delivery was exact, in tune and collected, striking a chord with the more discerning professionals in the music business.

The days immediately following her television début saw several features in the national and local press. For the first time, Frida had managed to make a strong impression on the media. Several record companies expressed an interest in signing her, and talent contest arranger EMI almost lost their new discovery. Producer Olle Bergman recalled: "I really fell for her in a big way and felt that she had everything you needed to get ahead in this business. We wanted to sign her immediately, on the night of the contest, but she sort of got caught up in all the excitement. All of a sudden she had disappeared and gone back home to Eskilstuna." Bergman called Frida up the following morning and drove from Stockholm to Eskilstuna to secure the contract with her.

On September 11, Frida entered a professional recording studio for the first time. She recorded four tracks, among them the two sides of her first single. Naturally, 'En ledig dag' was chosen as the A-side. The decade as a dance band vocalist had turned her into a professional, consummate singer, and she produced a perfect lead vocal track on the first take.

Olle Bergman and Frida shared a liking for jazzy material such as 'En ledig dag', which was one of the reasons Bergman wanted to sign her in the first place. But it certainly wasn't what was needed to further Frida's career in late Sixties Sweden. When the single was rush-released shortly afterwards it failed to become a hit, despite the television exposure in front of millions of viewers. Apart from becoming a recording artist, little had changed in Frida's career. The hesitant distance in her voice didn't endear her much to radio listeners and she failed to enter the important *Svensktoppen* chart.

One of the sides on her follow-up single was 'Du är så underbart rar', her Swedish version of the current Frankie Valli hit 'Can't Take My Eyes Off You'. It, too, failed to enter any charts, but was heavily featured on radio playlists. Low as the sales figures were, it was to remain her best-selling single for the next couple of years.

In hindsight, Frida's late Sixties recordings have aged better than many of the oompah *schlagers* and dronesome ballads that were major hits around this time. What lesser artists might have turned into shallow anachronisms, Frida managed to colour with a warmth and sincerity that lent credibility to the songs. Her vocal control was a quality that would win out in the long run.

With so little real success to her credit, leaving Anni-Frid Four was not an option for Frida at this point. The conflict between the safe and familiar life as a housewife and local singer in Eskilstuna, and whatever possibilities she may have had on a national level, remained. She was determined that her home should be in perfect order and spotlessly clean, while show business demands meant that she seldom got into bed before two in the morning – only to be woken by the children a few hours later.

"The offers were pouring in after my talent contest victory," she said at the time. "But my first priority was to be a mother to my children. I turned down many offers." It was like a mantra she kept repeating in interview after interview: "My duties as housewife and mother come first."

If Frida was unable to charm audiences through transistor radios or television sets, her qualities as a singer didn't go unnoticed. In early 1968, she appeared in a radio show together with the immensely popular singer Lasse Lönndahl. Charmed by her appearance and impressed by her voice, he asked her to come along for a six-week tour of the *folkparks* in the summer. Frida, who already had plans for a tour with another, less famous singer, readily agreed to Lönndahl's flattering offer.

The 40-date tour between May 22 and June 30 was certainly a useful experience that Frida remembered fondly as her first real show business venture. But it didn't seem to help her much in terms of increasing her popularity with the audience: two more singles were released in 1968 and both flopped. EMI did what they could to promote her, but to little avail.

Frida couldn't help but succumb to a nagging feeling of hopelessness. Here she was, with a record contract and a producer who maintained his faith in her despite every record dying a dismal death, as well as opportunities to go on tour with the biggest artists in Sweden. And yet she had to keep up her domestic duties in Eskilstuna, when what she really needed to do was to spend time in Stockholm to try to further her career as best she could. The equation simply didn't work out.

The ever-supportive Ragnar recognised a part of the problem, encouraging her to leave Anni-Frid Four, as she told reporters: "My husband says, 'Now you have the chance, Anni-Frid. Of course you should be out and about. You could have a career, you're simply too good to remain with us any longer.'"

For her own part she had also come to the realisation that whatever affection she felt towards Ragnar, it had never been true love. The bond between them had more to do with a special kind of friendship that arose from the comfort and security he provided for her, and from the shared experience of raising a family together.

In interviews during the months following her breakthrough, there was always a certain distance when she talked about Ragnar. Statements like "my husband is a wonderful father and spouse – much better as a husband than as a musician" sounded more like she was talking about a colleague at work than someone whose very being occupied her heart and soul. And despite the many practical advantages of playing in a band together, their professional collaboration was a strain on their relationship as well.

Insecure about her self-worth at the best of times, the situation threw her into a depression. "I discovered that Anni-Frid was in fact a totally different person to the housewife and mother that was about to dust herself to death in her sheltered existence," she later reflected. "I felt as if I had to jump straight off a cliff in order not to choke."

The final, decisive push came when Frida got an offer to work in a cabaret show with veteran pianist and entertainer Charlie Norman. Scheduled to open in January 1969, the show would entail engagements for several months at different venues all over Sweden. It would be impossible for her to come home to Eskilstuna in the evenings and act the part of a housewife. The romance in Frida and Ragnar's marriage had long since died. They had both reached the same conclusion: a divorce was inevitable.

But Frida worried about leaving her children behind. Six-year-old Hans and Lise-Lotte, not yet two, remained with their father in Eskilstuna, where he could give them a safe and secure upbringing. It was a heartbreaking decision for Frida, but at the same time one she made without much hesitation. "I've never regretted taking the step of moving to Stockholm," she said a year later. "In a way it was the first time I did something for *me*. But I will never give up on remaining in contact with my children."

Frida's move to Stockholm was not an especially happy experience at the outset and for much of the time she longed to return to her family life in Eskilstuna. She was living alone and isolated in Bro, several miles northwest of the capital, close to Charlie Norman and his family. "Of course I could go and visit Charlie, but . . . Being lonely doesn't agree with me – it was awful," she reflected. "It was the loneliest period of my life." Nor did being based in Stockholm mean any great improvements in her recording career. Plans to secure a West German record contract, like many other Swedish singers had done successfully around this time, came to nothing.

The only light in the darkness was her collaboration with Charlie Norman, which turned out to be long and successful. Opening their show in Gothenburg on January 7, Frida was to work regularly with Norman for the following 18 months. "He was a very good teacher, both musically and in terms of how to act on stage," she acknowledged. "He was something of a father-figure for me."

In March 1969, Frida was given yet another chance to achieve a breakthrough as a solo act. She entered *Melodifestivalen*, the Swedish selections for the Eurovision Song Contest, with a song called 'Härlig är vår jord' ('Our Earth Is Wonderful'). Although she only finished fourth, the song did bring her some small recognition when it became her first entry on *Svensktoppen*. Alas, the song remained in the chart for only one week and was nowhere to be seen on the sales chart.

One of the composers taking part in the contest was more successful. Benny Andersson had collaborated with singer and songwriter Lars Berghagen on an entry entitled 'Hej clown'. The song finished second, but became a major hit on the Swedish charts.

Benny and Frida later remembered saying hello at *Melodifestivalen*, but with all the hubbub surrounding the event, they remained preoccupied that evening. It was only on their second meeting a few days later that they had a chance to talk some more. The Hep Stars had recently started doing cabaret shows, and took their show to Malmö for a few days in early March. Their guitarist Janne Frisk had now left the group completely, and once again Björn Ulvaeus stepped in as a temporary replacement.

For their part, Frida and Charlie Norman were just concluding their own engagement at another venue in Malmö. One night they were having a late night supper at a restaurant when, quite by chance, Björn and Benny showed up to have a meal. Before long they had been joined by Svenne Hedlund and his fiancée Charlotte Walker.

It all turned into one big get-together, with everybody talking and enjoying each other's showbiz stories. The party continued at Björn and Benny's hotel, where the two young men were joined by Frida and Charlie. "We had coffee and booze and sat talking until seven in the morning," remembered Benny.

Nothing more happened at this first meeting. But when Frida left the boys' hotel on that chilly March morning, she felt like she had known Benny all her life. There was a warmth and kindness exuding from his eyes, and his combination of youthful attraction and authoritative gentleness was irresistible. Likewise, Benny was charmed by the attractive brunette with the infectious laughter.

Later the same month Björn and Benny met Frida again, when all three were part of a "jukebox jury" style panel in the radio show *Midnight Hour*. Benny was in a relationship with another girl, but couldn't resist the temptation of a brief fling with Frida. "We decided not to meet again, we were not at all supposed to fall in love or make any commitments," she remembered. "Of course, I was in love with him already, but it took some time before he felt the same about me."

Benny recalled: "My relationship with this other girl was nearing its end, but still I was going to Paris to see her. I felt sorry for Frida, who lived so far from central Stockholm, so I let her borrow my apartment. When I came home I told Frida that my girlfriend would be coming back to Stockholm in the autumn. Frida didn't like the sound of that at all, but she didn't say anything about it. Then it was time for her to move out. 'You can stay until the end of the month,' I said. But then she didn't move out after all, because all of a sudden I found that I didn't want her to do that."

Frida felt the same way. Despite her seven years with Ragnar, she was now truly in love for the first time – with Benny. Similarly, Benny found that he was serious about someone for the first time since Christina. Still Frida was wrapped up in a shell that wasn't easy to break through. Benny recognised that it would take time to get to know her. "She was so secretive at the time – unbelievably secretive," he said. "She was so serious. She'd talk and talk, but didn't really say anything about herself."

Frida recalled the clashes in musical tastes and expressions between the two. "I came from jazz, Benny from pop. At first, it was just confusion when we were supposed to meet musically in 'Moonlight In Vermont'. Benny didn't know the song, he thought the chords were strange." For several months the love affair was kept a secret from the press, but the tension and the differences made the relationship all the more exciting.

When Benny and Frida met for the first time in the spring of 1969, Björn and Benny's tentative songwriting sessions had already blossomed into a full-blown partnership. They were spending as much time together as possible, even going on a one-week holiday to the Canary Islands in December 1968. On their return home, they made an impromptu performance as a duo at a venue in Björn's home town.

While the pair was in Malmö the following spring a songwriting collaboration with Stig Anderson, 'Ljuva sextital' ('The Good Old Sixties'), was recorded in their absence by singer Brita Borg. It turned out to be their first hit as composers – the media was starting to recognise Björn & Benny as a music-making unit.

With the development of Benny's relationship with Frida, she also became a part of the duo's everyday life. Three quarters of what was to become Abba were slowly getting to know each other, and the final piece of the jigsaw puzzle was just about to enter the equation.

A year earlier, on January 10, 1968, Frida had appeared on a television show called *Studio 8*, performing her single 'En ledig dag'. But it wasn't Frida's performance that stayed in the minds of those watching the show that night. Instead it was another young singer, a 17-year-old, blonde girl with an innocent smile, who made the audience sit up and take notice.

Her début single was a song she had written herself, and when she performed it on television, it would send her spinning into national fame. Björn Ulvaeus, watching the show at home with his parents in Västervik, was mesmerised by the cute girl. As he recalled, he thought it was "cool with a chick who wrote her own songs. It was fairly uncommon at the time." He told Aina and Gunnar, "That girl's going to go far!"

It was the first time Björn set eyes on Agnetha Fältskog.

Chapter 8

"Dreamer, silly dreamer, they all call me, since I met you . . ." The chorus was insistent and repetitive, simple to learn and to sing along with. The energetic performance from the male lead vocalist lent itself particularly well to the uptempo arrangement of the song, as it rang out from the tiny speaker of the yellow plastic record-player. Complete with nonsensical "hush-hush-a-bye" backing vocals, it was a recording that belonged to the dumber end of the early Sixties Brill Building pop spectrum.

For all its annoying perkiness, in December 1964 the song seemed irresistible to 14-year-old Agnetha Fältskog. Both the single, Neil Sedaka's 'The Dreamer', and the record player were Christmas gifts she had received from her parents. Although she probably didn't think of it at the time, the song was a soundtrack to an important part of her life during those early teenage years.

For dreaming was what she was doing. Now that Agnetha had her very own record player she could spend hours in her room, just listening to music. Holding her hairbrush like a microphone, she'd sit in front of her make-up mirror, singing along to the lyrics, imitating every inflection and each breath to perfection. When she wasn't playing Neil Sedaka songs, she'd imagine she was someone like Italian singer Rita Pavone, or perhaps French songstress Sylvie Vartan.

Agnetha's real favourite, however, was Connie Francis. She was especially fond of love-lorn ballads like 'Who's Sorry Now?', 'Carolina Moon' and 'My Happiness', where the singer sounded like she was about to burst into tears any second. Connie Francis was Agnetha's idol among idols. It was her albums that spun most frequently on the little yellow record player, it was her she wanted to sound like most of all: she was the role model for all Agnetha's dreams. "I wanted to become a star, a celebrity. I wanted to be on television," she remembered.

So far, Agnetha's daydreams of fame and fortune hadn't taken her very far outside the borders of the town of Jönköping, where she lived in a four-room apartment with her parents and little sister. Situated at the southern end of lake Vättern in the county of Småland, Jönköping is primarily known in Sweden for being the nation's biggest stronghold for

Chapter 8

Christian Free Churches; a typical medium-sized Swedish town, with a population of around 50,000 at the start of the Sixties, its economy relying on a number of large industries.

It was into this environment that Agneta Åsc Fältskog was born on April 5, 1950. The "h" in Agnetha was added later in life, but her name has never been officially registered in this fashion.

At the time of Agnetha's birth, her father Ingvar was 27 years old. A store manager by trade, he had an outgoing personality and a keen interest in music and show business. Since his teenage years in the late Thirties and up until the end of 1949, he'd been writing and staging local amateur revues in Jönköping. Ingvar would write skits and songs for the shows, although they never made many waves outside the town borders. "I guess I lacked in both musicality and self-confidence," he said. "We covered our expenses, but not much more than that."

There were many practical problems involved with the staging, and it was particularly hard to get all the chorus girls to appear on the same night. "Their boyfriends would be mad because they never had any time off," explained Ingvar. After finally giving up the revues, he kept his ambitions in music and entertainment alive in more modest ways. Ingvar would arrange local parties or perhaps appear on stage as a singer with various small bands.

In October 1945 Ingvar married Birgit Johansson, who was 26 when her first daughter was born. Mild mannered and introverted, she remained a housewife until Agnetha and her sister Mona, born in 1955, had grown up. Birgit Fältskog was also musical and had a good singing voice, but despite helping out with her husband's revues on the practical side, she was never seen performing on stage.

The Fältskog home was warm, noisy and protective. As a child Agnetha always felt that outside visitors were unwelcome, and their presence would invariably lead to temper tantrums. "I'd scream out loud when we had guests. I wouldn't calm down until they left. Then I'd wave from the window, overjoyed."

Agnetha has also admitted to strong feelings of jealousy when Mona was born, but the five-year age difference between the two sisters soon ceased to matter very much: they both remembered being close as children. In the summers the family would go away on camping holidays, and Ingvar and Birgit were always supportive of their children's inclinations.

Both sets of Agnetha's grandparents lived nearby, further extending the close family environment. For the traditional Swedish midsummer celebrations the family would go dancing by the lake in nearby Axamo, while the children were playing and taking part in fun and games. Later in life Agnetha often reflected on her secure and idyllic childhood.

"Growing up under secure circumstances made me strong as an adult. By secure I mean that my mother was always at home, and we had firm routines and regular schedules that we lived by. When I got home from school my mother was there, and at ten past five every day daddy came home from work. And then you went to bed at a certain time and got up at a certain time."

Music came early in life to Agnetha, perhaps earlier than any of the other future Abba members. She made her stage début as a singer at the end of 1955, when her father arranged a Christmas party for the local angling club, of which he was an active member. Agnetha performed the traditional song 'Billy Boy', which had been a hit in Sweden earlier that year. Although Agnetha herself has no recollection of the event, the most memorable part of her performance seems to have been when the elastic of her panties snapped, causing them to slide slowly down beneath her dress while she was singing. She remembered the story her mother told her: "People were roaring with laughter. I'm surprised I ever dared go onstage again."

A duality in her feelings about appearing before an audience would follow her through life, well into adulthood. "The inclination to express my talents was there already during my school years," she recalled. "I thought it was awful standing in front of the class, reading an essay or singing. But although I wanted to sink through the floor, I remained until I was finished."

While her father used to sing and play the guitar at home, it was another instrument that was to strike Agnetha's fancy. In the spring of 1955, around the time of her fifth birthday, she heard magical sounds from the upstairs apartment. Music teacher Sigvard Andersson and his wife Enid had just invested in a piano, and Sigvard was trying out their new purchase. Wearing a light-blue dress, she climbed up the stairs to the Anderssons and rang the door bell.

The Fältskogs and the Anderssons would often socialise together, so Agnetha was warmly welcomed into the apartment. Sigvard lifted her up on to the piano stool; Agnetha put her fingers on the piano keys and started playing. She obviously wasn't able to play a genuine melody at this first attempt, but she was entranced by her ability to produce such intriguing sounds from the instrument.

Agnetha soon became a frequent visitor to the patient Anderssons. "[I] was there every single day. I'm sure I drove [them] crazy in the end," she recalled. Her piano skills gradually improved and she'd sit for hours on end, playing and singing to herself. After a while she was able to pick out her own melodies on the piano. At the age of six she wrote her first song, a simple little ditty entitled 'Två små troll' ('Two Little Trolls').

It was apparent that Agnetha's love for music was more than a passing infatuation, and on her seventh birthday her parents bought her a piano of her own. "I was so happy," she remembered. "I was glued to the piano every day from morning till night. I'll never forget it." Agnetha spent hours searching for notes, and even tried to learn how to read music.

Taking the usual tedious recorder lessons before furthering her piano-playing skills would have been a waste of time, so the ever-helpful upstairs neighbour Sigvard Andersson arranged for Agnetha to start taking piano lessons immediately. But it was difficult to learn to read music properly. "At first, I could only play with either the left or the right hand. It was hard for me to make them work together. But all of a sudden, I managed to produce the right sounds. It was music and it gave me an extraordinary feeling."

As a child, Agnetha was well liked and had many friends. A minor trauma occurred at the age of ten when she needed to have dental surgery to correct her teeth. After the operation she had to wear braces for four years, which perhaps wasn't the most fortunate way to enter into her teens. "I had an enormous complex about that," she recalled.

Around the same time Agnetha started writing songs for real. Most were never released on record, but she has kept them all in notebooks and on tapes. She was 13 when she formed a vocal trio with two girlfriends, Lena Johansson and Elisabeth Strub. Calling themselves The Cambers, the trio would appear in local variety shows, at the *folkpark* and at private parties. Much of their act consisted of Agnetha's compositions, which The Cambers would perform in three-part harmonies. "We were inseparable," recalled Lena Johansson. "We did everything together and had so much fun. Sometimes we went out dancing, but most of the time we kept to ourselves and would be singing together. Singing and music was our main common interest."

The Cambers' sights were already set far beyond Jönköping. "We could sit for hours and dream of what major stars we would become and the fantastic careers we'd be making," Lena remembered. At one point the girls sent a tape to the Swedish Broadcasting Corporation, hoping to secure a television appearance. The rejection letter arrived almost by return of post.

Agnetha was 14 when her piano teacher told her that he'd taught her all he could. It made her very proud. By then, she was already playing complicated Bach fugues on the harpsichord in her local church. "They weren't especially easy things; my level of ambition was high. At the same time I was a member of the church choir and we'd often sing together. It was a good choir."

For all her formal training it was European female singers and early

Sixties American and British pop that remained the focus for Agnetha's musical aspirations. Idols like Sylvie Vartan, Neil Sedaka and Connie Francis were later joined by Petula Clark, Cilla Black, Sandie Shaw and Dusty Springfield. On the male side she favoured P.J. Proby, The Beatles and The Beach Boys. "My biggest idols were often artists who wrote their own songs. And I'd be thinking about how they were living: 'I wonder what he or she's doing right now,' things like that."

Throughout her school years, Agnetha had been a good pupil, but found that she lost interest in her final years in the four-year junior secondary school. Graduating at the age of 15, her grades in maths, physics and chemistry were decidedly unimpressive though her results were better in Swedish, English, German and music.

Around the same time, engagements for The Cambers dried up and soon the group dissolved. Meanwhile Agnetha was going through her teenage revolt stage, seeking independence and discovering boys. She started smoking at 15, and became acquainted with the disadvantages of having a 10-year-old sister. "If she'd been mean to me, I'd say that I would tell on her," remembered her sister Mona. "But Agnetha would bribe me to keep quiet. I got a couple of kronor or a fiver every now and then to keep quiet. I must have earned at least 50 kronor on not saying anything about her smoking."

Mona would also follow Agnetha on the sly when she went dancing instead of going to the movies, like she'd told her parents. Agnetha would use a mix of pleas and threats to make Mona keep quiet. "But the most fun of all was when Agnetha started dating boys. Me and my friends would sneak after her and make our presence known at the exact moment when Agnetha and some boy would start kissing or cuddling. We thoroughly enjoyed watching their embarrassment and anger."

After her graduation in the early summer of 1965, Agnetha chose not to continue studying. Instead, she got a job working in the office and on the switchboard at a local car firm. She never forgot the long morning walks to her employment. Of course Agnetha didn't really care what kind of work she was doing, as long as she was able to go on with music in her spare time. During the weekends, she'd sometimes sing with different orchestras in Jönköping. But her big break didn't come until over a year after she'd left school.

In the summer of 1966 a dance band called Bernt Enghardt's Orchestra, hailing from the nearby town of Huskvarna, had just returned from a long engagement in Berlin. Originally formed as an eight-piece orchestra, the band started performing in public in 1964, and were slowly becoming one of the more popular dance bands in the area. By 1965, they were down to six guys plus a vocalist called Agneta Desilva, who'd sing the occasional song in Enghardt's largely instrumental act.

"We had quite a lot of jobs after a while and ended up at this American military base in Berlin," recalls Bernt Enghardt. "What they wanted to hear down there was soul music, so we tried to make that style work for us. We'd go to discotheques and clubs, hearing other bands play this kind of music."

By the time Enghardt's returned to Sweden, Agneta Desilva had become romantically involved with the band's guitarist and they decided to leave. In lieu of the guitarist an organist was recruited, but the problem of finding a new female singer remained. "One of the other guys in the band remembered this girl trio from Jönköping who used to sing at clubs and parties," says Enghardt. "One of them was Agnetha Fältskog and we asked her to come and audition for us. I can't recall that we tried any other girls. We fell for Agnetha immediately."

The band was especially impressed that Agnetha was able to learn both melodies and lyrics so quickly: it was important that she could take over much of Miss Desilva's repertoire. "She wasn't able to do the Spanish-style songs, like 'La Bamba', but the rest of the material posed no problem at all."

According to Enghardt, Agnetha effortlessly wrapped her mild, Swedish small-town girl voice around songs like 'Sunny' and 'Hallelujah I Love Him So'. Perhaps even more astonishingly, Agnetha would perform the lead vocal on the James Brown soul shouter 'I Got You (I Feel Good)'. "It sounded just fine," claims Bernt. "She could pull off things like that. That's one of the reasons we thought she was so great."

An additional advantage of having Agnetha in the band was that Enghardt's wouldn't have to print any new posters. The vocalist billing as "Agneta" could remain if they just pasted a picture of Agnetha over her predecessor's face. After a period of rehearsals, on September 17, 1966, Agnetha made her début as vocalist with Bernt Enghardt's at the Bellevue in the town of Karlshamn.

"To begin with, I don't think Agnetha sang many numbers," says Enghardt. "It was probably something like every fourth song." In addition to the band's soul repertoire Enghardt's act also featured a few jazz-oriented numbers, as well as the inevitable Swedish and European *schlagers*. "It depended on where you were playing. It was almost like you'd have to have a specific repertoire for each venue."

Agnetha was over the moon that she'd been chosen as the new vocalist for such an established band, but other members of the Fältskog household expressed concern. "I had to have long talks with her parents in the beginning, they wanted to know who I was," says Enghardt. "They were a bit worried, and who wouldn't have been? A 16-year-old girl cramped up with six young guys in a car, travelling all over Sweden."

For the first few engagements, Ingvar Fältskog accompanied his daughter out to the car, making his presence felt so that the boys wouldn't forget that Agnetha had a protective dad. Whether because of the shadow of daddy Fältskog looming large over them or because of Agnetha's own lack of interest, no romances developed between Agnetha and the band members. "I had promised Ingvar to keep an eye on things, which I did," says Bernt.

It didn't take long before Ingvar stopped worrying too much about Agnetha's trips with Enghardt's. With his background in revues, he was very encouraging about the band and his daughter's singing. It was actually harder for Agnetha's mother to come to terms with the situation. "There were many nights that I'd be lying awake and waiting: 'Three o'clock, four o'clock – isn't she back yet?' " Birgit Fältskog recalled. "It made me very worried. I can't help being a mother."

Birgit also feared that it would be too big a strain on Agnetha to work at the car firm Monday to Friday and then spend the weekends singing. A teenage girl needs time to do other things, she insisted – relax, go out and have fun with her friends. But Agnetha was determined: "No, I'm going to sing."

Joining Enghardt's hadn't stopped Agnetha from continuing her own songwriting, and by the end of 1966 she had amassed a catalogue of more than a dozen songs. Judging by the compositions that have been made public from this period, Connie Francis' repertoire was still an important influence as Agnetha worked out her songs at the piano. It wasn't the perky, uptempo Francis hits like 'Stupid Cupid' and 'Lipstick On Your Collar' that captured Agnetha's imagination; rather, the maudlin, doe-eyed ballads of broken hearts and unattainable boys offered the inspiration for the songs from her teenage years.

"You're often unhappily in love at that time of your life," she reflected. "I guess it was at such times that I wanted to express myself. I would write my songs when I was having strong emotions and feeling down. It felt good to do that." No more so, perhaps, than on a warm summer night in 1966.

For a while Agnetha had been going steady with a boy called Björn Lilja. The relationship had seen its ups and downs, even from the start. "For the most part, I was the one who broke up. But I regretted it every time, and then we'd patch it up again."

On this particular night the pair were in one of their off periods, and Agnetha was feeling depressed. She sat down at the piano and started toying with a melody to divert her thoughts. Half an hour later Agnetha had both words and music for a song she called 'Jag var så kär' ('I Was So In Love'), although the title doesn't actually appear in the lyrics. It was a slow, dramatic *schlager* ballad, heavily influenced by the most self-pitying pages of the Connie Francis songbook.

Agnetha felt especially pleased with this new composition, but she kept it under wraps for several months before mentioning it to Bernt Enghardt. Her urge to compose and express herself musically was often restrained by shyness and a lack of self-confidence: whereas boys her age could draw inspiration from celebrated teams like Lennon & McCartney, role models for 16-year-old girls who aspired to become songwriters were few and far between in the mid-Sixties.

Eventually she plucked up the courage to play the song during a band rehearsal. Sitting down at the piano, she drew a deep breath and started singing. "She was really shy," recalls Bernt Enghardt. "But we said, 'This song is great! We're going to write an arrangement for it and include it in our set.' 'No, really . . .' she said. 'Of course we will. This song could get you on the charts. You've got the feeling for this.' "

The band set to work. Organist Bertil Bodahl improved on the song's harmonic structure, and saxophonist Tom Edberg wrote a horn arrangement, including a jazzy break in the middle. 'Jag var så kär' was introduced in the act. "To begin with, the reaction wasn't that overwhelming," says Bernt. "When you play dance music you always have a 'first song' which you use to get the audience to start dancing. It was a long while before we could use it for that purpose."

Around the same time the band was putting out feelers for a record contract. Bernt Enghardt's wife was the cousin of former rocker Little Gerhard, now Cupol record producer Karl-Gerhard Lundkvist. The band leader made a phone call to Stockholm, asking if he could send Lundkvist a tape.

"He said yes, but told me that there was no chance unless we had material of our own. But we sent him a tape anyway, and a letter came back where he said that he wasn't that fond of the girl's voice: 'She's a bit young and she sounds like she has a cold.' But he said that we should try again when we had some original material."

In the spring of 1967, Bernt Enghardt and Bertil Bodahl got an offer to play with another, more professional orchestra, and left the band. Agnetha and the remaining boys persevered, even retaining the brand name Bernt Enghardt's. Before leaving the band, Bernt's Grundig reel-to-reel tape recorder had been used to make a second tape of the current repertoire in the music room at the Huskvarna school. By this time, Agnetha's 'Jag var så kär' was included in the repertoire. Several months later this tape, too, was sent to Karl-Gerhard Lundkvist.

The record producer still didn't express much enthusiasm for the music of the Huskvarna. "It wasn't good, it wasn't bad – it just *was*," he says today. But as luck would have it, Bernt Enghardt's demo had been recorded only on the left channel and on the right channel was music from the other side of the tape. While listening to the band's music, Lundkvist's attention was caught by the backwards sound of a girl singing and playing the piano on the right channel.

He turned the tape over and had a proper listen. The girl was singing a song called 'Utan dej' ('Without You'). Lundkvist pricked up his ears – this was more like it. But he didn't have a clue who the girl could be; it didn't really sound like Bernt Enghardt's anodyne vocalist.

It turned out that some of Agnetha's private recordings of her own songs had ended up on the Enghardt's tape – and there was a marked difference between the energetic vocals of her own demos, and her rather flat performance on the band's recordings. "The voice on the other side of the tape was exactly right for those times, it was in line with other popular singers," says Lundkvist. "And she sang very well. She didn't slide in on the notes, she nailed them bang-on." He felt that he could make good records with this singer, and decided to try to locate her. Eventually he discovered that it was the same girl singing on both sides of the tape. But Lundkvist also realised that it was Enghardt's who had sent him the tape, making the situation somewhat delicate. With the help of his wife, he managed to find the girl's name and her home phone number.

Agnetha recalled: "This guy called me at home one night, said that he was Little Gerhard and wondered if I wanted to make a record. I had this hang-up on celebrities and was certain that someone in the band was trying to pull my leg." She giggled and said, "Yeah, right," before slamming the phone down. Why would a famous rock idol call up a teenage girl in Jönköping? It was ridiculous.

Lundkvist was annoyed at her behaviour, but called her up again, telling her that this was serious business. "I said that I still didn't believe him," Agnetha remembered. "I wanted proof that he really was Little Gerhard. 'If I send you the tape back and enclose a greeting, will you believe me then?' he asked."

The tape was returned and Agnetha finally accepted the story. "I just couldn't believe it was true at first. That's how convinced I was that I couldn't accomplish anything of real value." It was as if the dream of stardom was always meant to remain a dream. No one had told her that small-town girls weren't supposed to be songwriters. Yet, it seemed to be beyond her imagination that she would get any serious recognition from something that she had created.

Her delight at getting the chance to make a record was somewhat clouded by the news that Lundkvist wanted to sign only Agnetha, and not the band. "It was a touchy situation and it was terribly hard for me to tell the guys that they would not be allowed to appear on the record," she recalled.

According to Karl-Gerhard Lundkvist, Cupol Records boss Helge Roundquist was disinclined towards modern music or young singers, and it was hard to get him to agree to new signings. Lundkvist conferred with top arranger Sven-Olof Walldoff, playing him Agnetha's tape. "He told me, 'She's great, you must record her. Don't mind what that old man says.'"

A session was booked for Monday, October 16, 1967 at the Philips Studio in Stockholm. Lundkvist decided to take a chance and record two singles at this very first session. Agnetha was heavily involved in the creation of three of these first four titles: 'Jag var så kär' and 'Utan dej' featured her own words and music, and she had written Swedish lyrics for 'Följ med mig', a cover of 'Hello Love' by British singer Julie Grant. Incidentally, the lyrics for the fourth song had been dashed out by the prolific Stig Anderson.

Agnetha's head was spinning at the prospect of her first proper recording session. The thought of going alone on her very first visit to the capital was too frightening to even contemplate, so her father promised to come along and they arranged to stay with his sister Maj. The night before the train trip to Stockholm, Agnetha could hardly sleep. In the morning, she got up much too early to fix herself up for the day. For such an important occasion, she wanted to appear the freshest girl in the world.

By the time father and daughter arrived in Stockholm and the Philips Studio, Agnetha was a wreck, feeling very much the country wench. "I had to take pills to keep my nerves in check. My legs were shaking and I felt really silly," she recalled. Dressed in boots and a green shift with large polka-dots and bell-shaped sleeves, clasping her father's hand tightly, she descended the stairs to the studio, the sound of string instruments being added to the backing track of 'Jag var så kär', her very own song, ringing in her ears.

Agnetha was overwhelmed with joy, her fears swept aside. Indeed, she would never forget the feeling of hearing a professional, full-orchestra arrangement of the tune she had written on her piano back in Jönköping. "It was the happiest moment of my whole career in music," she said later.

"It sounded exactly like I had hoped it would, Sven-Olof Walldoff captured it perfectly."

Agnetha added a plaintive, distinctively personal lead vocal to the tape, as Karl-Gerhard Lundkvist remembers. "She knew exactly what she was doing musically. When I asked her to add a harmony part, she did it like it was the easiest thing. But at the same time she didn't have much belief in herself. She was very mild and shy – it wasn't 'watch out, here I come!' but rather, 'okay, all right, whatever you say . . .' She couldn't believe it was her own song she was hearing."

During the recording session, a photo for the cover of the first single was taken. Agnetha was asked to climb up on the grand piano. "I was lying there in some kind of pose. It felt really corny," she remembered. With her long blonde hair and thick layers of mascara around shy-looking eyes, the photographer had clearly decided to make the most of Agnetha's image, an alluring blend of shy innocence and kittenish sexuality.

For their part, Lundkvist and Walldoff felt extremely satisfied with the recordings. "If Helge Roundquist had said that he didn't want the tracks, Walldoff and I would've released them ourselves. We agreed on that even in the studio." The recordings were mixed and brought to the Cupol offices for the approval of the boss. "At first he gave me a right telling off and said, 'You can't just go away and waste money on recordings like this!' But when he heard the songs, he changed his tune on the spot: 'This is really good. Is she still in town?'" Agnetha and her father were asked to come up to the Cupol offices to make the deal and sign a contract.

"The president of the company was absolutely delighted and everyone was really kind and helpful," Agnetha recalled. "But they had high expectations and said that it wasn't often that Cupol gambled on two singles by a new and inexperienced singer. That didn't exactly make me feel any more relaxed."

Ingvar Fältskog was a tough negotiator and saw to it that Agnetha, who hadn't yet come of age, was signed to the label on unusually good terms for a débutante in 1967: a 75,000 kronor (£5,200) guaranteed sum every year and a fixed monthly payment against a royalty rate of 21 öre (0.21 kronor) per single.

Ingvar also took charge of all other business arrangements and handled Agnetha's bookkeeping and tax returns for the first few years. "Agnetha was just so happy when the offers started pouring in," he recalled. "She was eager and wanted to say yes to everything immediately. 'But dad, we will never get more than 800 kronor (£55) on a Saturday night gig,' she'd plead." But Ingvar played it cool and managed to negotiate far better deals.

The recording session and contract signing over, Agnetha returned to

Björn Ulvaeus, the backbone of the group, its unofficial leader, evaluator, public face and, eventually, its astute lyricist. (*LFI*)

Alfred Haase, Frida's German father, circa 1943.

Synni Lyngstad, Frida's mother, in the mid-Forties.

Frida as a child, with her grandmother Agny who raised her in Sweden, pictured together in the summer of 1953.

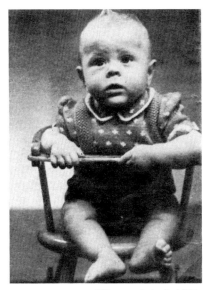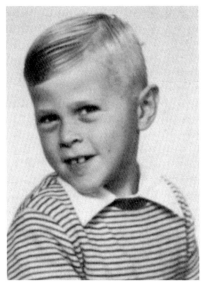

Björn as a baby in 1945, and aged around five years.

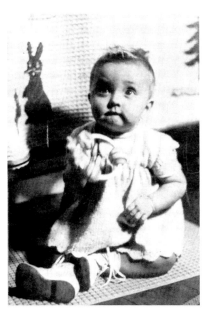

Agnetha as a baby in 1950.

Benny with his father, Gösta Andersson, circa 1950.

Björn, with his first electric guitar.

Stig Anderson in the late Fifties,
when he was a teacher in Stockholm.
(*Bengt H. Malmqvist/Premium*)

A 19-year-old Björn with the clean cut, well-mannered folk music group the Hootenanny Singers, in 1964, left to right: Johan Karlberg, Björn, Hansi Schwarz and Tony Rooth. Björn later said: "The Hootenanny Singers is the worst name that any band has ever had. It's just so ugly - possibly only beaten by Abba." (*Bengt H. Malmqvist/Premium*)

Agnetha, posing with two fans in the mid-Sixties. (*bigpicturesphoto.com*)

Benny, in his early Hep Stars days,
circa 1965. (*Sven Eric Delér/Premium*)

Frida at home in 1963. Note the picture of
her mother on the bookshelf.

Frida with the Gunnar Sandevärn's Orchestra in the mid-Sixties, left to right: Frida, Gunnar, and brothers Lennart and Ragnar Fredriksson. Ragnar was Frida's first husband. (*Gunnar Sandevärn Collection*)

Frida on stage with the Sandevärn's Orchestra. Gunnar Sandevärn recalls: "Frida didn't like it if you got slack or the breaks were too long, and she wanted us to rehearse constantly - all the things that mark out a real pro." (*Gunnar Sandevärn Collection*)

Hep Stars, 1965, left to right: Lennart Hegland, Janne Frisck, Svenne Hedlund, Christer Pettersson and Benny. The Hep Stars were Sweden's number one pop band of the Sixties, but "weren't actually very much to listen to," said Benny. (*Bengt H. Malmqvist/Premium*)

Publicity pictures of Agnetha in the late-Sixties during her pre-Abba career as a pop singer, aged 18 in 1968 (left) and 19 in 1969. Agnetha relished her first taste of success: "All of a sudden, everything you've fantasised about comes true. You're almost a celebrity." (*Ulf H. Holmstedt*)

Frida in the late Sixties. Despite several singles she failed to have any hits and contemplated leaving the music business. "I love being an artist, but I'm not sure that I'm among those who will survive," she said. (*Bengt H. Malmqvist/Premium*)

Jönköping. She carried on working at the car firm, singing with Enghardt's two or three nights per week. At the end of November, Agnetha's début single was released. 'Följ med mig' was the A-side while her own 'Jag var så kär' had been put on the flip. But it was Agnetha's song that caught the attention of radio producers. She recalled the very first time she heard a broadcast of the song. "One morning, as the family sat around the breakfast table, I heard my own voice on the radio. I took the radio in my arms and danced around with it."

Apart from the odd radio-play and a few signing sessions in local record shops, nothing much happened with the record at the outset. It would take almost two months before it was tested for entry on the all-important *Svensktoppen* chart. "It was hard for newcomers to *Svensktoppen* for a while," recalls Karl-Gerhard Lundkvist. "And I don't know if the record company was nagging at them a little too much. They may have been told to cool it a bit."

It wasn't until Agnetha secured her television début on the *Studio 8* show on January 10, 1968, that things started happening. Agnetha's aura of innocence reached right out of the screens into thousands of living rooms, and ten days later, 'Jag var så kär' was played on *Svensktoppen* for testing. There followed a tense week of sleepless nights for Agnetha, who was still thinking the worst. "I thought my song would finish last," she said.

Then, on the afternoon of Saturday, January 27, Agnetha received a phone call from show host Ulf Elfving. She was the highest new entry on the chart that week, at number three, and an interview was taped for airing when the show was broadcast the morning after. That was the final, decisive push the song needed: a week later, it entered the sales charts at number six, and by late February 'Jag var så kär' was number one.

Agnetha found it hard to believe what was happening. Tears of joy had streamed down her face when Ulf Elfving called her. "For an established artist I guess it's just an amusing little event to have a hit on *Svensktoppen*, but for me it meant everything," she reflected at the time. "I don't believe anyone can imagine what it feels like – all of a sudden, everything you've fantasised about comes true. You're almost a celebrity."

Life for Agnetha became increasingly hectic, with several press interviews and appearances on television and radio. "I don't even have a boyfriend," she said. "The guys give up after a while. I never have any time off."

Agnetha's second single, 'Utan dej', was scheduled for release in early February. She was writing a song for male singer Gunnar Wiklund, which she hoped he would perform as an entry in the Swedish selections for the Eurovision Song Contest (the song, 'Försonade' ['Reconciled'], was rejected and was instead released by Agnetha as a B-side). Shortly after signing her to the label, Cupol set to work drumming up interest in Agnetha from West German record labels. Her career was on a roll.

Somewhat surprisingly Agnetha kept up both her day job and the work with Enghardt's orchestra, but it soon became too much to handle. She recalled: "The trips we made with the band became longer and longer. Sometimes I would get home at five in the morning from a gig and then I had to be at the switchboard by eight. In the end I just couldn't take it anymore, I didn't get enough sleep."

Things came to a head one day in February. "One of the girls at work told me that I looked pale – that's the last thing I remember. Then I fainted." Agnetha came to as someone tried to help her up. It was clear that she had been working too late, eating too little and smoking too much. She took a few days off from work to rest.

Her mother was concerned, and gave Agnetha an ultimatum. "[She] told me that I had to choose: the switchboard or the singing. I chose the singing and I don't think my parents were too happy with that choice." But Agnetha was unstoppable, and as the month of February came to a close, she quit the car firm.

Her first few months as a full-time singer were a bit shaky. She kept performing with Enghardt's, but 'Utan dej' disappeared after two weeks on the *Svensktoppen* chart. Her third single, 'En sommar med dej' ('A Summer With You', a waltz written by her father), appeared on neither *Svensktoppen* nor the sales chart.

Meanwhile, despite Agnetha's initial reluctance, plans had been made for her to explore the possibilities of recording in West Germany. Many female Swedish singers had enjoyed a great deal of success there during the past decade, and it was an almost obligatory requirement that you should "try to go for the West German market". "She was blonde and Swedish – they loved that in West Germany," explains Karl-Gerhard Lundkvist. "It didn't matter if they could sing or not, just as long as they had long, blonde hair. The rest could be fixed in the studio."

A contract was signed with Metronome Records, and by May she found herself in a recording studio in Berlin. Both sides of her first single were written by 25-year-old songwriter Dieter Zimmerman, one third of the successful writer-producer team Zimmerman/Buschor/Meisel, who handled Agnetha's recordings.

Dieter, a handsome, stylish young man with dark hair and a lot of self-assurance, was struck by the appearance of the blonde Swedish girl. "I really believe in Agnetha," he stated confidently. "Her romantic and slightly melancholy style is exactly what is needed in West Germany right now." A spark ignited between them right there in the recording studio, and before long they were an item.

But Agnetha had commitments in Sweden that didn't allow her to remain in Berlin. Back home, she started a *folkpark* tour together with Enghardt's. On Thursday, May 23, 1968, the band had an engagement in a small place called Målilla in Småland. Although Agnetha's new-found status as a singing star meant that she received special billing – "Enghardt's with Agnetha Fältskog" – the act was still regarded as a dance band. They were expected to provide entertainment for several hours, as opposed to being afforded the status of a star attraction with a 30-minute stage show.

On that particular early summer night, it was the ever-popular Hootenanny Singers who were the stars at Målilla Sports Park. Agnetha had been in the audience when the group performed in Huskvarna a few years earlier. "All the girls were looking at Björn. My friends said, 'Isn't he cute?' But I said that Johan Karlberg was the cutest. I knew that in reality I liked Björn the most – I just wanted to stand apart from my friends."

Björn was delighted to finally meet the pretty blonde girl he'd seen on television. He was well aware that since then she'd had a number one hit on the sales chart, an accomplishment that had eluded even the Hootenanny Singers. When Enghardt's arrived at the park much later than scheduled, this first meeting between Björn and Agnetha didn't go well. With no live entertainment at all in the park, the Hootenanny Singers had to start their performance somewhat earlier than their 9.30 star spot. "They were really angry that we'd arrived late – our bus had broken down – and I was happy that they'd stepped in for us," recalled Agnetha.

The Hootenanny Singers were pretty disparaging towards Agnetha and her band. "We felt that we were the artists, and they were just a dance band who were in the way; we wanted to do our show and then get the hell out of there," says Hans "Berka" Bergkvist. "As I recall, Agnetha came in to our dressing room and we were joking pretty cruelly with her: 'What are you doing here? Get out, dance band singer!'"

Despite the insensitive jokes, Björn was mesmerised by Agnetha. "He was very determined: 'She's the right girl for me, I'm really going to work on this,'" says Hansi Schwarz. "He grabbed the opportunity to have a good talk with her."

Eyewitnesses in the Enghardt's camp recall that Agnetha was less than impressed by Björn and the Hootenanny Singers at the time, finding him sycophantic and the band pompous. Agnetha's own memories of Björn's attempts to chat her up were a bit rosier: "I was in seventh heaven. I had seen Björn several times on television and had a small crush on him."

At the time, Björn had just released his first solo single, 'Raring', a cover of the Bobby Goldsboro hit 'Honey'. Agnetha asked Björn to send her a copy of the single. "The next day we went to a record shop and bought the single, and then we mailed it to her," recalls Berka. Björn enclosed a letter, asking to see her again. "We went to see her perform later on, just him and me. It was all very hush-hush."

There were other fleeting encounters during the year: at one point, the Hootenanny Singers and Agnetha appeared on the same television show. But for the moment there was not much either of them could do to explore any romantic possibilities. Besides, Agnetha's mind and heart were already occupied by someone else.

Dieter Zimmerman arrived from West Germany a few days after Björn and Agnetha's meeting in Målilla, and he spent more than a fortnight tagging along on Agnetha's park tour. Her first foreign single, 'Robinson Crusoe'/'Sonny Boy', was just about to be released in West Germany. Agnetha and Dieter had also resolved to exchange songs: the plan was that she would be recording his songs in West Germany, and he would try to place her songs with artists in his country.

'Robinson Crusoe' was a pretty average *schlager*, and failed to become a hit, but this didn't seem to temper the affection between the two. On July 22, Agnetha and Dieter got engaged at the Fältskog's apartment in Jönköping. The engagement was celebrated with coffee and champagne, and Dieter stayed in Sweden until the middle of August. The news momentarily shattered Björn's hopes of getting together with Agnetha. "I was interested, but then I read in the papers that she'd got engaged," he recalled.

Less than a year after her début record, Agnetha's dream of becoming the Swedish Connie Francis seemed to have come true. She was a successful singer and songwriter who had topped the sales chart with her very first single – and she had written the song herself. She was also engaged to a young, attractive songwriter, and her career looked promising both in Sweden and West Germany.

On September 30, the tour concluded along with Agnetha's commitment to Bernt Enghardt's, and they went their separate ways. As if to celebrate her independence, her fifth single, 'Allting har förändrat sig' ('Everything Has Changed'), written by Karl-Gerhard Lundkvist, finally gave her a major hit again on both *Svensktoppen* and the sales chart.

This prompted Agnetha's decision to move to Stockholm. It was arranged that she could stay with the family of Lars-Johan Roundquist, the son of Cupol label boss Helge Roundquist. "I was no more than eighteen when I made the move and headed for the capital," she recalled. "It was pretty courageous and I sometimes wonder why I wasn't more uneasy about it. How could I have known it would be all right? Was I just naïve? But I've never felt any fear when it comes to work; one step comes naturally after the other. I've been lucky; things have always fallen into place in that area of my life."

Around the same time, she embarked on a three-week package tour with a few other high-profile Swedish artists. Before leaving, she enrolled in an acting school to improve her stage appearance. Part of the tour was filmed as a short television documentary, and judging by Agnetha's appearance as a backing singer for one of the other acts, some advice on how to perform on stage was sorely needed. She seemed to have a fondness for fluttery arm movements, and her attempts to perform a few simple choreographed steps didn't impress.

Agnetha found it hard to adjust to life as a recording star and professional artist. "I've reached the goal of my dreams, but I keep myself in check every day so that I won't become conceited," she said. For a teenage girl from the country, it was a challenge to try to fit in with the Stockholm show business crowd. Many were deceived by her innocent looks and tried to patronise her. They lived to regret it when they were confronted with her fiery side.

"Just because you're small and blonde it doesn't mean you're completely stupid," she said. "People shake their heads and say, 'You're so young and new, you can't have much in your head.' I don't like that." She was also offended by those who refused to believe she really wrote her own songs. "As if a girl of 18 shouldn't be able to do that," she spat.

Hep Stars singer Svenne Hedlund has a vivid recollection of the first time he met Agnetha, shortly after her move to Stockholm. "She talked like a guy would. In those days it wasn't that common for a girl to curse and use bad language like she did. I remember thinking, 'That's a really tough girl, she's got a mind of her own.' I guess she needed to be like that to make her way in this business, just because she was so young."

For the most part, Agnetha really enjoyed her status as a celebrity and was amazed by all the friends she was making. "They take me out to parties and are really helpful. It's important to go to parties. You have to be seen, otherwise people will forget that you exist."

During the autumn of 1968, parallel with the tour and the acting lessons, she was also doing her best to keep up the romance and musical collaboration with Dieter Zimmerman. One more German single, the inane 'Señor Gonzales', was released before the end of the year – several months later it made a brief appearance on the lower end of the charts. Agnetha later revealed that she was concerned about her German material.

"I tried to persuade the Germans to let me sing my own songs, but they chose songs for me instead. They were horrible songs and none of them became hits."

At the end of 1968, Agnetha released her first, eponymous album. It collected her five Swedish singles so far, plus two tracks exclusive for the album. From a credit point-of-view, it was an impressive début. Agnetha's name graced nine of the 12 tracks as composer, lyricist or both. The three songs she had written alone were among the best selections on the album. For all their heavily orchestrated naïvety and innocence it was clear that they came from her heart, and this gave them a certain charm that was lacking elsewhere. Her four collaborations with Dieter Zimmerman – he provided the music, she the lyrics – were fairly disastrous, however: the melodies were German *schlagers* at their very blandest and Agnetha's lyrics were unambitious, ranging between the soppily sentimental and plain whimsical.

"Many of the rhymes are just awful," she later acknowledged. "My excuse is that I was so young. When I hear songs like 'Skål kära vän' ('Cheers, My Dear Friend') and 'Snövit och de sju dvärgarna' ('Snow White And The Seven Dwarves') I just want to die – that's how bad the rhymes are."

Practice hadn't exactly made perfect yet, but the talent and the urge was there. During these early years of her career Agnetha was constantly writing songs. "The ideas kept coming all the time – on the town, in the tour bus, anywhere. I could hardly get pen and paper out fast enough," she recalled. When she got in the mood she would light two candles – preferably red – and then sit down at the piano. This would provide the right atmosphere to work those ideas into proper melodies, usually sad ones.

She was aware of the contrast between her perky personality and the melancholy nature of her songs. "I've written lots of happy songs, but it seems the public prefers my more tragic melodies," she said. Her theory was proved when she tried to record one of her more jaunty compositions. The song, 'Tag min hand låt oss bli vänner' ('Take My Hand, Let's Be Friends'), was left in the can for several months, and was eventually used only as a B-side.

Though Agnetha was brimming with creativity, most of the recordings immediately following her first album bore the mark of Dieter Zimmerman and his team – and they weren't interested in her songs. In the spring and summer of 1969, she released a further two singles in West Germany, one of which – 'Concerto d'amore' – rendered her a brief chart appearance. In June she entered a *schlager* contest in Berlin with Dieter's 'Wer schreibt heut' noch Liebesbriefe' ('Who Writes Love Letters Today') but didn't reach the finals.

Even in Sweden, most everything Agnetha released was a composition by Dieter, for which she had merely written the lyrics. In hindsight, it is clear that this domination by the Germans in general, and by Dieter in particular, was detrimental to her career. Nothing at all happened in West Germany, and for a 12-month period she only had one brief entry on the *Svensktoppen* chart. This minor success came with a particularly bland song called 'Fram för svenska sommaren' ('Here's To The Swedish Summer'). Agnetha's comment a decade later — "Did I really record this? Certain things leave no trace in the memory whatsoever" — perhaps said it all.

Her relationship with Dieter, a union founded on love and musical creativity, was rapidly souring. After a six-month engagement, the pair still couldn't agree where they should live. "He wanted me to move to Germany, but I didn't want to do that. There was no reason he couldn't have moved to Sweden just as well," said Agnetha. But neither wanted to budge.

Agnetha was also tiring of Dieter's attempts to guide her career. Karl-Gerhard Lundkvist recalls that Agnetha was the type of artist who knew exactly which songs she wanted to record and which she did not. "I met Dieter Zimmerman a couple of times, he was a nice guy. But it was evident he was the one who decided which songs should be recorded. He was very much in charge."

A clash was inevitable, and the physical distance between the two didn't strengthen their motivation to patch things up. "It didn't work when we saw each other so seldom," said Agnetha. "Both of us were jealous and kept wondering what the other one was up to. We had planned to get married eventually, but we never set a date. But we had acquired a few things for the home we were going to get. Still, after a while we realised it would be best to break off the engagement. I felt a bit low in the beginning: two people who have been engaged do have quite a few things in common."

By the spring of 1969 Agnetha was again a free agent, with her own plans for her career. Her songwriting continued in full force, and she was even asked to write for other artists. Singer Hans Smedberg, a new Cupol signing, released one of her songs on his début record. For the summer, Agnetha was scheduled to go on a *folkpark* tour with Smedberg and a stand-up comedian.

On May 4, she had been booked to start the filming of a television special. The roster included several of the more popular Swedish artists at the time. One name in particular on the list made her heart skip a beat. For working on this project would give her an opportunity to spend a considerable amount of time with Björn Ulvaeus.

Chapter 9

On the surface, the second half of the Sixties was fairly prosperous for the Hootenanny Singers. The individual members' plans for a future outside the group did nothing to stop them from touring, making records and having hits. The four young men were still good friends, but where once they had been a united force, they were now drifting apart. For his part, Björn was determined that whatever happened he would remain in the music business. "My biggest wish was that it would all continue," he said. "I remember sitting in the tour bus, thinking, 'It can't be over yet, just give me one more hit so that we'll have one more season.' "

By the autumn of 1967, while the other members of the group were studying in the southern regions of Sweden, Björn had finally moved from Västervik to Stockholm. He started studying business economics, statistics and law at Stockholm University and, together with Hans "Berka" Bergkvist, he moved into a rented one-room apartment in the centre of town. His enthusiasm for studies was fairly low, however, and his presence in Stockholm was motivated mainly by the opportunity to be close to the music industry. While Björn's passion for working in the recording studio was stronger than ever, the same could not be said for other members of the Hootenanny Singers.

The group's hit version of 'Green Green Grass Of Home' in early 1967 was something of a watershed careerwise. Stig and Bengt decided that more songs in this style would be a good way for the Hootenanny Singers to reinvent themselves and maintain their profile. Heavily supported by Björn, who recognised their commercial value, the recordings they made during the rest of the decade would be dominated by cover versions of American MOR and country hits.

Tony Rooth and Johan Karlberg were fairly indifferent to these developments, or at least didn't voice their concerns, but Hansi Schwarz hated this new direction. The arguments in the studio were many and heated. "Hansi thought I was too commercial, and that we shouldn't have recorded some of the stuff we did," said Björn. "But he was pretty alone in that, because the other two didn't really care and both Stig and Bengt were on my side."

Hansi had been fairly positive about Björn's attempts at pop music, but felt that the group couldn't remove themselves too far from folk music and still remain the Hootenanny Singers. Things came to a head when Stig proposed that the group should record a certain song, the mere mention of which practically sent Hansi through the roof. When he threatened to leave the group, the song was dropped. "But I was the only one who would fight about these things, and the normal outcome was that I lost and ended up feeling very sad," said Hansi. "I can hear it in my voice on some of those recordings: I was unhappy when we did them."

The connection to the Hootenanny Singers' folk music roots was upheld by the odd track on each album: songs like 'The Long Black Veil' and 'Greenback Dollar' were included primarily to appease Hansi. It was clear that as their recordings drifted towards country and *schlager*, only Björn could muster much enthusiasm in the studio.

Quietly observing the state of play from behind his mixing desk was a fresh-faced engineer at the Metronome Studio. Just 23, he'd begun his employment shortly before the sessions for the group's 1967 album *Civila* (*Civilians*) started. Michael B. Tretow, who would later come to play an important part in the Abba saga, had a clear view of the Hootenanny Singers at the time. "Björn was the only one who was doing any real work. The others were just eating sandwiches, drinking beer and reading porn mags. Björn was at them all the time, telling them that they had to do some work. He seemed to be pretty alone in really enjoying the studio work."

Despite the disinterest of the other members, the group had several hits with their country/MOR material over the following years. 'Början till slutet' (a Swedish version of 'Almost Persuaded') was a particularly well-made production that retained some of the group feeling, giving them a Top Five hit.

The country ballad repertoire fitted right in with the group's career direction at this time. In many respects, country was the Anglo/Saxon genre closest to European *schlager* music. They both shared simple, almost traditional, melodies with strongly sentimental arrangements, and the lyrics were frequently concerned with the plight of ordinary men and women coming to terms with the problems of their lives. Asked by American journalists to define the word *schlager* a few years later, Björn, Benny and Stig would refer to it as "country with a German beat".

Like most Hootenanny Singers recordings around this time, 'Början till slutet' featured Björn on lead vocals. Being based in Stockholm and representing the group in his dealings with Stig and Bengt, it seemed only a matter of time before he would branch out into full-blown solo recordings.

That time happened in April 1968, when his first solo single, 'Raring', a Swedish version of 'Honey', was recorded. It gave him a Top Ten hit. Parallel with the Hootenanny Singers' records, Björn's solo career continued until the end of 1969 with cover versions of songs like 'Harper Valley P.T.A.' and 'Where Do You Go To (My Lovely)'.

The B-side of the 'Raring' single was Björn's own 'Vår egen sång' ('Our Own Song'). Several Ulvaeus compositions found their way on to the Hootenanny Singers' album of that year – Björn's ambition's as songwriter hadn't died, even if the group's attempts to cross over into pop had fizzled out. His very last effort as a writer in collaboration with anyone other than Benny came in the spring of 1969: one of his solo singles was graced by the B-side title 'Gömt är inte glömt' ('Hidden, But Not Forgotten', featuring lyrics by Stig Anderson).

Björn's emergence as a solo star coloured the Hootenanny Singers *folkpark* tour of 1969, when a fair share of their repertoire consisted of his solo hits. Hansi and Tony even did a skit where they made digs at him for branching out. The group also performed a version of 'Ljuva sextital', a hit written by Björn and Benny, but never recorded by the Hootenanny Singers.

The final Björn Ulvaeus solo single, 'Partaj-aj-aj', an original Andersson/ Ulvaeus composition, was included on the Hootenanny Singers' album *På tre man hand* (*A Group Of Three*). This album was released in December 1969 and, as the title implied, the band had been reduced to a trio when Johan Karlberg left earlier in the year to take over his father's car firm.* Stig and Bengt's promotion of Björn as a solo act culminated on this album, which was even credited to "The Hootenanny Singers featuring Björn Ulvaeus".

It was clear the group was running out of steam, having trouble finding the right songs as well as the energy to commit to the project. With uninspired cover versions of titles such as 'Wichita Lineman' and an embarrassing novelty recording of The Beatles' 'Maxwell's Silver Hammer', the album marked the nadir in the group's exploration of the MOR market – even Björn had to concede that. "It's a really bad album, really tired. I can tell just from looking at the track listing," he said later. Never in the Hootenanny Singers' recording career had they released such an unsuccessful LP: the album spawned only two minor *Svensktoppen* hits, with no singles at all appearing on the sales chart.

Nevertheless, despite the in-fighting and Hansi and Tony's detachment from the music business in Stockholm, the affinity between the group members was still there. And recent slumps nothwithstanding, the demand

---

* Johan Karlberg died from heart failure in August, 1992.

for Hootenanny Singers' records remained. The future for the group would be to continue as a studio act: shortly before the *På tre man hand* album was released, it was announced that the Hootenanny Singers would give up touring.

Over the next few years they would record albums based around a folk-song theme or the work of a certain composer, which they'd already done successfully in 1965 and 1968. The European *schlager* songs for which Stig had acquired the rights, and which he insisted that the group should continue to record, were henceforth released only on occasional singles.

For Björn it seemed that the Hootenanny Singers were simply treading water. The only bright spot was his ongoing collaboration with Benny Andersson, which in many ways counterbalanced the lack of enthusiasm for the group. After a two-year break in the songwriting partnership, the second Andersson/Ulvaeus composition was recorded by The Hep Stars in the autumn of 1968. The ballad 'A Flower In My Garden' was an improvement on Björn and Benny's first attempt two years earlier, even if it wasn't exactly destined to storm up the charts. Hidden away as a Hep Stars single B-side, the song left few marks in pop history, but for Andersson/Ulvaeus it was the starting point for their more regular work as a composer team.

Around the same time, Björn enjoyed another stint as a stand-in guitarist for The Hep Stars. During a short tour of Finland in early 1969, the joy of playing pop music again – and having the chance to do it with Benny – was the wake-up call he needed. Björn finally decided to give up his half-hearted attempts at studying and give the music business his full attention.

Parallel with his studies he had already started working at Sweden Music, with a view to learning how the music business worked from the ground up. While his face continued to adorn the cover of teen magazines, and his Hootenanny Singers and solo records maintained their presence in the charts, Björn could be found at a desk in the offices, filling out copyright cards and doing other menial paperwork. "That was purely his own choice; he was starting to get interested in the business side of things," says Berka. "Stig also recognised his talent, and I think he wanted to groom him as a successor, or at least make him an integral part of the Polar set-up."

Björn's emerging interest for the music business was evident in his interviews around this time. He'd comment on everything from his and Stig's hunt for new songs for the group to record, to the difficulties of securing important television appearances. "You have to beg on your knees, and if you don't get to promote your record on television you might as well not release it at all," he stated in one interview. In another, the reader learned that "you have to view things from a commercial standpoint, give the people what they want and disregard cultural snobs like Fugs and The Mothers of Invention." It was almost like listening to a younger pop version of the Sweden Music head honcho.

With Tony and Johan now married, and Hansi engaged, 23-year-old Björn was the only bachelor in the Hootenanny Singers. But although he appreciated his status as a single man, he was starting to long for an opportunity to settle down in some form or fashion. He acknowledged that his attempts so far had been problematic. "It's hard to be together with a girl who has to get up and go to work at seven every morning if I want to stay out late and go partying. I've tried, but it hasn't really worked out. There were many things I had to show consideration for, even though I wasn't able to."

For nine months in 1968, he dated a girl called Marianne Åkerman, but even though they were interviewed as a couple, Björn was keen to stress his modern views on relationships with the opposite sex. "We meet when we feel like it. But there are no strings, we can each do what we want," he said. "Marriage is on its way out. For me it makes no difference whatsoever whether you're married or not . . . A marriage certificate doesn't make you more in love or more considerate." By the end of the year, the romance was over.

"When the others got married I just felt relieved to still be free, to be able to do exactly what I wanted," he reflected later. "I dated a lot of girls, but I guess none of them were right for me. My demands were probably very high."

Meanwhile, he was navigating through the ups and downs of his music career, accepting whatever work opportunities were thrown his way just to remain visible. In the spring of 1969, he was asked to participate in a tribute television special, dedicated to the recently deceased *schlager* composer Jules Sylvain. The songs included in the special were a bit old-hat, and Björn later viewed his participation as something of an embarrassment.

Shooting was scheduled to take place at various outdoor locations all over Sweden, starting on May 4 and continuing throughout the month. Even though most of the songs performed were solo numbers, the rest of the featured artists functioned as backing vocalists or "actors" in most of the scenes. Both recording of songs and filming, then, required the presence of almost everyone on the roster.

This gave Björn the opportunity he needed to explore his possibilities with that blonde newcomer, Agnetha Fältskog, who was also signed to take part in the filming. Agnetha was just as happy as Björn at this latest opportunity to develop the attraction both of them had felt in the *folkpark* a year earlier.

The final, irrevocable realisation that they had fallen for each other came when the entourage was down in Kungshamn on the west coast of Sweden, only a couple of miles from where Björn had lived for the first few years of his life. Among the numbers filmed in Kungshamn was Björn's interpretation of the song 'Titta in i min lilla kajuta' ('Come Around To My Little Cabin'). Björn was filmed standing on a fishing boat as he mimed to the song, and one of the girls who came "to his little cabin" was Agnetha. There was no mistaking the genuine spark between the two as he lifted her aboard and kissed her on the forehead in full view of the cameras.

Another scene filmed on the same location was for the song 'Vårkänslor' ('Spring Feelings'), sung by the whole cast. The sequence called for them all to walk down a road, hand in hand. Björn didn't waste the opportunity to grab hold of his Agnetha. "All of a sudden Björn appeared by my side," she remembered. "That's when I knew there was no going back."

It was the early spring, windy and chilly despite the watery sunshine, and the artists were required to run around in thin clothes for that genuine summery touch. Agnetha, wearing a thin yellow t-shirt and blue jeans, didn't try to resist Björn's attempts to keep her warm. "The next day it was still chilly and Björn had to go on keeping me warm," she remembered.

During a break in the filming, Björn asked Agnetha to take a walk with him. There was no use denying the attraction they both felt, but Björn was concerned that Agnetha was still seeing Dieter Zimmerman. "The papers hadn't written anything about our engagement being broken, so I had to be quick about telling Björn," she said. There was no longer anything to keep them apart, and after the filming was concluded it wasn't long before Björn and Agnetha became a couple. Berka moved out of the apartment he shared with Björn, and Agnetha started spending much of her time there.

Despite their attempts to keep their romance a secret, the papers broke the story in July 1969. It was quite a sensation that one of the most eligible bachelors in the Swedish music business had become involved with this up-and-coming singer, and a deluge of press interviews followed over the next few months. "The first thing I noticed about Björn was his eyes," gushed Agnetha. "The nice wrinkles around his eyes every time he laughs are just irresistible."

They both stressed how good it was to be in a relationship with someone who shared so many of their own characteristics, and even worked in the same business. But it was also obvious – even in these early interviews - that it was never going to be a smooth relationship, for those very same reasons. By their own admission, they would quarrel about almost everything. "[Agnetha is] individual and stubborn, just like me," said Björn. "We have to make many compromises, otherwise it would never work. But I wonder if she isn't a bit more irritable than I am after all."

Similarly, Agnetha was wary of suggestions that they should start a musical collaboration. "Our relationship wouldn't work if we did that," she said. "We are both very hot-tempered. The sparks would fly on stage. That's why we're afraid of working together."

Agnetha was adamant that she wouldn't be "one of those people who constantly get married and divorced". She was burned by the experience with Dieter Zimmerman, and was even hesitant about getting engaged. "I want to sow my oats before I commit myself to anyone," she said. "The next time I exchange rings with someone I want it to last."

By the autumn of 1969, things were looking a little brighter and more focused for Björn than they had in a long time. He had a new girlfriend and was in love like never before. "This time it's for real," he told the papers. And he was intensifying his friendship and working relationship with Benny.

For Benny Andersson, the dust was also beginning to settle after a turbulent couple of years. Back in the summer of 1966, his status as a member of The Hep Stars undoubtedly made him one of the more enviable young men in Sweden. With his strong musical talent, easygoing personality and role as "the second cutest member", the 19-year-old Benny was an invaluable asset for the band.

But his quick rise to the uncontested position as The Hep Stars' musical motor hadn't happened by design. "It's only small details, random things, that have led me on to this," he reflected a decade later. "I've never had any goals like, 'I'm going to make it big in music.' It was never like that, things have just kept on happening."

Svenne Hedlund, who also had strong opinions on the musical direction of the band, acknowledges Benny's exceptional qualities in this field even at this time. "As a rule I'd listen to what he had to say, because most of the time I agreed with him. Even though he was self-taught, he had musical authority."

With The Hep Stars' tremendous success, Benny and his band mates were able to live the lives of true pop stars. Benny himself had his own Ford Mustang car, a five-room apartment in central Stockholm, and he could pick and choose between the girls – in short, there was nothing to complain about.

Some of the money the band was making could also be put to good use by starting a production company, they reasoned. In June 1966 an organisation they called Hep House was founded. Much like The Beatles' Apple two years later, Hep House had the double function of handling The Hep Stars' business, as well as serving as publishing company for Benny's songs and a record label for other acts (the group themselves remained with Olga Records).

The Hep Stars' first year as a recording act had been characterised by a fairly primitive attitude to making records. Producing their own records with the help of engineer Gert Palmcrantz, most of their output was simply their live act transferred to disc in the recording studio. The group's second LP, the late 1965 release *Hep Stars On Stage*, was even a straight live effort.

But with the influx of more ambitious and complex records from Great Britain and America, notably those by The Beatles and The Beach Boys, Benny became more interested in the process of creating recordings from the ground up in the studio. "It's hard to achieve the same groovy sounds that they have on British and American records, but I have no idea why," he mused in an interview in January 1966.

During the course of the year, he started to take a more dominant role in the recording studio. He was also keen to have a hands-on involvement in the recordings Hep House released, and his piano-playing contributions can be heard on several singles issued by the label.

The initial Hep House output fared quite well in the charts. Benny and Svenne's production of 'Dum Dum (Marble Breaks And Iron Bends)' for a band called The Dee Jays was the very first release on the label and became a number three hit. A cover of 'Puff The Magic Dragon', produced by Benny for Hep House signing The Fabulous Four, reached the same position.

Within the context of The Hep Stars, Benny's development as a songwriter also continued unabated. As the group started sessions for their third album, his latest composition, 'Consolation', was committed to tape. A fine pop production with a mystical organ introduction and a catchy chorus, the single spent 10 weeks at number one on the charts on release in the autumn of 1966. Benny, always his own harshest critic, was sometimes unable to recognise the true merit of his material. Originally, he didn't see any potential at all in 'Consolation' and had to be persuaded by his fellow band members that the song should be recorded.

The new album, entitled *The Hep Stars*, was recorded in between mini-tours and other commitments in the autumn, with sessions mostly taking place at night. "We were in a hurry, because that album had to be completed as quickly as possible," recalls Svenne Hedlund. "And we had decided that we should have as much original material as possible on it."

For all the outgoing, party-loving parts of his personality, the other, introverted side of Benny would just as easily take precedence even in those early days. The need to come up with a decent LP could make a solitary, introspective composing session seem like a much more appealing prospect than a wild party. One night in late October the album project forced Benny to pass on a concert by The Who, one of the hottest acts on the British pop scene. While the rest of The Hep Stars eagerly went along to the gig at Club Nalen, Benny remained in the recording studio, composing the complex and atmospheric ballad 'Sound Of Eve'.

Convinced that he had the best ideas on how to record the material – not only his own songs – Benny could often be extremely stubborn in the studio. This often led to conflicts with the other members, reaching an impasse where they didn't do any work at all for several days. To let off steam during the quarrels, Benny would go off and play his accordion until things calmed down.

Work on the album wasn't completed until the end of a marathon recording session in early December, which started on a Saturday at midnight and finished at 9.30 the following morning. Rush-released two weeks later, *The Hep Stars* confirmed the group's astonishing popularity by becoming the first album ever by a Swedish act to enter the sales chart in those single-dominated times.

Certainly, there was much to enjoy on the album. Benny's songs, whether written alone or in collaboration with Björn or Svenne, were never less than solid. Other original material, like the track 'I've Said It All Before', had been brought in from composers such as the up-and-coming songwriting team of Arnold/Martin/Morrow. The trio's greatest success would arrive in the late Seventies with Barry Manilow's recording of their 'Can't Smile Without You'.

Compared to earlier efforts, the album was a quantum leap in terms of ambition. This was mainly due to Benny taking charge of the musical direction. But the success of the LP didn't give Benny any illusions on its merits in the greater scheme of things. "I wouldn't say that it's . . . better than The Beatles' *Revolver*, because musically that's a better album than ours," he admitted.

Benny was undoubtedly aware that The Hep Stars themselves were the weakest links in the chain. Svenne Hedlund was crucial to the group in his capacity as the nation's biggest teen idol, but his vocals at the time were often much too weak. While he did a good job carrying straightforward, uptempo songs like 'Bald Headed Woman' or 'Wedding', more complex compositions like Benny's 'Sound Of Eve' required a singer with a better command of his own voice.

As a collective, the band sounded more convincing on their version of Ed McCurdy's folk favourite 'Last Night I Had The Strangest Dream'. The Hep Stars had enjoyed huge success with the single release of a Swedish-language version of the song, 'I natt jag drömde', earlier in the autumn. It was their first recording in their native language, a somewhat controversial step for a band that wanted to retain their credibility with the pop audience. "We received an offer to appear on television," Benny recalled, "and since the show was good we were very anxious to do it. But there was one condition attached: we would have to sing in Swedish."

The Hep Stars interpretation of 'I natt jag drömde' on television went over so well that they released it as a single. It didn't hurt their standing one bit: on the contrary, it gave them access to a new audience. The single spent a total of nine weeks at number two and went on to become one of The Hep Stars' biggest sellers ever. Henceforth, the group's repertoire would contain a considerable amount of Swedish-language recordings.

Professionally, The Hep Stars ended what turned out to be their peak year of 1966 on a high. Their album was a success and three of their single releases during the past 12 months had spent a combined total of 19 weeks at number one. There was only one small, private matter that tarnished their image as Sweden's golden boys.

On November 2, the weekly magazine *Se* published an interview with Christina Grönvall, Benny's former fiancée who up until now had been a well-kept secret from most fans. Much less did the public know that Benny was also the father of two small children. "[Pop stars] shouldn't be married. It's part of our job not to be married," he had told a newspaper just before the news about Christina reached the press.

Christina claimed that during the final months of their engagement, Benny had refused to be seen in public with her. Not even when he visited her and the children in Vällingby would he consider being seen with a girl pushing a pram. "Once, at the start of The Hep Stars' career, a couple of us girls were allowed to come along for one of their shows. I've never been along on a tour since then. Also, that once, the condition was that we remained in the tour bus . . . while they were performing. And the curtains had to be drawn."

According to Christina, every public outing was simply unthinkable to Benny. They could perhaps go to the movies if it was a "serious" film that wouldn't attract The Hep Stars' audience. But going dancing was out of the question. "His argument was always, 'I have to think about my fans.'"

It was inevitable that some of the fans caught on to Benny's secret, and Christina had experienced the true measure of fan hysteria several times. Girls would call her up to tell her that they were pregnant with Benny's child. Others declared that they had to "have it out with Benny about what had happened". At 10 p.m. one Saturday night, just after Christina had put the kids to bed, the phone rang and a hysterical girl voice screamed, "Keep your bloody hands off Benny, bitch!"

"Benny broke off the engagement abruptly last summer, over the telephone," Christina related. "I never got a reasonable explanation." Her story was splashed all over the national press, and Benny, feeling that the whole thing had been blown out of proportion, tried to give his side of the story. He maintained that it was untrue that he refused to be seen in public with Christina, and pointed out that he'd always been wearing his engagement ring on stage. "Thousands of people every year decide to split up. Our decision to go our separate ways has nothing to do with my profession in The Hep Stars. It wasn't something rash that was over in one minute."

He continued: "With time I noticed that Christina and I were growing apart. It became especially apparent when The Hep Stars started touring. We'd see each other more infrequently and . . . Well, I guess that our love cooled off."

Benny desperately wanted to keep his private life private, so it was a painful experience for him to see the story blown up in the national press. At the same time, it gave him the opportunity to have everything out in the open and put a definite end to this chapter of his life. He would remain in touch with Christina and the kids over the years, but for now his priorities lay elsewhere.

The new year of 1967 meant new projects for The Hep Stars. Many of them seemed exciting on the surface, but would turn out to be nothing short of disastrous. Before the year was over, the band would have learned two hard lessons: sudden wealth brings with it the need to handle your finances properly, and plenty of people want a piece of the pie.

Chapter 10

Somewhere in an office in Stockholm, covered by a thick layer of dust, lie several cans of film. They represent the remains of a movie that has never been shown: it should probably never have been started in the first place. Several decades have passed since anyone even attempted to fit together the disjointed scenes, and it is unlikely that the project will ever be revived. "I won't waste another dime on it," said one of the stars of the film, Hep Stars singer Svenne Hedlund, in the early Nineties.

This ill-fated project was begun in late 1966, when The Hep Stars were approached by cinematographer Åke Borglund. The filmmaker had an idea for producing a wacky, Beatles-style feature film starring the group. Sten-Åke Lindström, the Managing Director of Hep House, went for the idea, and The Hep Stars were persuaded that this was a worthwhile project. They were also told that the movie couldn't possibly be made in Sweden.

"They said that we needed some interesting environments, and to start out with there was talk of sending us to Majorca or the Canary Islands," says Svenne Hedlund. "But all of a sudden that wasn't enough either. 'No, we need to make it bigger than that.'"

Eventually it was decided that the only location suitable for such a prestigious project was Nairobi in Kenya. The film acquired the working title *Habari-Safari*, and in February 1967 the entourage embarked for Africa to start shooting. The movie was financed largely out of The Hep Stars' own pockets, while Olga label boss Åke Gerhard, who was also supportive of the film idea, invested 280,000 kronor ($£$19,500) in the project.

Habari-Safari turned out to be a disaster from start to finish. Although Åke Borglund later made the absurd claim that he had completed a 600-page manuscript before the trip, in Nairobi everything was just chaos. "We hardly had any manuscript at all," says Svenne Hedlund. "It was sort of jotted down at the airport and on the plane down."

Many hangers-on came along for the ride – Managing Director Sten-Åke Lindström even found it necessary to bring his wife – all of which was paid by the Hep House company. And when prior commitments made it necessary for The Hep Stars to go back to Sweden after 16 days, Borglund and Lindström elected to stay in Africa for one more week. As Benny wryly recalled, "It turned out to be an expensive trip."

Later in the spring, additional shooting for the plotless movie was made during ten days in Denmark, and also in Stockholm and surrounding towns. "After that, the film was meant to be completed," recalled Benny. "And certainly, we had 5,000 metres of film. But there was no plot, and without a plot you can hardly release a feature film."

At one point, budding director Lasse Hallström was brought in. He was later to direct most of Abba's promo clips, as well as their feature film *Abba – The Movie*. At the time, he was making short pop film clips for television, and he did his best to somehow try to salvage this cinematic folly. Even some two years after the project was initiated, an enthusiastic Benny proclaimed that "the film is going to open soon!" But it turned out to be impossible to make the film work and it was never completed.

Åke Gerhard's investment in the film turned into a debt of almost 300,000 kronor (which he simply deducted from future royalties), and funds had also been bleeding out of Hep House as a result of the project. The one positive outcome of the Nairobi experience was that the group found a song called 'Malaika' while they were filming in Africa. Their recording of the song became a number one hit in May 1967.

With successes like this to their credit, on the surface everything still seemed satisfactory for The Hep Stars. Late April saw them start a successful four-month *folkpark* tour, encompassing 184 concerts. In October, they had their eighth and, as it turned out, final number one hit with 'Mot okänt land' ('Towards An Unknown Country').

Plans were also afoot to renew attempts at cracking markets outside of Sweden. Several singles had already been released in West Germany, and the group had made plenty of visits there, including television appearances. But the West German market remained impenetrable for The Hep Stars, and the results were never on a par with their efforts. On one occasion, the group and their entourage spent 15,000 kronor (£1,050) going to Berlin for a gig that paid just 750 kronor (£52) , and at another German club, Sweden's top act suffered the humbling experience of playing to 36 people on a Friday night. "No one knows who they are and, besides, no one comes here on Fridays," was the blunt explanation.

Similarly, there seemed to be a curse on the band every time they tried to have a record released in the UK. Before the 'Wedding'-related troubles with Kim Fowley in the autumn of 1966, the undoubted pop qualities of 'Sunny Girl' had impressed the people at Decca Records. The label prepared a single release of the song, and it was obvious they were trying hard to push it. " 'Sunny Girl' was played on Radio Luxembourg four times a night for a while, and I was so happy," remembers Svenne Hedlund. "To hear yourself on that station was like making the big time for an old Luxembourg fan like me." But as he found out many years later, the whole deal fell through because of a disagreement between Åke Gerhard and the record company.

"All of a sudden the record was withdrawn, and it turned out that Åke had been making a fuss about the royalty level. It was only something like a half per cent, but that was enough to make Decca lose interest completely."

In 1967, in an attempt to further their chances in Great Britain, The Hep Stars acquired the services of one Richard Reese-Edwards. The 22-year-old Englishman was one of the many who had begun swarming around them like flies. "Benny was sceptical, but I really believed in him," says Svenne Hedlund.

The relationship did get off to a good start. Reese-Edwards was given the chance to prove that he could make things happen and, in August 1967, he managed to secure The Hep Stars an appearance on the high-profile UK television show *Dee Time*, hosted by the popular Simon Dee. "It was really hard to get on that show, especially if you were unknown," says Hedlund. The Hep Stars were impressed by Reese-Edwards and his ability to secure this star spot. But the song that was performed on the show, Benny's 'It's Nice To Be Back', was never issued in Great Britain, rendering their appearance largely pointless in the long run.

Next, the young manager promised that he could arrange for the group to make a film in Great Britain. Shooting was scheduled to start in November 1967, reported the papers, but the deal fell through. Although Reese-Edwards remained on the payroll, it seems the *Dee Time* appearance was his sole contribution to the group's attempts to crack the UK market.

Meanwhile, in his capacity as sixth member, the resourceful Felle Fernholm had become even more important to the group as their tour manager, spokesman and general Mr Fix-it, and was pulling strings in another part of the world. Since the beginning of 1967 Felle had been trying to arrange for a tour and a possible record deal in the USA. Eventually, he managed to secure the interest of Steve Clark, the California-based business partner of legendary producer and songwriter Curt Boettcher. Clark mainly handled the financial side of their production company, Boettcher the studio work, and by the autumn of 1967 he had produced sunshine pop acts like The Association, Tommy Roe and Sagittarius.

But around the same time, the relationship between Steve Clark and

Curt Boettcher began to sour, as the producer felt that he didn't see enough money from all the success their company was generating. Clark, who had told Felle that he could see a potential for The Hep Stars in the US, ended up taking care of The Hep Stars' production himself.

One of his first decisions was to dispose of the services of founder members Lennart Hegland, Christer Pettersson and Janne Frisk. "He took a listen to our earlier productions and decided that what was interesting was Benny's keyboard playing, and the vocal performances from me, Benny and Felle," recalls Svenne Hedlund. "I don't think the other members of the group were too happy about that – I'm not even sure I was – but that's the way it was decided we should proceed."

For that bona-fide pop music flavour, recording sessions in "Swinging" London were scheduled for November/December 1967. The backing was provided by session musicians, augmented by Benny on keyboards. Steve Clark presented Svenne, Benny and Felle with a list of possible songs, mainly from previous Curt Boettcher productions, from which they made a final selection. Benny contributed only one song for the album, the title track 'It's Been A Long Long Time'. It was the first fruits of his collaboration with singer Lasse Berghagen, with whom he would write a number of songs over the following 12 months.

The resulting LP was a pleasant enough sunshine pop artifact, displaying the luscious harmonies and soft rock approach typical for that genre, but without any real standout track. The title song was released as the lead-off single in the spring of 1968, but was The Hep Stars' lowest-charting release to date, reaching number 14. And hopes of making it in the USA were shattered when only one flop single from the sessions, 'Musty Dusty', was ever released in America. Previously arranged plans for a US tour with star act Paul Revere & The Raiders were put on ice.

Svenne Hedlund has a clear view of the true machinations behind the album project: "I don't think very much was really done to get the album released over there. That was only something Steve Clark and the American record company were tempting us with: 'Let's do this, and we'll see what can be done for you in the USA.' In reality, they only wanted to jump on our bandwagon since it was likely the album would sell a hell of a lot in Scandinavia." No further attempts were made to conquer the American market.

For all their efforts over the years, outside the Nordic countries The Hep Stars only ever achieved any real success in The Netherlands. In the summer of 1968 they reached number four on the Dutch charts with 'Sunny Girl', but by that time The Hep Stars were already crumbling from the inside. Recent events, where three founder members had to suffer the humiliation of appearing on the cover of an album they didn't perform on, probably helped divide the band. However, the seeds of their demise were sown when the group first started getting hits.

In December 1967, newspaper headlines in Sweden trumpeted out the shocking revelation that The Hep Stars had been hit by a tax demand of 900,000 kronor (£62,500). The facts were astonishing: during the previous two years no one in the group had paid a single penny to the authorities, despite earning bucketloads of money. The members hadn't even submitted any declarations for 1966; instead their incomes had been established by the tax commissioner. When the Hep House people appealed against the authorities' decision, the tax commissioner decided to *increase* the outstanding tax debt.

No one apart from their record company boss Åke Gerhard had ever warned The Hep Stars of the perils of their reckless spending, but it was now clear to one and all that the time was ripe for implementing cutbacks. The three directors and eight office girls at Hep House were soon relieved of their positions, thus emptying the lavish new offices in a Stockholm suburb. Only one employee was left to take care of the band's concert bookings.

It was also revealed that Hep House had never had any proper bookkeeping, with income and expenditure mostly being noted on small pieces of paper. The Hep Stars acquired a new financial advisor, Lars-Henrik Ottoson, who commented: "They have naïvely just pumped money into the company and then not cared about managing it. They have appointed people but to no avail. I feel sorry for the guys."

In July 1968, Hep House was declared bankrupt with 260,000 kronor (£21,000) of debt and a meagre 15,000 (£1,200) kronor in assets. With the help of an accountant, Benny managed to decrease his personal debt from a staggering 174,000 kronor (£14,000) to 8,000 kronor (£645) over the following year. The joy was shortlived, however: a tax debt of 83,000 kronor (£6,700) for 1968 was next up. "Today I can only laugh at the total chaos that surrounded us," said Benny a few years later. "No one was responsible for anything. We shrugged our shoulders at every problem and said, 'It will all work out tomorrow.'"

For the moment The Hep Stars soldiered on, hoping to work themselves out of their problems. In the summer of 1968 they acquired a new singer, Svenne Hedlund's American girlfriend Charlotte "Lotta" Walker, who was to share lead vocal duties with him. Lotta had been a member of girl group The Sherrys, scoring a Top 30 hit on the US R&B chart with 'Pop Pop Pop-Pie' in 1962.

Although some consider Lotta's high-pitched, vibrato-laden voice an acquired taste, there can be little doubt that she provided The Hep Stars with considerable vocal authority. Svenne and Lotta duetted nicely on the group's delicious easy listening version of 'Let It Be Me' (complete with cheesy organ work by Benny), and her solo lead on the fine pop psychedelia of the Benny Andersson/Lasse Berghagen composition 'Songs We Sang' was simply terrific. "Lotta was a great asset for The Hep Stars," acknowledged Benny.

The only successes chalked up during the remainder of The Hep Stars' career were either Swedish language *schlagers* or cover versions of fairly lightweight material. Many of the group's old rock fans were less pleased with the increasing presence of Swedish language material and cabaret-style shows. "I guess we did betray them, although we didn't think of it like that at the time," remembered Benny. "We just jumped at whatever opportunity came our way. We were very young and very keen to remain in the business. The Hep Stars were popular for some four or five years, and that was simply because we acquired a new audience after a couple of years."

Certain members of the group agreed with the group's new direction only under silent protest. After a tour on the cabaret circuit between February and April 1969, Janne Frisk, who left the group at the end of February, Lennart Hegland and Christer Pettersson had all had enough. They were adamant that the group should return to their rock roots.

"The financial problems also contributed to our difficulties in holding together the group," remembered Benny. "Svenne and I both agreed that we had to get an accountant who could sort out this mess. We had to stop buying expensive diamond rings for our fiancées. There simply was no money available for extravagances like that. But it seemed not everybody in the group was able to understand that." In May it was announced that after this year's summer tour, Benny, Svenne and Lotta would leave The Hep Stars.

The group went through with the tour mainly because they couldn't afford to neglect the income from the lucrative *folkpark* circuit. It was not a happy event. When they were not on stage, Benny, Svenne and Lotta became "the others" as far as the remaining members were concerned. "We just argued all the time," remembered Svenne. "We were divided into two camps and hardly agreed on anything. It was a tough year."

It was a time of hardship for most Swedish high-profile pop bands. By the end of 1967, with discotheques taking over as night-club entertainment, the number of gig opportunities had decreased significantly. A year later, most bands had reached the point where the only option left was to call it a day.

The demise of the pop bands was hastened by a music industry that seemed less inclined towards further exploration and development of pop music. In an effort to sustain their careers, many acts aped The Hep Stars and reverted to cabaret-style shows, *schlager* music or oldies covers.

Ola & The Janglers, one of The Hep Stars' main competitors, were a good example of the latter approach. In late 1968 they enjoyed what turned out to be their biggest-ever hit with a cover version of Chris Montez' 'Let's Dance', which reached number one on the Swedish charts. Ola & The Janglers were also the first Swedish pop act to enter the US charts, when 'Let's Dance' reached number 92 in May 1969. This proved that Sweden didn't lack the talent necessary to compete on the international music market, but it was also obvious that no one had a clue what it took to promote their artists properly. The experiences of The Hep Stars and the Hootenanny Singers in that area were fairly typical – and trying to flog your wares to the pop Mecca markets in Great Britain and America was simply too intimidating for most Swedish music moguls.

Producer Anders Henriksson worked with the group Tages, who were considered the cream of Sixties pop in Sweden. Several decades later he summed up the situation: "You were a bit scared to talk with 'big brother' [at EMI] in London. I'd put the singles into envelopes and send them to the A&R guys. None of us would pick up the phone and say, 'We've got a great thing here!', trying to sell it like you do today. Instead, you'd check the mail every day to see if there was a reply."

The success of Ola & The Jangler's 'Let's Dance' cover also signalled that the initiative had been taken away from those that truly wanted to explore the possibilities within pure pop and rock music. Going for safe entertainment may have sustained a career for a few more years, but it was hardly likely to convince the rest of the world that you wanted to compete for the audience's attention on international terms.

With the demise of the Swedish pop band wave many of the chief players remained in the business one way or another, but went off into completely separate directions. When newcomer Pugh Rogefeldt released his Swedish-language début album in the autumn of 1969, it became a huge success and sent out the signal that not only was it possible to do rock music in your native language, it was virtually mandatory if you wanted to be taken seriously. The other wing went into light entertainment. They'd either concentrate their efforts on the cabaret circuit, *schlagers* and the *Svensktoppen* audience, or continue with straightforward pop music, mostly of the MOR variety.

After The Hep Stars played their very last gig in Stockholm on August 31, 1969, Benny, Svenne and Lotta decided to explore the possibilities of the entertainment side. Teaming up with Björn and comedian Finn Alberth, they put together a cabaret show that opened in Gothenburg on December 1.

The show was typical of the era with its concoction of lightweight diversions. The material ranged from Swedish versions of 'Little Green Apples', Ray Stevens' 'Gitarzan' and 'Maxwell's Silver Hammer' in the novelty interpretation originally recorded by the Hootenanny Singers, to Lotta's version of 'This Girl's In Love With You', interspersed with gags. Just like The Hep Stars' earlier forays into the genre the show got fairly good reviews, indicating that this could be an area worth pursuing.

But Björn and Benny had several other projects lined up for the future. With both of their groups dissolved for all practical purposes, they planned to intensify their collaboration as songwriters and producers. By the summer of 1969 they had already enjoyed two Top 10 hits as songwriters with Brita Borg's 'Ljuva sextital' and The Hep Stars recording of 'Speleman' ('Busker'). August and September saw further events that turned out to be important signposts to their future careers.

On August 18, on the opening night of Frida's latest cabaret show with Charlie Norman at Hamburger Börs in Stockholm, she and Benny got engaged. By that time, their romance had been going for almost six months. It had been a fiery period, with Frida looking to Benny to satisfy her desperate need for comfort and security. "I'd have fits of jealousy, without any reason," said Frida. "My jealousy originated in my lack of self-esteem. I couldn't believe that a wonderful guy like Benny could love me. It was simply unthinkable." Unwarranted jealousy ate away at Frida, and sometimes consumed her completely. "I don't know how many times a day I'd ask Benny if he really loved me and if so, why? Over and over again I forced him to tell me."

Despite the pressures in the relationship, Benny was in love with Frida and wanted to make a go of it. As he bid farewell to The Hep Stars, his most important partners over the past five years, he formalised his commitment to the new woman in his life. Before long, Frida had settled permanently into her fiancé's small studio flat in central Stockholm.

Benny's financial problems had forced him to move to a more modest home. Most distressingly, there wasn't even room for any keyboard instruments. "For the first time since I was a child, I was living in a house without a piano. I was forced to practise at friends' houses or before concerts," he recalled.

The small apartment also made it difficult for Frida and Benny to have their children visit, much less stay for long periods. They supported each other when the world was passing judgement on them for the way they had "abandoned" their families. "The kids will remain in Eskilstuna," Frida established. "I'm not going to drag them to Stockholm. What would be the point? I think they take this the right way. To them I'm still their mummy. It's not like I've really left them. They know I will always be back to see them."

"I used to believe that it was best for my children if they didn't see me at all," said Benny. "I wanted them to forget me, that they should get a new daddy. Now I've changed my mind, because I know they need me. Peter was old enough to remember me when I left my fiancée, he would talk about me. My ex-fiancée has met a new man, but Peter doesn't view him as my 'replacement'. Daddy is daddy and mummy's fiancé is mummy's fiancé."

At a recording session on September 10, 1969, Benny began his career as Frida's exclusive record producer, a position he would hold for more than a decade. Moreover, the A-side of the single he produced for her was an Andersson/Ulvaeus collaboration entitled 'Peter Pan'. It was an event of some historical significance, for it marked the first time that three future Abba members contributed to the same piece of music, but 'Peter Pan' wasn't a great record by any means. Apart from Benny's characteristically tinkling piano and Frida's competent vocals, very little of the future Abba magic could be traced in this opus – more than anything else, it sounded like a children's song for grown-ups. Released in October, 'Peter Pan' turned out to be yet another Anni-Frid Lyngstad non-hit.

Two days after the recording session for Frida, Björn and Benny teamed up for their very first official co-producing assignment. In Björn's case, despite his collaboration with Bengt Bernhag on the Hootenanny Singers' records, it was the first time he held the formal title of producer. For singer Anna-Lena Löfgren, one of the most popular female artists in Sweden at the time, the pair masterminded the recording of a Swedish version of the Bee Gees hit 'First Of May' and Björn's composition 'Så kom den där våren' ('Then The Spring Came'). This latter track became a *Svensktoppen* hit.

In October, despite their earlier protestations, Björn and Agnetha also worked together professionally for the first time since becoming a couple. The project was a month-long package tour called *Top 69* with other popular Swedish artists of the time. Originally, it was only Agnetha who was going to be a part of the tour, but she admitted to being jealous and wanted to spend as little time as possible away from Björn.

Björn was talked into coming along on the tour, but said that this was as far as their collaboration would go. Although Agnetha was eager that they should write songs together, he absolutely refused to do that, nor was he interested in producing her records. "I'm sure it would be fun as long as everything is going well and the songs become hits. But when they fail, who will she blame then? Me? No, I wouldn't want to experience that."

Meanwhile, Stig Anderson and Bengt Bernhag were watching Björn and Benny's career development with great interest. A few years earlier, Stig didn't have much faith in the Andersson/Ulvaeus partnership. "When the two of them arrived at the office, I really couldn't see what they could have in common because they had such different personalities," he recalled. It was true that Björn tended to be more organised and level-headed, while Benny was more of a bohemian with a carefree attitude to life. But they complemented each other, and their differences were an asset rather than a source of conflict.

By the spring of 1969, Stig's tune had changed. For one thing, a quick look at the charts over the past few years would have told him that Benny had a knack for creating major hits. Combined with the enthusiasm and talent of their protégé Björn, Stig and Bengt both recognised the potential in the collaboration. Stig's dream of selling Swedish music abroad, and not just import foreign hits, hadn't died with the failure to break the Hootenanny Singers internationally, and unlike so many of his colleagues, he saw no reason to feel intimidated by British or American music businessmen.

Similarly, Björn and Benny were planning a gradual withdrawal from their identities as performing artists in order to focus their efforts on songwriting and producing for the Swedish market. But Stig felt in his bones that the partnership had even greater potential. The talent of the two young men, combined with his own refusal to acknowledge the received wisdom that Sweden couldn't produce any international hits, was – he thought – an unstoppable combination.

"One day, the pair of you will write a song that becomes a worldwide hit!" he predicted. Björn and Benny laughed and said, "Yes, well . . ." This was their secret dream too, but they were by no means as confident as Stig. "It was very hard to maintain, even in your own eyes, that the song we were working on was just as good as the one that for example The Hollies were having a hit with at the same time," reflected Benny many years later.

Björn and Benny's first hit as songwriters, 'Ljuva sextital', featured lyrics by Stig and was released on the Polar label in the late spring of 1969. At the very least, it was clear that the Andersson/Ulvaeus team could look forward to a lucrative future as Swedish hitmakers. Stig remembered: "Nothing makes me as happy today as when Björn and Benny remind me that I believed in them. They didn't really believe that themselves! I said that we must start a publishing company together."

In October 1969, the publishing company Union Songs was founded. Stig, Bengt, Björn and Benny had a 25 per cent share each in the partnership. Benny, now 22, moved closer to the Sweden Music family when Stig's wife, the astute and dependable Gudrun Anderson, helped sort out his business problems. It took four years of being put "on pocket money", as Benny put it, but by then he was completely free of his tax debt. "Every single penny I paid back came from my own songwriting," he noted proudly.

Benny came to appreciate the value of belonging to a well structured organisation that could offset his tendency to drift off into introverted music-playing. It was a far cry from the chaos of Hep House. "The best thing that has happened to me was coming into contact with Stig," he said in 1976. "He has taught me the importance of straight economic thinking and an ordered life. And since we work together every day it is quite natural that he has influenced me."

With his usual fervour, once he'd hit upon an idea he believed in, Stig tried every avenue available to him to push the Andersson/Ulvaeus partnership. In the summer of 1969, there was talk of Björn and Benny recording a demo album of their material: not as a commercial release, but as a sampler that could help drum up interest on the foreign market. Unfortunately, this never happened, and instead their début recordings as a duo were made under somewhat less fortunate circumstances.

Never was the myth of "Swedish sin" stronger than in the late Sixties, when there seemed to be a large soft-porn market for everything connected with the Scandinavian countries. The 1967 movie *Inga*, made in Sweden by American cult movie director Joseph W. Sarno, had become a huge success on the international market. By the autumn of 1969, Sarno was planning a follow-up, adorned with the working title *Inga II*.

Shooting started in November and continued for one and a half months, with actress Marie Liljedahl reprising her title role as Inga. The male lead character was played by Tommy Blom, former lead singer with the defunct pop band Tages. Stig Anderson got wind of the project and approached Björn and Benny with the offer of providing music for the film, no doubt reasoning that it would provide them with international exposure. Björn and Benny were excited at the prospect of writing music for a movie and readily agreed. At one point, Björn was even considering taking a part in the film. Agnetha put the kibosh on that. "I don't think he would be right for the part," she said innocently.

The movie ended up featuring several Andersson/Ulvaeus compositions, most notably the songs 'She's My Kind Of Girl' and 'Inga Theme'.

In the spring of 1970, those titles made up the two sides on the first single released under the duo name Björn & Benny. Incredibly, post-production on this low-budget cash-in film was delayed to the extent that it didn't open until October 30, 1971, by which time its English-language title had become *The Seduction Of Inga*.

As a promotional opportunity for Björn and Benny's songs, then, the project was a waste of effort, and 'She's My Kind Of Girl' did not become a hit. Rather, the movie remains as a sad testament of the depths to which former successful Swedish pop stars like Björn, Benny and Tommy Blom had sunk by the end of the Sixties.

But if it was hard for them to adjust to life as ex-pop stars, relative newcomers on the scene, like Agnetha and Frida, were finding the going equally difficult.

PART II

The March To Waterloo

Chapter 11

On Saturday, August 16, 1969, at 7.15 p.m., a one-hour television special called *Räkna de lyckliga stunderna . . . (Count The Happy Moments . . .)* was broadcast on Swedish television. The show presented a little light entertainment in the shape of a bunch of familiar tunes performed by popular artists. It was also a manifestation of the romance between Agnetha Fältskog and Björn Ulvaeus that had developed during filming, and which had recently broken in the press.

Agnetha had to all intents and purposes moved into Björn's Stockholm studio flat during the summer, and a few months later the couple acquired a three-room apartment of their own. The new flat was located on Lilla Essingen, one of the smaller of the many islands upon which Stockholm is built. Between engagements Björn and Agnetha spent the autumn getting settled in their first proper home. Agnetha's dream of a "fairy-tale prince in a fairy-tale world where I'm a princess", as she sang on one of her early demos, had come true.

Where her career was concerned, however, things had slowed down considerably. It was now 18 months since she had her number one record with 'Jag var så kär'. Although Agnetha had notched up quite a few *Svensktoppen* hits in 1968, her last appearance on the sales charts had been 'Allting har förändrat sig', a number seven hit in October of that year.

In 1969 even *Svensktoppen* had failed her, and she had so far managed only one four-week appearance on that important chart. Nor had the focus on the West German market over the previous 12 months yielded appreciable rewards. No doubt Agnetha and her advisors in Sweden had come to the conclusion that it was her own songs that seemed to reach out to the audience – or at least the material she really felt for and could invest with genuine emotion.

Later, she reflected on an important aspect of her very first rush of success: "I really felt like I had succeeded, because they were my own songs. It wasn't like many other artists who borrowed material or had it especially written for them. I had a special feeling for it all from the beginning, since I had created it myself: both words and music."

This was certainly not true of the material recorded during her second

155

year of fame, when only one completely self-composed song appeared on record. In West Germany, the situation was even worse: despite her attempts to get her producers interested, Fältskog compositions like 'Utan dej', which she felt was right for that market, were ignored. Meanwhile, many of the titles she recorded in German, as well as other compositions by the likes of Dieter Zimmerman, were imported to her Swedish records.

It seemed as if Agnetha was the victim of a power struggle. Although her biggest hit so far had been the début single she had written herself, the male entourage that surrounded her felt the need to demonstrate to the teenage girl how the music business *really* worked. It was almost impossible for Agnetha to voice her opinions in the face of such formidable opposition – but now that Dieter was out of her life it was time to regain more control over her career.

Agnetha was performing one of her own new songs on her 1969 summer tour. As yet she had only a melody and, somewhat bizarrely, improvised nonsense words every time she performed the song. Eventually, lyricist Bengt Haslum was drafted in to come up with the right words for her uptempo, Central European-flavoured melody. The song was given the title 'Zigenarvän' ('Gypsy Friend') and was recorded in mid-June.

The track was released in the autumn with one of Dieter's songs on the flip side. "I believe more in 'Zigenarvän'," Agnetha stated confidently. She was proven right when the song finally gave her a convincing *Svensktoppen* hit again, reaching number five and spending six weeks on the chart.

But the success was immediately clouded by a controversy. The lyrics – about a love affair with a "dark-eyed gypsy with white teeth" – were branded "a tasteless exploitation". Reviewers and commentators felt that 'Zigenarvän' tried to capitalise on the then current controversy over the treatment of gypsies living in Sweden. One newspaper article even claimed that the lyrics' somewhat one-dimensional, romantic portrayal of "the gypsy character" had influenced a landlord in Eskilstuna to turn down 70 gypsies who wanted to live in his building. Agnetha's somewhat weak defence, was that she "hadn't written the lyrics".

The furore soon blew over, however, and 'Zigenarvän' was included on her second album, *Agnetha Fältskog Vol. 2*, released at the end of the year. The album repeated the formula of her first, and had a certain air of kitschy charm about it, but against the blandness of the dominant German *schlagers*, it was clear that 'Zigenarvän' was about the only song on the album with a truly strong hook. Agnetha's confidence in her own talents as a songwriter was further strengthened in the spring of 1970 when she spent 15 weeks on *Svensktoppen* with a brand new single. 'Om tårar vore guld' ('If Tears Were Gold') was yet another of Agnetha's sentimental, *schlager* ballads performed in her own, earnest way.

It is easy to smirk at the apparent banality behind the sentiments conveyed in Agnetha's songs from this period, but there's no question that both her songs and the way in which she sang them struck a chord with a large slice of the Swedish population. Parts of her audience identified strongly with the protagonist of 'Om tårar vore guld', a slightly more mature woman who'd been abandoned by her husband. "I got so many letters after [that song]," Agnetha recalled. "It was mostly older ladies who wrote, 'This could have been written about me. This is exactly how it feels.'"

Abba engineer Michael Tretow, who recorded several of Agnetha's early solo efforts, also recognised her natural ability to convince. He reflected on his first impressions of the young singer several decades later. "Of course, it was fun with a girl who wrote her own songs, but there wasn't much rock'n'roll in it. But there was one thing that made her stand out from others. You did actually believe in her although she sang [lines like] 'I would own millions if tears were gold'. The credibility in Agnetha's voice was something that she just had from the beginning."

'Om tårar vore guld' led to yet another controversy for Agnetha a few years later. In April 1973, Danish orchestra leader and composer Per Hviid filed a plagiarism suit for 35,000 kronor (£3,325) against Agnetha in the Danish court, claiming that 20 bars of the song were identical to one of his own songs. Agnetha refuted the accusation on logical grounds. "He wrote the song in 1950 – at that time I hadn't even started singing, much less listening to music. I'm sure that the melody is my own composition." It was hard to fault Agnetha's line of reasoning: 1950 was the year of her birth, and the Danish composition was still unrecorded at the time of the lawsuit. Instead she pointed out that both melodies bore a resemblance to the third movement of Shostakovich's sixth symphony.

But the lawsuit refused to go away and wasn't settled until 1977. To finally put an end to the affair, Hviid was offered a relatively modest settlement of 5,000 kronor against no further claims to the song. He accepted.

Meanwhile, Frida's career was limping along much as before. Although she continued working the cabaret circuit with Charlie Norman, her records failed to reach the charts. When the 'Peter Pan' single flopped, acquiring Benny as producer seemed to have made very little difference.

In March 1970, Frida recorded her second single with Benny. 'Där du går lämnar kärleken spår', a cover of the Edison Lighthouse UK number one hit 'Love Grows (Where My Rosemary Goes)', became her second-ever entry on *Svensktoppen* in the spring of 1970. Although it lasted for only two weeks, it was an indication that more pop-orientated material might be the way to go in the future.

Frida was well aware that her restrained style of interpretation didn't lend itself to the kind of songs that people wanted to hear on *Svensktoppen*. "I've tried a more cheerful style, but it doesn't work out for me," she mused in a newspaper interview. Nor did she rate her chances at remaining on the charts very highly. "It's not going to last very long. It's not the kind of song that people go for, that they think is cute."

But in the midst of all that exasperation a strong core of self-belief continued to shine through. "Of course, I'm too exclusive for *Svensktoppen*," she fired off. "But I like my records. At least there is some kind of quality to the songs." Full acceptance by the general public was still a few more years away for Frida.

Benny's role as an anchor in her life was growing in importance. Symbolic events in the spring meant that fewer ties than ever remained to her old life in Torshälla and Eskilstuna. In March, her divorce from Ragnar had become final, and on May 19, her grandmother Agny died at the age of 71. In later years they had become closer than before, with Agny taking much pride in her granddaughter's local and national singing career. The death of the hard-working woman who had abandoned her own family to raise her occurred while Frida was in the middle of a *folkpark* tour with Charlie Norman. Only a few days after the low-key funeral, Frida was back on the road again.

Frida's relationship with Benny led to a friendship with Björn and Agnetha as well, and in the spring of 1970 the four of them drew closer together than ever before. On April 5, Agnetha's 20th birthday, Björn, Agnetha, Benny and Frida left for an eleven-day holiday in Cyprus. Benny and Frida served as witnesses when Björn and Agnetha got engaged on the Mediterranean island.

The future members of Abba made an important discovery during this spring holiday. The guys had brought along guitars and in the evenings they would all sit around together, relaxing and singing songs. When Björn and Benny's voices, fairly unremarkable on their own, harmonised with the highly individual voices of Agnetha and Frida, they were astounded at the effect.

On a whim, they decided to road test their combined vocals in front of a live audience by performing for the United Nations soldiers stationed on the island. The response was positive, and an idea was born. Björn and Benny, who had toured their cabaret show with Svenne and Lotta successfully since last December, were committed to a summer tour with them. Now Björn, Benny, Agnetha and Frida discussed teaming for a cabaret show of their own in the autumn.

When the two couples returned home, Svenne and Lotta Hedlund were called to a meeting. "It was all very well presented to us," remembers Svenne. "Benny and Björn told us that they were planning to team up with the girls. Besides, they said, Lotta and I were such a strong entity as an act that we would manage perfectly well on our own."

While lyricists and gag writers Peter Himmelstrand and Bosse Carlgren were engaged to prepare numbers for the show, the quartet went about their usual business as individual artists. Frida started her *folkpark* tour with Charlie Norman, while Agnetha toured with comedian Bert-Åke Varg. Agnetha was starting to come into her own as a performer, further confirmation arriving when 'Om tårar vore guld' was a true hit. "It's amazing," she marvelled after one performance. "Each time I sing it, people start kissing. Wherever I looked tonight people were kissing." Even she was forced to realise that only when she sang about unrequited love was she truly able to hit a nerve with the audience.

For their part, Björn and Benny continued to have their fingers in several pies. As songwriters, the first few months of 1970 hadn't been very successful for them. Despite two major hits the previous year, artists weren't exactly standing in line to record their material. The few who did ended up going nowhere on the charts. There was at least some historical significance in the flop single that Björn and Benny produced for singer Billy G-son in February 1970. The raspy-voiced vocalist's reading of their song 'There's A Little Man' marked the first time backing-vocalist Agnetha Fältskog appeared on a Björn and Benny-related production.

By this time, the Andersson/Ulvaeus team was starting to build up a substantial stockpile of songs that no one wanted to record. With the encouragement of Stig and Bengt, they decided to record a Swedish-language album of their own songs as a duo act. Partly, the LP would function as a sort of demo album, similar to what they had intended to do the previous summer. It was hoped that this would be a more convincing way of presenting their work for potential recording artists. In June 1970, on days off from the park tour with Svenne and Lotta, Björn and Benny started sessions for the project.

Yet another milestone in the Abba story occurred fairly early in the working process. One of the songs recorded for the album was called 'Hej gamle man!' ('Hey Old Man!'), the affirmative zest of the melody inspiring lyrics about a Salvation Army soldier. Recalling the effectiveness of their combined voices from the spring holiday, Björn and Benny invited their fiancées to record backing vocals on the track. It was the first time all four appeared on the same record.

But as a whole, the completed album, titled *Lycka* (*Happiness*), wasn't an especially convincing product. It sounded like what it was – a demo album – and it was clear that the duo lacked focus with their music. One track found them aligning themselves with the Swedish folkpop movement, while on the next they were doing *schlager*, and on the next a novelty ditty.

The album was released around the time of the première of Björn, Benny, Agnetha and Frida's cabaret show. Labouring under the painfully punning title *Festfolk* (with its double meaning of "party people" and "engaged couples"), the show opened at Trägår'n in Gothenburg on November 1, 1970. Apart from two recent appearances on radio and television, this was their public début as a group.

Comments from the four before the opening were characterised by a sense of optimism at the prospect of working together. "It's logical that we team up on stage as well," said Björn, ignoring his recent doubts about a professional collaboration between him and Agnetha. Benny and Frida stated: "We two *have* to be together. If you work separately as artists the relationship ends sooner or later. You experience too much on your own and grow apart. We don't want to take that risk."

Masterminding the show was songwriter Peter Himmelstrand, who'd previously written most of the material for Björn, Benny, Svenne and Lotta's cabaret act. When at his most inspired, Himmelstrand had a knack for writing both storytelling lyrics and catchy songs with a clever twist. These were talents that came in handy for a show where the aim was to present more than just an ordinary concert.

On paper, the 45-minute *Festfolk* show looks like it should be a fairly entertaining night out, at least compared to other similar productions around this time. With backing from dance band The Lolas, Agnetha, Björn and Benny opened the act with a number called 'Skriva låtar' ('Writing Songs'), where a medley of their hits as composers functioned as the basis for a lighthearted look at songwriting.

Frida did 'Tre kvart från nu' ('Three Quarters Of An Hour From Now'), an effective ballad about a mistress contemplating her lover's day-to-day life with his family, less than an hour after their secret tryst. Agnetha and Frida performed a number called 'Vi är väninnor' ('We Are Girlfriends') in which they sang about what great friends they were. In a droll counterpoint, these mutual endearments were then contradicted by a pre-recorded background tape on which they expressed their true, less positive feelings for each other.

Björn and Benny had a duo spot in the bizarre number 'Arga unga män, förenen eder!' ('Angry Young Men, Unite!'), in which the two singers acted the part of two small boys at a daycare centre who were demanding their rights. It was all set to the music of 'The Internationale' and similar anthems and protest songs. The words were written by lyricist Bosse Carlgren (later to work extensively with Agnetha), who also penned new lyrics for Björn and Benny's 'Hej gamle man!' Under the new title 'Tyck om varann' ('Care For Each Other'), this was the show's grand finale.

Festfolk attracted good reviews and should have been a success, but something must have been inherently wrong in the set-up for the omens were discouraging, even at the very first performance in Gothenburg. "There were just a few scattered couples at the tables in an otherwise empty venue," recalled Agnetha.

The simple truth was that despite the combined popularity of the four members none of them were especially good at cracking jokes or performing comedy skits on stage. The nature of the restaurant audience didn't make their task easier. "It's a pretty undemanding crowd, but they eat and drink during the show," said Björn. "Just when you feel that you've reached the audience, someone says: 'Cheers!'"

Straightforward delivery of songs was certainly not the problem, but despite the efforts of director Thor Zachrisson they couldn't find the right chemistry to convince as all-round entertainers. As Björn recalled, "This was when we learned exactly what we should *not* be doing."

In December the show was taken to Stockholm for three weeks, followed by two short tours in January and February 1971. The lack of success, combined with the strain of two couples working together, turned what should have been a triumph into a disaster. Long trips in a small car on slippery roads during what Frida remembered as "a cold and nasty winter", did nothing to ease the tension.

While Agnetha and Björn were relatively unscathed by the experience, *Festfolk* almost led to the end of Frida and Benny's relationship. Plans for a collective summer tour were soon ditched, and in mid-January it was announced that Frida would instead tour with Benny's old songwriting partner, singer Lasse Berghagen. "A happy solution," said Benny, and Frida agreed. "It's not a good idea to both work and live together," she said. "It's easier to get in a bad mood. We sat in the car together, dined together, performed together, checked into the hotel together. It was just too much."

Although it's unlikely the show was as bad as they remember it, *Festfolk* has become a symbol for everything the group wanted to avoid. Björn cringes at the mere thought of the four "dressed up in brown unisex outfits and grinding away at some second-rate show", and often refers to it as an absolute low point for everyone involved. Memories of him and Benny dressed up as small boys with lollipops and propellers on their hats seems to be particularly embarrassing. "Luckily, the show was never recorded," he shudders.

When 'Hej gamle man!' became a hit in late November, it was performed with the original lyrics in the show and received a better reaction than any other number. "That's when we really knew that we should concentrate on doing our own material in the future – it was a kind of turning point," recalled Björn.

'Hej gamle man!' was the biggest hit any of those involved had experienced in well over a year, reaching number five on the sales chart and number one on *Svensktoppen*. In hindsight, it was a definite indication that they were on to something big with the group concept. "I don't think it would have become such a hit if Agnetha and I hadn't been on it," Frida reflected.

The combination of the four voices on record, not least the considerable increase in energy levels resulting from the addition of Agnetha and Frida's voices, stirred something inside them all. But with both girls tied to recording contracts with companies other than Polar, it would be difficult to form a permanent group. And the less than encouraging experience of *Festfolk* didn't exactly strengthen their resolve to pursue the matter for the time being.

Still, the working relationships between the four had intensified during 1970, and not just on the Björn & Benny album. In September Agnetha recorded her third album, *Som jag är* (*As I Am*). Björn's wariness at helping his fiancée in the studio vanished as he stepped in as her producer for the first time. He shared the credit with Agnetha's previous producer, Karl-Gerhard Lundkvist, but in truth it was Björn who was really in charge. "By then she'd already come so far that it didn't matter," says Lundkvist. "I had done my bit and it was time for her to move on."

In what seemed like an attempt to exploit the high media profile of the romance between the couple, Björn also duetted with Agnetha on the ballad 'Så här börjar kärlek' ('This Is How Love Begins'), written by *Festfolk* mastermind Peter Himmelstrand. The lyrics – a mawkish account of a couple meeting and then falling in love – were not among his stronger efforts.

Benny had already handled Frida's productions for one year when the Lyngstad and Andersson team started work on her début album in the autumn of 1970. After three years as a recording artist, Frida still hadn't experienced any real hits. It was to EMI's credit that they didn't drop her, but continued to believe that such a talent must achieve a breakthrough sooner or later.

The album that Benny produced for his fiancée, titled simply *Frida*, turned out to be the musical high point of her years with EMI. She excelled on recordings of songs from *Festfolk*, such as Peter Himmelstrand's 'Tre kvart från nu' and 'Barnen sover' ('The Children Are Asleep'), as well as Swedish versions of songs like 'Going Out Of My Head'. Her recording of Björn, Benny and Stig's ballad 'Lycka' was the definitive interpretation, putting the original version on the Björn & Benny album to shame.

Frida finally seemed to be moving closer towards pop territory: her association with Benny had opened her ears to a form of music she had previously ignored. "I'm almost ashamed to admit that I learned to listen to The Beatles at such a late date," she recalled. "I used to be a jazz broad. I listened only to jazz and said, 'The Beatles are just trash.'" Benny had convinced her there was some merit to pop music after all and this was reflected in the choice of material for the album. Swedish interpretations of Simon & Garfunkel's 'The Sounds Of Silence' and Leonard Cohen's 'Suzanne' were included though they both sounded a bit uneasy. Curiously, a stellar interpretation of The Beatles' 'The Long And Winding Road' was left off the LP.

As a whole, the *Frida* album was an artistic triumph both for Frida and for Benny as producer. The two years as a cabaret performer perhaps had something to do with fine-tuning her ability to turn singing into storytelling. She might not be a fully fledged pop singer yet, but she certainly knew how to make simple songs and superficially corny lyrics sound like believable statements.

Released in the spring of 1971, and attracting favourable reviews, the album lacked hit singles and as a result didn't exactly fly out of the record shops. It was ironic that in terms of musical and artistic integrity Frida far outshone Björn, Benny and Agnetha, yet their output was far more successful on a commercial level. The only single to be released from the project, the somewhat anachronistic 'En liten sång om kärlek' (a version of 'Five Pennies Saints' from the 1959 Danny Kaye movie *The Five Pennies*), was far from the best choice for an artist desperately in need of a hit.

Frida could look back on more than three years as a fairly well-known singer, but the statistics were unimpressive. Her new, accomplished album had suffered the same fate as all her singles. Only her cabaret performances with Charlie Norman had achieved anything remotely close to true success. Even her attempts at working with Benny on stage hadn't worked out.

Deep down inside Frida was struggling with the awful realisation that she might be unable to continue her career as a singer. Having graduated from school with mixed grades, singing was virtually all she knew how to do, so in the spring of 1971 she started studying again, this time by correspondence course. "It's not that I plan to abandon my career as an artist – at least not yet," she said. "But I think it's best that I prepare myself if I should have to quit."

When she reflected on her situation, it was clear that she hadn't yet found the inner peace she was looking for. "Sometimes I get the feeling that what I do is pointless . . . I try to find a meaning with life. Sometimes I succeed in doing that, but not always. It was on one of those occasions, when I felt like nothing was especially meaningful, that I decided to start studying. It fills part of the void I feel. I realise that I won't be able to solve the riddles of the world, but in some way it assuages my worries."

On June 25, Frida began a two-month summer tour with Lasse Berghagen. Despite her long experience with Charlie Norman, Berghagen couldn't help noticing that something was still lacking in Frida's stage routine. "She seemed a little distanced from the audience," he recalled. "You had the feeling that she never really reached across the stage."

Frida had been well aware of this problem for a long time. "I'm just impossible on stage," she said in an interview a year earlier. "I'm insecure and scared, and then I freeze up." She said she intended to do something about it, but 12 months on she had only come part of the way. It would be a while yet before she was able to reach an audience in a tangible way.

While Frida fought her own psychological turmoil, Agnetha, Björn and Benny went on a 60-date *folkpark* tour of their own, starting on April 30. Although Frida's absence from the mix was probably beneficial for the mood on the tour, Agnetha and Björn's patience with each other was also under strain from time to time. "I guess it's just too much, to both work and live together," said Agnetha. "You get on each other's nerves in the end. Even if you don't want to have a fight, you still do sometimes, and then it's hard to go on stage and look happy afterwards."

The trio performed at weekends only and had time for several recording sessions in the interim. A couple of Björn & Benny tracks recorded at this time, again with Agnetha and Frida on backing vocals, became hits on *Svensktoppen*. In the autumn, they reached number one on that chart with one of their recent recordings, 'Tänk om jorden vore ung' (later recorded by Andy Williams as 'If We Only Had The Time'). The song's success prompted its inclusion on a reissue of the *Lycka* album.

Agnetha also started working on her fourth LP, this time with Björn as sole producer. Released at the end of 1971, *När en vacker tanke blir en sång* (*When A Beautiful Thought Becomes A Song*) retained some of the soppy sentimentality of her previous efforts but in other respects was a significant step forward. While her earliest songs had benefited from the sincerity of her heart-rending charm, they had also been very simple in their structure. With the new album she demonstrated her ambitions as a writer, offering the first real signs of an ability to come up with uniquely personal melodies that somehow sounded quite effortless. The light-pop song 'Många gånger än' ('Many Times Yet'), one of the singles from the album, was her first truly strong track in this new vein.

She had also seen the wisdom of letting others write the lyrics for her songs. The prolific Peter Himmelstrand penned the lyrics for 'Många gånger än', a depiction of the everyday existence of a married couple, marked by a fine sense of detail. Easy to dismiss as lightweight pap, it was an indication of what would become a strong part of Agnetha's persona as an artist, both in her solo work and as a member of Abba.

Significantly, this celebration of marital bliss was recorded just a week after she married Björn on July 6, 1971. It was Agnetha who insisted that they had to formalise their relationship. "I'm so romantic. Björn is more relaxed about it," she said. The groom conceded: "The practical difference won't be that great, but we feel that it's a cool tradition."

The wedding took place at the parish church in the small village of Verum in the south of Sweden. The location was chosen primarily because Björn was friendly with the restaurant-keeper at the nearby Vita Hästen (White Horse) Inn, who was to handle the catering. Their rapport with assistant vicar Uno Wårdener, who conducted the service, got off to an unfortunate start. When Björn called him he was asked what the young couple did for a living. "We're artists," answered Björn. But Wårdener misheard. "I'm not sure if I want to wed any atheists," came the stern reply.

Despite attempts to keep the wedding a secret, the date leaked out and it attracted a good deal of attention from the media as well as curious onlookers. The wedding ceremony was scheduled for 4 p.m., but people started showing up as early as 10 a.m. Every man that could be mustered from the police force in nearby Hässleholm was summoned to guard the happy couple from the estimated 3,000 who gathered to watch. In the chaos, one of the horses that was to pull the landau taking the couple to their wedding dinner stepped on the bride's foot before the ceremony. A doctor was called to examine Agnetha's bruised foot but the ceremony proceeded as planned.

Agnetha's bridal outfit was a long, two-piece white dress with a wreath of flowers in lieu of a bridal veil. The wedding bouquet was a mix of pink roses and lilies-of-the-valley, Agnetha's favourite flowers. Björn was dressed in a black suit, white shirt and tie. Frida, on tour with Lasse

Berghagen in the north of Sweden, was unable to make the celebrations but Benny played Mendelssohn's traditional 'Wedding March' on the church organ as the bride and groom entered the church. Björn's best man was Hans "Berka" Bergkvist, while his sister Eva and Agnetha's sister Mona served as bridesmaids.

By all accounts it was a moving ceremony. When assistant vicar Wårdener asked if Björn wanted Agnetha to become his lawfully wedded wife, his "I do" resounded loudly throughout the church. Agnetha's reply to the corresponding question came out as a shy whisper. As the couple walked out of the church arm in arm, Benny played his and Svenne Hedlund's old Hep Stars hit 'Wedding'. Outside, pandemonium ensued. Just as Björn was about to give his wife a wedding day kiss, a handful of rice that had been thrown towards the couple landed in Agnetha's mouth.

Berka, who also acted as bodyguard, remembers another surprising incident. "The chairman of the Verum gymnastics club wanted to give Björn a sundial to congratulate them. But since I was standing so close to them, he mistakenly assumed that I was Björn, so he gave it to me instead." So many had gathered to watch the proceedings that the road was lined with onlookers for 200 metres. Said Björn later: "We wanted a wedding to remember, and I guess that's what we got."

The wedding supper was held at Wittsjöhus castle, with around 40 guests from family, friends and the world of Swedish entertainment. With Lotta Hedlund on drums and Benny on piano, the bridal couple's wedding dance was 'Sunny Girl', as performed by Svenne Hedlund.

Stig Anderson's wedding present was a clock-radio: he knew that both bride and groom had trouble getting up in the morning. Björn and Agnetha's parents brought with them a floor-lamp and a cookery book. Stig put together an improvised show with some of the many showbiz friends present. The show was performed on the balcony of the castle, where a large crowd had gathered. The couple was cheered all through the evening and, like royalty, had to go out and wave several times. The party continued late into the night, turning into one long celebration of love and togetherness. The guests were even treated to the sight of Björn doing a fiery tango with his father.

One guest was conspicuous by his absence. Stig's partner and Björn's mentor, Bengt Bernhag, had been forced to turn down his invitation to the wedding. Since 1963 Bengt had suffered from a colitis that severely affected every aspect of his life. As a result of the illness he had to wear a colostomy bag, causing him no end of embarrassment. He became reclusive, and to make matters worse during the past few years he had started drinking heavily to relieve the pain and the shame.

Bengt kept all his problems from the Hootenanny Singers, who had no idea that he was ill. But they, and everybody else who came into contact with him, couldn't help noticing his drinking. Michael Tretow recalls: "He'd disappear to the toilet and then when he came out again, he smelled strongly of after-shave lotion. Then he'd taken a swig of something."

Finally, the pressure of his illness and his alcohol problems became too much for Bengt. On the night of Björn and Agnetha's wedding, no doubt fuelled by remorse at being unable to attend, he went out to his garage, fixed a hose from the exhaust pipe through a window of his car, got inside, started the engine and gassed himself to death. He was 43 years old.

Stig Anderson got the call on the night of the wedding. He didn't want to spoil the mood of the party, so Björn and Agnetha weren't told until the next morning. Stig and Björn were devastated. Stig had lost a valued business partner, a skilful producer and a close friend. Björn never forgot how much Bengt had meant as a mentor and friend, teaching him the ropes of the music business.

The festivities of the night before were soon forgotten as the tragedy sank in. Decisions had to be made, and quickly. Stig and Björn rowed a small boat out into the middle of a nearby lake to talk in private. Stig's belief in Björn's songwriting collaboration with Benny was still strong, but it was primarily Björn that he and Bengt had groomed to bring into Polar. Björn would be a valuable asset as a producer, with his finger on the pulse of new music.

As the water lapped the sides of their boat, Stig offered Björn the post of house producer at Polar. His monthly wage would be 10,000 kronor (£800).

"I'd love to come to work for you," replied Björn, "but you've got to take on Benny as well. I won't take the job without Benny."

Stig cleared his throat. "Well, I really can't afford to hire more than one guy."

Björn gazed out over the lake and thought for a second or two. "If we split the salary, will you then take on the two of us?"

Stig mumbled a lame joke about "quantity discount", then agreed to Björn's unselfish proposal.

"It was a damned generous gesture on Björn's part," said Benny, who would always remember his friend's loyalty at that crucial moment. The pair started their employment as Polar Music house producers effective immediately.

The past few days had been one long turmoil of emotions, but no honeymoon was ever planned for Mr and Mrs Ulvaeus. With the ongoing park tour and upcoming recording commitments, there simply wasn't time for such luxuries.

Back in Stockholm, Agnetha and Björn's marital bliss suffered an early setback shortly after the wedding. Ever since their engagement the previous year, they'd been trying to have a child. "I have always had very strong maternal instincts," said Agnetha many years later. "Even as a child I'd cut out pictures of prams from newspapers and would imagine the feeling of pushing my own pram through fresh winter snow and seeing the tracks of the wheels behind me on the road."

It wasn't long before the couple realised that conceiving a child was not going to be as easy as they had hoped. Agnetha thought the problem may have something to do with her being on the pill since she was 16. Now they were married, the situation began to eat away at Agnetha. It didn't help that both her and Björn's parents were also wondering about when they might have a grandchild. "I have dreamt of having a child for so long," she said at the time. "Now I get startled whenever I see a pregnant woman or a pram. Everyone we socialise with has kids. Benny and Frida each have children of their own. Only Björn and I haven't got any."

When they realised that Agnetha might not be able to conceive, they looked into adoption. But there was a problem: Swedish law stated adoptive parents had to be 25 years old, and Agnetha was still only 21 at the time. "I think it's wrong," she thundered. "There is nothing that says that you're mature the day you turn 25. I have read lots of books about adoption and even the authors argue that it's a strange attitude." Still, the newlyweds decided it was too early to get seriously worried. For the moment, they would concentrate on adjusting to married life and developing their careers.

Meanwhile, Frida's career as a solo singer stumbled along like a bumpy fairground ride. The ever-patient Benny, eternally sympathetic to her mood swings, did everything in his power to help her achieve that elusive hit, and in the summer of 1971, he produced her single 'Min egen stad' ('My Own Town'), a Swedish version of an old song called 'It's Nice To Be Back' that he'd written for The Hep Stars.

To everyone's relief, the song became Frida's first big hit, reaching number one on *Svensktoppen* and giving her self-confidence a much needed boost. Encouraged by the success of the song, EMI added 'Min egen stad' as an extra track to a reissue of the otherwise hitless *Frida* album.

Further signs that things might be looking up for Ms Lyngstad came in the autumn when she was hired to appear in the revue *Mina favoriter* (*My Favourites*) at the Folkan theatre in Stockholm. Staged by one of Sweden's most popular and enduring revue writers, Kar de Mumma, the show was virtually guaranteed to become a surefire hit. Lasse Berghagen, already a three-year veteran of the Kar de Mumma revues, recommended Frida to the show's director Hasse Ekman. Berghagen stuck a copy of the *Frida* album in Ekman's hands with the recommendation: "Listen to this."

Mina favoriter opened on October 22, 1971 and ran for seven months. Frida was not exactly the star of the show, but she recognised the opportunity to learn from experienced stage performers. She had three major numbers, one of which was her Swedish interpretation of the old standard 'Me And My Shadow'. The show was a success and kept Frida occupied for several months.

For their part, Björn and Benny certainly didn't lack working commitments and during the summer they started work on a new duo album. The material remained within the *schlager* field that had been their chosen framework for the past two years, and sessions for the album continued on and off over the next 12 months. A more important commitment for Björn and Benny over the next two years was their work as house producers at Polar. In October, they began producing the début album for 15-year-old *wunderkind* Ted Gärdestad. Ted, who had an exceptional talent for melody, let his 23-year-old brother Kenneth write the lyrics.

The Gärdestad brothers had approached Polar two years earlier, but at that time Stig Anderson felt that Ted was too young. Also, he didn't believe the songs should be performed in English. "Start writing in Swedish and come back when you're a little older," he said.

That's exactly what the two brothers did. Ted and Kenneth turned up at the doorstep at Polar and Benny, who opened the door, was astonished when they refused to leave until he had listened to their tape. "They were pretty cocky and said, 'You have to listen now, otherwise we'll go somewhere else,'" recalled Benny. "But it was incredibly good." Björn remembered: "I'd never heard anything as obvious as this in all my life." This time there were no arguments: they had to sign the boy. Ted's début album, *Undringar (Thoughts)*, was recorded in an intensive six-week period in the autumn of 1971. Björn and Benny produced the LP and contributed backing vocals, as did Agnetha and Frida.

This excellent album, with its solid singer/songwriter pop songs, must have been an eye-opener for Björn and Benny. The truth was obvious: this fresh-faced kid was making better and more honest music than relative veterans like themselves. While Björn and Benny seemed caught in an "aim to please" trap, Ted wasn't even aware that songs came from anywhere other than the heart. "It happened on a few occasions that we recorded something we didn't like because we thought that the public might like it anyway," Benny confessed a few years later. "But they never did. You have to feel for the song yourself."

The sales figures for Ted's album spoke for themselves: after a false start on release in January 1972, it topped the charts for a staggering 10 weeks during the summer. On the albums market, neither Björn nor Benny had ever been close to such phenomenal sales. After Abba, Ted would be Polar's most successful recording artist during the Seventies.

While their own careers as recording artists in the early years of the decade had thus far been fairly uneven, Björn and Benny felt very much at home in their roles as songwriters and producers first and performers second. They'd spent the Sixties as home-grown stars, seemingly on a never-ending tour, and they were now only too eager to leave this aspect of their careers behind them. Over the next few years they would produce a wide variety of different acts on Polar: children's records, big band jazz, odd experiments with accordion and synthesizer, religious works and straightforward pop. The lessons they learned in recording studios in the Sixties were applied to these assignments, which in themselves provided invaluable experience for the future.

However, their track record as songwriters was somewhat less than impressive. Out of the eleven songs they had written for acts other than themselves (including The Hep Stars) since they first started collaborating with each other, few had become hits. In August 1971, they enjoyed success on the sales chart with the song 'Välkommen till världen' ('Welcome To The World'), recorded by popular singer Lill-Babs.★ Just like their own hits with 'Hej gamle man!' and 'Tänk om jorden vore ung', the recording featured prominent and energetic backing vocals from all four future Abba members.

Similarly, Frida's first-ever hit of any significance, 'Min egen stad', also benefited from Benny's production and backing vocals from the same line-up (minus Björn, who was doing his military refresher course). The signs did seem to be pointing in one specific direction but at the time it may have been hard to see, since they all seemed to have slightly different goals with their respective careers. And besides, they were still tied to three separate record labels.

Meanwhile, Stig hadn't lost his faith in Björn and Benny's future as songwriters for an international market. As was his habit, he did everything he could to further the boys' careers. Earlier in the year, the team had scored some success in a song contest in Málaga, where Björn & Benny performed 'Language Of Love' (an English version of 'Livet går sin gång', one of the better tracks on their *Lycka* album). Although they finished only sixth, the attention meant that Stig managed to sell the song to

★ A few years later the song was recorded by skiffle legend Lonnie Donegan as 'I Lost My Heart On The 5.42'.

170

nine different countries. French songstress Françoise Hardy was among the more prominent performers to express an interest in covering the song, although it seems no such recording was ever made.

The importance of international contests as a way to market songs was certainly not lost on Stig. Whereas the American and English music business sneered at his attempts to drum up interest in Scandinavian music, song contests invariably led to immediate, on-the-spot feedback.

Exposure was everything: that was perhaps the most important of the many lessons Stig had learned over the past decade. If the world had to learn about Björn and Benny's songwriting talents through a contest, so be it.

Stig was acutely aware of one other important factor. Small affairs like the one in Málaga were one thing but everybody in the business knew that at the end of the day, there was only one song contest that truly mattered.

Chapter 12

The televised entertainment spectacle known as the Eurovision Song Contest was born in the autumn of 1955. That year the European Broadcasting Union decided that a music competition, broadcast via the new Eurovision network, would be held the following spring. The seven participating nations entered two songs each, and the purpose was to determine which of the 14 titles was the best song.

One of the underlying reasons for the contest was to create an accessible and entertaining means of unifying the countries of Europe, which only a decade earlier had been torn apart by the Second World War. But primarily, the contest should serve to solidify television as a medium and, more specifically, the Eurovision collaboration.

Over the years the rules of the competition have changed many times, along with the number of participating nations. Though often derided as trivial, the Eurovision Song Contest has mirrored changing political climates and, in more recent times, even the wars plaguing Europe.

Since it began, the music featured in the competition has been virtually synonymous with the *schlager* genre, but considering Stig Anderson's status as Sweden's king of *schlager*, both he and his artists had a surprisingly limited presence in the contest for the first decade and a half of its existence. Nevertheless, Stig was there as a contender from the very beginning. The first year that Sweden took part, in 1958, a jury at Swedish radio simply chose the song they thought was the best out of the many submitted. Stig saw a chance to reach across the borders and entered one of his own compositions. Alas, it was turned down.

The Swedish entry finally chosen had a tenuous Abba connection, however, for the song was composed by future Hep Stars manager Åke Gerhard. Alice Babs performed 'Lilla stjärna' ('Little Star'), which finished fourth out of the 10 songs competing in the Eurovision Song Contest that year.

Up until the early Seventies, with the exceptions of 1964 and 1970, Sweden had taken part in the contest every year since 1958. By that time, the competition had grown to become an important and significant event for the light entertainment segment of the European music business, and many big hits had found their way onto the world's sales charts via the Eurovision Song Contest.

Over the years the original quagmire of dramatic, orchestrated ballads performed in an atmosphere of exaggerated solemnity had given way to a higher quota of snappy uptempo numbers. Among them was one of the internationally successful winners, Sandie Shaw's 1967 UK chart topper 'Puppet On A String'.

Ironically, many of the entries that didn't win had been more successful than those that did. Examples of well-known songs first making their mark in the Eurovision Song Contest include 'Volare', subsequently a US number one hit for singer and composer Domenico Modugno, and a number two hit on the UK charts in a version by Dean Martin. The 1967 entry 'L'amour est bleu' (aka 'Love Is Blue') was a US chart-topper for Paul Mauriat, and Cliff Richard's 'Congratulations' hit number one in the UK in 1968.

This fact certainly wasn't lost on Stig Anderson. In purely commercial terms, it was easy to conclude that it wasn't winning as such that was most important, but the exposure to an audience of hundreds of millions. If the song and the performance were strong enough, they would cut through everything else and find their way straight into the hearts and minds of the television audience, no matter what the juries thought.

Starting with the 1959 contest, Swedish Radio hosted a selection every year, eventually acquiring the name *Melodifestivalen* (*The Melody Festival*). The first hurdle was to get a song entered into those heats. Early attempts by Stig and the future members of Abba, in as far as they have become public knowledge, had led to mixed if encouraging results.

Agnetha's composition 'Försonade' was rejected for the 1968 competition, and the same fate was bestowed on Björn, Benny and Stig's 'Ljuva sextital' in 1969. Benny had better luck that same year with his and Lasse Berghagen's 'Hej Clown' which finished second in its interpretation by singer Jan Malmsjö. Also in 1969, Frida got a joint fourth placing with 'Härlig är vår jord'. Two years later, Björn and Benny suffered a double rejection: 'Det kan ingen doktor hjälpa' ('There's No Cure For That', featuring lyrics by Stig Anderson), subsequently a Björn & Benny hit, and 'Välkommen till världen', which also turned out to be a successful record.

It wasn't until 1972 that the Andersson/Anderson/Ulvaeus team finally got their break. The selection process for that year stipulated that composers should submit their songs for specific artists. The Swedish Broadcasting Corporation had already chosen these lucky singers, and among them was 17-year-old Lena Andersson, who'd achieved her big breakthrough as a Polar recording artist in 1971. It was therefore only natural that young Lena would choose as her entry a song written by Björn,

Benny and Stig. The song was a *schlager* ballad entitled 'Säg det med en sång' ('Say It With A Song', recorded in English as 'Better To Have Loved').

Convinced they had a winner on their hands, Stig decided that no energy or expense should be spared in recording the song in a manner that would sound credible on the international market. Great Britain, the home of modern pop music, ought to be able to provide the right atmosphere.

A backing track recorded in a Swedish studio was scrapped, and at the end of January, Björn, Benny and Lena travelled to London to record fully orchestrated Swedish and English versions of the song. Their arranger was Arthur Greenslade, who had previously worked with artists as diverse as Dusty Springfield, Genesis, Marianne Faithfull and David Bowie. The British backing choir had to learn the Swedish lyrics phonetically.

In terms of the contest, however, all these efforts were to no avail – the jury of music business people voted the song third in the selections in February. But Lena and her songwriters got a major Swedish hit out of 'Säg det med en sång'. As a Top 10 entry on the sales chart, and number one on *Svensktoppen*, it was far and away the most successful of all selection contenders that year. As Stig concluded, the song had the people's vote.

By the spring of 1972, most of those who would play an important part in guiding Abba towards worldwide fame had found their place in the extended Polar Music family. Sound engineer Michael B. Tretow, although formally employed by Metronome Studio, had emerged as an invaluable collaborator who shared Björn and Benny's ambition to explore all the possibilities of the recording studio.

Görel Johnsen was only 20 when she began working as Stig's secretary in September 1969. It was Gudrun Anderson who hired the shy small-town girl while Stig was away on a business trip in the United States. Görel was seated in a corner with piles of sheet music to file away and copyright lists to make up, learning how the music publishing business worked from the ground up. Stig returned to find a soft-spoken girl who curtsied for him and bashfully introduced herself. He was not impressed. Taking Gudrun aside, he hissed, "This is baby-snatching!" But Gudrun insisted that Görel should be given a chance.

"It was rough stuff from the word go," she recalled. "If Stig was angry he'd show that by throwing pens or yelling things." One incident that incurred his wrath related to one of the many lyrics he was pouring out at the time. It was no secret that Stig was extremely protective about his words and always wanted to make sure that everything turned out right.

"He would come down to the studio with a wild stare in his eyes and raise hell," recalls Michael Tretow. "It didn't matter if it was a lyric he'd written for an artist on another label. He was regarded as a real pain in the ass, because no producers really liked the lyricist to meddle with the recordings."

At one point, Stig had been working from home and phoned the office to dictate the lyrics to Görel. The song was to be recorded by a major artist signed to the Metronome label. "I happened to put a few words in the wrong place, so that the rhythm was disturbed," Görel recalled. "I'll never forget how angry Stig got, he looked like he'd need to overturn the whole town district to work off his anger. He roared that my mistake had made him the laughing stock of the whole business, and that Metronome already regarded him as finished . . . I suggested that perhaps we could phone [the producer] and correct the mistake? Oh no, that was unthinkable! It only made Stig even angrier."

Those who weren't broken by Stig's fits of rage instead developed an exceptionally thick skin. "In the beginning I'd lock myself in the bathroom and have a cry," said Görel. "But then I realised that Stig liked it if you answered back." It didn't take long before Görel became Stig's most valued associate at the office, his personal assistant who was entrusted with fairly complex assignments. By the mid-Seventies, she had acquired the title Vice President of Polar Music.

"Stig was generous with teaching you things and could give you incredibly demanding tasks, telling you, 'I know you can do this!' There are far too many competent secretaries that never get a chance like that. Stig taught me that it's not always so important who does what. The main thing is that the problem gets solved – in the best and quickest way possible."

For Stig, who'd had to rely on a strong, resourceful woman throughout his youth, there was nothing odd in his promotion of Görel – he didn't care if it excluded him from any boys' club. The unusual circumstances of Stig's upbringing had taught him that extraordinary results could only be achieved by ignoring rules that served no other purpose than maintaining the status quo. And contrary to many other, more traditional families, it was his wife who handled the finances both at home and at the office. "When I need to know how much money the family's got, I ask my wife," he said.

In later years, Stig took pride in pointing out that he was pioneering the concept of equal opportunity between men and women in the workplace. "I was one of the first in the economic life in the Seventies to make my secretary a managing director. That was because she was often treated as a

175

pretty young thing, especially by international business colleagues. Even though she was very knowledgeable. So when those male chauvinist pigs called she could put them in [their] place."

Stig was also starting up a close association with London-based music publisher John Spalding. It was Stig's Belgian partner, Robert Bosmans, who originally introduced the two a decade earlier. So far, the business had tended to travel in one direction. "I got him a lot of publishing, but of course, his Swedish tunes didn't mean a thing over here in those days," recalls Spalding.

John Spalding had started out working for London-based music publisher Eddie Kassner, then moved to a company called Dominion Music. "There were only about four of us worked in Dominion Music, and one week in the early Sixties we had seven of the hits in the Top 20. Obviously we were doing something right," he says. Dominion was eventually taken over by United Artists, and John Spalding became the head of that company, building it up in the UK. He was instrumental in helping Stig get the Hootenanny Singers' singles released on the company's record label.

From the beginning of their association, Stig and John got on exceptionally well, the two of them being birds of a feather. Spalding eventually became a trusted partner who'd accompany Stig on his many business trips around the world. His insights into drawing up contracts was especially valuable. "I was an asset for Stig, but we both rubbed off on each other. He could be Mr Nice Guy and I could be Mr Nasty Guy when all those deals were made."

As work on getting Björn and Benny's music known abroad continued, Björn, Agnetha, Benny and Frida were getting on with their lives as two couples, and socialising as friends. At the start of 1972, all four had moved into brand new town houses in the northern suburb of Vallentuna.

It was Agnetha and Björn who first decided to make their home in this neighbourhood, but Benny and Frida too were desperate to leave their small Stockholm apartment. After four rough years paying instalments to the tax authorities Benny was now back on his feet financially, which made the move possible. "They brought us out to the area," said Frida. "We thought it looked so cosy that we made up our minds on the spot."

They were keen to live near Björn and Agnetha, feeling a sense of comfort in having friends in this otherwise unfamiliar place. They also needed more room for the sake of their children. "They are all cheerful, lively kids who need a lot of space," said Frida. "They will get their own rooms and can visit us even more often. The kids can play outside the house without us worrying ourselves sick about cars."

Benny and Frida were looking forward to sharing more time with their children. At this point, both Ragnar and Christina had found new partners, and Hans and Lise-Lotte even had a new baby brother. Benny reflected: "When I left my family I was only 19 years old – 19, a father of two and right in the middle of The Hep Stars' success, which opened up an enormous world to me. I can never defend my actions, my only explanation is that I was so young . . . I'm grateful to the mother of my children that she's done everything to enable us to meet as often as possible. She could have reacted with bitterness and exclusion."

Frida sometimes dwelt on how people might view her after she'd given up her family life in Eskilstuna. "What hurts me the most is the slanderous talk that I'm a bad mother," she said. "That I've abandoned my children to lead a life in the limelight, a wild life with champagne and caviar. That I don't care what happens to them, that I only think about myself. It never ceases to amaze and sadden me how easy it is for people to pass judgement on circumstances they know absolutely nothing about."

The two young couples enjoyed an idyllic suburban life in their newly built dwellings. They cherished the nearness to surrounding forest areas where they could go for walks with Björn and Agnetha's bulldog, Ada, and Benny and Frida's soft coated wheaten terrier, Zappa.

Agnetha recalled those early days in Vallentuna with fondness. "We saw a lot of each other. The boys got going with the writing and we'd visit each other's houses, singing and playing together . . . We shared the same profession and our common interest in music forged a bond between us . . . [Frida and I] socialised a lot out there in Vallentuna." She sometimes found it hard to start acting the ideal housewife though. By her own admission she had a knack for making potted plants wither, and she called her and Björn's garden "the worst-looking in the neighbourhood". Nor was her first attempt at baking especially successful. "I used too much flour. You had to approach the loaves with a saw – they were hard as cement!"

In between the baking accidents, Agnetha continued writing songs for a new album and exploring other possibilities for her career. Encouraged by Björn, who'd always admired her songwriting, she became inspired by Carole King's *Tapestry* album which was just taking the world by storm. Here was the role model she had been lacking: a woman both singing and performing her own material. Moreover, soft rock songs like 'I Feel The Earth Move', 'It's Too Late' and 'You've Got A Friend' appealed to Agnetha, as King conveyed a sense of being deeply personal yet easily accessible at the same time. Agnetha decided that there was no need to rush the recording of a new LP. Only when she had songs she was a hundred per cent satisfied with would she go into the studio. "It's going to be a bit more complex than before," she said of her upcoming opus.

In the meantime a new challenge came her way. She was offered an audition for the role of Mary Magdalene in the Swedish version of the Andrew Lloyd Webber/Tim Rice musical *Jesus Christ Superstar*. It was a friend of Björn's who had seen a performance of the show in Copenhagen who thought that Agnetha would be right for the Swedish production.

Agnetha passed the audition, doing six of the nine scheduled performances, with two other singers handling the remaining three. The musical opened on February 18, 1972, at the Scandinavium in Gothenburg, less than a month after Agnetha had been asked to try for the part. But the critics were not especially pleased with the show. "[The] performance verges on amateurism," wrote newspaper *Expressen*. "Agnetha Fältskog . . . is a sweet young girl and she knows how to sing, but no more than that."

Despite such harsh reviews, Agnetha herself has always looked back with fondness on the *Jesus Christ Superstar* experience. Perhaps her Björn-produced Swedish version of 'I Don't Know How To Love Him' from the musical had something to do with it: the recording reached number one on *Svensktoppen*.

While Agnetha was enjoying herself in Gothenburg, Frida was having a disastrous time in Stockholm, suffering night after night during the seven-month run of the *Mina favoriter* revue. What had originally seemed to be an exciting career move – and an opportunity to develop as a stage performer – had rapidly turned into a nightmare. Frida's old onstage insecurity was to blame, and this time it had developed into a full-blown trauma. As a result, she convinced herself that she was completely inadequate and had no future as a musician. Wasn't that what the world was trying to tell her when, after 13 years as a singer, she still hadn't learned how to make an audience love her?

A month after the opening, in late November 1971, Frida registered with a tailor's school in Stockholm. Her grandmother had taught her how to sew and she had always made her own stage clothes. Anni-Frid Lyngstad was going to give up singing and become a clothes designer. "I'm no dreamer, on the contrary I'm very realistic," she said. "That's how I know that I'm not the kind of artist who is prepared to fight for their place in the spotlight at any price. The competition in this profession is incredibly hard, only the strongest and best survive. Despite the fact that I love being an artist . . . I'm not sure that I'm among those who will survive."

If it wasn't for Benny, Frida acknowledged, she would have given up a long time ago. When she was depressed, he was there to lighten things up, supporting and encouraging her in every way imaginable. What little self-confidence she had was completely thanks to him, she maintained. In January 1972, Frida recorded her last single for EMI. The A-side was Björn and Benny's 'Vi är alla bara barn i början' ('We Are All Just Children In The Beginning'). It was yet another in the row of 'Hej gamle man!' clones that the Andersson/Ulvaeus team was specialising in at the time.

The assured faith of the beat, coupled with the positive lyrics, seemed almost like a message of encouragement directed at Frida. "We are all just children in the beginning, on the road to great adventure, if we give each other a helping hand when tomorrow dawns," asserted the chorus, vocally backed up by her fiancé along with Björn and Agnetha. Stig's Swedish lyrics for the B-side cover of Carole King's 'No Sad Song' sounded as if they too had been written especially for Frida. The song opened with the lines: "Who are you, feeling low? Do you make a big thing of your sorrow? You have to take life as it is." Whether Frida felt she was singing about herself or not, the songs probably didn't help boost her sagging confidence: on release at the end of February, the single sank without trace.

Frida's future in show business looked bleaker than ever. To the stage fright that was already plaguing her at the revue was added the feeling that it was all becoming a boring drudge. Even with the benefit of a few years' hindsight she recalled the seven months at the theatre as "pretty difficult. Coming in and doing only three numbers each night doesn't agree with me. It's much too little to do under such a long period of time."

Her moods weren't helped by the fact that she was surrounded by people whose careers just seemed to thrive unabated. Agnetha had a starring role in *Jesus Christ Superstar*, was topping the *Svensktoppen* chart and had her first solo *folkpark* tour booked for the summer. Björn and Benny had secure positions as songwriters, producers and recording artists, scoring regular hits.

Even the Hootenanny Singers, who should have been dead and buried by now, continued to rack up hits despite a minimum of effort. Together with Benny, they were also scheduled to set out on a 70-date summer tour for the first time in three years. In the gang of close friends, Frida was the only one who didn't have anything scheduled once the revue closed at the end of May. It was too much to bear. She was heading for a deep depression and not even Benny's soothing words could rescue her.

Even at the best of times there was friction in the relationship. Benny's easygoing, harmonious approach to life often clashed with Frida's fretful nature and deep insecurity. They loved one another and wanted to live together, the pair said, but they just didn't function very well together. "Many times I've said something to Frida that I meant in a positive, warm way. But when my message reaches her she receives it in a way I could never dream of," reflected Benny. "It's as if she has a built-in transformer that converts my message to something completely different from what it was when I sent it. She gets hurt – I don't even understand why – and then we start to quarrel and get unhappy."

A miserable time ensued in their Vallentuna town house. With things at their worst, Frida even refused to get out of bed, sleeping her days away. She couldn't even handle the most mundane, everyday chores, and wanted only to escape from everything and everyone.

Benny was exasperated. It seemed impossible to snap her out of it. "I doubt everyone and everything, even Benny's love," Frida said of her depressions. "I mean nothing but misery for him, so how could he love me? Yet, he has shown me that he does so completely, standing by me and helping me in a way that no one else has done. Either through challenging me to activity, or through making me see reason in his gentle way, giving me comfort and warmth."

Benny and Frida's devastating *Festfolk* experience was nothing compared to the strain placed on their relationship during these months. Three years of ups and downs with Frida had given Benny food for thought about his own role in the drama. "For a while I was wondering if in some unconscious way I needed the excitement and all the dramatic interludes that followed our misunderstandings. Today I am one hundred per cent certain that I don't," he stated a few months later.

Frida admitted that her depression added to her reluctance to take a greater role in the upbringing of her children. "How should I, who cannot even take care of myself during my depressions, make any claims whatsoever on taking care of them? Don't they have it as good as they possibly could . . . with their confident father and his new family? Don't think it's easy for me, I miss them terribly. But I feel that their happiness must take precedence over mine, and that I've done exactly the right thing."

However, while Frida struggled with her insecurities a new dawn was breaking, even if at first it didn't seem to concern her personally. Stig Anderson's prediction of worldwide fame for Björn and Benny suddenly seemed to be coming true.

Chapter 13

Over the years, Stig Anderson had acquired a good, solid reputation on the international music publishing scene. Business associates from all over the world were astonished at his knack for taking their songs and turning them into lucrative hits in this small country in northern Europe. Apart from his own publishing corporation, he was also the Scandinavian representative for companies such as United Artists, Screen Gems, ATV-Kirshner, Palace Music and the Italian publisher Sugar Music. But Stig's real ambition was to reverse this process, and he refused to give up trying to sell Swedish music to the world, even though his efforts had yet to pay off in a truly convincing way.

It wasn't as if his Stockholm rivals had fared much better, for thus far the sum of Swedish presence on the important music markets was virtually nil. The first time a Swedish artist appeared on the US charts was when singer Siw Malmkvist duetted with Italian singer Umberto Marcato on the song 'Sole Sole Sole', reaching the US Top 60 in 1964. In Great Britain, beginning in June 1962, The Spotnicks had scored four Top 40 hits and a Top 20 album in the course of a year. A few other artists had entered the US and UK charts briefly over the years, but the eyes of the music business world weren't exactly turning to Sweden for "the next big thing".

Apart from his suggestion that The Spotnicks should record 'Orange Blossom Special', Stig hadn't even been a party to any of those odd fluke hits, although it certainly wasn't for lack of trying. Records by the Hootenanny Singers, the first-ever act to be signed to Polar Music, had been released in 12 different countries within two years of their first domestic hit.

In view of Abba's success and the subsequent export explosion of Swedish music in the Nineties, it is perhaps hard to realise that there actually was a time when it took a virtual truckload of self-esteem to approach the seemingly unattainable overseas markets.

Björn and Benny's favourite analogy over the years has been the imaginary A&R executive at a British or American record company throwing their demo tapes in the waste basket without even listening. "In the early days, there really wasn't any use trying to get your records released abroad, because the fact that we were Swedish automatically meant that no one really cared," reflected Benny.

In the spring of 1972, Polar Music suddenly experienced one of those fluke overseas successes that so far had eluded them. It kick-started a chain of events that would turn the world upside down for the ambitious Swedes.

Björn & Benny's 'She's My Kind Of Girl' may have been a flop in Sweden, but Stig still had faith in the song. At one point he had been planning the release of a soundtrack album for *The Seduction Of Inga* in America and Great Britain. As was his habit, he sent out copies of Andersson/Ulvaeus songs to all his publishing contacts, or simply left them at their offices while he was on a trip. So far the results had been fairly negligible, although a handful of songs had in fact been recorded by foreign artists.

In early 1972 Stig's perseverance finally paid off. According to legend, a Japanese publisher happened to hear the 'She's My Kind Of Girl' single at the office of a French colleague while on a trip to Paris. With its vaguely oriental-sounding intro and melancholy minor-key melody, the Japanese publisher felt it was just the kind of song that could become a hit in his country. He secured the rights to the record, which was released on Epic Records in February 1972. By the following month the single had reached number one on the charts, going on to sell some 250,000 copies.

It was fairly astonishing that a record by two artists famous in their own country had done absolutely nothing at home yet was a smash hit in a nation where they were completely unknown. But Stig was not surprised: even in the mid-Sixties he had noted how musical tastes were different all over the world. 'Karelia', The Spotnicks' version of a melancholy Finnish folk song, had become a major hit in Japan, and parts of 'She's My Kind Of Girl' touched exactly the same chord – it was perfect for the Far East.

In the quaint tradition of Japan's music business, the record was given the alternative Japanese title of 'The Little Girl Of The Cold Wind'. It was entirely unrelated to Björn and Benny's lyrics, but underlined the sad and wistful appeal of the melody to the record-buying public.

A follow-up was naturally required as soon as possible – if Epic Japan had their way, a whole album would be recorded especially for their market. Björn and Benny were surprised and delighted. This was the opportunity they had been waiting for. All of a sudden there was a demand for what they really wanted to do: English-language, contemporary-sounding pop music. This looked like their best chance of breaking away from the drudgery of *schlager* and cabaret where they had been marooned for the past few years. "We said, 'Let's do things we really want to do,' " recalled Benny. " 'Let's do it ourselves without anybody else involved. And exactly the things we most want to record.' "

The Japanese success led to a flurry of activity on several different fronts. There were Björn & Benny singles to be recorded for the home market – primarily Swedish *schlagers* – as well as tracks for their second Swedish album, by now a long-running project. In addition, they needed to record English-language singles and possibly also an LP for release in Japan.

It was an exciting time, where the safe road ran parallel and sometimes even intermixed with more risky endeavours. "The recordings seem to have been . . . planned in an almost haphazard from-day-to-day manner," as Björn and Benny accurately noted many years later.

In mid-March, Björn and Benny dug up an old unused melody of theirs entitled 'Grandpa's Banjo'. The lyrics were rewritten, and under the new title 'Santa Rosa' the song was recorded on March 21. Björn and Benny also wrote a brand new song called 'Merry-Go-Round'. As they have acknowledged, with its minor keys and oriental-flavoured intro, this song was more blatantly geared towards the Japanese market.

Their instincts also told them that there might be a way to use Agnetha's and Frida's voices in this pop concept. The winning combination of the four voices had been proved beyond doubt: the energetic sound of their backing vocals had helped push record after record up the charts over the past 15 months. The strong potential of their four voices just wouldn't leave Björn and Benny in peace. If they refrained from repeating the disastrous experience of going on tour together, there was no reason why the two couples shouldn't be able to collaborate smoothly in the recording studio.

British bubblegum groups like The Sweet and, more pertinently, Middle Of The Road provided a blueprint for their experiments in pure pop. "We listened to them and thought, 'We can do that just as well as they can,' " recalled Benny. But the real inspiration came from what in hindsight seems to have been almost a draft outline for Abba, at least in terms of their combined experience: Blue Mink, a British group comprised largely of qualified session personnel. From their very first hit 'Melting Pot' in 1969, the group's trademark had been an exchange of lead vocals between front-figures Madeline Bell and Roger Cook, both of whom – like all four members of Abba – were music industry professionals. Backing them in the studio was an impressive list of session names, Herbie Flowers on bass, Alan Parker on guitar, and Barry Morgan on drums.

There seems to have been one specific Blue Mink record that gave birth to the idea of shifting between male and female lead vocals, although today none of those involved can recall which one it was. In a way it doesn't matter, for almost every Blue Mink track was aligned with the theme Björn and Benny sought to emulate in their own songs: a plea for peace and harmony – racial, global or otherwise – delivered within a light-pop framework.

On Wednesday, March 29, 1972, Björn, Benny, Agnetha and Frida entered the Metronome Studio on Karlbergsvägen in the district of Vasastan in Stockholm. Helping them out with the backing that day was guitarist Janne Schaffer, bass player Mike Watson and drummer Ola Brunkert. All three musicians were veterans of the Sixties pop band scene, but had since emerged as highly competent session players. Michael B. Tretow was ensconced behind the mixing desk, while Benny played the piano and Björn contributed additional guitar.

When the day's work was over, two complete tracks had been recorded. One was that Japanese flirtation, 'Merry-Go-Round', conceived as a Björn & Benny record with the girls on backing vocals. The second song was their Blue Mink-style concoction. For this track, Björn and Benny shared the lead vocals with the girls, singing alternate lines and coming together on the chorus, just like Blue Mink did.

Agnetha and Frida certainly helped liven things up, their clear and zestful vocals contrasting sharply with Björn and Benny's more nasal tones. Which was exactly the idea: "Benny and I knew our limits as performers," Björn later said. The girls even came up with a somewhat quaint yodelling part towards the end of the song. After a long day's hard work, the very first Abba song, 'People Need Love', had been born.

Listening to the playback in the control room the quartet experienced an emotion they had never felt before. "I remember thinking that 'now we have made our first really good record', and I think Björn felt the same way," said Benny.

Today, 'People Need Love' is often dismissed as a piece of lightweight, superficial pap, the hit that no one wants to remember. But the song provides an important clue to the tradition and mindframe from which Abba sprang. It is true that at the time Björn and Benny were eager not to be identified as cabaret or *schlager* artists; they wanted to become internationally recognised writers and producers of credible pop music. Nevertheless, when they made their first pop record together with Agnetha and Frida, they didn't look for inspiration in glam rock, heavy metal or Philly soul, to name three contemporary trends. Instead, they allied themselves with a predominant trend in the MOR pop world.

Songs with a message have their roots in union movements and radical political groups the world over. Often banned by strict regimes, they came out into the open with the biting protest songs of the early Sixties, many of the best known stemming from the pen of Bob Dylan. By the end of the decade, the potency of subversive songs had travelled through the hippie landscape of peace, love and understanding, before finally ending up in the land of easy-listening. What had originally been a message of sincerely felt social concern had eventually been watered down to a worried wrinkle on the forehead of middle-class suburbia.

Examples in the more lightweight world of popular music were many. Originating in an advertising jingle for Coca-Cola, The New Seekers' message that they'd like to "teach the world to sing in perfect harmony" gave them a UK number one in 1971. On the other side of the Atlantic, the Canadian group Ocean reached the upper regions of the charts by urging the people of the world to "put your hand in the hand" of Jesus. In the case of Blue Mink, Roger Cook was a white man, while Madeline Bell was a black woman, an image that lent itself especially well to the easily palatable plea for racial harmony that was their breakthrough hit 'Melting Pot'.

With all this going on within their chosen field, it wasn't so strange that the budding Swedish foursome found it worthwhile to establish that "people need love" on their very first single release. The lyrics were peppered with words like "hope", "loving", "fellow man" and "harmony". Light social criticism and non-confrontational pleas for global harmony were also a recurring theme on the Swedish Björn & Benny singles around the same time. It was a favourite subject for *schlager* lyricists like Stig Anderson.

'People Need Love' was released as a single in Sweden in June 1972, with 'Merry-Go-Round' on the B-side. The record bore the credit 'Björn & Benny, Agnetha & Anni-Frid'. Abba legend would have it that there was a long struggle with Stig Anderson to finally allow the girls' contribution to be credited on the label. According to this myth, Stig continually resisted all attempts to give Agnetha and Frida proper recognition for their efforts, but this is obviously incorrect. On earlier collaborations, the girls' contributions had been limited to backing or harmony vocals. 'People Need Love' was the first song where they had lead vocal parts.

It is true that Stig Anderson was not especially fond of the group name 'Björn & Benny, Agnetha & Anni-Frid', but this was simply because the moniker was such a mouthful. Stig, who liked things to be simple and easily marketable, nearly exploded when Björn and Benny insisted that Agnetha and Frida should be billed alongside them on this record. "I said, 'You don't come to me and say we should call it Björn & Benny, Agnetha

& Anni-Frid!',", he recalled. But even he had to admit that the girls were as much artists on this single as Björn and Benny.

Another irritation for Stig was that Frida and Agnetha were still under contract to other record labels. Stig wanted to keep as much as possible under his own umbrella, but this full credit necessitated an annoying payout to other companies for the girls' services. He was also obliged to acknowledge their ties to the other labels on the record sleeve.

What the unwieldy credit primarily implies was the temporary nature of the collaboration – the two girls were in effect guests on the new Björn & Benny single, certain to be included on the boys' next album. When a song called 'Åh, Vilka Tider' ('Those Were The Days') was recorded by Björn & Benny in June, the session sheet shows that Agnetha and Frida were duly paid for their "backing vocals" contribution.

The quartet could not even be bothered to have a new photograph taken for the 'People Need Love' sleeve; instead they dug out a two-year-old picture from a *Festfolk* promotion session. With the benefit of hindsight, it is quite clear that Björn and Benny had far too many balls to juggle at the same time: their own career as a Swedish *schlager* act, new forays into the pop world – with and without their partners - as well as songwriting and production work for other artists.

The first indication that the budding group had a hit on their hands came on Saturday, July 1, when 'People Need Love' entered the *Tio i topp* chart at number five (it would eventually reach number three). It was the first time that any of the four singers had appeared on that pop music chart since The Hep Stars' version of 'Speedy Gonzales' three years earlier. For Agnetha and Frida it was their début entry. "We were surprised and insanely happy when it entered *Tio i topp*," recalled Frida. "At the time that was a little cooler than *Svensktoppen.*"

When news of this success reached them, Björn and Benny were out on their Hootenanny Singers tour while Agnetha was busy with her solo *folkpark* trek. Björn and Benny were also preparing the recording of a Hootenanny Singers album, scheduled to begin the following Monday. Their thoughts were centred on projects far removed from the pop music world.

But they were quick to capitalise on the success, and two weeks later the quartet made their public début as a pop act promoting the song on television. On July 25, 'People Need Love' entered the combined singles and albums sales chart, eventually reaching number 17.

It was the biggest hit any of the four had enjoyed as individual artists since 'Hej gamle man!' in January 1971. Take away all the albums from the chart on its peak date, and you have a number seven single hit for

'People Need Love' – a promising start and an indication that it might be worth pursuing the group concept.

The only thing that might have held them back was their disastrous experience as a collective 18 months previously. Frida certainly hadn't forgotten those problems but even she, the most likely pessimist amongst them, was hopeful. "We were living so closely and it was unavoidable that there were disputes. But now we know each other well and are able to adjust to each other. It's nice to be able to get along that way with your best friends."

Nevertheless, despite 'People Need Love' becoming a hit, no decision was made to form a permanent group. Recollections of discussions at that point, in as far as there were any, are long since lost in the mists of time. It's likely that Björn and Benny were still looking towards a future where they would be songwriters and producers only, not artists. They certainly didn't view this initial group success as any reason to make any drastic changes in their career management.

"Compared to what we had been used to, it was nothing," recalled Björn. "It wasn't like we were convinced that 'this is what we're going to do from now on.'" The time when all four would focus on one single project as recording artists was still some time off; for the moment, hedging their bets seemed like the best strategy.

It was probably Frida who benefited most from the 'People Need Love' experience at this point, as it marked her first-ever appearance on the sales chart. Before the record was released, her career as a performer had reached rock bottom, but attaining a hit single with her fiancé and their two closest friends gave her fortunes a rapid and long overdue upturn.

Soon after the release of the single, her EMI contract expired and she was brought into the Polar Music fold. This was in line with the family spirit surrounding the company: for Stig it was completely unnatural that the fiancée of Benny Andersson wasn't a Polar recording artist. For the first single on her new label, Frida was given a cover version of one of the Italian *schlagers* that Stig favoured around that time. The Swedish title of the cheerful number was 'Man vill ju leva lite dessemellan' ('You've Got To Live A Little Every Now And Then'). Stig's hit instincts proved to be spot-on again: the song became Frida's biggest *Svensktoppen* hit so far, reaching number one and spending 10 weeks on the chart.

Even more remarkable developments were taking place at the same time. Although Frida hadn't toured during the summer, she teamed up with jazz guitarist and singer Roffe Berg for a 30-date cabaret tour in the autumn, starting on August 22. Whether it was due to her recent pop success, or because the *Mina favoriter* revue had been a more valuable experience than she thought, the tour brought with it a sudden and quite dramatic release from her stage fright. "It was the first time I felt it was really fun to be on stage and that I wasn't scared anymore," Frida recalled. "The interaction between us was terrific. I don't know exactly why, but all of a sudden I just felt, 'now the pieces have fallen into place', and that made me feel secure for the first time." It was an extraordinary turn of events, almost as if she'd had to plunge to the deepest depths of depression to be able to fight her way back up again.

For Björn and Agnetha, the modest success of 'People Need Love' was largely overshadowed by another event that occurred early in the summer. After trying unsuccessfully to have a baby for almost two years, they had resigned themselves to adoption – and having to wait another three years, until Agnetha turned 25. Then, in May 1972, Agnetha felt the early symptoms of pregnancy. At first she thought it was another false alarm. Joy had turned into disappointment many times before, so this time she decided not to say anything to Björn. Instead, she waited as long as she could before she took a pregnancy test. Agnetha vividly remembered that fateful day.

"When the time came to take the car and drive [to the doctor] in Vallentuna town centre to get the answer, I had to ask a friend to come along. I thought, 'If the result is negative I will be so depressed that I won't be able to drive home. If it turns out to be positive I will be so happy that I won't know what to do with myself.' "

The answer was the one she hadn't dared hope for. "At first, it just didn't sink in, I thought they were joking with me. I couldn't believe it was true. I was so happy that I walked around in a daze the whole afternoon. I called Björn, who was at the office. When I heard his voice I found myself unable to speak, I had to cry for a bit. He was terrified and wondered what had happened. 'You have to come home,' I sobbed. 'You're going to be a father.' "

An ecstatic Björn rushed back to Vallentuna. He was so moved that he began to cry as well. When he got home, the happy couple celebrated with a bottle of sparkling wine. They talked to the media about their joy at expecting the baby they had wanted for so long. "We don't care what others are saying regarding how or why, if it's right to put children to this world and so on. If that's how they feel, it's up to them to not have children. We felt that we wanted a family. That's why we got married in the first place."

They also maintained that they still intended to go through with their adoption plans. "The fact that we're having a baby 'of our own' hasn't got anything to do with it," they said. "In the long run it wouldn't have mattered how we got our child. The next one we will adopt, as soon as we're allowed to."

Agnetha decided to take it easier after her park tour ended in August. It suited her perfectly, for it meant that she could concentrate on writing songs for her next album. A stop-gap release of a new single reached record shops in November: 'Tio mil kvar till Korpilombolo' coupled with 'Så glad som dina ögon' ('Ten More Miles To Korpilombolo'/'As Happy As Your Eyes'). Agnetha had written both sides herself, although in line with her habit of late she left the lyrics to others.

Meanwhile, Björn and Benny were busy dealing with the Japanese market and exploring the possibilities of extending their career there after the success of 'She's My Kind Of Girl'. It didn't look very promising so far. Epic Japan had released 'Merry-Go-Round' as a follow-up in June, with the sleeve notes cheerfully proclaiming: "The other day we received a letter from Björn & Benny, who are very busy in Sweden at the moment. They are very happy that 'The Little Girl Of The Cold Wind' has become a big hit in Japan. 'We . . . would love to visit some day. But we are very busy with our work, so for the moment we will have to abandon such thoughts', they write in their letter. . . . If ['Merry-Go-Round'] becomes a big hit, Björn and Benny may just come to Japan. That would really be nice."

Unfortunately 'Merry-Go-Round' failed to repeat the success of 'She's My Kind Of Girl'. It might have helped if Björn & Benny had gone there to promote it, but a quick glance at their schedule around this time, which was chock-full of Hootenanny Singers tour dates and production commitments, makes it clear that this would have been impossible. They had far too many disparate projects on their plate.

Following the 'Merry-Go-Round' flop, the record company concluded that it would be best to ensure that they and the Japanese public were given what they wanted. A song by Japanese composer Koichi Morita was submitted for the third single. Björn and Benny were trusted to come up with the lyrics, under strict instructions as far as subject matter was concerned. They were informed by telex that "lost love" was the theme that would captivate the Japanese audience.

The result was the unremarkable 'Love Has Its Ways', which was released as a single in Japan in the autumn of 1972. This effort didn't help matters very much, although it did appear briefly on the charts, albeit just outside the Top 20.

In November, a final attempt was made to salvage what little was left of Björn & Benny's Japanese career. The duo entered the Yamaha World Popular Song Contest in Tokyo, performing 'Santa Rosa', a leftover from the spring recording sessions. It was Epic Japan that decided that this exceptionally weak song would be suitable for the contest, a choice with which Björn and Benny did not agree. "That's a bad one," Benny later determined. "It's one of those we shouldn't have recorded." In Sweden, 'Santa Rosa' was relegated to single B-side status.

But they went along with the record company's decision and performed the song at the contest. Agnetha and Frida even accompanied them on the trip and helped out with the backing vocals. They might as well not have bothered: Björn & Benny were among those few acts awarded no prize whatsoever. After that flop performance, 'Santa Rosa' was never even released as a single, and Björn & Benny's Japanese career quietly fizzled out.

This probably didn't matter too much at that point, as their group career was rapidly gathering pace in Sweden. Sometime in the aftermath of the success of 'People Need Love' it was decided that Björn & Benny, Agnetha & Anni-Frid should record an album together. However it was still just one of many projects the four were involved with at the time – "a hobby", as Björn called it.

In accordance with the lack of focus and seemingly random nature of the recordings made during these months, the projected Swedish-language Björn & Benny album was cancelled. The tracks already recorded were for the most part junked or given to other artists. Likewise, plans for an album for release in Japan died along with their flop singles on that market. Instead, this brand new foursome album was intended to be an even mix of Swedish and English tracks. Presumably, some of the unused Björn & Benny recordings would have been used for that purpose. In the event, those plans changed along the way as well, with only one track recorded in the group's native tongue finding its way on to the LP.

Recording of the Björn & Benny, Agnetha & Anni-Frid album started on September 26, 1972. It marked the first time that a studio session sheet clearly stated that the recording was intended for a release which would be credited to all four. Björn recalled: "The managing director and the house producers of the Polar record company had simply decided that it would be much better to make an album with this constellation than with the two boys only, since the girls were much better singers."

In the course of the first month's sessions for the album, the group's next single was recorded: a gospel-influenced mid-tempo stomper entitled 'He Is Your Brother'. Maintaining the lyrical theme of reaching out to your fellow man, and again switching between male and female lead vocals, the song might easily have been 'People Need Love, Part II'. On release in November, 'He Is Your Brother' didn't enter the sales chart, but did go to number one on *Tio i topp*.

Stig's faith in Björn and Benny's talents as songwriters and producers was now stronger than ever. His enthusiasm moving into overdrive, he even managed to get 'People Need Love' released in the USA. Bearing the ludicrous credit "Björn & Benny with Svenska Flicka ['Swedish Girl']", the song was issued on the smallish Playboy Records, which lacked the clout to make a big hit out of the record.

Despite the low-key promotion, 'People Need Love' did show up just outside the Top 100 on some charts. It was Björn and Benny's first song to gain any momentum whatsoever in the USA, and if nothing else was yet another encouraging sign, however small, that they were on the right track with the group concept. The Swedish press was also noting the unprecedented forays into the international music market, reporting regularly on every small step Stig, Björn and Benny were taking.

Similarly, despite the many setbacks and the notable continued lack of interest from the Anglo-Saxon markets, everyone in the Polar team was full of confidence about what they were trying to achieve. The encouragement of their associates was invaluable for Björn and Benny at this time. "I just felt 'People Need Love' was so great," recalled Michael Tretow. "It had everything. I thought, 'This must become a worldwide hit.'"

It didn't, despite being released in countries as far ranging as West Germany, New Zealand, France, and South Africa. But the quest for worldwide success continued unabated. The Eurovision Song Contest still loomed large on the horizon and still seemed the best way to gain the exposure they wanted.

For the 1973 show, the Swedish Broadcasting Corporation had yet again changed the rules for selection – but this time it was to the advantage of the producer/songwriting team at Polar. No longer were composers invited to submit songs for specific artists. Instead, a number of record industry people were each asked to make a list of ten songwriters whom they thought could come up with a competitive tune. In November 1972 the team of Andersson/Anderson/Ulvaeus was finally chosen, and towards the end of the year newspapers reported that Björn & Benny, Agnetha & Anni-Frid would perform their contribution.

The Christmas and New Year's holiday of 1972 saw the songwriters retreating to their holiday island of Viggsö in the Stockholm archipelago. Stig had owned a summer house there for a few years. Björn and Agnetha had just bought their chalet, while Benny and Frida would follow suit a year later. This was where Björn and Benny would write many of Abba's best-known hits.

Slogging away in Björn's house during those winter days of 1972, Björn and Benny finally came up with a song which they gave the working title

'Klocklåt' ('Bell Song'). When Stig heard what they had come up with, he felt that this was exactly what they should be aiming for. "We wanted to do something poppy, something that reflected the popular music tastes of today," he recalled. "We wanted to get rid of all the pomp and circumstance surrounding the Eurovision Song Contest: the dinner-jackets and the evening dresses."

It fell to Stig to come up with the lyrics, and, above all, the right title – a skill in which he excelled. Just like Björn and Benny, Stig felt that the main purpose of pop music was to provide light entertainment through hook-laden melodies and catchy lyrics. Fifteen years older than his protégés, and a long-time jazz fan, it's not improbable that pop for him was virtually synonymous with strictly commercial, disposable bubblegum music.

He was certainly aware of how successfully this genre had been exploited around the world over the past few years. In 1969 his friend and associate Don Kirshner had enjoyed four weeks at the top of the US charts, and a staggering eight weeks in the UK, with 'Sugar Sugar', as performed by his cartoon creation The Archies. The bubblegum production team of Kasenetz-Katz had garnered a US and UK Top Five hit with 'Yummy Yummy Yummy' by Ohio Express the year before.

Stig had firm ideas about the significance of a good title: "It's extremely important that the title fits the song. You should get the impression that the title and the lyrics were born in the same instant as the melody." Repeating the same word a couple of times was obviously a good idea, he concluded. For this new song the right title turned out to be 'Ring Ring', echoing Björn's and Benny's associations to a "bell" feeling in the song.

The result, they all felt, was their best song yet. The next step was to give this new piece the right framework in the recording studio.

Chapter 14

Being a recording engineer in the Sweden of the late Sixties and early Seventies was a frustrating experience. Brilliantly made, cutting-edge recordings from Great Britain and the United States were flowing in across the borders, all of them demonstrating what could be accomplished with the right recording methods and a little patience.

Certainly, hour upon hour could be spent recording contemporary pop groups, the contenders to the position of Sweden's answer to The Beatles, The Rolling Stones or whoever else they wanted to emulate. But for the most part, those hours were necessitated by the inadequacy of the musicians, as they struggled to play in time, sing on key or nail instrumental breaks that were simply too difficult for players of often less than stellar calibre.

On those sessions devoted to *schlager* acts, a fairly set formula was followed: the electric bass was played with a plectrum for a snapping sound, while the double bass was used for a more rumbling effect; the drums were played with brushes for slow songs and sticks for uptempo songs; the piano should preferably be played in the style of American session giant Floyd Cramer.

Into this environment stepped 22-year-old Michael B. Tretow when he began working as a professional recording engineer at Metronome studio in January 1967. Michael, born and raised in the town of Norrköping, always had a touch of the mad professor in him. An interest in recording and experimenting with different techniques, trying out new sounds, had been a defining part of his persona ever since his teens.

Michael's Tandberg reel-to-reel tape recorder seemed to be running constantly. He had friends playing in local rock bands who would all cram into his room so that he could record them. Michael was musically talented himself and used to experiment with multi-overdub recordings of his own songs. He would sing and play all the instruments himself.

Those early pop recordings were of the zany, novelty variety which would render him several hits as a recording artist in the Eighties. It was all in line with his streak of restrained madness, full of whimsy and with a great affection for all kinds of electronic gadgets. If there was something to investigate within the world of technology, he was there to explore it.

At the end of 1965 Michael decided to send his tapes to a few record companies, and eventually he got a positive reply. The record label Knäppupp mainly released comedy records associated with the shows staged by label owner, composer and actor Povel Ramel. Michael's novelty material fitted perfectly with the rest of the Knäppupp roster. When the label wanted to release Michael's original demo tapes as they stood, Metronome studio head Rune Persson intervened and pointed out that there was too much hiss and noise on them. "You'd better let this Tretow come to Stockholm and make brand new recordings at a professional studio," he said. Michael was overwhelmed the first time he entered a real recording studio. "This is what I want to work with," he thought.

Michael's first EP didn't become a hit, nor did the further singles that he released over the next year or so. But even during that first session he managed to impress Rune Persson with his abilities to record and mix properly. A year after his first recording session he was employed as a recording engineer at Metronome studio. Michael's youth and interest in contemporary pop and rock naturally resulted in his handling most of the pop acts that used the studio. These were pioneering times, when new sounds and tricks were like state secrets, guarded by each studio so they might have the jump on their rivals.

Sitting in a Swedish studio it was almost impossible to obtain any information about what was going on in the rest of the recording world. Engineers, not only in Sweden, were lucky if they even got a credit on album sleeves. Magazine articles or books dealing with the technical aspects of modern popular music recording simply didn't exist. New techniques were passed on by rumour or word-of-mouth. Michael Tretow recalls how he learned about phasing, a suitably spacey effect that was popular on psychedelic recordings in the late Sixties. "The first time I heard it was on 'Itchycoo Park' by The Small Faces and we tried to figure out how on earth they'd done it," he says.

An engineer at a competing studio finally told him how the phasing effect was achieved. It was a complicated set-up involving four different tape recorders, he was told. "I was surprised that he let me in on that, though, because it should have been something of a business secret."

But the main problem for a young and eager engineer like Michael was the resistance against actually making use of all the technological advancements, and move with the times in terms of sound treatment. "Most of the time I could hear exactly what they'd done on those American records, it was just that they wouldn't allow me to do it here. The classic example is the drummer who wouldn't let me remove the drumskin on the front of his bass drum. The sound we got was 'boom, boom', and I knew that I could have achieved a muted, more modern sound."

Things didn't really change until Michael Tretow started working more closely with Björn and Benny. After recording the Hootenanny Singers and Agnetha extensively, and even doing one session for Frida, he bonded especially well with the two up-and-coming producers. Ambition and an unwillingness to accept that Swedish records couldn't sound just as good as American or English releases were characteristics they all shared.

From 1970 onwards, Benny had become an important presence on Hootenanny Singers' sessions. Although Bengt Bernhag was listed as producer, Björn and Benny had more or less taken over the actual work as Bengt's health problems forced him to take a back seat. "They knew exactly what they wanted, and worked much harder than anyone on achieving that goal," recalled Michael. "The fact that things didn't have to be done as quickly as usual gave me the opportunity to put the finishing touches to my end of the job." While Benny was struggling with his piano overdubs, Michael could move around his microphones in the quest for a perfect sound. It was a win-win situation for everyone involved.

The relatively fresh-faced Björn and Benny would even argue with the intimidating string section. "Their job had to be done quickly because they had to catch the bus or whatever," recalls Michael. "They were usually very unwilling to do retakes." Michael sat silently impressed as the young producers berated the venerable violinists, urging them to play a piece again and again until their musical vision became a reality.

Similarly, Björn and Benny were delighted to be working with an enthusiastic engineer. "Right from the first time I met Michael in the studio, I felt that here was a guy that thought that this was just as exciting as we did," recalled Benny. With 'People Need Love', the trio had collaborated on a truly contemporary-sounding pop recording for the first time. The opening backwards piano chord that draws the listener into the song was most likely a Tretow touch.

Despite this affinity with Björn and Benny, Michael was still frustrated by the lack of information about developments in international recording techniques. Current trade magazines were mostly filled with mathematical formulae and strictly technical advice. "It was dry as dust. It had nothing to do with music, nothing to do with sounds," he says. Serious books about rock music were also fairly uncommon in the early Seventies, even on an international level. It was even rarer for the few titles that were published to find their way to Sweden, and when they did, only a few select bookshops would bother importing them.

One of the more open-minded booksellers was located in central

Stockholm. Michael would pop in every now and then to see if any interesting titles were available. One day in the autumn of 1972 he finally found the book he'd been dreaming about. It was called *Out Of His Head: The Sound Of Phil Spector*. The author was Richard Williams, the assistant editor of the British music paper *Melody Maker*, and the volume had just recently been published. Michael didn't hesitate, and headed straight for the cashier with this find before anyone else snapped it up.

Björn, Benny and Michael were all roughly the same age, and like most of their generation had discovered rock through Elvis Presley. They were also big fans of the records made by the producer Phil Spector in the early Sixties. His "wall of sound" had been the foundation for dozens of legendary recordings he produced for several American girl groups, as well as artists like The Righteous Brothers and Ike & Tina Turner.

What Michael wanted to know was how Spector achieved that enormous sound. Although he wasn't entirely sure, he thought he had a hunch – and now *Out Of His Head* revealed all the secrets. 'Then He Kissed Me' by The Crystals had used "a whole gang of guitars", the book established. On the following page, a section about The Ronettes' classic 'Be My Baby' went into even greater detail. "The orchestra, outragously [sic] gigantic, had pianos and basses arrayed in ranks in the studios," wrote Williams, "and everyone joining in to play the percussion which Spector had arranged with almost militaristic precision."

Michael nodded to himself. "That explained why it sounded like five guitars," he recalled, "it was because Spector really did use five guitars." But having several guitarists, pianists, bassists and so on in the studio at the same time would have been far too expensive for comparatively low-key Swedish productions. If a similar effect was to be achieved, they would have to do several overdubs of each of the instruments instead. Michael knew he simply had to try it sometime.

The opportunity arrived soon enough, for the Metronome studio had been booked by Polar for Wednesday, January 10, 1973. That was when Björn and Benny were going to record 'Ring Ring', their new song for the Eurovision Song Contest selections. The night before the session, the three friends met at Michael's place, discussing the best way of recording the song. Michael told them what he'd read about Phil Spector's techniques. Wouldn't that be a good thing to try on this new song, to record the backing track at least twice? Björn and Benny enthusiastically agreed.

It was an important session and nothing was left to chance. Benny, Björn and the backing band – Janne Schaffer, guitar, Rutger Gunnarsson, bass and Ola Brunkert, drums – were playing away, hour after hour to find the right groove. It took half the working day just to come up with the catchy bass and guitar riff that runs throughout the song. Only then was it finally time to start recording.

When the first backing track had been committed to tape and it was time for the second overdub, Michael Tretow decided to try an additional effect he had discovered for himself. The Metronome studio had recently acquired a new tape recorder which allowed for the speed to be changed. Earlier in the month, Michael was hanging back in the studio one night, experimenting with an electric guitar and the new tape recorder.

He was thinking about guitars and mandolins with double sets of strings, where the sound of each note could be widened if the strings were just slightly out of tune with each other. What would happen, he thought, if he tried to achieve the same effect electronically? He recorded the sound of his ordinary electric guitar, and then did an overdub of the exact same part, but with the speed of the tape recorder changed ever so slightly. The result was simply fantastic. "It sounded like the world's biggest guitar," he recalled. "It was like stepping inside of a five feet high guitar. Then I thought, 'What would this sound like if you tried it with a whole band: letting everybody play their parts twice, but changing the speed between the overdubs?'"

Michael hadn't mentioned anything about this to Björn and Benny. But during the 'Ring Ring' session, when the first backing track had been recorded, he changed the speed of the tape recorder when it was time for the second take. "I changed it . . . on the sly," he remembered. "It was a risky thing to do considering the expense of the musicians and studio time that would be wasted if it failed."

Michael needn't have worried. "It was like the roof was caving in, Björn and Benny were ecstatic. And I can still remember the chills and how the hair stood up on my arms. It really was something else."

From an international perspective the resulting recording may not have been especially groundbreaking, but in the framework of Swedish recording techniques – mostly professional, but not very adventurous – 'Ring Ring' was nothing less than astounding. To their flair for a good melody and catchy lyrics, provided by Björn, Benny and Stig, and Agnetha and Frida's stellar vocals, was now added the third vital ingredient in the Abba formula: Björn, Benny, and Michael's quest for an internationally competitive sound – their own, Nordic version of the Spector approach. 'Ring Ring' rumbled and thundered, the percussion rattled, the guitar and bass riff ground its way into the brain, every space of the recording was filled with sound – quite simply, it had all the markings of a hit record.

That 'Ring Ring' really was a step away from what was expected from a Swedish record at the time was further illustrated by the way the lead vocals were handled, a typical Abba feature which was also borrowed from Phil Spector. Rather than being the focal point of the recording, they were almost buried in the mix and were treated as just another sound ingredient. On release, Polar received complaints from Swedish radio, who insisted that there must be something wrong with the record.

Certainly, Abba were not the only recording act to be inspired by the Phil Spector sound. There was a direct line to Benny's hero, Brian Wilson of The Beach Boys, who almost had a fixation on Spector. To Benny's thinking, The Beach Boys' output "sounded like real records", and that was what he was striving for as well. "When you hear a wonderful record like 'Do You Wanna Dance?' by The Beach Boys . . . and there's this marvellous sound, [that becomes] something that we [want] to do too: make the records sound great."

As for Spector himself, his feelings about being a major influence on a pop band from northern Europe remain unrecorded for the most part, although it seems he wasn't especially flattered. In a long and rambling speech at a Rock & Roll Hall of Fame ceremony in January 1990, Abba were mentioned by the eccentric producer who insinuated that they, along with Eric Carmen and Bruce Springsteen, had imitated his work.

With a possible worldwide release beckoning, it was important that the English lyrics of 'Ring Ring' sounded authentic. To ensure that the words were written by someone with a strong intuition for hits, Stig Anderson approached Agnetha's old idol, Neil Sedaka, whom he knew through his publishing contacts. It was an excellent choice: Sedaka had late Fifties/ early Sixties success behind him as a writer and performer working within the context of the Brill Building hit factory, and was responsible for hits like Connie Francis' 'Stupid Cupid' and his own 'Happy Birthday Sweet Sixteen' among many others. He accepted the assignment on the condition that he liked the song.

Sedaka received a tape with Stig's rough translation of the Swedish original. He was impressed by 'Ring Ring' and believed strongly in its chances of becoming a worldwide hit. Just a few days later the singer returned a set of lyrics he had written together with then songwriting partner Phil Cody. "We were very happy that such a famous artist as Neil wanted to help us," recalled Benny.

Stig was overjoyed with the outcome of 'Ring Ring'. This was the recording that would finally push open the barriers and put his act on the international music scene. He didn't waste any time, taking the 'Ring Ring' tape with him to the annual MIDEM music fair in Cannes in January. The reaction was overwhelming. More than 15 countries in Europe, Latin America and Australasia bought the rights to the recording.

All that was needed now was an appearance in the Eurovision Song Contest, and the world would be theirs.

On February 10, 1973, the Swedish selections for the contest were held, with 'Ring Ring' as the outstanding favourite among all the entries. For Björn & Benny, Agnetha & Anni-Frid, however, the broadcast was overshadowed by deep concern over Agnetha. Now highly pregnant, she had been scheduled to give birth on February 2. But nothing happened, and it was uncertain if she would be able to go through with the performance.

The previous nine months had been a life-changing experience for Agnetha. When she fell pregnant the previous May her focus had shifted virtually overnight, with her career becoming almost inconsequential compared to the child growing inside her. She read everything she could find about pregnancy and child rearing. "I could hardly think of anything else than the baby," she recalled.

The problems she and Björn had experienced getting pregnant in the first place made her worried, and even a little superstitious. "I knitted a pair of orange baby socks immediately after finding out that I was pregnant, but I haven't done anything since then," she said shortly after getting the positive test results. "I'm a bit scared of doing too much. I'm so afraid that I'm going to lose the child."

At the time she had just started her four-month summer tour, and it turned out to be problematic for her. "I suffered morning sickness and often had headaches . . . I couldn't show the audience that I was in a bad mood. But it turned out all right. Everybody I travelled with were understanding and didn't complain about me."

For Agnetha, getting pregnant was like the missing piece of a jigsaw puzzle. "The other day I felt something moving in my belly," she told a reporter in the autumn. "It was the first sign of life from the child, and then it felt much more real. Somebody who is able to move." Björn and Agnetha's parents were delighted with the news – it would be the first grandchild for all of them. Gunnar Ulvaeus made a cradle, his wife Aina crocheted a bedspread and Birgit Fältskog started sewing baby clothes.

Agnetha's pregnancy occurred during a period when she and Frida were closer than ever before. Being neighbours in Vallentuna had made them rely on each other for almost everything, and when either of them quarrelled with their man, they would turn to each other for support and advice. It was just a few minutes walk between their houses, and as her pregnancy began to show Agnetha took great comfort in Frida's experience and insights. All through those months, Frida soothed her best friend's anxieties about everything from the delivery to the responsibility of taking care of a child.

The experience caused Frida to reflect on her own situation as a mother, and parenthood in general. "If I should want a baby later on I'd rather adopt one," she said. She disagreed with Agnetha that it was unfair that you weren't allowed to adopt before the age of 25. "You have to think carefully before you have a baby," she stated. "I feel that it's only in the past few years that I've become mature enough myself."

In the spirit of the times, Frida worried about the future of the planet and was doubtful if she wanted herself and Benny to have a child together. They needed to further stabilise their relationship before they could offer a child a secure upbringing, she argued. A child wouldn't solve any problems or help to bridge any differences.

The last few months of Agnetha's pregnancy progressed without undue strain and only towards the end did the situation become somewhat problematic. It was especially annoying that such an important television performance clashed with the time of arrival. When the baby didn't appear as scheduled, Agnetha's doctor set a new date which couldn't have been less convenient, for it was February 10, the actual night of the contest. Prospects for the group's appearance in the Eurovision Song Contest selections were looking very bleak indeed.

Then a new pre-natal examination a few days before the fateful night brought another prediction: this time the doctor told Agnetha that the child probably wouldn't be born until well after the contest. And even if Agnetha didn't appear 'Ring Ring' had fortunately been arranged with the girls singing together all through the verses, with Björn and Benny joining in for the chorus. If necessary, Frida and the boys could actually manage on their own. "The difference won't be that great if I'm not there, even if the sound won't be as full," Agnetha reasoned.

The rehearsals at the television studios turned out to be stressful, although it wasn't Agnetha who lost her cool. "I wasn't too stressed out myself but everyone around me was more or less hysterical, especially one of the studio hostesses," she recalled. "On one occasion she happened to hear a child shriek, came storming down the corridor and yelled, 'Oh, my goodness, has it arrived?' She thought I'd had my baby in the middle of the television studio!"

On the night of the live broadcast, Agnetha found it hard to keep her nerves in check. Just as she was going on stage there was a particularly tense moment when she felt several wild kicks from the baby. "I tried to keep myself in the background so that I could leave the stage quickly if something happened," she said later. It was a false alarm, and the group were able to go through with their performance as planned.

The four who made their way to the studio floor didn't exactly look like they wanted to project a groovy pop image. Their appearance was more along the lines of an average European *schlager* act of the time. Björn was dressed in a purple velvet dinner jacket and bow tie, Frida wore a bright yellow blouse with matching cardigan and trousers, Agnetha sported a green maternity blouse with a pink flower pattern and white trousers, and Benny had chosen a dark suit and bow tie.

Apart from a line fluffed by the girls in the second verse, the group turned in an energetic and convincing performance of 'Ring Ring'. The studio audience was rapturous in their applause but the jury was less easy to please. The members could award each song one, three or five points, and only two of the 11 members gave 'Ring Ring' any points at all.★

Björn, Benny, Agnetha and Frida were astonished by the failure of 'Ring Ring' – and deeply disappointed. Stig Anderson, who had planned a major marketing campaign all over Europe, was furious and frustrated at having failed two years running. If the expert jury wasn't dispensed with, it was unlikely Andersson/Anderson/Ulvaeus would want to participate again, he thundered.

Ten years later, the memory still rankled: "We have a few experiences from what happens when 'experts' clash with the will of the general public: 'Säg det med en sång' by Lena Andersson in [1972] and 'Ring Ring' by Abba in [1973]. Both times we ended up third. Lena shot up to number one on *Svensktoppen*. Abba's song was an international success and was number one in six countries! Conclusion: never write your songs for 'experts' – because what goes on between the ears of 'experts' no one knows, least of all themselves!"

The winning entry in 1973, 'You Are Summer – You Never Tell Me No', was unquestionably a good song and, though it lacked the immediate catchiness of 'Ring Ring', it ended up fifth in the Eurovision finals. Many observers agreed that Björn & Benny, Agnetha & Anni-Frid would at the very least have bettered that position.

Ironically, one half of the duo Nova, who performed the winning entry in the contest, was Claes af Geijerstam. A veteran of the Swedish Sixties pop scene and a good friend of the Abba members, he would later become the sound engineer on some of the group's tours.

★ One of them was singer Peter Holm, who awarded the song his top score of five points. Later, this early champion of the Abba cause gained worldwide tabloid notoriety as husband of actress Joan Collins, whom he sued for alimony after their divorce in the late Eighties.

'Ring Ring' may have failed in the contest, but after the mid-February release, the record flew off the record shop shelves. The Swedish and English versions occupied the number one and two positions respectively on the sales chart. By late March, the two singles had combined sales of 100,000 copies, a figure rarely attained in Sweden. Now there was no question that the foursome concept was significantly more substantial than Björn's proverbial "hobby".

The statistics were truly mind-boggling: for two weeks in a row in April, the Swedish version of 'Ring Ring' was number one, the English number two, while the *Ring Ring* album was number three. The record was also a great success in many European countries. Although it may not have topped the charts in six countries, as per Stig's recollection, in Belgium 'Ring Ring' was number one for seven weeks, and featured in the higher regions of the charts in Norway and The Netherlands. It also fared well in Denmark, Finland, Austria, South Africa as well as several South American countries. A year after release, worldwide sales for the song were an impressive 545,000 copies.

Notable exceptions in this success story were Great Britain, the United States and Japan, the three most important record markets in the world. A change of record company in Japan, from Epic to Phonogram, improved the group's fortunes just slightly: 'Ring Ring' was passed on, but they reached number 21 with a song called 'I Am Just A Girl'. In the United States, the deal with Playboy Records had expired and wasn't renewed, and Björn & Benny, Agnetha & Anni-Frid found themselves left without any outlet at all on that market.

In Great Britain the single was issued by Epic Records, an imprint of CBS, but it took until October before it happened. It was almost a miracle that it was released at all, for by that time 'Ring Ring' had been turned down by several major record labels, among them Polydor, EMI, Decca, Pye and WEA.

It was Stig's publishing contacts that provided the solution. Indeed, he would often find the right record deal in the different territories through local publishers that he knew and trusted.

Paul Atkinson, former guitarist with Sixties hit group The Zombies and at the time a newly employed A&R man at Epic, had just such a connection to Stig: Sweden Music had handled The Zombies' Swedish publishing. Fortunately, Atkinson genuinely liked 'Ring Ring'. "I played it all the time in the office to the point of driving everyone nuts," he recalled. "It would be my first signing and it became a bit of a joke around the building that I wanted to sign this obscure Swedish group. Atkinson's Folly they called it."

Finally, he managed to convince his boss, Dick Asher, that they should give the group a chance. Abba were signed to Epic, including an option for America, for a £600 advance against a 10 per cent royalty rate. But the promotional efforts on behalf of the record company were at best half-hearted, and 'Ring Ring' failed dismally in the UK – it didn't even chart and ended up selling a measly 5,000 copies.

An additional reason for the disappointing results in Great Britain may have been the 'Ring Ring' sound: for all its Spector influences, it was grounded in a somewhat march-like beat. "We dissected the problem and reached the conclusion that 'Ring Ring' was a hit for the Germanic part of Europe," recalled Stig. "In terms of musical taste, there is in fact a dividing line that runs straight through Brussels."

Back in Sweden, the group didn't have to worry about any dividing lines. The *Ring Ring* album had been released in March, marking a slight group name change in that the "Anni-Frid" billing had been changed to Frida. It became the greatest album sales success any of the individual members had experienced up to that point, eventually peaking at number two on the chart.

It was not the greatest album the group would ever record though, even if it got by on its enthusiastic charm. A song title like 'Me And Bobby And Bobby's Brother' was made believable by the warm commitment in Frida's voice, which almost managed to turn a throwaway ditty into an engrossing piece of storytelling. Tracks like 'Love Isn't Easy (But It Sure Is Hard Enough)' (grammatical inconsistency and all) and 'Nina, Pretty Ballerina' had a joie-de-vivre that transcended their fluffy Europop origins.

But there was no escaping that *Ring Ring* was a patchy collection, assembled without a clear focus in mind. The various tracks had been scraped together from several different sources, recorded in several different studios and not always with Michael Tretow at the mixing desk. The decidedly non-rocking 'Rock'n Roll Band' was the brushed-up B-side of Björn & Benny's Japanese 'Love Has Its Ways' single. 'I Am Just A Girl' started out as a song recorded for a Swedish 1972 movie and had originally been sung by a male actor. The group simply recorded English language vocals onto the existing backing track.

The dirge-like 'I Saw It In The Mirror', featuring Björn and Benny on lead vocals, holds the dubious distinction of being the least-liked Abba track ever among the group's hardcore fans. The song itself was a left-over, originally released as the B-side to Billy G-son's 'There's A Little Man' in 1970. Despite the addition of a new bridge to the song, the updated version was far inferior to G-son's soulful, uptempo interpretation, and served only to shine a cruel spotlight on Björn and Benny's vocal limitations. 'I Saw It In The Mirror' had actually been recorded in great haste, along with two other tracks, less than two weeks before the album was released. Agnetha's sole songwriting contribution to an Abba album, 'Disillusion' (featuring lyrics by Björn), was also committed to tape during this period, but suffered from under-production.

Agnetha felt inadequate as a songwriter compared to Björn and Benny. "I guess I was rather proud that they wanted it on the album," she recalled, "but I remember being a little doubtful that it was good enough." Agnetha had nothing to be ashamed of: melodically, several songs on the album were far weaker than her singer/songwriter ballad. She would later record a superior, Swedish version of the song for a solo album.

The reason for the disparate nature of the tracks on the *Ring Ring* album was obvious. In March 1972, when sessions started for 'People Need Love', the oldest recording on the album, the group didn't really exist. As in the case of that first single, it could even be argued that the *Ring Ring* LP had been conceived as a Björn & Benny album with the girls as guest stars. On three of the album's tracks, the boys handled sole lead vocals, on a further four the leads were shared with the girls. Björn and Benny's vocal interjections were also prominent on several of Agnetha and Frida's lead songs. International versions of the album even substituted the Swedish version of 'Ring Ring' with 'She's My Kind Of Girl', upping the Björn and Benny quota by one further track.

Quite simply, the *Ring Ring* album showed a group who were feeling their way towards a distinctive voice. The notion of having an even mix of male and female lead vocals had yet to be abandoned. Judged on their own merits there were many strong melodies on *Ring Ring* – it's unlikely it would have sold more than 100,000 copies domestically otherwise. But the wall of sound production of the title track was the only recording on the album to truly indicate where the group was heading.

About a month before the album was released, Agnetha finally gave birth to her and Björn's first child. It had been a stressful three weeks between the scheduled birth and the final arrival. For Agnetha, that last period felt longer and more tedious than the previous nine months put together. "I got more and more worried about the delivery," she recalled. "And there were people calling me all the time, asking if the baby had been born yet."

The delivery turned out to be long and hard. Agnetha's doctor warned her that it wasn't healthy for the baby to remain in the womb any longer; he was going to induce the birth on February 23. "But on the night before, the contractions started. I'm sure it was out of pure fright," she remembered. "In the middle of the night we went to the maternity hospital – and then the contractions stopped again. They had to induce the birth anyway, on the day they had planned to."

Björn was with her all through the delivery, mopping her forehead and holding her hand. "It was the most fantastic experience I've ever had," he beamed afterwards. Agnetha suffered great pain during the birth, and had to have pain-killing drugs towards the end of the delivery. Even then the relief only lasted for half an hour. Yet the pains didn't come as a shock to Agnetha. "I had expected that it would hurt so much that I thought I was going to die – which it did," she said. "Although the pain was so incredibly great, it was still the happiest moment of my life."

On Friday, February 23, at 8.35 p.m., a daughter the couple named Linda Elin was finally born. Her weight at birth was almost seven pounds. Elin was the name of both Björn's and Agnetha's maternal grandmothers, while Linda was chosen "simply because it's such a beautiful name", as Björn revealed. When he finally arrived home after a very long 24 hours, Benny and Frida came over with a bottle of champagne and were the first to congratulate him.

Three days after Linda's birth, the press was allowed into the hospital to take the first pictures. Although the weeklies had fought for exclusive rights, Agnetha and Björn decided against it. Instead, for half an hour on a Monday afternoon, teams of photographers and reporters, dressed in yellow hospital gowns and wearing masks, were let into Agnetha's room in groups. The nurses at the hospital had to arrange a system with queue numbers to make everything work. "We thought it would be easier to have everybody here at the same time," Björn explained. "Otherwise the phone won't stop ringing when we get back home again."

Afterwards, Björn and Agnetha both regretted their decision. It felt like an invasion with all those camera flashes and intrusive questions. But Linda herself behaved perfectly: "not one scream despite all the flashes," reported one newspaper. The pride and joy radiating from both parents in the pictures was unmistakable.

"Sometimes I think, 'Should you be allowed to be this happy?' " reflected Agnetha. "That's when I get really scared that something's going to happen. I have nothing more to wish for, except that it will all remain the same. I have everything: Linda, Björn, our families, my work, good incomes and a house we enjoy living in. It's almost unfair that I've been given so much."

Not long after Linda's birth Agnetha started working on a song about her daughter, but for many months she was unable to strike the right chord. It wasn't until the summer of 1974 that she finally recorded 'Visa i åttonde månaden' ('Song In The Eighth Month'). It was a retrospective tribute to the child she had been expecting, expressing the fears and doubts of having children in a world plagued by war and famine.

Agnetha was secretly relieved that the group hadn't won the selection for the Eurovision Song Contest. It gave her a chance to remain at home and be with her baby during those first few, important months. She found herself incredibly weak for a long while after the birth – it was bad enough that she had to rush away to the recording studio only days after returning home with Linda on March 1. "I never expected that it would be such a drain on my strength," she said. "Sometimes my legs just collapse."

Fortunately, her mother Birgit was there to take care of Linda for the first two weeks when Agnetha and Björn were away working. Birgit was relieved by Björn's mother Aina, and then Agnetha's sister Mona stepped in. Even then, it wasn't as if Agnetha could keep a lower profile in the studio, for her own song, 'Disillusion', was recorded during this final, hectic period of sessions for the *Ring Ring* album.

Motherhood brought with it other adjustments as well: the arrival of a new member of the family wasn't entirely unproblematic. Agnetha hardly dared hold her daughter, who felt so small and frail. Benjamin Spock's child-rearing classic *The Common Sense Book of Baby and Childcare* was her constant companion and reference book. Agnetha spoke of feeling a connection to Linda that she'd never felt to another living being before. "In the beginning I'd run and check that she was breathing every five minutes. It was as if the umbilical cord hadn't been severed yet. The merest squeak would wake me up in a second."

She'd often pause to reflect on the wonder of what had happened. "At first I could hardly believe it was true – what I had wished for most of all in the world – to have a baby. That she was ours, a piece of both Björn and me. It's such a miracle. That she has lain there and grown in my belly."

Linda was only a few weeks old when Agnetha and Björn took her on a trip to Jönköping and Västervik to introduce her to relatives. Agnetha's focus on her baby daughter's well-being resulted in an astounding selflessness. "When we were going to Västervik I spent the whole day packing for Linda, thinking about what she might need. And then I packed a few things for Björn. It was only when we were about to go away that I realised, 'Oh, maybe I should bring something for me to wear as well!'"

Agnetha stayed at home during early promotional efforts abroad for 'Ring Ring'. The somewhat unusual solution to the problem of Agnetha's absence was to use a stand-in. Inger Brundin, a friend of Frida's, replaced Agnetha when the group were appearing on television across Europe. Inger had pretended to be Agnetha for the first time in January, when the group promoted 'People Need Love' in West Germany. Presumably, the individual members weren't sufficiently well known outside Scandinavia for anyone to notice the difference.

But by the end of April, Agnetha felt she wanted to resume work and not miss out entirely on the success of 'Ring Ring'. "Why would I give up working?" she said. "It wouldn't make Linda happier. It's possible to take care of both her and my work." Agnetha wanted the "real" Björn & Benny, Agnetha & Frida to go to Brussels in May to promote 'Ring Ring', and started to wean Linda from breast feeding.

Despite the overwhelming success experienced by the group, Agnetha still had no plans to extricate herself from her Cupol recording contract and abandon her solo career. The autumn saw the release of a new single, 'En sång om sorg och glädje' (her version of Middle Of The Road's 'Union Silver'), and a compilation album. Notably, neither side of the single was her own composition – Agnetha was saving those songs for her next album. But it was the very first time she produced her own recordings, marking her ambition to take an even stronger grip of her own career as songwriter and performer. "It made it a more enjoyable and important record for me," she noted.

Nor were Björn and Benny relieved of their production duties at Polar. No one thought it would be a good idea to place all their bets on something that still might turn out to be a fluke, and even the Hootenanny Singers were kept alive as a studio entity with sessions for a new album pencilled in for May and June. "Having it this way suits me perfectly," Björn maintained. "With the Hootenanny Singers I get the opportunity to sing folk songs, and in the other group I get an outlet for another type of music that also interests me a great deal." He was even mentioning the possibility of a Hootenanny Singers *folkpark* tour for the summer of 1974.

Frida was making plans for a solo album of folk-style songs written especially for her, but she needed Benny to produce it. With all his other production commitments the project was put on ice for the time being. Together with Stig and Polar label mate Lena Andersson, Frida travelled to take part in a song contest in the Venezuelan capital of Caracas only two days after the Swedish Eurovision selections. Then she returned to being a housewife and one quarter of the Björn & Benny, Agnetha & Frida constellation. After her long experience of failure on her own, she felt safer and more fulfilled within a supportive group environment.

With the breakthrough success of 'Ring Ring' to bolster their confidence, Björn & Benny, Agnetha & Frida embarked on their first *folkpark* tour on June 15. Although the tour had been announced the previous autumn, when they only had two relatively minor hits as a foursome to their credit, the preliminary dates quickly proved insufficient. Despite a resistance to overworking themselves, their itinerary was soon crammed with double and sometimes triple concerts on the same day. Although the group mainly performed at weekends only, by the time the tour ended on September 9 they had slogged their way through a staggering 80 performances in less than three months.

Touring with three musicians, in addition to Benny's electric piano, moog and mellotron, the 30-minute show was jam-packed with songs, but the programme did little to diminish the conflict that still raged within the group as to the direction of their career. The "pop" presence was strong enough: tracks from their recent album – the three hits 'People Need Love', 'He Is Your Brother' and 'Ring Ring' among them – were augmented by a version of The Beach Boys' 'I Get Around'. However, these songs sat uneasily beside the cabaret style material and Swedish *schlager* hits from Björn, Agnetha and Frida's back catalogue.

Although the cabaret image of their Eurovision Song Contest selections performance had been ditched in favour of glittery, sexy, bodyhugging outfits with stars and sequins, they had yet to rid themselves completely of their *schlager* act image. There were even a few remnants of *Festfolk* left in their act – the show featured choreographed dance steps, and one of the lyricists from their ill-fated cabaret venture had put together two numbers for the present tour. Benny did a Swedish version of the archaic 'Fairfax Rag' (as recorded by Harry Nilsson), where he sang and played the ukulele, and the whole group performed a medley of Swedish children's songs with ironic lyrics. It was a far cry from the average rock or even pop concert.

The reviews were polite if not unduly enthusiastic. This didn't seem to matter much to audiences who couldn't get enough of the group. As for their own feelings, Björn and Benny in particular had seen all they needed of the *folkparks* of the country. Benny acknowledged that they all shared a nostalgic longing for the park circuit, but in truth, being on stage no longer held any special attraction for him.

At the same time, what Björn & Benny, Agnetha & Frida needed to do was to raise their profile and build on the momentum of their newfound success. Yet, Björn and Benny were obliged to spend their time producing records by dance bands, religious singers and children's choirs, to name just a few of their chores during the weekdays that summer.

Was Stig Anderson determined to exploit his talented employees for everything they were worth – as artists, songwriters and producers – even if it meant running them into the ground? Did Björn and Benny still nurture a hope that they would eventually be able to withdraw from the limelight and work behind the scenes?

Both theories are probably true: everyone seemed to be hedging their bets. It was a tough summer for all four members of the group. The opening night on June 15 set the tone: to their originally scheduled Gothenburg concert, a further two were added in Lidköping and Anderstorp. All three towns are in the southern part of Sweden, but far enough apart for to make the shows seem more like a chore than the kind of pleasurable experience that making music was supposed to be.

Indeed, not much had changed from the Hootenanny Singers and The Hep Stars' gruelling treks of the Sixties: quick car rides between different *folkparks* were still the norm. Frida's reaction to the stress was to lose five kilos. No matter how much she ate, she didn't regain her normal weight until the tour was over. And again the foursome experienced the ups and downs of being two couples on tour. "You get tired and irritated. With Björn I don't try to act like everything's just fine," reflected Agnetha.

As for her feelings about being away from little Linda, she made fairly light of the prospect at the start of the tour. "It's only on the weekends. I will spend the whole weeks with her. We'll get a nanny and then Björn's and my parents will step in." A month later, her tone had changed. "When Friday comes and I must leave her, I just sit and cry. To cram myself into a bus and tear away to some *folkpark* stage is the last thing I want. But what can you do? If I stay at home the whole show will collapse. Everybody else will be without a job."

Linda joined her parents on at least one occasion on the tour. On July 6, Agnetha and Björn's second wedding anniversary, their daughter was christened in the church of St Gertrud in Västervik. Björn and Agnetha had asked vicar Uno Wårdener, who wed the proud parents, to travel to Västervik to officiate. There was no time for any long christening celebrations, however: in the evening, Björn & Benny, Agnetha & Frida were back on stage again.

It was full speed ahead and the foursome were exhausted. A newspaper team followed them for a few days to do a feature on an ordinary working week for the group. Calling their hotel on the phone for a photo opportunity, they ended up being snubbed by Benny: "We have to try to get some sleep today. It's so seldom we have the chance."

The hectic schedule and the pressure of the media at least confirmed that there was a future in the group concept, and as this became more and more evident everyone realised they needed a name. Stig Anderson had become exasperated at having to repeat the long-winded and unmanageable name "Björn & Benny, Agnetha & Anni-Frid" every time he spoke about them to the press. He had been toying around with different combinations of the initials of the members' first names, and started referring to them as "Abba". The press was amused – there was already a Swedish canned fish company of that name – and the name Abba started appearing as a joke in articles about the band.

Meanwhile, in February the Gothenburg newspaper *Göteborgs-Tidningen* had held a "think of a name for Björn & Benny, Agnetha & Anni-Frid" competition. "We want a good name, one that could work on an international level: a name that sounds right in as many languages as possible," said the group. "We've been thinking and thinking, but it seems we can't come up with anything ourselves."

At the end of March the result of the competition was reported in the newspaper. Several hundred letters had been sent in, some of them with long lists of names. The group stated that they liked three fairly ludicrous suggestions: Alibaba, Friends and Neighbours, and Baba. But no final decision had been made yet. "It's an important choice – we have to think this over carefully," the group said diplomatically.

Curiously, although band myth would have it that Abba was the most popular submission in the competition, this name didn't appear at all in the article about the results. The three suggestions favoured by the group members were the only ones revealed to the public. In any case, it was unlikely that Stig would have accepted any result other than Abba, whatever the outcome of any discussions or competitions. Frida later pointed out that the unofficial victor of the contest was probably called Stig Anderson. By the summer it had been decided that the group would be named Abba, the change coming into full effect on their next domestic record release.

The final obstacle was securing an okay from the other Abba, the fish company. Stig phoned the managing director, who said yes on the condition that the group wouldn't discredit his company. "Björn and Benny didn't like the name very much in the beginning," recalled Stig. "They thought the name Abba smelled of canned fish. But we soon agreed that it was an excellent name in an international perspective. You can say it in any language." As usual, simple solutions and common sense prevailed.

The heightened visibility, the increased momentum, the feeling that something really was starting to happen at long last, was vindication for all four members of the group, not least for Björn and Benny who wanted to prove themselves as a credible pop songwriting team. Frida had never been anywhere near success on this scale before. "Right now we can't imagine anything else than working together," said Björn. "We feel that we've found a new style, a fresh and youthful style. Benny and I will keep ourselves in the background, the girls sing so much better after all."

But Agnetha was already beginning to back away from the pressure of fame brought about by the focus on the girls. She felt uncomfortable with people staring at her wherever she went and was even contemplating getting a black wig and dark sunglasses to avoid being recognised. "It's just moving unbelievably quickly," she mused. "You almost get scared when something like this happens, everything grows out of proportion."

The attention bestowed on celebrities was troublesome enough, but in Abba's case another kind of unwelcome spotlight now focused itself on the group. Primarily, it was Stig Anderson who was the victim, and as he and Abba would soon find out, it would just not go away.

Chapter 15

"People are not as stupid as you think – they are even more stupid." How Stig Anderson must have regretted the day he uttered those infamous words. Although the foreign media didn't pick up on the remark at the time, it was to haunt him in his own country for the rest of his life. He'd be asked to defend himself in innumerable interviews over the years, and the statement was held up time and time again as a summation of everything he was believed to stand for: appalling cynicism and blatant contempt for the general public.

The remark originated in a major interview with Stig, published on February 6, 1972, in the Swedish newspaper *Expressen*. It was a typically frank conversation where he gave his honest opinions on his profession as a lyricist. He admitted that the job had made him disillusioned: many times when he had worked hard on a lyric and felt that he was saying something worthwhile, the song had flopped completely. Other times, when he had dashed off some inanity in an hour or two, the song had become a major hit.

The facts proved him right. One of the lyrics he singled out as his worst, 'Min greve av Luxemburg' ('My Count Of Luxembourg', a version of a typical German marching-beat *schlager*), reached number one on *Svensktoppen* and number three on the sales chart. One of his best lyrics, the translation of 'Little Green Apples', as recorded in a Swedish Grammy award-winning interpretation by singer Monica Zetterlund, went nowhere.

The interview was but one of many where Stig would work himself up and go a bit overboard with his statements – it was as if he couldn't help himself from being brutally honest. The reader learned how the past decade as publisher and "song manufacturer", as he called himself, had turned exasperation into cynicism.

"I've experienced how half the record buyers interpret a *schlager* lyric the way I wrote it – as a throwaway piece – while the other half takes it seriously," he said. Switching into full gear, he continued: "The Swedish population is programmed: just look at *Svensktoppen*. You won't sell a single record until it enters that chart. On the Monday morning [the day after the broadcast] it's suddenly a good song. Why is it good on the Monday when it was bad on the Saturday?" And then came the payoff: "If I do a good job and it's not appreciated, but people instead choose the things I've done as pure routine work, then I sometimes think, 'People are not as stupid as you think – they are even more stupid.'"

Remarks like this certainly didn't go unnoticed. From the late Sixties onwards, Stig became a focus for attacks on bad taste and what was perceived as deceiving people into buying records they didn't want. "He is dangerous and what he writes is shit . . . He and others like him are glorifying life and spreading opinions that are repugnant to me," wrote Swedish Academy member Lars Forssell.

The outraged criticism didn't just stem from esteemed intellectuals like Forssell. As the Sixties gave way to the Seventies left-wing, quasi-revolutionary organisations led by angry young men with long hair and beards were growing in strength and cultural importance all across Europe. Certain types of progressive rock music helped focus their energies – but what Stig and Abba were doing was like waving a red flag in front of them all.

The student revolt in Paris in May 1968 had its own more modest, Swedish variant later the same month. Students at Stockholm University occupied the students' union building for three days in protest against a proposal to implement a fixed curriculum. The proposal was viewed as an attempt by the Social Democrat government to take control of the higher education of the nation. Somewhat inevitably, the protest developed into a demonstration against capitalist society in general. It was all a part of the hangover the western world was suffering after the previous decades' relentless glorification of market economy values.

The late Sixties was also a time when many countries, Sweden among them, founded local wings of Vietnam's National Liberation Front. Sympathising with the North Vietnamese in their fight against the United States' imperialist intervention in the south of their country, the Swedish NLF became a part of the general leftist wave in the nation.

The Swedish NLF had a two-edged relationship with the government. On the one hand it wasn't thought to be radical enough in its stance, but on the other Prime Minister Olof Palme openly supported the many protests and demonstration marches against the American occupation, severely damaging Sweden's relations with the superpower in the process. With endorsement from such high quarters, it was hardly surprising that a general socialist and anti-American feeling left its mark on the debate at the time.

Other incidents attracting a high media profile included the so-called "elm tree conflict" in May 1971. The local government had decided that a subway station was to be built in Stockholm's Kungsträdgården park, necessitating the felling of 15 elm trees. Environmental activists protested that the station and the removal of the elm trees would severely damage the environment in Stockholm. The confrontation and public outrage eventually led to a victory for the protestors, which resulted in the authority of high-handed politicians being weakened and a general belief that civil disobedience was right and proper.

It was inevitable that such undercurrents in society exerted a strong influence on all aspects of cultural activity, including art, theatre and – not least – popular music. The Seventies in Sweden were deeply coloured by the so-called Music Movement, or as it was mostly referred to, the *progg*. "Progg" was short for "progressive music", which in the Swedish vernacular didn't necessarily mean long-winded symphonic rock experiments in the vein of British bands like Yes or Emerson, Lake & Palmer, although that genre was represented within the Music Movement as well. More than anything else, the *progg* was marked by an "everyone can play" attitude, to some extent presaging the punk aesthetics of the late Seventies. The roots of *progg* could be found in the most rural Swedish folk music, Sixties folkpop and artists like Bob Dylan.

Certain bands were also heavily influenced by trad jazz, which tended to betray these musicians' middle-class high school backgrounds. Just like Björn Ulvaeus, several members of the most prominent bands of the Music Movement started out as trad jazz musicians in the late Fifties and early Sixties.

The origins of the *progg* era can be traced to two music festivals held at the Gärdet field in Stockholm in 1970. They were a sort of Swedish version of the Woodstock festival, where everybody played for free and no one was charged an admittance fee. The Gärdet festival became an annual event over the next few years.

The most important defining traits of *progg* as a genre and movement were that it at all times embraced left-wing messages in lyrics and attitude, that the music wasn't "commercial" and that it professed to have aims beyond pure entertainment. Image-wise, it was more or less self-evident that the acts wouldn't dress up in anything other than their everyday wear, which meant jeans and work-shirts, let alone anything remotely glammy or glittery.

Abba and Stig Anderson were the antithesis of everything the *proggers* stood for. Where the Music Movement encouraged everyone to play, no matter if it sounded a little amateurish at times, Abba were striving for professionalism. Where Stig and his protégés simply wanted to entertain, the *progg* advocates insisted on a relevant, political message. Abba and

Polar Music made no secret of their aim to sell as many copies as possible of their records worldwide, but the Music Movement and its followers opposed anything that was blatantly commercial, whether in the creation of the music or in the marketing of it. This atmosphere lay behind the decision to abolish radio broadcasts of the sales chart in August 1975 – Sweden lacked any such chart completely for the following three months – and the total closing-down of the much-loved *Tio i topp* show the year before.

Stig Anderson would have none of it. He was on a constant collision course with the Music Movement, vehemently opposing their use of the word "progressive" in his inimitable style. "I feel that Abba's music is extremely progressive. The far left have more or less appropriated that word. But they are more ultra-conservative than anyone. With records that sound like they were made in the Thirties I can't understand how you can call yourself progressive."

By the mid-Seventies, entirely through the commercial success of Abba and one or two other acts, Polar boasted an impressive slice of the domestic record market. It was said that their share fluctuated between six and 10 per cent, whereas a multinational label like EMI, with an artist roster that included The Beatles and other top international acts, could muster only 20 per cent. Coupled with his confrontational statements and general high media profile, this made Stig in particular the symbol of everything the *proggers* deplored. "They needed a clear target, a convenient punchbag within easy distance," he recalled. "I had exactly the right measurements: a proletarian background, class traitor, professional cynic in the *schlager* business – and I didn't mind answering back. The result was big headlines."

If there was ever the remotest possibility that Abba, Stig Anderson and Polar Music would enjoy even a shred of credibility in the eyes of the Music Movement, an incident that occurred as early as 1971 ensured that the opportunity was lost forever. In February of that year Stig got a tip from a radio producer who told him to listen to a show featuring an up-and-coming group from Malmö called the Hoola Bandoola Band. "They're good and I think they could be something for you," said the producer.

Stig listened to the show and was impressed by what he heard. He called up 25-year-old band leader Mikael Wiehe and invited him to Stockholm to discuss the matter further, offering to pay for the train ticket. Around the same time, Wiehe was approached by the Stockholm-based MNW, one of the leading leftist record labels. Before finally going up to Stockholm later that year he went to a record shop to listen to some records released by the two labels. "All the albums from Polar had a large, syrypy *schlager* sound and were damned uninteresting," he recalled. The MNW records, meanwhile, featured artists and production values that really appealed to him. "I felt like that was where I wanted to be, on MNW."

Mikael Wiehe still accepted Stig's offer of a train ticket and went up to Stockholm. He was young and eager to have a record released, and decided not to make any decisions until he'd met everyone involved. An initial meeting was held with Björn and Agnetha at a restaurant. Mikael played Björn a few of his songs from a demo tape during a second meeting at the Polar Music offices a few days later.

Meanwhile, Wiehe had a talk with MNW and got on very well with them. The final word from MNW didn't come as quickly as expected, however, and Wiehe decided to go back to Malmö in the meantime. But he had made up his mind: whatever happened, he definitely didn't want to record for Polar.

Back in Malmö, he lost no time in sending a money order to Stig Anderson for the train ticket. His conscience told him it wasn't right to let Stig pay for the ticket in the first place; after all, he'd wanted to go with MNW all along. A short while later, he got a call from MNW label boss Roger Wallis, who told him that everything was settled: Hoola Bandoola Band were welcome to record for MNW if they wanted to. Overjoyed, Mikael Wiehe naturally accepted.

A day later another, less pleasant phone call came in. It was Stig Anderson, furious that Wiehe had left Stockholm without saying anything. He insisted that they had a binding, verbal agreement, which Wiehe denied. This just made Stig even angrier. He was going to stop Mikael Wiehe's career, the young musician was told. There wouldn't be a radio or television show that would have Hoola Bandoola Band on, no record label would be able to sign them and no club would be able to book them. The phone call finished with the words, "And besides, I want the money back for the train ticket!" Wiehe recalled: "To my unbridled joy I was able to tell him, 'I've already sent it.'"

Wiehe was shaken by Stig's call and the torrent of threats and accusations. "He behaved like a real prick towards me," he recalled. "[I] was young, unknown, ignorant – a nobody. He was the king of this business and had to crush me with his elephant foot. I never forgot that or forgave him."

This was Stig at his meanest, and he absolutely refused to let go of the affair. He held the view that once you'd been invited to join his "family", the game should be played according to his rules, one of which was complete loyalty towards him and his company. The rules were in themselves generous, allowing for creative freedom for those who were talented. But those who contravened them were not easily forgiven.

On August 11, Stig dictated a threatening letter to MNW. "You are well aware that Mikael Wiehe has a verbal agreement with Polar to record one album in English and one in Swedish. A verbal agreement is just as binding as a written one," he stated. Towards the end of the letter he wrote, "I don't believe we will be satisfied with just watching how Mikael Wiehe and you break a contract together."

Stig's bluff failed, and the whole sordid business eventually fizzled out. In the fullness of time, the Hoola Bandoola Band went on to become the leading band of the Music Movement, with three charting albums to their credit before they disbanded in 1976. Stig, Björn and Benny always singled out the band as one of the few musical entities of any worth in the *progg* era. Again, once he had seen reason, the other, more gracious side of Stig's personality surfaced. "It would have been meaningless to try to work with artists that didn't want to record for us," he said in 1976.

This was the conclusion an experienced businessman such as himself should have been able to draw five years earlier. But at that time the rift between Stig Anderson – and, by default, Abba – on the one side and the Music Movement on the other was rapidly becoming unbridgeable.

The left-wing culture and the demand for political awareness found voice in much of the Swedish media. Parallel with the wide-eyed, admiring reports on Björn & Benny's success in Japan and the sniff of a breakthrough in the United States, a sharper focus was put on the "entertainment" side of the music business. By 1973, the Abba members were fielding interview questions like, "Would you ever consider writing political lyrics?" Reports on the "calculating" attitude of the group and their music escalated in direct proportion to their growing popularity domestically and abroad. It was a far cry from the harmless questions about dream dates and favourite food in the teen magazines of the Sixties.

Benny later reflected: "I understand it very well. With the movement of 1968 and everything, when you have all these forces working to make things better in society, it can be very provocative with a band that just runs around in platform boots and plays music, and doesn't think about anything else."

In the eyes of the left-wing commentators, making "unpolitical" music was a political statement in itself. "There was a time when I almost envied Mikael Wiehe this burning ideological conviction," recalled Björn. "But I didn't feel that way. For me and Benny, and for the girls, the music was enough of a driving force in itself. We didn't have the need to convince on any other level."

There was little Abba could do except shrug their shoulders and soldier on. By the autumn of 1973 they were on a journey of their own, their sights set firmly on the international music market. It wasn't hard to ignore domestic squabbles when the growing scent of worldwide success was guiding them ever forward.

Although Stig didn't put all his faith in the Eurovision Song Contest, the competition still seemed like the only surefire way to get the international exposure he sought for Abba. The problem, as ever, was to crawl through the eye of the needle that was the Swedish selection process as long as the jury consisted of "experts". With 'Ring Ring', it was crystal clear that they'd had the people's vote if not that of the jurors.

Ever since the Eurovision Song Contest became really popular in Sweden in the early Sixties, it has continued to engage television viewers. At the time of both the selections and the actual contest, the major evening papers usually invite their readers to phone in and have their say on whether "the right song won" or not. In 1973, no less than 80 per cent of those calling one newspaper opined that 'Ring Ring' should have won. While the Abba song topped each and every chart in the country, the winning song enjoyed only a brief spell at number 12 on the sales chart.

The solution to this discrepancy was obvious, as Agnetha pointed out. "I believe they should change the voting system so that people from all over the country can vote. That way you will find out what the audience likes, and a hit cannot become a hit if the audience doesn't like it. After all, they're the ones who are going to buy the records later on."

For the 1974 contest, Agnetha's prayers were finally answered. Although the jury system for the selections had varied over the years, the single "expert" jury format had in fact only been preferred since 1971. The "new" system with 11 district jury groups, with 15 voters in each group, was more a return to order than a revolution, then. However, whereas previous district juries had contained a high quota of "experts", for 1974 the jury members were chosen from a cross-section of the Swedish population, selected by statistical means.

On November 14, 1973, newspapers announced which composers had been invited to submit entries to the Swedish selections of the 1974 Eurovision Song Contest. Again, the names Björn Ulvaeus, Benny Andersson and Stig Anderson featured on the list. The trio welcomed the challenge.

Stig Anderson already had a hunch that Abba would participate in the 1974 selections, and through discussions with international music business colleagues he had tried to determine what kind of song would be suitable for this year's contest. More important, though, was to come up with a song that was right for Abba.

Stig and the group still maintained that actually winning the Eurovision Song Contest wasn't the most important aspect of participating, it was the chance of exposure to a large audience that meant most. The 1973 contest had again proven this theory correct: while the Spanish and British runners-up became worldwide hits, the success of the winning Luxembourg entry was more modest.

Björn, Benny and Stig decided that the best bet for Abba would be a "happy", uptempo song. The invitation to participate in the selections came during recording sessions for the group's second album, with six tracks already in the can. None of these seemed like a suitable contender for the contest, however. Shortly after getting the invitation, Björn and Benny headed out to Björn's chalet for a week of songwriting.

The house on Viggsö was becoming an increasingly important haven for Björn and Benny. With all their commitments at Polar and their status as members of Sweden's number one popular music act, there always seemed to be someone who wanted their attention when they were in Stockholm. Not so on the island. "Out there you can concentrate completely on one thing," said Benny. "No unwanted telephone calls, no recording studios, nothing. We write, eat and have a beer or something a bit stronger every now and then."

Over the five years that Björn and Benny had functioned as a regular songwriting team, they had established a basic working method that would remain constant throughout the Abba years and beyond. With Benny at the piano and Björn strumming his acoustic guitar, they would play chords for hours on end, humming melody fragments, trying to come up with that elusive melody that was worth developing. Their quest for the strongest possible melody meant that all but a scant few of those fragments were left unused.

All through the songwriting session they'd be singing nonsense words in English, just to have some syllabic sounds on which to hang the melody. In most cases, this was the shape in which it arrived at the studio. The final lyrics would often be written only when the style and arrangement of the song had been determined, after a backing track had been recorded.

In the course of that week in November 1973, Björn and Benny worked intensely through long days and nights. When they were finished, they had composed four new songs, among them that catchy, up-tempo melody they were looking for.

If their goal was to keep in line with current British pop music trends, they had certainly hit on the right tune. The song was very much in line with the work of another Spector revivalist, Roy Wood, whose group Wizzard had topped the UK charts earlier that year with 'See My Baby

Jive'. That record had also been a Swedish Top 20 hit.

Björn and Benny recorded a demo of the new song. Singing their non-sense lyrics, they accompanied themselves on guitar, piano and the sound of their feet stomping on the floor. The tape was given to Stig Anderson who would come up with a title and write appropriate lyrics. Stig knew all too well that the right title was absolutely crucial. "I was looking for a word that wouldn't need a translation, something that everybody would be familiar with: something like 'Ring Ring'. I needed a three-syllable word that would fit the melody," he said.

It was an agonising process. Stig barely slept for a week and ended up with several different suggestions. "One of them was 'Honey Pie'. I was searching frantically in my wife's cookery-books to find out what a honey pie was. But the title still wasn't right."

He finally found the right title in the early hours of a Saturday morning in mid-December. Looking through the book *Bevingade ord* (*Familiar Quotations*) by Pelle Holm he suddenly chanced upon the elusive three-syllable word he needed: "Wa-ter-loo". It referred to Napoleon Bona-parte's legendary defeat by British and German forces at the battle in the Belgian town on June 18, 1815.

"Once I have an idea and a title, writing the lyrics is usually a pretty quick process," said Stig. He proved it by completing the lyrics on the afternoon of that same day, using the battle of Waterloo as a metaphor for a girl surrendering to the love of a persistent suitor. "I called Benny up, played the tape and sang him the lyrics over the phone," Stig recalled. Benny, and soon afterwards Björn, gave the lyrics their seal of approval.

Two days later, the 'Waterloo' backing track was recorded at Metro-nome Studio. With the aid of their regular backing musicians at the time – Janne Schaffer, guitar, who invented the catchy bass and guitar riff, Rutger Gunnarsson, bass, and Ola Brunkert, drums – and with Benny on key-boards, they found the right feel after a couple of attempts.

The day after recording 'Waterloo', backing tracks were also completed for the last two songs to be included on the new album: 'Sitting In The Palmtree' and a composition with the working title 'Who's Gonna Love You'. Listening back to the tape after the session, Björn and Benny got a feeling about that last song. It was a languorous, mid-tempo composition that would be just as suitable for the Eurovision Song Contest as the rocking rhythms of 'Waterloo'. Stig was just about to leave for a Christmas holiday trip to the Canary Islands, and shortly before driving out to the airport he was given a cassette tape with the backing track.

Stig was a genuine workaholic for whom there was no such thing as a real holiday. During the Las Palmas visit a great deal of time was spent coming up with the right lyrics for this new song. Help finally came from Spanish radio, where every night Stig would hear the announcer finish off the day's broadcast with the phrase "hasta mañana", meaning "see you tomorrow". "That's a good title," he thought.

Abba were eager to record the song as quickly as possible, and Stig shocked his fellow tourists when he dictated the lyrics very loudly down a crackly telephone line between Spain and Sweden. At the end of December, Agnetha and Frida were brought to the studio to record the vocals for this new ballad. At first, the session did not go well: however hard they tried, they just couldn't find the right way to interpret the song.

The breakthrough was typical of how the awareness of the female half of Abba would enhance the recording process. It was Agnetha who finally came up with the right idea: to colour her vocal interpretation with the style and mood of the music that had captivated her as a teenager. "We realised that neither of us were able to sing it and we had actually started to give up on it," she recalled. "Then I ended up alone in the studio and fooled around a bit, thinking that I might do it like Connie Francis would. I sang it in that really emotional way and then we found that we were on the right way."

Agnetha's slightly more mature interpretation of Francis' vocal style, combined with a melodramatic spoken part, was exactly what 'Hasta Mañana' needed. The result was Abba's first convincing display of their trademark amalgamation of Anglo-Saxon pop idioms and European *schlager* ballad traditions. It was also one of the strongest tracks from the ongoing album sessions.

Stig arrived back in Stockholm on January 5, just two days before the deadline for submitting entries to the Swedish selection contest. The next day, Björn and Benny came out to his house in the suburb of Nacka. It was time to make that crucial decision – which song would they choose?

At first they discussed 'Hasta Mañana', reasoning that this would be a better contender for the Eurovision Song Contest. After all, it was more in line with the previous four years' winning entries: a female solo performance of a slow to mid-tempo ballad. But was that really the image they wanted Abba to project? Wouldn't 'Waterloo' be the better choice precisely because it broke with the Eurovision tradition? The song focused on both Frida and Agnetha as lead vocalists, which meant that the actual performance of the song would work much better.

"I had already determined that it should be 'Waterloo'," recalled Stig. "I said to Björn and Benny, 'Let me decide about this. If it all goes wrong you can kill me afterwards.'" Stig felt that 'Hasta Mañana' might bring a short-term triumph, but the more up-tempo song would prove to be a winner in the long term. 'Waterloo' was the entry that was submitted to the Swedish Broadcasting Corporation.

Saturday, February 9, 1974 was the day of the Swedish selections. The show would be taped in the afternoon for broadcast later in the evening. After having finished third two years in a row, Björn, Benny and Stig were on edge, wondering if this would be the year when they finally achieved their victory.

They believed the new format with a jury of "ordinary people" ought to work in their favour. And their entry was markedly different to the other nine, being the only pop song in the line-up. "Perhaps our song is too rocky to be a hit with the public at large," mused Björn before the contest, "but 'Ring Ring' certainly did become popular."

The general public were on Abba's side when they ran onto the television studio stage and unveiled the Swedish version of 'Waterloo' to the audience. Conductor Sven-Olof Walldoff, Abba's string and horn arranger, was dressed like Napoleon to great effect. The group was outfitted in glittery costumes, created by clothes designer Inger Svenneke, that made an unforgettable impression on the viewers. Certain details on the costumes, such as the epaulettes, were designed to enhance the "military" theme.

Although the *folkpark* tour of the previous year had been marked by a certain amount of onstage glam, the startling outfits of the 1974 Eurovision Song Contest were the first to truly stick in the memory of the general public. "We owe a great debt to our costumes," confirmed Benny many years later. "The first outfits that we wore in [the Eurovision Song Contest] looked really great."

For energy, zestfulness and catchiness, none of the other artists could match Abba's performance. They were the clear winners, the jury awarding them 302 points – almost 100 points more than the runner-up. "It was about time that we won," said a gratified Stig.

Abba and Stig Anderson watched the pre-taped broadcast of the contest at the Anderson family house. They celebrated their victory with a party attended by some 50 friends, business associates and Polar employees. It was a triumphant and happy occasion. 'Waterloo' was played over and over again at the highest volume, the sound reverberating throughout the neigbourhood. Björn had bet that the song would not win, and had to hand over his silver platform boots to one of the backing vocalists used during the contest.

When the party was over at five o'clock on the Sunday morning it was back to business again. Only a few hours later the Polar offices were bustling with activity. Tapes of the English version of 'Waterloo' were copied at a rapid pace, and telegrams were sent to all the local record companies to prepare them for what was going to happen.

As they arranged the European launch of 'Waterloo', Stig and Abba realised that it had been a blessing in disguise when 'Ring Ring' didn't win the selections in 1973. The Polar organisation was far better prepared for success when the time finally came. Many years later, one Swedish jury-member was astonished when Stig Anderson thanked him for not giving the earlier song any votes.

'Ring Ring' had been released in a large number of countries, many of which had turned it into a sizeable hit. This made the local record companies interested in further product from the Swedish group. With the knowledge of exposure in the *Eurovision Song Contest*, they were especially eager to capitalise on the free promotion opportunity. In January, Stig had introduced 'Waterloo' at the annual MIDEM music fair and the reception was extremely positive. "They were fighting for the record," he said.

In the case of the important and trend-leading UK market, Abba didn't even have a record company at all until more than six months after the release of 'Ring Ring' in Sweden. Now, when they had an even stronger song to give to the world, they had a deal in place at the exact time they needed it. Unlike most other contest participants before or since, Abba were not going to be caught off-guard by a sudden demand for records after the event. As Björn pointed out, raising awareness of 'Waterloo' and getting it released abroad before the contest had been "like pushing a button".

Stig Anderson wasn't leaving anything to chance, insisting on having a hands-on involvement in the marketing of 'Waterloo'. On the Tuesday after the victory, armed with a bagful of 'Waterloo' tapes, group biographies and other promotional material, he set out on a three day trek to Copenhagen, Hamburg, Amsterdam, Brussels, Paris and Vienna. "Every radio station and DJ of importance will have a copy of the record. If you mean to really go for it, then that's what you should do," he said.

Stig returned home briefly to pick up a couple more promotional packs, and then flew straight to London. "The fact that everything got started immediately after we had won the Swedish selections made the whole thing much bigger," remarked Björn later.

Full-page ads were also placed in American business journals like *Cash Box* and *Billboard*, and some 250,000 kronor was spent on the promotional campaign. Stig was satisfied that it had been worth all the money and the effort. "The British always had an advantage on us because their records – through being in English – have been played on all the radio stations across Europe," he pointed out. "Now we suddenly eliminated that advantage."

The Eurovision Song Contest rules stipulate that once an entry has been selected, the song cannot be heard in public again until after a specific date. In 1974 the date was March 4, and that day saw the simultaneous release of the two singles in Sweden featuring the Swedish and English versions of 'Waterloo'. They were the first records to be credited to "Abba", although the old name "Björn, Benny, Agnetha & Frida" was retained in brackets. Other countries soon followed suit with the release, just as Stig had planned. In some of those territories, the UK for instance, Agnetha's name was changed to Anna for easier pronunciation.

The *Waterloo* album was released in Sweden on the same day as the singles. It retained some of the patchiness of the first LP effort, but unlike its predecessor it had been recorded with a clear focus in mind. The *schlager* influence was more a flavour than a predominant factor. Overall, the album seemed to vibrate with the joy the group felt at finally being allowed to concentrate completely on doing "pop music in English".

Some of the tracks on the LP flirted with glam rock, notably the Björn-led 'Watch Out', which, with its fuzz guitar riff and raspy vocals, was as rocky as Abba ever got. Other more convincing efforts, such as 'Dance (While The Music Still Goes On)', continued on the Phil Spector trail with a 'Be My Baby'-style beat and multi-layered wall of sound. The title track was a piece of glam energy filtered through Abba's Nordic Spector production values.

One weakness of the album was the continued insistence on sharing lead vocal parts between the boys and the girls. It was still more or less a 50/50 distribution between the sexes, and the tracks featuring lead vocals by Björn and Benny are not among those that have aged most gracefully. *Waterloo* is unique insofar as it is the only Abba album to feature a solo lead vocal by Benny. His performance on 'Suzy-Hang-Around' made clear why he chose to step back in the future. As he himself has put it many times, he sings "in tune, but it's an ugly sound".

His lead vocals on this track came about primarily because he had written the lyrics. In the early days Björn and Benny used to write half the number of lyrics each, but by the time they started writing songs for Abba albums Benny's contribution had already diminished considerably. His own recollection is that the words for 'People Need Love' were co-written by both, but only 'Me And Bobby And Bobby's Brother' (from the *Ring Ring* album), 'Gonna Sing You My Lovesong' and 'Suzy-Hang-Around' (both from *Waterloo*) were single-handed Andersson efforts.

Judging by 'Me And Bobby And Bobby's Brother', a woman's reminiscence of her childhood friends, and 'Suzy-Hang-Around', a somewhat incomplete story of a little girl who isn't allowed to play with the older kids, Benny had an affection for nostalgic flashbacks to uncomplicated childhood days. But he found writing a pain and envied the relative ease with which Björn dashed off effective lyrics. "He could actually write a decent lyric in one day, while I would struggle for two weeks and still not get any further than the first verse," said Benny. "In fact, I have never managed to write a good lyric, and in the end I think even Björn agreed that it would be better if he did all of them."

The light-hearted approach that still prevailed at this time underscored the secondary roles that lyrics played in their music. Beyond a catchy title, it seemed the words of their songs could say almost anything so long as they contained the right number of syllables.

As one might imagine, the standout tracks on the *Waterloo* album are mostly those that feature prominent vocals by Agnetha and Frida: 'Hasta Mañana', 'Dance (While The Music Still Goes On)', 'Honey, Honey', 'Gonna Sing You My Lovesong' and the title track. 'My Mama Said' has a jazzy, almost funky feel, lending it an aura of coolness that somehow manages to convince several decades later. Certain other tracks, like 'King Kong Song' and 'What About Livingstone', get by on their whimsical charm. Whatever the relative merits of the various tracks, in 1974 there was definitely a freshness and uniquely personal touch about Abba that stood out amid the rest of the Swedish music landscape.

Once again the group had the pleasant experience of watching the two singles and the album shoot to the top of the sales chart, battling it out for the top three positions. Four weeks after release the album had sold 125,000 copies domestically, said to be the highest number of albums ever sold in such a short time. *Waterloo* was number one on the chart for 12 weeks and by the end of the year it had sold 250,000 copies, more than any other album in Sweden up to that point.

It wasn't all a bed of roses, though. Certain sections of the public were hostile to Abba and took the opportunity to rain on their parade. 'Waterloo' was reported to the performing rights society for plagiarising The Foundations' 1968 hit 'Build Me Up Buttercup'. It wasn't even this song's composer or publisher who complained, merely a private individual who felt compelled to reveal Abba's shameless lack of originality. Björn and Benny rightly dismissed the accusation. "If 'Waterloo' is similar to 'Build Me Up Buttercup', 'Baby Love' by The Supremes is also similar to it," said Benny. "They all have the same rhythmic theme."

As both single and album did very well in the rest of Scandinavia, where the record-buyers had been won over the previous year, Abba shrugged their shoulders and concentrated on their work. There can be no question that the group were supremely confident in their ability to reach out with their music as they prepared for the trip to the English coastal resort of Brighton where the 1974 Eurovision Song Contest would take place.

For Benny, Björn, Agnetha and Anni-Frid the time had come to fulfil the promise of a Polar Music press release issued some six months earlier: "These talented and hard-working artists will no doubt be among the few Swedish artists who will have an international break-through. Their music and recordings will mean a lot all over the world."

PART III

The Time Is Right

Chapter 16

Stig Anderson was pondering Abba's chances of success in the upcoming Eurovision Song Contest. "I'm certain we will come out of the experience in one piece, but surely, no one really expects us to win?" he told a reporter. He knew that experts had deemed 'Waterloo' "a bit too aggressive" for the contest, but he didn't care much anyway: Abba would be seen by hundreds of millions of viewers, and that was good enough for him.

The date for the contest was Saturday, April 6, the place Brighton, on the south coast of England, famous for its Pavilion, an ornate white palace constructed by fun-loving King George IV that would not be out of place in Disneyland. The entourage – Abba, Stig, Hans "Berka" Bergkvist and tour promoter Thomas Johansson – left Sweden for England the preceding Monday. Everyone was in good spirits for the upcoming challenge, though Agnetha had been suffering from a sore throat and was still on penicillin.

At Heathrow airport the Abba party were met by representatives from Epic Records who sped them to London in a white Rolls-Royce. It was a confident team that arrived in England's capital city for an initial meeting with the press. BBC Radio was playing 'Waterloo' frequently, even more than Britain's own entry, Olivia Newton-John's 'Long Live Love'. A couple of weeks earlier, the group had received an offer to appear on *Top Of The Pops*, the UK's principal chart TV show.

Their earlier, domestic popularity had instilled in the four members of Abba a degree of level-headedness in regard to their prospect of worldwide success. "It's not a matter of wanting a lot of new things – limousines and houses," mused Björn. "I don't want to become nouveau riche, like many of the English artists. They wallow in luxury, they don't know what to do with their money." The group as such seemed to be but one of many projects on Björn's mind. "I'd like to continue making Hootenanny Singers records. It's cool to be doing as many things as possible."

Before leaving Sweden, Björn and Benny assessed their chances of ending up the winners of the contest. "We will probably get several votes from northern Europe and possibly also from England. It's harder with the

Italians, the Spaniards and the French; in those countries they want their ballads. But we are working this with the intention of winning. That's the only way to do it."

Demonstrating his confidence, Stig bet £100 that Abba would win. The initial bookmaker odds on Abba placed them among the favourites: along with Italy they were at 6–1, with only Luxembourg and The Netherlands on shorter odds.

Abba arrived in Brighton on the Tuesday. By a baffling coincidence, they had been booked to stay in the 'Napoleon' suite at the elegant Grand Hotel on the sea front. The entourage was joined in Brighton by drummer Ola Brunkert and bassist Rutger Gunnarsson, who were to back the group on stage. John Spalding and Carole Broughton, the co-director of Spalding's publishing company Bocu Music, were also on hand.

The venue for the contest was the Brighton Dome, originally the royal stables, erected in the early 1800s, which sported a glass dome roof and had been converted into a conference centre and concert venue. The legendary Katie Boyle was going to present the show, her fourth time as Eurovision Song Contest hostess, a record unbeaten to this day.

Brighton was bathed in spring sunshine, with flowers blooming everywhere. The town was full to bursting, with no less than 800 visitors representing each of the 17 participating countries. Journalists and photographers made up an additional 300.

There were threats directed at three participating countries, Israel, Greece and Ireland, which necessitated the presence of several hundred policemen and security people. The horrific events of the 1972 Olympics in München, when 14 Israeli athletes were killed by Arab terrorists, were still fresh in the world's memory. As a result the participants from these nations were all housed on the same floor of the hotel, described by one journalist as "hermetically sealed". There was a policeman outside each room, one on every staircase and even one by the dumbwaiter. Those who entered into the Dome passed through a metal detector.

During the first rehearsals on the Wednesday Abba experienced sound problems. Since the rules allowed for a pre-recorded backing track to be used – provided that all musicians on the tape were present on stage – Abba had brought along drummer Ola Brunkert and bassist Rutger Gunnarsson to "mime" their parts. Presumably they figured Björn and his star-shaped guitar would render Janne Schaffer's participation superfluous.

From the group's point of view the sound just wasn't loud enough at the rehearsals. They were after the full impact of a backing track and vocals punching through the television screen, and after four straight run-throughs, each punctuated by complaints from Björn and Benny, they still didn't have the mix they were after. 'Waterloo' was considerably more full-tilt rock than anything previously performed in the Eurovision Song Contest, which may have been the reason why technicians initially refused to raise the volume. Finally, inevitably, Stig Anderson lost his temper and rounded on the representatives of the Swedish Broadcasting Corporation. Someone with authority in the Swedish team must tell those reluctant BBC technicians to set the volume according to Abba's wishes, he snapped.

The very last dress rehearsal in the afternoon of April 6, the day of the contest, was to be broadcast to the jury members in the 17 participating countries so that it could be taped. In reality, juries would decide how they would cast their votes from this performance. Luckily, everything finally came together almost as Abba had wanted, but their fingers were still itching to take charge of the sound themselves.

Although Abba began as one of the favourites, by Thursday their odds had lengthened considerably on the bookmakers' lists, down to 20–1. The main competition, according to the bookmakers, were Italy's Gigliola Cinquetti with the ballad 'Si', the Dutch duo Mouth & MacNeal and their catchy 'I See A Star', plus the UK, represented by Olivia Newton-John and 'Long Live Love', their umpteenth 'Puppet On A String' copy. Taking advantage of the situation, Stig bet a further £20 on Abba.

Many years later, Agnetha remembered that she was far from sure of winning. She felt the strongest competition came from The Netherlands and Great Britain. "I thought they both had a better chance than 'Waterloo' which, frankly, I think was one of our poorer songs!" Everyone in the Swedish entourage shared Agnetha's fondness for the Dutch entry and saw it as the main challenge to their own song. Self-belief was certainly not lacking in the Mouth & MacNeal duo themselves – after all, they were already an internationally successful act with the US Top Ten hit 'How Do You Do?' to their credit.

At a party arranged by a music publisher on the night before the contest, the male half of the duo, Willem Duyn ("Mouth") drank freely. The gigantic, long-haired and bearded singer was running around, telling everybody that he "was going to win!" "We had a fight," remembered Frida. "I thought he was so self-important and I got really angry with him. I told him off in my own brand of English, which was a bit curious at the time." Eventually the over-confident singer found himself face to face with Agnetha. "Who are you? Abba?" he rambled. "Don't think you're the strongest – I'm the strongest!" Seconds later he had lifted a less than amused Agnetha up in the air. Embarrassed representatives of the Dutch team had to intervene, leading away Mr Mouth.

Apart from the 2 p.m. dress rehearsal, the members of Abba spent the hours preceding the night of the contest in an unusually relaxed fashion. Frida, who had begun an intensive course in high school English and French, even found time for a bit of language study before it was time to go to the Dome. While the others in the group remained calm, Björn was nervy – and it didn't help that his costume was so tight that he couldn't sit down. At the time it was said that the trousers had been "incorrectly sewn", but years later Björn remembered the real reason. "It was terrible. I cursed myself for not slimming a bit before that thing . . . And afterwards, of course, I went on the strictest diet you can imagine." He memorably described his onstage appearance as "a fat Christmas Tree".

Abba appeared in the contest as number eight in the line-up, between a nondescript entry from Yugoslavia and Luxembourg's oompah stomper. From the moment conductor Sven-Olof Walldoff appeared onstage in his Napoleon outfit, they had the laughing and applauding audience at the Dome on their side. The group entered the brightly coloured stage together with their jeans-clad wax-dummy-like backing musicians. Their own sequinned, glittery costumes and platform boots shone and sparkled: a major contrast to the cocktail dresses and sensible suits worn by other contestants. Frida and Agnetha's beaming smiles flashed from the stage like high-powered halogen lights.

"I immediately thought about the 500 million viewers," recalled Benny. "And then everything just mixed up in my head and I felt the stress disappear. The fact that there were four of us helped a lot since we kept giving each other encouraging looks from time to time." There can be no question that Abba's confident, zestful performance, their colourful clothing and the song itself made a big impression on the viewers.

After Italy had performed the final entry it was time for the voting. By now Björn had become so nervous that he elected not to watch the proceedings. In the end though, he couldn't keep himself from grouping around the monitor together with Benny, Agnetha and Frida, biting his nails all the way through. "No one can imagine the tension of such an event," he said. "Your skin crawls, your stomach knots up and your throat gets all dry. You want to run away from it all, at the same time as you're standing there transfixed and spellbound. Believe me, it's a real ordeal."

In the 1974 voting system, the individual members of each country's jury of ten had one point to award as he or she saw fit. The omens were good for Abba when the Finnish jury started out by awarding them half the nation's allotted points. As the voting continued, no other country came close to threatening Abba's dominance. Down in the auditorium,

Chapter 16

Berka Bergkvist was watching the scoreboard with mounting tension when Thomas Johansson leaned over to him and said, "Goddamn it, I think we're going to win."

Sixteen minutes and 30 seconds after the voting had commenced the Italian jury concluded their score. A nervously giggling Katie Boyle announced that Abba were the victors of the 1974 Eurovision Song Contest. Quite apart from the group's own triumph, it was also the first time that Sweden won the contest.

The only countries that failed to bestow any points whatsoever on 'Waterloo' were, surprisingly, Great Britain and Belgium, two of Abba's most loyal strongholds in the future, as well as Greece, Monaco, and Italy. Because of the low amount of points distributed among the participants, Abba's total score was an unimpressive-sounding 24 points – but it was enough to win.

Stig rushed onstage to accept his songwriting award and proceeded to repeat the phrase "thank you" in the languages of several of the participating countries. He had rehearsed the phrases earlier in the afternoon when he thought he should prepare in some way for the eventuality of winning.

The awards ceremony became somewhat anticlimactic for the other two songwriters. When Björn and Benny tried to get on stage, they were held back by security guards who insisted that "only the composers are allowed on stage" for the ceremony. The guards were holding on to their legs as they were trying to climb the short steps leading to the stage. "The guard [said], 'You're not a writer, you've misunderstood this, you dumb Swede! You have to wait,'" Björn recalled. "The way I was dressed he would have thought, 'He can't be the writer.'"

Benny eventually managed to fight his way onto the stage, but the guards absolutely refused to let go of Björn. Stig, who had tried to explain his two co-composers' no-show by saying that they were "probably shocked" by their win, cracked up laughing in front of the hundreds of millions of viewers when Benny told him what had happened.

Björn never made it to the awards ceremony, for broadcasting time was quickly running out and it was time for Abba to perform the winning song again. He didn't seem to mind too much, though, as he let out a triumphant "yeah!" before the first chorus. 'Waterloo' had turned out to be a winner in every sense of the word.

In the hours after the contest, most of the group were swept away as if in a hazy dream. Björn and Benny remembered how they were both convinced that someone would soon tell them that the votes had been incorrectly calculated. Agnetha called her parents in Jönköping, crying with joy down the telephone line. Only Frida managed to keep her cool in the midst of the excitement. "I was surprised at myself because I believe I was pretty ice-cold," she recalled. "The reaction didn't come until afterwards. It was hard to believe that we had won this major contest."

Stig called his home in Nacka where the celebrations were in full swing. The employees at Sweden Music and Polar had gathered in the villa to watch the broadcast. When Stig accepted his award a perplexed Gudrun Anderson was heard to exclaim somewhat irrelevantly, "But . . . he's wearing the wrong shirt!" Now, though, everybody was cheering wildly and wanted to talk to Stig, who was blissfully unaware of his sartorial faux pas. "They sounded happy," was his understated comment after the call.

Phone conversations concluded, Abba and Stig went on to the official banquet arranged by the BBC. Frida had finally been hit by the realisation that they had won, and was puffing away on a celebratory cigar. The group later went on to another party, where, at three o'clock in the morning, Frida and Stig were approached by a team from the Swedish news show *Rapport* (*Report*).

It was a time for celebration, for the nation to salute their heroes who'd fought so well and triumphed in the *schlager* battle. Reporter Ulf Gudmundsson thought otherwise, however. According to Sweden's unofficial media agenda of the time, it was inappropriate to treat Abba or Stig simply as winners of a competition, as a sports reporter would have treated a victorious athlete. Instead, Gudmundsson's opening statement was, "Last year you made a song about people phoning each other, this year you did a song about how 40,000 people died, cynically speaking."

Stig's jaw dropped and for a second or two he didn't know what to reply. For once he was so dumbstruck that he didn't even lose his cool – but nor was he able to come up with a crushing reply. "That was extremely cynically spoken, because that's not at all what we meant," he improvised. "Waterloo is a concept the world over and stands for a historical event. It doesn't have anything to do with people dying. That was really putting a spin on it, I must say."

When the camera was turned off Stig exploded, telling Gudmundsson to "go to hell before an accident happens!" He told a newspaper reporter: "Don't these people know anything? . . . I can just about accept that they don't read the lyrics properly before they ask their questions, but not that they think we'd literally sing about the slaughter on the battlefield at Waterloo. Do they think we're idiots?"

It was typical of their confrontations with the media. Often Stig or Abba were asked to defend statements they hadn't made, things they hadn't done and opinions they didn't have. The incident was soon forgotten, and the celebrations in Brighton continued. The group didn't get into bed until 6 a.m. the following morning.

Three hours later they had to get up again: Epic Records had arranged a champagne breakfast at the Bedford Hotel, with numerous media representatives invited. Even Agnetha, who was getting her flu back, enthusiastically answered all the reporters' questions. The breakfast was followed by several hours of photo sessions at the beach.

When the group finally withdrew to their hotel suite, finding time at last to collect themselves after the whirlwind of events, the sense of euphoria remained intact. John Spalding recalls this brief snapshot of undiluted joy as one of his most treasured memories of Abba. "It was just the four members, Stig, myself and Carole Broughton," he recalls. "We stayed in the hotel the whole day and just drank champagne and read about a hundred odd telegrams." The group was genuinely touched by all the greetings that had been sent by everyone from family and friends to music business colleagues and total strangers.

The team was also discussing the numerous offers that were pouring in: requests for newspaper interviews, radio shows and, most importantly, television appearances. "We'd decided to keep ourselves very cool and let everything calm down," recalled Stig. "I had to make decisions and keep track of everything so that we didn't do anything in haste."

It was a time when Stig's loyalty to those who had believed in the group before they were Eurovision Song Contest winners shone through. Although the important British market was Abba's main priority, Stig didn't back down on a promise he had made to Dutch television producer Eddy Becker who had been impressed with the group during rehearsals and offered them an appearance on his television programme, *Eddy-Go-Round*. He just jotted down the date of the show on a business card and offered them plane tickets. After the victory, Becker was worried because his offer had only been verbal, but he was reassured that they would honour their agreement. "I have rarely seen such integrity from artists and their manager," he said.

On the Monday, Abba left for London and further promotion. There was no question that overnight they had become one of the hottest acts in the country: during their limousine ride they stopped at a petrol station and were immediately swamped by autograph hunters.

The British media hadn't failed to notice that the winners of this year's Eurovision Song Contest differed in many ways from previous winners. Even before the event, the usually Euro-suspicious *New Musical Express* had declared 'Waterloo' the best pop song of the contest. Now the daily press followed suit, praising Abba as a welcome breath of fresh air to the staid proceedings.

Björn even went so far as to confidently predict that artists like David Bowie or Roy Wood's Wizzard would be entering the Eurovision Song Contest after this first pop victory, but it was not to be. Abba's triumph influenced Eurovision only insofar as a greater influx of groups with more pop style songs would compete over the following years.

There was no mistaking Björn, Benny and Stig's joy at being taken seriously by the British music business. "England is the world's toughest record market, the homeland of pop music and all that," they beamed. "That our victory should take place here and our records get a proper chance is nothing less than fantastic – Sweden has never achieved anything like it before."

A hectic few days of interviews and other promotion activities followed, crowned by the taping of their first *Top Of The Pops* appearance on April 10, for broadcast a day later. Agnetha's flu had returned in full force, complete with a sore throat and rising temperature. The British musicians' union rules stipulated that miming wasn't allowed, so Agnetha simply had to be able to sing for the group's very first British television appearance.

A doctor's appointment was hastily arranged and things worked out fine in the end. By the time of the *Top Of The Pops* broadcast, Abba were already on their way home to Stockholm, having flown via Hamburg, on West Germany's north coast, for yet another TV appearance.

Winning the Eurovision Song Contest changed everything for Abba.

Frida, who'd begun studying languages simply because she was bored being a housewife, had her courses in French and English to consider. "At the end of April our school group was supposed to go to England and stay with families in order to really get into the language. But I don't know if I'll be able to do that now," she reflected naïvely. It seemed she still didn't fully realise the impact this international breakthrough would have on her life.

Furthermore, Frida and Benny planned to get married in the summer of 1974. Frida had sewn her wedding dress while she was studying at the tailor school back in 1972, and it had been hanging in her closet ever since. The couple was adamant that they didn't want a media wedding, such as Björn and Agnetha had endured. With the added attention bestowed on the group after Brighton, they knew there would be no way that they could escape intense media attention. Benny and Frida decided to wait until after the worst of the Abba fever had died down a bit.

In some respects it was curious that Abba ever took part in the

Eurovision Song Contest in the first place. For one week, in April 1974, it was as if they stepped into a completely artificial world, becoming a huge part of all that Eurovision is about: a pompous, ceremonious, overblown event for something as trivial as deciding which three-minute ditty is purportedly the best in Europe. After all, the truly great songwriters of the era, from Lennon & McCartney downwards, would no more enter Eurovision than record an album of nursery rhymes.

Abba meant it only as a parenthesis, a launching pad for their international aspirations, but instead it became the single most famous episode in their entire story. Although it was highly incidental, an aberration in the long-term, they and their career became intrinsically linked to the Eurovision Song Contest, and it to them.

The moment they decided to step into those Euroglam space suits and participate in a high-profile event dedicated to the inconsequential, their place in rock history was decided for them. They weren't aware of it at the time, but in the two minutes and 46 seconds that it took to perform 'Waterloo', they effectively lost all chance of ever being taken seriously by the cognoscenti. It was the price they paid for becoming far and away the most successful group ever to have competed, and the way Eurovision has developed over the past few decades, Abba's joy at being so strongly associated with the event hasn't increased. "Musically, it's a catastrophe," said Benny in the early Nineties. "It was better in the Fifties and the Sixties. [These days] it's a fun TV show, maybe, but it has nothing to do with music."

For Stig, the victory meant that an already hectic life became even more stressful. "I will have even less time for my family after this," he admitted. "Our seven-year-old son is still a small child, but my wife will have to take the blows . . . This is in my blood. I can't just let go of it, even if it means rush and tear and wearing myself into the ground. I love this job and the competition for the top position."

The celebratory party in the Anderson house in Nacka had been tempered by the knowledge that tomorrow would bring a hard day's work. "It was a big party, but at the same time it was, 'Tomorrow it's back to the office and push all the buttons that Stig has prepared,'" recalled Görel Johnsen. "Apart from Stig and Abba, I believe we were all at the office the next day."

Back in Brighton, Hans "Berka" Bergkvist had a similar experience. Since the late Sixties, he had been working at the record distribution company GDC, owned by Polar together with several of the other major record companies. It was a job arranged for him by Björn and Stig. Berka was a hard worker and had advanced swiftly through the company. Stig liked ambitious people, and as a thank you for giving his all to his job, Berka was invited to come along to Brighton.

"Right after the victory Stig said to me, 'Now you're going back to Stockholm to take care of this. You're going to start working at Polar,'" he recalls. Berka became Polar's label manager, handling all the contacts with the pressing plants, printing companies and everybody else instrumental in manufacturing records. With the added demand, the company needed one specific person to take care of this job.

Stig was also aware that success would bring financial complications. Sweden Music and its associated group of companies were already healthy businesses, with 15 employees and an annual turnover of 15 million kronor (£1.5 million). Thus far, it was the international publishing deals and the ongoing acquisition of other domestic publishing companies that formed the basis of the company's fortunes.

There were many advantages to being a small company enjoying big success and keeping as much of your business as possible under one umbrella: larger profits for the owner of all these rights, for one thing. However, with a big turnover and few costs, those profits could become so large that almost everything disappeared in tax. Something had to be done, especially since Abba's success was likely to bring with it a river of money flowing in at an even more rapid pace. "In my opinion, we have a hell of a problem and a lot of work [ahead of us]," said Stig when he phoned Sweden Music's accountant, Stig Engqvist, from Brighton.

Engqvist had met Stig through Benny, whose tax problems he had initially tried to sort out in the late Sixties. His contact with Sweden Music was initiated when he represented Björn and Benny in the negotiations for their employment at Polar. With the escalating revenues for Sweden Music, and the prospect of future high income at Polar, the plan was now to invest the profits in other companies and real estate. Gudrun, still responsible for the company's financial affairs, would handle this together with Engqvist.

While business matters were dealt with away from the spotlight, Stig and Abba concerned themselves with immediate career plans. Now that they had achieved an international breakthrough it was natural that the group's priorities shifted away from the domestic market. It was vital that they took every opportunity they could to promote themselves abroad and build on the momentum that 'Waterloo' had created.

Earlier in the year, Abba had made tentative plans for a tour of the Swedish *folkparks*, including a visit to Denmark. Beginning in the second half of June, they were going to play 25 venues in one month. The group was viewing the summer tour as a "warm-up" for a European trek in the autumn. They were planning to upgrade the presentation from the 30-minute entertainment formula of their earlier stints, to a proper, full-length rock show with impressive sound and spectacular lighting. As early as the Swedish selection victory in February, however, they were starting to have second thoughts about the preliminary bookings for the summer tour. After all, there could be a sudden demand from abroad if everything went according to plan.

The weekend after returning home from the Eurovision adventure, the four members of Abba retreated to the Viggsö island where, away from the pressure, they could talk things through amongst themselves. They knew that numerous visits to European countries loomed over the following months. Björn and Benny were also committed to oversee several record productions on behalf of Polar Music. The previous February Benny had begun work on a solo album for Frida, and sessions were scheduled to continue sooner rather than later. Agnetha had pencilled in the first sessions for her new album in July. Despite the recent breakthrough, Abba was still but one of many projects on their agenda.

Moreover, the extensive travelling was interfering with their private lives. This was felt especially by Björn and Agnetha, who were horrified by the reaction of their one-year-old daughter when they were reunited with her after the two weeks away entering Eurovision. "Björn and I longed like crazy for Linda all the time: every day, every hour," Agnetha related. "And of course we thought that she was longing as much for us, that she'd throw herself in our arms when we finally returned home. But when we walked through the door she didn't recognise us! She became shy and scared and stretched her hands out towards the nanny instead."

Agnetha started to cry. "We were all so worn-out and exhausted, so I guess I was extra sensitive. Björn and I promised each other to never, ever again stay away from Linda for such a long time." Over that April weekend on the island, they made their final decision: there would be no tour of Sweden that summer.

A few days later, Stig issued a press statement that all the preliminary bookings had been cancelled. The *folkpark* organisations and the newspapers were outraged and said that Abba were "terribly immoral", letting down the Swedish audience that had supported them throughout the years. Although no contracts had been signed, the *folkpark* managers argued that there were other binding agreements.

Eigil Svan, the head of artist booking at the Tivoli amusement park in Copenhagen, wrote an angry letter to Abba's tour promoter Thomas Johansson at the EMA-Telstar agency. "This is quite simply the biggest insult I've ever experienced during my many years in this business. I have engaged the biggest international stars and then I have to be ridiculed by a gang of Swedish amateurs, who have become too big because of a sudden hit and who are certain to be forgotten a year from now." Mr Svan hinted that the real reason was probably that the concert fee hadn't been high enough. "Every future letter from you will be returned unopened," he concluded.

Stig was relieved that the group had cancelled their engagements. He rarely saw the point in long, expensive concert treks – as far as he was concerned it just stole valuable time from songwriting and producing. Besides, common sense told him that strategic television appearances were easier to handle and, most importantly, could reach millions in one single broadcast.

While the storm was blowing over, Stig had other, more interesting challenges to take on. When 'Waterloo' was released across Europe in March and April 1974, the United States was the only major market where Abba didn't have an outlet for their records. The Playboy deal back in 1972 had lapsed after the limited success of 'People Need Love' and one or two further releases in the following year. A planned television appearance in November 1972 had also failed to come off.

It was a disappointment for the group, who kept talking about the American market in their interviews. Frida revealed that she dreamed of appearing live in front of thousands of people at Carnegie Hall in New York. "Right now we're mainly setting our sights for Europe," said Benny, "but of course somewhere in the long run we have hopes for the USA. I guess everybody has that dream."

By the spring of 1974, CBS had yet to pick up the option for the American market that had been available to them under the terms of Abba's signing to their Epic label in Great Britain. After the failure of 'Ring Ring' to become a UK hit they seemed to have lost interest, even though – by a curious coincidence – Swedish music was making a breakthrough in the USA. On the day of Abba's victory in Brighton, the group Blue Swede had become the first Swedish act to top the US charts when they scored with 'Hooked On A Feeling'. But even after the 'Waterloo' victory, when Stig had further talks with the American branch of CBS, they were still pretty uninterested in this Scandinavian pop group.

"They had a very strange attitude," recalls Michael Tretow. "Before the contest, Stig played 'Waterloo' for them, but they just said, 'Yeah, yeah.' Then he called them and said, 'We won! Surely you'll release it now?' 'Ah, we'll see.' They were cool as ice."

Stig was frustrated when CBS let their option drop, but kept up a brave front. "We'll take it easy as far as America is concerned," he sniffed. "The value of having a big hit on the American charts is exaggerated, you don't earn much money on that."

Meanwhile, he asked his friends in the Swedish music business for help. The Metronome record label, also owner of the studio Abba usually used, was the Swedish distributor of the WEA group of labels. The "A" in WEA stood for Atlantic Records, the legendary home of numerous soul and R&B artists, including Ray Charles and Aretha Franklin, and distributor of Stax, the Memphis-based label of Otis Redding and Wilson Pickett. Since the late Sixties, Atlantic had been signing top-drawer rock bands, including Crosby, Stills & Nash and Iron Butterfly from the US and The Rolling Stones and Led Zeppelin from the UK.

When Stig asked his colleagues for help, Metronome co-founder Börje Ekberg contacted Atlantic. Phil Carson, who was the label manager in Great Britain, listened to the 'Waterloo' single and liked what he heard. He, in turn, sent the record to Atlantic President Jerry Greenberg in New York. "Phil mentioned in his letter that CBS had passed on the North American rights of this song," recalls Greenberg. "I happen to be a big fan of Phil Spector and everything that he did. When I first heard 'Waterloo', to me it sounded like a Spector record: it had this kind of echoey drum sound. I didn't know anything about the people singing on the record, but to me it was a hit."

At the end of April, Stig and John Spalding flew to New York to meet with Jerry Greenberg. Spalding recalls how keen Atlantic were to get the deal, sending limousines to pick up Stig and himself for the luncheon meeting. "Stig was a really tough negotiator," says Greenberg. "A gentleman, but a very tough negotiator. He knew what he had, and he knew what he wanted, and he was experienced in the music business. This guy wasn't going to make a bad deal for his artist."

There was some interest from Mercury and MCA as well, but Stig valued the personal rapport he struck up with Greenberg. When he returned home at the beginning of May, he had a US contract for Abba with Atlantic Records.

The relationship between Polar and the American label got off to a flying start. Almost before the ink had dried on the contract, Atlantic had a pre-order of 30,000 copies for the single. Additionally, 'Waterloo' was singled out as a "special pick" by influential radio tipster Bill Gavin. On June 1, the song entered the *Billboard* charts.

The following week brought further encouragement for Abba's American career. Once again it was Stig's publishing contacts that brought an opening, rather than his connections in the record business. The legendary impresario and promoter Sid Bernstein got a tip from Lou Levy, head of the publishing company Leeds Music. Bernstein had worked with numerous famous acts over the years and had been the manager of The Rascals in the Sixties. However, he was best known for his relationship with The Beatles. Bernstein was the first to book the band for a concert in the United States in 1964. Famously, he had also arranged their appearance at Shea Stadium the following year, the first stadium concert in rock history, breaking every attendance record at the time.

"Lou called me after the Eurovision Song Contest," recalls Sid Bernstein. "He said, 'Sid, you've got to fly to Sweden and sign this group, they are amazing.'" After a phone call with Stig, it was decided that Bernstein should come over and meet the group and their manager.

Bernstein arrived in Stockholm in early June. He and Stig took a motor boat out to Viggsö and the group's summer houses. Björn and Benny had just begun writing songs for the next Abba album. There were no food stores on the little island, so Stig brought a big supply of provisions for himself and the group. Bronx-raised Sid Bernstein, a big city boy in every bone of his body, was in for a small adventure.

"We took this little boat, and just as we loaded up it started to storm really bad," said Bernstein. "Stig said, 'This is kind of rough, you want to go back?' I replied, 'No, I've come this far, I'm not going back. We're going.'"

On the stormy trip out on the open sea, the boat passed what seemed like several hundred virtually identical pine forest and flat rock islands. "There were so many islands on this trip. I kept saying, 'Which one, Stig, which one?' 'There's a lot more to go.' I said, 'Oh, my gosh!'"

As if by a miracle, when the two men arrived at Viggsö, the clouds broke and the sun came out. Bernstein got off the boat and was greeted by Björn and Benny. The two composers were just about to move their piano to a small cottage in the grounds of Björn's house where they planned to hold songwriting sessions. Sid Bernstein, who barely had time to recover from the traumatic boat trip, offered to pitch in. Stig, Björn, Benny and Sid all struggled with carrying the heavy piano up a steep hill and into the songwriting cottage.

His back aching, the world-renowned impresario was introduced to Agnetha and Frida. Sitting down with the group and their manager, he listened to their music and talked things over. Bernstein fell in love with Abba instantly and felt the group's image would work extremely well on the American market. "I liked them all. The guys I thought were wonderful, the girls were lovely. Very feminine and sweet girls." Sid Bernstein returned to the United States with a three-year contract to represent Abba in his country. Stig told him afterwards that the fact that he wasn't above chipping in with the piano had been a deciding factor why they'd wanted to sign with him.

Over the summer, the 'Waterloo' single slowly climbed the American charts. Obviously, Abba would be required to fly over as soon as possible. They needed to meet the press and make personal appearances on television to help promote the single in the world's most important record market.

In reality, things were happening far too quickly for Abba at this time. Between mid-April and the end of May they visited several European countries for promotion purposes, including a visit to the town of Waterloo in Belgium. "If things start happening in the USA at the same time as we're working on Europe, well, then I don't know what we'll do," said an exasperated Stig. Things did start happening and what Abba did was to stay in Europe.

Björn and Benny were writing songs for the next album, which the group hoped to have in the shops before the end of the year. For Agnetha's part, she wanted to stay at home to be with Linda as much as possible. That was a valid enough reason not to go on promotional trips. To that was added Björn and Benny's roles as Polar Music house producers, which still took precedence over almost everything else. And then there were Frida and Agnetha's albums.

Despite the decision not to visit America in the summer, 'Waterloo' eventually peaked at a very credible number six position on the *Billboard* chart, eventually selling 800,000 copies. For now, Abba's presence in the US market seemed to be taking care of itself.

Stig Anderson was certainly rubbing his hands together in glee over this development. "He loved the fact that CBS had passed on the record, and that he gave it to somebody else," says Jerry Greenberg. "He could walk around and really give it to them: 'You stupid idiots in America, you could have had this!' "

But the conflict between the demands made on the group for promotion and their reluctance to leave Stockholm remained. A solution of sorts was reached in the summer, when Abba decided to make film clips of 'Waterloo' and 'Ring Ring'. It was a fortuitous decision which would have significant consequences, putting Abba at the forefront of a development in pop music that would not become fully felt until the mid-Eighties.

"Film clips" had been used to great effect by major artists like The Beatles since the mid-Sixties: make a short film of the group performing the songs and send that film out all over the world. The television companies get to show moving pictures of the artist, the group gets to stay at home – everybody is happy. These promo clips have, of course, been known as videos since the Eighties – nowadays all artists with serious chart aspirations make videos to accompany their singles, but back in the Seventies the film clips were merely a convenience for those who were reluctant to tour or, indeed, travel in general.

"We had a look at something called a 'promotion film' from a record company in America," recalled Björn. "It was one camera, one shot; very badly done. We said it must be possible to do a thing like this, but much, much better."

Budding director Lasse Hallström, who'd been making pop film clips for television since the late Sixties, was enlisted to help Abba with these productions. It wasn't actually his music experience that attracted the group to Hallström, but the short comedy skits he directed with two comedians at the time. These skits were much-loved by Swedish television audiences.

The budget for the Abba clips was minimal, and they were pretty straightforward films. Nevertheless, even at this early stage they were clear about one thing. "We wanted to do videos where they [the fans] could actually see us," remembered Björn. "There were many videos that were very, very obscure and artistic but you couldn't actually see the group at all."

At the end of September, Abba were finally persuaded to make their first visit to the United States, although it lasted only three days. A reception was arranged by the prestigious, Government-run Swedish Information Service, and was hosted by the Swedish consul to New York, Gunnar Lonaeus. Judging by the press Abba was getting, Sid Bernstein's hunch about the band was absolutely right.

Where Abba were reviled by parts of the Swedish media and the Music Movement for making "blatantly commercial" music, Americans weren't lumbered with any such preconceptions. Instead, many writers pointed out how rock had been evolving into a sometimes pretentious and grandiose art form. These critics seemed to perceive Abba as a breath of fresh air who added a Scandinavian slant to the Phil Spector and Beach Boys productions of the early Sixties.

"Abba's emergence is one of the most cheering musical events in recent months," wrote Ken Barnes in a review of the *Waterloo* album in *Rolling Stone*. Barnes pointed out the debt of 'Dance (While The Music Still Goes On)' to The Beach Boys' 'Don't Worry Baby', as well as the Byrds-guitar-like clavinet sounds on 'Suzy-Hang-Around'. "With their concise, upbeat pop creations, Abba is much closer to the essential spirit of rock & roll than any number of self-indulgent hotshot guitarists or devotional ensembles handing down cosmo-dynamic enlightenment to the huddled masses," the review concluded.

Other reviewers echoed his sentiments, opining that 'Waterloo' (the song) "slices through the morass of soul ballads and country cornflakes on the airwaves with laser beam ease", or hailing it as "the first real girly group-singing since maybe Martha [& The Vandellas'] 'Jimmy Mack' or some late Supremes stuff."

During their three days in the United States, Abba talked to the media and appeared on the children's television show *Wonderama*, as well as *The Mike Douglas Show* in Philadelphia. Sid Bernstein was adamant that they must play concerts in America as soon as possible, and Frida again expressed her eagerness to stretch out. "Sweden is a very small country," she said. "This [the 'Waterloo' experience] has been very successful; this is much more exciting."

The group was indeed planning US concert appearances in February or March 1975, but didn't want to commit to anything. "They are trying to do it so we could come here and be a headline group," said Benny. "We probably need another hit." Abba's second single on Atlantic, 'Honey Honey', was climbing up the charts and would eventually peak at a respectable number 27.

The 'Waterloo' single was released in a mind-blowing 54 nations, reaching number one in many European countries as well as South Africa. It was a Top Five hit on most other charts, but while things were looking up in the USA and elsewhere, Abba's fortunes in Great Britain were about to take a rapid downturn.

In Björn and Benny's hearts, the biggest moment of pride came when the song spent two weeks at the top of the UK charts in May. "It's just like an incredible dream," Björn told *Disc*. "It's always been our ambition to get a record to number one in Britain – it means more than a number one in the States to us. You see, for years Britain has been at the top – the headquarters of pop music."

So, how to follow this success? Many other countries decided to release 'Honey, Honey', as per Polar's own release plan. In the UK, Epic wanted it differently: even before 'Waterloo' was released, they had decided that they wanted to make a new attempt with 'Ring Ring' should the Eurovision entry become a hit. After all, this was the record that made Paul Atkinson want to sign them in the first place.

Atkinson suggested beefing up the recording by adding a bit of saxophone to remind listeners of the 'Waterloo' sound. Björn later admitted that they weren't exactly opposed to the suggestion. "In the early days there were quite a few suggestions from England on how things should be or not be. But in this case, I think we felt ourselves that we could give the recording a bit more punch."

With 'Waterloo' residing at number one on the UK charts in early May, Paul Atkinson flew over to Stockholm to oversee proceedings. The saxophone he requested was overdubbed, as well as an additional fuzz guitar, giving the song more of a rock edge. The recording was also slowed down a bit. Atkinson took the 16-track tape with him back to Great Britain to take care of the actual remix himself.

On June 21, this brushed-up version of 'Ring Ring' was released as Abba's follow-up single to their number one smash. The group spent a few days in London at the end of the month, trying to promote themselves and their new single. It didn't start well: a scheduled *Top Of The Pops* appearance had to be cancelled because of a technician's strike.

Although they appeared on many radio shows and did quite a few press interviews, it was to no avail. The remixed 'Ring Ring' did have some added forcefulness, but the saxophone overdub sounded superflous and out of place. Another UK visit in mid-August saw an appearance on *The Tommy Cooper Hour*, but it made little difference. The single reached only number 32 on the chart.

Meanwhile, the 'Honey, Honey' single was a Top Five hit in Germany, Switzerland and Spain, reaching the Top 20 in several other countries. To add insult to injury, the British duo Sweet Dreams also recorded a cover of the song. Released in the UK around the same time as Abba's 'Ring Ring' remix, their version of 'Honey, Honey' was a Top 10 hit.

While Abba had spent much of the summer relaxing after a fashion, they had also kept working very hard. Sessions for Frida and Agnetha's albums continued on and off, and Björn and Benny were busy with their Polar assignments. At the end of July, they set to work on yet another Hootenanny Singers album, *Evert Taube på vårt sätt* (*Evert Taube Our Way*).

The previous year's LP with the folk group, *Dan Andersson på vårt sätt* (*Dan Andersson Our Way*), was an organic effort that came to life as a collaboration between all involved. From the point of view of the members, it turned out to be one of their very best albums. In comparison, this year's production was marked by a lack of commitment from Andersson and Ulvaeus. With the pressure the producer pair was under, the Hootenanny Singers' album had become but one of many assignments.

"It was a ready-made product and we just came up to Stockholm and did our vocal overdubs," says Hansi Schwarz. "It wasn't an album that evolved within the group, but a Björn & Benny production with pre-written orchestral arrangements." It was the group's very last LP with Björn in the line-up, and today he doesn't even recall making it.

It was clear that Björn and Benny were mentally moving away from their roles as Polar Music house producers, saving their energy and long working hours for Abba. Songwriting sessions throughout the summer had produced ideas for a couple of new songs, and on August 22, recording sessions were started for the new album.

Abba were also making plans for their autumn tour. However, due to the many commitments and the explosion in interest in the group all over the world, much of what they had planned to do in 1974 turned out to be postponed. The tour, originally pencilled in for the last week of October, was rescheduled for mid-November. The album, which would be released before the end of the year according to optimistic predictions, acquired a new, indefinite release date in the new year.

The autumn of 1974 was an anxious time for the group in many respects. In terms of record sales, they had most of the European countries in a firm grip, but the British market seemed to be slipping out of their hands. The *Waterloo* album, which had been a European success of some measure, managed only two weeks in the UK Top 50.

In November, Abba released the first single from the recent sessions. 'So Long' seemed to be a safe choice: out of the five or so tracks that were finished so far, it was an up-tempo, shuffle rocker that adhered most closely to the 'Waterloo' formula. In Great Britain, no one was very impressed and the song didn't even chart.

Björn and Benny's hearts sank as the hotly coveted UK market seemed to slip from their grasp. "Groups like ours that had been tagged as 'Eurovision' were not meant to have more than one hit," recalled Björn. "We felt that 'they have decided that Abba are something which we simply aren't!' "

Epic's loyalty to the group declined rapidly as they failed to sustain the success of 'Waterloo'. It almost seemed the follow-up singles were released as a matter of courtesy and that everyone expected the group to disappear from the British pop scene in the manner of previous Eurovision winners from Continental Europe.

Abba had originally planned to visit London on their autumn tour, but those plans were cancelled as interest in the "one hit wonders" dropped dramatically. John Tobler, their press officer at Epic at the time, recalled meeting the group at their hotel during one of their UK visits. They were telling him about their plans for a concert at the London Palladium. "My response must have displayed guarded enthusiasm," recalled Tobler. "It seemed uncertain whether they could fill a bus, let alone the Palladium, but it would have been rude to say as much."

Abba still persevered with the remains of their tour plans. Surely, they would be a popular attraction in the countries where they had enjoyed such convincing success? At the end of the two-week trek, they would know.

Chapter 17

When Abba emerged as an entity on the pop music scene, the public and the media perceived them as the characters in a fanciful fairy story. They were two couples united in their love of one another and in the making of joyful pop music. All four lived in the same neighbourhood in an idyllic suburb, just like one big, happy family. It was an image perpetuated by Sweden's weekly magazines, which printed feature after feature stressing the group's togetherness. Over Christmas 1972, one magazine even published a big photo spread on the four friends, portraying them as if they were celebrating the holidays together, all dressed in red.

The first year in Vallentuna had indeed been marked by a certain togetherness. But Björn and Benny were no longer happy bachelor buddies, roaming the streets of the city and partying all night long. And Agnetha and Björn had become parents of a young daughter, giving their private lives a different focus than that of Benny and Frida. Also, as their popularity as a group increased, they were all working more closely than before, and the need to keep a distance off-hours became gradually greater.

"At the most, we borrow the lawn-mower from each other," Benny told a magazine in the spring of 1974. "Sometimes it's happened that we've gone to the movies together, but it's not like we're constantly running back and forth between our houses . . . We work too much together to stand each other after five."

The distance increased when both couples decided to leave Vallentuna. In October, Björn and Agnetha moved to a villa in the celebrity-infested suburb of Lidingö, while Benny and Frida acquired an apartment in Stockholm's picturesque Gamla stan district ("Old Town") a few weeks later.

Although Benny and Frida had joined the Ulvaeus and Anderson families on Viggsö and built a house there in the autumn of 1973, their chalet was on the other side of the island. It was a practical solution: they were close enough to get in touch when they needed to, yet sufficiently far apart not to have to sit in each other's laps.

The relationships within each of the two couples were sufficiently volatile without the extra tension of socialising as a gang of four around the clock. Luckily, whatever problems they had as a group had mostly been solved by the time of the 'Waterloo' breakthrough: the real ordeal had occurred during the *Festfolk* period three years earlier. "In the beginning there were a lot of conflicts," admitted Agnetha. "Especially on tour it's tiresome to socialise constantly. It's like a marriage with four people involved. But it's easier now that we know each other so well."

It's likely that this was also the period when the personal, out-of-working-hours relationship between Abba and Stig Anderson was beginning to wane. "The people that made up Abba are clearer in my memory than the music they made," said Gudrun Anderson later. "I remember Abba's emergence, how we'd all feel each other out in a fine spirit of community. In the beginning we socialised quite a lot, perhaps mostly with Benny and Frida. It was unbelievably entertaining when Frida and Stig's temperaments were up against each other – oh dear!"

When Abba finally embarked on their tour of Europe in November 1974, it had already been postponed at least twice. Since the 'Waterloo' victory, nothing had worked out as planned. "We're totally behind schedule," said Stig Anderson. "All our plans have collapsed. The Sweden part of our tour should have been over by now. We should have been on tour in England now. Our album should have been released. All the songs haven't even been written for that one. The tour of the United States has to be completely cancelled."

The group's extravagant plans for concerts all over Europe had been severely cut back. Dates in England, Scotland, The Netherlands, Belgium, France, Turkey, Israel, Greece, Yugoslavia and Spain had been abandoned, and only Germany, Austria, Switzerland and the Nordic countries remained.

The most heavily promoted reason for the shortened itinerary was that the group simply didn't have time. The full truth contained a few more shades: the Abba schedule was very cramped, certainly, but the lack of demand for a group with so few hits to their credit was an equally dominant factor. The five to six concerts that were planned for Great Britain, for instance, were simply not feasible.

Agnetha and Björn both felt guilty every time they left Linda and as a consequence insisted that the group should never be away for more than two weeks at a time. The solution was to split the series of dates in two parts: Denmark, Germany, Austria and Switzerland in November, the remaining Nordic countries in January.

The tour was arranged by promoter Thomas Johansson at EMA Telstar. The company was founded in the late Sixties and was rapidly becoming the leading concert promoter and booking agency in Scandinavia.

Anni-Frid "Frida" Lyngstad, the dark beauty with the wondrous voice, a mixture of fortitude and vulnerability born of a rags-to-riches life that defies belief. (*Retna*)

Frida and Ragnar Fredriksson, with their children Hans and Lise-Lotte, in late 1967. "I think I was looking for security," Frida later reflected.

Christina Grönvall and her children with Benny, Peter and Heléne, in October, 1966."Benny was terrified that it would be known that he was engaged and the father of two children," said Christina.
(*Sven-Gösta Johansson*)

Stig Anderson and his wife Gudrun, in 1974. Gudrun was the "mother figure" at Stig's Polar Music. (*bigpicturesphoto.com*)

"A fine and true romance": Björn and Agnetha mingle with the crowds after their marriage at Verum on July 6, 1971. (*bigpicturesphoto.com*)

"This was when we learned exactly what we should not be doing." Björn, Agnetha, Benny and Frida do their best on their failed *Festfolk* cabaret show, Gothenburg, November 1970. (*Bror Augustsson*)

Agnetha, Björn and baby Linda, shortly after her birth on February 23, 1973. "It was the happiest moment of my life," said Agnetha. (*bigpicturesphoto.com*)

The moment of triumph: Abba with Stig Anderson and conductor Sven-Olof Walldoff in his Napoleon outfit after winning Eurovision with 'Waterloo', April 6, 1974. (*Hulton Getty*)

Abba pose for photographers on the Brighton sea front after their Eurovision victory.
(*Popperfoto*)

Agnetha and Frida on stage at the Konserthuset in Stockholm, January 11, 1975.
(*Bengt H. Malmqvist/Premium*)

Abba in the studio in 1978 with Michael B. Tretow, their engineer, a key member of the recording team. "The first time I met Michael I felt that here was a guy that thought that this was just as exciting as we did," said Benny. (*Bengt H. Malmqvist/Premium*)

Benny with Polar recording artist Ted Gärdestad and Stig Anderson.
(*Bengt H. Malmqvist/Premium*)

Benny and Frida, and Björn and Agnetha relax on the island of Viggsö where they maintained holiday chalets and where many of Abba's best known songs were composed. (*Bengt H. Malmqvist/Premium*)

However, it's unlikely EMA Telstar would have managed to pull off a tour on this scale all on their own. Johansson had to draw on the expertise of Danish promoter Knud Thorbjørnsen, who at that point had more experience and important international contacts on the touring scene. Thorbjørnsen had promoted The Beatles' concerts in Denmark in June 1964, and had since become the European contact for The Rolling Stones and other major acts.

Thomas Johansson was to become one of Abba's most valued associates on their journey out into the world. The connection had begun with Björn and Benny, but Stig soon came to appreciate Johansson's personal qualities. He especially recalled an incident where he had been on the phone with the promoter, who found himself at a hotel where a visiting rock band was staying. Johansson mentioned, almost in passing, that the window had been smashed and a piano had been thrown on the ground outside. "Then I thought, 'This man is someone I must get to know better.' He was cool as a cucumber."

Johansson organised all of Abba's subsequent tours, and also accompanied them on many of their early promotional trips. Similarly, much of his experience and good reputation on the international music scene came from his association with Abba. Although seldom very visible in the group's entourage, he was one of its more important members, and the close relationship with the individuals has continued through the decades.

Abba had been working hard on preparing this the first large-scale rock concert presentation by a Swedish act. Their PA system was worth 200,000 kronor (£20,000) and the lighting equipment was especially imported from West Germany. It was the most expensive tour anyone from Sweden had ever attempted. Rehearsals kicked off at the beginning of October. Björn and Benny were scuttling between sessions for the new album and rehearsals in the auditorium of the Rudbeck school in the suburb of Sollentuna.

Agnetha and Frida visited choreographer Graham Tainton for two hours every day for two months, rehearsing their choreography and exercising to become fit for the hard onstage work. The collective weight loss for the group during the rehearsal period was 19 kilos, out of which the previously podgy Björn contributed no less than 11. "But now he's almost too thin," said Agnetha.

For the last ten days before the start of the tour, Abba shifted rehearsal locations to the Jarla Theatre in central Stockholm. By then, the group had assembled a programme of between 15 and 20 songs, a fair number culled from the as yet unfinished new album. One of the new melodies was the instrumental 'Mama', later released on record as 'Intermezzo no. 1'. A combination of rock and classical influences, the number was a popular showcase for Benny on this and every subsequent Abba tour.

Experiments in applying classical music to a pop format were very much in vogue at the time but although 'Intermezzo no. 1' showed a sense of musical ambition, this particular opus, along with other works in the same genre, have come to seem a little dated. Benny's classical influences were more effectively expressed in the shape of flourishes and fills on Abba's more hit-orientated pop songs.

The design of the stage costumes was handled by the firm Artist Dressing, which consisted of Owe Sandström and Lars Wigenius. Artist Dressing was Sweden's leading company in stage costume design at the time. Up to this point, the band members' own ideas had formed the basis for their costumes, and would sometimes do so in the future as well. However, from now on the input from Abba would mostly come from Frida, the member who took the greatest interest in this particular aspect of their presentation. She had been used to making her own garments for more than a decade and would discuss the different concepts with the designers, often contributing original suggestions of her own.

In the Sandström/Wigenius partnership it was mainly the former who contributed the ideas, while Wigenius provided the tailoring skills. For the rest of the decade, this pair would be responsible for the outrageous costumes worn by Abba, creating the image of colourful absurdity that has become permanently etched in the public's memory.

On the autumn 1974 tour, Agnetha wore a body-hugging white jumpsuit with flounces from the knees down and a green cape with ostrich feathers. Frida sported a similar cape, a white bustier and a mini skirt which was made up of 18 four-inch wide strips of cloth, designed to be teasingly revelatory during wild dancing movements. "Curiously, it was Agnetha's jumpsuit that attracted all the attention," recalled Owe Sandström. "That was the costume that gave her the tag 'the sexiest bottom in pop', while Frida's skirt, which was actually much more risqué, went virtually unnoticed."

Björn and Benny were both outfitted in tight, sequinned, blue trouser costumes, leaving room for displaying virtually bare chests if they so desired. Benny often opted to wear a tiger-skin jacket, but Björn had nothing more than a cape with which to shield himself. In hindsight, he has found it hard to come to terms with many of the costumes he wore during those days, singling out this year's tour outfit as especially repulsive. "For a while I thought, 'the more outrageous, the better'," he recalled. "Some of the things I wore in 1974 and 1975 are just insane. They are so ugly that nobody has ever been as badly dressed on stage."

While Abba have been singled out as a symbol for everything that smacked as bad sartorial taste in the Seventies, it is worth remembering that much of their inspiration came from contemporary British glam rock acts like Gary Glitter, The Sweet and Slade. "One mustn't take away the work that Owe and the others did," Benny noted. "They did just what we asked them to do."

By mid-November, the group was all set to go, finally on the verge of being able to confirm their popularity in the places they were visiting. But the signs were slightly ominous, even at the first concert in Copenhagen on Sunday, November 17. For their opening date, two gigs had been tentatively scheduled, should demand for tickets become exceptionally high. As it turned out, the group was some 150 seats short of selling out even the first performance in the 2,150 seater Falkonerteatret venue, and the second concert was scrapped.

Attendance aside, the show itself was a success, attracting reviews that ranged for the most part between good and excellent. By all accounts, their stage act was professionally executed both musically and visually. The dance routines got a mixed reception, however. "To be quite honest, the girl's dancing was a bit too ambitious: a strain both on them and the audience," wrote one reviewer.

Frida's ongoing transformation was quite remarkable. Just three years earlier she was noticeably inhibited on stage. Now she was all over the place – even go–go dancing on a podium – and was singled out by the reviewers as the biggest onstage attraction. While Agnetha confessed that she didn't especially enjoy performing in front of an audience, Frida had grown to love the interplay with an ecstatic crowd. "I think its dead fun being onstage," she said. "That's where I experience the happiest moments of my life. When I stand there I'm completely naked and open. I turn myself inside out and have nothing against exposing myself. I feel secure because I enjoy what I'm doing."

Alas, after the Copenhagen concert it was all downhill. It started with a small mishap. Someone at the concert agency had miscalculated the driving distance between Copenhagen and Hanover in West Germany, which was the next destination. To ensure that the girls arrived on time to wash their hair before the concert, they were dispatched with a Swedish media team. The rest of the entourage travelled in the bus driven by tour manager Hansi Schwarz, Björn's friend from the Hootenanny Singers.

Realising they were behind schedule, Hansi stepped on the gas with just a little too much enthusiasm, and 27 miles short of Hanover the bus was caught speeding. Björn, Benny and backing group The Beatmakers were delayed for half an hour before they could reach their destination, thus cancelling out efforts to catch up the missing time.

Arrival in Hanover didn't bring any encouraging news either: the concert venue, the 1,500 seater Kuppelsaal, had not been sold out. In fact, whereas none of the venues on the tour – with one exception – seated more than 2,800 people, not one single concert was played to a capacity house. The next stop was Munich, where Abba attracted 1,900, leaving more than 500 seats unsold – and so on.

It did seem that the gap between the Eurovision label that Abba had been tagged with and the "pop" credibility they so desperately sought was much too wide for their new-found European audience. "It was a bit of a crisis sometimes," recalled Björn. "We didn't even have a full house in Austria, even though we had had four or five hits there."

The group kept up a brave front on stage, but it was clear that the mood within the entourage wasn't especially happy. Tempers frayed within the couples, and interview comments didn't display much enthusiasm for the venture. "Eating is really the only fun you have on a tour like this," said Benny lamely. "You roam from place to place, from hotel to hotel, from stage to stage – and what you remember afterwards is what you've eaten in the different cities."

Michael Tretow was handling the tour sound together with Claes af Geijerstam. A reluctant traveller at the best of times, Tretow claims to have blocked out most of the trip. "After you'd stayed at the Hanover Hilton, the Frankfurt Hilton and then the Munich Hilton, it was just a mess of Hiltons. I only have two memories. At one of the hotels there was an automatic breakfast machine. You'd enter three coins and then instant coffee and a sausage came out of the wall. And then, at one of the concerts, there was a German father who came up to us and shouted, 'louder, louder!' while making a downward motion with his hand. It was awful."

There were certainly plenty of mothers and fathers in the audience during the tour: the average age of audiences was much higher than expected. Where Abba were expecting screaming teenyboppers, they got a much less ecstatic crowd around the age of 25 to 30. "Even though musically speaking the show started to rock every now and then, nothing much happened with the audience in their seats," noted one West German reviewer. "They sat there and hardly moved. Clap-along attempts and lets-get-excited efforts were quickly suppressed. The only reason Abba still managed to make it to the encore, was that the encore was called 'Waterloo', and that was, of course, what everybody had been waiting for."

The autumn 1974 tour was the only occasion when Michael Tretow was present to engineer the onstage sound. For someone who was madly in love with exploring the studio and experimenting with new and undiscovered gizmos, working with live sound was fairly pointless. "It was so hard to do anything with the sound that it was no fun at all going on tour," he said afterwards. "For me, touring is the major downside of what Abba are doing. I will certainly not be a part of this again."

As the tour progressed, disaster followed upon disaster. The concerts in Düsseldorf and Zürich – the only performance in Switzerland – were completely cancelled due to poor ticket sales. Frida was suffering from chorditis throughout the tour, and the concert in Wels, Austria, was cancelled to give her a chance to rest. Austria was also the scene for the most depressing attendance record: the Stadthalle in Vienna seated 5,600 people, but only 1,200 showed up.

"Touring on this scale was a fascinating experience, because it was something completely new for a Swedish act," says Hansi Schwarz. "But it was just too early for Abba to do a tour like that, they were too hurried to get on the road. In both Munich and Hamburg I remember giving away free tickets to fill up the venues a bit more."

Financially, it was clear that the tour had been a resounding failure, but the group had counted on this from the beginning. The tour was seen more as a promotion trip, although with so few people showing up the commercial worth has to be debated. It was with a sigh of relief that Abba returned home to Sweden on December 1.

Stig, who didn't see much point in touring in the first place, threw up his hands in exasperation. "Of course I want Abba to make personal appearances," he said, "but the disruptions in our production schedule that followed as a consequence of the tour were too huge. It's more trouble than it's worth. [We lost a great deal] when everything at home – recording sessions, songwriting, etc. – lay dormant while they were away."

Stig may have had a point. If Abba had been more readily available for promotion of the 'So Long' single – which was released around the time of their tour – it's likely it would have become a greater international hit. In Sweden, where almost everything that the group released stormed up to the top of the charts, it took two months after release until the song crept into the Top 20 – and then only after the group had performed it on television.

Meanwhile, Stig was out doing what he did best. Over the course of two weeks in November 1974 he visited several countries, relentlessly promoting Abba and making plans with local record companies. His zeal was remarkable and the international music business was truly amazed at what Stig and Abba had achieved during the year. Against all odds, he had managed to turn a Swedish pop group into an international phenomenon.

At the end of December it was announced that the American trade magazine *Billboard* had chosen him as one of 11 recipients of their Trendsetter Of The Year award. Only one European, Beatles manager Brian Epstein, had ever received it before. Stig, wrote the magazine in their announcement, was awarded because he had demonstrated "that Scandinavia can produce an internationally accepted act like Abba." None of the many awards, prizes and plaques he received over the years would make Stig prouder than this one.

One of the countries he visited on his long business trip in November 1974 was Australia, where Abba had been signed to a record contract the previous year. Both the 'Ring Ring' single and the album of the same name were released at the end of 1973. As usual, Stig didn't necessarily choose the record company that offered the biggest advance. He was more concerned about fostering a good relationship with the label, and he was shrewd enough to realise that a higher share of the royalties would offer better long-term benefits than a big, seductive advance. The first deal with RCA Records was signed against an advance of just $A1,500.

Stig was able to do this because he already had a successful business. Had he and his artists been in desperate need of cash, they could easily have fallen into the trap of accepting lower royalties and a short-term "handout". Instead, as contracts were renegotiated over the years, Stig would always prefer more royalty points over the lure of a big advance.

Many in the music business raised their eyebrows when Stig signed with different record companies all over the world, instead of simply letting one major label handle the group worldwide. That, however, was the whole point. Stig's theory was that no company could be strong in every territory in the world. Therefore, Abba's sales figures might be better served by working with the label that had the most impressive presence in each market. There was the matter of rivalry, with each major label competing against the others to prove it was superior to the rest, a situation that could only benefit Abba, especially as their global popularity escalated.

"We decided that this was the best way, although it was time-consuming," says John Spalding. "It would have been so easy to have done what The Bee Gees did and give it all to PolyGram for the world and then start moaning about all their accounts afterwards: 'Where is this and where is that?' Our agreements were direct between Polar and these other companies and that really paid off."

Stig wanted to sign with companies that really liked Abba and were prepared to work hard to promote them. However, this system also meant that Polar had to have individual relationships with a myriad of companies, entailing a lot of extra work for everyone. Just to deliver masters for singles and albums to all the different companies the world over could be a gigantic undertaking. "We had to do some 25 different shippings every time instead of giving the one master, say, to CBS and you'd make copies and run with it," recalls Spalding. "We wanted to make it work, and it did. But there were a lot of late nights."

The contracts would usually run for three years at a time, which was also beneficial for Polar. As the contract neared its end, Stig and John would be aware of quirks that were specific for that territory and could see to it that the contract was adjusted accordingly for the next term. Abba's consistent popularity was obviously also working in their favour. "We were lucky, because we were always going good at the end of the three-year period," says Spalding. "We had a situation where we could raise things. We could either ask them for more money or get some better clauses in the contract. Some artists don't last that long, so when the renewal comes up they'd not even be asked to renew. We never experienced that with anybody."

Just as Stig placed a high premium on loyalty from those who worked with him, so he extended a similar loyalty to those he enjoyed working with and who had been generous to him over the years. When the *Waterloo* album was released in Great Britain in May 1974, the different publishers who had given him good copyrights over the years were rewarded with publishing rights to cuts on the album. Two tracks ended up with United Artists, which was still run by John Spalding, and a further four with Spalding's own Bocu Music. However, the remaining six tracks all had different publishers. It was certainly a most unusual way of doing business. "He gave it to them for no advance and for ten years," says Spalding. "He was very fair on things like that."

ATV Music, who'd been given 'Honey, Honey', certainly tried to make the most of their acquisition. It was their record company arm, Bradley's, that put together the Sweet Dreams duo and released the UK Top 10 cover of the song. That was just fine with Stig: Abba's recording was never a single in Great Britain, and so it didn't present any competition. He was doubtless less pleased when the Sweet Dreams version was released in the United States as well, at the same time as Abba's own single. Atlantic president Jerry Greenberg relished the challenge.

"Jerry sent in all of his troops to beat the Englishmen," recalled Stig. "He personally called 25 very influential disc jockeys at the larger radio stations, explained that 'Honey, Honey' by Abba was a given hit and advised them to place the song on their playlists." As a result, Abba's version entered the Top 30 on the chart, while Sweet Dreams peaked at number 68.

The loyalty and personal relationships with associates the world over sometimes paid off in even more manifest ways. At one point, when the time for a payout to Polar was imminent, Managing Director Robert Cook at RCA Australia gave Stig a call. "He said, 'Look, we're gonna send you your money early,'" remembers John Spalding. "'Ooh, that's nice, why is that?' 'Well, I think they're gonna devalue the Australian dollar in about a week's time.' And that's exactly what happened. He sent all that money out and we made a bit of a killing. I don't know how he knew. I've told the story to other Australians, and they say, 'I wish he'd have told *us!*' It didn't make any difference to him – it was the same amount that went out – but we got a much better exchange rate."

After 'Ring Ring' had a brief look-in at the tail end of the Top 100, 'Waterloo' became a number four hit in Australia in 1974. It was clear that this was a potentially lucrative market for Polar. Stig's trip down under at the end of 1974 was ostensibly to promote Abba, but he also took the opportunity to drum up interest in some of the other Polar acts, like Svenne & Lotta, Ted Gärdestad and Lena Andersson.

Svenne & Lotta had joined the Polar roster in the autumn of 1972, and enjoyed a huge Scandinavian success with a covers album the following year. Ted, Lena and the duo – all of whom were produced by Björn and Benny – had rapidly become the next most popular acts on the label after Abba. Stig managed to secure an Australian release of Svenne & Lotta's versions of 'Dance (While The Music Still Goes On)' and 'He Is Your Brother' on a single.

In the autumn of 1974, Svenne & Lotta were in the midst of recording their second album for Polar. With Björn and Benny busy with their Abba commitments, they had been handing over much of their production chores to other producers, although they were involved in this album as well.

Björn, Benny and Stig had been invited to submit a composition for the Swedish selections for the 1975 Eurovision Song Contest. There was never any talk of Abba appearing in the contest again, so Svenne & Lotta were instead given this chance of valuable international exposure. A song called 'Bang-A-Boomerang' from the ongoing Abba album sessions was rewritten and reworked a bit, and submitted to the selection jury. On February 15, the selections were held in Gothenburg. Unfortunately, Svenne & Lotta finished only third in the competition, so they couldn't compete in Eurovision.

At this point Stig, Björn and Benny made a strange decision. Instead of letting the song remain an exclusive Svenne & Lotta recording and pushing it for all they were worth, they decided to put their own vocals on the track and include it on the new Abba album. At the same time attempts to break Svenne & Lotta abroad continued, and their version of 'Bang-A-Boomerang' was issued as a single in Australia and several European countries. "But when our single was finally released the DJs said, 'ah, but this is just an Abba cover' and threw it aside," says Svenne Hedlund. "We'd charted with our cover of Dion's 'Sandy' in Austria and done some television in the Benelux countries, so things were happening there. And 'Bang-A-Boomerang' would've done even better." As it was, apart from Scandinavian success, Svenne & Lotta's version didn't make many international waves at all.

It's unclear exactly why it was necessary for Abba to make the song their own. Presumably, they didn't want to let a catchy track go to waste, but it also seemed to suggest that Abba's success was already threatening the careers of Polar's other acts.

Svenne & Lotta's original version of 'Bang-A-Boomerang' was recorded just days before the second, Scandinavian leg of Abba's tour commenced in Oslo on January 10, 1975. This part of the tour was considerably more successful than the trek to West Germany and Austria – the concert in Gothenburg sold out its 7,000 capacity quite easily – and restored some of the group's confidence.

Expressen journalist Mats Olsson, in his review of the Oslo performance, was responsible for Agnetha's "sexiest bottom" tag. Writing about her "enormously tight, white overalls" he noted that "Suzi Quatro will have some competition for the title of 'the most handsome backside in pop.'" From there on, the comment snowballed until the matter was brought up at virtually every Abba press conference over the next few years.

The concert at Stockholm's prestigious Konserthuset was a nervy affair. The house was full of friends, relatives and music business colleagues. In addition, Sid Bernstein had flown over to assess the group's onstage appearance. Much was at stake that night for Abba. Everything went well, except for a mishap during 'King Kong Song'. At one of the percussion breaks in the song, one of the girls started singing in the wrong place. Artists and backing band fell out of synch with each other and the song just collapsed. "It's the worst onstage moment that I have ever experienced," Björn remembered.

Despite this mishap Sid Bernstein was impressed and became even more eager to promote Abba in the United States. "They are among the best in showbiz right now," he told a reporter after the concert.

The group's own enthusiasm was more muted. Against Stig Anderson's wishes, Abba had announced that they would tour the Swedish *folkparks* in the summer. But after that, they said, it was unlikely they would ever do any major tours again. "First of all you have to do a lot of rehearsals," said Björn, "and life on the road is much too hard. Financially, the losses are so huge that you hardly make ends meet."

There can be no question that the long *folkpark* treks undertaken by Björn and Benny during the Sixties had killed any enthusiasm they might have had for touring. They wanted to remain at home in Stockholm and devote their energy to creating music in the studio.

By the last week of February, Abba were back in the studio for the final sessions for the new album. Even by Abba's previously swift standards – the *Waterloo* album was virtually completed in three months – it had been ludicrous to expect the group to have their third album out before the end of 1974 when sessions only commenced at the end of August.

By this time Abba's level of ambition had risen considerably, and the new album was the first to be produced according to the group's "it'll be ready when it's ready" philosophy. Whereas sessions for previous albums hadn't produced any unreleased recordings, the track listings included one or two songs that perhaps would have been left in the can had there been more time to write and record new material for those projects. Now, however, Abba's working situation had changed in several ways. "The success with 'Ring Ring' and 'Waterloo' means that we don't have to be as serious as we used to be," said Björn and Benny. "There is time enough to play around. We can afford to do that."

Michael Tretow had left his employment at Metronome Studio and was now working at Glen Studio, owned by arranger and producer Bruno Glenmark. The competition with other labels for the use of the Metronome Studio had been fierce, with only one day per week allotted to the various companies, but Abba were able to book Glen Studio extensively for their explorative sessions. Unlike at Metronome, Michael Tretow now had the right to freelance on the side if he so desired, which allowed for even greater flexibility. There was no question that Björn and Benny wanted Michael as their engineer.

Glen Studio was where most of the new album was to be recorded, but it wasn't always to benefit the end results. Benny later complained that the acoustics at the studio, which was located in the basement at the Glenmark family home, weren't exactly the best. "The recordings [we did there] almost never turned out that well," he said, feeling that the sound on a Glen Studio track like 'So Long' was "much too hard and sort of 'steely'."

Even before Abba went out on tour they had scrapped no less than four songs from the sessions. The pressure was on to move forward, to come up with something new, to develop their songwriting and production. No longer was there any room for tracks that felt weak. The group was fiercely determined not to become a one hit wonder, nor did they want to release albums with just two hits and a lot of filler material.

"Obviously, we can't get by on the strength of 'Waterloo' much longer," said Björn towards the end of the sessions for the new album. "We're aiming at becoming a good album act . . . Our [previous] LP got good reviews in the USA, so I think that we'll be able to make it in the future. We won't say no to a hit single, but we don't want to go in for singles to any great extent."

The new album, simply titled *ABBA*, was released in Sweden on April 21, 1975. It was an instant success, entering the charts at number one and staying there for the better part of the year. It was clear that the group's new-found ambition had paid off: the LP was a giant leap forward and the first to truly showcase Abba as an entity with the potential to leave an imprint on pop music history.

The opening track, 'Mamma Mia', the last song to be written and recorded, gave a clear indication that Abba were finding their own voice, and were much less dependent than before on earlier influences. Many of the aesthetics they had picked up along the way remained – filling the musical spectrum with sounds à la Spector, harmonising vocally in the vein of The Beach Boys – but Abba were now using their very own tools to apply them.

In many ways, Abba created music that suggested that the past ten years hadn't happened: genres such as psychedelia, progressive rock and heavy metal were virtually untraceable in their output. Instead the group's music recalled some of the innocence of early Sixties pop, adorned with a framework of modern production techniques. It was a form of displacement that was both effective and unexpected in the popular music landscape at the time.

As a song, 'Mamma Mia' was expertly structured and arranged, and no aspects of it suggested that its creators were anything less than in full control of their craft. The possibilities of the recording studio were explored for all they were worth. On the spur of the moment, Benny decided to try playing a marimba that was in the studio to "find out what that sounded like". The verdict was positive and the tick-tocking marimba figure became one of the identifying factors of the 'Mamma Mia' recording.

Michael Tretow, always stimulated by the lust for discovery and refinement in the studio, grabbed the opportunity to try out new tricks and methods. For 'So Long' he placed the guitar amplifier in the Glenmark family's tiled pool hall, using it as an echo chamber. On 'Man In The

Middle' he fed the sound of Björn singing the phrase "in the middle" through one of guitarist Janne Schaffer's effect boxes.

Michael's sound ideal at the time was current American soft rock records made by the likes of James Taylor, The Eagles and Fleetwood Mac. "They were certainly more of an ideal than the English records, which I felt sounded much tinnier and rattling," he said. "We were exponents of our time: everyone within the recording business wanted as much hi-fi as possible; high quality and forcefulness. Everything should sound good and strong and well-defined."

Abba and Michael were on a journey together, but the developments they pioneered were taking place on all levels within the group. As a solo artist Agnetha had been impatient, wanting to go into the studio, do her vocal overdub and then get out. Now she was beginning to realise the value of working long hours just to get everything to sound exactly right. "When I first met her, Agnetha was singing off-key quite a lot," says Michael Tretow. "But with Abba she was given a musical guiding that alerted her. Björn and Benny were like her musical mentors, and she realised the importance of working an extra half hour on one single note. It was something that was awakened in us all when we discovered that it was possible to do proper records, when we all pulled ourselves out of the *schlager* swamp."

To Michael's way of thinking, Frida was already an expert performer when Abba came together. "She was in charge of her craft from the beginning, but with Björn, Benny and Agnetha there was a parallel development – they were like their own little entity moving upwards and forwards within this system."

The downside of the long hours in the studio, and the insistence on constant retakes, was the strain they put on the relationships within the couples. According to some onlookers at the *ABBA* sessions, the air turned blue at the language used by Agnetha and Frida when Björn and Benny demanded that yet another vocal detail should be adjusted. "[Frida and I] are alike in one respect," admitted Agnetha at the time. "We are easily irritated and both of us get fired up equally quickly, even if it fades away just as swiftly. But perhaps Frida has more patience – that's something I lack completely! This is not a problem between the two of us. Rather, it's between me and Björn that the conflicts can arise, and between Frida and Benny. Obviously, it can sometimes be difficult to both live and work together."

It wasn't just because the group didn't want to be disrupted in their work that they seldom allowed journalists to visit them in the studio. "We don't want people to get the wrong impression of us, so we firmly turn down all requests of recording session features," said Björn. "Of course we fall out every now and again. Especially when we're doing the vocal overdubs – sometimes there can be four different opinions on the best way of doing it."

A specific source of conflict was the boys' insistence on pushing the girls' voices up to the highest register, almost beyond their capacity. "Sometimes they'd drive us crazy, because there was always that demand that we should be singing way up," recalled Frida many years later. "When you are couples, like we were, you say what you think in a way that you perhaps wouldn't do otherwise."

Benny in particular was adamant about the high register sound, almost to the point of "obsession", as Björn put it. One of Benny's childhood favourites was the girls' choir Postflickorna (The Post Girls) who conveyed a softer variation of that sound on their records. This fondness for soprano choirs might have had some bearing on Abba's working methods. However, Benny had also learned an important lesson way back during the time when Elverkets Spelmanslag became part of Guy & The Turks for a few gigs. The manager for Guy & The Turks, Silas Bäckström, was rehearsing the act when he suddenly stopped the proceedings.

"He said, 'No, goddamnit, that's the wrong key, you need to raise it!' " Benny recalled. " 'What do you mean, raise it?' 'Well, you've got to place a song so that you get way up. The singer should be forced to sing for all he's worth, with the highest note on the max.' 'Uh-huh, okay,' we said. And that's something I've remembered through the years. With Abba, the girls were always on the max. The highest note was as high as they could manage, and then the rest was adapted to wherever that note was. It gave everything some kind of extra energy."

As an Abba recording technique, it had been emerging step by step on the *Ring Ring* and *Waterloo* albums: on the third album this philosophy was applied with full force for the first time throughout a whole LP. With the multi-overdubs of the vocals, it certainly did make for a rich and energetic sound.

This layer upon layer of the girls' harmony vocals, and the "third voice" that emerged through their combined forces, quickly became one of Abba's most important trademarks. Indeed, the choral backing was mostly recorded before the lead vocals, underscoring their importance for the combined vocal soundscape. It may sound surprising, but producing these complex textures was apparently a part of the recording work that was concluded fairly quickly.

"I guess we were quick learners and also pretty talented," Frida reflected later, "and of course we acquired a certain working routine over the years.

Also, when we were in the studio, we worked very hard from nine o'clock in the morning until lunch, and then continued until we dropped, as it were. There was a lot of improvisation going on[.] When you kept hearing the melody over and over again, you started getting these little ideas for a suitable harmony phrase or something."

There was no question that *ABBA* was the group's strongest effort to date. The equilibrium between male and female vocals had been abandoned, and Björn had only two leads on the album. The first, 'Man In The Middle', is quite possibly the weakest track on the collection: a plodding attempt at a funky feel that falls far short of its intentions. 'Rock Me', featuring Björn imitating Slade's Noddy Holder, was better, an adequate representation of Ulvaeus lead vocals on the album.

The girls had many strong collective tracks, but Frida was awarded only one solo number. 'Tropical Loveland' had a fine melody, although the attempt at a reggae feel was somewhat misguided. Even Frida herself has called it "a pretty uninteresting song".

As far as solo parts were concerned, it was clear that the album belonged to Agnetha. The ballad 'I've Been Waiting For You' was a knock-out track, a multi-layered tour de force where Agnetha sounded as if she was constantly on the edge of falling off key, thereby demanding the attention of the listener from start to finish. But the absolutely strongest recording on the album was 'SOS'. This was Agnetha's first "heartbreak classic", where her ability to "cry with her voice", as Michael Tretow once put it, met a hundred per cent match in the gorgeous melody and Benny's semi-classical keyboard flourishes.

Here, the voice that had first captivated an audience by declaring that she "would own millions if tears were gold" was finally given a framework worthy of her abilities. The moog and guitar riffs that run throughout the song were only added at the last minute, when Björn and Benny stayed back in the recording studio late one night. It would be a while, though, before 'SOS' got the chance to capture the imagination of the world's pop fans. When Abba released the second single from the sessions, just before the album hit the shops, they made another choice.

'I Do, I Do, I Do, I Do, I Do' was a recording heavily coloured by the *schlager* music of Björn and Benny's youth. The saxophone sound, and, indeed, the song itself, was a tribute to American bandleader Billy Vaughan, who'd hit it big in Europe in the late Fifties. The melody was strong enough, but as a production the track hasn't held up too well. Here was a rare occasion when the insistent wall of sound aesthetics worked to Abba's disadvantage: combined with the high-register singing the recording feels like a laser drill on the eardrums.

The single met with widely opposing fates on the world's major music markets. In Great Britain it did very little to restore interest in the group, bettering the performance of 'So Long' by at least entering the charts, but its peak position of 38 was still unimpressive. It was clear that Abba's status as a Eurovision one hit wonder was hard to overcome. The *Melody Maker* review of the single – "so bad it hurts" – didn't exactly help.

While the Swedish left-wingers dismissed Abba on the grounds of being politically incorrect, the British media were just as guilty of rubbishing them for what they perceived as their embarrassing image. The judgement of the reviewer in *Disc*, for example, was certainly clouded by preconceptions. There's no other way to account for the absurd claim that the only good tracks on the *ABBA* album were 'Bang-A-Boomerang', 'I Do, I Do, I Do, I Do, I Do' and 'So Long'.

Even UK record company support seemed to be lacking in a most blatant way at this time. "When 'Waterloo' was a hit, we were driven around in a Rolls-Royce, and put up at a first class hotel," recalled Björn. "Then, for every single that bombed, we got picked up at the airport by a gradually less classy car and were put up in a gradually less classy hotel. That's how crass it was."

At the end of April, Abba teamed up with Lasse Hallström to make four promo clips of the songs they felt had the strongest hit potential on the album: the current single, 'I Do, I Do, I Do, I Do, I Do', was an obvious choice, along with 'Mamma Mia', 'SOS' and 'Bang-A-Boomerang'. These four clips were the first Abba promos since the previous year's films for 'Ring Ring' and 'Waterloo'. Despite the enormous promotional value of the music clips, Lasse Hallström was never permitted extravagant budgets for his work with Abba. Polar as a company was notoriously tight with its money, and Stig would question each and every krona that was spent.

For Hallström, many of the assignments for Abba actually meant filming two songs on the same day. That had been the case with 'Waterloo' and 'Ring Ring', and it was also true of his latest efforts. The combined cost for the four films was less than 50,000 kronor (£5,500), infinitesimally small potatoes compared to the lavish video budgets that have been the industry standard since the Eighties.

Fortunately, Lasse Hallström had been used to making the most of modest resources ever since he'd started putting together short pop film clips for Swedish television. Whether it was local Swedish acts or guesting foreign rock stars, Hallström had one or two hours at the most to complete his films. Necessity being the mother of invention, he'd become skilled at coming up with unusual ideas and mastering the art of editing to create some kind of visual excitement.

These new Abba clips were the first to present the iconic video image of the group, establishing many of Lasse Hallström's typical trademarks. The 'Mamma Mia' film, for example, introduced the frequently used close-up shots of two members, one of whom was shown in profile. Hallström also began grouping the four individuals in different combinations of pairs, contrasting one against the other. 'SOS', meanwhile, made full use of Agnetha staring sadly into the camera, as she would in numerous other films throughout Abba's career. The concerned faces of the other group members, along with shots of bare trees, helped underscore the song's melancholy feel.

When the clips were made, Abba had already visited several European countries for personal television appearances, and would continue to do so for the rest of the spring and the early summer. The four film clips were primarily made for far-off countries that were just too inconvenient to visit, such as Australia and New Zealand. They were fresh off the editing board when they were dispatched to Australia and shown on television, just as intended.

But not even Stig at his most confident could have predicted the impact that these simple screenings would have in that corner of the world.

Chapter 18

Stig Anderson protested wildly, but Abba were adamant: they were going to tour the Swedish *folkparks* in the summer of 1975. They felt they owed it to the Swedish audience to compensate for the cancellation of the previous summer's dates. Stig's agenda was somewhat different, however. He wanted the Andersson/Ulvaeus team to write new Abba hits and let some of their magic rub off on other Polar acts.

Björn and Benny had already cut down drastically on their outside production chores. After working on sessions for Svenne & Lotta parallel with the last few tracks for the *ABBA* album in February and March, they would produce no one outside Abba for the next few years. The one exception was Ted Gärdestad, still only 19, for whom they felt a certain responsibility. Besides, he wrote all of his own material, and therefore made no demands on them for songs.

In truth, the group's enthusiasm for the tour was also somewhat muted. Except for Frida, they were all in agreement on the pointlessness of the excercise. Björn and Agnetha, as before, worried about leaving Linda at home while they were away but in the end they decided that it was best that she didn't come along with them. Agnetha was so dismayed at the prospect of further live engagements and long periods of separation from her daughter that she wanted to put a permanent stop to it. "I can promise you that this will be the last Abba tour," she told a reporter.

The 14-date trek around the country commenced on June 21 and was scheduled to continue until July 7. The itinerary had been carefully planned so as to cover the whole of Sweden, from the northernmost areas to the south. No one was going to be able to complain that Abba didn't come to their part of the country.

The programme was basically the same as the tour of Europe, with two numbers replaced by their latest singles, 'I Do, I Do, I Do, I Do, I Do' and 'SOS'. The Beatmakers again handled the backing, augmented by guitarist Lasse Wellander, who'd begun his association with the group on the *ABBA* album. Henceforth, he would take over from Janne Schaffer as the band's main session guitarist.

During the tour, Abba were seen by a total of 100,000 people. At the amusement park Gröna Lund in Stockholm, the 19,200 spectators broke records for a Swedish pop act. No tickets had been sold in advance – concert-goers simply had to pay at the entrance to the park – and the mad rush to see Abba live created unexpected traffic chaos in the central parts of the city.

Before the tour commenced, the *folkpark* arrangers had been shocked by Abba's demand of a guaranteed sum of 15,000 kronor (£1,650) against 60 per cent of the admittance fees. It was unprecedented in Swedish show-business history, but Stig Anderson was well aware of the group's worth at this point. "In the USA it's not unusual with 70 per cent among the biggest names," he ascertained. "We've been offered 60 per cent over there, so that's what we'll charge at home as well."

Due to this wise decision, the 1975 *folkpark* tour earned Abba 500,000 kronor (£55,000) and as a whole, the 1974/1975 touring eventually made a profit. But after expenses, there was only 250,000 kronor (£27,500) left for the four members to share, which could hardly count as a major success. For Abba, touring was always going to be a matter of goodwill and promotion.

"There is only one place on earth where you can earn any money on touring, and that's the United States," Björn remarked. "Possibly Australia also. There you have the arenas for 20–30,000 people that are needed if you're going to make a profit. In Europe there is no touring pop group that makes any profit."

The summer tour attracted the same favourable if not wildly enthusiastic reviews as the previous autumn/winter trek. Some old-timers were a bit overwhelmed by the sheer ambition of the show with its soap bubbles and fireworks; a far cry from the usual straightforward, small-scale, 30-minute *folkpark* performances.

Abba's professionalism was applauded, but their somewhat stilted stage appearance was seen as a let-down. Of course, among the reviews there were also a few classic examples of Abba-bashing. "In an artificial cloud of neon, Abba appeared onstage and disappeared in the same way. Afterwards these four people seemed just as unreal and elusive as the smoke that stayed behind at the stage," began one insightful highlight.

"A perfect show with well-directed spontaneous laughter and musicianship. Nothing personal that could disturb Stig Anderson's consummate hit products," the review continued. "Abba are the *schlager* broilers of the computer age. The songs are built on simple harmonies and multinational repetition . . . 'I love you', Abba sing and point towards the audience. But it's a lie. Abba don't love us. They love the 20 kronor they can steal from us when we've been swept away by the Abbamania and lose our grip on reality for an hour."

As usual, Abba were far too busy with the logistics of the tour to be bothered by such criticism. Two concerts had to be cancelled and re-scheduled at the tail end of the trek. Agnetha, who had long suffered recurring throat problems, had been feeling unwell since the end of the rehearsals. Ten days into the tour she got hit by an infection of the respiratory passages and was taken to hospital with a temperature of almost 40° Celsius.

The doctor told her not to sing for at least a week, but after only two days rest she was back on her feet again. It wasn't until just before noon on the day of the concert in Malmö that the doctor finally authorised Agnetha's appearance. She was still not well, but the show must go on and she took a plane down to perform at Abba's 9 p.m. concert.

Agnetha remembered this particular show as her worst onstage experience ever, calling the performance "a nightmare. My legs were shaking and 10 minutes before going on stage I broke down in tears in the dressing room. Luckily, I managed to keep going until the end of the show. Our doctor . . . was waiting backstage in case something happened to me."

Minutes before she was due on stage she still hadn't applied her make-up, but finally she managed to pull herself together. She knew that cancelling simply wasn't an option at that stage. The experience did little to alter Agnetha's already dismissive feelings about further touring. Even as early as her first *folkpark* summer back in 1968, nine engagements in the middle of the tour had to be cancelled when Agnetha suffered throat problems. It was clear that something had to be done about this problem in the near future.

At the end of the *folkpark* tour Abba retreated to Viggsö for a few week's seclusion. Meanwhile, things were stirring elsewhere in the world. The recent promo clips were doing a much better job as a representation of the group than they could have imagined.

In 1974, a one-hour TV show called *Countdown* started airing on the government-owned ABC network in Australia. It was hosted by Ian "Molly" Meldrum, and as the title suggested it featured a countdown of the week's Top 10 on the charts – a sort of Australian version of the British *Top Of The Pops*. *Countdown* also included performances of new songs that were thought to have hit potential on the Australian market.

After the success with 'Waterloo', a Top Five hit in August 1974, Abba's fortunes in Australia had been mixed. 'Honey, Honey' had reached number 30, but the singles that followed had made only brief appearances in the mid to low regions of the Top 100. However, on July 7, 1975, 'I Do, I Do, I Do, I Do, I Do' entered the Australian charts at number 83, starting a slow climb up towards the Top 10. The interest of the producers at *Countdown* was piqued when the song began to take off in the local Brisbane charts. This was a good enough reason to feature it in the programme.

Full-time colour television had arrived in Australia only a few months earlier, and the show was desperate for any kind of programming in colour. For a one-hour broadcast like *Countdown* it was inevitable that some of the features were filmed. Those acts who took the trouble to supply clips of their songs therefore stood a good chance of having them aired on *Countdown*.

The show's producers contacted RCA Australia to find out if there was a film clip available for 'I Do, I Do, I Do, I Do, I Do'. RCA had received copies of the four recent films that Lasse Hallström had directed, and these were now submitted to the show. The *Countdown* producers took a look at the clips. The song they had asked for was wonderful, certainly, but there was another song that seemed even more catchy and commercial: 'Mamma Mia'.

'I Do, I Do, I Do, I Do, I Do' was screened nationally on August 3, and 'Mamma Mia' the following week. The response was incredible: requests for repeat showings of 'Mamma Mia' flowed in, and although it wasn't a single, the clip was shown again the week after.

The combination of catchy pop music and arresting visuals caught the attention of *Countdown*'s mostly pre-teen audience. The tick-tock opening of 'Mamma Mia' effectively pulled them into a song that was simple and direct with easily understandable, clearly pronounced lyrics. Agnetha and Frida looked like a pair of dolls, two slightly surreal beauties in outlandish costumes – the same that had been used on the 1974/1975 tour – while Björn and Benny came over as fresh and healthy male support, backing up the women on guitar and piano.

The clips were one hundred per cent in accordance with the group's philosophy that they should be clearly visible. And not only that: the Abba members were not facing sideways or posing with an attitude, they were looking straight into the camera, their eyes interlocking with the viewers. Both the music and the visuals were invitingly bright – it was as if Abba were made for colour television.

Indeed, the group's image was based on accessibility. Despite Benny's years with The Hep Stars, none of the Abba members had any great affinity with rock star attitudes. While their peers were experimenting with soul-searching, introspective rock as the Sixties turned to the Seventies, Björn, Benny, Agnetha and Frida were out doing cabaret shows. Their credo was to entertain and make everyone feel welcome and included: "we aim to please" was the motto.

Australian fans went into record shops, asking for the 'Mamma Mia' single – but there was no single to buy. Polar had just selected 'SOS' as the next single from the *ABBA* album, and didn't want to issue any further tracks. When RCA Australia asked for permission to release 'Mamma Mia' locally the reply was, surprisingly, a prompt no. "Our resistance was because the Australians had already released so many goddamn singles," said Stig Anderson. "We felt that we were over exploited."

The four clips hadn't necessarily been made to promote individual tracks, but were meant to create interest in the *ABBA* album as a whole. As Stig knew very well, the big money was to be earned through album sales. If they kept on releasing singles, he reasoned, interest would be directed away from the more profitable album.

Still, the demand wouldn't die down, and RCA persisted in their requests to release the song. Finally, Polar relented, allowing 'Mamma Mia' to be issued as a single. The fact that a clip had been produced for the song indicated that Polar was aware of the strength of the track, and now they were forced to conclude that it would be foolish to persist in their refusal. "We wanted to find out what the potential of 'Mamma Mia' was, how strong it was," Stig recalled.

What happened next was nothing less than amazing. With 'I Do, I Do, I Do, I Do, I Do' just having entered the Top 10 after its 12th week in the chart, 'Mamma Mia' appeared just outside the Top 50 at the end of September.

On October 13, 'I Do, I Do, I Do, I Do, I Do' hit the top of the charts, remaining there for three weeks and lingering in the Top 10 for a further month, having been replaced at the top by 'Mamma Mia', which occupied the number one position for a staggering 10 weeks. Meanwhile, 'SOS' was also released as a single in Australia, and with 'Mamma Mia' still at number one, 'SOS' parked itself at number two for four weeks. When 'Mamma Mia' finally gave up its top position, 'SOS' hit number one for one week, before settling at number two for a further four weeks. In addition, the *ABBA* album had been racing up the charts, going on to spend a total of 12 weeks at the top.

It's difficult to explain this rapid and phenomenal acceptance of Abba in Australia. Other countries also lapped up the group with great enthusiasm – the strong songs, the expertly executed arrangements and productions, the vocal and visual appeal of the girls – but it was still nothing compared to the reception on the part of the Australian public.

The short timespan within which the three number one singles were released was probably an important factor: for five or so months Abba's presence on radio, television and the charts was constant. They seemed to be coming up with catchy new songs at a breathtaking pace, even if those tracks had simply been taken from the *ABBA* album.

The continued exposure on a high-profile television show like *Countdown*, which had a two million viewer rating, also meant that it was hard to escape Abba. In the country regions, there were only two channels available: a commercial one and the ABC, which hosted the show. At the same time, there was still an enigma surrounding the group: despite their inviting and accessible image, information about them was scant and superficial.

It was as if their success during the final months of 1975 was taking place in a universe parallel to the rest of the pop and rock scene. While Abba were enjoying their 14 week run at the top of the singles charts, coverage on them in the leading Australian music magazines at the time, *Juke* and *RAM*, was negligible. Except for chart listings, Abba didn't appear in *RAM* at all from August to December. *Juke* mentioned Abba only once: as part of a competition where the group was pictured and readers were asked who they were and which country they came from. Abba were even ignored in the magazine's list of nominees for best act of 1975, nor were they a prediction for biggest act of 1976.

At one point during the same period, the daily music column of the Melbourne paper *The Sun* noted with some disinterest that Abba had "the two top spots on the [charts] for the second week in a row". At the end of the year, the column somewhat lamely pointed out that Abba's contribution to the 1975 pop scene was to prove that "there is still a place for good time rock'n'roll". There was no mention whatsoever of their almost saturation-style presence in the country's music landscape.

This lack of media coverage created a tension between Abba and their Australian public, which served only to heighten the interest in this mysterious group from the other side of the planet. The audience could spin their own fantasies around Abba's slightly unreal, almost too perfect appearance. The absence of information even gave birth to a couple of bizarre rumours: Agnetha and Frida were supposedly not the real singers, but just two attractive models hired to mime to the records.

Much has been made of Abba's status as pop video pioneers. Although they were not the first to do promo clips – as has sometimes been stated – they might have enjoyed an advantage in that virtually all of them were made by the same director, giving the films a uniform look in terms of editing style and visual aesthetics.

Also, they were certainly pioneering the art of promotion through massive television exposure. With the exception of groups such as The Monkees and The Partridge Family, whose music was marketed through especially created television shows, the Abba/Australia phenomenon was probably the first instance where a pop act achieved superstar status solely through pre-filmed television performances of their songs.

Abba's image was also perfectly acceptable to older generations, meaning that they were welcomed by parents and even grandparents. Not only was the group perceived as "nice and clean" compared to other more rowdy rock acts at the time, but their two couples image portrayed them as symbols for healthy family values. "To adults, it's a pleasure to be able to enjoy watching a group their youngsters like, a group without unpleasant gimmicks like pop star Alice Cooper's killing chickens," wrote one Australian reporter. "With Abba, adults can feel reassured because their young are watching two nice clean-cut heterosexual couples."

"Abba have introduced new people to record-buying – we're getting people right across the board, who've never bought records before," said a record shop assistant.

Whatever it was that the Australian public craved from their music idols, it seemed Abba had it in abundance. They were the first group since The Beatles to have three singles simultaneously in the Australian Top 20. The analogy with the British Fab Four was appropriate. What happened in Australia mirrored the way The Beatles had knocked out the American audience with a well-placed appearance on *The Ed Sullivan Show*.

While all this was happening, Abba had already started tentative work on their next album, in between promotion engagements all over Europe. Simultaneously, Agnetha and Frida were putting the finishing touches to their long-running solo albums, while Björn and Benny were also producing sessions for Ted Gärdestad's fourth album.

Apart from Ted, and to some extent Svenne & Lotta, Polar were allowing acts to falter as their energy was devoted to advancing Abba's career. Teenage discovery Lena Andersson is a good example. Lena had achieved her breakthrough in 1971 with a number two single and Top 10 album. Only 15 years old at the time, she had a high, clear voice, which, coupled with her blonde and innocent looks, made her a sort of Swedish version of Mary Hopkin.

In the spring of 1972, she'd achieved yet another major hit with the Andersson/Anderson/Ulvaeus song 'Säg det med en sång'. Her first two years as a recording artist had seen the release of three albums, the latter two of which were produced by Björn and Benny. After that, however, things had slowed down considerably. It was partly because Lena herself wanted to devote a bit more of her time to studies, but it was also clear that she was sliding down Polar's list of priorities.

In the autumn of 1975, she'd had no album out in three years, and her only recent hit of any note had been her Swedish cover of Abba's 'Hasta Mañana', which reached number one on *Svensktoppen*. Certainly, anyone would be happy to get the chance at an Andersson/Ulvaeus song at the time, but this move bore all the signs of a stop-gap hand-me-down, rather than being a part of any long-term career development plans for Lena.

"Not much has been heard from her, and that's our fault completely," admitted Stig Anderson earlier in the year. "We've had our hands more than full with Abba, Svenne & Lotta and our other artists. Unfortunately, we haven't devoted the time that we should to Lena. It takes time to write songs and find other good material that suits a particular artist, and we have had no opportunity to do that in Lena's case. But now we will get a grip on ourselves. We'll make a new album with her."

Even after this public pledge, no new album was forthcoming, nor even any domestic single releases. Instead, Lena was sent to the studio to record further cover versions of Abba songs, this time in German, which gave her a few hits in West Germany. Meanwhile, her career in Sweden came to a standstill. It wasn't until the spring of 1977 that a new album was released – but it went nowhere on the charts and turned out to be her last record for Polar.

"There was no time to work with the other artists in the way that should have been done," says Berka Bergkvist. "There was also the problem, as new producers took over from Björn and Benny, that although the recordings were good, they didn't quite measure up to their standards. Abba was the yardstick, everything we did was supposed to sound as good as they did. If Svenne & Lotta released an album, you could always hear exactly which tracks Björn and Benny had been involved in."

Andersson and Ulvaeus were still under incredible pressure. Not only were they responsible for Abba's career and required to take part in all the promotion as full-time members, but they were also expected to spread their fairy dust on recordings made by other Polar Music artists.

Everything was continually postponed. In August 1975, the group began working on tracks for their next album, but the sessions saw only the completion of one recording. It would take another six months before they had the time to concentrate on the project in earnest. The equation didn't work out: after the completion of Ted Gärdestad's album the following spring it was 100 per cent Abba.

Parallel with developments in Australia, things were finally starting to look up in Great Britain. In September, 'SOS' entered the UK charts, eventually reaching number six at the end of October. The group felt vindicated. "The strongest memory I have of 'SOS' is that it was the song that brought us back in England," said Björn many years later. Indeed, there can be little doubt that this was Abba's first truly classic pop single.

'SOS' was also making progress in the United States, prompting Abba's second promotional visit to the other side of the Atlantic in November 1975, though, as yet, no concerts were on the agenda. America beckoned, but there were specific problems to contend with, the most obvious being their lack of profile. Jerry Greenberg's enthusiasm aside, the fact that they were signed to Atlantic Records gave them an unfortunate image problem on the strictly classified US radio. "On the radio stations that primarily play middle-of-the-road music we've encountered some resistance," admitted Stig Anderson. "They are wary of the Atlantic label, they believe that the record must necessarily contain heavy rock or black soul."

Abba also had a problem with LP sales in America. They had been successful with their singles, but it had proved difficult for them to cross over to the albums market. Despite the positive reviews for the *Waterloo* album, it had only managed to reach 145 on the *Billboard* chart. Again, the problem was largely down to radio formatting. Abba were considered a "pop" singles act for AM radio, and were shunned by the album-oriented "rock" stations on the FM network.

Atlantic was aware of the problem and was hoping that things would turn around with *ABBA*. After release in August, however, it had yet to appear on the charts two months later. The record company's advertisement in the trade press reeked of desperation: " 'SOS' – the single Top 40 DJs are taking home with them. From *ABBA* – the album progressive rock DJs are taking home with them."

Sid Bernstein's hopes of arranging a 25-date, three week tour for the group earlier in the year had been quashed, but his enthusiasm was still high. "Abba are going to be major superstars after this visit to America," he said. "Their records have already been selling here, but their real chance at a breakthrough comes now when the big audience gets a chance to see what they look like."

Bernstein had secured appearances in several major television shows, *The Merv Griffin Show*, *Don Kirshner's Rock Concert*, *American Bandstand* and *Saturday Night* (the precursor to *Saturday Night Live*) among them. Despite this exposure not much changed for Abba in the United States. 'SOS' eventually reached a respectable number 15 position on the *Billboard* chart, but the group still failed to capture the albums market.

The "progressive rock DJs" mentioned in Atlantic's ad may very well have taken home their free promo copies of *ABBA*, but despite continued positive reviews, public interest in the LP remained low. Although vastly superior to *Waterloo*, *ABBA*'s chart performance was far less impressive: it spent three weeks in the Top 200, reaching only number 174. It was hugely disappointing for the group, especially since they were so desperate to be taken seriously as an albums act.

Abba did get a kick out of finding themselves in the middle of the American showbiz scene, however. While their motives were consistently questioned in their own home country, it was refreshing to be in an environment where success was applauded. "They have an altogether different attitude towards music in the USA," said Björn. "There is much more respect for those who actually make it. They are very much aware of the tough competition."

Meanwhile, back in Sweden, the attacks and the mauling continued unabated. In September, a 30-minute documentary on Stig Anderson was produced for Swedish television. The title of the programme was *Mr Trendsetter*, a reference to the Trendsetter Of The Year award Stig had received from *Billboard* earlier in the year.

The programme was produced with full co-operation from Stig, and set out to depict an ordinary week in his life: at the office, at home, out at Viggsö and on travels across Europe. "Our aim hasn't been to do a programme of cheap nastiness, but just to describe Stig Anderson's reality as it appears to him," said producer Rolf Nordin, presumably with a straight face.

To anyone watching the documentary it was clear that the producer's agenda was altogether less honourable. The programme opened with a sombre-sounding woman reading a text. "Music used to belong to the people," the viewer learned, "but then someone discovered that it could make you rich." All the while, "genuine" folk-style music was playing in the background. Later on Stig was filmed performing his own 'Tivedshambo', accompanying himself on acoustic guitar. Reaching the end he plays the wrong chords, and immediately asks for a retake. But no retake was included in the programme – instead, the fluffed performance, including Stig's request, was screened. Another long sequence featured Stig out jogging in slow motion, while a kitschy synthesizer version of 'Honey, Honey' played in the background. At the end of the film, a slightly tipsy Stig is filmed talking about the current left-wing tendencies in the Swedish cultural climate. His speech is intercut with the camera sweeping across drink glasses.

Viewing the documentary a quarter of a century later, it is hard to understand why so much energy was devoted to discrediting someone who was, after all, a relatively minor player on the music scene. It speaks volumes about Stig's perceived influence on the entertainment industry and demonstrates clearly how controversial a figure he was to many people.

Around the same time, a huge victory was scored by those who opposed everything that seemed blatantly commercial or trivial. When Abba triumphed with 'Waterloo' at the Eurovision Song Contest, the Swedish Broadcasting Corporation were obliged to arrange the 1975 competition in March. Held in Stockholm, the contest attracted wild protests, demonstration marches and even an alternative festival. A song called 'Doing the omoralisk schlagerfestival' ('Doing The Immoral Song Contest') was recorded, containing defamatory couplets like, "And here come Abba, dressed up in plastic, just as dead as tinned herrings/They don't give a damn about anything, just want to make a quick buck." Stig got a line of his own, naturally, and was described as "a cynical swine".

At the time, he was engaged in televised debates with people like Roger Wallis, head of the *progg* label MNW, who was adamant that Sweden should pull out of the contest. Again, with the perspective of time, it is hard to comprehend how something so trivial as the Eurovision Song Contest could evoke such anger.

Combined with a reluctance to win the contest again – it had been quite expensive to arrange the 1975 broadcast – the influence of the left-wing protestors ensured that the Swedish Broadcasting Corporation withdrew completely from the 1976 Eurovision Song Contest. It was a triumph over the contest, but was also seen as a blow against Abba, its most famous exponents.

Apart from Stig's frequent appearances in the media, raving and shouting against those who opposed him, the reality was that he and Abba didn't take much notice of what was going on. For one thing, they didn't have the time: they were preoccupied with production and songwriting commitments, and the business aspects of their enterprise were growing ever larger and more complex every day.

Being the sole owner of a music empire was a mixed blessing for Stig. The road to riches had been lined by tragedies, with two of his closest business associates, Robert Bosmans and Bengt Bernhag, both taking their own lives.

Bosmans' death led to Stig assuming complete ownership of Bens Music, which gave him the foundation he needed to expand the publishing side of his business. When Bengt died, Stig gained absolute control of Polar Music. With the Swedish record market growing by 35 per cent between 1973 and 1974, and the recent international success of Abba, it was turning into one of his most profitable companies.

Though he much preferred to control everything himself there was a team player side to Stig, and he saw the value of rewarding those who were important assets to his companies. On April 1, 1975, 50 per cent of the shares in Polar Music were transferred to Harlekin, the company set up in the late Sixties to handle Björn and Benny's income from their work as musicians and performers. It was Stig's way of giving something back for the pair's considerable contributions to his success.

"From the beginning we discussed whether Björn and Benny should have a share in the company," he said. "'If our collaboration turns out well we'll raise the issue again in a few years,' I said when they first started working for me. And it turned out that we complement each other very well. It often happens that we have differing opinions, but we discuss everything and try to convince each other. The three of us must always be in agreement on a decision." At the same time, Stig bought Björn and Benny's 50 per cent in the publishing firm Union Songs. At the stroke of a pen, the business ties between the three had become closer than ever before.

In the summer, the Sweden Music group of companies moved to refurbished new offices in one of the more upmarket areas of central Stockholm, where several embassies were located. The building and the address, Baldersgatan 1, became symbols of the ever-expanding business empire that was controlled by Stig Anderson.

Many believed at the time that the Abba fortune had enabled Stig to cough up the 2,475,000 kronor (£247,500) for the building, originally the residence of the founder of a large Stockholm department store. At this point, however, not even the royalties from the sales of 'Waterloo' had reached their accounts. It was Stig's successful publishing business that paid for the house.

Except for the two top floors of the four-storey building, which Sweden Music rented out to an insurance company, the house was occupied by Stig and Abba. Björn and Benny's offices were located on the ground floor, alongside a room where Agnetha and Frida could practice their jazz ballet. Stig, Gudrun, Görel Johnsen and Berka Bergkvist made up the hub of the organisation on the first floor, handling the administrative side of the enterprise. Gudrun, still looking after the companies' finances – together with two assistants – also handled the Abba members' private affairs.

Sweden Music and Polar encouraged a family spirit and Gudrun became a sort of mother figure for everyone who worked there. Employees would talk of the offices as a second home. "It doesn't feel like work," reflected

Görel Johnsen, "it's more like a way of life." "Many of us were in our twenties, had moved to Stockholm and perhaps didn't have much else going on," explains Berka Bergkvist. "We didn't have any relationships, so we stayed behind at the office where we had a lot of fun. Whenever we did something, we did it together. We were all pretty tight."

Polar and Sweden Music employees were always invited to Christmas office parties and midsummer celebrations out on Viggsö, which led to a unique sense of community. "That was the difference between Polar and other record companies: we had a family feeling they didn't have," says Berka. "For the other labels it was just work, because they were so big and had so many different departments: marketing, advertising and so on. At Polar, we would take a hand in most everything."

In all this, Gudrun was the one who looked after the staff, helping them with their problems and seeing to it that they didn't overwork themselves. "Stig didn't always have the time, he was out on a race of his own. But she would always take time out to have a talk; she was the one who'd say, 'Right, it's time for lunch' and things like that."

As 1975 drew to a close, Agnetha and Frida were finally able to release their solo albums. Sessions for both projects began 18 months earlier, but Abba's success in the meantime meant that the albums had to be recorded in breaks between group commitments.

Frida's album, *Frida ensam (Frida Alone)*, was first out on the market and reached Swedish record shops on November 10. Produced by Benny, it was an eclectic mix of Swedish language covers and one or two tracks of domestic origin. The earlier concept of an LP of folk-style songs written especially for Frida had been dropped along the way.

In terms of style, the new album was a radical departure for Frida. She'd reinvented herself, eradicating the old jazz *chanteuse*, housewife and mother of two and substituting a new persona, a modern singer and high-flying pop star. Distancing herself completely from the material she previously released on EMI, she stated: "*En ledig dag* [the first song she recorded] is one of the few of my early singles that I can bear listening to these days. The rest I'd rather forget."

Frida ensam saw Frida tackling everything from country hits, such as 'The Most Beautiful Girl', to The Beach Boys' classic 'Wouldn't It Be Nice' and even David Bowie's 'Life On Mars'. "On the album I've included a lot of things that I wanted to do, but was unable to sing with Abba because we're a group," she said. As a whole the album was excellent, a fine showcase for Frida's ballad style and the interpretative skills she had acquired over the years.

With Benny as producer, there was the inevitable risk that Abba's sound and style would colour the album to a large extent, and to avoid this Agnetha was deliberately not asked to contribute backing vocals. Similarly, only one track on *Frida ensam* was an original composition, written by Björn, Benny and Stig. 'Fernando' had been recorded at the time of the first sessions for the forthcoming Abba album, but was originally intended only for Frida's LP. The track was never released as a single in Sweden, but quickly became the most popular song on the album, topping the *Svensktoppen* chart. As a result, those who wanted a copy of 'Fernando' had to buy *Frida ensam*, which occupied the number one spot on the albums chart for six consecutive weeks the following spring.

Agnetha's album, *Elva kvinnor i ett hus* (*Eleven Women In One House*), had also been a long time coming. While the first four years of her recording career saw one LP per annum, four years had now elapsed with only three singles and a compilation album released. Abba's career, and taking care of her young daughter, had given Agnetha plenty to do, and this accounted for some of the delay. An additional, more important, factor was that she didn't want to rush the songwriting this time around.

Agnetha was hoping that this album would be a less lightweight project than her previous efforts. The love-lorn, starry-eyed teenager, performing a mix of sad Connie Francis-style ballads and German *schlagers*, was gone forever, replaced by a married woman and mother in her mid-twenties with plenty of experience under her belt. Recent interviews had seen Agnetha cite singer/songwriters like Carly Simon, Elton John and Carole King as her influences. Her ambition was to create something more personal and substantial along those lines for her own new album.

Her unwillingness to write lyrics led to experienced wordsmith Bosse Carlgren collaborating on the new project. He had been one of the contributors to the *Festfolk* show, and was also the only outside writer to contribute to Abba's 1973 *folkpark* tour. His first lyrics for Agnetha were written for three of the songs on her last album, *När en vacker tanke blir en sång*, back in 1971.

Carlgren lived in Vallentuna, so when Agnetha and Björn moved out there in 1972 they began socialising on a more regular basis. At one point he suggested a concept that would mean they collaborated on the whole album, specifically 12 songs which each represented a different female character. The idea was presented to Agnetha in January 1974, and received a favourable response.

The original suggestion for the artwork was quite grand, involving a gatefold sleeve with drawings by Carlgren that introduced each of the 12 different women. The concept allowed for a degree of creative freedom, for Agnetha to step outside of her own personality, yet retain enough of her own point of view to give the album a personal feel.

The album was slowly pieced together between Abba engagements over the next 18 months. Agnetha had been working on new melodies since 1972, and the close collaboration with Bosse Carlgren turned out to be perfect for her. Her songwriting method was most unusual. She would take the lyric sheet from another artist's album and use those words as the starting point for her own melodies. "[On her demos] you can hear some lines from Simon & Garfunkel, or a Paul Simon song," recalled Carlgren. " 'I hear a song to this one,' she would say." Out of these songwriting sessions came ideas that usually formed the basis for the final lyrics. Agnetha's English demo title 'The Boy Is Waiting' turned into 'Och han väntar på mej' ('And He's Waiting For Me'), while 'Come Into My Garden' became 'En egen trädgård' ('A Garden Of My Own').

The new album was Agnetha's final obligation to Cupol Records, which had merged with CBS a few years earlier. As the project progressed, Abba's career was exploding and Cupol knew that Agnetha would be leaving them when the contract expired at the end of 1975. As Agnetha involved herself more with Polar and Abba, so her relationship with Cupol deteriorated.

The first fruits to emerge from Agnetha and Bosse's collaboration for the new album was an English-language song called 'Golliwog', recorded in the spring of 1974. It was issued largely because Cupol hoped to capitalise on the new-found pop audience Agnetha had attracted through Abba, the thinking being that a track like this could become a hit on the *Tio i topp* pop chart. The song failed to make an appearance there, but, against Agnetha's wishes, the label decided to release the song abroad. "I couldn't stop them," she said.

As time passed the label began losing interest in the album project. "It became so small in comparison to what had to be done for [Abba's] international career," recalled Bosse Carlgren. "We had to fight to get the album completed and we couldn't get the money to make it as advanced as we really wanted to . . . It was a dream for both of us to get this album afloat. For a while it was like, 'What will happen? Will we ever finish it?' We didn't want to jeopardise that because it really was important for her to do her own album, not just to be another Abba member."

The ambitious gatefold sleeve plans were abandoned: Bosse Carlgren and Agnetha had to settle for a simple sleeve with photographs of the singer on the front and a generic apartment building on the back. Also, the 12 tracks were reduced to 11, one of which was Agnetha's solo version of 'SOS', included at the insistence of the record company.

"She was, at first anyway, disappointed," remembered Bosse Carlgren. "She had wanted it to be her own music through and through. Maybe it came to the point where everyone told her, 'If you want to make this solo album you've got to have a well known Abba song on it because we want to sell records' . . . It didn't fit into the concept with the women living [in a house], the character gallery of women with different types of personalities. It's more of an ordinary pop song lyric. This one is a very anonymous person."

The Swedish lyrics for 'SOS' were written by Stig Anderson, who also had a hand in the English original. As business commitments took precedence, his lyrical output had diminished drastically in recent years, slowing down to a point where he would contribute words to Andersson/Ulvaeus songs only. His lack of interest in lyric writing was reflected in the Swedish lyrics for 'SOS' : where once he would come up with inspired storytelling, often with a clever punchline, the lyrics for 'SOS' were workmanlike and dull, relying on simple solutions and an archaic vocabulary that jarred against the song's modern pop sensibilities. It was certainly not worthy of him, nor of Agnetha.

Ironically, through its Abba connections, 'SOS' was probably the song that initially sold *Elva kvinnor i ett hus* after release on December 1. It was the opening track on the album, and was also its first hit single, reaching number four on the chart. The rest of the album, however, made clear that Agnetha had undergone an extraordinary development. She had produced the album herself, relying on Michael Tretow's engineering experience to get everything exactly as she wanted, and had truly come into her own as a writer and performer. The melodies were original and inventive, varied throughout the album, yet with a uniquely personal touch that gave the album a pleasing consistency. Agnetha had mastered the art that every ambitious composer strives for: making songs sound as if they had been born in the moment, without being blatantly derivative or predictable.

As Michael Tretow has pointed out, working with Björn and Benny had evidently been inspirational for Agnetha. Whereas her early songs hadn't shown many signs of serious editing, the last few years had seen her working much harder on her compositions. "All of a sudden my demands on myself have become so high," she said halfway through the sessions for the album. "Everything has to be perfect and I write a lot of songs that I just throw away. I believe I have ten half-finished songs that I don't want to complete."

Similarly, Bosse Carlgren's lyrics lent a special quality to the songs. If Stig's words for 'SOS' were anonymous and boring, Carlgren's ministories gave Agnetha something to emote on, and he managed to structure them so that they seemed to be Agnetha's own thoughts. It was a collaboration, but it didn't take away from the personal statements in the songs. *Elva kvinnor i ett hus* didn't sound like any other Swedish pop album.

At the time, the reviews were mixed, however, and the concept of Agnetha acting the part of different women on the album was wildly misinterpreted. Some reviewers felt it made the album less personal, and one of the songs even raised some controversy. 'Tack för en underbar vanlig dag' ('Thanks For A Wonderful Ordinary Day') was about a naïve girl giving thanks to the Lord for all that had happened to her during the day: everything from finding a nice pair of shoes to getting a leaflet advertising a good price on coffee in her corner shop.

The song was meant to be ironic, a wry comment on the implausibility that any such woman could exist. Of course, in the Serious Seventies the song was taken literally, as if Agnetha and Bosse really thought that people should give thanks for such trivial occurrences. One newspaper even argued that the song was part of a religious "wave" in popular music that tried to exploit God and Jesus for commercial gain. Admittedly, the earnestness of Agnetha's delivery lacked traces of irony – perhaps this was a case when her ability to infuse songs with believability was just a little too convincing.

The album spent a total of 26 weeks in the chart, eventually peaking at number 11. Although total sales were less than half of Frida's album, which sold 130,000 copies, it was still Agnetha's greatest commercial album success so far.

Of course, neither of the girls could match the phenomenal achievements of Abba. By the end of 1975, the *ABBA* album had sold 450,000 copies in Sweden, a figure that in itself broke the previous domestic sales record set by the *Waterloo* album.

Taking into consideration that neither Agnetha nor Frida did very much promotion for their albums, the sales figures were certainly more than creditable. In the spring of 1976, Frida was scheduled to appear on a television show, performing songs from her album, but Benny, Björn and Stig advised her against it on the grounds that Abba's group image needed to be projected at that point.

It was a disappointment for Frida, and it seemed a somewhat unnecessary decision. "In Sweden people knew who we were from the beginning, before Abba got together, and that's why it's okay to do solo albums on the side," she pointed out. However, she acknowledged that it could be a little confusing with solo projects and group albums from the same people. Just as Björn and Benny abandoned their outside production work, henceforth Agnetha and Frida would also concentrate completely on Abba.

Agnetha viewed the closure of her Cupol contract, and with it the motivation to come up with new solo material, with mixed feelings. Certainly, juggling her main responsibility for Linda's upbringing and the demanding Abba career was difficult enough without having a third commitment hovering over her. "Whenever I'm abroad I promise myself that I'm going to devote all my time to Linda when I return home," she said during recording of the album. "But once I'm home I have to write songs, and that takes time. Linda cries, pulls my trousers and wants me to come and play with her. Then I put her in my lap and sing with her."

At the same time, she was forced to abandon her own ambitions as a songwriter. Without the incentive of an album project as a work in progress, it was unlikely that Agnetha would be able to sustain any enthusiasm for composing, especially now that the demands on her were so overwhelming. As most songwriters will testify, it is dangerous not to write on a regular basis – the muse needs to be kept alive through constant work – but at this point, it was a sacrifice she was prepared to make.

With the release of *Elva kvinnor i ett hus* taken care of, Agnetha had other issues to confront. A week after the album hit the record shops, she finally checked into hospital to have her tonsils removed, maintaining complete silence for two weeks after surgery. Although she feared that the operation would change her voice, she came out of the experience unaffected.

While Abba were taking a break from most public appearances, the success of 'Mamma Mia' in Australia had prompted its release as a single in the other major markets as well. It proved to be an intelligent decision, for the song restored the group to the top of the British charts for the first time since 'Waterloo'. The statistics were no less impressive in other countries.

Meanwhile, Björn and Benny were putting the finishing touches to the one track they had begun recording for Abba in the summer, its working title 'Boogaloo'. With Abba's somewhat conventional European background, they often found it difficult to apply the right kind of dance rhythm to their music. While they all admired soul and funk, they were well aware of their limitations in reproducing this kind of feel. 'Man In The Middle', from the *ABBA* album, was a good case in point: a "funk" attempt that failed to come off.

'Boogaloo' seemed to call for a dance rhythm in the backing track, and for inspiration they listened hard to George McCrae's disco classic 'Rock Your Baby', thus managing to find the right feel. Both Michael Tretow and session drummer Roger Palm were fond of the drumming on Dr John's 1972 *Gumbo* album, and this elastic New Orleans ingredient was now applied to the dance groove they were putting together. As a final touch, Björn fed his electric guitar through a tape echo, thereby lending some metronomic structure to the proceedings. The basic backing track of drums, bass, guitar and piano was ultimately completed to the satisfaction of the two songwriters.

When Benny played the recording to Frida at home, she was captivated, so much so that she broke down in tears. Agnetha recalled how they all "knew immediately it was going to be massive". Clearly, this song was going to move people, one way or the other, but the icing on the cake came from Stig who gave it the title 'Dancing Queen'. He also wrote the original set of lyrics, but in all likelihood these were later extensively rewritten by Björn. Work on the track continued throughout the autumn and early winter.

The recording of 'Dancing Queen' had started at the same time as Frida's 'Fernando'. It didn't take long to realise that 'Fernando' was also a cracker of a track – it simply had too much hit potential for a Swedish-language only solo release. Without further ado, it was decided that this would be turned into an Abba recording as well. Stig, who wrote the original Swedish lyrics, sweated for several weeks over the right title, but like his words for the domestic version of 'SOS', the rest of the lyrics showed signs of having been dashed off in an afternoon. The title didn't inspire him to come up with anything better than an ordinary love story: the girl of the song directing herself to the brokenhearted Fernando, again with a choice of words that sounded a bit old hat.

For the English lyrics, Björn invented a completely new theme. "After thinking a while," he recalled, "I got this strong vision in my head of two old revolutionaries in Mexico, sitting outdoors one night, reminiscing." It was an obvious way to go, but it had completely eluded Stig.

Björn had picked up a trick or two from Stig in terms of lyric writing, always acknowledging his knack for coming up with catchy song titles, but by now the apprentice had surpassed the master. The only difference may have been that Björn devoted more time to his craft, but the fact remained that Stig's lyrics were no longer very imaginative.

By the start of 1976 *ABBA* had been pretty much milked dry of singles, and it was high time to release one of the brand new recordings they had in the can. Both 'Dancing Queen' and 'Fernando' were completed, mixed and ready to hit the shops. There could hardly be any better illustration of the roll the group was on at the time. It echoed the situation in which The Beatles found themselves a decade earlier, when they had to decide whether John or Paul's song should go on the A-side of their upcoming single release.

Although they knew there is no such thing as a guaranteed hit, Stig,

Björn and Benny were optimistic about both songs. Indeed, the hit potential of the two recordings was so great that most acts would have given their right arm just to get one of them. But the trio could afford themselves the luxury of sitting back and juggling between them: they were both theirs, and it was only a matter of which to release first.

"Björn and I felt that 'Dancing Queen' was the best thing we'd done," recalled Benny, "but Stig didn't see it as an option to release that one before 'Fernando'. Not that 'Fernando' is a bad song, but maybe it was a bit too much of a *schlager*, and Björn and I felt that 'Dancing Queen' was such a progression." Berka also recalls the discussions. "I believe it was a strategic decision. The previous single was 'Mamma Mia' and they decided to break the trend from an up-tempo song and go for a slow song, instead of releasing two up-tempo songs in a row. There was a lot of tactic in that, a lot of smartness."

'Fernando' was chosen as Abba's next single and was issued in March in most countries, shooting to the top of the charts almost everywhere. Bass player Mike Watson recalled an incident on a trip to England for a *Top Of The Pops* performance: "We were picked up by a limousine at Heathrow and driven to a really nice hotel. When we arrived, Frida and Agnetha refused to stay there. The record company had to quickly find rooms at another, even nicer hotel." Watson interpreted this as Abba's "revenge" after Epic's lack of faith in them during their earlier slump.

Because 'Fernando' had originally been released as a Swedish solo recording by Frida, the plan had been not to release Abba's version at all in Scandinavia.★ It was as if they naïvely underestimated the combined power of Abba and their own strong songs. "I guess we'll be forced to release it, even though Frida has already done it," sighed Björn. "If people hear it played on Radio Luxembourg, there might be some here who want it as well." One or two people were indeed interested in the song. On release in April, the group version of 'Fernando' shot to number two on the Swedish chart.

By that time, Abba had already returned home from their first visit to Australia. Their clever strategy of sending out promotion clips to far-off countries, so that they wouldn't have to visit those places in the flesh, had backfired on them. Instead of appeasing the demand for the group in Australia, the clips had created an interest in the group that bordered on frenzy. The Australian public just couldn't get enough of Abba, and the trip had brought their popularity to a new, unprecedented level.

★ Due to the lack of Top 40 radio in Sweden, which meant limited airplay for hit music, many of Abba's biggest singles were never released in their home country. They were usually issued in the rest of Scandinavia, however.

Chapter 19

The telegrams, telexes and telephone calls flooded in. It was late 1975, and Abba and their manager were beginning to realise, much to their bemusement, that they had suddenly become the most popular act in Australia. Their local record company, RCA, was pleading with them: "You've just got to come here!"

The group refused to go. It was too far, too long, too much. They wanted to stay at home in Sweden and work, be with their families, take care of business. And despite their reluctance at performing live, they'd already made tentative plans for a concert tour in Australia later in 1976. That would have to be the time for their first visit.

But the requests just refused to die down. Soon afterwards, television companies started calling as well – they wanted to produce a special completely devoted to the group. That was when Abba finally relented: it was an offer too good to refuse.

In mid-January 1976, while the group was in London promoting 'Mamma Mia' on *Top Of The Pops*, they met with representatives of production company Reg Grundy Productions. After hard negotiations with Stig, the Australians managed to secure an appearance. The price tag for the privilege was a reported $A10,000, plus free plane tickets and accommodation. Some reports claimed the company actually had to pay 10 times as much.

The television special was produced as part of the pop show *Bandstand*. It was to be titled *The Best Of ABBA*, to tie in with a recently released compilation album of that name. While in Australia, Abba were also scheduled to take part in several other television shows.

The news of Abba's forthcoming visit and television special was mentioned in virtually every newspaper in Australia. "Abba, the hottest pop group in the world, will make a one-hour *Bandstand* special in Australia next month," trumpeted the *Daily Mirror*. Another paper renamed the nation ABBAustralia. The country seemed to be bustling with excitement now that these slightly unreal pop stars were actually going to be there in the flesh.

On Thursday, March 4, Abba stepped off the plane that had brought them to Sydney. On arrival, masses of jubilant teenagers greeted the group. It was a shock: Abba's success in Europe had been convincing and calmly solid, but had never led to anything like hysterical airport receptions. Beyond the fantastic sales figures they were getting accustomed to, the Australian visit was Abba's first tangible glimpse of true international superstardom. It was also as good an example as any of how Abba were perceived by the general public and the archetypal roles played by the two women, who were obviously always the main focus for the group's public image.

There can be no doubt that Agnetha was and remains the most popular individual member of Abba. With her long, blonde hair and open smile, she seemed to embody both the older, more archaic image of the blonde girl as a sweet "ice maiden" and the modern interpretation as a sexually available woman aligning herself with the myth of "the Swedish sin".

Frida, while certainly not playing some eternal second fiddle to Agnetha as has been suggested elsewhere, had an image that was just that little bit less attractive and accessible. She also managed to embody two different myths: the antiquated, where the brunette was the mature, sexually available female, and the contrast to the sinful blonde that emerged during the 20th century: the motherly and faithful homemaker.

The actual five-year age difference between the two seemed to underline this image: Agnetha still had an air of virginal schoolgirl about her, while Frida had passed into adulthood. One was an innocent girl, the other a sophisticated woman; each attracted hysterical adulation, with Agnetha enjoying just a slight edge.

On the day after their arrival in Australia, Abba attended a press conference and gold record award ceremony at the Sydney Hilton Hotel. Most of the visual attention was naturally focused on the girls and put their different roles into sharp focus. Dark-haired Frida's elegant appearance in a fur shrug contrasted with Agnetha's long, blonde hair and summery white, almost folk-style dress – it was as if she'd just taken a temporary break from the milking stool to give the press her attention for half an hour or so.

As usual, it was Agnetha who attracted most of the attention. One report, while making no mention whatsoever of Frida's appearance, gushed that Agnetha was "looking beautiful in white. She was shoeless and explained she had no shoes that fitted." Agnetha's outstanding status was underlined towards the end of the visit, when a photo was cabled out of the "lithe blonde" alone, hands on hips and gazing sexily into the camera with a hesitant smile. The shot was printed in newspapers all over the world.

At the press conference, much was made of the fact that a press release had stated that Frida and Benny were married, when in fact they were not – they had been too busy, they explained. This revelation challenged their nice and clean couples image slightly, but in reality it added just a hint of extra spice to the overall group image.

Attention again turned to Agnetha, who was asked if she was aware that her bottom had been nominated as the sexiest in pop. "She blushed, hid briefly behind Frida, and then said: 'But what about my feet?'" a newspaper reported.

The media were frantic: they wanted to find out everything they could about the group. "You have to understand us," said Channel 9 producer Lyle McCabe to Abba. "As individuals, Abba are just as unknown to us as Adam's pyjamas. That's why Australia wants to know all about you."

That was certainly an accurate summary of the situation. Whereas *RAM* had finally published their first major article on the group a few weeks before the visit under the headline "In Search Of Abba", *Juke* had their first feature shortly after the Australian trip; tellingly, it was headed "Abba Revealed". On the evening after the press conference, every news show on every television channel had a report on Abba's arrival in the country. Throughout their visit and beyond, the brand new promo film for 'Fernando' was shown over and over again on television.

Lasse Hallström always felt that on this particular clip his visual imagination had let him down. Contrary to his earlier films, in 'Fernando' he wasn't really able to overcome his time and budgetry restrictions. "It looks pretty poor," he said many years later. "They're sitting there around a fire, playing guitar with some kind of 'starry sky' behind them – it's kind of pathetic. I really don't think that one's very good, it's much too conventional." However, 'Fernando' was Abba's first clip since 'Mamma Mia' and the three other tracks off the *ABBA* album, and in Australia it was lapped up just as eagerly as the previous films.

Everything was just a whirlwind of events from the moment the group arrived in Sydney. Thomas Johansson accompanied them on the visit to explore the possibilities of a concert tour later in the year. On that first day, he got offers from six different local promoters.

Monday saw Abba fly from Sydney to Melbourne, where they were scheduled to appear on a couple of television programmes. If possible, the reception was even more hysterical than in Sydney. The airport was filled with people waiting for the group, and fans were waving banners reading, "Welcome Abba". The group had to wait until last before they could leave the plane, and were escorted by police through the back of the airport and all the way to the hotel. "When we stepped off the plane in Melbourne I looked at Frida," recalled Agnetha. "Her eyes were filled with tears, just like mine. That's how moved we were by the reception." They had never experienced anything like it.

Things didn't ease up at the hotel, which was besieged by fans. Abba were forced to sneak out through the garage to reach the television studio where they were appearing on *The Don Lane Show*.

It was all so different to the situation back home in Sweden, the only country so far where Abba's popularity was on the same scale. Their stardom at home had evolved slowly from the members' individual careers before the group was founded: there was nothing explosive about Abba's emergence on the Swedish music scene.

By now, their albums were breaking all sales records, their concerts were always sold out, and the major evening papers devoted extensive coverage to their doings. A whole generation of children were "playing Abba", alone in front of the bedroom mirror or together with other friends. Miming to the records with skipping ropes as pretend microphones, they'd be quarrelling about who was to be Frida or Agnetha. There was no question that the group was immensely popular.

The difference was that the Swedish fans wouldn't do things like go to the airport to greet them when they returned home from their trips – it just wasn't in the nation's psyche to afford domestic pop stars that kind of attention. The voices that strongly disapproved of Abba exercised a disproportionate amount of control over the media, and so far there hadn't been any exclusive television specials centred around the group. Certainly, Australia had its Abba detractors, but their voices weren't as loud as their Swedish counterparts.

After fulfilling their Melbourne obligations, the group travelled back to Sydney to spend a few days filming the television special which was the main reason for the trip. In front of a studio audience, Abba performed 11 of their hits: from the very oldest, such as 'Ring Ring', to their current single, 'Fernando'.

Other television appearances followed before it was time for Abba to return to Sweden. A week later, on Saturday, March 20, at 6.30 p.m., *The Best Of ABBA* was broadcast on Australia's Channel 9. The transmission was truly the event of the week. People who didn't own colour television sets visited neighbours and friends to view the broadcast in all its visual glory. Abba's staggering 14 weeks in a row at the top of the singles chart paled in comparison with the effect of this special.

More than half of Australia's viewers sat glued to their television sets that Saturday evening: 54 per cent according to contemporary reports. The previous viewer ratings record – the 1969 moon landing – was shot to pieces by this 45 minute performance by a Swedish pop group.

The show in itself was nothing especially spectacular. Abba performed their songs, changed costumes a couple of times, went through a few dance routines and talked in stilted English between certain numbers. Björn and Benny introduced and interviewed the guest star, singer Lucky Star. That was all. But to the audience it was enough just to see the group live, in a special produced for their very own television screens. The romance between Abba and the Australian public blossomed into a full-blown love affair.

When the papers wrote about the *Bandstand* television special they openly acknowledged the sex appeal of Agnetha and Frida as one of the group's main attractions, something that was also pretty unusual in the Swedish media. "The girls are two of the sexiest looking ladies in show-business," the *Daily Telegraph* established. "Usually they appear in long dresses or trouser suits . . . but for the Sydney spectacular they [brought along] a knock-out outfit they wear while singing their first big hit 'Waterloo'. In mid song they rip off the bottom of their long gowns to reveal two of the shapeliest pairs of legs in the business."

Bizarrely, before the "strip tease" performance, Agnetha had invited the children in the audience to clap along to the song in her best pre-school teacher style, lending a somewhat questionable slant to proceedings. But that was also part of Abba's unique attraction: that they managed to simultaneously play on their sex appeal and their clean, wholesome image.

Agnetha and Frida's indisputable status as flag bearers drew attention to an odd disparity in the group's chemistry and image. Abba is probably the only group ever to attain fame on a massive level whose most popular members do not make up its creative core. Whenever they were interviewed collectively, especially by non-Swedish media, it was mostly Björn and Benny who replied to the questions. To a large extent, this had to do with Agnetha and Frida's comparatively limited command of English. However, it also pointed to the fact that beyond their roles as vocalists and onstage front figures, the creation of Abba did not emanate from the two women. And yet, they were the ones who had to handle most of the attention and the pressure.

During the Australian visit, their already easily irritable temperaments were not assuaged by having to attend press conferences, struggling to find the right English words, while their bodies had to overcome adjustments to a ten hour time difference. They tried to keep up a brave front, but when the media was out of sight their moods could change at the flick of a switch.

As usual, it was their partners who faced the temper tantrums that followed. Early nights watching television in their hotel suites behind slammed doors were the norm. "The girls have it worst," Björn and Benny admitted. "We can always manage. We don't have to fix our faces, think about our hair, be models even in private."

The success of the Australian television special was so great that it received a prime-time repeat in most cities within a few weeks. Channel 9 was swamped with offers from overseas television stations who wanted to buy the rights to broadcast *The Best Of ABBA*. According to programme manager Lynton Taylor, the station would probably "go close" to getting back what they paid for the rights to produce the show.

The promotional visit inevitably sent Abba's popularity skyrocketing to even greater heights in Australia. Newspapers and magazines, who'd previously had but scant coverage of the group, continually printed interviews and cover stories about the four Swedes. On the singles chart, 'Fernando' knocked Queen's 'Bohemian Rhapsody' off the number one position to initiate a record-breaking 14 week run at the top – only The Beatles' 'Hey Jude' had managed as many weeks. Earlier singles also flooded on to the charts, with the 'I Do, I Do, I Do, I Do, I Do' single achieving another round in the Top Five when the B-side, 'Rock Me', caught the fans' attention. At one point in May, Abba had four albums in the Australian Top 20. The compilation album *The Best Of ABBA* spent 16 weeks at number one on the charts, eventually selling over 1.1 million copies – more than any other album in Australia before or since.

The knowledge that the group would tour the country in November just added to the interest. Reg Grundy's company had made a merchandising deal with Stig Anderson and were producing everything from T-shirts to posters, lunch boxes and bubble gum cards. However, it seems this deal wasn't too favourable to the Swedes: two years later, Stig claimed that their worldwide earnings on merchandise so far wasn't more than a comparatively puny one million kronor (£130,000).

After returning to Sweden, just a little over a week passed before Björn and Benny entered the recording studio to finally continue their work on the next Abba album. Since completing 'Dancing Queen' and 'Fernando' three months earlier, no songs had been written and not one single recording had been made.

Sessions began with a song called 'Knowing Me, Knowing You'. It was, perhaps, the first Abba song to truly acknowledge that the group consisted of four adults. Whereas previous lyrics about love troubles had been more generic, couplets like "in this old familiar room, children would play" indicated that 'Knowing Me, Knowing You' dealt with the collapse of a marriage, as opposed to any old teenage romance.

The title came from Stig Anderson, but the rest of the words were written by Björn. He has since denied that the lyrics had any bearing on his own situation at that time. "Even if the roots are somewhere deep inside, from something that has happened to you, it's still 90 per cent fiction," he said. "I was just working from images. I saw a man walking through an empty house for the last time as a symbol of divorce. I just described what I saw. I hadn't been through that myself then."

This was certainly true, but there was no denying that there was plenty of friction in the Ulvaeus household at this time. Whereas at one time the tension between Björn and Agnetha had contributed a spark to the relationship, it was now turning into a problem. From the beginning Agnetha had felt inferior to Björn in almost every respect: he had high school studies behind him and came from a home where reading, studying and trying to advance yourself intellectually was encouraged. Her own background was different. She never went to high school and when the pair met she didn't even like to read novels – it was something Björn encouraged her to do.

On her *folkpark* tour of 1970 Agnetha studied psychology on the tour bus, and the shadow of Björn's influence seemed to loom large in the background. At the time she could even make statements like, "Perhaps I'm not very intelligent. I take every day as it comes, I don't think much about the future."

It had taken Björn and Agnetha several years to truly get to know each other; when they first met they used to quarrel about almost everything. They had gone through the stages of domestic adjustments that most couples do: Björn was sloppy and would leave things lying around, while Agnetha had to do most of the cooking and cleaning. Agnetha's self-absorption when the two first met had been tempered, and they had both become better at compromising. Outwardly, not only were they a happily married couple with a daughter of three, but they were also part of a pop music phenomenon that was giving them creative and financial rewards most other couples could only dream about.

But it was as if they were too much alike to ever find a true balance and harmony in the relationship. "We are both very sensitive and enormously self-centred, so of course we clash violently at regular intervals," Agnetha confessed. "My worst side is my jealousy. I can create terrible scenes if I see Björn together with another girl."

The sexy, fun-loving girl with whom Björn had fallen in love and married had changed completely since becoming a mother: Agnetha wanted to stay at home with Linda and give her a secure upbringing. Björn's mind was primarily on his career, and his attention was focused on exploiting the potential of Abba to the full. "His worst fault is being a workaholic," Agnetha complained. "He thinks about work all the time and often doesn't hear a word I say."

Even at this stage, Agnetha was unwilling to go on promotional trips. Her inclination to remain at home with their child was joined by a strong fear of flying that complicated matters even further. Björn, meanwhile, took the promotional duties as par for the course. "Agnetha *really* didn't want to go anywhere," he recalled. "I thought, 'It's necessary. We have to, we can't miss this. We'll regret it for the rest of our lives if we just don't bother anymore.' So . . . between Agnetha and myself [it] was always difficult, because I wanted to go and she didn't want to."

There was still a strong bond of love between them, motivating them to try to make the relationship work, but it seemed at times that there was just too much pressure on them. Björn writing a lyric about divorce – one that said "there is nothing we can do" – when his own marriage was fraught with problems may not have been pure coincidence. It was obvious the couple's growing differences would have to be resolved one way or another sooner or later.

A month after 'Knowing Me, Knowing You', Abba started recording a song which was to showcase a fundamental area of Björn and Benny's working methods. When the songwriters and their backing musicians entered the Metronome studio on April 26, they had a Fats Domino-style song with the working title 'Why Did It Have To Be Me' on their hands.

Toying around with the song in the studio, they moved away from rock territory and arrived at some kind of Hawaiian feel. Stig put together a first draft lyric, and the result was titled 'Happy Hawaii'. A steel guitarist was called in to do an overdub, the sound of crashing waves in the intro was achieved with the help of some white noise from a transistor radio, and then Agnetha and Frida were called down to record a joint lead vocal. The recording was completed and mixed.

As album sessions wore on, however, Björn and Benny were getting cold feet. 'Happy Hawaii' – what kind of silly concept was that? The lyrics told the tale of a girl going to Hawaii to forget the lover who jilted her but this seemed a bit inconsequential. "There was nothing especially wrong with the recording," recalled Björn, "but the lyrics were just too damned corny." A more countrified arrangement of the song was then recorded, entitled 'Memory Lane', but that didn't feel right either. The boys had to admit defeat: towards the end of the album sessions they returned to the Fats Domino rock framework, adding a short burst of Beach Boys-style falsetto backing vocals to great effect. The original working title, 'Why Did It Have To Be Me', was also brought back in, and a third version was recorded with Björn on lead vocals. That was how the song was presented on the finished album. 'Happy Hawaii', meanwhile, did gain an eventual release, as the B-side of the 'Knowing Me, Knowing You' single.

This experience showed not only how the one and same basic composition would often be tried in several, widely different styles, but also how Björn and Benny were drifting apart from Stig on all levels. Their relationship had been at its closest in the years up to the 'Waterloo' victory in Brighton. At that time they were all unified in their quest for reaching out into the world with their music: 'Waterloo' was a team effort on every level, with all three on the same wavelength.

But now, only two years later, their journeys were running on two diverging tracks: Stig was occupied with the further marketing of Abba and handling all the business that their success generated, while Björn and Benny wanted to develop and further themselves musically. They were aiming at goals far beyond Stig's bubblegum approach to pop music, not to mention his slightly old-hat lyric concepts. The 15-year age difference was making itself felt with full force.

Stig certainly did have his hands full with a rapidly expanding business. Both he and Abba were now beginning to realise the financial rewards of their enormous success. The financial year of 1975/76 and the income from the *ABBA* album had led to a turnover of 18 million kronor (£2,340,000) and a profit of 4.5 million (£585,000). It was a quite extraordinary turnover/profit ratio.

However, Swedish income tax for high earners like Stig and Abba was a punitive 85 per cent at the time. If the company profit was just dished out and declared as salaries, most of it would disappear to the state. No one could know for certain when the Abba bubble would burst, so everyone involved – especially the group members – had to consider investments for the future: it would be nice to have something left when the day came when they were no longer international superstars.

Such intricate financial schemes were a bit too complex for the basically self-taught Gudrun Anderson, who had handled all financial matters so far. "We have to invest and do something sensible with the money," she said. "I don't know how to do that. I don't have the education – I'm a weaving teacher."

Stig sought advice from lawyers and financial experts, who advised them all to leave the country and live somewhere more beneficial for high-income earners. That wasn't very popular with anyone. "Gudrun, I and the Abba members were in total agreement about this," remembered Stig. "We would not let ourselves be run out of the country and let fiscal reasons and tricks decide where we should live."

Their advisors pointed out to them that their line of work had very few investments that would reduce their taxes – there were only so many music business ventures they could do that were low-risk in terms of actually retaining the capital, which was the whole point of the exercise. "That meant that we had to reconstruct the whole company to adjust it to the handling of profits according to the tax law. In other words, we had to invest our money in some kind of financial venture – spread our risks by safeguarding the real value of the capital that was accruing in our bank accounts."

So far, investing in real estate had proved to be a good move, but other, different solutions were also needed. In the spring of 1976 the decision was made to form a new company as an umbrella for all the different business ventures. The plan was that this corporation should eventually get listed on the stock exchange. The tentative name of the new company was Abba Invest.

Stig realised that it would take a few years before this investment business was viewed as solid and dependable enough to get listed. Some of the company's plans for the moment were to open an art gallery and art shop, found a book publishing firm and a television production company, as well as buying a building somewhere in central Stockholm to build "the best recording studio in Europe", as Stig said. For these initial investments, the aim was to keep most of them confined to the art and entertainment sphere.

While the income was building up into unmanageable amounts, the attention on Abba as a phenomenon was equally hard to control. In May 1976, a bizarre rumour spread through West Germany, and then across Europe, that all the members of Abba except Frida had been killed in a plane crash at Tempelhof airport in West Berlin. As with all stories of this kind, it wasn't clear exactly where the rumour originated. It was said to have started when a certain Jürgen Blaus called a radio station, stating that he had heard the details of the crash reported on East German radio.

The group tried to quash the rumours by giving several interviews confirming that they were indeed alive and well. Still, it took some time before the tens of thousands of devastated Abba fans, jamming the switchboards of Polar and other record companies, were finally convinced that there was not a single grain of truth in the story.

The incident echoed the famous rumour in 1969 that Paul McCartney had been dead for several years, and been replaced in The Beatles by a look-alike. Abba's plane crash rumour proved beyond any shadow of a doubt that they had now achieved true superstar status, an eminence that inspired fantasies – not necessarily healthy ones – to be spun around the group and its individual members.

Chapter 20

In August 1976 – a full year after recording had commenced – Abba finally released 'Dancing Queen' as a single. The group was clearly at the height of their creative powers, with one song after another pushing the boundaries established by the previous release.

Somewhat incongruously, in June the group had performed this discotheque celebration at a special gala before Sweden's King Carl XVI Gustaf and future Queen, Silvia Sommerlath. The gala was televised on the night before the couple's wedding, with Abba as the only pop act on the roster. At first they were in a quandary about which song to perform, toying with various recently recorded tracks, but in the end the choice was obvious. "If you have a song called 'Dancing Queen', you naturally choose to perform it on an occasion like that gala," said Benny.

And that's what they did, dressed in baroque outfits appropriate for the gala, which was transmitted from The Royal Swedish Opera in Stockholm. Ludicrously, many assumed afterwards that the song about a teenage girl on a dance floor had been written as a tribute to Queen Silvia. At 33, Ms Sommerlath may still have been fairly "young and sweet", but she was certainly not "only seventeen".

The group had truly found their voice in the past 18 months, a progression that reached some kind of summit with 'Dancing Queen'. Agnetha and Frida's voices cut like laser through the soundscape, Benny's piano tinkled jubilantly in the high register, while the groove pumped along. 'Dancing Queen' reached number one almost everywhere in the world where charts were compiled – it seemed it never fared worse than the Top Five anywhere. Through the decades, 'Dancing Queen' has continued to fill dance floors all over the world. In pure commercial terms, the song remains Abba's most popular track.

'Dancing Queen' was the first Abba release to feature the group logo with the inverted B. This famous trademark symbol was designed by freelance art director Rune Söderqvist, and was based on the group's foundation as two couples, which made it natural to turn each "B" towards each "A".

Rune's first sleeve design for Abba was the Swedish version of the

Greatest Hits album in late 1975. Henceforth, he would do the artwork for all Abba album sleeves, and in keeping with the Polar Music family feeling, Rune became a trusted collaborator and friend of Stig and the Abba members. He and his common-law wife, Lillebil Ankarcrona, were especially close to Benny and Frida, with the two couples socialising a great deal.

As an indication that the left-wing grip on the cultural climate in Sweden was easing up just slightly, Abba were the subject of both a television special, entitled *Abba-dabba-dooo!!* (aka *Abba From The Beginning*), and a five-part radio series in the autumn of 1976. Still, the mood in the nation made itself felt in both productions. The narrator of the radio series had to justify the broadcasts by saying that the producers "thought that it was motivated" to do a series on such a popular group as Abba. And in the interview segments of the television special the members had to defend themselves against the usual accusations of speculation and cynicism.

Abba's fourth album, *Arrival*, was released on October 11, 1976. If the previous LP had seen the group find their voice and their own unique sound, *Arrival* was the first album to finally abandon all remnants of vocal democracy and blatant *schlager* aesthetics. The *schlager* influences were still there, of course, but most of the silly lyrical concepts had been abandoned by this time. "We had become much more conscious about things like that," remembered Björn.

There did seem to be one unfortunate exception in 'Dum Dum Diddle', although perhaps the culprit here was the nonsensical title rather than the lyrics as such. The concept of a woman hoping to replace a violin as the object of her loved one's affection was obviously not politically correct, and the imagery was certainly strained, but the words were no more infantile than those of the opening track, 'When I Kissed The Teacher'. Decades later, however, Björn found almost everything about the song hard to stomach, especially the lyrics, which he admitted to have written out of pure desperation at five o'clock in the morning. "It might as well have been '*Dumb Dumb* Diddle!'" he said.

Björn also regretted the decision to abandon the original, slow and heavy feel that marked the song's composing session. In the course of recording the backing track in the studio, it became more Euro-lightweight. Frida agreed with Björn's retrospective assessment: "A silly song – I don't like it!" Their regrets aside, beyond any unfortunate connotations its title may have evoked, 'Dum Dum Diddle' was the same expertly crafted pop that marked the rest of the album.

While the cream of the previous album's solo vocal performances belonged to Agnetha, it was now Frida's turn to shine. Where Agnetha

Benny Andersson, the group's musical motor, an intuitive tunesmith, the easygoing bloke in the midst of an eternal flow of melodies. (*LFI*)

Abba's extravagant dress sense became a characteristic of the group that aroused passionate opinions. On stage in 1975, these 'big cat' designs appeared as emblems on long white skirts which were removed in mid-concert to reveal similar designs on short white dresses beneath. (*Bengt H. Malmqvist/Premium*))

Björn and Benny in the studio with Polar singer Lena Andersson.
(*Bengt H. Malmqvist/Premium*)

Björn and Benny writing together, head to head, in their songwriting cottage at Viggsö.
(*Bengt H. Malmqvist/Premium*)

Frida and Agnetha in their matching outfits and blonde wigs during the "mini-musical", *The Girl With The Golden Hair,* which closed their concerts in 1977. (*Rex*)

Frida with her daughter, Lise-Lotte, and son, Hans, in the background (right). "It's taken a long time and many talks to sort out our relationships," said Frida. (*Bengt H. Malmqvist/Premium*)

Agnetha with her second child, Christian, shortly after his birth on December 4, 1977. Agnetha later said this was "more important than anything else that happened to me in 1977." (*Bengt H. Malmqvist/Premium*)

Björn, Agnetha and Linda with Björn's parents, Aina and Gunnar, in 1976. (*Tor Wiklund*)

A cheerful outtake from the photo session that produced the famous 'park bench' shot that appeared on the first edition of Abba's *Greatest Hits*. In the original Agnetha looks solemn while Björn, unconcerned, reads a magazine – a strangely apt comment on their stagnating relationship. (*Bengt H. Malmqvist/Premium*)

Agnetha covers her eyes when asked about having "the sexiest bottom in pop" at the press conference at the Sebel Townhouse in Sydney, on February 28, 1977, the day after Abba arrived for their hectic Australian tour. (*PM ART Australia*)

Agnetha's rear, the source of much comment in the press. (*PM ART Australia*)

Abba bubblegum (top) and socks. About 20 million ABBA bubblegum cards were printed in Australia during 1977 and those remaining are now quite collectable. The socks were advertised as "100% nylon"! (*PM ART Australia*)

The sea of umbrellas at Abba's first live performance on Australian soil at the Sydney Showground, on Thursday, March 3. All of Abba recall this event as the most memorable show of their entire career, not least because the heavy rain failed to dampen the spirits of more than 20,000 of the most enthusiastic Abba fans in the world. (*PM ART Australia*)

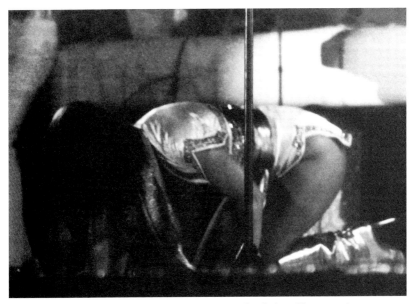

Frida slips on the rainswept stage during the amazing Sydney Showground concert.
(*PM ART Australia*)

Frida, without make-up, and her father, Alfred Haase, in September, 1977, when he reappeared in her life after his niece read about Abba in *Bravo*, a German pop magazine. (*Hans Gedda*)

had been devastated and pleading in a song like 'SOS', Frida's *chanteuse* style added a more mature slant to the divorce proceedings in 'Knowing Me, Knowing You'. This crucial difference between the two vocalists would henceforth serve as a guide to which one should handle which song.

Frida's superior skills as an interpretive singer came to the fore on the cabaret inflections of 'Money, Money, Money'. Within the confines of a three minute format, this was a sublime performance, opening in the tradition of European theatrical music combined with a basic Anglo-Saxon pop rhythm, and finally topped with Frida's dramatic delivery.

The genesis of 'Money, Money, Money' was similar to 'Why Did It Have To Be Me', insofar as it ended up being released under its original working title. Björn, who felt that "there were enough 'money' songs around", came up with a set of working lyrics entitled 'Gypsy Girl'. "But that came out a bit awkward, somehow," he recalled. "In the end, I had to go back to 'Money, Money, Money' – that simply sounded best." This philosophy was endemic to Abba and fundamental to their success: whatever their ambitions the group never forsook simplicity and direct communication with their audience.

In any event, the storytelling, musical-like layers of 'Money, Money, Money' made it Benny's favourite track on the album. "Of all the things we have done, that one is the best ever," he said. "It's a very basic recording; you could say that it's constructed like a stage number. I imagine someone else doing it, not necessarily us: someone standing on a platform, singing these lyrics."

As usual, the album sessions were marked by the odd temperamental outburst, especially during vocal overdubs. "It only helps to have a slightly heated recording atmosphere," said Benny. "It gives some spirit to the song." Frida's strident delivery on 'Money, Money, Money' suggests that the sparks were indeed flying when this particular recording was made.

Agnetha's plaintive, dramatic ballad 'My Love, My Life' added to her public persona as a vulnerable woman, constantly despairing over matters of the heart. Her solo lines on the opening track, 'When I Kissed The Teacher', graced one of the final examples of Abba's trick of creating pop that could have come from the early Sixties yet was enhanced by a Seventies aural environment. Solo spots aside, it was still the energetic joint vocals on tracks like 'Dancing Queen' and the rocky 'Tiger' that gave the album its identity.

Although it was Björn and Benny's vision that guided Abba's work, Agnetha and Frida were no mere puppets when those magic vocal tracks were put down. "Sometimes it has been hinted in books and articles about us that 'the girls didn't have much to do with the work in the studio', or that 'they simply did as they were told', but of course this isn't true," Agnetha reflected later. "When you work as a producer yourself, like I have done, and spend that much time in the studio, you learn a thing or two. I know that I have contributed lots of ideas and arrangements, harmony parts, gimmicks, and solutions to several problems over the years."

The title track, 'Arrival', was the second in what threatened to become a series of instrumentals, after 'Intermezzo no. 1' on the *ABBA* album. Along with the intro to 'Dum Dum Diddle', 'Arrival' was also the first time that Benny's fondness for Swedish fiddlers' folk music overtly coloured an Abba album track. At one point the title of the song was 'Ode To Dalecarlia', referring to the Swedish county most closely associated with this particular strand of folk music.

There were some discussions about whether such experiments really belonged on an Abba album. But Benny insisted. "Michael and I stayed late one night and did some work on it with the mellotrone and the mini-moog so that we could make a convincing case of it," he recalled. "It's much easier to get your way if you can say 'listen to this!' instead of humming your way through a half-finished idea."

In many ways, *Arrival* was as much a triumph for Michael Tretow as it was for Abba. As well as adding to the pleasant working atmosphere with his light-hearted personality, the trust that had developed between him and the group members was of vital importance for the sessions. "Michael is a great source of inspiration, and has so many ideas," said Benny. "You can leave so much to him. We can concentrate on our 'art' and the musical side of things, the feeling . . . There are never any problems between us, he knows what we think and we know how he likes things to be. Without him it wouldn't be as easy to produce an album that leaves you as satisfied as this one."

Arrival was the last of Abba's albums to retain the innocence and sense of wonderment at actually succeeding in the dream of making internationally relevant pop music. Björn and Frida were now both in their thirties and before the year was out Benny would also turn 30. Songs like 'Knowing Me, Knowing You' marked a transition: there were more serious, more grown-up aspects of life to deal with in the future.

In Frida's case, growing older didn't necessarily add to her sense of well-being, and at the time of the release of *Arrival* she was on her way out of a year-long depression. At the time of the release of her solo album she spoke of having finally reached an equilibrium, but despite the sense of purpose that came from being a part of Abba and interacting with the audience during live concerts, Frida's old insecurities had come back to haunt her. "I think it is something most women go through around this age," she reflected a few years later. "I read somewhere that at 20 you make up your mind what you want from life and at 30 you change and question everything. Everything was upside down for me. I had no confidence in myself. At the same time, you must go on working."

Frida realised that she had to bite the bullet and seek psychiatric help if she was ever going to get to the bottom of what was troubling her. "Benny was a great help to me, too," she said, "although he couldn't understand everything. Now I feel very strong, very confident. I know what I want to do. I have to listen to myself, not to what everyone else tells me. And Benny had to change, because I was a new woman. So our relationship changed. It is much stronger than before."

After completing the *Abba-dabba-dooo!!* television special at the beginning of October, Abba set out on a series of promotional trips for the *Arrival* album. The first of these took them to Poland, the purpose of the visit being to tape yet another television special devoted entirely to the group. So great was the group's popularity and so important their visit that they were collected in Stockholm in a special plane and then flown back to Poland (all except Agnetha, who'd gone the day before).

Both the *Waterloo* and *ABBA* albums had sold very well and Abba were now the hottest property in the country. When the address of Abba's Swedish fan club was printed in a Polish newspaper in 1975, the offices had been swamped with tens of thousands of letters. The Polish fans sent gifts in the shape of handiwork with images of the group. In the first few batches that reached the fan club, many of these items depicted Björn with breasts – for some reason, quite a few Poles thought that he was a woman.

The entire annual Polish budget for 1976 for importing Western pop records was spent on the 800,000 copies of *Arrival* that were eventually pressed. In Poland and other Eastern Bloc countries, however, the demand for Abba exceeded the amount of western currency the various countries were allowed to allocate to western pop music. This was a problem for Stig: 250,000 copies of the *ABBA* album had been purchased in Poland but many thought it could have sold at least one million. In the Soviet Union, so far they had been able to import only 25,000 Abba albums – Polar's own Swedish pressings – at one single instant. Finding a way to solve that problem – to allow the various countries to procure as many Abba records as were actually needed to meet the demand – was a conundrum now taxing the minds of the business brains at Polar.

The group barely had time to return from Poland before they flew out on a two-week visit to the USA and Canada, Abba's third promotional visit across the Atlantic in as many years. They did the usual round of television appearances and interviews with press and radio in Los Angeles, Vancouver, New York and Philadelphia. The most memorable incident of the promotional trip took place in Los Angeles, when the group guested on *The Dinah Shore Show*. Ms Shore, shocked by the fact that Frida and Benny had still not wed after seven years of engagement, offered them the opportunity of marrying on the air. The couple politely declined.

As yet, however, no concert tour was on the cards. "My only disagreement with Stig was that he wanted to hold off bringing Abba here until they had at least three number one records," says Sid Bernstein. "I said, 'Stig, don't hold off. One is enough in America. They're very special, they're a very attractive group. America will love them.' "

Of course, it wasn't only Stig that didn't want to tour America. The group were naturally disinclined towards live performances anyway and, in the case of America, there was the added problem of whether or not interest in live concerts by Abba was sufficiently high. Bygone dreams of becoming a huge success in the United States and playing Carnegie Hall didn't seem so exciting anymore. Why should Abba spend all the time and effort cracking the American market – perhaps even as an opening act – when the rest of the world seemed to lap them up like crazy? The disastrous experience of the autumn 1974 tour of Germany and Austria was still fresh in their minds. They had vowed never to tour anywhere where there wasn't a clear, solid market for them, and they would not change their minds.

"There is no demand for us as headliners in this country but that's the only offer we would accept," Benny told the *Los Angeles Times*. Björn remarked bluntly: "In Sydney we play for 40,000 people, so it would be a step back to be a supporting act here, especially when we don't need it."

Because the United States was always lagging behind with their Abba releases compared to the rest of the world, it was also hard to co-ordinate promotional efforts with the group's grand-scale international plans. 'Fernando', which had been a hit in Europe and Australia six months earlier, had just started its climb up the American charts at the time of Abba's visit. *Arrival* wasn't scheduled for release until January.

There was no getting around the fact that it would take far more than a couple of television shows on an annual two-week visit for Abba to make any real impact on the American market. "Their Los Angeles stopover was hardly front page news," as one magazine put it. "Abba are . . . not quite faceless, but nameless."

It all boiled down to the tour that they refused to make. Two and a half years had already elapsed since they first signed with Atlantic Records, and yet they hadn't performed one single live concert. There was also the ongoing dilemma of the group's image as an AM radio pop act and the consequential negative attitude towards them by progressive, album-oriented FM stations.

A national promotional campaign by Atlantic Records for the group's current American album, *Greatest Hits*, had little impact. The record company proclaimed a "National Abba Weekend" to capitalise on the tail end of the group's visit, but it failed to impress record buyers. Something else was needed before Abba would be accepted as a "serious" albums band in the land of Uncle Sam.

After a couple of weeks' rest, Abba continued their promotional campaign with a visit to Great Britain. The *Arrival* album had been released on November 5, and ten days later the group arrived in London. The visit coincided with the UK release of the second single from the album, 'Money, Money, Money'.

Any earlier disapproval of the group had been completely eradicated during the past 12 months, at least as far as the UK record-buying public was concerned. Abba had enjoyed three consecutive number one hits and their *Greatest Hits* album spent a total of 11 weeks at the top of the albums chart, selling more than 1.25 million copies by the end of the year. Globally, *Greatest Hits* was one of Abba's top sellers during their time as an active group.

For this, their first major promotional visit – where their arrival was an anticipated event as opposed to yet another attempt to push open the doors – it was decided to hold an extravagant press conference aboard the ship *The Mayflower* on the River Thames. Moreover, to tie in with the *Arrival* album cover art, which featured the group in white overalls seated inside a helicopter, they would fly from Heathrow Airport to the boat in a helicopter, dressed in the same outfits. Unfortunately, due to dense fog on the day, their arrival on the boat was delayed by an hour. The helicopter idea was abandoned and an ordinary limousine had to suffice.

When the *Arrival* album was released, it topped the British charts for a total of 10 weeks. The UK music scene was captivated by Abba in much the same way as the Australians had been, simply because the four Swedes were providing the British public with a type of quality pop music that was virtually unavailable elsewhere. At a time when the cognoscenti declared that pop and rock should have something relevant to say, Abba catered to those who simply wanted straightforward pop music with a high gloss finish. No pop band in the UK seemed able to match the songwriting skills of Björn and Benny or the vocal talents and sex appeal of Frida and Agnetha.

The competition in the UK, historically a breeding ground for all that was world-conquering in pop, seemed almost to have retired from the contest. Björn and Benny's role models, Lennon & McCartney, no longer worked together. Lennon had moved to America in 1971 and gradually lost interest in his music career, and by 1976 had withdrawn completely from public life. After a shaky start to his post-Beatles career McCartney was enjoying success with his group Wings, although in truth they were little more than his backing band. By the mid-Seventies, McCartney – and Elton John – were arguably Abba's biggest rivals in providing well-produced popular music.

Other high-profile British Sixties pop stars had fallen into oblivion and some had even become drug casualties. Those that survived, generally those at the hard rock end of the spectrum, were concentrating their efforts on long stadium tours in the United States. "The Seventies was a time when English pop music lost all its nobility and all its pride, and went to America," as Ray Davies of The Kinks noted. "Abba came along and it was a very innocent music."

The difference between Abba and much of the other more lightweight music of the time was that Abba took their lightweight music seriously: they spent hours and hours composing and recording their finely crafted pop hits. The average Europop group or cabaret act were more geared towards quick, disposable recordings, almost as if they expected to be one hit wonders.

Unknowingly, Abba exploited the comparative absence of good, solid pop music on the British market. They didn't believe in the accepted wisdom that a new album should be followed by a tour, concentrating their promotional efforts instead on strategic visits and appearances on popular TV shows. It was a unique combination of pop sensibility and career planning that crushed all opposition.

British rock journalists were baffled by this development. Since rock music first broke through on a large scale in the late Fifties, it had followed an almost linear path. The innocence of the early days was followed by the political awareness of the mid Sixties, and by progressive experiments and the androgynous glam rock of the early Seventies. There was therefore a sense of gleeful anticipation about the next exciting, forward-moving, step.

It was a huge disappointment when it turned out that the biggest group mid-decade was a Swedish cabaret/*schlager* act who just wanted to make hit records and . . . entertain. Abba was a group that could be unreservedly enjoyed by the whole family, truly worthless as role models for teenage rebellion and breaking free from the constraints of suburbia, the traditional function of rock stars. Abba *were* suburbia.

Consequently, most British rock journalists gave Abba a hard time. Simply by virtue of being European, the group had committed the unforgivable crime of lacking origins in, or acknowledgement of, rock's blues and soul traditions. "They say we have no soul, but in Europe, and especially in Sweden, it's a different kind of soul," countered Björn, but it seemed that influences from Swedish folk music and Mediterranean heartbreak ballads wouldn't cut it with the rock critics. Grammatical slips like "since many years I haven't seen a rifle in your hand" in 'Fernando', coupled with Swedish accents, studied diction and mispronunciation of certain words, didn't earn them any extra goodwill.

In extreme cases it seemed Abba were viewed as a pan-European threat, as if the British music scene was facing the possibility of a Germanic invasion, spearheaded by the four Swedes. The blitzkrieg tactics of the Second World War had been supplanted by a more subtle but equally menacing attack of cheesy oompah beats performed by "well coiffured and sexlessly hermaphroditic" Euro-rockers.

Several concert reviews from Abba's tour of Britain in February 1977 lend credence to this theory. The group was churning out "single after single with robot-like precision", noted one writer, while another called them "shrewd manipulators". Others singled out the "lack of warmth [and] almost glacial atmosphere" of the "technically perfect" live shows. In a highly dubious outburst of reverse prejudice, *Record Mirror* even saw fit to remark that Gambian percussionist Malando Gassama was "the only non-Aryan member" of the backing band.

The success of MOR act The Brotherhood Of Man, who scored two consecutive UK number ones with their quite terrible 'Fernando' inspired 'Angelo' and the Euro stomper 'Figaro', seemed to suggest that there was indeed an unpleasant side to Abba's dominating influence on current popular music. "[They] thought they had to have a Spanish name for every title," noted Björn wryly.

The Seventies just weren't like the Sixties, when the biggest-selling band – The Beatles – was also the band that broke down barriers and led the cultural revolution, embodying both cuddliness and rebellion at different times. In the present decade that heritage was split in two: it was Abba who ruled the charts with their melodious and well-produced records, while protests and political awareness were handled by the punk movement.

In a sense, Abba and punk/new wave were aesthetically united in knocking down the rock dinosaurs and purveyors of symphonic rock like

Yes and Emerson, Lake & Palmer. Their forms of expression may have been different, but they were both bringing back pop as a means of direct communication. Although punk and new wave is generally looked upon as the complete antithesis of everything that Abba stood for, many of the more famous punk rockers have often name-checked the four Swedes. Glen Matlock of The Sex Pistols has even admitted that the riff in 'Pretty Vacant' was lifted from 'SOS'. "I heard the riff on it, one simple repeated octave pattern," he recalled. "All I did was take that pattern and alter it slightly." Matlock was replaced in the Pistols by Sid Vicious who turned out to be an Abba fan as well. At one point, Vicious ran into Abba at an airport, drunkenly staggering up to shake the hands of a startled Agnetha and Frida.

Respect for Abba might have been thin on the ground among critics but the more perceptive musicians, regardless of their age, were considerably more astute. Elvis Costello picked up on Abba's direct pop sensibility and enjoyed his biggest hit on the UK charts with 'Oliver's Army', which was adorned by a very Benny-like piano figure. Pete Townshend, too, was impressed. "Abba was one of the first big, international bands to actually deal with sort of middle-aged problems in their songwriting," noted The Who's principal songwriter. "And it [seemed to be] what was going on among them – that song, 'Knowing Me, Knowing You'."

After four days in London, Abba returned home to Sweden to start rehearsals and other preparations to tour the world. With sessions for the *Arrival* album taking longer than expected, and with unexpected additional promotion activities to handle in the course of the year, the tour of Australia planned for November had been postponed. Instead, the European part of the tour, due to commence at the end of January, became the first series of dates, with the Australian leg following in March.

It was also decided that promo clip director Lasse Hallström should produce a full-length Abba feature film while in Australia. The movie was to be based on concert footage, but would also serve as some kind of documentary of the tour.

While the world's love affair with Abba escalated to unimagined heights, it was still politically incorrect in Sweden to admit to liking the group and their music. It was a perverse contradiction: an inexplicable conflict between their domestic chart success – 12 consecutive weeks at the top with *Arrival*, to name only their most recent achievement – and a dominant media attitude that bordered on derision.

The attacks came from all places at all times, recurring characteristics being loose assumptions and illogical conclusions that were somehow allowed to pass as fact-based arguments. Many of the comments were similar to the complaints lodged by the British rock press, though the Swedes put their own curious slant on the subject.

"Abba's music seems much too calculated, it doesn't feel spontaneous," said Christer Eklund, the managing editor of youth programming at the Swedish Broadcasting Corporation when asked for his opinion about the group. "Their music doesn't express any feelings, and a sort of product thinking shines through. The music becomes a cold and unemotional, targeted product that is commercially marketed. And then I don't like their lyrics either; they are so unrealistic as to be virtually cynical."

At the time Christer Eklund was freelancing as a musician, parallel with his work at the radio, and he had appeared on several Swedish records. It has to be assumed that his dislike of Abba wasn't quite so strong in January 1974 when he gladly accepted payment for the spirited saxophone performance that graced 'Waterloo'.

In the climate of the times, it wasn't so strange that Eklund found it necessary to distance himself strongly from his work with Abba. Other musicians had experienced quite extraordinary reactions because of their association with the group. Guitarist Janne Schaffer, a recording artist in his own right, had been forbidden to perform at certain venues controlled by the Music Movement. The period that bass player Mike Watson spent in Schaffer's band didn't exactly help matters – Watson was also a frequent session player for Abba. Saxophonist Ulf Andersson, who even went on tour with the group, was a member of the jazz group Egba, whose music in itself was acceptable to the Music Movement. But just like Schaffer, Egba found themselves banned because of Andersson's "crime".

The atmosphere was strange, inexplicably judgemental. Abba and Polar had no choice but to distance themselves from much of the Swedish music business. The thinking of the Music Movement was certainly isolationist: to consciously work hard in order to reach beyond the borders of Sweden was just unthinkable. There was a clear division between the blatantly "commercial" records ("manufactured" to be "sold") that Eklund described, and "non-commercial" music. In the contrary logic that ruled the arguments at the time, "commercial" could only be bad, while "non-commercial" was good simply by virtue of not being commercial.

As a result, efforts to emulate what Stig was doing, to learn from his example, were very limited in the contemporary music business, even from those other labels that might be described as commercially oriented. The main exception was probably Abba's good friend Björn Skifs, US chart-topper with 'Hooked On A Feeling' under the name Blue Swede, and Bengt Palmers, Skifs' producer and co-writer. Palmers was also the producer of Harpo, who in 1976 gained an international hit of some note with the song 'Moviestar'.

Thus did the experience and knowledge gained by Stig and Abba remain almost solely within the extended Polar and Sweden Music family. Stig and Abba certainly opened doors to the international music scene through which other Swedish artists might follow, but very few artists or record companies took advantage of this opportunity after Abba had passed through. The main link from this closed world was tour promoter Thomas Johansson who, through his association with Abba, eventually became a conduit for other Swedish acts from the mid Eighties onwards. By then, of course, the climate had changed.

But at the end of 1976 Johansson and Abba were still on a journey together throughout the world, and the next stage was Abba's first major tour. The countdown towards the première date of January 28, 1977, had begun.

Chapter 21

How quickly the time had passed since Björn and Agnetha first met, and how different things had become between them. By the time 'Dancing Queen' was released, more than seven years had elapsed since they became an item during the filming of that banal television special.

Back then, Agnetha was just 19, an up-and-coming singer, relishing her new found fame and all that it brought her. She drove around Stockholm in her very own white Triumph Spitfire with red upholstery, the car she had bought with the first money she earned as a star. Björn was 24, a songwriter just like Agnetha, a handsome, eligible bachelor with neat sideburns. Music was his life, and he was establishing himself as a genuine force within the Swedish music scene. Björn was Agnetha's teenage fantasy come true.

It had been a time marked by excitement: flirting, falling in love, moving in together. Both loved to party and were living an almost bohemian, irresponsible life in central Stockholm. Sometimes they'd forget the keys to their one-room apartment. Luckily, it was on the ground floor so Björn could climb in through the window. In another situation it would have been an annoying mishap, but for the two lovebirds it was just an amusing incident, a shared memory to laugh over as they poured a glass of wine.

And now, just seven years later, they were international stars, millionaires who were selling records by the bucketload. They had been married for five years and were the parents of a three-year-old daughter. In November 1976, they moved from their first villa to a new home, still located in the affluent suburb of Lidingö.

Both sets of parents-in-law were crazy about their childrens' chosen spouse. "Björn is the ideal man – he's fantastic!" gushed Birgit Fältskog. "There is nothing he can't manage at home. He's actually better at cooking than Agnetha. Whenever we visit he takes care of us like you wouldn't believe. He spends hours in the kitchen, conjuring up the most amazing dishes. We're very impressed, especially by the wonderful way he takes care of Linda. There can't be a better man than him!"

Everything should have been just fine in the idyllic Fältskog/Ulvaeus household – but it wasn't. After the difficult early years, when Björn and Agnetha had struggled to get to know each other, ironing out the rough spots, they had reached an equilibrium of sorts. But paradoxically, instead of growing closer when they had figured each other out, they found that they were beginning to drift apart.

Although Björn could be stubborn and testy, he was a miracle of calm and reason compared to Agnetha's violent mood swings. The storm would blow over as quickly as it had started, but how painful it was while it lasted. And the difference in their outlooks on life was growing bigger, not least in terms of how to balance Abba's extraordinary career with their responsibilities as parents.

Agnetha's resistance to promotional trips and concert tours was becoming more determined by the day. Her love of music was still solid, but career obligations would never take precedence over her role as a mother. Although Björn shared Agnetha's reluctance to tour, he was determined to fulfil all promotional duties. "I just thought that we could have both," he recalled. "I thought, 'We have a nanny. If we're away for two or three days, what difference could that make?' But that wasn't her view."

Björn and Agnetha had long resisted having a second child. They wanted to wait until they felt the time was right: taking care of Linda and balancing their growing career demands was more than enough responsibility. However, now that their marriage felt less solid they began to believe they were lacking something to unify them, something that could give their relationship a renewed sense of purpose. Was one more child what was needed? Linda was almost four years old, so the time was ripe for an addition to the family. Björn and Agnetha made their decision: they were going to try for another child.

Life was calmer, if not exactly placid, on the other side of the Abba equation. After the years of frustration, success on this scale was an elixir for Frida. It was as if the girl without an identity, the orphan stranger in a strange land, had simply stepped through the looking glass and become someone else entirely. Gone was the housewife and jazz-vocalist and in her place was a dazzling pop star, but the inevitable question remained: who was the real Frida? For all the confidence she exuded, somehow it seemed she still didn't know exactly who she was.

To a greater extent than Björn and Agnetha, who had a child to take care of, Frida and Benny thrived on being pop stars. They socialised more and were often seen out nightclubbing. In November the couple had moved out of their central Stockholm apartment and into a stately villa in Lidingö, where Agnetha and Björn already lived. Their children were visiting on a regular basis and would soon start living in the house semi-permanently. Nevertheless, Frida still harboured a guilty conscience over Hans and Lise-Lotte. Although she remained convinced that she did the right thing when she left Eskilstuna, she had strong regrets over missing out on so much of their upbringing.

Now Frida was determined to build a more trusting relationship between herself and her children, one in which she could become a natural base in their lives. She realised that it was going to take a while. "I used to be very scared of doing the wrong thing as a parent, and many times that made me a bit inhibited," she reflected. "Loneliness has been my constant companion in life and I've perhaps found it hard to give them that genuine thing that I never experienced myself."

As she admitted later, the fact that she was still mainly looking out for her own needs complicated her attempts at developing a better relationship with her children. Outwardly she may have been a regally elegant, confident pop star, but inside there was still a little girl looking for true emotional fulfilment.

Benny remained the centre of Frida's life, the anchor who would pick her up when she fell into her depressions. She wasn't unhappy, far from it – following her most recent depression her life was very much in tune with her personality, and the love she felt from Abba's audience was filling the void that she had felt inside her since childhood.

In the midst of all the Abba chaos, Frida was also becoming more reflective. She was starting to recognise the danger of constantly relying on another person or outer surroundings for her emotional stability. Slowly but surely, she began a quest for getting to the core of her own being.

As Björn and Agnetha, and Benny and Frida, tried to sort out their personal lives and grappled with their insecurities, they were all obliged to continue their leading roles in the phenomenon that was Abba, with all that this entailed. Next on the agenda was the tour of Europe and Australia. After three years as pop superstars, it was to be Abba's first truly international tour, an unprecedented lack of presence on the stage circuit for an act of their stature.

This absence may also have been one of the keys to their longevity: the group worked very hard, but they didn't run themselves into the ground in quite the same way as their peers. A look at what some of the most successful contemporary American acts were up to towards the end of 1976 puts Abba's situation into perspective.

The Eagles, for instance, were struggling to finish *Hotel California*, one of the quintessential albums of the Seventies. Because the group had a major tour scheduled, the album had to be completed after the tour had already begun. The group was flying back to the studio between concerts to record all night and then flying out to the next gig the following day. "We did a lot of work on drugs in The Eagles," drummer and lead singer Don Henley later admitted. "Our schedule was just so gruelling we didn't have the stamina otherwise." The *Hotel California* experience effectively killed the band, and they only released one more, lacklustre album before breaking up acrimoniously.

Fleetwood Mac, meanwhile, were working their way towards completion of the *Rumours* album, another milestone of the decade. Marked by cracking relationships within the group, they toured before, during and immediately after the making of the LP. Needless to say, recording sessions were fuelled by excessive drug consumption and band morale went from bad to worse.

Even a supposedly clean and wholesome act like the Carpenters were buckling under the pressure. Since 1969 they had released one album virtually every year, but still devoted inordinate amounts of time to touring and long spells in Las Vegas. Richard Carpenter, a songwriter of some ambition in his collaboration with lyricist John Bettis, regretted not having the time to write more original material for the group's albums. His sister, Karen, was sliding into ultimately fatal anorexia nervosa, while Richard himself was developing a pill addiction to keep him going.

Abba, however, took the pragmatic and sensible route: they never indulged in any of the usual rock star hard drugs like cocaine or heroin, and were even ambivalent to soft drugs like marijuana. Björn pointed out that whatever experience he had of such substances had been limited to his young and curious days as a teen idol in the Sixties. "It was worse back then, when cannabis started coming," he recalled. "Because it's obvious that you tried it a couple of times. But when you heard about brain damage and things like that you quit."

Thanks to holding back on touring and other outside commitments, Abba were able to produce regular albums of high production value which consisted entirely of original material from the group's two songwriters. It also meant that they would come out of the experience alive and without any drug addictions to shake off.

After a year's preparation and two months of rehearsal, Abba finally set off on the first leg of their 1977 tour. The itinerary would take them to Norway, Sweden, Denmark, West Germany, The Netherlands, Belgium and Great Britain, commencing with a concert at Ekeberghallen in Oslo, Norway on Friday, January 28. The schedule didn't leave room for many

312

hiccups: they had crammed 17 concerts at 14 venues into 17 days. Abba would be appearing before a total of 84,000 people. All the shows were sold out months in advance.

This time the group and tour promoters EMA Telstar experienced the exact opposite problem they had encountered on their 1974 trip, massively underestimating the demand to see Abba in concert. Famously, London's Royal Albert Hall received a reported 3.5 million ticket applications for a total of 12,000 tickets available for two concerts. Ironically, only six months earlier, Abba had been thinking of booking the much larger Wembley Empire Pool, which could seat as many as 11,500 but, burned by previous tour experiences, they were worried that they wouldn't be able to fill it.

The autumn 1974 trek had been the most ambitious concert venture attempted by a Swedish act up to that point, but the new tour set unprecedented production standards. It was said that in terms of the size of the production, it was the biggest tour anyone had ever undertaken in Europe apart from The Rolling Stones. One aeroplane, a bus and four especially constructed trucks were needed to transport the entourage of 52 people and 30 tons of equipment.

"Our expenses are as high as our income, at the very least," said Thomas Johansson. "The tour might very well make a loss." Which indeed it did – it was hoped that the Australian leg would recoup the loss to even things up or, with a bit of luck, turn it into a profitable venture.

People from EMA Telstar had scrutinised each and every venue of the tour. Abba themselves had prepared every last detail, with Agnetha and Frida taking jazz ballet lessons twice a week to get themselves in the best possible shape. The backing band on the new tour consisted for the main part of session musicians who had appeared on their records, plus two additional keyboard players and a trio of female backing vocalists.

Even as the line-up of musicians was put together, Abba had a taste of the domestic, politicised resistance to their methods and music. Highly respected percussionist Ahmadu Jarr was invited to come along on the tour, but when his wife threatened to leave him if he did, he turned down the offer. Instead, Malando Gassama, who had previously contributed percussion to Abba's records, took his place.

The purchase price for a seat at the Oslo première concert had been 40 Norwegian kroner, but in the days before the performance, black market prices had skyrocketed to 500 kroner. Expectations were high, and the start of Abba's first major tour was fraught with nerves and plenty of tense moments. Journalists had flown in from all over Europe: this was the concert that everybody was going to review, the one that would set the tone for the rest of the tour.

Two days earlier, the Abba entourage arrived in a cold and wintry Oslo with temperatures well below freezing point. To the dismay of the many reporters the group wasn't available for any interviews whatsoever during their whole time in the Norwegian capital.

Despite persistent attempts from the media they were kept at arms length all the time by tour arrangers EMA Telstar or Stig Anderson himself. "We want to do a good job, and to be able to do that we need peace and quiet," he snapped. "Besides, what is there to talk about? There is nothing to say that hasn't already been said . . . Our schedule is so tight that we need every last minute to relax." At one point, the somewhat overzealous security men were even on the point of throwing out the official photographer hired by Polar.

A full week before the concert, fans had begun circling around the Grand Hotel where Abba were staying. An entire corridor at the hotel had been blocked off for the group and was supervised by diligent guards. When Abba finally arrived, no children between the ages of nine and 15 were even allowed into the hotel without special permission. The fans instead directed their attention to the rehearsals, waiting in the cold outside the venue, climbing on ladders, window sills and even each other to try to get a tiny glimpse of their idols.

Even when Abba tried to relax a bit in Oslo, it turned into a minor nightmare. A horse-drawn sleigh ride had been arranged for the whole entourage the night before the concert. On a curve, the sleigh with Stig, Berka Bergkvist and Görel Johnsen turned over and they all flew out into the snow. Stig hadn't even dressed properly for the event, having on a pair of summer shoes. Furious, he refused to get into the sleigh again. He changed his mind when he learned that it was another two and a half miles before they reached their destination. "It was horrible," he fumed afterwards. "It's pure luck that no one got hurt."

In addition to their pre-concert nerves, some of the musicians were struck down with colds. Lena Andersson, who was one of three backing singers, lost her voice completely. Abba's doctor, on permanent stand-by back in Stockholm, had to fly over quickly to get everyone back on their feet and in good shape.

At 8 p.m. on the Friday, Abba finally appeared on stage before the 5,300 strong audience, including Norway's Crown Prince Harald and Crown Princess Sonja. The group was fairly choking with nerves. "Fifteen minutes before we were due to go on we were so nervous we were not talking to each other," said Björn. "I felt like saying, 'Let's forget the whole thing. If this is what touring means, let's not bother.'"

Abba's show was suitably lavish. Both stage and costumes were predominantly white, with blue curtains and large vases filled with red roses at various spots to add a dash of colour along with the lighting effects. The costumes worn by the Abba members were brightened up with golden trimmings of varying size.

Each performance began with the rocky *Arrival* song 'Tiger', preceded by the sound of a helicopter booming through the speakers. It was all meant to connect to the *Arrival* cover theme, although some bemused concert-goers thought it sounded more like a train. The helicopter effect was so loud that at the Oslo concert, the royal couple were seen to put their fingers in their ears for the duration of the introduction.

Presumably, they were placated when Abba performed a few lines from the Norwegian song 'Vi har ei tulle med øyne blå' ('Our New-born Baby Girl Has Eyes Of Blue') as a special tribute. In 1976, the children's song had been released on a single by Crown Princess Sonja duetting with Norwegian artist Wenche Myhre. This certainly wasn't going to be a traditional, wild rock concert.

But Abba did work very hard during each performance. Standing to the left, Björn seemed to be acting out his rock guitarist fantasies, while at the other side of the stage Benny was bouncing up and down on his piano stool, pouring all his Hep Stars experience into the performance. Agnetha and Frida were all over the stage, improvising their movements one moment, dancing according to Graham Tainton's choreographed steps the next.

With four albums to their credit, the group had ditched most of the material from the *Ring Ring* and *Waterloo* LPs: only 'He Is Your Brother', 'Waterloo' and 'Sitting In The Palmtree' remained in the 25-song, two-hour performance. Instead, the bulk of the programme consisted of songs from the *ABBA* and *Arrival* albums. Incidentally, the live version of 'Sitting In The Palmtree' ended with a fade-out, extremely unusual for a live performance.

The Oslo audience was enthusiastic if not exactly ecstatic. When the group urged the crowd to sing along in 'Fernando', they were met with an embarrassing silence. "If you don't know the lyrics, you can just hum along," the group tried, but apparently to no avail. For future concerts, asking the audience to just sing the word "Fernando" in the chorus solved the problem.

It was evident that Abba's nerves were on edge during the première performance. A number written especially for the tour, 'I Am An A' (aka 'A Simple Four Letter Word'), wherein the four members introduced themselves and each other in an unusually ironic and self-deprecating manner, was delivered at a forced pace compared to later, more relaxed concerts.

'Why Did It Have To Be Me' was performed as a duet between Frida and Björn, and Frida showed off all her best moves, playing around with the microphone stand in true rock star fashion. The "jazz broad" of yesteryear was now unquestionably a "pop girl". Sound engineer Claes af Geijerstam dubbed her "Abba's Rod Stewart", referring to her stage antics and interplay with the audience. "Agnetha probably wouldn't have toured at all if she could have avoided it. Frida's opinion was the complete opposite. She really liked being on stage and before each concert she was impatient and expectant."

Preparing for the 1977 tour, Abba wanted to offer something more than just a run-through of their hits and assorted album tracks. Björn and Benny had long nurtured a dream of writing a musical: stretching their abilities to see if they could make their music work within a dramatic format. The *Arrival* track 'Money, Money, Money' was an exploratory venture into that kind of territory.

As they prepared for the tour they decided to dip their toes a little deeper into the water and put together what they called a "mini-musical". The 25-minute opus *The Girl With The Golden Hair* had a thin storyline about a small-town girl leaving her hometown to achieve stardom as a singer, only to find herself trapped by fame. It would close the show, and Frida and Agnetha both donned blonde wigs and identical costumes to indicate that they were both playing the same character. In some respects, the plot could have been based on their own lives.

The Girl With The Golden Hair opened with 'Thank You For The Music', where Agnetha had the solo spot. "I've been so lucky, I am the girl with golden hair", she sang. The somewhat naïve celebration of the joys of singing while the whole world is listening seemed to mirror her own teenage daydreams and subsequent rise to fame as a peroxide blonde singer in the late Sixties.

Frida took over for the second number, the dramatic show-stopping ballad 'I Wonder (Departure)'. The words about leaving the security of a small-town life partly echoed her own experience in breaking up with Ragnar and the children. "Leaving now, is that the right thing?" the song asked. The conclusion, "But who the hell am I if I don't even try?" corresponded almost literally with Frida's real-life decision to break away.

Together, in 'I'm A Marionette', where the protagonist had been caught up in her own success, the two women sang about feeling "pushed around". The final number, 'Get On The Carousel', was all about shunning the music business that had made the girl with the golden hair famous. Certainly, placing the story within the context of the showbiz world was a self-evident solution for Björn and Benny. But the theme of being trapped by fame was hardly coincidental, even if the idea may have been triggered on a subconscious level.

The Girl With The Golden Hair used narration as a time-saving device to advance the plot between songs. For Björn and Benny, it was important that the narrator had a genuinely British, theatrical voice. Francis Matthews, a 24-year-old Royal Shakespeare Company actor, was hired through a theatrical agency. Appearing onstage in heavy make-up as a sort of Faustian version of the Harlequin character, Matthews struggled to lend dramatic authority to the thin story line. Björn and Benny themselves admitted that both plot and narrative text were weak.

Even during the tour, Matthews spoke quite frankly about the oddness of his place in the entourage. "This world is alien to me. It's with pretty mixed feelings that I walk onstage," he said. The actor, who had written a few short stories and a play himself, saw his participation as a career opportunity. "I think that Abba's first attempt at a musical is very promising from a musical point of view, but the story is thin. It would be fun to give them a reasonable text to work with." Alas, the 1977 tour would be the full extent of his work with Abba. Francis Matthews later became the director of the Greenwich Theatre in London.

Reviews after the first concert were mostly favourable, though the group was criticised for their stilted between-song banter. It was that old cabaret entertainment spirit shining through again. The group was panned for their somewhat lame jokes and clunky introductions for the duration of this tour and, indeed, all of their subsequent live concerts. Nor did the mini-musical meet with much more than a lukewarm response for the most part. Audiences had never heard the songs before, and grew impatient, waiting for it to end. Critics pointed out that the story was flimsy and clichéd.

At one performance, Frida had been in such a hurry to get her wig on that she didn't have time to fasten it properly. In one of the wild dances the wig fell off when she threw her head forwards, exposing the unflattering stocking cap she had used to flatten her own hair. When she desperately attempted to put the wig back on as quickly as possible, it ended up back to front. Such incidents didn't help the ambience Abba's composing team hoped to achieve with *The Girl With The Golden Hair*. "You tried to build up a special mood in the course of the musical – it was supposed to end on a certain note – but that blew it all away," Benny noted wryly.

The composers were aware that the plot left a lot to be desired, but blamed time restrictions; indeed, it was a miracle that they had time to come up with anything at all in the short timespan between the end of *Arrival* promotions and the start of tour rehearsals. "I think it was I who came up with this concept, which was simple and flexible enough to fit almost any type of song," Björn recalled. "I remember that someone asked us why we didn't extend it to a full-length musical. Well, I don't think the story was *quite* good enough for that!" When the musical songs were recorded in the studio later in the year some of the more clunky lyrics had been rewritten, most notably in 'Thank You For The Music'.

After the tour had ended, the musical song 'I'm A Marionette' was the subject of some controversy. Swedish singer Harpo, of 'Moviestar' fame, accused Abba of utilising his idea of the song. For the past few years Harpo had been working on an as yet unrecorded musical of his own, entitled *The Story Of Peter Blue*. The project included a song called 'I'm A Marionette', which the singer sometimes performed during his stage shows.

"In the summer of 1975, Abba and Stig Anderson [watched me in concert]," Harpo related. "Afterwards they went up and congratulated me especially for the marionette number. When they go and write a song along the same theme, and let Frida and Agnetha jump around on stage according to the same jerky moves as me, it's no goddamn coincidence!"

Benny absolutely refuted the accusations, although he admitted having vague memories of the number in Harpo's show. "But our marionette hasn't got anything to do with his," he said. "We knew that the third song in the musical was to deal with the girl ending up in a situation where she felt like she had no control over her own life. To associate to a marionette at that juncture is hardly unique – Harpo is not the first to make poetry about marionettes." The controversy died as soon as it had started.

All in all, Abba's tour première in Oslo had come off successfully. Reviewers noted that Agnetha had become much more animated onstage and didn't come off as stiff in contrast to Frida as she had on earlier tours. "I had forgotten how tremendously exciting it is to appear in front of a live audience," noted Björn afterwards. Abba celebrated with an all-night party after the concert.

Their lack of drug use didn't mean that they didn't know how to wind down and have fun after a performance. On the contrary, long experience had taught them how to knock back quite a few drinks before the night was over, even if they never wrecked any hotel rooms or threw television sets out of windows in true "rock star" style.

Due to the nation's restrictive alcohol policy Swedes don't have much of a pub or bar culture. When they do party, however, it traditionally turns into quite wild booze-fests, with a great deal of alcohol being consumed. These behind-the-scenes festivities were in sharp contrast to the wholesome aura that Abba projected, and which to a degree was forced upon them by the media. "No doubt we had a clean-cut image, but we did have a few wild times on the road," as Agnetha later put it.

The day after the Oslo première, Abba headed for Gothenburg for the tour's two Swedish concerts. Things got off to a bad start, even before they had left the hotel. Going down to the garage and the waiting limousines, the elevator got stuck between floors. It took 25 minutes before they could finally drive out to the airport.

The group immediately ran into further logistical problems. The Gothenburg area was in the throes of a bad snowstorm, they were told, and all flights were cancelled. Landing at Torslanda airport was an impossibility. With Abba's tight schedule, flying was the only chance to get to the venue on time. The plane had originally been due for take-off at 1.50 p.m., landing at Torslanda 40 minutes later. This would have given them ample time for a soundcheck at 6 p.m. before the concert at 7.30.

Thomas Johansson pleaded with Scandinavian Airlines and the air-traffic controllers that an exception should be made for Abba's plane. Finally, an okay was given and the flight, loaded with the Abba entourage and a mass of reporters who were covering the group's European tour, could take off as scheduled. But it still wasn't certain that the plane would be able to land at Torslanda.

They reached the Gothenburg area at 2.30, but the weather was too bad to allow for any landing. The pilot went into a holding pattern, waiting for conditions to improve. There was talk of landing in Jönköping instead, perhaps Malmö or even Copenhagen. If that happened, there would be no chance that the concert – in front of 9,500 – could begin on time.

An hour later, the plane still hadn't landed. Abba and their friends remained calm, however, with Stig Anderson sipping champagne and raving about the previous night's good reviews. Through enormous efforts by the ground personnel at Torslanda, the runway was finally cleared of snow. At 3.40, the flight could touch down without violating safety regulations. Everyone on the plane applauded as the pilots completed the tricky landing, and the Abba members personally went into the cockpit to thank them. No other planes were allowed to land at Torslanda for the next several hours.

While Abba were whisked away to their hotel in limousines, the musicians and backing vocalists faced another obstacle. The bus that was to transport them and their equipment had been caught up in the bad weather and slid off the road into a ditch. After a long delay the bus arrived at the airport, but the backing band had to go directly to the Scandinavium concert venue and the soundcheck.

In the end everything worked out, and the first Gothenburg concert went off without a hitch – a walkover victory with the concert-goers. One notable quirk with the Abba concerts on much of the tour was the lack of hysteria on the part of the audience. It really was a family-type crowd, and even the teenagers remained fairly calm. Abba simply didn't attract a riot-inducing audience.

The group played a second Gothenburg concert the day after, and then went on to Copenhagen where two concerts had also been scheduled. Mechanical problems continued to dog them. The brake valves broke on the bus carrying the 15 people responsible for sound and lighting. Five taxi cabs had to drive the crew the rest of the way: the total cost was 4,500 kronor (£585), an expensive way to travel even if it was a drop in the ocean in the total tour budget.

Abba had their own snags to contend with. Because of the continuous bad weather and a heavy fog over the airport, EMA Telstar didn't dare rely on going by plane this time. The solution was a 160-mile limousine ride to Copenhagen, which meant that the group arrived three hours late and had no time for resting at the hotel – it was straight on to the concert venue. With all these problems, the performance still wasn't delayed by more than half an hour.

Less than a week into the tour, the four members of Abba were already feeling the strain, with tour fatigue familiar to all rock stars setting in. The insides of hotel rooms and concert halls were far from stimulating, even if the two hours on stage were as exhilarating as anything life had to offer.

Abba were the most popular recording act in every country they visited. The statistics pointed to one long row of singles in the top regions of the charts. In The Netherlands, for instance, the group had been proclaimed the best-selling group in the entire history of the Dutch record industry. Inevitably, such success inspired an inordinate amount of attention. "We haven't been able to take one single step," Benny complained. "There are fans waiting outside every hotel entrance. Frida and I managed to sneak out to the Munch museum in Oslo, but that's all. For the most part, we're forced to stay locked up in our hotel rooms. It's unbearably boring." Benny wasn't exaggerating the physical pressure from the fans: at one point, Frida almost got a pen in her eye from an ardent autograph hunter.

In Gothenburg, Agnetha and Björn were going crazy being confined to their room – they just had to get out. The main entrance was besieged by fans and it was only with the aid of the hotel staff that they were able to sneak out through the hotel's basement. "But that kind of maneuvre is too much like hard work in the long run," sighed Björn. "You end up staying inside instead."

Björn continued to express his doubts about the wisdom of touring. He'd experienced a strange, queasy feeling in his stomach in the weeks running up to the début concert in Oslo. "We're in the middle of an enormous machinery that just *has* to work," he said. "Then there is all this other pressure, from journalists and fans . . . This is not the reality. The reality is to be home with Linda and live like everybody else."

The tour management attempted every trick imaginable to outsmart the fans, often re-directing the group's routes at short notice. On the West German leg of the tour, Abba travelled between cities in limousines or by train, instead of scheduled plane flights. Many a disappointed fan was left standing at the airport with their cameras and autograph books.

Even though the musicians and roadies enjoyed accommodation far more luxurious than was common on rock tours, they never stayed at the same hotel as Abba. The reason was that the colourful Abba trucks attracted too much attention and would invariably make the fans seek out nearby hotels in the hope of a glimpse of the group.

The pressure and sense of living in a twisted version of reality didn't ease up when Abba reached Berlin on February 2. There they were greeted by the latest issue of British tabloid the *Sun*, and an article headed "Secret Catfights of Abba's Angels", purporting to tell the inside story about the group. The *Sun* informed its readers that "tensions within Abba often boil over into full-scale rows. In particular, the two girls go for each other's throats in spitting, screaming catfights."

The writers had apparently picked up on a year-old article from *Expressen*, written by a Swedish journalist travelling with the group on their promotional visit to Australia. He revealed the sensational titbit that the punctual Agnetha was occasionally displeased by having to wait in hotel lobbies because Frida was sometimes three or four minutes late. In the *Sun*'s version of events, Agnetha was "obsessional about being on time for rehearsals and being ready in costume on time for stage appearances. Frida is constantly late."

The tabloid was closer to the truth when it claimed that Frida found it easier to learn new songs than Agnetha, who "doesn't grasp the musical points being made by Björn and Benny as quickly as Frida". However, the writers applied the in-band conflicts to the wrong pairing when they tried to establish that, "In rehearsal, Frida's exasperation with Agnetha's slowness bubbles over and the two girls really let fly at each other."

Björn and Benny were confronted with the article just before Abba's first West German concert, in Berlin. They saw to it that the feature was kept from Agnetha and Frida until after the performance. But when the two singers finally did get to see it Agnetha burst into tears, maintaining that it was all lies. "This is going to be repeated all over the world," she exclaimed. "Of course Frida and I are two hot-tempered personalities. But we've never come to blows. We are the best of friends and can talk about everything." Frida laughed off the accusations, pointing out that it was ridiculous to think that a group would hold together if the members actually hated each other to that extent.

The *Sun's* exposé was the first major story to detail rumours of conflicts between Frida and Agnetha. These stories would pop up now and again over the years, and even long after the break-up of the group it has come to be established as a "fact" that the two girls had never got along. "Certainly, the girls are very different and are both highly temperamental," said Stig Anderson a few months after the feature in the *Sun.* "But these days they get along fine because they are aware of it. They find it much easier to co-exist now than they did five years ago. Now they know each other and have learned to show consideration for each other."

Agnetha and Frida themselves always denied the animosity between them, describing their relationship as that of two siblings. It followed, therefore, that sibling rivalry might occur – and the exaggerated attention on Agnetha from fans and media no doubt fuelled these feelings – but the retrospective portrayal of Frida as "the other one", or even "the ugly one", is quite clearly a grossly inaccurate depiction of the situation. An ill-advised perm or two aside, Frida was a classic beauty whose features contributed greatly to Abba's sex appeal.

However, the women did acknowledge certain differences. "I don't want to hide the fact that Frida and I had opposite backgrounds, temperaments and personalities," Agnetha admitted many years later. "Nor did we get ourselves going or wind down in the same way. We could get furious and tired with each other, so we had our moments but, surely, it would have been strange if we didn't. It went on between all the members of the group."

Claes af Geijerstam noted that it was quite natural that there was a bit of tension in the extreme conditions of a tour. "You must realise, they were always in the same room," he said. "To snap at each other was a pressure release."

Perhaps the more interesting question is why it was always more attractive for the downmarket media to try to find evidence of quarrels and even outright hatred between Agnetha and Frida when the major conflicts throughout Abba's career actually occurred within the two couples. The obvious reason was, of course, that as lead singers they were the front figures of the group. As such, they competed for the audience's attention –

it was all for the better of the performance, adding a bit of tension between the two, some of it no doubt real. "We pushed each other along," Frida confirmed later. "Anything you can do I can do better!"

This part of their charisma seemed to harbour the roots of the animosity rumours. Overt competition was expected between men: in school, in the workplace, on stage – in fact in every social context imaginable. However, the rules for women have always been different. Whereas support and competition aren't expected to be mutually exclusive in a male friendship, modern culture determines that animosity must lurk somewhere beneath the surface when two women compete for the same space.

In the case of Abba, Agnetha acknowledged that there was a fight for the spotlight, but dismissed all other allegations as "pure nonsense. During our years with Abba we always supported each other onstage. If one wasn't on form the other stepped in and took over."

Despite their predominantly soft and mild appearances, as well as their silence in group interviews and press conferences while Björn and Benny prattled on, there was always a slight aura of self-assuredness, a "don't try to mess with us" attitude, emanating from Agnetha and Frida. It's possible that this tiny inflection in their image posed something of a threat towards the patriarchal culture and, indeed, the self-image of women who had accepted their designated roles within that culture.

When the kind of competition that appeared "natural" between two men showed itself between Agnetha and Frida – for the best songs, the audience's affection, the onstage attention – society had no way of handling it unless the two women were also perceived as mortal enemies or "catfighters". In that way the "flaw" in their characters could be pounced upon to neutralise the challenge their image presented.

At the end of the day, Agnetha and Frida enjoyed a solid friendship, getting a buzz out of hearing the combined forces of their voices, creating intricate harmony parts together. Certainly, they also recognised the advantage of sharing the experience of being the focal point of a world-famous group: contrary to the experience of isolated solo performers, in Abba one lead singer always knew what the other was going through as the pressure became overwhelming.

An article like the one in the *Sun* wasn't exactly what was needed to break the mood of isolation and the feelings of unwanted attention. "It's pure death, it really is," said Björn. "Unbearably boring. Same thing all the time. And new people constantly who only wish you well – *too* well. They want to show us things and are so accommodating and want us to do this and that. And the only thing we want is to be left in peace."

But there wasn't much peace to be had for the duration of Abba's week in West Germany. A loyal territory ever since the days of 'People Need Love', *Arrival* had topped the albums chart for 14 weeks. A month after the European tour ended the Germans would give Abba their sixth consecutive number one single with 'Knowing Me, Knowing You'. The attention was just as overwhelming here as in the rest of Europe, if not more.

This had some unfortunate consequences in Hanover, where a photographer from the tabloid *Bild Zeitung* insisted on taking unwelcome photographs of Abba. The group protested that they were tired and worn-out, asking to be left alone. The request was ignored, which provoked a violent reaction from tour manager Bosse Norling, since 1975 an invaluable bodyguard cum all-round fixer on Abba's tours and promotional trips.

"I punched him in the stomach," recalled Norling, "but unfortunately I hit the Leica he had hanging there. So I was hurt, not him. That didn't stop him from lying floored on the ground for 15 minutes with a satisfied grin. The day after I could read about myself described as Abba's lethal gorilla who was knocking people out left, right and centre. A mad bulldog, that's what I was."

As a peace offering, the photographer was given an exclusive, private photo opportunity with the group. However, the matter was still pursued afterwards and wasn't settled until two years later, when Norling was ordered to pay an 800 kronor (£88) fine.

For Agnetha, the pressure of living the surreal touring existence was becoming unbearable. The feelings of displacement experienced by so many other pop stars in her situation started getting to her. "The travelling is very, very hard," she reflected a while later. "One day when I woke up [I thought,] 'Where am I? In which city?' It's terrible."

Agnetha desperately needed to see Linda, the symbol of everything that was solid and real in her life. She was planning to fly back to Sweden and be with Linda after the last West German concert in Hamburg on February 8. Then she would fly out to Birmingham for the first British concert two days later. Logistically, it would have been impossible to make it work. Instead, Linda was brought to London, joining her parents who were staying with friends in a private apartment. "Without her we wouldn't have managed to go through with our work," said a relieved Agnetha.

The group concluded the European part of the tour with five concerts in Great Britain, opening in Birmingham on February 10. Special precautions had been taken for the British leg, with four bodyguards hired especially to protect the group from their fans. "It's necessary," said

Thomas Johansson. "The audience is more forward there, they want to get close to their idols and touch them."

At the first show, at the Birmingham Odeon, concert-goers were all body searched before entering the venue because of recent IRA attacks on two pubs in the town. The rush for tickets had been as great as ever. The Odeon could seat 2,500 people; ticket applications topped 50,000. Despite the successful first week of the tour, pre-concert tension was as high as ever. It was especially scary to be performing in front of a British audience. "We were terribly nervous," said Agnetha about the first concert. "After all, it's classic ground in terms of pop music."

Things didn't seem to improve very much the day after. Before the performance in Manchester, Benny was seen pacing up and down his and Frida's suite, while his fiancée read a book and hardly spoke a word for several hours. Agnetha, meanwhile, had locked herself in the bathroom.

The tour concluded with the two concerts at London's Royal Albert Hall. The prospect of performing at this prestigious venue was quite overwhelming – opera singer Jenny Lind was the only Swede before Abba to have been the star attraction in the concert hall, but at least Frida's nerves had been calmed down by this point. "The only thing that bothers us is that we'll do two concerts in one night," she said. "We hardly have the time to take a shower in between."

Although the hall could seat 7,000, Abba wanted everyone to be able to see the show properly, so only 6,000 seats per concert were sold. After a slow beginning with reserved audiences in both shows, the group managed to win the crowd over. Afterwards they felt that the Albert Hall performances were the high-point of everything they had experienced in their careers so far.

Agnetha did admit to having been pretty nervous throughout both concerts. "During the first show I never let myself go at all, I just felt rigid and strange," she said. Björn concluded: "It will take at least two and a half years before we do another tour of Europe. It's too much hard work, takes too much time and costs too much. But it's been fun and the experience is worth the hard work." Even the tour-reluctant Stig Anderson was beaming: "I guess this is what I wanted and was dreaming about."

The tour of Europe was Abba's first hands-on experience of living under the pressure of their enormous fame for a prolonged period of time. They found it difficult to deal with, perhaps more so than they had expected. Still, it was a mere walk in the park compared to what was waiting for them when they arrived on the other side of the world.

Chapter 22

When the plane carrying Abba and their entourage touched down at Kingsford-Smith Airport in Sydney at 8.50 p.m. on Sunday, February 27, 1977, it was the start of two of the most intense weeks of madness in the entire history of the group. The day after their arrival, the headline of the tabloid *Daily Mirror* simply trumpeted "THEY'RE HERE!" above a photo of the four Swedes. No further explanation was needed – all of Australia knew exactly who "they" were. The headline proved beyond any doubt just how completely Abba had been adopted by the nation.

Walking the streets in any of the major cities offered endless reminders of the group's almost incomprehensible popularity. "There was Abba – Abba – Abba – everywhere," says Michael Tretow, who accompanied the tour to record the group's concerts. "There were pictures of them on every corner, wherever you went. I got really tired of their photo faces. The overload was so great that it just went into the red."

Abba's tour of Australia would certainly leave its mark on both the nation and the group themselves. Agnetha later recalled it as "the most incredible of all the things that I experienced with Abba."

The group's arrival in Australia was almost on a par with a state visit. The nation's ambassador in Stockholm, Lance Barnard, personally met with the group to bid them farewell before they flew to London for a night's rest in preparation for the long flight to Sydney. Queen Elizabeth II, visiting the country at the same time as Abba, actually found herself playing second fiddle to the group as far as media coverage was concerned.

Two Australian states, Tasmania and Queensland, would not be visited by the tour, which led to a great deal of controversy. While Abba were in California for promotion the previous autumn, they had received a telegram from Bill Know, Deputy Premier of Queensland at the Parliament House in Brisbane. "On behalf of thousands of Abba fans in Queensland I urge Abba to include Queensland in their Australian Tour next March," wrote Know. "The group would be assured of a warm and enthusiastic welcome by the Government and people of Queensland." Their plans remained unchanged, however.

Nor would Abba play any concerts in Canberra, the Australian capital, prompting Prime Minister Malcolm Fraser to urge the group to at least pay a short visit there. When Fraser was turned down, as a last desperate measure he offered a free trip on a private jet, paid for by the authorities – in other words, the tax payers. A storm of protest broke out: the Prime Minister's offer was especially provoking since he'd recently lectured the population on the virtues of financial prudence.

Not everyone was quite as delirious about the group's presence in Australia, however. One of Bill Know's esteemed colleagues in Parliament had apparently overdosed on the myth of "the Swedish sin". Concerned about the risk of indecent behaviour by the members of Abba, he now questioned their clean-cut image. "Nude bathing is the 'in' thing in Sweden. One look at our glorious beaches could excite this 'wholesome group' into wanting to bathe as the Swedes do back home. It could cause a furore," he averred, evidently in all seriousness.

This in turn inspired a woman from Brisbane to write to a newspaper, complaining that Benny and Frida set a bad example for Australian youth by living together despite still being unmarried. "These people, with their indecent costumes, have freely admitted that two of them are living together without the blessing of God's holy matrimony. While this may be accepted in socialistic Sweden . . . this thinly disguised pornography [must be barred] from entering our Christian state and protect us from the spread of communistic anti-Christianity."

Such piquant protests aside, there was still a public outcry when it was clear that Abba would not visit Brisbane. Some fans were even out demonstrating in the streets in protest, but no one was able to persuade Abba to extend their itinerary. Björn and Agnetha refused to stay away from Linda for more than two weeks, and nothing would change their minds.

The demand for Abba's presence was so high that it seemed the group could have continued touring forever. Offers ranged from the incredible to the ludicrous. One telegram in particular, cabled by a somewhat naïve Singapore promoter shortly before the tour, caused quite a few smiles at the Polar offices. "Understand you conclude your Australian tour in Perth," wrote this hopeful individual. "Interested in arranging an Abba concert in Singapore. You can depart Perth so you arrive Singapore 4.00 p.m., so concert can take place 7.30 same evening. Departure Singapore thus possible Tuesday morning. Please confirm your interest."

It has to be assumed that the promoter had absolutely no idea of the size and scope of the venture. The tour had been planned for months in advance, and it would have been impossible to travel the distance from Perth to Singapore, prepare the stage and then perform a professional concert, all within the space of a few hours.

The European part of the tour had been huge enough, but the Australian trek surpassed even that operation. Indeed, the 106-strong entourage made it the biggest tour ever attempted in Australia. Apart from Abba and everybody else contributing to the actual shows, the core gang consisted of Stig Anderson, John Spalding, Thomas Johansson and tour manager Bosse Norling, as well as people from RCA Australia and local concert promoter The Paul Dainty Corporation.

There was also a group of 17 string players, necessitated by the Australian Musician's Union who demanded that at least as many local musicians were employed as were already on stage. The Abba members, actor Francis Matthews, the musicians and the back-up singers numbered exactly 17. This must have been one of the most expensive string sections ever to appear at a rock concert, their services being required for just a few bars here and there, in 'Dancing Queen' and the mini-musical song 'I Wonder (Departure)'. Adding to the extra costs was a hydraulic platform that raised the string section into view for a brief spotlit moment during 'Dancing Queen'.

The largest part of the entourage comprised the film crew involved in making a movie out of the tour. This project had been instigated by Reg Grundy Productions in Australia, who supplied 25 per cent of the budget while Polar financed the rest. Certain Abba members were not too enthusiastic about the film, especially Benny to whom it smelled overmuch of previous, unfortunate experiences in movie making. "I had my reasons, because of the flop we had with the Hep Stars film," he explained. "It didn't leave much desire to get involved with [movies] again." Perhaps it was mostly to assuage Benny's worries that Stig Anderson confidently told reporters the film wouldn't be released if they didn't like it.

In truth, it seemed incredible that so much money and energy would be squandered on a project if there was ever a real possibility that it could be scrapped. Benny was persuaded to approve of the project, but his suspicions remained long after shooting had commenced.

Abba promo clip director Lasse Hallström – still with only one full-length feature film and one television movie to his credit – was in charge of this new production. As usual with Abba, Hallström didn't have the time to spend on planning and pre-production that would normally be set aside for a film extravaganza with a substantial budget. At first, the intention was to put together a straightforward 16 mm document of the concerts that could function as a television special. It was only at the end of 1976, less than two months before the tour commenced, that the project grew into a big budget 35 mm Panavision cinema release.

To Hallström's relative inexperience as a movie director was added the somewhat overwhelming prospect of working abroad for the first time. "In other countries they often have different ideas on how you should act as a director," he worried. "And then you don't always know the terminology in their language. What do you do if a camera breaks down or something else falls to pieces?"

Along the way, the director decided that the film would work better if it had some kind of plot. "I've seen lots of concert films, with long heavy numbers on stage and that just gets boring," he said. "I think even the most devoted Abba fan couldn't stand a full-length film with only music performed on stage." To this end Hallström himself came up with a somewhat flimsy five and a half page screenplay: his plot dealt with an Australian country music radio DJ, Ashley Wallace, who is charged with the well-nigh impossible task of securing an in-depth interview with Abba as they tour Australia.

The live concert footage making up the bulk of the film would be interspersed with the main thread of the movie: Ashley's attempts at hunting down the group as they travel from city to city, constantly eluding him, at the same time as he's trying to get a grasp of the Abba phenomenon. Some new, studio-recorded songs were to be added to the mix after the group returned to Sweden.

In January 1977, the director spent a week in Australia, checking out the various locations where the film would be made, and meeting the local production team. "The script wasn't even written," recalled Shelley Bamford, Production Co-Ordinator on the movie. "Lasse was writing the script as we were travelling. We had paper everywhere: it was on backs of cigarette packs and on brown paper bags." Returning to Stockholm at the end of the month, Hallström followed Abba on tour to get an idea of what their stage show was like.

What Abba and everyone involved in their entourage had to contend with for their two weeks in Australia was not only performing a total of 11 concerts in front of 145,000 people[*] but also dealing with the media, the mass hysteria and the fans. Facilitating and making themselves available for the shooting of a movie simply added to the already inconceivable pressure. The clearer heads amongst them must have realised it would take a Herculean effort to make it all work.

When Abba finally arrived in late-summer Sydney, the mania was already on the boil. Despite continuous announcements on the radio that, for security reasons, the group would not be able to greet any crowds at the

[*] More than one per cent of the Australian population at the time.

airport, 1,500 fans made their way there, hoping for a glimpse of the four Swedes. Because of the late hour, some parents had even brought their young children dressed in pyjamas, ready for bed, to meet the group.

The pandemonium started the moment Abba stepped down on Australian soil. One 12-year-old fan was trampled as the crowd of fans heaved against a police barricade. As the girl tried to get to her feet, she was knocked down by the crowds and hurled against a wall. Police had to carry her into the airport's immigration reception room. As luck would have it, Abba were due to appear for a short photo session in that very room at that exact moment. Disappointment turned to euphoria, and the shock of being trampled was soon forgotten. "I still think it was worth it, especially now that I have seen Abba in person," the girl beamed.

The rest of the fans waited in vain, however. Abba, exhausted after the long flight, were whisked from the aircraft straight through immigration, then into the reception room where they posed for photographs for less than a minute. As usual in these slightly tense situations, it was the boys who came to the rescue, smiling for the cameras. The girls were clearly not in the mood to play pop stars. Agnetha managed only half a smile, although she did join Björn and Benny in waving to the cameras. A pale Frida kept her hands stuck resolutely in her pockets, a positively grim expression clouding her features.

After the quick photo opportunity, Abba were escorted through a rear exit and out of the terminal. Hundreds of fans were still at the airport an hour after the group had left. At the hotel, the Sebel Townhouse, 40 fans were waiting. They didn't get much more than a glimpse of Abba, however, as the group entered the hotel through a side door.

This *modus operandi* set the pattern for the remainder of the tour. Everywhere Abba went or were rumoured to be going, there was a crowd: at the airports, lining the streets, surrounding their hotels, outside the concert venues. There was complete mania on all levels at all times, with absolutely no limit to how far people would go to get close to the group. "A mother ran up and put a baby down on the highway so that [the] caravan of cars would stop – only to get an autograph," remembered Thomas Johansson. "That was to the extreme, but that sums up how mad and totally crazy the whole thing was."

The Abba entourage was constantly chased and under some form of surveillance. During limousine rides between airports and hotels, helicopters from four competing television stations fought desperately to get the best shots. While choppers buzzed above, motorists would drive closely behind them, beside them, in front of them, in the middle of the road, even straight ahead at oncoming traffic – anything to get a glimpse of Abba. "At the same time they held their children out through windows so they would get a better view – at a speed of 90 miles an hour!" remembered sound engineer Claes af Geijerstam. "We just sat there in the limousines, completely powerless, and watched people risk both their own and their children's lives."

It was pure luck that no one got seriously hurt. "I was often worried that someone would get run over when they threw themselves in front of the car or hurled themselves at it and began pounding on it," Agnetha recalled. At one point a large crowd of enthusiastic fans climbed all over the car and started rocking it back and forth. "Sometimes it got frightening, when we were forced to use excessive speed to get through the crowds."

The day after Abba's arrival in Sydney, the group held a press conference at the Sebel Townhouse, attended by 250 invited media representatives, additional gate-crashing journalists and some curious fans who somehow managed to evade security. Björn, pale, jet-lagged and queasy after a bout of food poisoning, applied some extra make-up for the television cameras. In an attempt at creating a Swedish atmosphere to proceedings, the room was adorned with yellow and blue curtains (the colours of the Swedish flag). Flashbulbs were popping everywhere and news crew cameras circled like vultures.

Perhaps inevitably in view of the tense atmosphere, the conference was a bit stilted and the group faced a series of dull, often banal, questions. Their blank faces and bemused looks betrayed their own feelings about the affair and, as usual, Björn and Benny offered more lengthy responses while Agnetha and Frida did the best they could with what they were given. When Agnetha was asked if it was true that she had the sexiest bottom in pop, she replied, "How can I answer that? I don't know, I haven't seen it." At least one press reporter expressed embarrassment at the lame or downright inane questions and silly behaviour of her colleagues.

The crew from the Abba movie were also present at the press reception. Indeed, they had started filming from the moment Abba arrived at Sydney airport, and would be ever-present until the group left for Sweden. Robert Hughes, a 29-year-old Australian actor, had been cast in the role of DJ Ashley Wallace at very short notice; less than a month before filming commenced, the production team was still auditioning authentic radio DJs for the part. In the end common sense prevailed and a professional actor was hired.

For the sake of credibility the identity of Robert Hughes was not immediately revealed to the Abba members. For a couple of days they remained puzzled by the seemingly crazy journalist who kept turning up at their public appearances, trying to get their attention in every way imaginable. "I wondered who this odd, pushy journalist was," recalled Frida. "He kept desperately asking strange questions all the time and always wanted us to 'go someplace where it was a little quieter'!"

Likewise, Tom Oliver, who played the role of Abba's bodyguard in the movie, was initially not introduced as an actor to the group's real security people. When Oliver began pushing Robert Hughes around in scenes filmed on the steps outside the Sydney Opera House, the bodyguards joined in for real. "I got clobbered right away and a glorious fight started," remembered Hughes. "I was glad when someone eventually convinced those guys I was the actor." Despite effectively being Abba's co-star in the movie, everything was so hectic that he barely said hello to the four Swedes throughout the duration of the tour.

Even Lasse Hallström found that making the movie was far harder than he expected, not least because when they weren't performing Abba demanded to be left alone, away from all the pressure and craziness. "I wanted access to them all the time," Hallström recalled. "I wanted to be in their faces as they were waking up, going to bed. [But what we got was] a couple of doors . . . shut in front of us." Björn later pointed to other reasons why the movie lacked dialogue from the group. "The girls were dead scared of speaking English on screen," he recalled. "They just didn't want to do it."

Amid the constant chaos, the security men also gave Hallström a hard time every now and then. "I found myself forcibly restrained from getting close on several occasions and I got just a little tired of having to explain that I was there at Abba's own request!" he remembered.

The Australian leg of the tour was arranged by EMA Telstar in collaboration with The Paul Dainty Corporation, and was said to have cost $A750,000. It would certainly have been even more expensive had Abba not signed a $A1 million deal for an advertising campaign with the Japanese electronic hardware manufacturer National. The campaign was centred around five campy television commercials, filmed in Stockholm the previous August. To the tune of 'Fernando' – with new lyrics penned by a copywriter – Abba sang the praises of record players, transistor radios, toasters, vacuum cleaners and television sets. The opening line of the song, "Can you hear the drums, Fernando?" had been changed to "There is so much more to National", and it went downhill from there. In later years, Björn and Benny have come to view the commercials with embarrassment. Watching them today, however, Abba's exaggerated delight at the wonders of National products makes it patently evident that they had their tongues firmly planted in their cheeks during filming.

In a similar deal, the Volvo trucks that had been built especially for the European part of the tour came free of charge. In return, the Swedish car manufacturer was allowed to use Abba's name and image in their advertising. With all this financial support, the Australian tickets were still said to be the most expensive ever charged for a rock concert in that part of the world – the top price during the tour was $A12.

All the planning and preparation, the excitement and the chaos, reached a climax on Thursday, March 3, the date of Abba's first live performance on Australian soil. Alas, the Gods were against them and the first concert at the Sydney Showground, in front of more than 20,000 people, was engulfed in disaster, heavy rains having reduced the grounds to a virtual quagmire. There was even concern that the venue would be destroyed after being trampled down by a mass audience.

The weather had also upset Abba's rehearsal schedule, their early arrival in Australia having been partly motivated by the need to rehearse with the new crew, including the string section. However, the insistent rain left them with no opportunity to rehearse. "We hardly had time for a sound-check, so we were just praying to God that everything would work," said Benny. "It was a bit of stress."

The seats weren't numbered, and fans anxious to get a good seat for Abba's Australian début had been queuing for 24 hours. Despite the constant rain, the atmosphere was electric as the hours ticked away before Abba's arrival on stage. Fans were playing transistor radios, and every third song played seemed to be an Abba song, which added greatly to the anticipation. When the gates finally opened at 4.30 p.m. there was a mad rush for the best seats – followed by another wet four-hour wait.

The group and their close associates were astonished that the crowd could wait so patiently in such dreadful conditions. "Can you believe that?" an agitated Stig Anderson asked a radio reporter. "We never saw that in our lives! . . . How can people love them that madly? How can they be here not only for two hours, because that's the concert, but for, three, four, five and six – and more?"

Backstage, Stig had other matters on his mind beyond the fans' discomfort. As the rain poured relentlessly down, Abba were forced to consider cancelling the show. The stage was drenched, making the floor exceptionally slippery, and there was also the danger of electrocution. But Abba's itinerary was too cramped to allow for any rescheduling – the concert *had* to go ahead. Besides, to cancel would have meant too many logistical and financial problems, not to mention disappointing this immensely loyal and fervid audience.

Shortly after the scheduled starting time of 8.30 p.m., the show finally commenced. The opening helicopter sounds were not used at outdoor venues, and instead Abba's very first live concert in the country that had taken them to their hearts more than any other began with the long thunderous drum, bass and guitar intro to 'Tiger'. When the group rushed out on the stage, it was as if every single person in that more than 20,000 strong audience joined together in one deafening shriek of ecstasy. "We have probably never received such a rapturous reception anywhere," Agnetha recalled. "It seemed the ovation would never end."

Stagehands were constantly running across the stage, trying in vain to mop the floor, and throwing out towels. "Even Stig was crawling around on all fours on the floor, mopping up the water," recalls Michael Tretow, who watched the diligent efforts of the Polar Music Managing Director on a monitor in the mobile studio bus.

The group members also had to do their utmost to keep the stage and themselves free from water – Frida cleverly incorporated her towel in the routine when she and Björn performed 'Why Did It Have To Be Me'. The only serious mishap occurred in the third song, 'Waterloo', when Frida slipped and fell over, bruising her hip and injuring two fingers. Although she was in pain there was nothing else to do but to pick herself up, smile and keep up a brave front: the show must go on.

"We were terrified," said Björn afterwards. "We could have been electrocuted ... But we were determined to play because the people had waited for hours in the rain." Somewhat inadvisedly, Björn jocularly promised the audience that as a thank you, Abba would shake the hands of everybody attending the concert backstage afterwards. When the crowd cheered with delight he had to tell them that it was a joke, to the great disappointment of many a naïvely innocent fan.

As Abba performed their hits, the chaos continued. Those in the front rows stood on their chairs to get a better view, blocking the view for those behind. All the umbrellas exacerbated the sight-lines problem. A young man selling drinks slipped on the steps and had to be taken to hospital with back injuries. Lasse Hallström thought the dramatic qualities of the event would enhance his movie, and rubbed his hands together in glee. "We will get some fantastic scenes from that rain disaster concert," he said after shooting was completed. He had yet to discover that the rain had leaked into the film canisters, destroying much of the footage from this first concert. In the film, the opening number from the Sydney première had to be spliced together with sequences from at least one other concert.

The rain never held up throughout the show. It flowed into the sound system, wreaking havoc with amplification equipment and blowing out speakers. Reportedly, the sound was dreadful during the first hour, with vocals disappearing intermittently. Yet despite these appalling conditions, it was as if the rain and the sound problems mattered not one iota for the majority of the audience that night: they simply adored Abba and loved the show unreservedly. It stands as a highlight in Abba's career and over the years, Björn, Benny, Agnetha and Frida have all remained deeply touched by the loyalty of their Sydney fans on that wet night. "Imagine 25,000 people standing outdoors in the pouring rain, holding 25,000 umbrellas, and then, when you step out onto the stage pandemonium breaks loose!" said Björn. "It almost makes your heart burst. You wonder what you've done to deserve this. I can't describe the feeling."

A few thousand rain-soaked fans did elect to leave before the show was over, and several complaints were lodged, leading to the Minister for Consumer Affairs stating his department was investigating ways of protecting the public. Several journalists, as well as promoter Paul Dainty, pointed out that the real problem was that a city the size of Sydney didn't have an indoor venue that could hold an audience on that scale. Abba's concerts had already been split from the originally planned single performance for 40,000 people, into two 20,000 shows.★

Reviewers also had a few issues with the show, jumping on Agnetha's tendencies towards singing off-key, a problem that would follow her for the remainder of Abba's live career. The two women's dance routines and overall stage movements led one critic to comment that "a good choreographer wouldn't go astray". One infamous headline after the first show read "Agnetha's Bottom Tops Dull Show". The comment referred to Agnetha's habit of repeatedly turning her back to the audience, displaying her famous rear end. When the newspaper was held up in a scene in the movie, the word "dull" was conveniently blocked out by Benny's thumb.

Frida was extolled as the life of the performance, while Agnetha, by her own admission, came across as more restrained. "You watch yourself [on film] with very critical eyes: 'Why didn't you do it like that instead? Why didn't you move a little more there?' " she said. Agnetha was just unable to ever feel truly comfortable on stage, and called her own appearance "unimaginative". "One thing I particularly noticed in Australia was that it makes no difference whether there are 5,000 or 50,000 in the crowd: I was still just as stressed and nervous," she reflected some two decades later.

The enormity of the 1977 tour only alienated her more. "It seems the greater your success the greater the audiences' expectations and impatience, while at the same time you demand more and more of yourself.

★ In actual fact, thousands more attended each concert.

The machinery that surrounds you becomes incredibly complicated, with more and more people involved – people you never really get acquainted with or even learn to recognise."

No one could fault the musical tightness of Abba's performance, however. There had been much speculation and rumours along the lines of the group being "manufactured" – the old theory that Frida and Agnetha were only miming was still alive and well. They were not a "real" rock group and, therefore, they wouldn't be able to cut it live. But faced with the show as it actually was, even the most suspicious reviewers had to acknowledge the group's musical prowess. Also, contrary to most of their attempts in the studio, on stage Abba really knew how to rock. Their live sound was vividly energetic and rumbling, with many extra, half-improvised piano riffs from Benny and on-the-spot vocal ad-libs courtesy of Frida. Unfortunately, by the time Abba's live recordings reached movie screens, television sets or record players, they had often been polished and corrected into sterility. The discrepancy between the loose feeling of the basic performance jarred against the attempts to somehow "upgrade" them into studio recordings.

As ever, the most problematic part of the show was the between–song banter, which appeared stilted and "rehearsed". Infinitely small variations from night to night proved that it had in fact been pretty much pre-written, though proceedings were enlivened one evening when Björn made an unfortunate improvisation, calling Benny "a bastard", an expression considered far too strong for Australian family audiences. More than two decades later, Björn still recalled the shocked silence of the audience and the embarrassment of his inadvertent faux pas: "I only meant to say, 'You silly man'."

The Australian weather would play further tricks with the concerts. Although no other shows were marred by rain, at one point the warm summer night gave the group another problem to contend with: their white costumes and white-on-white stage, illuminated by 120,000 watts of overhead light, attracted thousands of flying bugs. Benny's white piano was turning all black, covered by large insects, as was the floor. "It was pretty nasty," recalled Agnetha. "We were doing 'SOS' when suddenly I saw this swarm coming towards us – black, huge things. I thought, 'What on earth is that?' They hit our faces and legs, and were all over us. Benny and I are just as scared of insects, and I saw him going all stiff at the piano."

One of the bugs crawled down into Agnetha's décolletage just as she was struggling with her solo parts on 'SOS'. "I thought, 'I have to get rid of this creature in some way.' I actually panicked a little. I turned my back to the audience, put my hand inside, got it out, and finished the song."

After completing 'SOS', there was a short break so that the bugs could be swept off stage.

On Saturday, March 5, Abba boarded their chartered Boeing 727 and flew to Melbourne to continue the tour. The airport reception was somewhat quieter than in Sydney – only about 100 fans greeted Abba this time, but it turned out to be the calm before the storm, for once they reached the city a truly amazing welcome awaited them.

At 12.30 p.m. Abba were scheduled to attend a Lord Mayor's reception in the Melbourne Town Hall. The event had been announced in the media well in advance, which explained the absence of fans at the airport – they knew where the real fun was going to happen. When Abba arrived at the town hall in their Rolls-Royces, an estimated 6,000 people stood cheering and screaming at them, many having waited for the group for several hours. "First, when you drive out from the airport and you see the street actually lined up all the way from the airport to the city, you don't even believe your eyes," recalled Frida. "And then you understand, 'This is actually a reception for us, nobody else. It's not the president coming.'"

The Abba entourage stepped out of their cars, entered the building and climbed the stairs to the balcony to greet the crowd. Excited radio reporters were covering the event live on the air, blow by blow: "Here they come now. I can see them! They're inside. They're just about to come on their way out. They're coming out onto the balcony now . . . It should be in two to three seconds . . . And here they are!"

When Abba finally stepped out on the balcony, the crowd erupted. All the group had to do was to stand there and wave. For the five minutes while they appeared on the balcony, the screaming never died down. The scenes outside Melbourne Town Hall constituted irrefutable proof that Abba's popularity had exploded far beyond ordinary fame. In Australia, if not quite elsewhere in the world, it was clearly on a par with The Beatles during 1964, when they too had appeared, Popelike, on that same Melbourne Town Hall balcony to greet streets full of frenzied fans.

Afterwards, the group was meant to stay and mingle with guests at the reception, but they were too exhausted and were escorted back to their Rolls-Royces. But when they got to the cars there were no drivers – the group wasn't expected back for another 20 minutes. Abba had to wait in the cars for five very long minutes surrounded by watching crowds before the drivers returned. In the meantime, they were more or less forced to chat to the media and sign a few autographs.

In the evening, 14,500 people watched Abba's performance at the Sidney Myer Music Bowl while a further 16,000 tried to listen outside the fenced-off concert area. The whole area was full to bursting several hours in advance. Two sections of fencing were knocked down by the crush of fans when the gates were opened. Those without tickets were climbing up on cars or anything they could find to try to catch a glimpse of Abba. A teenage boy, who'd made his way up to the top of a tree to watch the concert, fell and had to be taken to hospital with suspected head and internal injuries. Otherwise, the audience was well behaved: as ever when Abba played, the age span stretched from six to 60 – and beyond.

Having been thoroughly soaked at the opening concert in Sydney, Björn was suffering from a sore throat throughout the Melbourne visit. Although the group's doctor tried to improve his condition by spraying his larynx several times during the first performance, some of Björn's lead vocal numbers had to be cut from the show.

Prime Minister Malcolm Fraser attended the concert together with his wife, two daughters and a son. When Abba's schedule didn't allow for any trips to Canberra, Fraser had to bite the bullet and travel to meet up with the group himself, the political prestige in being photographed with such a popular act being just too good to miss. However, Fraser's attempts to curb inflation by trimming government spending and discouraging large wage increases had not made him especially popular with the general public. When his entrance was announced at the Music Bowl, he was roundly booed by the audience.

In another eerie reflection of The Beatles in 1964, further evidence of the insanity of Abba's popularity was afforded by the fate of their bed sheets from the Old Melbourne Motor Inn. After they left, the hotel manager cut up the sheets Abba had slept on, stamped them with a special commemorative message and distributed them through the newspaper the *Sunday Observer*. Incredibly, the offer was announced while Abba were still staying at the hotel. No one bothered asking the group how they felt about it all – they were just confronted with the situation and had no say in the matter.

After Melbourne, Abba's triumphant tour continued to Adelaide, where the mania was as strong as ever. Bosse Norling recalled it as "sheer hysteria. When we went from the airport to the hotel, there was an un-believable media posse. On the car radio we heard all the stations giving live reports of our journey, even how *I* was waving to the reporters." One television channel in Adelaide had a five-minute slot every day that the group was in Australia, giving updates on the tour and the group. There had even been a proposal to allow children the day off school so they could line the streets to welcome the group, but the authorities said no.

At the hotel, Norling managed to shut off the entire premises so that

Abba could swim in peace in the pool, a luxury they hadn't yet experienced on the tour. The group made no secret of their relief at being left alone, if only for a brief moment or two. "It's nice to have enthusiastic fans, but it's also nice to be away from them for a while," as Benny diplomatically put it.

In Adelaide, the group performed one concert at West Lakes Football Stadium before 21,000 people. To this record-breaking attendance figure came an estimated additional 10,000 who enjoyed the concert for free outside the arena. The usual scenes of frenzy surrounding the event were repeated in Adelaide: masses of people gathering, live radio reports during the hours leading up to the concert – some journalists had even gone up in a helicopter to cover the event and give a bird's-eye view report of the proceedings.

After a week, the insanity began to get to the group. For the duration of the tour they had two bodyguards on constant call, but there was only so much they could do when Abba were swamped by crowds everywhere. "There was fever, there was hysteria . . . there were sweaty, obsessed crowds," Agnetha remembered. "Sometimes it was awful. I felt as if they would get hold of me and I'd never get away again. It was as if I was going to be crushed. On occasions they would grab hold of us in the most unpleasant ways, and there were times when we burst into tears once we were inside the cars."

Odd or annoying things would be happening all the time. In Sydney, a jeweller's store called to inform them that "the jewellery that Frida had ordered was ready". The only problem was that she hadn't ever visited the store, much less picked out any jewellery.

The group did their best to accommodate the media at all times. If a microphone was shoved in their faces while they were on their way somewhere, they answered politely, even if their eyes and facial expressions often betrayed their complete disinterest in the conversation. "They were utterly co-operative," recalled Patti Mostyn, the group's Australian publicist. "There was none of this 'Let's run to the car!' or 'How dare you take a photo of me?' They realised that it was the media [and] the fans that got them [where they were]. They were quite prepared to do [what was required of them] and never shirked their responsibility on that level at all."

Sometimes even the stoic and public relations-minded Swedes bucked under the pressure from the media. One evening the group and their closest associates were out enjoying what they thought would be a quiet dinner. Alas, it was not to be. "There was a journalist at another table who really wanted to upset Frida for some reason," recalls John Spalding. "He was just trying to see how far he could go. In the end it worked, because she just up and left the dinner."

As a last desperate measure to escape the choice between incessant crowds and confinement in their hotel suites, the group went on boat trips. "Because nobody's at sea, right?" Benny said. But he was proved wrong on that account: television news teams would not only sniff out their whereabouts in the harbour, but would actually follow them out to sea in their own boats, filming them and pestering them for an interview.

When the media sharks weren't after them, there were other real, live dangers awaiting in the waters. "We rented a yacht, anchored up and then dived in to have some fun," remembered Bosse Norling. "That is, until the captain appeared on deck, screaming hysterically. We were in shark-infested waters! We got out of the water as quickly as we could."

It seemed there wasn't much point attempting boat trips when they just led to problems and annoying incidents. In the end the four Abba members were forced to remain cramped up with each other at the hotel most of the time, with all the added stress to the relationships this entailed. Some outlet from the pressure occurred at the parties thrown throughout the trip – everything from barbecues to more private, hotel-based get-togethers. Some of the local crew in Australia had been informed that all was not well between Agnetha and Björn. It was noticed that they stayed apart from each other more than would be expected during these shindigs.

At the press conference in Sydney, the group had admitted that even if they didn't take any drugs they weren't above having "an occasional drink". Those who thoroughly believed in Abba's clean image might have experienced slight shocks when they encountered the group's partying side on the tour. Sometimes it would even get just a little out of hand.

"They'd all had a few drinks one night, and all of a sudden we couldn't find Björn," recalls John Spalding. "We got a bit worried that he wasn't in his room. We were getting serious with the police and everything: 'Has he been kidnapped or what?'" The frantic search ended in Lasse Hallström's room. "It turned out that Björn was absolutely drunk, and he was on the bed with Lasse. They both had taken a load of drink to their room and didn't tell anybody, and then drunk so much that they just passed out on the bed."

The incident was effectively quietened down – it was absolutely necessary that the press didn't find out, as Spalding remembers. "'Oh, he's in bed with Lasse Hallström! That's all the papers need, you'd better forget that!' But for about half an hour we were very worried that he'd been kidnapped."

In the midst of all this chaos, work on the tour movie continued unabated. There had been far too little time to put together a proper screenplay, so many of the scenes were improvised on the spot. This failed to please dialogue writer Bob Caswell, who'd been hired by Reg Grundy Productions to do additional work on the manuscript. Caswell would later go on to write the screenplay for films such as the 1988 Meryl Streep vehicle *A Cry In The Dark* (aka *Evil Angels*).

For Lasse Hallström, however, the addition of a local screenwriter was not so welcome. The prospect of "a guy in Australia, sitting there writing some kind of dialogue", was just another pre-production worry for the director. Once shooting commenced, Caswell found that he didn't enjoy himself that much either. "He was really upset, because everything was moving too fast and he didn't have time to write anything," remembered Robert Hughes. "Most of the scenes I did were shot on my own and were ad-libbed. There was no rehearsal." It was all in line with most of Lasse Hallström's film work around this time, which was marked by an improvised *cinéma vérité* style.

Many ideas for scenes were thought up on the spot. Robert Hughes remembered initiating a sequence in Perth, where the Ashley character is seen walking along a beach at sunset. "We were driving along and I saw a line of seagulls hanging in the breeze. I suggested putting a long lens on the camera and I walked towards it through the seagulls." The constant improvisations and whims on the part of the director truly put the crew to the test. "Lasse was very, very demanding," recalled Shelley Bamford.

Perth was the location for the last concerts of the tour. Five shows, each attended by a relatively manageable 8,000 people, were scheduled at the city's Entertainment Centre. It was the only indoor venue on Abba's Australian trek, and the more easily controllable surroundings facilitated the film crew's work a great deal. Consequently, although the movie supposedly featured an equal amount of songs from each town, the Perth shows were in fact used to masquerade as other venues.

As is evidenced from the completed production, the cameras were sometimes very close to the onstage action throughout the tour; too close as far as Benny was concerned. "My attitude towards the film was so negative that I didn't want to allow Lasse to shoot on stage during the concerts," he admitted. "I thought the film crew disrupted us and the audience."

Robert Hughes remembered vividly the sight of cinematographers doing close-ups on stage, obscuring the view for those who had actually paid money to watch Abba in concert. "A lot of people complained about that and I can understand why," said the actor.

As if there hadn't been enough drama on the tour already, Perth brought a most unwelcome surprise for Abba. With only 30 minutes left to go of the first concert, a woman called the venue and announced there was a bomb in the arena. It was scheduled to go off at 8.05 p.m., just after the two-hour show ended. Benny, who was at that moment concentrating on his 'Intermezzo no. 1' solo spot, wasn't informed of what happened at first. After the number was finished, he noticed that all the musicians had left the stage. Dumbstruck, he just sat there, wondering what had happened. After a while he was motioned off and the audience was asked to leave the premises. The audience wasn't informed of the reason for the break, however, and most of them simply thought it was an intermission.

Meanwhile, every available policeman was rushed to the arena to remove the crowd and control the scenes outside. As the audience left the complex, the following concert's audience was arriving at the venue, which made things even more chaotic and difficult. "It was absolute mayhem," said a police inspector afterwards.

While dogs were searching the venue for bombs, Abba and the band had to wait in an enclosure outside the building for 20 minutes. Separated from the audience by only a fence, Benny decided to offer some entertainment. "He played the accordion, I borrowed someone's violin, and Stig Anderson was playing spoons," recalled keyboard player Anders Eljas. "We played old folk songs, and it was a lot of fun because everything was just so confused outside. The audience was wondering what the hell we were playing. 'These aren't Abba songs!'"

Eventually, the audience was ushered in again to enjoy the final part of the show. It says much for the spirit of those involved that the second show that night was delayed by only 30 minutes.

Exhaustion and relief flooded through Abba and their entourage as the plane taking them back to Sweden took off from Perth at 7.30 p.m. on Sunday, March 13. The final escape from this surreal experience was tinged with incredulity as much as anything, with the group themselves as amazed as anyone at their own popularity. But nobody doubted it had just become too much.

Success on this level went far beyond what they had counted on or even dreamed of. The members of Abba had to ask themselves why they had entered this business in the first place. They all agreed that it certainly wasn't to be transported around the world like some kind of exhibition object.

The two-week drama of the Australian tour seemed to have an especially fundamental impact on Agnetha. "No one who has experienced facing a screaming, boiling, hysterical crowd could avoid feeling shivers up and down their spine," she said many years later. "It's a thin line between ecstatic celebration and menace. It can turn around in a flash. I don't think anyone could stay the same after such an encounter. It affects your personality. Something changes within you and it can be the source of phobias."

After the tour, Agnetha, who had already become increasingly protective about her private zone, tried to take further steps back from the limelight. She was, without a doubt, the most popular individual member of the group, and the public wouldn't let her get away that easily. It seemed the more she tried to project herself as unassuming and "ordinary", affecting a low-key appearance, the more the fans and the media were drawn towards her.

Björn and Benny were mostly displeased at being uprooted from their songwriting cottage and beloved recording studio. Hysterical adulation and figuring out ways to outsmart maniacal fans had been fun in the Sixties, but that was then. They'd grown older and they seldom looked back on that part of their pop star existence with affection.

It was as if their complete outlook on live performances had changed. In Australia Björn complained that "it's a bit of an asocial life on tour. You just eat, sleep and go on stage, and nothing more. It kills creativity in a way that I don't like."

Even with the distance of time, later in the year his tune hadn't changed much. "I find it very hard to believe that we will tour again. After every tour the pressure and expectations grow enormously. If we're to do another tour it has to be bigger than the last one. The whole set-up just grows and grows. In the end it will attain mammoth proportions – and then it's better to chuck it in."

His songwriting partner echoed these feelings. On tour with Abba, Claes af Geijerstam remembered Benny as "incredibly nervous before the concerts began. If it were up to him, he would have preferred to hide behind a screen. Benny wanted to be heard, but not to be seen." The introspective side of his personality had taken over almost completely from his outgoing Hep Star persona.

Only Frida, who hadn't even been close to true stardom before Abba's breakthrough, thrived on their enormous success and developed a genuine love affair with the audience. As a woman she had already been through the child-rearing phase and could devote 100 per cent of her time to being an Abba star. Although she later singled out the 1977 Australian tour as her most treasured memory of the Abba years, even she had been a bit overwhelmed, recalling the surrounding hysteria as "nasty".

After the group returned home to Stockholm, the pressure eased up a little, but it didn't exactly die down. There were so many expectations on them from everywhere, so many demands. According to plans, both the movie and the brand-new studio-recorded album were scheduled for release in October. Except for the numbers in their mini-musical, nothing had yet been written. And despite some 50 hours of film being shot in Australia, it would only cover about half of the projected 100-minute movie.

The group would not only be required to take part in additional scenes, but also had plenty of work to do doctoring the soundtrack to studio standards. According to Michael Tretow, it was basically only drums and audience cheers that remained authentically live. "That's the way you usually do live recordings," he pointed out. "Their voices would disappear from the microphones because they couldn't possibly concentrate on singing when they were so busy putting on a show. They were jumping up and down and dancing, and it was raining and whatnot, so it was hard to get a good sound."

Leaving the Australian madness behind only served to shift the pressure and the stress that came from other directions. Before Abba embarked on the tour it had already been decided that they wouldn't be doing any promotional trips or major interviews once they returned home. Nevertheless, the movie and album deadlines loomed. It really did seem that the harder they worked, the more work was heaped upon them.

While Abba themselves pondered the price of fame, the rapidly accruing revenues from their success were creating another kind of problem that would come to occupy more and more of Stig Anderson's attention, ultimately creating an insurmountable wedge between him and the group. Like the rain in Sydney, money would soon shower down on Abba with relentless force, and although no one could have known it at the time, this would eventually prove to be the Achille's heel in their relationship with their manager.

344

Chapter 23

The letter was one of the best Christmas presents Stig Anderson had ever received. "May I take this opportunity of saying that I, as the official representative of Sweden, am pleased and happy about Abba's enormous success over here," wrote ambassador Per Lind at the Royal Swedish Embassy in Canberra, Australia. "The excellent PR which Abba provides for our country facilitates to a great extent our efforts in furthering Sweden's reputation and interests."

The letter arrived at Polar's offices in December 1976. After reading it, Stig beamed with pride, promptly including the missive in a newsletter issued by the company.

Stig had long been annoyed at the lack of official recognition for Abba's enormous international success as representatives of Sweden, and for all the export income their record sales and publishing royalties generated. "If we had been British, we would have been honoured by the Queen a long time ago," he used to point out, no doubt thinking back to the prestigious MBEs (Membership of the Most Excellent Order of the British Empire) The Beatles had received in 1965.

So far during the Seventies, the climate in Sweden had been opposed to any official declarations of support for Abba. Apart from all the political and highbrow cultural resistance against them, there was simply no precedent for recognising an internationally successful pop music act. Taken altogether, Abba's achievement seemed to land somewhere between the realms of export business phenomena and culture, an area which didn't exist before their arrival on the scene.

At the time, Sweden had many other structural and individual symbols of national pride on an international level. Certainly, the country had several problems: along with the rest of the western world it had been hit by a recession, caused by the oil crisis. However, Sweden was still regarded as a role model in terms of social security and equality, and the nation enjoyed one of the highest living standards in the world.

Olof Palme, the former social democrat Prime Minister who was in opposition for six years from 1976, was a highly respected politician on an international level. Well known for his work in protecting the interests of

345

small nations, he served as an intermediary link between national movements in the Third World and Social Democrats in the West. Palme became a living symbol for Sweden's international role as the planet's peaceful conscience.

In the world of sports, tennis star Björn Borg became one of the most highly regarded and famous athletes ever after winning the Men's Championship at Wimbledon five years in a row. Alpine skier Ingemar Stenmark created a sensation by becoming the most successful performer in the history of the sport. In most Swedish schools, lessons would stop every time he had a race so that everyone could watch it on television. When Stenmark retired at the end of the Eighties, he had won more World Cup races than any other skier.

Abba's international presence was just as great. Indeed, it's likely that more people were aware of the group's music than the achievements of any other Swede. On travels to foreign countries, Swedish tourists were amazed and surprised to hear Abba's music played in the farthest corners of the earth. Whereas individuals like Borg, Stenmark and Palme – admittedly a hotly debated figure domestically – were lauded for their achievements in putting Sweden on the map, Abba would enjoy little public goodwill during their time together. Whenever the media reported on the enormous revenue generated by Polar Music, it was almost exclusively focused on the personal fortunes of Stig and Abba. In some respects they had contributed to this state of affairs themselves: unusually truthful about their affairs, they willingly allowed reporters to study their balance sheets and replied fairly honestly to questions regarding their business.

"With the taxes we're paying I believe it's primarily the state that benefits from our success," sniffed Stig at one point. But accurate observations such as this were mostly ignored by the media. "Lining their pockets" was a more commonly used phrase than "contributing to the trade balance".

Stig never apologised for being proud of his success and his journey from the shack in Hova to his impressive villa on the posh island of Djurgården, his residence from October 1977 for the best part of two decades. However, his honesty and directness came at a price: in the same way that his opinions on music rubbed the Music Movement up the wrong way, truthful statements about his fiscal fortunes were seen as bragging, his pride regarded as arrogance.

High taxation was a very real problem if Stig and Abba were going to hold on to their earnings. One single example illustrates the situation very clearly. In the late Sixties, Björn and Benny had founded a company called Harlekin to handle all the income from their activities as performing artists, which now also included Agnetha and Frida's shares of the Abba revenues. Since April 1975, Harlekin in itself owned 50 per cent of Polar Music, and it was Harlekin that paid the four Abba members' salaries.

For the financial year of May 1, 1975 to April 30, 1976, following the breakthrough of the *ABBA* album, the Harlekin turnover had skyrocketed to 3.4 million kronor (£442,000). The running expenses were just 460,257 kronor, exceptionally low for a company of that size.

With no other write-offs beyond a measly 1,681 kronor for musical instruments, the Harlekin surplus was 2.9 million. After taxes a profit of 1,063,921 kronor remained. This enormous sum was consolidated since the company didn't actually need the money for anything: had it been taken out as income most of it would have gone in taxes too. Clearly, it was necessary to start implementing Polar's investment plans as soon as possible.

Some of the ideas they were able to think up for themselves. The purchase of the art gallery AH Grafik was a natural investment since both Stig and Benny were interested in art. The new recording studio was also an obvious project: although Polar knew that a studio in itself would probably not be very profitable, it would make Abba's increasingly time-consuming recording work so much easier.

Other types of investments also needed to be made, but this was just too complex for Stig and Gudrun. Instead of the previously planned "Abba Invest", Polar Music was restructured, acquiring the new name Polar Music International. Under the umbrella of this new company the income generated by record sales was to be transformed into profitable investments.

The decision was also made to hire an experienced Vice President who would be in charge of all such matters. Leif B. Bengtsson, formerly a financial manager at a major magazine publisher, began his employment on May 1, 1977. Around the same time, Björn and Benny assigned half of Harlekin to Agnetha and Frida so that all four members each ended up with 25 per cent of the shares. Harlekin in itself already owned half of Polar Music International.

Leif B. Bengtsson's task was to find ventures close to Polar's own line of business: entertainment, recreation, leisure. Shortly after starting employment the new Vice President hit upon a solution to an old problem: meeting the demand for Abba records in the Eastern Bloc without having to rely on the limited supply of western currency in these countries. Bengtsson suggested that Polar should purchase a company called Wimab Sport, which dealt in imports of sports equipment, primarily from West Germany and France. However, an Eastern Bloc country such as Poland was also a major manufacturer of similar items.

To Bengtsson's way of thinking, the import of actual goods would mean that Polar could trade those for the valuable licensing rights for Abba's records. In that way they would free themselves from the dependency on Polish access to foreign currency. On paper it looked like a wonderful idea – but in reality it turned out to be a gigantic flop.

The purchase of 92 per cent of the shares in Wimab was executed on September 1. For Wimab, the sale was attractive since new capital was needed to facilitate growth. Then, just before Christmas, it became clear that the company was in bad shape. The previous, snow-free winter had a detrimental effect on the sales of winter sports equipment, while summer-related items, such as tents and fishing tackle, had also been harder to sell than expected. The company would require even more capital just to survive.

Stig was furious. Fortunately, the conditions of acquisition had included a clause whereby the company's balance sheet had to be in the black at the end of the year. When Wimab proved to be on the verge of bankruptcy, Polar excercised their right to revert the purchase. The investments Polar had already made would remain in Wimab, however, and Leif B. Bengtsson would assist the sports company in restructuring their business. In the long run Wimab was doomed: six years later, they went into liquidation.

The affair had a seriously detrimental effect on the relationship between Stig and Bengtsson. Stig's plan was that Polar Music International should be listed on the stock exchange within a few years. When the company took its first steps outside the entertainment industry, it was vital that it was taken seriously. For Polar Music International to fall flat on its face with its very first major deal was an intolerable humiliation. Within a few months, Bengtsson had left the company. "I will always get the shivers whenever I see rucksacks and sleeping bags," said Stig later.

While Polar Music was busy with investment schemes, the source of its income – Abba – experienced a no less hectic time. After returning from Australia, they enjoyed a break of just a few weeks before heading back to work again. In June 1977, Robert Hughes and Tom Oliver were scheduled to arrive in Stockholm to shoot the additional scenes in the upcoming movie. The group had to write and record a couple of new songs that were going to appear on the next album, as well as taking part in the scenes to be filmed in Sweden.

Björn and Benny were also involved in the construction of Polar's projected new recording studio. In May, they went to Los Angeles together with Michael Tretow and Berka Bergkvist to check out state-of-the-art equipment for the facilities.

348

It was an excellent time for them to visit the United States. At the end of 1976, Abba had received their first gold album for the *Greatest Hits* LP. A few months later, on April 9, they topped that achievement with their first number one on the singles chart with 'Dancing Queen'. At that moment Abba finally acquired "top act" status on both sides of the Atlantic, and it looked as if this was the definitive breakthrough needed to solidify their American career.

"Up until then Abba were very much considered a straight pop act," says Jerry Greenberg, "but 'Dancing Queen' became a disco favourite, which I think really helped turn the image of the group around. They gained a new audience. All of a sudden Abba were getting played in the clubs: they were hip." There obviously was a market there to be exploited, but whereas other acts would have dashed over to the United States as quickly as they could, Abba elected to play it cool and stay back in Sweden.

The success with 'Dancing Queen' pushed the *Arrival* album up to a number 20 peak position on the albums chart. It was the best result for an Abba LP so far, so there was optimism that this was the start of more glorious things to come. The synchronisation problem with the American single release schedule had also been solved. 'Money, Money, Money' was skipped as the follow-up to 'Dancing Queen', an additional reason being that the song was "more European than American", as Björn put it. Instead the next single became 'Knowing Me, Knowing You'.

The concert tour that Abba really needed to do was scheduled for 1978 at the earliest, but a three-week promotional visit to the United States had been set aside for the autumn. At least some kind of presence was planned in the not too distant future. Things looked promising.

When Björn, Benny, Michael and Berka arrived in Los Angeles, Atlantic made no secret of their hopes for Abba's future career in the United States. For Berka, who was used to Polar's relatively modest, casual operation – Swedish workplaces have a less hierarchical tradition than is common in countries such as Great Britain and America – the exceptionally warm welcome they received was a somewhat overwhelming experience.

"Jerry Greenberg came flying down from New York just to say hi to us," he recalls. "Then I remember being picked up in a special Cadillac that was to be at Björn and Benny's disposal in Los Angeles. At my hotel room there was a huge fruit basket and a bouquet of flowers." Berka was nonplussed at all this romancing – after all, they were only in town to have a look at some tape recorders and microphones, and he himself wasn't even a pop star. Björn explained what it was all about.

"The contract with Atlantic was about to expire and the point was that we would go back to Stig and tell him that we 'simply had to re-sign with Atlantic, they're fantastic!' I believe that was a typically American way of doing business. They were great people with whom we worked well over the years, but that was just their way. Björn taught me not to be so impressed by that."

Whatever success was coming their way, breaking the US market remained a low priority on the group's part. When work on the new album and upcoming movie turned out to take up so much time, the planned promotional trip was quickly cancelled. The prospect of adding to the kind of adulation they enjoyed in Europe and Australia, as would certainly be the case in a country so obsessed with the cult of celebrity, did nothing to heighten their enthusiasm. "I'm a little afraid of America," said Agnetha. "I think the people are open and friendly, but I don't think working there will be as relaxing as it's been around the rest of the world."

The promising relationship with Sid Bernstein had come to an abrupt end at the beginning of 1977. When the contract was up for renewal Stig let it lapse, much to the regret of the enthusiastic impresario. "My belief was, after seeing them in concert and the television exposures, that they could have been as huge as some of the British groups that I brought over in the Sixties," says Bernstein. "But it was all down to their absence when they should have pursued the key markets. I had a three year contract with Stig, but the minute it ended, he ended our relationship."

It was not as if there had been a flurry of activity for Bernstein during the past three years – three short promotional visits was hardly the same as arranging major tours across the nation. Bernstein had seen the writing on the wall long before the contract expired. "At that point I was already working on other things. I brought The Bay City Rollers to America, helped break them here. The energy I wanted to put into Abba I gave to others; I just had to keep busy. When Stig ended the contract I was already involved with two or three other acts. But I reluctantly saw them leave, I adored the group."

Nevertheless, Stig found it intolerable that the US market couldn't be cracked like the rest of the world, and Björn and Benny would have been delighted to add America to the scalps that dangled from their belts. But if they were going to do it, it had to be on their own terms. Much thought went into finding a way to accomplish what they wanted, yet without having to do too many personal appearances, much less concert tours.

Songwriting for the new Abba album had commenced in April 1977, but it was only after the trip to Los Angeles that Björn and Benny came up with the first completed songs. The mood of this new music was a direct

350

result of the mellow, laid-back Californian music climate of the time. The composing team also followed a more ambitious streak in their music. The success of the *Arrival* album hadn't made them complacent: there was still an urge to break down boundaries.

On May 31, recording sessions started with a tune provisionally titled 'A Bit Of Myself'. The song was centred around a bass and synthesizer riff which sounded remarkably like a slower version of its counterpart in Stevie Wonder's 'I Wish' (from his current *Songs In The Key Of Life* album). Wonder was among Björn and Benny's biggest favourites at the time.

With this riff as a centrepiece, the rest of the song was then built up as a six-part structure, in itself a completely new step for the group. Stig Anderson took a listen to the backing track and came up with the phrase 'The Name Of The Game' as the song's final title. Björn then completed the lyrics.

'The Name Of The Game' was Abba at their absolute best. The song rested on a sunny Californian, laid-back chug-along rhythm, tightened-up by Abba's icy Scandinavian sensibilities, while a 'Penny Lane'-style synthesized piccolo trumpet added a whiff of late Sixties British pop to the mix. The different sections of the song made perfect use of Agnetha and Frida's voices as musical instruments: they each had their own parts, but also drifted in and out of joint sequences – magically harmonised – in an unusually compelling way. 'The Name Of The Game' far transcended its Los Angeles inspirations. In fact, the song didn't sound like anything else on the music scene at that time.

The day after this latest masterpiece was started, the backing track for the next song to be influenced by Björn and Benny's Los Angeles trip was recorded. The majestic 'Eagle' had some heavy metal patterns in its chord structure, although again, most of those strokes were camouflaged by Abba's pop inflections. Björn found the inspiration for the lyrics in the Richard Bach novel *Jonathan Livingston Seagull*. "I was trying to capture the sense of freedom and euphoria that I got from reading that book," he said.

Björn had taken the criticism levelled at him for Abba's weak lyrics quite seriously. "It's important that the words go well with the music. They must have the same sort of rhythm," he mused in an interview. "But I guess the content has suffered because of that. This is something we're going to get into, which is an interesting new step. Now we want to say something with the words as well."

'Eagle' also meant a chance to hear Agnetha and Frida sing together throughout a whole song, an arrangement that had been important to the group's early success, but which would in fact occur on only a handful of songs after the current album. The more the lyrics were individualised, the more vital it became for them to emanate from a single voice.

These two new songs made for a promising beginning to sessions for the next album, which for the most part was recorded at Marcus Music Studios in Solna, just outside Stockholm. While Abba were waiting for their own studio to be completed, which would take another year, they made the decision to hire a studio that they could block book for longer periods of time. With the long and painstaking working methods they had arrived at, combined with a rapidly approaching deadline, it was absolutely necessary that they weren't impeded by any limitations of studio time.

During these early sessions, the group also attempted a studio recording of the mini-musical song 'Thank You For The Music'. They removed themselves slightly from the loose cabaret mood of the live version, arriving at an arrangement characterised by a slight ragtime feel. Agnetha put in a solid, Doris Day-inspired lead vocal performance and the whole group added backing vocals. This was as far as the recording got, however: it was still not the right way to present the song, and the track was shelved.

At that point the group had to direct their attention to the completion of their as yet untitled movie. Actors Robert Hughes and Tom Oliver joined them in Stockholm for the additional takes needed to finish off the film. Many street scenes, which in the movie were supposedly located in Australia, were in fact shot in the Swedish capital. Similarly, a bit in the film where the group read concert reviews in their hotel room in "Perth" was actually staged at Stockholm's Sheraton Hotel.

Just before this period of shooting commenced, the news that Agnetha was pregnant again reached the press. Her condition affected all the group's plans for the rest of the year, not least the filming. "At first I panicked a little," Lasse Hallström admitted. "How would it look if Agnetha suddenly appeared pregnant in the middle of the movie and then was thin again at the end, in the scenes that are already filmed?" The problem was solved by Agnetha wearing clothes that hid any bodily changes, and also by mostly filming her head and shoulders. Still, in certain sequences it was hard not to notice her obvious pregnant state.

Among scenes filmed in Stockholm was a corny sequence, set to 'The Name Of The Game', where the Ashley character dreams of securing his Abba interview. The premise of the scene was that Ashley has become the centre of the group's attention: he is Björn and Benny's best buddy, while Agnetha and Frida can't get enough of him, constantly kissing him and clinging to his body.

The point of the sequence was rammed home pretty quickly, and the

Abba members' constant attention to Ashley even had some bizarre inflections. The sexual overtones of Frida's and Agnetha's overly physical behaviour seems slightly dubious in the light of Björn and Benny's hearty relationship to the DJ, as if they were happy to let him "borrow" their spouses. Fortunately, the lovemaking stops short of an orgy. "After all, it's a family movie," said Agnetha innocently. "You have to think about the young children." It was not the most successful sequence in the film.

Also filmed in June was the scene towards the end of the movie, where Ashley finally runs across Abba in an elevator and gets his interview. The actual interview is never seen, but instead the viewer gets a fantasy sequence where the group performs 'Eagle'. A brand new effects machine called the "flutter box" created the impression of a surreal elevator ride. The flutter box had been invented for the currently in-production movie *Superman*, but the Abba film was the first to actually use it. When the 'Eagle' sequence was filmed, the group members had to stoop in a 45 degree angle, all the while singing and trying to look natural.

Lasse Hallström, who was used to making simple, no-tricks comedies rooted in everyday life, relished the opportunity the Abba movie gave him. "Looking back on it, it was really like a film school to me, to play around with all the equipment we had," he said many years later.

Similarly, throughout filming Robert Hughes was continually amazed at his luck at landing the part of Ashley and all that it brought with it: his visit to Sweden was the first time he had ever been outside Australia. He remembered thoroughly enjoying every moment of the filming, despite the sometimes chaotic circumstances. "It's the best thing I could ever do," he enthused shortly after filming began. "I still can't believe it. If it's released in the United States it will be the biggest break I could ever have." Unfortunately, the movie didn't open in America until the autumn of 1979, and failed to become a box office smash in that part of the world. Robert Hughes never had any US opportunities to speak of, although he went on to have a successful acting career in Australia, especially as the title character in the television comedy series *Hey Dad . . .!*

By the time the final scenes were shot, the optimistic October date for the première of the movie and release of the new album had been moved to the end of the year. In July, Lasse Hallström and his team set to work on editing the movie – indeed, with the wafer-thin synopsis and the improvised or downright chaotic production circumstances, the film was virtually "created" at the editing board. Hallström was very much an intuitive filmmaker, and this was a part of his *modus operandi* at the time.

The 50 hours of film shot in Australia, plus the additional Stockholm footage, were to be condensed down to 90 minutes that made some kind of sense. Considering what the director had to work with the final result was fairly creditable, despite the many continuity clangers. Hardest to swallow was the logical leap towards the end of the movie, where Ashley misses out on his final interview opportunity at Abba's hotel. The group has left for the airport, he is told. But when he despondently returns to his own hotel and enters the elevator, he finally meets the group, begging the question: what were they doing at Ashley's hotel, and shouldn't they be on a plane headed for Sweden anyway?

It must also be said that although the Ashley character was a clever device to move the film forwards, he doesn't elicit much audience sympathy. Alternately clumsy and unprepared or smugly complacent, he annoys rather than makes the audience empathise with his plight at getting his interview. The improvised dialogue tends to grate on the viewer's patience, most obviously in the overlong opening scene where Ashley gets his assignment to interview Abba. The rambling conversation between the DJ and his station manager could easily have been cut by half without losing any impact.

These objections aside, the film remains as a valuable and vibrantly vivid document of the group's stage show, as well as the Australian Abbamania phenomenon. Lasse Hallström cleverly juxtaposed songs like 'I'm A Marionette' (from the mini-musical) and its lyrics of being trapped by fame, with shots of Abba talking to reporters and signing autographs, edited so that the same movement was continuously repeated, marionette-style. "The way the film describes that is reality," said Björn.

It was also an intelligent decision to minimise the Abba members' straightforward acting in the film. Although Agnetha recalled the group's few acting scenes as "not too embarrassing", it was clear that their talents in this respect were somewhat limited. "You have to keep the group out of the actual film text," noted Lasse Hallström. "Abba are no actors – and that's something they're aware of."

When shooting for the movie ended, half the year was already behind Abba, but there were still plenty of commitments. Although three of the mini-musical songs were slated for inclusion on the album – easing the pressure on Björn and Benny to come up with new tunes – the songs still needed to be recorded to their satisfaction. As the first, failed attempt with 'Thank You For The Music' proved, this wasn't necessarily going to be so easy.

Of the brand new songs, only two had been completed so far, and they needed to write and record at least another four. The film work had made it impossible for Björn and Benny to concentrate on any composing whatsoever in June. By early July, they were ensconced in their songwriting cottage, grinding away for hours to come up with new melodies. "We haven't got over the threshold yet, but we have a few good ideas," said Björn. "It's always like this. Every summer we sit out here, labouring over songs when we should be having a holiday. But we keep postponing the songwriting all the time, and this is our punishment."

There was also the film soundtrack that needed to be attended to. Off-key and off-mike singing, bum guitar notes, the odd slip on the keyboards — all the mistakes indigenous to live performances had to be corrected before the group would allow their concert sound to be heard in the movie. However, there was no point starting the doctoring work before the film had been edited and the final choice of songs determined.

The hectic lifestyle of the past two years, and the traumatic experiences of the Australian tour, had brought about a basic change within the group. Despite their history as domestic stars before Abba, there was always a touch of fresh-faced wonderment at everything that had happened to them as they conquered the international arena. Notwithstanding the odd beef at having to tour, deep down inside they were immensely proud of what they had achieved, thriving on their success and being taken seriously as a force on the pop music scene.

But even in 1976, as the first signs of overwhelming pressure began to take root, their tone started to change whenever they talked seriously about their future. The girls' roles as focal points made them especially vulnerable: Frida was suffering recurring nightmares, and Agnetha had trouble sleeping.

"It's terrible," she said. "You lie awake thinking and the longer you stay awake the more desperate you become. I have to get up early for Linda's sake, I know that I can't be lounging in bed until 12." Both attributed their problems to outside pressure: the demands of maintaining Abba's high standards — preferably improving on them — as well as the stress and the long and boring journeys.

Agnetha couldn't escape, not even when she visited her parents in Jönköping. She'd try to disguise herself to avoid detection, putting up her hair and wearing sunglasses. Nevertheless, if just one young fan happened to recognise her, she was soon surrounded by a hundred children asking for autographs. The fans would stand below the balcony of the Fältskogs' apartment building, shouting for Abba.

At home, in relatively secluded Lidingö, the situation wasn't much better. Having moved to a new house as recently as November 1976, by the following summer Agnetha and Björn found that they were forced to move again. "The location of the house is too open," said Björn. "The most excited fans just walk straight in." By October they had moved to their new, more unassuming-looking villa, also located in Lidingö. The price tag was still a hefty 900,000 kronor (£117,000).

Frida and Benny suffered similar problems, and the pair found it especially disturbing now that their children had moved in to live with them. "The fans would suddenly come striding along through the back door while the children were standing there," recalled Frida many years later. "Everyone who shows up is not entirely healthy. In that respect I'm damaged, it was rough for my children."

There were numerous chilling incidents. One night, Benny and Frida were woken by noise from the kitchen. With their hearts in their mouths they tiptoed down the stairs to find that there were people on their porch. A family from West Germany had put up a camping table and were having coffee in cups they had borrowed from the kitchen.

Sometimes it seemed as if there was nowhere to escape for any of them: with papers and magazines continually printing reports on Viggsö, fans or other curious people even made their way out there in the hope of meeting one of them. With Björn and Agnetha's marriage under perpetual strain, these pressures of fame just added to their dilemma. By now, the situation was also starting to colour the group's music more overtly.

In mid-July, Björn and Benny had finally written one more song for the new album. The working title, 'Sjömansvisa' ('Sailor's Song'), betrayed its origins in the Stockholm archipelago, but when the tune was arranged and recorded at Marcus Music studio it had turned into a soft rock ballad. A few months later Björn wrote the lyrics. Retreating to the recreation room in his and Agnetha's new house, he lay down on the floor and put together a story about a couple struggling to save their marriage. He gave the song the title 'One Man, One Woman'.

A recent piece like 'Eagle' may have been more ambitious lyrically than the "dum dum diddle"-isms of Abba's earlier work, but the result still didn't move far beyond the new age fantasies of the novel that inspired Björn's words. 'One Man, One Woman' seemed to be the first time that Björn's lyrics clearly emanated from his own life experience: an honest report on where he and his wife were at.

An earlier song on a similar theme, like 'Knowing Me, Knowing You', had been effective enough in its use of the absence of familiar sounds as a metaphor for lost love. The imagery in 'One Man, One Woman', however, was more painfully literate. The opening line, "No smiles, not a single word at the breakfast table," carried a potency like nothing else Abba had ever written before. It was patently clear what the subject of this song was going to be. This was not the rush of romance when a couple falls in love, nor was it the devastated cry after the break-up: this was the struggle to keep it all together when the dizzying feelings of love had turned into dull routine, the resistance to throw it all away after so much effort.

The husband of the protagonist leaves for work and "slam[s] the door", leaving his wife to contemplate their situation. "Daydreams of a better life, but I have to wake up/The sound of a key in the door" – the couple have to face each other again in the evening. The last verse ends on a hopeful note: "You smile and I realise that we need a shake-up/Our love is a precious thing/Worth the pain and the suffering/And it's never too late for changing."

Was Björn putting his own situation into words? He has usually dismissed all suggestions that any of the "marriage crisis" lyrics he wrote during the first half of Abba's career were a reflection of any real-life despondency. But coming so soon after a declaration of intent to make a better effort with the lyrics, it is hard to escape the feeling that 'One Man, One Woman' was a heartfelt depiction of what went on in the Ulvaeus/Fältskog household. The words were too real, too specific, the imagery too unerring not to have been a sincere outpouring of the wordsmith. As if to underscore the sensitivity of the matter, it was not Agnetha but Frida who ended up handling the lead vocals on the track.

Without diminishing Björn's talent for writing simple and direct hit song lyrics, 'One Man, One Woman' was the first time that his words sounded truly genuine. He was emerging as a master of the art of describing life as it is, facing up to the realities of everyday problems, as opposed to the rock myth of escaping from the dullness of a small-town existence.

By mid-August, backing tracks for all the songs on the album had been recorded, but the group was still under pressure to meet all their deadlines. There was still a great deal of work to be done with overdubs, not least the girls' vocal contributions, and so far not much work had been done on the movie soundtrack either. Agnetha's pregnancy only added to the strain.

In the midst of all this, when the four members needed all the peace and quiet they could get, Stig Anderson made an unexpected statement to the press. Following a recent report that Polar Music and its affiliated companies were the most profitable enterprise in the country, Stig announced that Abba were seriously contemplating moving abroad for tax reasons. "We have discussed the high tax pressure quite a lot," he said. "It has now made us consider leaving Sweden for good. It's not as if we're stupid."

They were all considering moving to Monaco, Switzerland or Lichtenstein, he related. "Abba can function just as well with any of these countries as a base, perhaps even better . . . Everyone in the group has been a part of the discussions . . . If the tax situation worsens we will not hesitate at implementing our plans to move."

Such plans were certainly news to the group, who firmly denied that they were going to leave Sweden. Taken unawares, they were forced to break their decision not to do any interviews until the album was completed and make a statement for themselves. "We have discussed the possibilities of moving abroad on a strictly theoretical level," explained Björn, "but only in passing." Agnetha was more forceful in her dissociation from Stig's statement. "Those views will have to stand for Stig," she fumed. "If he has implied that we four are thinking of leaving the country, that's wrong." What she said next marked the first time any member of Abba deliberately drew attention to the difference between their own views and those of their manager: "It's scary when people believe that Stig speaks for us all. It seems like everybody thinks that he *is* Abba. We're also able to think for ourselves."

Stig did indeed have the habit of referring to the group and himself as "we" more often than not when he spoke to the media. "We" are making a new record, "we" are going on tour, "we" are opposed to the taxes – his way of expressing himself had clearly contributed to the image of Stig and Abba as one entity.

Perhaps this was fine with the group when their own music-making talent rubbed off on Stig's public image, but it was evident that they weren't so keen on having to support every controversial statement Stig made in his frequent interviews. The day after his "exile threat", he was forced to tell the press that he and the group had no plans to leave the country. It was almost as if he tried to make out that he had never said any such thing.

That everything wasn't as it should be within the group came shining through in interviews. "I was a damn sight happier ten years ago, there's no denying that," Björn reflected. "It's like I've been constantly worried for the past six months." Agnetha added: "We work so hard in the studio. I think that's the reason. Everything has just been piling up for us."

Certainly, it was a time of unreasonable pressure on all members of the group. The responsibility of delivering "product" to eager record companies all over the world, and the constant carping from the Swedish press was bad enough – Abba certainly didn't need any further unnecessary problems to deal with.

Agnetha, who had to be careful about the baby she was expecting, still worked as hard as she could with vocal overdubs, often putting in 12-hour days. That was when disaster struck. Six months into her pregnancy she almost had a miscarriage and was rushed to the hospital. For Agnetha, it was an omen: a flashback to the problems of getting pregnant with Linda all those years ago. "I started wondering if I wasn't meant to have children," she said. Luckily, the doctors managed to stabilise her, but she would always remember her second pregnancy as "difficult".

Naturally, this crisis had consequences for all of Abba's current work. They were in the midst of vocal overdubs and final tweaking of the recordings, and though Agnetha would pitch in to the best of her abilities, for four weeks in September her doctor advised her not to sing at all since this could induce the birth. It was absolutely vital she took it easy and remained sitting or lying down, limiting her physical activities to the absolute minimum, but with the deadline for the movie rapidly approaching, she felt she had no choice but to be present in the studio. To facilitate her work, a deck chair was brought in so that she wouldn't have to stand up while she was singing, but could lie back in repose.

Even with all the film work completed, it looked increasingly unlikely that the album would be ready in time for a pre-Christmas release. In September it was announced that the album would be postponed until February 1978. The only official reason given at the time was that Agnetha "needed to take it easy", with no reference to the drama surrounding her pregnancy. Unfortunately, this only led to further speculation in the press that she was seriously ill.

When relatives read the stories and began calling to check how she was, even Linda got wind of the rumours. Finally Agnetha blew her top. "I'm used to a lot of writings, but sometimes you have to react," she snapped. "It's pretty normal for a pregnant woman to take it easy. It feels pretty silly to be labelled 'seriously ill' when I'm in perfect health."

It was almost as if there was a curse on the band as they tried to finish their album: shortly after Agnetha's near-miscarriage, Frida slipped on the staircase at home and broke her collarbone. But this physical incident was nothing compared to the emotional punch that fate had in store for her just a few days later.

Chapter 24

On Sunday, August 28, 1977, a 15-year-old West German Abba fan called Andrea Buchinger was reading the latest issue of the pop magazine *Bravo*. For the umpteenth time, the magazine had published profiles on each of the four members of the group. But this time, when Andrea read the text about Frida, she was startled. The article detailed Frida's background, stating that her father was one Alfred Haase, who was thought to have perished after the war. Alfred Haase was the name of Andrea's uncle.

Andrea showed the magazine to her mother, who was intrigued by the fact that her husband's brother had the same name as Frida's lost father. She knew also that he had been stationed in Norway during the war. It was too much of a coincidence. She picked up the phone and called her brother-in-law, who lived in the town of Karlsruhe. On this particular night, however, the phone in the Haase household was out of order. Eventually the news reached Alfred Haase's 30-year-old son Peter, who lived close to his parents.

At 11 o'clock that night, Peter went over to confront his father. Haase, who had turned 58 just two days earlier, was a distinguished gentleman with white hair and a well-trimmed beard. His 34-year-old daughter, Karin, had made him a grandfather, and he earned his living as a pastrycook for a large food company. That evening, Alfred and his wife were at home in their two-room apartment in Karlsruhe watching sport on television. Suddenly his son stormed in and said that he had to speak to him urgently, in private.

When the door closed behind them, Peter got straight to the point. "Does the name Synni Lyngstad mean anything to you?" he asked. The shock of hearing that name again after all these years stunned Alfred into silence. "Did you know her or not?" his son insisted. Alfred was still lost for words. "Where did you hear that name?" he finally whispered. It was all Peter needed: his question had been answered. He held up an Abba poster from the current issue of *Bravo*, pointed to Frida and said: "Congratulations – this is your daughter."

Alfred's head was spinning. He barely knew who Abba were, but sat down and studied the picture in total amazement. "Anni-Frid resembled her mother so much," he recalled. "The same forehead, the same hair. And Peter thought that she had my nose and cheekbones."

His feelings of joy were tempered by the knowledge that he now had to inform his wife, Anna, of his love affair with Synni in Norway all those years ago. Alfred took the bull by the horns, and went in to his wife. "What do you think about this girl," he asked, pointing to the picture of Frida. Anna, a great admirer of Abba, replied that she was very beautiful. "Small wonder," said Alfred. "After all, she's my daughter." After the feeling of shock and disbelief had died down, Anna was philosophical about the situation. "I have forgiven Alfred for his liaison," she said a short while later. "The times were unnatural back then. People didn't act in a natural way."

Before long Alfred had the phone number of Polar Music in Stockholm and had plucked up the courage to contact his daughter. But when someone claiming to be her father suddenly started calling the office, Frida initially told the office girls to dismiss him: her father was dead, and that was that. "I thought it was just a crank caller," she recalled.

In the mid-Fifties, Frida's aunt Olive Lunde had tried to investigate the fate of Alfred Haase. "We learned that the German authorities would pay 30,000 marks to foreign women who'd had a child by a German soldier," she recalled. "I felt that Anni-Frid . . . deserved that money." On a holiday in West Germany, Olive and her husband sought police assistance and tracked down a man called Alfred Haase, who might have been the right person. When they went to visit him, only his young son was at home. His dad had a job in insurance and was away on business, they were told. The Lunde couple didn't have the time or money to remain in West Germany until Alfred returned, so they were never able to confirm that they had reached the right household. However, Olive had a hunch that she had been close to the truth.

The winter after that trip, she made a visit to Ballangen, the childhood village she had left over a decade earlier. There she happened to speak to a woman who was certain that the ship taking the German soldiers out of the Narvik area had been sunk by the Allies. After that the Lyngstads abandoned their inquiries, but the lack of conclusive evidence about her father's demise had been fodder for Frida's childhood daydreams of meeting him one day. With time, she had lost hope, resigning herself to the fact that she was never going to know her parents.

More than a week passed before Frida finally decided to talk to the man claiming to be Alfred Haase. "Hello, my girl, this is your father speaking," said the voice on the other end of the line. She was still suspicious, but there were so many things he knew that he wouldn't have known unless he had some connection to Ballangen and her mother.

Several phone calls followed, and in all of them Frida's questions were met with plausible replies and detailed stories. "When it turned out that he had a copy of the exact same photograph that I had of him as a young soldier, that settled it," said Frida. She was convinced enough to invite Haase to Stockholm for a meeting.

Benny called Frida's Aunt Olive to inform her of the news. He told her that she had to come over: only she would be able to determine if it was the real Alfred Haase. A couple of days before Alfred was due to come to Stockholm, Olive arrived at the Lidingö villa so that they could prepare themselves. Since Haase spoke only German, and Frida had scant knowledge of that language, former Hootenanny Singer Hansi Schwarz was mobilised as an interpreter.

On Friday, September 9, less than two weeks after Andrea Buchinger first read the article in *Bravo*, Alfred Haase arrived at Stockholm's Arlanda airport. Frida was too nervous to face her father there, so Benny and Olive had to go out to meet him. Meanwhile, Frida and Hansi waited back at the house.

To avoid drawing attention to the airport pick-up, Alfred was met in the VIP lounge. "It was like a CIA operation," recalled *Bravo* photographer "Bubi" Heilemann, who accompanied the trip in the hope of getting some good shots of father and daughter embracing. "The plane landed, the doors opened and some guys took Alfred with them and I was left alone. [He] was 'kidnapped' out of the plane."

Alfred didn't know who was going to meet him, but the moment he laid eyes on Olive, he said: "Oh, you're Synni's sister!" He had never seen Olive in the flesh before, but recognised her from photographs that Synni had shown him.

When Benny, Olive and Alfred drove up to the Lidingö villa, Frida was outside, standing on the steps to greet them. Alfred was just as nervous as his daughter as he slowly walked up to her and handed over a bouquet of roses. No words were spoken as they embraced, both of them crying silent tears. After a while, Alfred quietly whispered, "*Mein Gott, mein Gott, ist es wirklich!*" ("My God, it's for real!") When she had composed herself, Frida welcomed her father in broken German.

Dinner followed. This was make or break time for Alfred to dispel all doubts that he really was Frida's father and not just someone who was after her millions. Olive placed some photographs on the table. Without hesitation Alfred pointed to the pictures and said, "That's Synni – and that's her mother."

"On the back of one of the pictures of Synni, Alfred had written something," recalled Olive. "We compared the handwriting. There was no doubt. As one piece of evidence after another established that the man sitting among us really was Anni-Frid's father, the tears were streaming down the cheeks of all of us."

Father and daughter also compared their index fingers and toes, which in Frida's case were bent in a way unlike anyone else in the Lyngstad family. They laughed when Alfred Haase's hands and feet turned out to be shaped exactly the same way.

Amidst all the emotion, Olive Lunde wondered about Alfred Haase's insistence that he hadn't known that Synni was pregnant when he left Norway. She felt that despite the joyful atmosphere, there were questions that remained unanswered. "Frida was a bit reserved towards her father," recalls Hansi Schwarz. "She wondered why he had never bothered to find out what had become of her. There were certain barriers, certain reservations."

That first night, Frida and Alfred sat up talking until four in the morning, but having to rely on an interpreter made conversation difficult. There were certain matters she wanted to broach that she felt were just between herself and Alfred. Frida told her father that she was going to learn to speak German properly.

On the Saturday, Frida and Benny took Alfred out to the atmospheric Gamla stan district in Stockholm, where they had been living until just a year earlier. They dined at a restaurant, still talking, asking questions, sussing each other out.

During the weekend, Frida and Alfred were photographed together, and two shots were sent to the press. The first showed the pair out walking, gazing into each other's faces with joyful smiles. The second was a stunning close-up portrait of father and daughter in a half-profile, contemplative pose. Both pictures showed Frida without make-up, looking more vulnerable and emotionally naked than ever before. Gone were the regal poses, the half-suspicious eyes, the shield that protected her from the misfortunes visited upon her: what remained was simply Anni-Frid Lyngstad, the little girl who was still trying to discover herself, connecting to the roots that had been snatched away so early in her life.

When the three-day visit was over, Frida drove her father out to the airport, both of them aware of the complicated and sensitive situation. "We did get to know each other a bit," recalled Frida. "But it's difficult to get a father when you're 32 years old. It would have been different if I'd been a teenager or a child. I can't really connect to him and love him the way I would have if he'd been around when I grew up."

They decided to try to develop the relationship one step at a time, exchanging phone calls and letters. Alfred invited them all to visit him in Karlsruhe. "We plan to get together so that I can meet the rest of the family," said Frida, "but if we don't get along for some reason we can't force ourselves to have any artificial feelings." They had an emotional farewell at Arlanda, and Alfred flew back to West Germany.

As she watched Alfred's plane disappear into the clouds, so many conflicting emotions raged inside her that she hardly knew what to think or what to feel. "It's like my entire background comes back, flowing over me," she reflected in an interview. "It's only now that the tension has been released – the reaction came the other night when I lay awake crying for several hours." It would take time to come to terms with this new situation. Six months later Frida referred to the meeting as the most significant event of her entire life. "It still feels unreal: to have a father who is like a stranger," she said.

The whole episode surely contributed to Frida's sense of living in a cartoon version of the real world. Ordinary people would find lost relatives through enlisting the help of private detectives or conducting painstaking research in official archives. For Frida, it was something as superficial and irrelevant as a brightly coloured West German pop magazine that had enabled her to get in touch with her father. It can only have added to the almost impossible dilemma of keeping her private identity separate from the public pop star persona.

Immediately after her father's return to West Germany, Frida joined Björn and Benny on a week-long visit to Bohus Studio in Kungälv near Gothenburg. The group were smitten with the idea of the luxurious recording studio: with living quarters in the same building as the studio, artists could work round the clock if they so desired. Agnetha was in no shape to travel and stayed behind in Stockholm, but the rest of the group went down together with their core group of musicians.

With all the backing tracks for the album completed, the purpose of the trip was mainly to do overdub work on the film soundtrack. As it turned out, the glamorous, night-long rock'n'roll lifestyle sessions never happened. "It really wasn't for us," remembered Björn. "No one wanted to record in the middle of the night anyway." Instead, most of Abba's Bohus week was devoted to the complicated mix of 'The Name Of The Game', slated to become the next seven-inch release.

There had been some debate as to which song to issue as the lead-off single from the upcoming album. Up until shortly before the Bohus trip, a rocky recording called 'Hole In Your Soul' was seriously considered as the best candidate. Indeed, in Australia, it had already been assigned a catalogue number by RCA. It was thought to be an excellent choice for the Australian market: the high energy level and direct approach of 'Hole In Your Soul' was very much in tune with the singles that had led to Abba's breakthrough in the first place.

Polar's decision to change the single to the more complex and muted 'The Name Of The Game' was not very popular with RCA. Since the insane success of the tour in March, Abba's fortunes on the Australian market had gone into a rapid decline. In many ways, this development was as inexplicable as the country's love affair with the group in the first place, but ominous signs were on the horizon immediately after the tour, when interest in Abba was at its highest. Logically, the current single, 'Knowing Me, Knowing You', should have enjoyed a walk-over success. Instead, six consecutive number one singles★ were followed by a number nine "flop".

Part of the explanation was obviously that 'Knowing Me, Knowing You' had already been available on the *Arrival* album for several months. Although this hadn't stopped the single from topping the UK charts for five weeks around the same time, John Spalding argues that the Australian market worked differently. "It was definitely an album market, that," he says. "I think the kids quickly realised they could get all the hits by buying the albums."

However, when 'The Name Of The Game' was released at the end of October, it wasn't available on any album. In the UK, the single hit number one three weeks after release, holding on to its position for four weeks. 'The Name Of The Game' should have shot to the top of the charts in Australia as well: instead it began a long and slow climb to a number six position, which it reached only a full three months after it was issued. This clearly wasn't worthy of a group that had a maniacal following across a large section of the population.

There are many theories about the decline in Abba's Australian popularity. Some suggest that their exposure between the 1975 breakthrough and the tour of March 1977 was just too high. Stig Anderson, who was very familiar with the old showbiz adage "always leave them wanting more", had feared this development all along. With the group being shoved in the population's faces day in and day out, a backlash was inevitable.

Others argue that everything was just too quiet in the seven months that elapsed between the end of the tour and the release of 'The Name Of The Game', and when the single finally came, it was the wrong type of song for the Australian market. Likewise, whereas the movie had originally been scheduled for an August première, it was postponed until October, and

---

★ Disregarding the re-emergence of lower-charting earlier releases during this period.

then finally to December. Some observers claim this was far too long a gap to capitalise on the interest generated by the March visit.

A feeling that it was "uncool" to be an Abba fan had somehow emerged at the time of the tour. The group's kids-and-parents core audience had inspired many of the initially enthusiastic teenagers to turn their backs on them, and sections of the media that had once ardently helped build Abba's career were now just as fervent in their condemnation of the group.

Powerful *Countdown* host Ian "Molly" Meldrum was a good example. At the height of Abbamania he had proudly boasted the show's role in introducing the group to Australia, even travelling to Sweden to make an exclusive Abba documentary in September 1976. By the time the group's *Super Trouper* album was released in 1980 his enthusiasm had dropped below zero. During his review spot in the *Countdown* show he held up the cover of the album, said "there's a new Abba album out", and then immediately threw it over his shoulder.

"A lot of adult people working within the music industry really had a great admiration for the group," recalled Australian music writer Glenn A. Baker. "But it was very difficult to express it, because their fan base appeared to be about eight years old. No adult with any sort of pretensions to cool was ever going to bat for a group whose fanbase was in fact children."

A song like 'The Name Of The Game', then, fell between two stools. It was slightly too sophisticated for the children and adults who preferred the accessible singalong qualities of the group's earlier material. At the same time, because it was Abba who delivered the song, the progressive nature of the record was largely ignored by critics who now routinely dismissed the group's releases.

When the new LP was released in Australia in January 1978 it reached a creditable number four position. Nevertheless, after three consecutive number one albums with record-breaking sales figures, it was well below expectations and proved that Abba had lost their overwhelming grip on the albums market as well. Although the group never scored another number one album or single in Australia while they were together, their loyal fanbase still sent their records into the Top 10 on a regular basis. But the time when Abba had the attention of the entire nation was gone.

In November 1977 Abba suddenly reversed their earlier decision to postpone the new album. The release date for Scandinavia was now fixed at December 12, although the rest of the world still had to wait until the first few months of 1978 until the album reached record shops.

The sudden change of plan had been made possible when, unexpectedly,

Agnetha was able to attend recording sessions more extensively. The group had also acquired more studio time than anticipated. When the originally scheduled sessions overran, Marcus Music studios hadn't been available to the extent that they hoped. The last few months had seen the group skip around between different facilities – clearly, it would be a great relief when their own studio was finally opened.

However, with the decision to rush-release the album another logistical problem arose: finding enough pressing plants to meet the demand from record shops at such short notice. Before Abba emerged on the Swedish music scene it was unusual for anyone to sell more than 50,000 copies of an album, and even that was very rare. For every new Abba LP, the group broke the sales record set by the previous release. *Arrival*, the most recent album, had sold an unprecedented 740,000 copies. "Our motto was that we would never run out of records," explains Berka Bergkvist. "When we found ourselves in a situation where there was a great demand for records we should always be able to deliver, which we did."

In the case of the current LP, four different pressing plants in the greater Stockholm area were used to manufacture the required number of albums. However, it seemed the rush did have some unfortunate consequences: a large number of albums shipped to record stores had the A-side songs pressed on both sides.

The LP was entitled *ABBA – The Album*, co-ordinated with the film title which was *ABBA – The Movie*. It had taken a while to come up with this fairly unimaginative but ultra-distinct solution. At one point Abba and Polar had toyed with *Thank You For The Music* as a title for both productions. Originally there had also been plans to extend the project synergy by making the record a budget-priced double album with one disc a live recording from the tour.

Considering the title, it was ironic that *ABBA – The Album* had a less cohesive "album" feeling than any of the group's LPs since *Ring Ring*. It seemed to consist of separate chunks of music with fewer unifying factors than usual. Although Abba had always prided themselves on their variety and versatility, the songs on *Arrival*, for example, had been tied together by a bright and shiny overall sound.

By way of contrast, on side one of *ABBA – The Album*, the group shifted somewhat uncomfortably from the "high, high" new age-isms in 'Eagle', over the bouncy bubble-gum pop of 'Take A Chance On Me' and the soft-rock inflections in 'One Man, One Woman', to the Euro-Californian experiment of 'The Name Of The Game'; breathtakingly brilliant tracks all of them, but in many ways sounding as if they had emerged from four different artists. The sole connection between the songs was Agnetha and Frida's ever sparkling voices, pointing to an obvious but often overlooked truth about the group's music.

"When you start talking about concepts like 'the Abba sound' you certainly have to mention the songs, the way we arranged them, Michael's contribution and all that," reflected Benny later. "But take away Frida and Agnetha and let two other girls sing their parts, and 'the Abba sound' goes out the window immediately. Their voices were simply the most important ingredient of our overall sound structure." On *ABBA – The Album*, perhaps more than on any other Abba LP, it was the girls vocals, together with Benny's own keyboard work, that identified the tracks as emanating from the same group.

The disparate nature of the album was further emphasised by the inclusion of the three mini-musical songs which closed the second side of the LP. It was as if the original album stopped after the first six songs, with the musical numbers tagged on as bonus selections. These latter tracks were also marked by somewhat different production aesthetics, the aim seemingly being to make them sound like stage recordings.

In at least one case, Björn and Benny's wish to present a polished sound had a detrimental effect on the outcome. A live version of 'I Wonder (Departure)' had been the B-side of 'The Name Of The Game', and the recording was put together under somewhat shaky circumstances. The piano solo, which was not part of the song during the original live performances, was not even recorded on the multitrack tape. Instead it was added during the mixing stage as the band were in a hurry to get the single out. According to Michael Tretow, this was the only time that short cuts like this were used during Abba's career. In the event, the slight roughness actually made this recording sound more warm and urgent than the too-perfect studio interpretation.

All in all, the mini-musical songs lent a somewhat heavy slant to *ABBA – The Album*, perhaps moving it a bit too far away from the straightforward pop that was the group's forte and main *raison d'être*. "I can understand why many felt that *The Album* was too difficult," Agnetha agreed. "That mini-musical worked well on stage but not so well on record."

Along with a release date that was too close to Christmas, the complex nature of the album perhaps also contributed to lower domestic sales than expected. Out of the 760,000 copies delivered to record shops, 100,000 remained unsold several months later. Although it spent four weeks at number one, many therefore branded *ABBA – The Album* a "failure". However, as Björn pointed out, "We've still sold 660,000 copies. Is that a failure?" The remaining copies found buyers in the end, even if some dealers had to radically reduce the price to unload their overstock.

When her work on the album was complete Agnetha retreated to her home, awaiting the birth of her second child. The arrival was expected in November, but as had been the case with Linda, Agnetha went several weeks over time, which put added strain on her already stressful life. It wasn't until three o'clock in the morning on Sunday, December 4, that Agnetha's labour started kicking in. Some 18 hours later, at 8.45 p.m., she finally gave birth to an eight pound five ounce baby boy. As with Linda almost five years earlier, it was a long and complicated delivery, and Agnetha was in terrible pain from dawn until it was all over. This didn't stop Björn from filming the birth with his Super 8 movie camera. "It's with sound and everything," he enthused. "I filmed Agnetha when she was lying there in labour, and then the boy when he sits rocking on her belly. Also Linda when she runs around at home in pure bliss. Great footage!" During the actual delivery he put the camera aside, however. "At that time I had other tasks to attend to," he explained.

Despite the pain, Agnetha was over the moon at becoming a mother again. Then there was the question of what to call the boy. Little Linda suggested Peter, or perhaps Fredrik. In the end, her parents settled on Peter Christian – the latter was daddy's middle name, although he spelt it Kristian.

Björn and Agnetha wanted at all costs to avoid the media frenzy that followed Linda's birth. This time they selected one photographer who would be allowed to take pictures, a selection of which would then be made available to anyone who wanted to publish them. The lucky recipient of this assignment was veteran record sleeve photographer Bengt H. Malmqvist, who had worked with the group on many occasions. The *Ring Ring* cover was among his more well-known work, along with the classic park bench picture that adorned the sleeve of the *Greatest Hits* album.

Malmqvist waited on stand-by for three days after Christian's birth before he finally got the call. In one intense 20-minute session, he snapped 70 colour and black and white pictures of Björn, Agnetha and Christian in all positions and combinations thinkable. The short time in the hospital room became his most lucrative assignment ever. "I earned 125,000 kronor (£16,250) on those pictures, which was just unbelievable," Malmqvist recalled.

On December 15, while Björn and Agnetha were getting acquainted with the new member of the family, Stig Anderson travelled to Sydney to attend the world première of *ABBA – The Movie*. Together with all four Abba members, Stig was also present at the Swedish gala opening in Stockholm on December 26.

Reviews for the film were mixed, with many critics unsure whether to regard *ABBA – The Movie* as one long advertisement for the group, or an attempt to make a piece of memorable cinema. The "interview hunt" plot was universally panned, but at least one reviewer picked up on the possibility that its effect may depend on one's viewpoint. Whereas Ashley's endeavours quickly became tiresome for the adult part of the audience, younger viewers empathised completely with the quest to get near their idols. "It was very clever to make us mysterious and unapproachable, because that's exactly what we were to that reporter," said Björn many years later.

Many observers also noted how the film concentrated a great deal on Agnetha's backside, leading to further musing about that part of her anatomy. "Don't they have bottoms in Australia?" the exasperated singer had asked in the movie, little knowing how much the film would add to the media's obsession with this subject. "I had no idea they were filming it that much," she said later. "I swear that it wasn't anything conscious on my part. I don't mind if people find it sexy, but the interest in my bottom in Australia and England is ridiculous. It was fun up to a point, but when they're having contests in England to determine whose behind looks better than mine, that's just plain silly."

The budget for the film was said to have finished at a cool 5 million kronor (£625,000), a considerable sum for a Swedish production at this time. However, after a preview in November, the rights for the movie were sold to the Nordic countries, West Germany, Belgium, The Netherlands and Israel, with Warner Brothers picking up the rights for the rest of the world, excluding Australia and New Zealand.

Whatever the subsequent financial rewards for local licensees, the deal meant that Polar and Reg Grundy Productions quickly recouped their investment. All in all the movie turned out to be a box office success, especially compared to the many flops that make up the history of "rock movies". A year after the première it had been seen by more than five million people, and at that time it still hadn't opened in North America.

Robert Hughes was later to complain that the monetary compensation for his role in *ABBA – The Movie* should have been higher. "I didn't get paid a lot of money for the film," he said in 1993. "I haven't had any residuals from overseas sales or anything. I just got a fee for each week of work and that was it . . . There's a bone of contention over the contract, which nobody seems to find."

In Australia, public enthusiasm for the film was muted. "*The Movie* has been described as being 'reasonably successful' in Australia," noted the fan-based Abba Appreciation Club newsletter somewhat coolly a few months after the première. "This means that the film has been successful but not to the extent that the producers had hoped for." The disappointing box office receipts were embarrassing proof of the extent to which the Abba fever had died down.

The group themselves were pleased with the movie for the most part, even if some of Benny's original objections to the project remained. "I don't like seeing myself on the screen," he was heard to mutter after the première. Being a public figure seemed to interest him less and less.

The movie premières brought 1977 to a close. It had been a crazy year for Abba, marked by a major sell-out tour amid scenes of outright hysteria, a series of hit singles – including their first US chart-topper – a brand new album, and a movie. Nevertheless, everyday life in Stockholm remained at the centre of their existence.

For Agnetha, her role as a mother took priority over anything else. In *ABBA – The Movie* it wasn't the thrill of seeing herself on the screen that caught her attention, but tellingly, a few scenes with children who struggle to put their admiration for Abba into words. "Having children of your own makes such scenes really funny," she said. Later she made a point of singling out the birth of Christian as "more important than anything else that happened to me in 1977".

The events of the past 12 months had only increased her determination to keep a lower profile. "I'm not tired of Abba, but I feel that I have to keep away now. I've got to get some time to find myself as a private person again, and not always be just a quarter of Abba."

She reflected on the pressures of being an international star. "I've become reserved these days, and perhaps that's because people seem a little scared. I mean, my career has been so great and there have been so many writings about money and success that you almost frighten people in your role as a part of Abba. It's going to be such a relief to withdraw from the public when all this business with the album and the movie is over. That's what I need right now."

For the whole of January and the first weeks of February 1978, Abba mostly went into hibernation. Björn and Benny's appetite for musicals had been whetted by the experience of *The Girl With The Golden Hair*, and they were considering the possibility of putting together a full-length production. But they weren't able to find the right idea, and since they also wanted to keep up their Abba work parallel with any musical work, the idea was shelved soon enough.

While Agnetha devoted her time to her newborn baby, the remaining three members accompanied Stig to the MIDEM Festival in Cannes to promote the film and the new album. During the press conference, they were asked what they would later recall as the most stupid questions they had ever faced as a group. "How to make a hit?" was a highlight from one reporter, while another delivered the classic, "Do you like music?" In a rare public show of anger, Frida was so annoyed that she up and left the podium.

In mid-February, the group went to London to promote the new album and attend the première of *ABBA – The Movie*. From the hands of Princess Margaret they received the Carl Alan Award for the second year in a row. The second single from *ABBA – The Album* was also released around this time. 'Take A Chance On Me' rapidly became Abba's seventh UK number one. If 'Money, Money, Money' hadn't stuck at number three, it would have been the seventh in an unbroken string of chart-toppers.

The making of 'Take A Chance On Me' pointed to an interesting dimension in the Andersson/Ulvaeus partnership. Although Benny was undeniably the primary musical motor of Abba, it is worth remembering that the collaboration between him and Björn was never strictly divided between music and lyrics. "In some of the melody lines in Abba's early production I believe I can actually hear, 'That one came from Björn!'" claims Tony Rooth of the Hootenanny Singers.

By his own admission, Björn contributed less and less of the musical ideas as the partnership progressed, but one shouldn't underestimate his role as editor of the tunes that flowed from Benny. As in almost everything the two composers produced, they both took the pragmatic route: it wasn't important who came up with the idea, the only thing that mattered was the end result.

"When someone had something they liked very much which the other one wasn't sure about," Björn recalled, "the technique we used was to bring it up again, and again, and again . . . 'No, I still don't like that fucking thing' . . . and again. Wear each other out. In the end it would either be discarded or it would be, 'Yeah, maybe you're right.' I remember that Benny didn't like the verse to 'Take A Chance On Me' very much, 'We could go dancing, we could go walking'. But in the end he went with it."

After a two-day promotional trip to West Germany, following the London visit, Abba returned to Sweden, after which Björn and Benny began tentative songwriting sessions for the group's sixth album. They failed to come up with anything new, however. In mid-March recording sessions commenced with the backing track for a song adorned with the curious working title 'Dr. Claus von Hamlet'. It was an attempt to make a

372

rock song out of a folk-style melody they had written a few years earlier.

But the track didn't come out as they wanted and was quickly scrapped. It was an ominous sign for the album sessions. Where time pressure had been the major hurdle for Björn and Benny to overcome during previous albums, the new project presented a much more serious and hitherto unfamiliar threat: writer's block.

Chapter 25

For those that crossed his professional path, as employees or outside collaborators, working with Stig Anderson was never a smooth and easy ride. By the late Seventies, his opinions on how things should be done remained as strong as ever: the implicit argument was still that his point of view was the only valid one.

Nothing irked him as much as wasting money and resources, and he supervised the daily goings-on at the Polar and Sweden Music offices with hawk-like diligence. The Abba millions may have been rolling in, but Stig remained adamant that no one should ever throw away a single paper clip – literally. He'd also insist that his employees always used the back as well as the front of every single sheet of paper. Old documents that needn't be kept should be torn in pieces and used for writing notes.

"I'm far from stingy, but it's important to be economical in the right way," Stig said. "You shouldn't throw away things that can be used." It was the young Stig Anderson talking, the boy from Hova who at the age of 13 left school to deliver groceries and who had no choice but to look after every single penny, to eke out a living any way he could, to make sure absolutely nothing ever went to waste.

Similarly, he would fret over every single outside cost incurred by the contractors Polar used. For the duration of his association with the company, someone like Lasse Hallström continued operating on a minuscule budget for his promo clips. Art director Rune Söderqvist would receive irate phone calls whenever he submitted an invoice for the sleeve of a multi-million selling Abba album. Fortunately, he had realised from the beginning that this was a company that liked to see where the money went, so he kept all his time reports and expense sheets in perfect order.

"Stig would hit the ceiling and ask me to get over and explain the invoice," Rune recalled. "I'd break down the figures for him: 'Well, this part of the job cost 2,000 kronor.' 'That's not very much, I guess.' 'And this cost 10,000.' 'Okay, perhaps it's worth that much,' and so on. Then I'd say, 'Well, if you add it all up it becomes quite a large sum.' I believe his reaction was mostly a matter of a conditioned reflex, actually."

Stig's firm control of matters had a positive effect on those who dealt with Polar. "He demanded that we held a very high level of service towards everybody," says Berka Bergkvist. "If the phone rang more than three rings we had to pick it up, no matter who received the call. No one should have to wait for longer than that. Our standards should be higher than anybody else's. It was a part of our image, and it was something we succeeded with."

Delegating tasks did not come easy to Stig, which was why he seldom relied on anyone apart from his very closest collaborators. He hadn't forgotten the experience of his mother's confectionery kiosk when he was a young child: if someone was entrusted with a responsibility they'd better get it right. The problem was that, from his viewpoint, few people ever did.

The high demands Stig placed on himself and others didn't ease up with Abba's success and the added pressure of taking care of their escalating revenues, nor had his hot temper softened over the years. Violent explosions were a constant occurrence in the Polar office. "You always knew when he wasn't in the mood for discussing a problem," Berka recalls. "Then you'd wait for 15 minutes. Sometimes we'd be having a meeting and he'd blow his temper for some reason and throw us all out: 'I don't want to see you!' Then, five minutes later, we were having a new meeting because by then he'd cooled down. We all knew that he could be mad as hell for a few minutes, but it blew over just as quickly, so that never really bothered us."

His outbursts notwithstanding, Stig was no slavedriver who cared little for the well-being of his employees. Every two weeks there would be a staff meeting to discuss problems or matters that could be improved. He had a strong sense of loyalty, and would never publicly embarrass an errant employee. "We felt a total support from him," says Berka. "He would back you up completely. Whatever you'd done, he was behind it as far as the outside world was concerned. He'd never blame you and tell you that you were fired or anything like that. I admired him for that. I learned incredibly much from him, he was the tops."

Stig loved his job and seldom complained about being overworked, but with time his lifestyle took its toll. Ever since he was a young child he'd been working constantly, seldom taking it easy or really enjoying a work-free holiday. Like most workaholics, it was the work itself that gave him the greatest pleasure, not the status symbols he could acquire as a consequence, the grand mansions and luxury cars.

"I've grown out of the 'swimming pool phase'," he said. "After a while you realise all the work it entails, not to mention all the other things you surround yourself with. You have boats that won't run. You've got strange machines that don't work. And you've got swimming pools that you've got to clean, and so on." In a curious attempt to avoid coming across as nouveau riche he even disguised his first Rolls-Royce to appear as a Bentley.

Going out to Viggsö very rarely gave him an opportunity to relax: on the contrary, during his days as a lyricist the main advantage was that he could write in peace, and he often finished off several songs simultaneously. By his own admission, his family had been neglected. "I fear that Stig will work himself to death," said Gudrun Anderson. "I worry that his tempo is much too high. Now I feel it's wrong that he hasn't had the time for us and I almost regret that I've always backed him up in everything."

Later in life his daughter Marie would joke that she was about seven years old when she met her father for the first time, but there was a sad truth behind the jesting. "Stig hasn't grown into the family," Gudrun reflected. "He's always been sitting by himself in his rooms and worked. It makes me sad on his account. He hasn't said anything himself, but I realise that he has missed out on this whole bit with the children growing up. His interests have always been focused on something else."

Ever since the Sixties, Stig had been in constant motion, travelling the world, always alert regardless of time-zones. "Half the year I was flying," he recalled. "For a while I almost had a punch-ticket on the flights to Australia." Together with John Spalding, who'd left United Artists and was now the International Vice President of Polar Music International,★ Stig did indeed put in countless hours on scrutinising, negotiating and renewing the deals with local licensees. The sheer number of labels they had to monitor added immensely to their exhausting schedule.

"[In the] middle of October Stig will be going on a trip around the world together with our international vice-president Mr John Spalding from London," noted Görel Johnsen cheerfully in a typical itinerary, as presented in a Polar Music press release from September 1978. "They will start off in Tokyo from October 15 to 21 . . . From there they will continue to Taipei, Taiwan (October 21 to 23) and to the Philippines – Manila (October 23 to 26). They will stop in Hawaii for a few days on their way to Los Angeles, where they will be from October 30 to November 3. Next stop will be . . . Miami Beach (November 3 to 7) before they return home via New York on November 9."

"It was a very time-consuming thing, but we wanted to make it work –

★ Spalding was still based in London, where he ran his publishing company Bocu Music.

and it did," says John Spalding today. "We did many hours together before having our business meetings and I'm sure this paid off. We'd go through the contracts line by line on some of these things. I don't think Abba really knew how much work we were doing to secure them the best deals."

Eyebrows were often raised in receptions of luxurious hotels when Stig and John checked in, carrying a coffee pot. It wasn't that Stig wanted to save money by making his own coffee: the explanation was that because of time differences the pair often worked at four o'clock in the morning, when it was difficult to get room service. If they wanted their coffee, Stig reasoned, he'd better bring his own pot.

Such were his commitments that Stig was virtually working around the clock and had been doing so for two decades. Sooner or later something had to give. When your head is buzzing, your body tense, and you need desperately to relax and sleep it's all too easy to reach for the bottle. Stig had long since become used to winding down with a drink or two. Over time, those drinks had been growing in number: by the late Seventies, the bottle had become his constant companion. Visitors to his office couldn't help noticing the whisky bottle that was always present on his desk. At first, Stig wouldn't admit to his dependency on alcohol, much less face up to it as a problem. Those around him could see clearly how far it had gone, though, and sometimes his lack of control would lead to fairly embarrassing situations.

At office parties, Stig's already hot-tempered personality was often fuelled by excessive drinking, and he'd end up firing every single one of his employees. The only people worth anything at all at Polar and Sweden Music were himself and Görel, the rest could just go to hell, a raging, rambling Stig would tell them. The day after, Gudrun would have to apologise to everybody, while a sheepish Stig tried to pretend that nothing had happened.

Paradoxically, despite his regular drinking and the conflicts that went with it, Stig's personal problems seldom affected his long-term relations with colleagues and associates, nor did it impair his business judgement. He always stood by the promises he'd made, in whatever state he had made them.

And he did have a great deal in the way of business matters to consider. Parallel with the failed Wimab affair, Polar went into partnership with the hugely successful industrialist and financier Anders Wall, owner of a prominent investment company called Beijerinvest. Together they formed a company called Sannes Trading, which was designed to deal in barter transactions, much along the lines of Wimab Sport. In this case, however, the scheme would not limit compensation for Abba music to one type of goods, but expand it to "everything from oil to cucumbers and horses", as Stig put it. It was the type of business in which Beijerinvest was already involved so, in effect, the scope of their venture would only be expanded by the influx of new capital. For Sannes Trading, the prospect of being involved with the lucrative oil market was the main attraction.

Stig saw the partnership as an opportunity to play with the big boys. His involvement in the musically creative side of his day-to-day business had trickled to a minimum. Abba's music formed the basis of his activities, but more and more of the practical matters relating to the group were handled by Görel Johnsen and Berka Bergkvist. The sound of Stig shouting for "Gööööörel!" was legendary at the Polar Music offices.

ABBA – The Album was the last Abba LP to feature any songs with Stig's lyrical contributions, and by now they were limited solely to song titles. As if to mark the extent to which his involvement had diminished, the sleeve featured a special credit to Stig, who "helped us with the lyrics on 'The Name Of The Game', 'Move On' and 'I Wonder (Departure)'." Soon afterwards Stig stopped writing lyrics permanently.

The challenge of selling Abba to various territories around the world still remained, but Stig's interest was gradually moving over to Abba's role in the greater scope of his ventures: investing the capital, making the "lightweight" entertainment business work for him in such a way that he would become a real and recognised force as an investor and financier, much like Anders Wall. Stig was already respected internationally as a music businessman; now he wanted to work towards respect as the head of a group of companies that were listed on the stock exchange.

Experienced, Poland-based Swedish businessmen scoffed at the idea of getting into the oil business. "The Poles have no reason to trade oil against Abba records," they said. "Of everything they have to offer, oil is the easiest thing to sell in the west – and they get paid in Western currency. Even if Abba are popular down here, they would never be favoured over Western currency."

They were proved right. The barter trading never really got off the ground, quite simply because no one could find the right kind of goods with which to trade. The items offered by the Eastern bloc countries weren't attractive to the Swedish market. The attempts continued, but the credibility of Polar Music International was not helped by the Wimab fiasco.

When Leif B. Bengtsson finally left Polar in June 1978, a 33-year-old banker called Lasse Dahlin took over as Vice President. Dahlin was hand-picked by Stig and Gudrun from the Stockholm offices of the relatively small Skaraborgsbanken. With characteristic loyalty, Stig had put his business through this institution for years, simply because they had once given him a small loan to buy his first typewriter.

Dahlin came from the same part of the country as Stig, the county of Västergötland, and despite his banking background he fitted well in the relaxed Polar atmosphere. Bengtsson, who found it hard to reject the formal suit-and-tie business tradition, never really adjusted to the company's style.

From now on Polar Music International would avoid ventures that brought with them responsibility for many employees, as Wimab had done. With Lasse Dahlin at the helm, their new direction was dealing in purely capital investment: stocks, leasing and the already successful real estate business. No more experiments – security and common sense was the motto.

Everything that Abba and Polar did created major headlines in the Swedish press, and the media were especially obsessed with all the money that the Abba records generated. Within this there was an unfortunate tendency to simplify the reports, so that it was "Abba" who bought and sold companies, and made investments, when in reality it was Stig and the financial advisors at Polar Music International. Abba's collective interest was only 50 per cent, and they certainly didn't run the business.

This led to a misconception that the four members of Abba were preoccupied with business, as if Björn, Benny, Frida and Agnetha spent most of their time around a boardroom table, poring over investment plans and studying balance sheets. In reality their interest in the business side of things remained on a peripheral level, which is not to say they weren't sometimes curious about where the money went. "It was kind of exciting in the beginning," Benny admitted later. "It was interesting: a new world, a lot of money in circulation and so on. And we had a certain interest in finding out what happened to our money."

The point of the set-up was to protect the group from these matters so that they could concentrate on being Abba. "Others take care of that," explained Björn. "Although of course, we make the big decisions – it's not like our fate rests in the hands of our accountants. It's the details of the investment business that we're not involved in. It's too boring. And if we did that, we wouldn't have any time for the music."

Such statements were mostly overlooked in the flow of headlines that built up Abba's image as cold financiers. Media allegations of crass commercialism were intrinsically linked to their creativity. Back home in

Sweden, away from the glare of the rest of the world, it still wasn't easy being Abba.

In the spring of 1978, making music was proving tough for Björn and Benny. After the first aborted attempt at recording the new album in mid-March, it took them six weeks to come up with two more songs deemed worthy of committing to tape. However, only one of those, 'Lovers (Live A Little Longer)', ended up on the next album, whereas 'Lovelight' was relegated to the B-side of a future single. The ongoing difficulty in creating satisfactory material was worrisome.

With two new tracks in the can it was time for Abba to turn their attention to the big challenge of 1978: conquering the American market. Instead of accomplishing this simply by touring, however, they would try a middle way more in line with their usual methods. The plan was to start off with a major promotional campaign in the spring and summer, including personal TV appearances and extensive interviews. Once the new album was completed and released at the end of the year, the success generated by the marketing campaign would hopefully have laid the ground for a concert tour to take place in the spring of 1979.

Although Abba's success has often been held up as a marketing phenomenon, the truth of the matter was that Polar's advertising budget was fairly small up to this point. A fair amount of money had been invested in the vital 'Waterloo' campaign back in 1974, but since then most of the success had been self-generated. Local licensees may have indulged in marketing campaigns, but interest in Abba from the media was so great that free TV and editorial coverage sold their records, just as it had sold Beatles records in the Sixties.

In West Germany, for example, the homogenous media landscape of the Seventies meant that one single appearance on a popular television show like *Star Parade* was sufficient to notify millions that Abba had a new single out. That was it – the job was done, and the rest was just a matter of seeing the records soar up the charts. The costs involved for Polar were mainly logistical: plane tickets, hotel bills and so on.

Stig had long refused to believe that the American market couldn't be conquered in similar fashion. But the three autumnal promotional visits between 1974 and 1976 hadn't broken the group in the same way as the rest of the world. They could have chosen to build on the number one success of 'Dancing Queen' in April 1977, but when they were completely absent during the whole of that year, the momentum died down.

"The albums never sold commensurate to the way the singles were breaking and the way the singles were getting airplay," says Jerry

Greenberg. "Stig was very, very frustrated about that, and so were we. When the Abba explosion happened he'd call me up and go, 'In Australia one out of every three families owns an Abba record! How come you're not achieving that?' We were doing okay, but they were nothing like they were everywhere else. Everywhere else it was like The Beatles."

Together with the band, Stig decided it was time to bite the bullet and make a real cash investment to break Abba in America by advertising. This wasn't necessarily to Jerry Greenberg's liking. "Atlantic operated differently than, say, a Warner Brothers or a Columbia.* Columbia was used to spending a lot of money on marketing costs and TV things. But Stig convinced us that we had to do a big TV time-buy, and we did it."

Polar and Atlantic split the costs, enlisting the help of notorious promoters Scotti Brothers, with whom they worked out a detailed US$500,000 (£275,000) promotional campaign. Kicking off at the end of March 1978, the campaign continued well into August. Abba's actual presence in the country would be limited to a two-week visit at the end of April, continuing into early May which had been declared "Abba Month". A giant billboard featuring the slogan "The largest selling group in the history of recorded music" was erected above Sunset Strip in Los Angeles.

Although hype is a prominent feature in the American way of doing business, the backlash was predictable with the media immediately questioning the validity of the statement on the billboard. How could Abba, who still hadn't enjoyed any multi-million sales in the United States, the world's largest record market, claim to have outsold acts like Elvis Presley and The Beatles in only four years? Atlantic Records argued that by their account, Abba had sold 120 million records worldwide. Further investigation revealed that the record company had applied a somewhat unusual method of counting every two tracks on an album as one "record", since there were two tracks on a single. Polar's own official figure at this point was a comparatively modest 53 million singles, vinyl LPs and cassette tapes.

The *Guinness Book of World Records* claimed at the time that The Beatles were the all-time number one act, with total sales up to 1972 of 545 million records. So even with Atlantic's method of calculating, Abba's 120 million was still far short of The Beatles' alleged sales, making their claim even more puzzling. Discussions regarding who has sold the most records worldwide have been raging ever since. In truth, all these figures are to a large extent based on estimates made by the record companies themselves,

---

* Many of Atlantic's biggest acts in the Seventies – Led Zeppelin, Yes, Crosby Stills & Nash etc. – had sold records through extensive touring.

and once sales reach stratospheric levels above 100 million it becomes a fairly pointless exercise anyway.★

During their American promotional visit of May 1978, Abba kept all questions of record sales at arm's length: they had their plate full as it was. Apart from a myriad of interviews, the group would also tape a high-profile Olivia Newton-John coast-to-coast special, with Andy Gibb as fellow guest star. This was exceptionally suitable company: all three acts had the same clean-cut image, and at the time of the broadcast date on May 24, Olivia Newton-John was enjoying an unusually high profile through her participation in the hit movie *Grease*.

For his part, Andy Gibb had two consecutive number one hits to his credit and was about to get a third chart-topper with 'Shadow Dancing' in June. To appear in the same television special as these two star acts at the peak of their popularity could only have beneficial consequences.

The campaign did achieve some significant results. The current single, 'Take A Chance On Me', reached number three on the charts, Abba's best chart placing so far after 'Dancing Queen'. Measured in sales and other statistics 'Take A Chance On Me' actually remains as the group's biggest American hit. *ABBA – The Album* became their greatest success on the albums chart, peaking at number 14 and achieving sales of one million. The campaign also stimulated sales of the compilation album *Greatest Hits*, pushing total sales over the one million mark.

It was still far from the statistics achieved in most other countries, but Stig professed to be satisfied with the outcome. Jerry Greenberg, however, was disappointed. "It didn't kick the record like it should've, like it did in every other country," he says.

As it happened, whatever momentum the campaign had created collapsed like a house of cards in the last few months of the year.

★ As if to settle the dispute once and for all, in 1985, the official sales figure for The Beatles was suddenly upped to "more than 1 billion", which must certainly have been a great exaggeration. In Abba's case, the authorised figure went from 180 million records in the early Eighties to 250 million ten years later. In 1999, the official number of records sold jumped to a staggering 350 million. Even with the revival success of the Nineties, the spearheading *ABBA Gold* compilation had sold "only" 15 million copies at that point, and it seems unlikely that catalogue sales of the group's regular albums and budget compilations would have accounted for 85 million copies. Misleading statistics aside, Abba did sell an enormous amount of records and belong firmly in the upper regions of all-time record sales lists.

Chapter 26

The first track to be completed in Abba's Polar Music Studio, which opened in May 1978, was 'Summer Night City'. But instead of being a triumphant beginning to their work in the new studio, the recording was surrounded by an air of disappointment and frustration: 'Summer Night City' was Abba's true problem child of 1978.

In August it had been decided that Abba should release a new single as a taster from the upcoming album. 'Summer Night City' was the only suitable track they had to work with at that point. Björn, Benny and Michael Tretow spent a week attempting numerous mixes, but to their way of thinking there was something inherently wrong with the recording: too slow, too fast, too many overdubs, too few overdubs – whatever it was, they couldn't put their finger on it.

An enormous amount of compression was applied to the mix, to give it a more pumping sound. When this wasn't enough, a dramatic 45-second string, piano and vocal introduction was cut from the recording to give it a more direct opening. "That was a bit silly, because you can really hear that there's been an edit," said Michael later. "We tried every way imaginable to get something from the tape that simply wasn't there."

Although Björn and Benny weren't completely satisfied with the outcome they decided to issue the song anyway. "Sooner or later you have to make a decision," Benny reflected. "Either you release the song as it is, or you record another song, and then you have to wait another four weeks before you can release the record. You never release anything that you think is completely worthless, but one or two years later you can still end up thinking, 'We shouldn't have released that one.'" Björn later called the recording "really lousy".

The problems didn't stop there. 'Summer Night City' was Abba's first release in Sweden since *ABBA – The Album*. After the LP sales had been lower than expected – although they were in fact still exceptionally high – many Swedish record shops didn't dare order too many copies of the new single. Some thought that Abba's time at the top was over.

On release in September, one major retailer ordered only 10 copies of the single. However, his fears of low sales were quickly proved wrong when those few copies were snapped up in no time. When he tried to re-order to meet the demand, the new copies didn't arrive as quickly as he hoped. "We have to wait an extra long time because we ordered so few to begin with," the retailer claimed. "It's Stig's way of getting back at us. He's a bit sulky in matters like this, that's well known throughout the business." Once record shops had received the required stock, the single became Abba's biggest Swedish hit since 'Dancing Queen', topping the charts for two weeks.

'Summer Night City' was an energetic, disco-influenced track, which would have been perfect for the American market in the autumn of 1978. It was the year of The Bee Gees and *Saturday Night Fever*, and Björn later admitted that the recording was inspired by the success of the brothers Gibb and what he called "the pulse of the Seventies".

On hearing the track, Jerry Greenberg dashed off a telex to the Polar Music offices. "Everyone here feels that 'Summer Night City' will be number one on the charts. Absolutely fantastic!" he enthused. "But is there any possibility that you can guarantee us an album at the end of November? We'd hate to have a number one single without releasing an album immediately afterwards."

Abba could guarantee no such thing. Everything seemed to be moving along at a much slower pace than before. The group was determined to enjoy a proper summer holiday in 1978, and had awarded themselves a well-deserved seven weeks in June and July.

Moreover, by early September, the product of the album sessions so far wasn't encouraging: eight songs recorded, out of which only half were eventually completed and released. The likelihood that there would be a new Abba album released before the end of the year was slim. As a result, the US release of 'Summer Night City' failed to happen, a planned television appearance on the high-profile *Dick Clark's Live Wednesday* show in November was cancelled – and that was that as far as Abba's 1978 attempts to crack the American market were concerned.

The full-length version of 'Summer Night City' was slated for the upcoming album, but with all the negative undertones attached to the recording, it was ultimately left off the track listing. Worldwide placings for the single were also less impressive than usual: it was, for example, the first Abba single for three years to peak outside the Top 3 in the UK.

The song's status as a "failure" is completely undeserved, however. The pumping, driving rhythm of 'Summer Night City' and its compressed mix combined to make an unusually captivating track. The lyrics' celebration of big city nightlife, and its dismissal of those who scorn its existence – "we don't miss them when they're gone" – added an undeniable edge to the song. Any imperfections in the recording only served to give it a strong sense of liveliness.

Ever since 'Summer Night City' was released, it's been alleged that one of the lines in the chorus, "walking in the moonlight", was actually sung as the decidedly more risqué "fucking in the moonlight" during the fade-out. Although the slurred diction and muddled sound do create this impression, it's unlikely that Abba would consciously risk their actively upheld clean image, and Björn has denied it several times. But the uncertainty and ambiguity added to the song's sexually charged drive.

The problems with 'Summer Night City' were typical of the snags that delayed the troublesome new album, and the opening of the new studio in May was one of the few bright spots during the initial sessions. Polar Music Studio was the studio of their dreams: the company had cash to spend, and every wish, every imaginable gadget Björn, Benny and Michael Tretow could think of, was now available in this one facility.

For instance, having two 24-track tape recorders in the same studio simply didn't exist elsewhere in Sweden at that time, but Polar could boast such a luxury. Likewise, every small detail that made the recording process that much more easier was also installed. "We wanted a gadget that we hadn't seen in any other studio," recalled Benny. "A little mixing console for each musician's headphones so that they would be able to have the sound level of each instrument as loud as they preferred it. Normally, the musicians would want to hear their own instruments a little louder than the rest, and that was very hard to achieve in those days."

The state-of-the-art Polar Music Studio immediately attracted the attention of top-flight international acts. Atlantic recording artists Led Zeppelin, one of Abba's few rivals for the title of best-selling group of the Seventies, were the first foreign star act to use the studio, spending two weeks there in November 1978 while recording tracks for their *In Through The Out Door* album. "Led Zeppelin appreciated Abba's music, they really did," says Jerry Greenberg. "They loved the sound."

Indeed, although it would seem that Zeppelin's blues-based hard rock was miles away from Abba's European pop, they shared more aesthetic traits than was apparent on the surface. Strong melodies, expert musicianship and highly energetic, upfront lead vocals were all characteristics shared by the four Swedes and several prominent hard rock and heavy metal outfits. Jimmy Page, who produced all of Zeppelin's work, was quick to appreciate top level production techniques when he heard them.

Having a studio of their own was a kick, but Björn and Benny were still up against the lack of inspiration that had set in during the sessions for the new album. "I can tell from the look in Björn's eyes when he gets home how the day's work has been," said Agnetha. "Many times the boys have been working for ten hours without coming up with one single song."

By November, two months after the release of 'Summer Night City', they had completed only two further tracks worthy of inclusion on the new album, which actually left them with no more than four finished songs. Polar had to announce that there definitely wasn't going to be any new Abba album before Christmas.

Considering the pressure from the outside world to come up with new hits, it's something of a wonder Björn and Benny managed to remain so cool and simply keep going back to the drawing board in the face of such adversity. "I suppose this is something that everybody goes through when they have been in the business for as long as we have," reflected Benny later. "All of a sudden you dry up a bit, and then you need fresh impulses in order to get going again."

Björn complained that the Swedish music climate was hardly conducive to creating current, internationally compatible pop music. With every kind of chart banned from the airwaves, and scant few pop shows, there wasn't much inspiration to be had from Swedish radio.

Though Benny and Björn both got a real kick out of being taken seriously by the international music business, the wide-eyed wonderment had long since been replaced by a realisation that they were now the ones with a finger on the pulse. On one of their US visits, a meeting was arranged with their hero, Brian Wilson of The Beach Boys. This was during a time when Wilson's psychological problems were at their worst, turning him into a virtual recluse whose behaviour could become decidedly erratic without warning.

The meeting took place at the home of a mutual acquaintance. Wilson was escorted in and sat on a chair. To the perplexity of Björn and Benny, the only word the former creative genius uttered during the entire encounter was a low-groaning "huh . . . huh . . . huh" with regular intervals. When they left, the host said, "How wonderful that you got to meet Brian, because tonight he was really on form." For a major Beach Boys fan like Benny, it was a huge disappointment. Nevertheless, the incident clearly symbolised the difference between Abba, who had risen to become a relevant force on the international music scene, and their ultimate role model, who at that point had very little access to his glorious creative powers.

Lately, Björn and Benny were becoming more interested in pursuing the American market for real. Each time they visited Los Angeles, it felt like a breath of fresh air. Everything revolved around music, and no one even thought of criticising them for being crassly commercial – hell, that was the whole point of almost everything that went on in America, including its music business.

The boys and Frida were all enthusiastic about spending a couple of months each year in Los Angeles, for the inspiration as much as for the furthering of Abba's career. "Sometimes I feel offside in Sweden," Björn said. "If we'd been right in the middle of things, in Los Angeles, I'm sure that we would have conquered the USA a long time ago." He even noted that if he hadn't been married to Agnetha and if they hadn't had two children, he probably would have been living in Los Angeles.

"If he hadn't been married to Agnetha . . ." Maybe one or two readers raised an eyebrow at the fact that he was even contemplating such a situation. But when Björn made the remark in April 1978, the general public knew nothing about how bad the situation had become in the Ulvaeus/Fältskog household. After a short period of happiness that followed the arrival of a new baby, things had taken a rapid turn for the worse.

It was now affecting Abba's work as well. Where the occasional conflicts in the studio had at one time added spice to the sessions, the crisis between Björn and Agnetha was now detrimental in the extreme. Shouting matches and accusations that had previously been confined to their home were now an increasing occurrence in the studio. "There were a lot of pressures," Björn remembered. "As they got worse we tried to disguise it but things just became impossible."

Right up to the end Björn and Agnetha seemed unable to make the final break, holding on in the improbable belief that they could work things out, but it had reached the point where they couldn't communicate any more, where they were just talking at cross-purposes. Neither party could point to specifics, could explain how their love had died, or what had killed the attraction between them. As Björn and Agnetha drifted apart, it seemed they had opposing outlooks on life, eternally conflicting opinions about what was important and what was not.

"The problems were piling up," recalled Agnetha. "I felt trapped in our marriage, locked up, walled up. We ran out of love, quite simply, and started wearing each other down . . . There's something weird about marriage. You devote all your time to each other. The framework becomes too constricted and suddenly you stand there, wondering what happened. You haven't added much to your personal growth, and you start looking around, feeling the panic set in."

Like so many other couples who had met and fallen in love while they were barely out of their teens, Björn and Agnetha suddenly woke up to the realisation that they were married to strangers. "You shouldn't be allowed to get married so young," reflected Agnetha later. "It's not so strange that you develop in different directions."

In the summer of 1978 the situation got so bad that a separation seemed the only way out. Even the quarrels had lost their spark; what remained was destructive irritation that simply sapped at the strength of what was left of their relationship.

Agnetha later admitted that she wasn't the easiest person to live with. "No, I guess I'm not," she said. "Maybe someone thinks I am. Björn didn't think so. It has to do with different personalities." Björn acknowledged that it had reached the point when he didn't even want to see his wife: "When I found that I no longer wanted to go home in the evening and would try to delay it as late as possible, hoping that Agnetha would have gone to bed, then I knew I had to do something about it."

As a final attempt to resolve their differences they began regular visits to a marriage counsellor, psychologist Håkan Lönnqvist. "We wanted an outside person looking at us, in case it should have been something about our relationship that we both couldn't see," explained Agnetha. But too many harsh words had been spoken, too many wounds inflicted: Lönnqvist had to admit that the couple already had a clear view of the situation. When they weren't able to patch things up even after professional help, the couple had to face the inevitable conclusion. In the autumn, Agnetha Fältskog and Björn Ulvaeus finally decided that they would put an end to their marriage.

For Agnetha, who idealised the circumstances of her childhood, the family life with a mother and a father who symbolised comfort and support, the collapse of her own marriage seemed like a devastating personal failure. "Children are so vulnerable in a divorce," she said. "Sometimes I'm struck by the thought that I've broken up a nice and secure family for them – the kind I had myself when I was small – but I have to shake off those thoughts. You can never repair a thing like this; we will never be mother, father and children again. One day I might meet someone I want to live with, but that still won't be like a real family for the children."

For the time being, however, Björn and Agnetha kept up a brave front. To the outside world, everything was as idyllic as usual in their relationship. In spite of all the unhappiness, they both knew they were doing the right thing by splitting up.

In an ironic twist of fate, their decision to break up coincided with Benny and Frida finally getting married after a nine year engagement. On Friday, October 6, 1978, virtually without telling a living soul – Björn and Agnetha included – the pair wed in the Lidingö church, near their own home. The only witnesses to the ceremony were the verger and a lady called Bitte, Benny and Frida's housekeeper.

The couple were more or less forced to keep the affair low-key. The more people that knew about it, the greater the risk of media and fans finding out. They wanted their wedding to be about the manifestation of their love, not an official event where they were reduced to "Frida and Benny of Abba".

The couple had already invited 25 of their friends to a party in their villa the following day, but had not told them about their marriage plans. The press got wind of the wedding shortly after the ceremony, however, and so their friends learned what had happened as well. Despite their efforts to keep everything low-key, the newly-weds were showered with gifts that the party guests had rushed out and bought. Among the guests were Agnetha and Björn, Stig and his family – Stig was one of the few who knew about the wedding beforehand – Benny's sister Eva-Lis, Frida and Benny's children, as well as associates like Michael Tretow, Thomas Johansson, Claes af Geijerstam, Görel Johnsen and Berka Bergkvist.

The wedding didn't change anything practical in the Andersson/Lyngstad household: they had been living as man and wife for almost a decade, and were regarded as such by the media. Perhaps this was why the wedding was seldom if ever brought up in subsequent interviews.

In November Abba turned their attention to the second major promotional campaign of the year. Attempts to conquer the United States had been only partially successful, and if the truth be told, Abba's fortunes had been similarly shaky in another of the world's major record markets.

Since Björn & Benny's number one hit with 'She's My Kind Of Girl' in 1972, Abba had enjoyed the occasional Top 10 single on the Japanese chart. The highest position any single had reached so far had been 'Dancing Queen', which peaked at number two, but the general statistics weren't even close to the results in Europe and Australia.

Stig Anderson recalled: "The Japanese had been telling us, 'Oh, the success you're having in Europe and Australia is simply amazing, but really, you could never achieve anything like that in Japan.' I thought, 'You just wait and I'll goddamn show you.'" It was another of those instances where Stig's belief in himself and Abba worked wonders. A detailed 10-day campaign for mid-November 1978 was worked out, encompassing several strategic television appearances – including the group's very own television special – and plenty of interviews with press and radio.

A week after the visit, Abba got their first Japanese number one hit with 'Summer Night City', the first of four consecutive chart toppers.

Meanwhile, *Arrival*, *ABBA – The Album* and a compilation package were all in the Top 20 of the album chart. Five months later Abba had sold more than 1.5 million records in Japan. Once again, an important market had failed to resist Abba's music and charms. "You've got to believe in what you're doing," as Stig so aptly put it.

Abba's Japanese record company, Discomate, had proved that they were a good choice as a partner in this territory. Stig had decided to leave Phonogram for this much smaller label in 1976, again after advice from their local publishers. "They were a small independent company but were ready to do a major job," recalls John Spalding. The theory was that a small, hungry label with motivation to fight for their artist would really give their all, and it paid off.

Returning to Sweden, 10 days were spent working on new songs for the album before it was time for another promotional trip. This time the group went to Great Britain, where they were scheduled to tape television appearances on the *Mike Yarwood Christmas Show* and *Jim'll Fix It*.

Björn and Benny had long been annoyed at the British Musicians' Union rules for playback performances on television. While playback performances as such were allowed, the backing track should preferably be recorded by British musicians. Since Abba's records were made with Swedish musicians, they weren't allowed to mime to their own master tapes like most British bands could do. "Once when we appeared in a television show at ITV in Manchester we were on just before Queen," Björn recalled. "Queen were doing a playback performance while we hardly had any time to rehearse at all. The outcome was obvious: our song sounded like crap while theirs sounded great."

Recently, Abba had found a sneaky way around this problem. On *Mike Yarwood*, the group was scheduled to perform 'Thank You For The Music' and 'If It Wasn't For The Nights'. The latter was one of their new, as yet unreleased songs, tentatively scheduled to become their next single.

Guitarist Janne Schaffer, a real musician's musician and a recording star in his own right, was offered the chance to appear on television with Abba on the December 1978 trip to England. "Normally, I didn't want to do these playback things because I felt that I had more important things to do. I thought it was just the pits," he recalled.

He was told that it was extremely important that he joined the group, since Abba needed to do new recordings of the two songs they were going to perform: they had received an okay to use their own Swedish musicians this time. When Schaffer and the other musicians (drummer Ola Brunkert and bassist Christian Veltman) had been assured that they were actually going to do some real playing, they accepted.

However, when the three musicians arrived at the London recording studio they were told that they wouldn't actually be playing a note, nor had this ever been the intention. Abba had decided to simply do new mixes of their original backing tracks, made in Stockholm. By removing all strings and whatever else had been added to the recordings, they could pretend that these were brand new tracks. "When the controller from the Musicians' Union came to the studio, we sat there and did some fake playing," Janne Schaffer remembered. "After he made his notes he left – and that was it." No one knew the difference, and the *Mike Yarwood* performance came off exceptionally well. Abba did a silly skit with the host and performed their two songs, offering no clues whatsoever that anything was wrong between Björn and Agnetha.

In London, the couple stayed in separate hotel rooms, but in Sweden they were still living under the same roof. The relief that followed the decision to split had taken much of the tension out of their relationship, and they were slowly winding down to the day when they would finally go their separate ways.

Their respective parents were the first to be told, followed by Benny and Frida. "It didn't come as any major surprise to them," said Agnetha. "They've been so close to us, seeing how we interact." The hardest part was to break the news to Linda, who was only five and a half years old at the time. "We agonised so much over it before we could tell her. We ended up crying, all three of us."

There was a meeting with the group and Stig to discuss what this would mean for the future of Abba, if anything. Stig was saddened and startled by the news of the divorce, concerned about what might happen to his greatest asset. His shock reflected the growing personal distance between him and the four members. "He hasn't been living as close to us as Benny and Frida," explained Agnetha.

The meeting established that Björn and Agnetha wanted to go on working together as usual. Their professional relationship wasn't at the root of their problems, it was a case of incompatibility on a human level. If it hadn't been for the group, the divorce would probably have happened much earlier, they said. "Once we had made the decision to part it eased a lot of tension in the group," Björn claimed. "It helped Abba in the end, even though we knew it would get a lot of attention. The split had to come. It was a case of a parting of two egocentrics."

Björn and Agnetha proved their commitment to the group in mid-December, when Abba completed yet another track for inclusion on the album: 'Chiquitita'. In accordance with the difficult nature of the current sessions, a version of the song, entitled 'In The Arms Of Rosalita', had been recorded just prior to their London visit. Frida and Agnetha shared the lead vocals on that first attempt, but when the song turned into 'Chiquitita', Agnetha took the more prominent role.

Session tapes reveal that Agnetha's presence wasn't simply a matter of just popping in to add vocals and then rushing out again. On the contrary, she was in the studio for much of the recording, relaying her opinion as Lasse Wellander worked out his acoustic guitar intro. An interim version of the song with different lyrics, entitled 'Chiquitita Angelina', was also recorded along the way. The long and hard work to achieve what they both considered a perfect recording necessitated a close working relationship between Agnetha and Björn throughout most of December.

The truth of the matter was that everything was flowing so much easier now that the pair were no longer man and wife in anything other than name. Agnetha was one of the singers in Abba, not Björn's wife, and he was one half of the group's songwriting and production team, not Agnetha's husband. "The tension that used to exist when we were working in the studio is gone," said Björn. "Today I can correct and criticise Agnetha without having to consider that she's my wife."

Björn and Agnetha spent Christmas Eve, the most important day of the Swedish holiday season, together as a family one final time. They had their Christmas dinner, exactly as they always did. Linda and Christian, who'd just celebrated his first birthday, received their gifts. On Christmas Day, Agnetha packed her bags, climbed into the car with her children and drove to her new home, just seven minutes away. It was a house owned by Polar Music and used for important guests. It was to be Agnetha's home for the next decade.

Björn stayed at the house that he and Agnetha had bought just a year earlier. It is not difficult to imagine his thoughts as he watched through a window as his wife and children drove into the distance, then turned to face the silence and emptiness they left behind. It was the lyrics of 'Knowing Me, Knowing You' brought to life: "In these old familiar rooms, children would play . . ."

They had agreed to share the custody of Linda and Christian, so he would be able to see them often enough. Living so close to each other, there would be no practical problems on that account, but it wasn't the same as everyone being together in the same house, all the time. "As soon as Agnetha and I split up I realised that I wanted to fall in love again," Björn recalled. "I knew that I couldn't make it as a bachelor."

On New Year's Eve he was invited to a party at Benny and Frida's home. The house would be full of mutual friends and acquaintances and the party was certain to be fun. Among the guests was a tall, thin, blonde girl called Lena Källersjö, not unlike Agnetha in her general features. She was not new to their circle of friends: formerly engaged in a relationship with record producer Bengt Palmers, she had been escorted to Frida and Benny's "wedding party" in October as the girlfriend of Claes af Geijerstam. Lena worked in the advertising business and was close to Frida. She also knew Agnetha quite well.

During the party, Björn and Lena talked more than ever before. It was as if there was an instant rapport between them: Lena shared Agnetha's tenderness, but not her hot temper. Where mutual stubbornness had proved incompatible in Björn and Agnetha's relationship, there was a more complementary interaction between Björn and Lena.

So it was that at the beginning of 1979 Björn was already involved in a new relationship. "I was only a bachelor for a week," he would later quip, sounding almost astonished himself at how quickly the romance had progressed. Indeed, the swiftness of it all underlined how his emotional commitment to Agnetha had long since disappeared.

In mid-January, Agnetha and Björn finally announced their divorce to the media. They had dreaded the moment because of the inevitable attention that would follow. *Expressen* journalist Mats Olsson was called to the Polar Music offices for an exclusive interview that would break the news to the world. "It's important to stress that this is a so-called happy divorce, if such a thing exists," said Björn. Agnetha added: "When you find that you've talked through absolutely everything and you still fail to get through to each other, then you must accept the consequences." After the interview they shook hands, said goodbye and drove off to their respective houses.

The news spread like wildfire all over the world. Björn and Agnetha soon realised that the press weren't going to let them get away with one simple statement. "It began right from the day after the divorce was announced," Agnetha recalled. "When I opened the blinds that morning I was met by a wall of photo flashes and couldn't go out into the garden all day. That wasn't very enjoyable."

Abba fans and the media were equally shocked. It seemed like a devastating blow to everything that the group was supposed to uphold: two happy couples, united in their love for making music, living their perfect lives in nice, suburban houses - and now such a crack in the façade.

The image of two couples – unique in pop - was an important device in the marketing of Abba, although they hadn't really gone out of their way to cultivate it themselves. Once the media had cottoned on to the fact that it was possible to identify them as different groups of pairs – singers Agnetha and Frida, songwriters and producers Björn and Benny, and then the two marriages – the angle was clear.

The "two happy couples" concept had been fuelled by regular magazine reports on how they all lived so close to each other, both during the early days in Vallentuna but especially out on Viggsö. Over the years, several photo reports on the couples had been shot on the island. The 1976 *Abba-dabba-dooo!!* television special featured extensive Viggsö footage, and even *ABBA – The Movie* contained a few shots.

Agnetha now felt able to kick down that part of the myth as well. "I will leave Abba's island in the Stockholm archipelago for good," she said, "but the others will spend time out there exactly like before. For me the island hasn't really meant very much. It was pleasant to be out there when the weather was nice, but it isn't all the time and then you feel isolated. You can only get away from there by boat and I just crash into the bridge."

Although both couples had spoken quite freely about conflicts within their respective marriages, this aspect of the group's interrelations was mostly ignored by the press. "That whole bit about an 'ideal image', 'married bliss' and things like that has been created by the media," Agnetha established. "At least it's not us Abba members who have done that. We have been as we are and now there is a divorce – that's also a piece of our reality."

Speculation was rife that the split between Björn and Agnetha must mean the end of Abba, and the group's local record company licensees were concerned. "I was nervous and didn't know what was going to transpire," recalls Jerry Greenberg. A lot of energy was spent assuaging worries all over the world, the general message being that what had happened was sad, but everything was fine and the group was working together better than ever.

"It was very difficult before Agnetha and Björn separated," Benny commented. "They were getting on very badly, it made things very difficult for the rest of us and created a lot of friction."

Now it was a different kind of working relationship to which all four members would have to adjust. Their roles within the group had changed, their outward image was different: one chapter had closed, and a new one was opening.

Chapter 27

'Chiquitita', Abba's first single of 1979, was released in Sweden on January 16, exactly 10 months after recording sessions for the upcoming album began. Five years earlier the group would have finished two albums in that time, but by the late Seventies the demand they placed on themselves had grown to almost unbearable proportions.

The current project had so far resulted in only five recordings slated for the LP, no more than half of the required songs. Many melodies in various stages of completion had been recorded and scrapped. In one case – a track called 'Dream World' – a whole recording was completed and mixed, only to end up left in the can.

'Chiquitita' was selected as the new single in preference to 'If It Wasn't For The Nights'. As part of the United Nations' 1979 Internationational Year of the Child, the song was premièred at a UNICEF benefit concert a week before release at the General Assembly Hall of the United Nations in New York. Furthermore, all publishing royalties for 'Chiquitita' were donated to UNICEF. The Bee Gees, Earth Wind & Fire, Olivia Newton-John, Rod Stewart and Donna Summer were among the other participants in the gala.

The concert included an all-star singalong to Abba's fairly obscure 'He Is Your Brother', much to the amusement of Benny. "None of the other artists was familiar with that song," he recalled. "Perhaps there was someone who'd listened to all our records and had learned it, but Earth Wind & Fire definitely didn't know 'He Is Your Brother'."

Despite this undeniably high-profile American promotion opportunity, Atlantic inexplicably chose not to release 'Chiquitita' as a single, thus losing even more of whatever momentum remained from the previous year's Abba campaign. When it was belatedly released in October 1979 it reached the Top 30, but it's likely it would have become an even bigger hit had it been issued to capitalise on the exposure from the UNICEF gala.

In the rest of the world, 'Chiquitita' restored whatever faith in the group may have been shaken by the slightly less impressive chart performance of 'Summer Night City'. The new single reached number one in at least nine countries and came close to the top in several more – as was now expected from a new Abba single.

The new album, previously postponed to February, was now put back to April. For the rest of the tracks, Björn and Benny decided that something radical had to be done, not least because Swedish radio offered next to nothing in the way of inspiration for anyone with an interest in contemporary popular music.

By the late Seventies the Music Movement had just about collapsed, a consequence of growing disinterest from the public, the rise of the equally politicised but more energetic punk music, and destructive infighting. Reality outside the confines of sheltered Swedish society came as a shock to the orthodox wing of the Music Movement when a group of musicians visited Cuba. Anticipating an exchange of ideas about revolutionary left-wing music, they were met by enthusiastic inquiries about Abba.

"It proves that our music works," said Björn. "They like our music on Cuba without us doing any promotion or marketing campaigns or any advertising. Surely, that proves that it's the music that's important?" What it did prove beyond any doubt was that music is primarily communication with the heart and the soul, transcending literary criteria and political agendas. Manipulation alone could never have resulted in Abba's music reaching into the hearts of so many listeners for so long, if there hadn't been something genuinely captivating about it.

Many of the musicians within the movement had a much less rigid and dogmatic attitude to music and its role in society than their self-proclaimed spokesmen, but the philosophy behind it still exerted an inordinate amount of influence on the domestic cultural hegemony. As late as June 1978, the Top 10 sales chart presented in the popular radio music show *Skivspegeln (The Record Mirror)* was banned. A complaint had been filed to the Broadcasting Commission by a school teacher, who was especially angered by the way Abba supposedly benefited by the airing of the chart music.

Clearly, this atmosphere was not conducive to musical creativity on the international arena where Abba operated. Therefore, in mid-January 1979, Björn and Benny embarked on a trip to the Bahamas. It was the first time they had gone abroad specifically to write new material, and it was only then that they were able to free their writer's block and finally come up with the songs they were looking for. The composers stated that this was largely because they finally had access to the kind of popular music radio that wasn't available in Sweden.

"There was music available round the clock, whichever type you wanted to hear," explained Benny. "It goes without saying that it's incredibly inspiring when you get to hear a lot of fresh stuff that you like. You get a kick to do something yourself that is just as good as the things you hear."

Two songs were finished in the Bahamas, both driven by a strong disco beat. Inspired by the musical climate, Björn and Benny wanted to continue tapping into the American music scene. Their proximity to Miami and Criteria Studios, where The Bee Gees, among others, made their records, suggested to them the idea of recording a backing track for one of their new compositions right there. Michael Tretow was brought over for one day to ensure that the recording would be compatible with the recording techniques at Polar Studios.

The myriad of producers and engineers on hand made up a virtual who's who of the American music business. The most prominent name was perhaps Tom Dowd, the legendary engineer and producer, who had worked on well-known recordings by Otis Redding and Aretha Franklin, as well as Dusty Springfield's classic *Dusty In Memphis* album, and more recently with Eric Clapton and Rod Stewart. Engineer Don Gehman was the house engineer at Criteria Studios and would go on to become a successful producer in the Eighties and Nineties. Ron and Howard Albert were also Criteria engineers who had lent their talents to Crosby, Stills & Nash, The Allman Brothers Band, Aretha Franklin, Donny Hathaway and countless others. The backing band consisted of members from the disco group Foxy, who'd recently enjoyed a US Top 10 hit with 'Get Off'.

With Björn, Benny and Michael supervising matters, this diverse line-up put together a tight backing track for what was to become 'Voulez-Vous'. Also tried, apparently at the spur of the moment, was a new version of 'If It Wasn't For The Nights', which Björn and Benny thought was the kind of song that might be enhanced by this rhythm section.

This was where Abba's European, melody-centred preferences complicated matters, however. "It didn't turn out too well," recalled Benny, "because that song has so many peculiar chord changes in the verses. I think that made it hard for them to get into a groove like they were used to."

The Miami/Bahamas experience offered Björn and Benny the fresh perspective they needed to re-energise their songwriting. When they returned to Sweden, no less than half of the songs on the album were completed within two months. Apart from 'Voulez-Vous' and 'Kisses Of Fire' – the two songs that had been written in the Bahamas – they now came up with 'As Good As New', 'I Have A Dream' and 'Does Your Mother Know'.

While Björn and Benny were off on their songwriting excursion, Frida spent a few days in Spain filming her début acting role in the Swedish movie *Gå på vattnet om du kan* (*Walk On Water If You Can*). She accepted the assignment for a token payment: the main attraction was the challenge of trying out an acting part.

The film itself, directed by Stig Björkman, was a fairly unglamorous love story set against a political backdrop in the Argentina of the Seventies. It was a lifeless concoction, where Frida played the part of "Anna", the wife of one of the main characters. She was on screen for only two and a half minutes, and it was hard to draw any conclusions about her acting abilities from these short scenes. Suffice it to say that she said her lines fairly convincingly, but didn't seem to stray too far from her own persona in her interpretation.

Frida was nervous on the set, but enjoyed the filming experience. Like the critics she was less impressed by the movie itself, however. A few years later, when Abba guested on the UK television show *The Late Late Breakfast Show*, she was asked which was the worst film she had ever seen. Björn suggested that "the one you were in" might be a good candidate, to which Frida laughed and said, "Yes, that's true actually."

Frida's life was getting better and better every day. She was feeling stronger and more secure than ever before, the hardships of her childhood and her early struggles now distant memories as her life finally came good. The uncertainties of the past few years as she coped with her rise as a world famous singer had been followed by a kind of personal settlement, a deep satisfaction that communicated itself in the way she related to the other members of the group and their immediate circle.

Even though she admitted to an ongoing fear of one day being abandoned, she had overcome the pangs of jealousy that stemmed from her deep rooted insecurity. She and Benny had formalised their commitment to each other by getting married. She had met her father and was slowly coming to terms with his role in her life: he could never become a father figure, but she felt it was worthwhile to continue exploring the relationship.

Frida was also developing her relationship with her children, a process greatly helped by having them living in her house. "[Benny and I] had our house in Lidingö and our four children," she remembered, "and it was unbelievably wonderful to come home to all that after the long tours when you lived in some kind of strange fantasy world. It was almost a prerequisite for being able to cope."

She knew it would take time to truly regain their trust and confidence. "There was a time when my daughter denied that I was her mother," she recalled many years later. "I'm afraid the feelings of loneliness I experienced with my grandmother were passed down to my children. Like her, I'm not a very physical person."

With the whirlwind period of Abba's rise to stardom behind them, Frida discovered a strength that enabled her to do some real soul-searching. She re-evaluated her existence and began considering her role in the greater scheme of things. She became a vegetarian and began reading the writings of the Indian spiritual leader Krishnamurti, which was a great help to her during the most hectic experiences with Abba. "I did as he recommended and concentrated on one thing at a time. Right in the middle of all this noise I could sit and devote myself completely to lifting a glass of water."

Frida returned home from Spain on virtually the same day as Björn and Benny came back from Miami. Together with Agnetha they all dived head first into completing work on the new album. It was ready by the end of March, and on April 23 Abba's sixth LP, *Voulez-Vous*, hit the Swedish record shops.

There is a theory that says a troublesome recording process makes for great albums. If this is true, *Voulez-Vous* proved it well: it was one of Abba's very best LPs. Where *ABBA – The Album* had been slightly schizophrenic, virtually all the tracks on the present collection were tied together by contemporary disco beats and dance rhythms, funky guitar riffs and pop strings, giving it an unusually cohesive feel. At the same time it was an album of contrasts, where Benny's keyboards had to fight for space with, for Abba, unusually prominent electric guitars.

Voulez-Vous was an album charged with strong sexual undercurrents, where heartbreak mixed with lust in one and the same track. The album opener 'As Good As New' set the pace. Agnetha's yearning lead vocals were backed by a relentless beat and a mix of baroque-style strings and funky rhythm guitars. Frida was coolly contemplative in 'The King Has Lost His Crown', while her seductive warmth was perfect for the sly references to dirty deeds in 'Lovers (Live A Little Longer)'.

In other instances, the anguish of being abandoned was made to sound jubilant, as in 'If It Wasn't For The Nights'. Even Björn chipped in with 'Does Your Mother Know', a daring tribute to cross-generational flirting in big city nightclubs. The whole album gave off the feeling of being showered with the 'Kisses Of Fire' that gave the closing track its title. It was pure and classic pop.

The tension between Agnetha and Björn that had ultimately destroyed their marriage had a beneficial influence on *Voulez-Vous*, as Agnetha admitted. "I wonder if the record didn't turn out better because of it," she said. "We work with feelings. We also communicate with our lyrics. Many of the lyrics on *Voulez-Vous* are very personal . . . A lot of things happen on a purely emotional level onstage, in the studio and strictly privately, and it shines through on the records."

The dance feel of the album was also a pretty accurate reflection of where the other half of Abba were at. Agnetha and Björn were more the homebody types around this time, staying in to be with their children, but Frida and Benny were often out clubbing in Stockholm with their friends. "[We] used to hang out at the Atlantic nightclub," recalled Claes af Geijerstam. "Frida and I were dancing to Earth Wind & Fire while Benny sat in the bar with his buddies." No doubt the pulse of the dance floor rubbed off on everyone involved.

Those responsible for the visual side of the group also picked up on the disco vibe. Lasse Hallström's videos for the two upcoming singles, 'Does Your Mother Know' and 'Voulez-Vous', both went for a club atmosphere with Abba performing in front of a dancing audience. Sleeve designer Rune Söderqvist, meanwhile, decided that the cover picture should be shot at the trendy Alexandra discotheque.

The group themselves were anxious that their album sleeves looked attractive, but were usually too busy in the studio to pay much attention to these matters. Participating in photo shoots and album designs was seldom a priority – especially for Björn and Benny – and more often than not they were put together at the last minute.

Rune felt that the pictures from the *Voulez-Vous* sleeve sessions, featuring the group posing as elegant nightclubbers, hadn't turned out too well. However, he wasn't going to ask them to come back and do it all over again during the last throes of mixing the album. His solution was to fly to London to add some gleam and sparkle to the picture at a company specialising in such matters. The outcome still wasn't completely satisfactory to Rune, but it was deemed good enough to be used for the cover.

Disappointing packaging aside, there is no doubt the record was of an exceptionally high standard: it was the group's old accessibility and high energy levels combined with a certain maturity and real-life honesty. If the stage musical experiments and literary influences on *ABBA – The Album* were Abba trying to pose as grown-ups, *Voulez-Vous* was the original spirit of Abba in a context that was grown up for real.

Of course, as if to prove the point they had to include a track like 'I Have A Dream', which somewhat spoiled the unity of the album by reverting a little too much to their *schlager* roots. The track even included the abomination known as a children's choir, the first time that any voices other than Abba's own appeared on their records, making the recording even more unusual. "There were many who thought that was a bit over the top," said Björn, "but I don't agree – it felt right to have them there."

Still, the song couldn't be faulted for its strong melody. "I remember that I was at home working on the lyrics for 'I Have A Dream', and when I had finished them I rang Benny up," recalled Björn. "He and Frida were having a party, and he told me to come on over. When I got there, we ran the song through on the piano in front of the other guests. After a while they were all singing along, because it was so easy to learn."

Voulez-Vous also marked a change in Michael Tretow's financial arrangement regarding his work with Abba. From this album onwards Björn and Benny decided that he should receive a 0.5 per cent royalty on all Abba recordings as a reward for his loyalty and invaluable contributions over the years. "Can you believe that? It was kind of unprecedented," Michael says, obviously still touched more than two decades later. "And it wasn't because I asked for it, they were the ones who said, 'You should have that.' I've never heard of anything like it. I honestly can't say that I feel it was well deserved."

As the new album hit number one in country after country, Björn and Agnetha were still coming to terms with their lives as divorcees. Meanwhile, the press was trying to sniff out if there were any new romances lurking in the wings. Only two weeks after the separation was announced the British press had ludicrously paired Agnetha up with the couple's marriage counsellor, Håkan Lönnqvist.

Agnetha flatly denied the story. Her own theory was that the rumour started because, to avoid being spotted, she had consulted Lönnqvist at fairly unusual hours. "The divorce has been a great strain," she said. "Now I want to savour my freedom and not be linked up with a lot of different men. Neither the children nor I can handle that."

Björn wasn't so easily let off the hook either. In February, when Abba were making a television programme called *Snowtime Special* for the BBC in Leysin, Switzerland, he was snapped having a conversation with Boney M singer Liz Mitchell. The West Germany-based group was also in Leysin for the filming of a television special, and the photo inspired a ludicrous gossip press story that they were having an affair.

On the contrary, Björn's relationship with Lena Källersjö had turned out to be serious. After he had been seen in public with her several times, the romance reached the press in March. "I think divorced men are very prone to meet someone very quickly, much more so than women," Björn reflected later. "Lena and I hit it off right away, which was incredible."

Björn and Agnetha wanted desperately to discourage questions and speculation about their divorce. At a press conference in Leysin they did the best they could to fend off all queries. "We've sorted out our situation," said Björn. "We don't see each other too often and try in every way to avoid meeting outside work." He even made an attempt to make light of the situation: "We've long been thinking of changing Abba's image. Now we've succeeded in doing that. Frida and Benny have got married and we are divorced." But however much they tried, it did little to diminish the media's curiosity about how they could go on working together when their personal relationship had collapsed.

Agnetha was less off-handed in her comments about life as a single woman. "Of course it gets lonely sometimes," she said, "especially when the children are at Björn's. I feel like climbing the walls, walking from room to room like an animal in a cage." A few months later, she reflected on her chances of finding a new love of her own: "I wonder how attractive a single mother of two really is? I don't believe it's that simple, really. I question my existence."

By the time the interview was published, she was in her first relationship after Björn. The object of her affection was 29-year-old elite ice-hockey player Lars-Erik Ericsson, whom she met at a party in the Atlantic club. The romance turned out to be a temporary fling, however, and a few months later it was all over.

With the *Voulez-Vous* album completed and released, Benny devoted time to outside production work for the first time in more than three years. He had met Norwegian singer Finn Kalvik at a song festival the previous summer. "We became friends and I liked his songs, so I suggested that we should record an album," Benny recalled. "It was nice to do something else for a change."

By this time, however, Polar had more or less become an exclusive Abba label. Though the label issued records by other artists, only Abba enjoyed any serious commercial success. One of the songs on the Finn Kalvik album rendered the singer a major *Svensktoppen* hit in the autumn of 1979, but the album itself mustered only two weeks at number 50 in the charts.

Still, they were better statistics than most of Polar's output around this time and, indeed, for the duration of the label's existence. A quick glance at the Polar discography from this time up to the present day reveals few successful releases that weren't directly related to Abba: as a group, as solo artists or as writers/producers.

Svenne & Lotta, who'd previously enjoyed many huge hits, found that the label had lost interest in them completely by the end of the Seventies.

Michael Tretow had been handling their latest productions, but after a low-charting album in 1978 and a flop single the year after, it all went very quiet. "Nothing happened," says Svenne Hedlund. "There were no more productions made at Polar, and we realised that we weren't considered that interesting anymore. Michael told us, 'If you find another label I think you should go for that, because it doesn't seem like there will be many efforts made on behalf of Svenne & Lotta.'"

Apparently, word was out in the music business about the duo being dropped: before long they received a phone call from producer Ola Håkansson, formerly lead singer with Sixties band Ola & The Janglers. Now working for the Sonet record label, he felt he'd found the perfect song for them. A major Italian success which was translated into Swedish, 'När dagen försvinner' ('When The Day Disappears') gave Svenne & Lotta a number one hit on *Svensktoppen* in 1980, followed by a further chart topper and a number two placing within the following 18 months. With the right repertoire and attention from their record label, there was obviously plenty of life left in the duo's career.

"If Björn and Benny had been able to set aside a little more time and done some productions with us I'm sure it could have worked out great at Polar," notes Svenne Hedlund. "Michael was a fine producer on his own, but Björn and Benny just had that special something that was needed to make it stand out. What it boiled down to in the end was that Abba took up all their time – there was nothing left for the rest of us."

Career development for other formerly successful Polar artists was similarly disappointing, though Stig had put plenty of effort into breaking acts such as Ted Gärdestad on the international market. As a songwriter, Ted had encouraging success in 1976 when one of his songs, 'Jag ska fånga en ängel', was translated into English as 'I Wanna Make You My Lady' and turned into a hit on the Australian chart by local star Mark Holden.

Ted usually had one or two English-language tracks on his earlier albums, but in 1978 he recorded an LP in Los Angeles with all songs in English. The resulting album, *Blue Virgin Isles*, was issued in a number of European countries as well as Australia, but didn't seem to please anyone. Ted also appeared as a guest star in Abba's *Snowtime Special*, which was broadcast in several territories. This exposure and Stig's faith still didn't help matters very much.

Ted's uniquely personal singer/songwriter style was rooted in a particularly Swedish, summery universe. When he sang in English and produced his music in America he was reduced to one among many artists working within the same genre. His first four albums never charted below number three in Sweden, but *Blue Virgin Isles* only reached 29. His last Polar album, a Swedish/English mix called *Stormvarning* (*Gale Warning*), was released in 1981 and peaked below the Top 30 mark.

Outside Abba, the only truly successful artists on Polar in the future would be those who'd been groomed on other labels and were already stars. Tomas Ledin, for example, who joined Polar in 1979 when he became the boyfriend of Stig's daughter Marie, already had three Top 10 albums to his credit at that time. For a record company that was branded as "blatantly commercial" the results weren't especially impressive.

From a purely financial point of view the failure of Polar artists other than Abba made little difference in the great scheme of things. Abba was such a gigantic cash cow that these disappointments were merely a ripple in the tidal wave. For the financial year of May 1, 1977 to April 30, 1978, the profits at Polar Music broke a new record, exceeding 50 million kronor (£5,500,000) on a turnover of 86 million kronor (£9,460,000). In comparison, their business partners for the Eastern bloc trades, Beijerinvest, had virtually the same profit, but in their case the turnover was 7.2 billion kronor (£792,000,000) and their employees numbered 10,100 – Polar had around 30 people working for them.

Other statistics were just as staggering. Polar had a 70 per cent profit on the working capital. During the same period, the corresponding figure for a gigantic corporation like the Volvo car company was a more normal five per cent. It was these figures that gave birth to the oft-repeated rumour that Polar was a more profitable company than Volvo. In terms of pure cash they weren't even close, but in percentage terms they beat the car manufacturer by a mile.

It was during 1978 that Polar Music International, under the guidance of Lasse Dahlin and with the help of several heavyweight financial advisors, finally got on the right track with their investments. Among the more high–profile ventures was the launch of a leasing firm called Invest Finans Infina, which soon became highly successful. By the spring of 1980 the company owned leasing properties worth around 100 million kronor (£10 million) – everything from excavators to computers – which were leased to some 450 different clients.

A few more speculative deals were implemented, most of them by accountant Stig Engqvist, who was becoming an increasingly important figure on the business side of Polar's activities. In January 1979, a limited partnership called Särimner, owned by Stig and the four Abba members outside Polar Music, bought a major Swedish bicycle manufacturer called Monark. The affair had been planned for over a year as part of a long-term scheme to further avoid heavy private taxation.

Stig Engqvist's idea was that Harlekin – the Abba-owned company which in turn owned their half of Polar Music - would subsequently be sold to Monark. According to Swedish tax laws, the Abba members would then be able to take out income from Harlekin without having to pay the 85 per cent income tax. Since the money had technically been generated by a sale, they would only have to pay capital gains tax: a mere 35 per cent. It was all perfectly legal, but there were many question marks surrounding the affair. In all truth, Abba and Stig Anderson had no interest whatsoever in Monark as a business, the deal was constructed simply for tax benefits.

Benny worried about their responsibility towards the workers at Monark, and Stig was violently opposed to the deal from the very beginning. A key factor in the new investment philosophy implemented after the Wimab fiasco was that Polar shouldn't become involved in companies that required responsibility for a number of employees – especially not within a field of business they knew very little about. The Monark deal seemed too "smart", too speculative and it didn't sound entirely honourable. The whole affair could end up damaging Polar's reputation and make it problematic for them to acquire their desired listing on the stock exchange.

Despite the initial hesitation, on January 3, 1979, Björn, Benny and everybody else involved decided to go along with the deal. The advantages seemed to be greater than the possible risks. Stig was on holiday in Hawaii and was informed about the decision by Lasse Dahlin over the phone. "I guess you might as well make me a part of the deal," he sighed, "since I will have to take all the shit when it all goes wrong and ends up in the newspapers."

While all these tax schemes were being implemented, the export earnings, music industry achievements and general goodwill generated on an international level by Stig and Abba were finally recognised beyond occasional fan letters from far-flung Swedish ambassadors. On March 8, 1979, Stig, Gudrun and the four Abba members attended an official dinner hosted by the King and Queen at the Royal Palace in Stockholm. The other guests were mainly members of the government, high-profile politicians and industrial bigwigs.

Finally, after five years of international success on a scale matched only by Elvis and The Beatles, Abba and their indefatigable manager were on their way to being recognised in their own country as something more than an insubstantial, money-grabbing, flash-in-the-pan pop group.

Chapter 28

After the *Voulez-Vous* album had been released, Abba skipped their usual round of promotional trips. They were simply unnecessary. The world media were only too eager to hop on a plane to Stockholm to do interviews, or talk with one of the four Swedes on the phone. Whatever their personal feelings about the venture, the group were concentrating their thoughts and energies on preparation and rehearsals for the last big hurdle, the long postponed début American concert tour.

The complete itinerary of the 1979 touring season was originally meant to encompass the Far East, the Eastern Bloc, North America and Europe, but when *Voulez-Vous* took so long to finish, most of the Far East countries were junked and the Eastern Bloc completely cancelled. Abba were considering Japan for the following spring, but nothing was decided. Notably, Australia, where Abbamania had raged only two years earlier, was never even on the cards.

What was left for the autumn was a three and a half week tour of Canada and the United States commencing in mid-September, followed by three weeks in Europe from mid-October. While the European part of the outing presented no worries whatsoever, the true test lay in America. It was a challenge they were now willing to face. Björn admitted that the United States had "a different mass media structure. You have to tour [there]. We've finally come to realise that."

Although three and a half weeks sounded like a fairly substantial trip, only 14 concerts were scheduled in the United States. The remaining four were in Canada, where Abba's popularity was far more entrenched. Based on a sales to population ratio, some of their albums sold three times more in this territory than in the US. The theory was that Canada, despite its proximity to the United States, was actually closer to Europe in its temperament and musical tastes.

The US part of the tour schedule had originally been more extensive, but as planning progressed several dates were removed. With such a scaled down itinerary, no one really expected that this relatively modest tour would achieve any major breakthrough in the USA. "I'd say to Stig, 'How come Led Zeppelin can sell three million albums and Abba only sell

800,000?'" recalls Jerry Greenberg. "'I know the music is different and we can't compare it, but I have to tell you, Led Zeppelin doesn't get played on Top 40 radio, which is the biggest avenue of exposure in America. We're able to get you that, but Led Zeppelin tours. Every two years they come to America and they play every nook and cranny.' And he'd reply, 'Well, Abba are not gonna do that.'"

The 1979 outing was very much a question of too little too late. With the release of *Voulez-Vous* postponed for six months, and not even a new single on the American market for an entire year, the impact of the tour as the second part of the promotional campaign started in 1978 was considerably diminished. There was still hope that interest in the group would be boosted to some degree – if nothing else, it would at least prove beyond doubt that Abba were four real live musicians and not some manufactured creation like The Archies, an image which still dogged them in certain parts of the US.

Polar and Atlantic had certainly prepared themselves to capitalise on the trip as much as possible. During the weeks leading up to the tour Stig and Abba gave up to 50 interviews for radio, a much more important marketing tool in America than in Europe, where television was the most effective way of reaching audiences. Reporters from newspapers and magazines such as *Rolling Stone*, the *New York Times*, *Washington Post* and the *Los Angeles Times* visited the tour rehearsals in Stockholm.

Tentative preparations with the band, consisting mainly of Abba's most loyal session musicians, started on May 13. A few days later the group performed two surprise concerts at small clubs in the towns of Landskrona and Norrköping, just to see how the band functioned. The outcome was satisfactory, and later in the summer three backing vocalists were added to the line-up.

The group was certainly apprehensive about the tour. They commenced rehearsals early not just because they hadn't played live in two and a half years, but also because they were going somewhere where they'd never performed any concerts before. They'd reluctantly reneged on their vow not to go until they'd had several number one singles and chart-topping albums, so there was some doubt whether they would be able to sell out the venues. No one wanted a repeat of the 1974 European fiasco.

Before Thomas Johansson drew up the itinerary for the US part of the tour careful analysis was done as to where Abba were selling the most records. According to Atlantic, Abba had enjoyed around seven number ones locally in Boston and topped the Los Angeles charts up to ten times. In accordance with this data, most of the cities chosen were located in the northern American states. As a result certain major markets – cities such as Miami, Dallas, Atlanta and St. Louis – were bypassed in favour of "safe", but minor, choices along the lines of Omaha and Milwaukee. It was instructive that unlike Australia two years ago, officials from those states not visited failed to petition Abba to change their minds.

The group also took very few chances in terms of venue sizes in these places. For example, The Music Hall, chosen for the Boston concert, could seat only 5,000. "It's easier to get contact with an audience of 5,000 than an audience of 50,000," said Björn. "And besides, to be quite honest, we don't want to risk having to play in front of half-empty arenas."

As a collective, the group's feelings about the tour hadn't changed: yes, it can be a kick to be onstage for two hours and experience the electricity in meeting their audience, but the travelling and all the other preparation was time-consuming, tiring and boring. As usual, only Frida was truly longing to meet Abba's audience, insisting that singing live was actually her favourite aspect of being in Abba.

For Agnetha, who had yet to find stability in her new role as a divorcee, the upcoming tour was nothing less than an unwanted intrusion into her daily routine. She wanted to be at home with the children and concentrate on building a new life for herself, but instead she was forced into the unreal and generally disagreeable life on tour. It truly was the last thing she needed at this time.

Her memories of the tour were not especially rosy. "It was important and successful, but for me it was horrible. Björn and I had separated and I had torn myself away from the children. I just wanted to go back home, home, home. But I had no choice. Björn and I were agreed about doing this tour together, despite the divorce, so we had to form a new relationship with each other and work together in a new way. It was an unfamiliar situation for all four of us – an ordeal. I had no one to talk to. So I mourned alone. The whole time I ached inside for the children and from homesickness."

Björn and Benny occupied the middle ground. Both preferred to be at home or in the studio but realised that the life of a professional pop musician involved more than this. Being on stage for two hours in front of an adoring audience was still a thrill but creating the live Abba experience was a big job, a huge responsibility which they could have done without. They also suffered from a form of creeping stage fright which manifested itself in odd ways.

Björn, as usual, felt the full weight on his shoulders from the very beginning, fretting over every little detail. He had been virtually sleepless for the two weeks leading up to the tour. "Sure, everything has gone well and it's easy for people to say that this is nothing to worry about, but I do worry," he said. "In my head, I run through the songs and the show time and time again, and I wake up at nights worrying about starting to sing in the wrong place or forgetting lyrics." In the hours just before the opening concert he professed to having lost both sight and hearing due to nerves. "Edmonton is an important concert," he noted. "The town may be a hole, [but] a lot of important people will come to the show. We can definitely not see Edmonton as a 'warm-up'."

Benny who professed to be completely cool up until shortly before the show kicked off, suddenly became a bundle of nerves. "When the curtain was about to be opened I was all shattered and breaking out in a cold sweat," he said. "It felt like we had no control over events."

In this frame of mind the members of Abba stepped on to the stage on September 13, 1979, shortly after 8 p.m., for their first ever North American concert in Canada, at Edmonton's Northlands Coliseum. Opening the tour in a country where they already had a stable following was crucial in building the group's confidence. The 15,000 tickets had sold out in one day when they went on sale in early August. According to the local promoter, Abba could have filled the arena three times over: on the day of the concert the black market ticket prices had risen to Can$200 (£80).

Visually, the set design of the tour was centred around a Nordic, "icy" theme. The backdrop was an iceberg-shaped construction. The shades of blue, white and purple and all the nuances within that spectrum would combine to give a northern lights feel, presenting a group that came from "the top of the world", as stage designer Rune Söderqvist recalled. Söderqvist worked in close collaboration with costume designer Owe Sandström to arrive at this theme. "We used the last three colours of the rainbow – blue, indigo and violet – as the starting point for our designs," Sandström recalled. "It's not an exaggeration to say that we looked at several hundred different shades of those three colours. That led us on to the almost pink-purple shades that you see in the sky when the sun goes down, which gradually turn into violet and then dark blue."

Frida, Agnetha and Björn were all outfitted in tight, body-hugging spandex overalls, showing off their shapely figures, while Benny wore a more loose-fitting blue jacket and white trousers outfit. The theme of mountains and lakes in northern Sweden served as the basis for almost every idea in the costume design. A couple of capes with a V-shaped pattern, worn by Frida and Agnetha at the opening of the show, were meant to resemble the reflection of mountains in a lake, in reference to the mountain shapes in the stage backdrop. The diagonal lines on the girls' tricot outfits were inspired by glacier rivers.

The show itself took on a Swedish theme, opening with Benny playing a few bombastic bars of an old Swedish folk song on his synthesizer in the darkened arena. Then, as the lights rose, the show kicked into life with a rousing version of 'Voulez-Vous', segueing right into the equally energetic 'If It Wasn't For The Nights'.

Unfortunately, this full-pelt opening was followed by a somewhat stilted welcome introduction by Björn, which hinted too much at Abba's cabaret roots even at this late stage in their career. Particularly ill-advised was his introduction of the third song in which he tried to make light of his and Agnetha's divorce, casually referring to her as "still 'As Good As New'." In Sweden, audiences were unlikely to read much into a joke like this, seeing it as a sign that Agnetha and Björn really were still able to get along, but this was not the case in middle America, where marriage is regarded as a sacred institution. Concert-goers couldn't possibly know to what extent the couple had resolved their differences, and squirmed in their seats at Björn's flippancy. "Ugh!" as one reviewer wrote.

However, those who went along on the tour testified that there really were no signs of conflict between Björn and Agnetha. "There is absolutely no way you could notice on stage," recalled keyboard player Anders Eljas. "I couldn't notice, and being on tour with them, if I couldn't notice, how could anyone in the audience?"

The concert programme consisted of around 25 songs, and it took a few performances before the show was properly knocked into shape. Originally, no songs whatsoever were included from the first two albums, and only 'Rock Me', 'SOS' and 'Intermezzo no. 1' harked back to the period before the *Arrival* album. Frida's 'One Man, One Woman' was ditched from the line-up after the first Edmonton performance for unspecified reasons: the song just failed to come off as it should. Towards the end of the American trek, 'Thank You For The Music' was also removed, while 'Waterloo' was added as an encore. One problem with the 1979 show was the high intensity level throughout the performance. By this time, Abba simply had too many hits that audiences expected to hear. "Where other bands have one or two standout songs, Abba had over 20," recalled *Expressen* journalist Mats Olsson, who accompanied the tour. "It was a bit heavy."

Abba's generosity in giving room for their backing band was reflected in their decision to invite backing singer Tomas Ledin to perform his latest single, 'Not Bad At All', as a solo number in the show. It was all part of

Polar's plans to break Tomas on the international market – indeed, this was one of the reasons he joined the label – but as with most other attempts outside Abba, it failed to come off.★

There were other unusual choices in the show that set it apart from the average rock show. On 'I Have A Dream', Abba had a specially rehearsed children's choir from each city where they performed. Although the choir was meant to be a heart-warming moment with small kids, it didn't quite turn out that way at every concert. "In some cities they had interpreted the 'children' concept a bit generously," recalled Björn. "They were just as tall as we were!"

On some shows, the choir also performed on 'Thank You For The Music', and altogether the presence of children on stage rendered a special atmosphere to the proceedings. "I loved the concert, but it was a family show," says Jerry Greenberg, who flew up to see one of the Canadian performances. "It was mothers and fathers and their kids: a very clean, family-oriented musical experience. I mean, I could walk into Madison Square Garden at an Emerson, Lake & Palmer or Led Zeppelin concert and just get a high off all the dope in the auditorium. I remember making jokes with the other guys from Atlantic: 'Ain't like a Stones show, is it?' We had a big laugh at that."

In Los Angeles, influential critic Robert Hilburn quipped that the audience demographic queuing to get in to the show "looked just like the lines you see in the Disneyland parking lots, waiting for a tram ride back to their cars".

The wholesome atmosphere was perpetuated off-stage as well. As usual, the Abba tour gang was very clean-living: no scandals, no wrecked hotel rooms, no drugs, at worst a harmless prank here or there. In one city Atlantic arranged a party with local strippers, assuming – as they would with Led Zeppelin, to name an obvious example – that this was the kind of party that rock stars enjoyed. Abba weren't interested, however, and withdrew to their hotel suites for their own private party.

The usual late-night shindigs were as bad as it got. "The press were a little surprised that we didn't have bigger rave-ups than we did, but instead could often be found jogging and exercising," recalled Agnetha.

Abba continued to take good care of their musicians and road crew, and everybody else who worked with them. "They were used to being treated

★ Tomas did go on to have one or two stray hits in isolated territories – most prominently the Agnetha duet 'Never Again' in 1982, where one suspects that it wasn't necessarily the male half of the duo who attracted the sales – but that was as far as it went. Summing up his international ventures, Ledin recalled being "a bit disappointed".

like shit by most of the other big acts," remembered Anders Eljas, "but with Abba it was different. The road crew should have their food, and we mustn't start the party before they had arrived, and so on, because those guys were working really hard. They thought that this was the best tour they had ever been on."

The opening show in Edmonton received encouraging reviews, if sometimes marked by a certain bemusement. Graham Hicks of the *Edmonton Journal* called the group "very human and very nervous". However, he noted that the first half of the show was a bit . . . "shaky. The pacing was slow, the songs delivered in a cautious, unfeeling way. The performance teetered, at times, on the edge of monotony."

According to Hicks, the show picked up later on: " 'Does Your Mother Know' and ['Hole In Your Soul'] were excellent. The girls loosened up, [Björn] paraded around the stage as he ought to have done all evening. Benny had a fine time, throwing out rockabilly licks on his white electric piano. It all clicked . . . The band began to let the music flow, rather than searching for an impossible perfection. And for five minutes, the crowd went crazy, in a polite Abba way."

There was always an air of awkwardness about Abba's live shows. It was as if they wanted to offer inoffensive family entertainment and a wild rock show at the same time – an impossible equation. None of the group were natural stage performers either, which put an additionally curious slant on the concerts. "I don't think that Abba were good enough as a live band," Agnetha would later summarise. "Perhaps I'm looking too critically at our performances. They weren't choreographically well-planned, we mostly worked on spontaneity and feeling." But she also recognised that the lack of slickness often worked to the group's advantage. "No doubt it had its charm, being so unrehearsed stagewise. A lot of spontaneous things happened and you can quite clearly see on the filmed performances whether it was a good or bad day."

It often seemed that the flaws in their stage appearance – Frida's long-winded choreographed dance routines, Björn's self-conscious running-around on stage, Agnetha's wavy arm movements – helped to endear the group to the often undemanding crowds that flocked to see them. The shows occasionally took on the look of amateur theatrics, something those watching might have felt they could pull off themselves, but at the same time included just sufficient glamorous sheen to lend a kind of star quality to the performers themselves.

The American tour was accompanied by several Swedish journalists. Some, like Mats Olsson of the basically Abba-friendly tabloid *Expressen*, were given special privileges. Olsson was treated to an exclusive preview

412

of Abba's as yet unreleased new single, 'Gimme! Gimme! Gimme! (A Man After Midnight)' among other things.

Less fortunate was Leif-Åke Josefson of *Aftonbladet*, a tabloid that certainly covered Abba a lot, but which was traditionally much more critical of the group, focusing on the "moneygrabbing" aspect of things. Josefson was already high up on the entourage's own PITA ("Pain In The Ass") list, and when word got out that he had written a bad review of the opening concert in Edmonton, Stig Anderson exploded.

"We felt that the première was a true success," recalls Rune Söderqvist, "but then, when we called back home they said, 'Oh, I'm so sorry to hear that it didn't turn out too well.' They had read the *Aftonbladet* review. So Stig told me, 'Go down and ask *Aftonbladet* to go to hell!' It was no use that they tagged along, he said, because they weren't going to get one single interview."

Björn had agreed earlier to talk with Josefson, but the journalist was now told to forget it – "now and for always!" When the hapless reporter approached Tomas Ledin for an interview, he was sheepishly told that nobody in the entourage was allowed to talk to him. Josefson was devastated – he knew that he had written a fairly positive review. In fact, only one phrase at the beginning of the article, added by the editor in Stockholm – "Success or fiasco – perhaps somewhere in between" – could be construed as even remotely negative. After a few days Björn got hold of the article himself and realised that it was all a misunderstanding. Josefson finally got his interview.

Meanwhile, Agnetha was struggling with her own demons. Being away in a different part of the world with constant feelings of homesickness was a deeply alienating experience. The farewell scene with her children before flying to Canada had been devastatingly emotional. The sight of other children playing in a hotel pool during the tour gave her a painful stab of longing.

"I don't know how I managed," she said many years later. "The others were in a different phase and held up better. They didn't have children at home who had just gone through their parents' divorce. It was me who had to live with a constant bad conscience. No one understood how painful it was. It's still difficult to talk about it."

Throughout much of the tour Agnetha kept to herself. When the rest of the gang went out on a boat in Vancouver, she stayed back at the hotel. She called her children on the phone every day and brightened up considerably when Linda came out to visit when the tour hit Los Angeles. Like other acts of première league status, Abba made the city their base for a week, renting holiday flats instead of staying in a hotel, and flying out to different venues and back the same night. Six-year-old Linda even made her stage début during 'I Have A Dream' at the Las Vegas concert.

Björn was compensated for his loneliness not only by Linda's presence, but by Lena who also came out to spend time with him in Los Angeles. Together with Linda and Agnetha, the couple visited Disneyland, which demonstrated to anyone who might be watching that they all got along just fine in their new situation. The children had taken well to daddy's new girlfriend. Lena, though, found it difficult to handle the attention that followed her relationship with Björn. "I don't give a damn about it, but for Lena it's hard," said Björn. "To not be able to sit together with me without attracting attention. She doesn't exactly want to be famous because she lives together with me. After all, Lena has got a career of her own."

As the tour neared its end Abba could look back on a fairly successful and largely routine outing. By way of meticulously arranged logistics, they had been able to withstand the pressures. Most of the concerts had come off well, with a good audience response. Reviews were mixed, but there was a high quota of positive comments among them. Agnetha may not have enjoyed the experience very much, but at least she was holding up. Then disaster struck.

Wednesday, October 3, was the day after Abba's triumphant sold-out concert at New York City's Radio City Music Hall. For transportation between cities, the group had chartered a private jet which had belonged to eccentric billionaire Howard Hughes. For the sake of their children, Björn and Agnetha usually didn't fly together in case anything should happen. On this particular afternoon it was Agnetha's turn to board the private plane for a flight to Boston and their next concert, scheduled to take place that same evening.

Not long after take-off the small plane flew headlong into a bad storm that suddenly appeared north of New York. It was no minor weather problem: in Connecticut a tornado swept across the landscape, wreaking havoc with buildings, cars and trucks, killing one person and injuring 300. The damages were estimated at more than US$100 million (£45 million).

The bad weather meant that the plane was unable to land at their designated airport. In fact, the airfield had been completely obliterated by the tornado, and the pilot decided to turn back to New York. Nerves were fraying as everybody on board became concerned that they would have to cancel the concert. This prompted the pilot to return to Boston again in the hope that the weather had improved, only to find that it hadn't. The decision was then made to circle in the air before attempting a landing. Matters took a turn for the worse when the pilot noticed that he was running out of fuel and was forced to make an emergency landing in the small town of Manchester, New Hampshire.

For Agnetha, who suffered from a fear of flying at the best of times, it was a horrific nightmare. "When we were almost down on the airfield, all of a sudden they flew back up again," she recalled. "Our lives were in mortal danger – that's how it felt for me – with flashes on the wings and without being able to see anything. Everything was just black and the plane was shaking something horribly. I prayed to God that I wouldn't die."

Tour manager Bosse Norling, also in the private plane, remembered how everybody thought this was the end. "Agnetha was hysterical, and I don't blame her. As if the terrible weather and the wobbling plane wasn't bad enough, the airfield lights were out – it was completely pitch-dark – and the pilots had a rough time bringing the plane down."

Thanks to the skill of the pilot the landing was completed safely, and on unsteady legs the Abba party climbed into waiting cars and drove away to the concert venue. The bad weather didn't have the same disastrous consequences in Boston as in the nearby state of Connecticut, but the roadways into Boston were still flooded and traffic was jammed for hours. The rest of the Abba entourage, travelling by regular flights, had also run into trouble because of the weather and were even later arriving. As a result, the concert was delayed by 90 minutes and didn't commence until 9.30 p.m.

Agnetha was in a terrible state, but somehow – remarkably – she went through with the concert. None of the 5,000 strong audience noticed there was anything amiss with the blonde singer that night.

The reaction didn't come until afterwards. The original plan had been to fly directly to the next stop on the tour, Washington, after the concert, but in deference to Agnetha the group stayed overnight in Boston instead. "[Agnetha] was completely devastated," recalled Bosse Norling. "She had to take sleeping pills in order to sleep that night."

The following day Agnetha refused to get into the small jet, and opted for a regular flight. But she was unable to put the incident behind her: negative feelings about touring combined with memories of the dreadful experience on the plane continued to come crashing down on her with relentless force. When she arrived at the hotel in Washington the full impact of the ordeal truly set in. Agnetha locked herself inside her room, refusing to leave it, much less let anyone from the tour entourage inside.

"I went to find Stig," remembered Norling, "and I told him that there might not be a concert. Agnetha was still in a state of shock and wouldn't let anyone inside her room. He flew into a rage . . . and tried to get into her room. She refused to open the door."

The hours were ticking away and no one knew if the group was going to go through with the concert or not. There was a financial worry as well: the tour had been insured with Lloyds of London, but if they cancelled the show they needed a doctor's certificate to prove that Agnetha was too ill to perform.

Agnetha agreed to let in the doctor – but only him. When the doctor re-emerged he announced that Agnetha had a 40 degree temperature, was vomiting and suffering from diarrhoea. The shock – in combination with a virus – had brought on the flu.

The concert could be cancelled without fear of repercussions, and everybody drew a heavy sigh of relief. The cancellation was announced on the radio, but it was too late to inform the 3,000 disappointed concert-goers who still showed up at the venue.

After Agnetha had rested at the hotel for another day, Abba flew to Montreal on the afternoon of their concert there. "I wanted to show up at any price for the audience there, although my legs were unsteady," she recalled. "They also showed up for me and that carried me through. When 12,000 people in Montreal get up and wave and applaud, a wave of energy hits you. You are given strength and are rewarded for all the hard work and it feels fantastic."

In a remarkably coincidental poignancy, Abba's 1979 show included a song performed by Agnetha called 'I'm Still Alive'. It was a completely new ballad that she had composed especially for the tour. The lyrics – about coming to terms with the end of a love affair – were written by her ex-husband. Agnetha sang the song at the piano, with thousands of cigarette lighters flickering in the dark at some concerts. She would remember it as the most touching moment in the show.

After one final concert, in Toronto, Abba arrived back in Stockholm on October 9. A week's rest awaited them before the European leg of their tour.

No one was likely to admit it at the time, but there was little doubt that the North American campaign had failed in its short-term aims. The expected boost in record sales failed to happen, at least for their current releases. When Abba arrived in the United States, the *Voulez-Vous* album had already reached its peak position of number 19 and was sliding down the charts without regaining any significant momentum. The current single, 'Voulez-Vous', had reached no higher than number 80. In an act of desperation it was flipped over to promote the B-side, 'Angeleyes', instead. Still, the single never climbed higher than 64, despite Abba's presence in the country.

"Our tours were a disappointment," admitted Stig. "We were told that touring was necessary to get the record sales going. But it didn't increase very much after the touring. Financially, the rewards are also very small considering all the time it takes."

There had been quite a few sold-out shows in the United States, but just as many miscalculations. The biggest flop was the show in Minneapolis. The St Paul Civic could seat 17,500 – it was the biggest venue of the tour – but many tickets failed to find buyers. By way of contrast, in New York, Abba played to a sold-out Radio City Music Hall, but the demand for tickets was so high that they could probably have filled the 20,000 seat Madison Square Garden.

Abba were never able to conquer the American market completely. Although there was talk of a television special to be made in 1980, Abba did not return to the United States as a group. Stig continued arguing with Atlantic that they should be able to break Abba without the touring exposure. Despite the mutual frustration he never made the decision to leave the label, nor did Jerry Greenberg ever consider dropping the group.

However, later in life Stig couldn't help reflecting on the wisdom of staying with Atlantic after all. "[Success] can depend on which label you're on . . . We were with Atlantic, which was mainly a black label. But we stayed with them because Atlantic were the first to give us a break and because of that we wanted to be loyal towards them." As usual, loyalty and personal relationships was Stig's first priority.

The tour of North America lost a reported US$200,000 (£90,000), but Stig was confident that they would break even after the European leg. There were no fears of empty seats here: Europe and Great Britain remained the biggest markets for Abba. At the start of the tour, only Vienna and Paris hadn't been sold out, but the last few tickets were snapped up by showtime.

The first concerts on the European leg, in Gothenburg and Stockholm, were hugely successful, with the Stockholm audience being especially ecstatic in their reception. "You might wonder what the hell you're doing in the USA when it's like this at home," said Benny, underlining the group's growing complacency in terms of conquering new territories. They had what they had and that was more than enough.

Beyond Abba's efforts to go on developing as recording artists, it was as if they had abandoned all further ambitions. There were no longer any plans to move to the United States to be smack in the middle of the music scene, and any tentative thoughts about becoming tax exiles had long since faded.

"We had a big talk about possibly moving to New York," recalled Benny a few years later, "but all four of us were completely agreed upon staying in Sweden. We feel that Sweden is the best country in the world. For example, we've come farther than anyone in terms of equality between men and women. The taxes are high, certainly, but the money goes back to the people." With typical Swedish modesty, the Abba members often pointed out that even with 85 per cent tax there was still plenty of money left for people in their income bracket.

The European trek encompassed Sweden, Denmark, France, The Netherlands, Germany, Switzerland, Austria, Belgium, England, Scotland, finishing in Dublin, Ireland. When the tour was over, more than 300,000 people would have seen Abba in concert in North America and Europe. This last leg of the tour served merely to confirm Abba's enduring popularity. Agnetha was much happier: when Abba played Wembley Arena in London for a record-breaking six nights in a row, she was able to have both her children with her for the whole week.

The atmosphere was marked by peace and harmony with none of the stress that visited the American dates, and the operation ran particularly smoothly. The British press were astounded at Björn and Agnetha's relaxed attitude to their divorce. An eyebrow or two was raised when the ex-marrieds were spotted at a restaurant together with Lena Källersjö.

The reviews that didn't shower unequivocal praise upon the group were the usual complaints about machine-like coldness, sly observations on cross-generational audience demographic and a sometimes begrudging respect for Abba's hit-making ability. Such cultural elitism was not shared by their peers in the music business who recognised a good thing when they saw it. In the VIP box at the Wembley concerts, members of hard rock bands like Led Zeppelin and Deep Purple were seen hobnobbing with Justin Hayward of The Moody Blues and even Joe Strummer of The Clash.

As usual, the late night hotel parties were Abba's main outlets for winding down. Representatives of their British record company, Epic, were astonished by how the group could out-party rockers with the most hardened reputations for after-hours fun and games.

The six concerts at Wembley were filmed by a team from Swedish Television for an "in concert" television special. Some behind the scenes footage had also been shot on the American part of the tour. The programme was so attractive for Swedish Television that although all profits from future sales were split in two with Polar Music, the broadcasting company paid the entire 3 million kronor (£300,000) production costs themselves. The reasoning was that Polar Music had already made a financial contribution by supplying the live show in itself, plus Michael Tretow's 24-track recordings of the concerts.

It turned out to be a highly profitable venture for both parties: the television special was picked up by several countries and was later released on video. More than two decades after it was first broadcast in the spring of 1980, worldwide interest in the programme was still healthy, much to the astonishment of the Swedish Television sales department.

The recordings of the concerts also resulted in a radio special, and plans were afoot for a live album in the first few months of the new year. Michael Tretow, whose enthusiasm for live recordings was normally very low, professed to be unusually satisfied with the recordings. He was even talking about turning it into a double album but the group's indifference towards live recordings put the kibosh on those plans. They argued that a live package would repeat much of the material on the recently issued *Greatest Hits Vol. 2*, and the project was shelved.

After the last concert in Dublin on November 15 – Frida's 34th birthday – the group celebrated the end of the European trek with a big party. The tour had been a huge success and even Agnetha said she felt a little sad at the thought that it was all over.

Abba had just enjoyed a big hit with a brand new single, 'Gimme! Gimme! Gimme! (A Man After Midnight)', which was recorded shortly before they embarked on the tour. The track was yet another of the disco-inflected numbers in which Abba excelled during 1979. Agnetha delivered a typically yearning lead vocal, unwittingly adding another layer to her public image as a lonely, abandoned woman.

On Abba's return home from the tour, 'I Have A Dream' was rush-released as a souvenir single of the 1979 tour and a fitting conclusion to the International Year of the Child. The children's choir may have been too much to handle for some sensitive ears, but there was no denying the song's commercial potential: number one in The Netherlands, Belgium and Switzerland, number two in the UK, Top Five or Top 10 in several other countries. Abba's image as one big, happy family might be slightly tarnished, but their stronghold on the world's record-buying public was as convincing as ever.

Chapter 29

The new decade introduced a new Abba to the world.

Their outward image had changed completely. Björn and Agnetha's divorce not only shattered the "happy couples" myth, but affected the group in a more literal way. The fantastic costumes by Owe Sandström that culminated in the body-hugging blue chill spandex of the recent tour were packed away for good, and with them Abba's iconic image as Seventies clotheshorses of sometimes questionable taste. There would be no more gold lamé capes, no more bizarre blouses adorned with drawings of animals, no more cat dresses decorated with especially imported pearls, no more costumes in blue satin with painted-on flower patterns.

What emerged in the new decade was a group of individuals. Although Benny and Frida were still married, the interpersonal relationships between all four changed when Björn and Agnetha went their separate ways: there were still two songwriters and two singers, but now there was only one couple. Abba's function as a unifying project, four people on an exciting journey towards an unknown future, had lost its relevance. Now, more than ever, it was a job: a pleasurable job, certainly, but the thrill of becoming international pop stars was no longer there.

It was also the beginning of a new era as far as Abba's contact with the general public was concerned. Enthusiasm for touring remained as muted as ever, and although Björn noted that it was easier for him and Agnetha now that they were divorced, after half a decade as one of the world's biggest acts, it all seemed fairly pointless. Abba had already agreed to tour Japan in March. There was a demand for a South American trek, but it was unlikely it was going to happen. All that remained for the group was writing songs and working together in the studio.

During the troubled United States tour the previous autumn, Agnetha had announced her intention to cut down her commitments to Abba during the upcoming year. It was particularly important for her to have time off in August, when Linda would be starting school. "My career means so little these days," she reflected.

In the spring of 1980, Agnetha elaborated on her situation. "My children come before everything else," she said. "Björn calls me a mother hen and I guess that's fairly accurate . . . I am a bit unstable sometimes. I'm around 30 years old and many people say that things are supposed to change at that time. You re-evaluate and question things, you develop. All the dreams you had when you were young – marrying and settling down – they don't really work out." Her current dream, she added, was to take a year off to spend with her children. Balancing her commitments as a mother against the demands of being a quarter of Abba was an impossible equation.

The campaigns to conquer different territories that ran parallel with Abba's musical development ever since 'Waterloo' would be put on the back burner for the most part. They were happy to continue releasing records and making promo clips, but that was basically it. "My musical home is the studio, not the stage," as Agnetha remarked many times. Promotional visits to other countries, let alone concert tours, were reduced to an absolute minimum. They had already had more success than they could handle.

The immediate task was to commence work on this year's LP, scheduled for release in the autumn. Björn and Benny's songwriting excursion to the Bahamas the previous year had produced fine results, so the experiment was repeated in January 1980. This time, however, they headed off to Barbados. The two songwriters rented a house where Paul McCartney and his family had stayed in the summer of 1978 at the same time as Benny and Frida were there on holiday. Benny remembered that it had been quite a luxurious abode, and thought it would provide a creative environment.

Meanwhile, Agnetha, Frida and Michael Tretow busied themselves with another project. At the end of 1978, Abba had yet to achieve a major breakthrough in Spanish-speaking countries, particularly South America. As usual, some thought went into what was needed, and Buddy McCluskey, an employee at RCA Records in Argentina, Abba's South American licensees, suggested they should record one of their songs in Spanish.

The perfect opportunity arrived with 'Chiquitita', already Spanish-flavoured in both arrangement and title. McCluskey put together the Spanish lyrics in collaboration with his wife, Mary, and the single was released in Argentina in April 1979. It stormed up the charts, hitting number one, while the English version was pulled along in the excitement and reached number seven. Within a few months the Spanish 'Chiquitita' had sold half a million copies in Argentina alone, and was said to be the biggest hit in South America in 25 years. Once again, it seemed that when Abba decided to make an impact in a specific territory, there was no stopping them.

In the autumn of the same year they released a Spanish version of 'I

Have A Dream', titled 'Estoy Soñando'. When that also became a success, the idea was put forward to release a whole album of Spanish versions of Abba songs. Björn and Benny were not too keen on the project, but said that if Agnetha and Frida were prepared to re-record all their vocals, and Michael wanted to produce it, they really had no objections.

In January 1980, while Björn and Benny were basking in the Barbados sunshine, the singers and Michael remained in chilly Sweden to work on the album. Sweden-based Spanish journalist Ana Martinez del Valle was enlisted to help out with the pronunciation, which led to some quite unpleasant consequences for her. Martinez del Valle was working at the Spanish department of the foreign broadcast services at Swedish radio, still run by judgemental left-wingers with no time for Abba. Her colleagues were upset that she was going to "sell" herself to Stig Anderson.

"I was called to an inquisitorial meeting," she recalled. " 'What kind of bourgeois nonsense is this!' . . . 'But I'm only going to help [Abba] with their Spanish pronunciation . . . Surely, that can't be too detrimental for the people of South America?', I defended myself. But the inquisitors were relentless. The price for my working relationship with [Stig] was expulsion." Fortunately, Ana Martinez del Valle was able to ride out the frosty atmosphere, and later in the decade she became a popular media personality in Sweden.

The album of Spanish Abba songs was released under the title *Gracias Por La Música* (*Thank You For The Music*) in the spring of 1980. The selected titles were mainly those songs with a Spanish/Latin flavour – such as 'Hasta Mañana', 'Fernando' and 'Move On' – as well as some of Abba's most familiar hits. *Gracias Por La Música* was a highly successful venture, reaching the Top Five in both Spain and Argentina – the most important South American market – and even charting in Japan.

The male half of Abba remained unconcerned. "I must admit that I have never ever listened to the Spanish album, except to okay it when it was finished," Benny said later. Nevertheless, when Abba released their next two regular albums in South America, both contained two tracks with vocal overdubs in Spanish.

Benny's hunch about going to Barbados had been correct – their visit turned out to be even more fruitful than the previous year's Bahamas trip. When Björn and Benny returned to Sweden they had no less than five songs completed: 'Happy New Year', 'Andante, Andante', 'The Piper', 'On And On And On' and 'Elaine'. 'Happy New Year' had its roots in the ever-present dream of writing a musical, and came to them while the pair were on the plane to Barbados. Their concept was to structure the plot around New Year's Eve. "We thought it would be a good framework: a few people in a room, looking back on what has been, thinking about the future, that sort of thing," remembered Benny.

On Barbados, they happened to meet up with the British comedian John Cleese, the star of *Monty Python's Flying Circus* and *Fawlty Towers*. Björn and Benny were huge fans, and over dinner they suggested that he write the book for the musical. Cleese wasn't too keen about that prospect, however, and soon enough the whole concept was ditched. All that remained of Björn and Benny's idea was a wistful ballad that was included on the new album.

At the beginning of February the two composers spent a little over a week recording the backing tracks for the first batch of songs. With the basis for five tracks in the can, Abba were in an unusually well advanced position after just a month's writing and recording work.

After that they took a break from the album and spent a few weeks preparing for the upcoming tour of Japan. The show and the personnel for the Japanese performances were virtually identical to the previous year's outing to North America and Europe. The only significant changes were that one of the backing singers had been replaced and that parts of 'I Have A Dream' were sung in Japanese.

Otherwise, just like the European trek, the tour merely confirmed the group's mind-boggling popularity, seen through with customary Japanese efficiency. The biggest drama occurred during the tumultuous arrival at Narita Airport when around 100 photographers stormed through a wall of 200 policemen who struggled to guard Abba from the attention.

More than 100,000 people saw Abba perform during 11 sell-out shows, six of which were at Tokyo's celebrated 10,000-seater Nippon Budokan Hall. The first of the Budokan concerts almost ended in disaster when the six-ton steel rig holding up the lights was on the verge of collapsing only hours before the concert. "It was pure luck that it happened before the première," said Thomas Johansson. "I hardly dare think what might have happened if it had occurred during the performance. Abba are standing directly under this equipment and it could have crashed down upon them."

Like all groups performing in Japan for the first time, Abba were surprised by the muted reaction of the Japanese audience. The concert-goers would clap along to each and every number in the show, except the ballads, before erupting at the end of the performance, when 'Dancing Queen' was played. Although Abba were used to fairly well-behaved audiences, this was a bit too quiet even for them. After a while an explanation was given: in Japan, cheering and dancing simply wasn't permitted during concerts.

Abba returned to Stockholm from Japan on March 29 and never toured again. A "never say never" attitude prevailed for a while, but there was nothing in their actions over the next few years that suggested they were ever seriously considering any more concert tours. Vague plans to tour South America in April were quietly shelved: the future held little prospect for such complicated and time-consuming ventures.

The wind had gone out of their sails during the Japanese trek, which ended on a sad note. Bosse Norling, the ever-faithful tour manager at EMA Telstar, fell out with Thomas Johansson, whom he felt "meddled too much". The situation got so bad between the two that Norling simply quit the Abba entourage in mid-tour.★ The incident simply emphasised that this would have to be the end of the road. It just wasn't much fun anymore.

After a short break on their return home, Abba spent the last three weeks of April recording vocals and finishing off the first five songs for the upcoming album. As the group concentrated on intricate harmonies and innumerable keyboard overdubs, the financiers at Polar were juggling increasingly complex business issues to the best of their ability – with mixed results.

On February 1, Abba's company Harlekin had been sold to the bicycle manufacturer Monark – which they owned as individuals together with Stig Anderson – according to the plan drawn up by Stig Engqvist and their other accountants a year earlier. This action freed a lot of cash for the four Abba members, and allowed them to avoid the high income tax. It was the first time they had executed a business transaction that served no purpose other than a short-term tax saving, a marked contrast to previous long-term investment plans which would also eventually save on taxes.

However, even before the Harlekin deal, the purchase of Monark had proved fortuitous, far beyond Stig and Abba's own motives. When the company was acquired it was in very bad shape, the victim of bad management for a number of years. However, continued high oil prices, coupled with the health craze of the late Seventies and early Eighties, led to a greatly increased use of bicycles. In August 1979 Monark's share price rose from 82 kronor (£9) to 106 kronor (£11.50) in one month. The profit for Stig and Abba just on this rise was 3.6 million kronor (£396,000).

Polar's ventures into the oil business were less successful, however. When the collaboration with Beijerinvest to do barter trading in the Eastern Bloc fell through, Beijer sold their part of the joint venture Sannes Trading to Polar Music International. Sannes Trading then changed its name to Pol Oil, concentrating completely on the oil business. Harry

---

★ Bosse Norling died in the spring of 2001.

Holmberg, the former president of a major Swedish oil company, was hired to handle these affairs.

In January 1980 Pol Oil bought 55,000 tons of crude oil on the spot market in Rotterdam at US$40 per barrel. The oil was meant to be sold – almost immediately after it was purchased – to a country where there was a shortage of oil, and at a higher price. This was common practice, but for Pol Oil the whole affair ended in disaster.

The oil was bought at the wrong time, when the price was exceptionally high due to unrest in Iran. It also turned out that the oil itself was of an unusual kind that was very hard to sell. Although Holmberg thought he had a prospective buyer, the interested party pulled out of the deal. The oil remained unsold – with exorbitant storage charges – and during the spring the price dropped by more than US$5 a barrel. "The prices went down – down down down down down," as Björn recalled. The whole sordid affair ended with Pol Oil selling the oil at a much lower price than they had paid for it. The total loss was a staggering 30 million kronor (£3.3 million).

By June 1980, Pol Oil had closed down, and the company's owners were deeply aggrieved. Although the monetary loss was painful, it said something for the riches accumulated by Polar that it was little more than a storm in a teacup for the company's financial stability. "We are not short of a few pennies," said Björn. "We are not exactly bankrupt." Over the past years private fortunes had also been stashed away in tax havens such as Switzerland and Jersey, so there was little fear that anyone would end up in the poorhouse.

More serious was the loss of credibility in the financial world. The Pol Oil experience brought home to Stig that much of Polar's investment business was on the wrong track. The financial structure with several different companies being owned or co-owned by Stig and/or the Abba members – and those companies in turn owning several other companies – was much too convoluted. "We've had a constant jackpot, which has led to the company being built up much too quickly," he said. "Now we have to straighten everything out and co-ordinate the whole enterprise . . . Only when we have done that will Polar Music International be a contender for the stock exchange. But there's a long way to go before we reach that stage."

For Stig, who had such a firm grip on the strictly music-related side of the business – the international licensing deals, the strategic promotional visits – it was annoying to be portrayed in the newspapers as some kind of dilettante. Established industrialists were laughing behind his back, saying that he was out of his depth. A working-class *schlager* lyricist born in a shed in Hova wasn't supposed to become a respected businessman. "It's just a matter of conservative thinking," Stig mused. "To be allowed to succeed you have to pass this or that exam; you have to walk a certain path."

Honesty, integrity and keeping all his business transactions in perfect order was Stig's motto. "We employed an English auditor called Raphael Attar to check up on the figures in our dealings with the licensees in most territories," recalls John Spalding. "He was very good – without giving away any secrets he did find some six figure sums." Sometimes Attar's diligence worked the other way around as well. "He was very honest to the extent that in Australia he found that RCA had paid us $A4,000 too much in one period. So we had to return this amount, in addition to paying all other expenses involved in returning it."

By the early Eighties little of this diligence was reported in the press anymore, it was the blunders and the half-failures that created headlines. Abba tried their best to keep the ups and downs of the business at arms' length – indeed, that's what the likes of Lasse Dahlin and Stig Engqvist were paid for. In the eyes of the media, however, it was still "Abba" who did the business: by now their names were mentioned in the press in conjunction with oil and leasing companies more often than with their music. The group watched this development with increasing dismay, not least when the phenomenon spread to the international press.

"Of course the journalists thought that was interesting," Björn recalled. "No English group would say a word about money. Then, all of a sudden, a group appears with a manager who tells the media exactly where the money was to be invested and what we were going to do. We would have preferred if there had been no talk at all about that side of it. That would have been the natural thing, because that's no image you want to give a pop group who's trying to do good stuff, that it just revolves around money. It wasn't good for us."

Björn was quite correct in his judgements. No British or American rock performers, regardless of their status, *ever* discussed their financial affairs with journalists, not even the most loquacious and forthright interviewees like John Lennon or Pete Townshend. Nor did the journalists, be they from the music press or elsewhere, presume to inquire, not least because in most instances they'd have been told in no uncertain terms that the topic was not on the agenda. It was as if a tacit understanding had been reached between the two parties on the matter, and even when a rock star invited comment by flaunting his wealth in the manner of, say, Elton John, it was generally accepted that this was merely a facet of Elton's loveable eccentricity, a virtue rather than a vice. In this respect, Abba were unique in

Agnetha Fältskog, the blonde, homely girl who became a reluctant superstar, the purveyor of heartbreak, the group's sex symbol. (*LFI*)

"You look like a movie star": Frida and Agnetha with actor Robert Hughes in a scene from *ABBA – The Movie*. (*Bengt H. Malmqvist/Premium*)

Stig Anderson with Abba at the opening of Polar Music Studios in 1978. (*Bengt H. Malmqvist/Premium*)

"The lights are gonna find me": Abba on stage in 1979, the autumn of their years as a touring band. (*Anders Hanser/Premium*)

Frida and Benny with Atlantic Records chief Ahmet Ertegun at a party following the New York premiere of *Abba – The Movie*. (*Rex*)

""When all is said and done": A shot from the last photo session that Abba undertook as an active group, in 1982. (*Anders Hanser/Premium*)

Agnetha with Gunnar Hellström in a scene from the film *Raskenstam*, her screen acting début. (*Hulton Getty*)

Björn and Benny with lyricist Tim Rice, with whom they collaborated on the musical *Chess*. (*Rex*)

Björn with his second wife, Lena Källersjö, and Benny with his second wife, Mona Nörklit, at the première of *Chess* in May 1986. (*Rex*)

Frida with Stig Anderson at
the London Première of the musical
Abbacadabra in 1983. (*Rex*)

Agnetha, looking distraught, leaving Solna
courthouse after the hearing involving
stalker and former boyfriend, Dutchman
Gert van der Graaf, October 11, 2000.
(*PA Photos*)

Björn and Lena's two daughters,
Emma and Anna, at the London *Mamma
Mia!* premiere, April, 1999. (*Rex*)

Björn and Lena in the Nineties. (*Rex*)

Frida in 1996 at a charity concert
in Helsinki. (*Rex*)

Frida with her son, Hans, at the Polar Music
Prize in May 2001. (*bigpicturesphoto.com*)

Frida and her third husband, Prince Ruzzo
Reuss, standing on the steps of the Cirkus
Theatre, Stockholm, where Björn and
Benny's musical Kristina från Duvemåla was
playing in 1998. (*bigpicturesphoto.com*)

Björn and Benny at the London premiere of
Mamma Mia! at the Prince Edward Theatre
on April 6, 1999. (*Rex*)

"The way old friends do": The last known occasion - June 21, 1999 - when all four members of Abba were together, the 50th birthday party of Görel Hanser, who has worked for and with the group since their inception. Clockwise, from top left: Björn and Lena; Frida and Benny; Frida and Görel; and Agnetha and Görel. (*bigpicturesphoto.com*)

their apparent willingness to discuss their financial affairs with reporters. The price they paid for their honesty was to be damned as avaricious materialists when in reality their attitudes to money were no different from those of every other successful recording act.

It is ironic that while the catastrophic Pol Oil business was collapsing, Abba was in the midst of a brilliantly creative phase that had absolutely nothing whatsoever to do with the cold laws of mathematics and economics. In early June, Björn and Benny went into the studio to record three new compositions for the present album project.

One of the songs was a country-flavoured melody called 'Burning My Bridges' which never went beyond the demo stage. Another was the wistful Frida-vehicle 'Our Last Summer'. Björn's lyrics, inspired by a teenage romance he had experienced long ago in France, pointed to his recent tendency to put more of himself into his songs. "It was that kind of melancholy memory of 'the last summer of innocence'," he recalled.

The third song was destined to go down as a true classic in the Abba annals, arguably the best recording they ever made. When the current sessions started, on June 2, the melody carried the working title 'The Story Of My Life' and was the first of the new pieces to be recorded. Even at the writing stage, sitting together head to head, Benny at the piano and Björn with his acoustic guitar, they sensed they were on to something special.

The first attempt at a backing track was an up-tempo arrangement with a regular, insistent beat. It sounded fine, but the songwriters felt it wasn't exactly what they were after. Benny recalled the track as "much too stiff and metrical". Listening to a rough mix of the recording in the car on their way back home, they decided to try again. "We felt that it was a really important song, and we wanted to make sure that we didn't 'lose' it," Björn remembered. They let the song rest for a few days, in the meantime devoting their attention to 'Burning My Bridges' and 'Our Last Summer'.

Four days later, on June 6, Björn and Benny were back in the studio with the musicians for a new attempt at 'The Story Of My Life'. Benny provided the key for the new arrangement when he came up with a "*chanson*-style", descending piano line, loosening up the structure considerably and giving the song a better flow.

As a guide demo for this new arrangement, Björn put down a vocal track with a French nonsense lyric. Someone even suggested that this new song could perhaps be performed by the lyricist himself. "It's a good thing I didn't," he sighed later, much relieved at having avoided such poor judgement. This was clearly a song that called for expert singing by one of the girls.

As was his habit at this stage in Abba's career, Björn went home with a tape of the backing track in order to write the lyrics. "I wanted there to be some kind of ambience in the recording," he recalled, "because then I would get a clearer picture of what the song was 'saying'. There was more pleasure in that than listening to some tape of me and Benny banging away on a piano and acoustic guitar."

The layers of French *chanson* in the arrangement suggested something that called for a touch of the melodramatic: strong feelings about an emotional subject. On this particular night Björn opened a bottle of whisky, and drank freely during the writing process. The alcohol went to his head and fuelled his creativity; it was the quickest lyric he ever wrote and also one of the best.

"I was drunk," he recalled, "and the whole lyric came to me in a rush of emotion in one hour. And that never works. You think it's wonderful at the time but it looks terrible the next day, but that one worked." When he was finished he had come up with the words for 'The Winner Takes It All'.

The lyrics dealt, of course, with the break-up of a relationship, always the subject at which Björn excelled during his years with Abba. He would freely admit that the heartbreak with Agnetha inspired 'The Winner Takes It All', although the words weren't meant to be taken literally. "Neither Agnetha nor I were winners in our divorce," he pointed out.

Nevertheless, the choice of lead vocalist was obvious, and Agnetha put in what unquestionably ranks as her best ever performance on record. Whether or not Agnetha was acting a role when she recorded her lead vocal, as Björn and Benny insist, is anyone's guess. It is naïve to imagine, though, that being in the same room as her ex-husband, with whom she had experienced a painful break-up a mere 18 months previously, didn't in some way affect her interpretation of his words. Tears flowed in the recording studio after Agnetha had recorded her lead vocal, and with good reason.

Agnetha herself called 'The Winner Takes It All' "the best of all Abba songs[.] The lyrics are deeply personal, and the music is unsurpassed. Singing it was like acting a part. I mustn't let my feelings take over. It was quite a while afterwards before I realised that we'd made a small masterpiece."

Indeed. Anyone wanting a lesson in pop song structure, and a near-perfect blend of music, lyrics, arrangement and vocal performance, need look no further than this recording. "As a melody, [it's] the simplest ever," Benny remarked. "There are only two different melody lines in it that are repeated throughout the whole song, and yet I think we managed to avoid a feeling of repetition." This was achieved by making the limited variations work to their advantage, contrasting changes in lyrics and melody against constant changes in the arrangement.

After the short intro, the first verse sets the tone in the present by declaring, "I don't wanna talk/About the things we've gone through," accompanied only by piano and acoustic guitar, playing gently in the background. Then, after the first chorus, the full backing kicks in, as the protagonist moves her story out of the present and begins reminiscing ("I was in your arms/Thinking I belonged there"). An emotional crescendo in the second chorus is followed by a reflective, toned-down third verse – still with bass and drums driving the song – wherein the singer questions the validity of her former lover's new relationship. In the fourth verse, the song is brought back to the present and the tone of the opening declaration, accompanied only by piano and hesitant strings, before creating the most dynamic contrast in the whole piece: the launch of the fully arranged explosion of emotions in the final chorus. Fade-out.

It was here that Abba's collective roots in the emotionalism of European *schlager* music fulfilled its perfect marriage with Anglo-Saxon pop tradition. Two disparate elements hitherto regarded as impossible to combine walked hand in hand as if it was the most natural thing in the world. 'The Winner Takes It All' silenced once and for all any accusations that Abba's music was little more than cold calculation.

It was a song and recording that had truly evolved from the heart, and everyone who ever heard it would sense this for years to come.

On June 18, 'The Winner Takes It All' was completed and mixed. Listening to the seven tracks in the can so far, it was clear to Björn, Benny and Stig that this was the obvious contender for a single. In mid-July Abba visited Marstrand, on the west coast of Sweden, to spend five hours shooting the promo clip for the song. The location was chosen because Lasse Hallström was filming his new movie there.

Björn had brought Lena with him to the location, while Agnetha was accompanied by Dick Håkansson, her new boyfriend. Håkansson was the well-dressed and handsome 34-year-old director of a ladies clothes manufacturer called Dots Design. The pair had met earlier in the year through Benny and Frida, just like Lena and Björn.

Considering the energy Björn has put into stressing how the lyrics for 'The Winner Takes It All' are not meant to be taken as a literal description of the break-up of his marriage to Agnetha, it's surprising that the group went along with Lasse Hallström's concept for the film. The director cast the group members in roles that corresponded fairly closely with their real-life situations. Agnetha, as the lead singer, performed the part of the jilted woman in the film, her face a picture of melancholia, the odd girl out. Meanwhile, Björn laughs and jokes with Benny and Frida, suggesting that he has found happiness after the break-up. Only in the flashback sequences does Agnetha appear to be having just as much fun as the other three.

Hallström even opened the clip with a collage of black and white pictures of Abba – the real group, not the "characters" in the film – which, by his own admission, was an attempt to "create some kind of nostalgic shimmer of memories of times long past". It was Abba themselves, the film was saying, who had once experienced those happier times. The last picture before fading into the colour footage of Agnetha singing the first verse was a shot of Björn out jogging, as if he was running away from his ex-wife. In a poignant coincidence, the promo clip for this song of heartbreak was made only 10 days after the marriage between Björn and Agnetha was finally dissolved in court.

For the general public, who didn't have the time to split hairs about who left whom or under what circumstances, much less whether parts of the lyrics were pure fiction or not, the song and its accompanying visuals left only one possible interpretation. Agnetha was singing about her own pain in splitting from Björn and that's all there was to it.

The lyrics of 'The Winner Takes It All' burst forth from radios and hi-fi systems at the end of a decade which had seen a dramatic rise in divorce rates, the culmination of an accelerating increase since the middle of the century. Mainstream movies such as the 1979 Meryl Streep and Dustin Hoffman vehicle *Kramer vs. Kramer*, highlighted how the issue had become an everyday reality in many parts of the world.

'The Winner Takes It All' – the song as well as the promo clip – struck a familiar chord across the planet. Here was a group, two members of which were divorcees, acting out the psychodrama not only of their own experiences, but of millions of couples across the globe. Agnetha, with her washed-out perm, blue eyeshadow, red blouse and trousers that were far removed from the sexy-bottom pantsuit of yore, looked just like an ordinary woman – indeed, as ordinary as the rest of the group.

Not surprisingly, 'The Winner Takes It All' became one of Abba's biggest worldwide hits, their first number one on the UK charts in two and a half years and the last of the group's three Top 10 hits in the United States.

When the promo clip for 'The Winner Takes It All' was made, Benny and Frida were on a boating holiday along the Swedish coast, making it quite convenient for them to stop over in Marstrand for a day. To the outside world it certainly looked like smooth sailing in the relationship: Benny was calm and steady as ever, Frida had finally found inner peace. "At least one couple in Abba has to be married at all times to keep the fans happy," Björn cracked during the group's US tour the previous year.

Lately, though, Benny and Frida were feeling uneasy about their relationship. There was a growing lack of commitment to their marriage, a feeling that they were staying together out of habit. Their earlier, passionate conflicts had put a special slant on their involvement together. Bosse Norling remembered a row that took place on one of Abba's tours. "Frida got so mad that she scratched Benny on the face. He came in to me and said, 'I can't take this.'" A room at another hotel was arranged for Benny that night, and the morning after everything was fine again. "With a little make-up no one could notice the scratch marks on his face."

Neither of them missed those incidents, but perhaps some of the spark went out of their marriage as they reached this equilibrium. With Frida off on her own self-reflective journey, they began to grow apart, and the passion that had brought them together was slowly ebbing away. "It was a terribly frustrating time," recalled Frida. "We both wanted something else and yet, as members of the group, we had to present a happy, united front to the public. It got to the point where we forced ourselves to go out every evening just because we couldn't stand to be alone at home together." But as yet, neither was prepared to take that final, decisive step out of the relationship.

Meanwhile, Agnetha's relationship with Dick Håkansson had already run its full course. After an article in the tabloid *Aftonbladet*, which hinted that everything wasn't exactly perfect between the two, Polar Music issued a bizarre statement on behalf of the couple. "Not unlike other relationships there are *some* differences between us," they said. "We have decided not to socialise *as intensely* as before, but let time decide how the future will turn out between us."

Apparently, Agnetha wanted to try in every way imaginable to halt speculation in the media regarding her relationships. It was as if she thought co-operation with the gossip press, issuing statements about the finer details of her romances, might put paid to the more wildly inaccurate reports. Either way, the romance between Agnetha and Dick soon died out completely.

After two failed relationships within 18 months of the end of her marriage, Agnetha's role as a singer in Abba seemed to reflect the reality of her life. So far, almost all her solo numbers in the group's oeuvre – those in which the lyrics dealt with collapsing relationships – portrayed her in one way only: as the abandoned woman, lying in a crying heap on the floor, begging her man to come back, unable to deal with the situation. It was inevitable that this image rubbed off on the Agnetha Fältskog who now became the star of a running series in the weekly gossip press. Her repertoire for the remainder of her time with Abba would only serve to strengthen that image.

Agnetha herself denied that her portrayal as a frail, lonely, jilted woman had anything to do with reality. "I see someone in the tabloids that I don't recognise, someone with whom I can't identify," she told author Brita Åhman. "They say that I am weak, but I am strong and down-to-earth. They describe me as some kind of fool, always alone and abandoned. But I have never been abandoned! This distorted picture of me is, ultimately, an unpleasant experience."

For all these strong feelings, it seems Agnetha never really made the connection between the message she conveyed in Abba's songs and promo clips, and the way the media depicted her. Nor was Björn aware of the tendency in his lyrics to portray Agnetha as weak and devastated and Frida as a more resolved woman in charge of her own destiny. "Of course, I always knew when I wrote the lyrics which song Frida would sing and which song Agnetha would sing," he said. "It might be that I thought Agnetha had more of a plaintive quality in her voice, but apart from that, I never consciously adjusted the mood or theme of the lyrics to their respective voices."

By September, the group was back in the studio for the last few recording sessions for the new album. It had already been decided that the LP was to be entitled *Super Trouper*, although no song of that title existed. In the meantime, Rune Söderqvist and photographer Lars Larsson were thinking of ideas for the album cover.

Super trouper was the colloquial term for the gigantic spotlights used in stadium concerts, but for Söderqvist and Larsson the association went more in the direction of a circus environment. From that basic concept grew the idea to take a picture of Abba surrounded by a large group of circus performers. "We knew that we would have quite a high budget for the album cover since a promo film was to be made at the same time," recalled Rune Söderqvist, "and then we had the idea that we should do the photo shoot at Piccadilly Circus in London." The location was chosen for no other reason than the "circus" pun.

Söderqvist flew to London with Thomas Johansson to arrange for the photo shoot, but the pair immediately ran into trouble. To begin with, the authorities feared that the photo shoot would cause chaos. "We said,

'We'll just shoot it at three o'clock in the morning when nobody is there,'" remembered Söderqvist. "My intention was that we would leak the information anyway, because I wanted there to be as many people as possible."

But the whole idea died when they were informed that there was a law against entertainers or animals appearing in central London, designed to discourage publicity stunts in the theatre district. Suggestions to take their chances and go through with the shoot anyway were quickly killed. "The group was very determined not to be mixed up in any scandals, so London was out," said Söderqvist.

A cheaper and more easily manageable alternative was to book the Europa Film Studio in Stockholm and arrange the photo shoot there. On the evening of October 3, members of two circuses assembled at the studios along with several friends and acquaintances of the Abba members. Even this occasion got off to a shaky beginning, however: the two circuses were enemies, causing one of the troupes to storm off the premises.

In the end everything worked out fine. Among the friends appearing in the picture was Görel Hanser (formerly Johnsen, but now married to photographer Anders Hanser, who became a new recruit to the Polar "family" in the process), Berka Bergkvist, Tomas Ledin and Stig Anderson's youngest son, 14-year-old Anders.★ Lasse Hallström also shot "festivity" scenes for the video for the upcoming Abba single. The only problem was that at this point nobody knew what that single was going to be.

Although the album was considered a completed project, just a few days earlier Björn and Benny got a last-minute inclination to come up with one more song for the album: a track they could release as a single, "something that was a cut above the rest," as Björn recalled. The composers succeeded with their mission, and on the day of the photo shoot, they recorded a backing track for this brand new song. When Björn sat down to write the lyrics, he found that the title 'Super Trouper' happened to fit perfectly. However, he remembered it as a bit of a challenge to come up with a complete set of lyrics about "some damned spotlight". The logical solution was to focus the story around a tour experience.

The last overdub on 'Super Trouper' was made on October 14. Three weeks later the new album was available in Swedish record shops, with the UK following on November 21. *Super Trouper* was yet another new step for Abba. If *Voulez-Vous* had seen the group coming of age, but retaining an excitement and tension in their outlook on life, the new album showed

---

★ Berka and Tomas are seen holding hands in the foreground of the sleeve picture.

them as mature and perhaps a little jaded. It was more a matter of perfecting a craft they had now mastered than a joyous journey of discovery.

Where the sparks had seemingly flown from the juxtapositions and contrasts in the arrangements on the previous effort, on *Super Trouper* Abba sounded more homogeneous. The keyboards weren't really battling it out with the guitars anymore; instead Benny's physically and aurally gigantic Yamaha GX-1 synthesizer dominated the soundscape completely on virtually all the tracks.

On some recordings, such as 'Happy New Year', guitarists are credited, but are all but inaudible. In that particular case it made no major difference, but rock attempts in the vein of 'On And On And On', would have benefited from the heightened energy level provided by some prominent electric guitars. Raw rockers had never been Abba's true forte – "I can't think of any rock song of theirs that has turned out any good," said Michael Tretow – and this was even less so during their mature Eighties phase.

'On And On And On' was otherwise notable for its inclusion of some Beach Boys-style falsetto backing vocals, courtesy of Benny and highly reminiscent of those in his heroes' 1968 hit 'Do It Again'. The arrangement caught the attention of the group's lead singer Mike Love, who recorded a lacklustre cover of the song for his 1981 solo album, *Looking Back With Love*.

Although the dominance of Benny's synthesizer layers became a bit tiresome for a whole album, the keyboard work did come into its own on recordings such as 'Lay All Your Love On Me'. This sequencer-driven dance track sounded very much like a blueprint for much of the more inspirational electro music that emerged a few years into the decade.

Björn's maturity as a lyricist was showcased in songs like 'The Winner Takes It All', and the hidden gem, 'Me And I', featuring an Eartha Kitt-inspired lead vocal by Frida, showed a hitherto secluded side of Björn's imagination. Its split-personality theme – "I am to myself what Jekyll must have been to Hyde" – combined with Frida's forceful delivery put a welcome, darker spin on Abba's largely bright and wholesome universe. It was a more literal version of the broodiness that coloured songs like 'SOS' and 'Knowing Me, Knowing You'.

Other lyrical subjects new to Abba included that of fascist threats, as introduced on the medieval-sounding 'The Piper'. The words were inspired by one of the main characters in Stephen King's 1978 novel *The Stand*, a charismatic leader in the Adolf Hitler mould. "The lyrics deal with the fear that there will come a time when people will want such a leader again," Björn explained.

The title track, 'Super Trouper', was released as a single in conjunction with the album, and became a huge hit. The song aligned itself more with Abba's earlier, classic style, showing that despite their aspirations towards maturity and complexity, they hadn't forgotten how to string together a catchy verse and chorus.

The *Super Trouper* album became another huge commercial success for Abba, topping the charts almost everywhere, just like all their albums since *Arrival*. In Great Britain alone it received record-breaking advance orders of 1 million copies. Less than two months after release the worldwide sales were already way past 4 million.

Björn, Benny and Michael Tretow have all singled out the album as the most artistically pleasing in the Abba canon. "It stands up as an album in itself, not only as a collection of songs," Michael said. "Also, from my own point of view, I felt that by this time I had really got a grip on the Polar studio. All the gadgets were in place, and I felt like I was in control of the studio equipment and could get all the sounds I wanted from it."

It was also the first album where Abba were taken seriously by the majority of reviewers. Perhaps it was the more overt maturity in both music and image – the most outrageous costumes had been ditched once and for all – that made it easier to take the group to heart. The honest sentiments conveyed in 'The Winner Takes It All', combined with its knock-out production values, was a turning point for many who had previously dismissed the group as insubstantial fluff. As critic Barry Walters noted many years later, Abba had become "a discofied Fleetwood Mac".

Several strategic promotional ventures for the new album were planned during October and November. On October 21, Abba arrived in Paris for two days of promotion. In November they were scheduled to go to Great Britain and West Germany, where they were going to tape a television special which would also be sold to other interested countries.

Such productions would enable them to cut down drastically on other promotional visits, just as they wished. "A lot of stuff is written about us just because we're members of a world-famous group," said Frida. "Even if it's just an insignificant little piece, there are headlines . . . That's when you pull the brakes and decide that it's time to lay low . . . and that's what we're doing right now." Agnetha and Björn were especially eager to stay at home to support seven-year-old Linda, who had started school in August.★

The itinerary was cut short even more drastically when a kidnap threat was directed at the group. About two weeks into November a tip about

★ Swedish children start school at seven, not five as in the UK.

the threat was received by the producers of the West German television programme *Show Express*, where Abba were scheduled to appear later in the month. An unspecified member would be kidnapped in conjunction with the group's performance and then held hostage for a ransom.

All four members were shocked and frightened. "When that sort of thing becomes a reality it's awful," Björn recalled. "Suddenly it dawns on you that there might be some crazy bastard out there." Everyone in the group was immediately put under police protection and advised to stay in Sweden. The trips to West Germany and Great Britain were quickly cancelled.

However, the production team behind *Show Express* were determined to have Abba on their programme. They simply brought the necessary props to one of the studios of Swedish Television in Stockholm, where Abba performed three songs from the new album: 'The Winner Takes It All', 'Super Trouper' and 'On And On And On'. The whole appearance was broadcast live via a link-up as a 20-minute segment in the West German television show.

The security company guarding the studios had called in extra personnel to protect the four members. Ten policemen watched all entrances to the building, while dogs searched the premises for bombs. The guests at the studio – around 20 of Abba's friends – had to pass through three control stations before they were let into the building. Fortunately, the threat was never executed and the protection of the group was gradually relaxed.

A foreign television crew going to the trouble of a live satellite link-up, just to make sure they had Abba on their show, was irrefutable proof that the group's relatively low profile during the year had not hurt their popularity one bit. It was also a reminder that the challenge of conquering new territories no longer existed – although they kept their promotional trips to a minimum, most countries simply could not get enough of Abba.

As the future would prove, the lack of challenge also curbed their creative inclinations, and, ultimately, sealed the fate of the group.

Chapter 30

When Björn Ulvaeus married Lena Källersjö on January 5, 1981, the circumstances couldn't have been more different from when he married Agnetha. The ceremony – a top secret double wedding with Björn's sister Eva and her boyfriend Leif Asterhag – took place in a 17th century church in a small village called Grythyttan. There were only 12 guests at the wedding: the couples' parents and siblings, and young Linda Ulvaeus – not even Stig Anderson had been informed beforehand. After the ceremony, the small entourage retreated for dinner at a nearby luxury restaurant. Discretion and exclusivity were the keywords.

Three weeks later, on January 25, the celebratory mood continued when Stig turned 50 and threw a lavish party. To mark the occasion, Björn and Benny wrote the tune for a song called 'Hovas Vittne' ('Hova's Witness', a pun on his place of birth) as a special gift for him.

The affectionately sarcastic lyrics, penned by the four Abba members, Michael Tretow and Rune Söderqvist, referred to all sorts of quaint characteristics exhibited by Stig. One example was his habit of switching on a vacuum cleaner when he decided it was time for his parties to end. "When he got tired of his guests – no matter who it was – he would bring out the vacuum cleaner and announce loudly: 'The taxi cabs are here!' Because he had called for cabs as well," recalled Rune Söderqvist. "Of course, it was a bit embarrassing to stay then."

The record was pressed on 200 red vinyl copies only, and featured an instrumental version of Stig's first hit, 'Tivedshambo', on the B-side.[*] Also, on the day before Stig's birthday, a special video, featuring Abba wearing their 1974 'Waterloo' costumes and singing 'Hovas Vittne', was made.

Stig's birthday party was held at his magnificent mansion in Stockholm, and was attended by dozens of friends and acquaintances. As a prank, Stig was given the publishing contract for 'Hovas vittne' in the course of the

---

[*] This was the second of Abba's two exclusive birthday records. The first was a one-sided 12-inch single called 'Sång till Görel' ('Song For Görel'), made for the 30th birthday of Görel Hanser in 1979. Both records are among the most valuable Abba items on the collectors' market.

437

evening, but it came attached with a condition. If the song was ever recorded by anyone else, the original lyrics must be kept intact.

'Hovas vittne' was a highly melodic tune and certainly no throwaway: even when a song was written to be heard only on one isolated occasion, Björn and Benny couldn't help being catchy. Stig, ever the music publisher, later complained – only half-jokingly – that it was a shame that such a strong melody should be doomed to obscurity.

A few weeks after this happy occasion, Abba-related news of a very different kind hit the newspapers. On February 12, large, black headlines announced that Benny and Frida were getting divorced. It was as surprising as it was shocking, not least because Frida had only recently been asked in an interview whether it was hard to both work and live with Benny. "Since I've both worked and lived with him almost from the beginning, for almost 13 years, it would feel very strange *not* to work and live together with him," was her reply. The reality conveyed a completely different message.

It was Benny who finally broke the stalemate in their relationship, falling for a 37-year-old television reporter called Mona Nörklit. It wasn't as if Mona had suddenly appeared from nowhere: she was the sister of Lillebil Ankarcrona, Rune Söderqvist's common-law wife. Lillebil and Rune were, of course, close friends of Benny and Frida.

Reportedly, it was at Lillebil's 40th birthday party in the autumn of 1980 that things clicked between Mona and Benny. A brunette with a mixture of gentleness and determination in her features, Mona was not far removed from Frida in general appearance. Like Benny, she was already a parent, with a 12-year-old son from a previous marriage.

Frida and Benny's decision to go their separate ways hadn't been made out of the blue, however. Along the way they had visited a marriage counsellor to try to sort out their problems, and as late as November they bought a new summer residence together. But as Benny's feelings for Mona became stronger, his situation with Frida became unfeasible. What they had once shared was now dead.

Something in Frida's observation about living and working together for 13 years hinted at a reason why their love had died. Benny and Frida had always believed their working relationship was an asset to their private life, stressing the positive aspect of sharing life with someone who understood about the music business. But their rapport was evidently linked too closely to their career, and when some of the spark went out of Abba as a group, a spark disappeared from their relationship. "I don't know exactly what went wrong," Frida reflected later. "Maybe it was the strain of working together, living together, never having time for our private life.

We were never able to sit down as two individuals and decide what we wanted from our lives. It was a mixture of everything . . . Abba took a great part of our lives." Benny later echoed Björn and Agnetha's sentiments, observing that if it hadn't been for the group, the marriage would have ended sooner.

Just as their wedding had been far more low-key than Agnetha and Björn's, so Benny and Frida kept their initial comments on the break-up to a minimum. Instead of inviting a trusted reporter to an interview, as their colleagues had done, they simply issued a short statement. "The decision has been made after careful consideration and on the best of terms," they said. "We're aware that there will be a lot of speculation in the media but we'll have to take that. Our private life is our own business and no one else has anything to do with that. This step doesn't affect Abba's continued collaboration in any way, but is of a strictly private nature. We don't wish to make any further comments."

The breakdown of his relationship with Frida was sad and distressing for Benny, but the gap was bridged quite smoothly when he met Mona. Once he had broken the news to his wife that he was in love with another woman – and the two had reached an agreement on how to handle the situation – Benny continued unfazed on his life's journey, typically content and unruffled. "Wouldn't you feel good if you were me? I'm sure you would," he told a reporter shortly before the split. "You know what I like: to write and play music . . . If you get the opportunity to do exactly what you want, chances that you will feel good are greater than if you're doing what someone else wants you to do."

For Frida, always less secure in herself than Benny, the situation was quite different. She kept up a brave face in the statement that she and Benny issued, but inside she was in turmoil. The confidence she had developed dissolved around her as her whole life was turned upside down yet again.

The reality of what had happened and the consequences it would have for her as a celebrity hit her on the very day that the news broke in the press. Frida was about to step into her local supermarket to buy some milk when she saw the placards outside with the picture of her and Benny alongside the word "divorce". She couldn't face going in to the store, and returned home instead. "I didn't go out for a week – I couldn't take it," she recalled.

Benny moved out of the grand Lidingö villa, and by March he was living with Mona in an apartment in central Stockholm. As Frida watched Benny leave, the pain was unbearable. "When you realise that he's walking out the door for the last time, then it hurts," she said a while later. "Then you get scared: will I be able to deal with my life? There are so many things that you have to handle. Everything from mundane matters to the most intimate physical and psychological needs."

Frida, for whom life seemed to present nothing but challenge, faced yet another psychological trial.

When the divorce was announced, Björn and Benny had just begun songwriting sessions for the next Abba album. They also hoped to come up with at least one song that could be released as a single later in the spring. By mid-March they were ready to go into the studio to record three new titles. The least significant of these songs was 'Two For The Price Of One', sung by Björn, with lyrics that told the bizarre story of a man answering an ad in the personal columns, placed by a girl – and her mother.

The two other titles were more personal. The relentless drive of 'When All Is Said And Done' made it one of the stand-out tracks on the upcoming album, and was directly related to recent occurrences in the group. "I was a bit cautious because of the lyrics," Björn recalled. "Frida and Benny had just got divorced, and that's what the song dealt with, more or less."

Frida had no objections. On the contrary, for her it was a cathartic experience to express all the regret and sadness she felt. From the sound of her vocals, Frida was truly vibrating with pent-up emotion as her performance was committed to tape. The song was a fairly accurate description of what had happened: much as Benny and Frida would have wished for a different turn of events, their love had died and their relationship along with it. Faced with such a situation there is nothing else to do but to deal with it and move on.

'When All Is Said And Done' would have made an excellent spring single for Abba but, unfortunately, it was one of those tracks that took quite some time to get right. Many overdubs were added and subtracted before the song reached its final state in late autumn.

The other standout track from these first sessions was the ballad 'Slipping Through My Fingers', which perhaps offered the most obvious glimpse of Abba's private lives. With lyrics by Björn and a lead vocal by Agnetha, the song dealt with their mixed feelings at seeing their daughter Linda grow up. Agnetha singled it out as the track on the album she had enjoyed recording the most, saying that it "felt very 'true' to do".

"I can remember the exact moment when I got hit by the fact which formed the basis for the lyrics," Björn recalled. "I was watching Linda going away to school, turning around and waving, and I thought 'now she has taken that step, she's going away – what have I missed out on through all these years?', which is a feeling I think every parent has."

Of Linda's parents, perhaps the song had the strongest significance for Björn. While Agnetha had made a conscious effort to stay at home with the children, he had devoted more time to his Abba career: long songwriting periods, round-the-clock sessions in the studio, business appointments, lyric writing, all those interviews that the other members of the group shunned. "Along the way I did not take care of those moments that I should have taken care of," he admitted.

After basic work on the first three tracks for the album had been completed in mid-April, it seemed that the further changes in the group's interpersonal relationships were unlikely to affect their work in any serious way. On the contrary: the advantages of being two couples, and the perfect understanding they each had of their partner's situation in life, brought with them a detrimental corollary in that there was too little distance between them all as songwriters, producers and singers. "When the fuss died down it was actually a relief that we no longer had to keep up any pretence," said Frida. "Once you're not involved emotionally it is much easier to work together. It becomes easier to concentrate. Everything is more efficient, because there is none of the blah-blah-blah – you just do your job and then go home. You don't get on each other's nerves when you don't see each other all the time."

Before long Frida had also found a new partner. Her new man came from her circle of friends: 38-year-old businessman Bertil "Bobo" Hjert who'd become a billionaire through his company Scandecor, which specialised in producing posters, the largest such business in the world. When he decided to finance a brand new fashion magazine called *Clic* in the spring of 1981, the editorial staff was a virtual who's who of Frida's friends. She posed on the cover and wrote a report on a trip to the island of Eleuthera in the Atlantic Ocean.

However, she was adamant about not letting the media know that Bobo Hjert was her new boyfriend. "I've learned from my mistakes in the past," she said. "I don't want my new man facing all the publicity and the questions and that's why I'm keeping his name a secret . . . I realise now that it's important to develop interests outside show business."

Frida visited Eleuthera in April, and on her return to Sweden Abba turned their attention to a television special, taped at the end of the month. The special was originally meant to be a 10-year retrospective of the group's career, mixing old videos with new material, but somewhere along the way that format was ditched. Instead, American talk show host Dick Cavett was brought over to Sweden to conduct an informal interview with the four members, which was followed by a nine-song live concert. Again, the idea was to produce a special that could be shown in as many countries as possible and, with the live performance, curb any demand for tours.

In the event, *Dick Cavett Meets ABBA* turned out to be a pretty lack-lustre show. There seemed to be no real affinity between Cavett and the four group members, and the tone of the conversation remained on a fairly trivial level. "Damn it, I forgot to ask about the divorces," Cavett said jokingly after the taping.

Swedish television producer Gunilla Nilars was not impressed. "This was more toothless than necessary," she noted sternly. "We don't learn anything about Abba that we didn't know already." Even the members themselves felt they were let off the hook too easily. "[The interview] was much too mediocre," said Frida. "Dick was too mild on us." Nor was the ensuing live performance an especially exciting experience. Visually it was static, as the members remained fixed in their positions, and musically it was flat and uninspired for the most part.

Songwriting and recording sessions for the new album resumed through-out May and early June before the group took a summer break, the first for more than a decade that all four members would spend apart. Frida and Agnetha retreated to their new summer-houses, holidaying with their children and friends.

On the surface, Frida's relationship with Bobo Hjert seemed to be perfect for her. "I'm together with a man I love and it's a free relationship, free of demands, and that's the way I like it," she said bravely. But although she enjoyed the male companionship Bobo offered, in reality Frida wasn't feeling especially good about herself. Finding a new life after security had been snatched away once again was tough going. As usual, her solution when faced with a crisis was to charge ahead, accepting new challenges, tearing up much of her old life by the roots.

In August, she accepted an offer to co-host a television series together with Claes af Geijerstam. Apart from his occasional duties as Abba's live sound engineer, af Geijerstam was mostly known in Sweden as a popular DJ and radio personality. The four part series *Lite Grand i örat** had a simple but attractive concept: let some of Sweden's most popular artists perform their own material and a bunch of cover versions in an unpreten-tious atmosphere. Frida herself performed one solo number, a version of Pat Benatar's 'Fire And Ice', as well as a duet with singer Tommy Körberg on Earth Wind & Fire's 'After The Love Has Gone'.

---

* A play on words – the show was taped at the Grand Hotel – loosely translated as *A Little Something For The Ear.*

Chapter 30

Unfortunately, *Lite Grand i örat* wasn't a very enjoyable production. Self-indulgent, with desperately unfunny skits and lame jokes serving as artist introductions, it was uninspired variety show television. Nevertheless, the series offered a gentle reminder of Frida's modesty in contrast to her status, a trait she shared with all the Abba members, at least in their own country. Frida may have been an international star, selling zillions of records all over the planet, but she wasn't above pitching in with back-up vocals for several of the artists in the show. It was a far cry from the Vegas-style, hierarchic production environment which would probably have characterised an American counterpart to the series.

By early September, Abba were back in the studio, recording the new album. The group hoped to have it out before the end of the year, but the time when they would kill themselves to meet an imposed deadline was long since gone.

"When we have got ten new songs together that we are satisfied with, we will release an album," said Benny. "I guess all the record companies will be very happy if we [have the album ready by Christmas], but what really matters is that we are satisfied with what's on it, so we can't tell when it's going to be released until we know it's good enough. There is a possible chance that we will have it out by late November. That is possible but I wouldn't bet on it."

In the spring the Polar studio had acquired a new 32-track digital tape recorder, replacing the 24-track analogue tape machine that Abba had used for the past five years. For Michael Tretow, who felt that he was finally in total control of the studio when *Super Trouper* was recorded, adjusting to digital recording was almost like beginning everything all over again. The digital tape recorder would cut off all sounds very sharply, leaving little in the way of lingering notes or delay. This gave the recordings a very dry and cold sound, so Michael worked on ways to outsmart the digital "perfection".

On the present album he was only half-successful in his endeavours. The contrast was especially evident in a recording like 'Head Over Heels' – one of the new songs made in the autumn – where the gap between the song's ostensibly joyful tone and the cold sound made for a curious listening experience. The song was like a refrigerated version of the spirit of 'Bang-A-Boomerang' or 'Take A Chance On Me'.

Simply blaming unfamiliarity with digital recording techniques is too easy, however: there was something inherently wrong with the conception and arrangement of the song. Björn and Benny's search for musical perfection and complete control seemed to lead them up the wrong path for much of the new album. Also, the rather trite theme of the lyrics – about a shopping-crazy and party-mad high-society woman rushing through life to the consternation of her exasperated husband – probably had a distancing effect on the listener. This "droll" description of life for the privileged classes – an extension of a theme introduced in the previous album's 'On And On And On' – jarred with Abba's penchant for tapping into the joys, hopes and fears of "everyday people". "I do write about things I have experienced myself," Björn admitted. "It's inevitable that we retreat from an 'ordinary' life."

When the song was released as the second single from the album in the spring of 1982, the public was mostly unmoved. It was Abba's least successful single since 'So Long', and was the first to peak outside the Top 10 on the UK charts since 'I Do, I Do, I Do, I Do, I Do'.

Sessions for the new LP, now entitled *The Visitors*, were concluded by mid-November after all, and it was released in Sweden at the end of the month. There were probably sighs of relief all round when work on this album was concluded – Benny would later remember the recording period as one long "uphill struggle". Despite numerous claims that the members were all getting on just fine during recording sessions, there have been just as many suggestions that something wasn't as it should be with Abba as a musical entity.

"It could be frosty [in the studio] sometimes," Björn acknowledged. "[After the divorces] it was getting harder to say, Please do that again [without hearing] 'No, I don't want to!'" Working in the studio as Abba had turned into a double-edged sword for the group. On the one hand, the separations had relieved them of many unwanted conflicts, and their professionalism and love for music made it possible for them to go on almost as before. At the same time, the divorces and the diverging ambitions within the group had robbed Abba of their *raison d'être*.

"When you've gone through a separation, like all of us had done at that time, it puts a certain mood on the work," Frida elaborated retrospectively. "Something disappeared that was so fundamental for the joy in our songs, that had always been there before. Even if the song itself was downbeat, there was always a joy somewhere.

"But on *The Visitors* I believe we were all a bit tired of each other. We had already gone through so much together that there was no joy left. The recording became more of a routine experience. We had grown apart and began developing in different directions and the unity that had always been a part of our recordings was gone. I don't know – perhaps there was a bit of sadness or bitterness that coloured the making of that album."

It certainly was a barren LP, made even more so when, for the first time on an Abba album, Frida and Agnetha didn't sing in unison in the verses on any of the songs. It was Björn who insisted on this. "The lyrics had suddenly become more real to me," he said. "I could 'hear' what they were singing, whereas in the early days that hadn't mattered as much. To have two voices singing this kind of lyrics would have been completely unnatural."

The arrangements on many of the songs seemed more downscaled than was usual for Abba – it was as if they reverted to the aesthetics of the *Ring Ring* days, albeit in a more sophisticated version. This was in accordance with Benny's new and ongoing philosophy: that the songs and the performances in themselves should convey the emotion and not be drowned in a wall of sound. He was more hesitant about the wisdom of letting every single track become a solo statement. "I didn't think that was such a good idea," he recalled, "although I understand Björn's point of view as lyricist, that it becomes more personal. But when the sound of Frida and Agnetha together disappears it becomes a bit more 'ordinary'."

The Visitors was a sort of cold war album for Abba, in both a literal and figurative sense. It was marked by a cold sound, and what little heat it had to offer came in the shape of the masterful 'When All Is Said And Done', where Frida's heartfelt vocal performance was successfully married with maturity and razor-sharp lyrics, in much the same way as 'The Winner Takes It All'.

The more literal cold war connotations were to be found in the heavy waltz 'Soldiers', as well as the title track. 'The Visitors' featured a raga-flavoured melody in the verses against a backdrop of synth-rock, with lyrics dealing with the dangerous situation for dissidents in the Soviet Union of that time. "I was trying to imagine what it must feel like to sit and wait for that ominous knock on the door," recalled Björn, "never knowing when it would come, and never being able to be sure of anything." Quite possibly the lyrics were also a reaction to the slightly uniform way of life in Sweden at this time, as perceived by people of Björn's liberal right-wing persuasion. "I had a constant feeling that others, the invisible powers that be, made the decisions over my head," he remembered.

Rune Söderqvist, as usual, put a slightly different slant on his interpretation of the "visitors" concept when he conceived the album sleeve. "I knew that it was going to be called *The Visitors*," he recalled, "and for me those 'visitors' could very well be angels. I knew that the painter Julius Kronberg had painted a lot of angels in his time, so I located his studio – at the Skansen park – which contained several of his paintings." Söderqvist has also mentioned the title of the album's desolate closing track, 'Like An

Angel Passing Through My Room', as an inspiration for this celestial theme.

The sleeve picture was shot in November, when the unheated studio was ice-cold. The atmosphere during the photo session wasn't very much warmer. In all previous Abba sleeves, the group had been photographed as a close unit, but the cover for *The Visitors* depicted the four sitting and standing in the semi-darkness of the studio, with a marked distance between them. "The relationship within the group wasn't very hearty at the time," Rune confirmed. "Without anyone of us being aware of it, it looks like they're living in separate worlds on the sleeve."

Many observers outside the group, as well as those working closely with them, were starting to wonder if this might in fact be the last Abba record. "You had the feeling that 'this won't last very much longer'," recalls Berka Bergkvist. "I remember talking with Björn about it, and he said, 'We might not go on working with this forever. We've emptied ourselves of everything we've got to give.' "

The first single to be released off *The Visitors* was 'One Of Us'. With its "love-affair-gone-sour" theme as performed by Agnetha, and the poppy melody, it was a fairly safe bet as a single and didn't give too many clues as to the band's new direction. When the decision was made about which single to release first, Benny and Stig were both doubtful, and only Björn was completely in favour of it.

For a number of years, Abba had used a small reference group of record company personnel around the world – in countries such as the United States, Great Britain and The Netherlands – for listening to the album tracks before release and giving advice on which would be the best singles. Although Björn, Benny and Stig made the final decision, it was mostly the track receiving the most votes that ended up as the single. In this case, 'One Of Us' was the favourite for most of the record companies, which led to the song's release in seven-inch format.

In the ever-loyal West Germany, Belgium and The Netherlands, this choice proved to be spot on when the song topped the charts. In the UK, 'One Of Us' reached number three on the chart accepted by the record industry, although it hit number one on some less heavyweight charts. 'One Of Us' was Abba's last major worldwide single success.

As an album, *The Visitors* reached the top of the charts in a fair number of territories, but it wasn't the overwhelming success that previous albums had been: indeed, *Super Trouper*, the most recent, was one of their all-time best-sellers. *The Visitors* also irrevocably crushed the myth of Australia as an eternally loyal stronghold for Abba, becoming their first LP to peak outside the Top 20.

The joy that exuded from 'Mamma Mia', the audiovisual experience that gave Abba their breakthrough in Australia, was nowhere to be seen on *The Visitors*. The few smiles the album had to offer came in the shape of the frozen grin of 'Head Over Heels' and the cleverness of 'Two For The Price Of One'. The message from record-buyers was clear: they just didn't want any excessive bleakness or maturity on their Abba albums.

Chapter 31

As 1981 neared its end, much was changing for Abba and those around them. Benny and Frida's divorce had shattered the last vestiges of the "Polar family", with Stig and Abba at the centre and their friends and associates making up a close inner circle. The symbolic change in atmosphere could be traced to the difference between the festive together-ness depicted on the *Super Trouper* cover and the dark isolation on *The Visitors*.

"Around the time of Benny and Frida's split, Rune Söderqvist and Lillebil also broke up," recalls Berka. "Everyone in this gang went their separate ways. I had also been in a long relationship that ended at the same time. The pieces fell apart, and it was actually quite tragic. Everything just ended – bang! – like that."

In November, Polar Music moved out of the building at Baldersgatan – the scene of so many dramatic and exciting events during Abba's story – and into offices on the more centrally located Hamngatan. The building had been bought by Stig and the four Abba members 18 months earlier and was as much an investment as a way to create more space for the 35 staff working for the growing company.

While Abba were struggling with the ups and downs of their relation-ships in the midst of difficult album sessions, Polar Music International and its affiliated companies were out on their parallel trek, with Stig at the helm in as far as he was able to control matters. With the business expand-ing, not least the real estate side, several industrial heavyweights were elected to the company's board of directors. A turning point had been the purchase of 87 per cent of the shares in the real estate company Stockholms Badhus in June 1980. Soon afterwards, all the real estate owned by Polar had been transferred to this company.

It was thought that with influential and experienced businessmen along for the ride, it would be easier to further boost the company's credibility and help Stockholms Badhus get listed on the stock exchange. The attrac-tion of a listing was obviously not because an influx of money was needed at the moment – the most common reason for such an action – but to ensure the exportation of capital in the long run. Also, most importantly, it was a way of freeing substantial amounts of cash for the owners: the Abba members and Stig Anderson.

When real estate mogul Birger Gustavsson – said to be Sweden's richest man at the time – joined the board in January 1981, the value of the Stockholms Badhus shares rose from 175 kronor (£17.50) to 280 kronor (£28). A week later the value of the shares rose to 400 kronor (£40) – when Polar bought the company the value had been a mere 85 kronor (£8.50). Stockholms Badhus became a listed company at the end of 1981, with Polar's highly profitable leasing company Invest Finans Infina following the year after.

The recent restructuring of the Polar group of companies was supposed to make the whole set-up easier to control and clearly separate the different lines of business activity from each other. However, the profits were escalating in a way that was virtually impossible to control. For the financial year of May 1, 1981 to April 30, 1982, the profit for Polar Music International and all its affiliated businesses was 100 million kronor (£9 million): it was more than double the profit just five years earlier.

The media interest in the business aspects of the Abba/Polar set-up had always been just as great as their inclination to report on the group's career as pop stars. The lower the profile of Abba as a music-making unit – and the more they moved away from their old pin-up friendly glam image into their wealthy thirtysomethings – the more the media focus shifted towards their role as "investors".

The release of *The Visitors* in November 1981 was a perfect example of how withdrawn the pop-star side of Abba had become. For the first time, the group made absolutely no promotional trips or related concert tours in support of the new LP. Instead, a press conference for the international media was held in Stockholm and teams from various television companies around the world were dispatched to do interviews on location. That was it.

The family roles and living arrangements within the group were also undergoing drastic changes at this time. "Linda wants to be with Björn right now," Agnetha said in an interview in the spring. "I can understand that she thinks it's more fun over at his place: there are two grown-ups there . . . When I was going out one night, Linda said: 'I wish you'd meet your Prince Charming tonight.' I guess she feels it's a bit lonely at my place."

When Agnetha's romance with 38-year-old police inspector Torbjörn Brander broke in the press at the end of September, it seemed she might have found the dream man Linda was wishing for. The couple had met at the police station in Lidingö. It all started when a crazed fan was banging on Agnetha's door at 3.30 in the morning. When the same man appeared outside the Polar studio a few days later, Agnetha was scared and reported the incident to the police.

The tall and responsible-looking Torbjörn Brander was the inspector in charge of the case. Meeting him, Agnetha said, was love at first sight. Brander moved into her house during 1981: the story fitted nicely with the mythical picture of Agnetha as a helpless woman in constant need of protection.

Similarly, the framework of Benny's social situation was subject to several symbolic changes at the end of the year. On November 26, his divorce from Frida was finalised. A week later, on December 3, Mona and Benny got married in a simple ceremony. Furthermore, Mona was pregnant and expecting a baby in mid-February. It was the same with Björn and Lena whose first child was expected around Christmas. In December, they finally moved out of Björn and Agnetha's old house and into a new villa in Lidingö.

Coincidentally, neither Björn nor Benny's child was born at the expected time. Lena went a week over time and the Ulvaeus couple's first daughter, Emma, was born on January 3, 1982. Benny and Mona's son, Ludvig, was born four weeks early, on January 10. Both Björn and Benny were determined to give ample time to their children, and the first few months of the year were mostly devoted to their new families.

Everyone in the Abba organisation had known for a long while that Andersson/Ulvaeus would be unavailable once their babies arrived, so in the summer of 1981, Frida began contemplating a solo album. It was inspired by her need to rediscover herself but was also an effort to launch her second career as a solo singer at a time when the future of Abba started to look slightly shaky. The late autumn had seen her emerging with a completely new hairstyle, a sort of high-society version of a punk look, which the general public was first confronted with on the cover of Abba's *The Visitors* album.

The decision with whom and under what circumstances she would produce her solo album had also been made in the summer, when she was spending time at her country house and discovered Phil Collins' 1981 solo album, *Face Value*. 'In The Air Tonight', the first hit single off the album, was brought to Frida's attention by her daughter Lise-Lotte. The song and recording "sounded more fresh than anything I'd heard for a very long time," she said.

The divorce theme that ran through many songs on Collins' album also struck a chord with Frida, and she played the album over and over again for months. The Genesis drummer emerged as the only viable choice of producer. Phil Collins recalled his first meeting with Frida in England: "She said, 'I love what you do and I think you'd be sympathetic to what I want to do, because I'm just in the process of going through a divorce.'"

One and a half months of sessions were booked at Polar Music Studios, kicking off on February 15, 1982. On the first day of recording, Frida was a bundle of nerves. All the old self-doubt crept up on her: was she good enough to face up to this challenge? Would she be able to cut it outside the security of the Abba environment?

The musical meeting between Frida and Phil Collins got off to a cautious start. After the first studio session, Frida was reportedly so sick with nerves that she had to stay at home for a day. Everything, except the studio, was a new experience for her: a new producer who had brought his own musicians and engineer, and everyone was speaking English, which made communication just a little more difficult. On top of this, the producer was constantly drinking whisky, a marked difference to Abba's clean-living working methods. However, to Frida's astonishment, there were never any signs that Collins was drunk or that it affected his work.

Initially, she found it hard to suddenly have to make so many decisions. Frida, used to being an instrument carrying out Björn and Benny's visions, almost drove Phil Collins crazy with her insecurity when he tried to make her a more active participant in the process. "The first week she was, 'I don't know, what do *you* think?' but I said, 'Listen, it's your album, baby, it's not mine.' And after two or three weeks, she really started to come through."

Although the album was a superstar "priority" project and the company certainly didn't want for money, according to true Polar philosophy the sessions had a fixed budget which was not to be exceeded. Nevertheless, Collins and his entourage still got a taste of the rich man's world, Frida style. One day when they wanted to go for a sauna Frida recommended Sturebadet, an exclusive bath house in central Stockholm. When Collins protested that they weren't members, Frida replied, "That's OK – I own it." This was in fact the bath house that gave its name to Stockholms Badhus ('Stockholm's Bath House').

Song selection had been a tricky process. A couple of months before the sessions started, Frida listened to hundreds of tapes without finding much that took her fancy. Phil Collins remembered how hard it was to agree on songs they both liked: submissions from British songwriters like Chris Difford and Glen Tillbrook of Squeeze, Joe Jackson, Elvis Costello and Phil Lynott of Thin Lizzy were all rejected.

Nor did the album's duet between Frida and Collins elicit fond memories in the producer. 'Here We'll Stay' was a failed entry to the 1980 edition of *A Song For Europe*, the UK selection for the Eurovision Song Contest. Collins called their joint performance "a complete lapse of taste on my part! I think it's hideous too!"

The producer had offered to sing on the album, and while he was coaching Frida for the 'Here We'll Stay' lead vocal he was coaxed into doing this particular song as a duet. Collins soon realised that the key of the song was actually too low for Frida and too high for himself and regretted his decision. But now he was committed to it, so he went along with the recording.

However, when the track was to be released as the third single off the album in the spring of 1983, Collins put his foot down. "I said, 'No way! I don't wanna be associated with this as a single.' We used the record company excuse that Atlantic, Virgin and Charisma [Collins' various labels around the world] would cause a fuss because it was my voice." The solution was for Frida to re-record the vocals as a solo performance, but on release the single sank without a trace. A shame, for it was, in fact, one of the better songs on the album, with a lively backing track and a spirited contribution from the Earth Wind & Fire horn section.

Otherwise, much of the album sounded like a fairly uneasy meeting between Phil Collins' drum-based aesthetics and Frida's attempt to rock out in the vein of American singer Pat Benatar, one of her role models at the time. The style didn't suit her very well, and it was on the more relaxed tracks – such as Collins' songwriting contribution, the bitter divorce ballad 'You Know What I Mean' – that she really came into her own.

Despite the problems, Frida came out of the experience in one piece and was proud of the album. Entitled *Something's Going On*, it was released in September 1982, preceded by the single, 'I Know There's Something Going On'. Stig Anderson claimed he couldn't hear any singles when they all listened through the album at his home, but this first release was an impressive Top 15 hit in the US. The album peaked at number one in Sweden, also reaching the UK Top 20, and ended up selling 1.5 million copies worldwide.

Björn and Benny had been asked to contribute to the album, but found it difficult to come up with something that would suit a Phil Collins-produced Frida album. Towards the end of the album sessions they made a demo of a potential contender, but it was never attempted by Collins and Frida. It's likely that a song from the hit pens of Andersson/Ulvaeus was Stig's idea rather than Frida's. A Björn and Benny tune was likely to guarantee a strong hit on the album, which in turn would generate greater sales. Afterwards Frida professed to be relieved that no song of theirs was included – this was *her* album, not an Abba project.

However, during the making of the album she also experienced the reverse problem with one of the songs she really wanted to record. Stig's old adversary, Mikael Wiehe, who'd gone on to a rewarding solo career after his time with the Hoola Bandoola Band, had recently enjoyed popularity with an atmospheric, synth-driven song called 'Flickan och kråkan' ('The Girl And The Crow'). Frida liked the track and asked for permission to have it translated into English and to record it for the album.

For Wiehe the matter had political implications. In the spring of 1979 Frida had participated in a high-profile advertising campaign for the Swedish Employers' Confederation, published in newspapers, magazines and pamphlets. Under the slogan "Put your faith in yourself", various successful, youth-oriented role models posed for the camera and told their life's story in condensed form. The moral of the stories was that it was possible to get ahead for those who really applied themselves, and that the youth of today needed to pull themselves out of their supposed lethargy.

The message of the campaign was highly controversial for many at the time, not least those youths who were unable to get a job. Perhaps even more importantly, in the collective-minded atmosphere of the Seventies, the philosophy of putting yourself first promoted a blatant egoism that definitely wasn't *comme il faut*.

For her part, Frida was very honest about her liberal right-wing sympathies and belief in the driving force of the individual. Certainly, her own life-experience had taught her that collective entities – such as the people of Ballangen or her schoolmates in Torshälla – were not something you could rely on for comfort and security. It was from the basis of smaller units – a dance band, for example, or the closest of your friends: the "families" you created yourself – you could reach your goals. And even then those units could be snatched away from you in a flash, leaving no one to turn to except yourself.

Mikael Wiehe hesitated for a long time: he had got it into his head that there was a chance that his musical hero, Paul McCartney, would hear the song if it was included on an international release like the Frida album. He gave a preliminary go-ahead to the recording, even supervising lyricist Fred Lane's work on the English translation.

In the end, the thought of Frida recording his song – an artist whose view of life seemed so far removed from his own – and releasing it on Polar, which had caused him so much harm ten years earlier, was too hard to swallow. The day before the scheduled recording session, Wiehe finally said no. "I respect his position, but I also feel it's sad when politics come before music," said Frida. "Especially when these are the consequences, for 'Flickan och kråkan' is wonderful poetry."

It was rare that Abba openly declared their views or took sides in current issues, but a few weeks before the *Something's Going On* sessions started, they were involved in a political controversy of their own. In the process, the group almost managed to fall out of favour with both of the world's superpowers at the same time.

On December 13, 1981, the Soviet-supported General Wojciech Jaruzelski declared martial law in Poland in an effort to crush the Solidarity movement and restore economic stability in the country. A few weeks into the new year, the American government put together a television gala called *Let Poland Be Poland* in support of Solidarity and the Polish people. The gala would be broadcast for free in those countries that wished to air it.

Abba were asked to appear at the gala, and although they didn't have time to go over to the USA, Björn and Benny taped a message on video and sent over their promo clip for 'When All Is Said And Done', the first US single from *The Visitors*. Although the Swedish population sympathised deeply with the Polish people, it was a controversial decision for Abba to take part in an America-funded gala which would even include an appearance by then President Ronald Reagan.

To mark their independence, Björn and Benny decided to include a few words in their statement about other nations where human rights had been violated. "There are many other countries in the world – for example, Chile, El Salvador, Afghanistan and Iran – where people are not able to express themselves openly and freely like we're doing now," a serious-looking Benny said on the video tape.

The Abba segment was duly dispatched to the producers of the show but pulled from the broadcast at the last minute. Although those responsible claimed this was because broadcasting time had been miscalculated, many thought that it was the references to the US-supported dictatorships in Chile and El Salvador that caused Abba's appearance to be removed from the show.

Before the broadcast, there had also been some critical voices raised in the Soviet papers about the show and Abba's participation in it. But the whole situation died down once Abba's segment was pulled. However, *ABBA – The Movie*, which had recently opened in Moscow, quietly disappeared from theatres in the Soviet capital during the course of the year.

This incident was but one of many occurrences that marked 1982 as a highly unusual year for Abba. The actions they took, the decisions they made, the moments when they suddenly reversed those decisions – it was all very far removed from their usual structured *modus operandi*.

The month of May saw Björn and Benny go back into the studio to begin recording a new Abba album. Initially, there had been quite elaborate plans for a double album with one disc being made in the studio and the other consisting of the cream of recordings from five or six live concerts at an unspecified venue somewhere in Europe. The live album part of the project was ditched along the way – "a bloody stupid idea", was Björn's retrospective comment – and the decision was made to simply make a new studio album.

But something was still not right. Even at the songwriting stage things seemed more uphill than ever for Björn and Benny. It was as if their energy had now run out completely. When they finally came up with a few songs, they found that the recording sessions were also marked by a strong lack of motivation. It was clear to all that the problems experienced during the making of *The Visitors* were more than a temporary setback.

"Even when everything is working great, you have these 'down' moments every now and again, so at first you don't take it as a sign that you're getting tired of the whole thing," Björn reflected later. "It's only after a while that you notice that every time you go into the studio, it gets harder and harder."

Three tracks came out of the sessions, but almost immediately after they had been completed, the group decided to cancel plans for an album in 1982. Abba needed to let themselves off the hook for a while if they were to regain the inclination to go on as a group. Two of the three completed tracks – 'Just Like That' and 'I Am The City' – were held over for possible inclusion on an album to be recorded the following year. The third, 'You Owe Me One', was not a track Björn and Benny were especially enamoured with. It would be a future single B-side, at best. Indeed, for better or worse, many of Abba's 1982 recordings sounded like a step back. The group reverted to joint lead vocals, multi-layered arrangements and more impersonal lyrical themes. It was clear that they were all a bit disorientated, unsure of Abba's place in their own lives as well as the current musical scene.

Much of the songwriting team's growing disinterest in Abba had its roots in their ever-present dreams of writing a musical. After several aborted ideas and attempts to drum up interest from people like John Cleese, Björn and Benny had been introduced to lyricist Tim Rice, at the time primarily known for his collaborations with Andrew Lloyd Webber on musicals such as *Jesus Christ Superstar* and *Evita*. In December 1981, Rice visited Stockholm to meet the two composers. They clicked instantly on a personal level and decided to develop one of Rice's musical ideas: the game of chess as a metaphor for a love story, as well as the East-West relationship during the cold war years.

Whether they would actually go ahead with the project or exactly when it would commence was another matter entirely, but suddenly the musical dream had become just that bit more real to them. It wasn't just some vague inclination they were going to explore some day when they had the time. In Rice they had an eager partner waiting for them to commit to the task.

This did nothing to strengthen Björn and Benny's resolve to go on working with Abba. When the album sessions collapsed, Polar decided to issue a stop-gap package in the shape of a warmed-up idea dating back to 1979. In the autumn, Abba would release a double album of their singles so far, and include two brand new tracks on it.

On August 2, Björn and Benny were back in the studio again, with two new songs to be recorded. 'Cassandra' and 'Under Attack' were both fairly good songs although the composers doubted that they would both work as single A-sides. They needed another track, something that could truly defend its place on a single. Very few Abba songs were ever written in the studio, but with rapidly approaching deadlines Björn and Benny were a bit desperate. They had just completed 'Under Attack' when they decided to afford themselves the luxury of "wasting" expensive studio time on the writing process.

Benny had an embryo of a song which he started playing on his Yamaha GX-1 synthesizer. Michael Tretow recorded everything on his tapes, with Benny playing "right out of the blue", as he recalled. The tape captured the process of the song taking shape: less than an hour later the whole melody was completed. The new song had the working title 'Den lidande fågeln' ('The Suffering Bird'), but would be released under the title 'The Day Before You Came'.

At this point, Björn and Benny made another unusual decision. They didn't call in any other musicians, but decided just to let Benny play the song on the synthesizer all by himself, using the drum machine in the GX-1 for rhythm accompaniment. It was a recording method perfectly in tune with the times.

Following the pioneering work by artists such as Kraftwerk and David Bowie, over the past few years synthesizer-based artists like Gary Numan, The Human League, Soft Cell and Depeche Mode had overturned the world's popular music landscape. Punk, new wave and disco faded as these new groups captured the imagination of young record buyers with their electronic sounds. However, it wasn't the fat chord layers of Benny's usual playing style that marked these new British records, but rather a more sequencer-driven, shrill blipping sound. Michael Tretow, whose ears were always open to current recording trends, suggested that they should try to push the arrangement more in that direction.

By gateing the sound of Benny's normal long-chord playing he achieved a sequencer effect, letting the beat of the snare drum or the hi-hat determine at what moments in the song the synthesizers would be heard or not. The result was great, driving the song along in a distinctive way, providing a pulse as a contrast to the reflective mood of the song. The only other instruments heard on the track were a snare drum overdub by percussionist Åke Sundqvist – to beef up the drum sound – and Björn's faint acoustic guitar.

Writing the lyrics for this song presented a special challenge for Björn. His idea for a theme was a woman recounting all the dull, ordinary things she "guessed she must have done" the day before she had a life-changing encounter with a man. "I already knew that the melody was such – from a technical point of view – that the lyrics had to be constructed so that they would lead up to the 'day before you came' place in the melody," he recalled. "Then, when I got the idea for a theme, I wrote down all the everyday incidents and things I could think of that would happen to someone leading a routine kind of life. It was very difficult from a grammatical point of view to get it all to fit together, because it would all have to be logical, there was no place for hitches."

The lead vocal was allocated to Agnetha, who was told by Björn and Benny to put down an "artless" vocal, sounding more like the ordinary woman she was portraying than the professional pop singer she really was. It was all in accordance with their increasing interest in "theatrical" music, but the two producers later regretted this decision. "I think perhaps that it would have been better to let Agnetha remain a singer, instead of making her act the part of the woman she is singing about," Benny reflected.

There seemed to be an underlying sense of closure during the vocal overdub session, which took place just as August turned into September. Michael Tretow recalled the occasion as "very emotional. There was a feeling that this was the end. Agnetha . . . did her lead vocal track with the lights down. The song still brings tears to my eyes." Although no one knew it for certain at the time, 'The Day Before You Came' was indeed Abba's very last recording. This captivating mini-melodrama was a more than worthy conclusion to a recording history that had taken its first shaky steps 10 and a half years earlier.

However, when the song was released in October as the first of the two autumn singles, much of the record-buying public failed to respond to the record. It did reach the Top Five in several important Abba markets – Sweden, Norway, Finland, The Netherlands, Belgium and Switzerland, for instance. It was a worrying sign, however, when 'The Day Before You Came' reached only number 32 on the UK charts. After all, as far as Björn and Benny were concerned, England was the home of pop music, the arena where important trends originated.

At this point even the United States were subject to what was referred to as a second "British invasion" (the first had of course been spearheaded by The Beatles two decades earlier). The American charts would soon be full of youthful synth and new romantic acts such as The Human League, Duran Duran and Culture Club, paving the way for the escapist Eighties. In the light of this development, Abba's complex, chorus-free and downright theatrical story of the drab life of a woman in her thirties, lasting for almost six minutes, seemed somewhat incongruous.

"If we at least had let Agnetha sing it more beautifully I believe people would have found it easier to take the song to their hearts," Björn reflected later. "We were simply starting to get out of touch with the pop music mainstream . . . You can only manage to be a part of that mainstream – that remarkable, mysterious force that is so hard to define – for a limited number of years." Abba had lost most of their internal energy, now they were rapidly losing their audience as well.

On September 21, the video for 'The Day Before You Came' was shot. This filming marked yet another change in the group's working routine. Lasse Hallström, whose last clip for Abba had been 'Head Over Heels' earlier in 1982, was replaced for the first time. "I believe the producers at shows like *Top Of The Pops* felt I was a bit antiquated," the director recalled. "There was probably a suggestion from somewhere that new blood was needed." Hallström, who had emerged as one of Sweden's leading movie directors, went on to score an international hit with the 1985 film *My Life As A Dog*. This success gave him the ticket to a Hollywood career and movies such as *What's Eating Gilbert Grape*, *The Cider House Rules*, *Chocolat* and *The Shipping News*.

As new producers of Abba clips, director Kjell Sundvall and cinematographer Kjell-Åke Andersson were drafted in by Björn after a tip from his wife, who had collaborated with them on an advertising project. At the time, Sundvall and Andersson were an up-and-coming film-maker team. Kjell Sundvall had very much been part of the Seventies *progg* movement and was one of Abba's old adversaries. Now he had to swallow his pride – this was work, after all – although he made a conscious effort to keep his association with the group quiet.

Later in life, what he remembered most from the video shoot was the

458

strange atmosphere within the group. "It didn't really feel like we had been working with a group, but with four individuals," he said. When Abba started their promotional campaign for the singles and the compilation album *The Singles – The First Ten Years* in November, they did indeed appear less as a collective than ever before. The positive effect was that they seemed more forthright than usual in their interviews, almost as if they knew the game was up.

An appearance on the Swedish television show *Nöjesmaskinen (The Entertainment Machine)*, for instance, saw the four relaxed and joking, meeting questions with honest and reflective replies. Frida and Agnetha opined that at the end of a relationship, men were more prone to throw themselves into new affairs immediately, being too afraid to be alone. Björn and Benny sheepishly half agreed.

In early November the group went to England and West Germany for television promotion and other meetings with the media. In mid-November they reunited with Sundvall and Andersson to make a dismal-looking, dry ice-laden video for 'Under Attack', the second single from the compilation album. The video ended symbolically with the four members walking away in the distance.

'Under Attack' didn't set the charts alight much more than 'The Day Before You Came' had done. Although it crept into the UK Top 30, only the ever-faithful Belgium and The Netherlands made 'Under Attack' a Top Five hit. On December 11, 1982, Abba appeared on BBC TV's *The Late Late Breakfast Show*. Live from Stockholm via satellite, they endured an inconsequential interview with host Noel Edmonds and conducted mimed performances of 'I Have A Dream' and 'Under Attack'.

No one knew it at the time, but this was to be the group's last ever collective appearance as a musical entity. The door to their life as Abba was slowly but surely closing behind them, and before long it became clear that neither Björn nor Benny, Agnetha nor Frida, were inclined to push it open again.

PART IV

That's Our Destiny

Chapter 32

Journalists profiling Stig Anderson in the Seventies were often divided in their opinions of him. Some were in awe of his achievements, recognising his sometimes brutal honesty, his forthright opinions, his diligence and belief in his own capabilities. Others portrayed him as nothing less than a money-grabbing cynic who would do anything for a quick buck.

Whatever their view of his philosophies, one thing that always shone through in articles was Stig's almost inhuman capacity for work, the strength he mustered to see him through his workaholic lifestyle. The bags under his eyes may have been more prominent than usual for a man yet to turn 50, but above those bags were a pair of alert eyes: piercing, energetic, astute.

At the beginning of the Eighties, however, those profiles of Stig were acquiring a few shades hitherto unseen. A reporter visiting his offices in December 1980 pointed out Stig's capacity for juggling several balls at the same time, noting that he was going through his paperwork while the interview was being conducted. At the same time something was obviously not quite right with Stig. "I see his hands trembling," the reporter wrote. "He doesn't seem to be in very good health, almost in the risk zone for a heart attack."

Stig's lifestyle – the constant hard work, the drinking – was catching up with him and sooner or later something had to give. His deteriorating health finally forced him to acknowledge that he had a drinking problem. He even began alluding to it in interviews: "With the life I lead I may not live to be very old," he smiled wryly in a television programme. In the official book written about him in 1983, Stig was even more blunt. "I drink too much," he stated laconically.

The wild-eyed Stig Anderson of the Seventies – his hair unruly and often standing on end, always ready with a provocative comment for the newspapers – was giving way to a less animated, neatly trimmed and rather tired version of the same man. On the positive side, he would no longer blow his top ten times a day: he was calmer, more sensible. On the downside, the "man on a mission" persona that inspired so many of his colleagues to excel in their own work, was disappearing fast, replaced by a daily routine more in keeping with accountancy than pop music.

Abba had become a self-perpetuating machine, its members showing no interest in further promotional efforts, especially Agnetha who was more determined than ever to stay at home with her children. Stig was no longer needed to promote their career and their day-to-day affairs were in the now expert hands of Görel Hanser and Berka Bergkvist, who were effectively running the administration at the Polar Music offices. This left Stig with nothing to do other than focus on the investment and tax-avoidance schemes.

There is little doubt that Stig was experiencing delusions of grandeur, visualising himself as the head of a business empire on a par with large-scale industries. Spectacular presentations for the share investors' club – with showbiz style light shows and special effects – were a part of his strategy to attract interest in the ventures of Polar Music International.

Lately, though, his partners in the company – the Abba members – were becoming disillusioned with his schemes. Those first bad deals, the Wimab debacle and the Pol Oil fiasco, occurred when they were just dipping their toes in the water, and had been fairly easy to handle. On the plus side, companies like Monark and Invest Finans Infina had turned out to be extremely healthy in their own right.

During 1982, however, things started going downhill rapidly. In February, Polar Music International, along with Stig and Abba as private individuals, acquired 65 per cent of the shares in an investment company called Kuben. Both the Chairman of the Board, Christer Brandberg, and the new President of the company, Rune Andersson, were typical of the experienced industrial heavyweights circling around the cash cow that was Polar at the time.

Within a year, the purchase of Kuben proved to be a miscalculation. A series of complex business deals led to a substantial loss as the company overstretched itself with too many investments. In March 1983, after a dramatic power struggle which interested readers could follow blow by blow in the press, both the President and the Chairman of Kuben left, and accountant Stig Engqvist took over as president of the company. Andersson and Brandberg both continued their successful business careers elsewhere. "I wasn't up to the mark for Stig Anderson's empire," Rune Andersson noted sarcastically in 1990, adding that Stig was "one of the biggest clowns I've ever seen".

The members of Abba already felt that their business interests attracted too much coverage in the media, and the Kuben affair was yet another irritating example of how the commercial side of Polar had escalated to a disproportionate level in relation to their musical interests. Established originally with the sole intention of allowing Abba to retain a larger slice of their vast income, the investments had taken on a life of their own: they had become a hydra, a monster that was growing out of their control.

The symbolic shift from music company to investment house could be traced back to Polar's move from their offices in the warm and atmospheric turn-of-the-century building at Baldersgatan, to the cold, steely façade of Polar's new headquarters in the city centre within spitting distance of several major banks. Björn and Benny had a rehearsal studio built in a tower room at the top of the building, but whatever took place on the floors below was increasingly alienating to them.

"In the beginning it was this gang of friends who were working together," says Berka Bergkvist. "Then, when we had the new offices, all these big affairs started happening and a lot of outside people were moving in. It had very little to do with music. Those of us who had been there from the start were basically music people, so there was a cultural clash – to say the least. But they didn't really care about us and we didn't have anything to do with them. It happened that they complained that we were playing music too loud. We maintained that it was a music company and not some bank."

While Stig thrived on his role as businessman, the Abba members fought hard to protect their integrity as musicians, which served only to increase the lengthening distance between the group and their manager. Some of the statements Stig made on their behalf over the years had been maddening enough, but most had been pretty easy to clear up and smooth over. By the summer of 1982, however, Abba had almost completely lost interest in covering up Stig's blunders.

Much to the dismay of the Swedish business community, the Social Democrats had declared that if they won the general election in September they would establish a wage-earner investment fund. It was one of the most hotly debated issues in Sweden during the early Eighties, and several protests were staged to raise support for the movement against the implementation of the fund.

In July 1982, Stig announced that he and Abba would arrange an "anti-fund" gala at the Gröna Lund amusement park in Stockholm. "The Abba members are not going to perform as a group, but they will appear as individuals," he stated firmly. The announcement was reported widely in the media over the next few weeks, much to Abba's personal irritation since they had no intention whatsoever of taking part in the gala, much less helping to arrange it.

Polar issued a statement from the four members, denying their involvement – and Björn didn't mince his words when asked for a personal comment. "Stig Anderson and Abba are two different things," he determined. "We dissociate ourselves completely from [his gala]. None of us would support a stunt like that. Politics should be pursued through words, not with artist galas and balloons. Participation in [this event] would lend an air of ridicule to Abba. We haven't even been asked to appear. This is Stig Anderson's own idea from start to finish."

Stig tried to back-pedal by issuing a statement of his own. "There's a slight difference in our opinions and the gala is my own idea completely," he said diplomatically. "I believe that artists that are opposed to employee funds should appear in the gala, but I respect that the Abba members feel otherwise."

It was a glaring crack in the façade, with Stig failing to realise that he could no longer represent himself and the group as a unified entity. Frank and distancing statements about Stig from assorted Abba members would pop up regularly over the next few years. "I suppose it's been easiest for outsiders to push us together," Benny reflected in 1983, "but the fact is that Stig has never represented Abba. At the most, he has a tendency to say 'we' when he means 'I'." Even for Stig, such statements must have made it patently clear that even if there had ever been a "we", it had gradually ceased to exist during the first few years of the Eighties.

Indeed, there wasn't much unity left within the group itself at this point. For Frida, the divorce from Benny had been a turning point in more ways than one. That fateful day in February 1981, when she was confronted with the newspaper placards outside her local supermarket, planted the seeds for her next move. She was sick and tired of living in Sweden, of being constantly held up in the press either as some kind of fantasy figure or as a ruthless businesswoman.

Frida had watched in sympathy while Agnetha had suffered through a kind of hell during the past two years, reading constant reports and bogus interviews in the gossip press, much of it erroneous and intrusive speculation about her personal life. She knew that the same fate awaited her unless she did something drastic. There were other, more intangible reasons for Frida's growing unease with Sweden. The more positive attitude towards Abba and their music in the current cultural climate had brought with it a feeling of bitterness about the way the group had been treated at the height of their fame.

A fairly prestigious cultural award bestowed upon Abba by the newspaper *Expressen* in November 1982 signalled an about-turn that made Frida suspicious. Doubting the sincerity behind the prize, she found it hard to attach much value to it. "It was like we'd been rehabilitated," she recalled.

"Now we were good enough, now we were distinguished enough. I didn't accept that award with any great joy: it was like they were feeling which way the wind was blowing. All of a sudden it was fine to give us an acknowledgement."

The insulated, Swedish perspective on the world felt increasingly alien to her now that she was striving to broaden her own horizons and break out of every imaginable constriction. So, 18 months after splitting with Benny, Frida decided to implement a physical, practical and psychological distance from everything that Polar and Sweden represented. She was going to move to London.

Much had occurred during these 18 months, and it was a radically different Frida that had emerged in the interim. The soft perm look she had affected for a couple of years had given way to a spiky-haired, tough, independent image at the end of 1981, and a new, more outspoken personality to go with it. She had completed her first solo album in seven years and, even though it had been an edgy and somewhat overwhelming experience, she had seen it through. Her initial comments about the album oozed confidence: "My ambition has been to do the best I can with the material we have chosen, and if that isn't good enough there isn't much I can do about it. All I know is that I have paid attention to every single detail."

In September 1982, she went on a promotional trip for the album with Görel Hanser. It was a relief to travel in such downscaled circumstances: no compromises with four different temperaments and inclinations, just her own will. Notably, she visited no less than eight different European countries during her trek, and spent nine days in the United States and Canada. Clearly, of the four Abba members it wasn't Frida who had in the past insisted on staying at home instead of going on promotional trips.

In late November, all practical details regarding Frida's move abroad had been settled. She sold all her shares in Polar Music – and whatever other companies she had an interest in – to the other Abba members and Stig. Before the year was over, Frida had settled into an apartment in the exclusive Mayfair district of Central London.

By a stroke of luck, when Frida emigrated and divested herself of all her business interests in Sweden, she managed to sell her shares in the ill-fated Kuben at exactly the right time. The value of the shares had fluctuated dramatically ever since they were purchased at 35 kronor per share. When Frida sold her shares the price was 255 kronor (£22.95), and she made a killing on the deal.

The rest of the group wasn't so lucky. The ousting of the original management in the spring of 1983 failed to stabilise Kuben. When Stig and the remaining three Abba members finally sold their shares in October 1983, the price had fallen to 25 kronor (£2.125) per share, lower than the purchase price. Together they received a total of 5.2 million kronor (£442,000) – the highest total value of their combined shares had been 62 million kronor (£5,580,000). "It will be a relief to get out of the business world," sighed Björn.

It wasn't just the complex business deals and the negative feelings towards Sweden that Frida felt a need to resolve at this time. The events of the early Eighties made her question several relationships in her life. She'd kept in touch with her father since their first meeting, but five years later she had cut contact down drastically. Frida explained that she hadn't met him "in a long while. It was hard work to enter into a whole new family life. It felt more like a strain than a stimulation. It was like meeting any kind of stranger, despite the fact that he was my natural father."

Later she revealed that there were other, stronger reasons why she failed to stay in touch. Frida never forgot her aunt Olive's belief that Alfred Haase had known Synni Lyngstad was pregnant. Along the way she sided with Olive, and there could only be one conclusion to the matter: Alfred was promptly ostracised from her life. "I prefer to spend my time with people who won't let you down," she said curtly.

While Frida was adjusting to her new life in London, Agnetha was walking in her footsteps by making a solo album of her own. She had already branched out a little by recording the 1982 duet 'Never Again' with Tomas Ledin, enjoying a sizeable international hit in the process.

In August she spent a few weeks making her début as a movie actress in the film *Raskenstam*, which dealt with a lonely-hearts racketeer in Thirties Sweden. Agnetha had a major part as Lisa Mattsson, an innocent fisherman's daughter whom the title character swindles. It was a surprisingly convincing and human portrait of the character. Though no one was likely to suggest that Agnetha was a major acting talent, she pulled off this role with an effective, natural interpretation. "In everything else I've done I've been Agnetha of Abba," she said, "but when I watched the movie I saw another person: I saw Lisa."

All these new ventures signalled Agnetha's first few significant steps out of the Abba fold in a long time. Her next major project would be a solo album at the beginning of the following year. It was time to establish herself firmly as an internationally viable artist on her own terms.

Agnetha was a huge fan of Barbra Streisand's *Guilty* album, which had been produced by Barry Gibb of The Bee Gees. Discussions were initiated with Gibb to work with Agnetha on her first English-language solo album, but the talks collapsed when Agnetha refused to leave Stockholm and Polar Studios to record the album in Miami, where Gibb lived. Negotiations reached a stalemate, and the subject was closed.

Instead, Agnetha turned to another light-pop expert, Mike Chapman, who'd done everything from glam-pop with The Sweet to new wave with Blondie. Chapman eagerly accepted, though it was his smooth balladeering and MOR pop as writer and producer for acts such as Smokie that attracted Agnetha, and it was in that spirit that much of the album was conceived.

Sessions commenced in mid-January 1983 and continued for two and a half months – a full 30 days longer than Frida had spent on *Something's Going On* the previous year. Mike Chapman had a completely different approach to recording than Agnetha was used to with Abba, where you went into the studio and worked hard while you were there and then went home. "Everything took so long," recalled Michael Tretow, who engineered the sessions. "He was funny that way, because he wanted everything to be so cool. The musicians would say, 'Can't we start playing now?' and he'd answer, 'No, take it easy, play some pinball, cool down . . .' It took forever, it seemed like the album would never be finished."

The resulting record, *Wrap Your Arms Around Me*, was released at the end of May. It was a slick enough product, but it was hard to detect any strong personality shining through, from either Agnetha or Chapman. *Wrap Your Arms Around Me* suffered from the same problem as so many other albums conceived in the same way: fairly bland songs picked out of various publishers' catalogues, professionally performed by a bunch of efficient session musicians, neither disturbing nor exciting anyone very much.

There were one or two highlights: the seduction-fest on the title track took Agnetha's sex-icon image and ran with it to great effect. Tellingly, it was Mike Chapman's sole contribution to the album as a songwriter, showing that he had a clear understanding of what could be done with her as a solo artist. A full-blown meeting between Chapman's shamelessly commercial tunesmithery and Agnetha's voice would probably have resulted in a more interesting end-product.

Another success was Russ Ballard's rocky 'Can't Shake Loose',★ which earned Agnetha a US Top 30 hit. The calypso-flavoured opener 'The Heat Is On' was a Swedish number one, also charting high as a single in Belgium and The Netherlands. But far too many songs fell into the trap of the cod-reggae of 'Take Good Care Of Your Children' or the lame Sixties

★ Ballard was also the writer of Frida's 'I Know There's Something Going On'.

girl-group pastiche 'Mr. Persuasion'. Perhaps the strained jollity of the latter track was necessary for Agnetha to break away from her image as the maudlin, abandoned woman of her vocal performances on Abba's records. "We wanted . . . a positive spirit," she said. "Not just tragic ballads about someone having left you, or that life is difficult."

Commercially, Agnetha was still a favourite with Swedish record-buyers. The album entered the charts at number one, selling 100,000 copies in two days and eventually notching up well over 350,000. World-wide sales stopped at an impressive 1.2 million. Despite promotional efforts during the year, Agnetha failed to set the UK charts alight, however: the album crept into the Top 20, but its singles charted considerably lower.

During her promotional trips, Agnetha travelled by bus as often as poss-ible, her fear of flying being as strong as ever. She was on her way home from London on a dark October night when disaster struck. Shortly after arriving in Sweden her tour bus was involved in a bad accident, and she was thrown from the vehicle. "The bus began to sway violently from side to side," Agnetha recalled. "There were screeching brakes and upset voices. I was thrown around and hit myself hard on the head and legs. The moments when I first realised that we were having an accident were frightening. I couldn't see anything because I was back in the sleeping compartment. But I do remember the last awful thump when we over-turned and span around, and the crashing of glass."

Holding on to the mattress on which she had been lying, Agnetha flew through a broken window, ending up in a ditch. The mattress protected her from the shattered glass. By a miracle, everyone on the bus survived the crash, suffering only relatively minor injuries.

One of the other passengers on the bus was journalist Brita Åhman, who was working on an authorised book about Agnetha. The accident would have fatal consequences for the project. When the gossip weeklies got hold of the crash story, they alleged that Agnetha was pregnant and suffered a miscarriage through the accident. There was no truth in this whatsoever, but Agnetha, tired of such reportage about her and always keen to file complaints about anything she considered a violation, clammed up and went off the book plans in a flash. Åhman had to break the contract with the publisher since it became impossible to write the book. However, she continued to do official, exclusive interviews with Agnetha over the next few years.

The crash occurred just at a time when things were looking promising in Agnetha's private life. In September 1983 she got engaged to Torbjörn Brander, following a recent reunion after a year-long break in the relationship. In yet another curious attempt at collaboration with the gossip press, Agnetha let Brita Åhman interview her and Brander, and photograph them embracing one another. The report was then published in one of the weeklies.

Alas, the engagement wasn't destined to last, and before the end of the following year, the pair split permanently. With bus crashes and on-again, off-again romances, Agnetha's gossip-rag image as a restless, doomed and eternally forlorn figure was as strong as ever.

While Agnetha was recording and promoting *Wrap Your Arms Around Me*, Björn and Benny had been virtually invisible, except for those occasions when their names were coupled with the latest Polar business drama. In November 1982, when Abba promoted *The Singles* in London, the pair finally decided to move ahead with their plans for a musical with Tim Rice.

At first, Björn and Benny considered working on both a new Abba album and the musical as two parallel projects. They soon realised this would be impossible and cancelled all plans for a new group LP in 1983. Instead they would devote all their time to writing the musical *Chess* and turning it into a concept album. If this turned out to be a success, the ultimate goal would be a stage version. Composing began in January and continued until the autumn. Many unused melody lines from discarded Abba songs were resurrected. The chorus of the member-introduction song 'I Am An A', from Abba's 1977 tour, turned into 'I Know Him So Well', one of the better known numbers from the musical. Part of the preparatory process was a bout of demo recording sessions, the purpose of which was to hear how the melodies sounded when they were sung by actual singers. During these sessions Agnetha pitched in and put down a vocal for a song called 'Every Good Man', which ended up as 'Heaven Help My Heart' in the completed musical.

In November 1983, recording sessions proper commenced at Polar Studios. After long and hard work – including sessions in London with the London Symphony Orchestra – the album was finally wrapped up at the end of September 1984. The creative process between Björn, Benny and Tim Rice was so entangled that they decided to credit the musical evenly to all three, although the basic distribution of work was music by Andersson/Ulvaeus, words by Rice.

The floating roles between the three were exemplified by many of Björn's demo lyrics being included in the final libretto. "[Björn] used to give me lyrics which were meant to be nonsense lyrics, but they always had wonderful lines in them, which I was able to nick and save myself many hours of pain," remembered Tim Rice. The line "One night in Bangkok makes a hard man humble" from 'One Night In Bangkok' was one of the more poignant instances as far as Rice was concerned. "I have been told by so many people that this was a complete summary of my brilliance – but Björn wrote it!"

There were four major parts in the musical: Swedish singer Tommy Körberg tackled the role of the Russian chess player, while British musical star Elaine Paige, with whom Rice was in a relationship, was Florence, the American player's second who falls in love with the Russian. Singer and actor Murray Head, a veteran of both stage and screen, was the American player. The role as the Russian's wife, Svetlana, went to musical actress Barbara Dickson.

Chess was a bigger and more unwieldy project than anything Björn and Benny had previously undertaken. Enough music was recorded to fill a triple album, but for marketing reasons the work was cut down to a two-record set. On release at the end of October 1984, *Chess* went on to sell two million copies worldwide. The musical yielded two major hits in the Paige/Dickson duet 'I Know Him So Well', a UK number one for four weeks, and Murray Head's 'One Night In Bangkok', which reached number three on the American charts. The album received mostly good reviews in the press: in Sweden, it was the first time that the critics treated Björn and Benny's work with full respect. "It was about time," said Benny proudly.

Musically it was hard to fault *Chess* for what it attempted to be: a modern musical in the tradition of Andrew Lloyd Webber, although it contained more hits and catchy melodies than was usual in the work of Björn and Benny's peers. The album was rich and varied in its styles and influences, reflecting the sense of freedom that Björn and Benny probably felt at being released from the constraints of what "pop" was supposed to be about. It was the theme of the project and the dramatic requirements that decided what kind of music was needed, not what people expected from an "Abba" album or any such other brand names.

However, the downside of this versatility was a certain lack of consistent tone. Although the signature of Andersson/Ulvaeus was unmistakable, the many pastiches of styles – everything from Gilbert & Sullivan in 'Merano' and 'Embassy Lament' to rap in 'One Night In Bangkok' – gave an unclear impression of the creators' musical language.

When *Chess* was staged at the Prince Edward Theatre in May 1986, the problems inherent in Tim Rice's plot concept became blatantly apparent. The staging had gone through several dramatic changes in the last few months before the première. American musical wizard Michael Bennett, the man behind musicals like *A Chorus Line* and *Dream Girls*, was the original director of *Chess*, but in January 1986 he pulled out of the production at short notice because of health problems. It turned out that Bennett was seriously ill, and he died of an AIDS-related disease a year later.

At the end of January, Trevor Nunn, the director of the Lloyd Webber hit musical *Cats*, stepped into the production. With less than four months to go before the opening, it was too late in the day for him to do much else than put his own slant on the staging as already conceived by Michael Bennett. The technical gadgetry that formed a cornerstone of Bennett's production continued to cause practical problems right up to the première date. On the personal side Tommy Körberg collapsed and had to be taken to hospital just a few hours before the very first preview performance. Körberg, making his London stage début, was exhausted by nerves and long rehearsals – miraculously he pulled himself together enough to go through with the performance.

More serious, however, were the problems with the musical itself. The embarrassing truth was that the story simply didn't hold up. "We spent many nights trying to analyse what was wrong," said Benny. "There was an imbalance in the plot: the human relationships were overshadowed by the more intellectual sub-plots: the actual chess game and the East-West relationship."

Anders Eljas, one of Abba's keyboard players on their tours, had graduated to the role of arranger and orchestrator on the *Chess* project. With last-minute plot changes, he had serious problems to overcome. "It was only decided exactly how the second act should be on the day of the première," he recalled. "The theatre was so small that the foyer was the only place with room enough for writing the notation. So while the audience was watching the first act, we had ten notators on their knees out there – some of them were really old men – rewriting the music for us."

The mixed reviews after the première set the tone for the musical's future. In London, the strength of the music and the performances as such, combined with a devoted audience of Swedish tourists, ensured that *Chess* ran for almost three years. It didn't make a huge profit, but the £4 million production costs were covered after the first two years.

When *Chess* opened on Broadway in April 1988, the production wasn't so fortunate. Björn and Benny felt the show had been improved when book writer Richard Nelson was brought in to add some structure to the plot. But success on Broadway is traditionally reliant on the word of influential reviewers, and this particular staging fell into the hands of Frank Rich of the *New York Times*. Rich was known as "The Butcher" – and butcher *Chess* is exactly what he did.

"[The] evening has the theatrical consistency of quicksand – and the drab color scheme to match," he wrote, adding that the show's book and lyrics "are about nothing except the authors' own pompous pretentions". The music was described as a "characterless smorgasbord of mainstream pop styles".

Within two months *Chess* had closed, incurring painful financial losses and injured self-esteem for the writers. Three Knights, the production company formed by the two Swedes and Rice, had invested US$2 million (£1.1 million) in the show, representing a third of the production cost. For Björn, the name Frank Rich became a dirty word and more than a decade later his bitterness still rankled. "I've never seen as bad a review as the one that this man wrote," he fumed. "Everyone I've ever spoken to felt it was completely unfair . . . [Perhaps] he felt that 'the musical is an American invention and the Europeans should stay out of here.' "

However, Björn did admit that much of the blame probably rested with the musical itself. "We should have chosen one of the other ideas Tim presented to us, but we felt – erroneously, as it turned out – that the chess concept was the most interesting. The story is just too weak."

Despite this failure – the only major flop in Björn and Benny's career – interest in *Chess* hasn't died down, and many regional stagings have been produced over the years. Even more popular, perhaps, is the *Chess In Concert* concept, performed regularly in Sweden by Tommy Körberg and others who were involved in the original recordings. Work to make the actual musical convince on stage has continued over the years. At the start of the 21st century the three writers are involving themselves in further productions, the first Swedish staging premièring in Stockholm in February 2002. Not only was this reworked version of *Chess* a sell-out success, but it will also form the basis of planned productions in London and New York.

In many ways, the *Chess* project served a transitionary function for Björn and Benny, an opportunity to branch out from their identity as members of Abba and to move away from their close business relationship with Stig. When they went into partnership with Tim Rice, they had formed a separate production company, Three Knights Limited, in which Stig played no part. The musical that "we" were going to write, according to Stig's vernacular over the past five years, was entirely removed from Polar's business sphere.

With this new company Björn and Benny negotiated a deal for the release of the *Chess* concept album, separate from their roles as Abba members. If Stig wanted the album on Polar he'd better be prepared to pay: the Polar Music boss later called the *Chess* deal "very tough".

However, in the process he did acquire the rights to negotiate a deal with RCA for the rest of the world.

Stig wasn't quite so hasty in granting Abba what they wanted in a new contract between the group and Polar Music. The time when Stig, Björn and Benny could sit down and have an informal talk about the way to progress Abba's career was over. In June 1982, around the same time as Abba cancelled their plans for a new album, they began negotiating a new deal for the group's recordings.

The first long-term contract was signed on July 1, 1975, wherein it was stated that Abba would get a royalty of eight per cent on all records sold in Sweden, and three per cent on sales throughout the rest of the world. This deal had been in operation since then, the only significant change occurring on July 1, 1980, when a separate contract was signed, according to which Björn and Benny would receive an additional 2.5 per cent "producer's royalty".

In September 1980, a contract covering the period July 1, 1982 to June 30, 1983 was signed by the group, along the same lines as the earlier agreements. It was this present deal that Abba now wanted to renegotiate. The group felt that a three per cent royalty was unreasonable in the light of the profits they had brought to Polar Music International over the years. Although they each had a stake in the company, giving them considerable revenues from the Abba record sales anyway, this only represented 12.5 per cent for each Abba member. Stig, meanwhile, had 50 per cent all to himself.

Since the future of the group was in doubt at the time, it was also necessary to construct a new deal that was better adjusted to a time when one or all the members of the group no longer had joint business interests, much less in Polar. Compared with the 2.45 per cent Stig had given the inexperienced Hootenanny Singers some two decades earlier, the three per cent for a top international act like Abba was derisory. Split into four, the individual royalty for each member was a measly 0.75 per cent, which seemed even lower when compared to Michael Tretow's 0.5 per cent. The matter was especially topical at this point, since everybody involved knew that Frida was on the verge of selling all her Swedish business interests.

Without a stake in the company, the higher royalty rate was fundamental for a fair distribution of the future income generated by Abba's music. What they now wanted was a nine per cent royalty for the group, roughly constituting half of Polar's revenues from the record sales. On top of this, Björn and Benny wanted to keep their 2.5 per cent producer's royalty. In effect, with this new deal the Abba members' total income from record sales would remain on roughly the same level even if they sold their Polar shares.

On January 11, 1983, a meeting was held at the Polar Music offices between Björn, Benny, Stig, Gudrun, Görel Hanser and Polar accountant Lou Talamo. The meeting was characterised by a sense of urgency: there were several deals that needed to be sorted out, and the failure over the past six months to reach an agreement on Abba's future royalties had not improved the mood between the participants.

By this time it was clear that Stig would not have a stake in Björn, Benny and Tim Rice's recently formed Three Knights production company, but Polar were still eager to acquire the rights for the *Chess* concept album. It was a trump card for Björn and Benny, who were now so annoyed with Stig's wilfulness that they threatened to sign Abba to another record company unless their demands were honoured.

Their efforts to reach an agreement were complicated by the uncertainty over Polar's other investments and tax schemes, which were running parallel with the record deal negotiations. Contract drafts continued circulating between Polar, Stig, Abba and their lawyers for more than a year without a final deal being settled upon.

Things finally came to a head during a meeting between Björn, Benny and Stig on April 25, 1984, when the male half of Abba insisted that Stig concede to the important clauses they wanted to include in the contract. Apart from the royalty adjustments, the new deal was to encompass any future recordings Abba might make, as well as being applied retroactively to all sales of old Abba recordings from January 1, 1983, onwards.

Stig, who still held out hope that Abba had a future as a recording act, finally relented – and the protocol from the meeting was signed. No actual agreement was inked as yet, however, but during the following months the final contract was drawn up. As far as Björn and Benny were concerned, document or no document, it was a done deal and Abba's rights as performing artists had been adjusted according to their demands.

At the end of 1983, in conjunction with the disastrous end of the Kuben affair, Agnetha had followed in Frida's footsteps and sold her shares in Polar. Björn and Benny secretly wanted to leave as well but felt that they should stay on a while longer, "for old time's sake", as Benny put it later. However, with the negotiations on the terms of the new record contract brought to a successful close, they were now free to leave Stig and Polar without fear of any financial repercussions.

There were indeed many reasons for them to get out of Polar and all its affiliated businesses as soon as possible, the Kuben affair being just one in a long line of investments that had gone wrong over the past two years.

Around the time of the Kuben acquisition in early 1982 Polar tried to buy a major wholesale business called Ahlsell. However, due to the many high profile deals over the past years in which Polar's investment philosophy had so clearly been geared towards avoiding taxes, the intentions behind the proposal were questioned. The venture was interpreted as an unfriendly take-over bid, and the deal fell through. Additionally, connections to a "shallow" pop group were viewed upon with some distaste whenever Polar's accountants and businessmen tried to conduct their affairs. "The Ahlsell deal collapsed because of our lack of credibility," said an exasperated Stig Engqvist. "We have acquired an unserious image which it will take years to wash away."

It wasn't just newspaper reporters who remarked unfavourably on the goings-on at Polar: even Volvo boss Pehr G. Gyllenhammar, a powerful and highly influential figure in Swedish business affairs, saw fit to comment on what had happened. To his way of thinking, Polar's deal-making strategies were part of an irresponsible new business trend wherein companies were juggled back and forth without any regard to the well-being of the nation's industry as a whole. "I don't begrudge Abba the right to earn money on their music," Gyllenhammar said, "but I do share the opinion of the board of Ahlsell when it opposed Abba's entry into the company. It's hard to see what Abba's contribution to Ahlsell would be." To make his point absolutely clear, he described the proposition as "a transaction that is profitable for those involved but not for the country".

With every failed deal and scandalous affair, the Abba members felt a growing displeasure at being constantly singled out as greedy and ruthless tax avoiders. They were adamant that the business needed to be restructured so that they could remove themselves from all the deal making. "It would be worth a lot to rid ourselves of all this," Benny told a reporter. "If Stiga [one of the companies purchased by Polar] cuts back on 10 per cent of their labour force, does that mean that it's Abba who have fired them? I don't want that kind of responsibility for other people's jobs."

Behind the scenes the exchange of opinions was considerably harsher. "We had confrontations with Stig about it," Björn recalled. "We told him, 'You've got to put a stop to all this, goddamnit!'" Stig, who had suffered plenty of public humiliation as a result of the failed deals, finally realised that the situation had got out of hand and resolved to take steps.

In October 1982 Abba and Stig sold 70 per cent of their shares in Polar Music International to those who were actually running the day-to-day business. Retaining a smaller cut, they would still be able to gain financially from the deals made, but without being so strongly associated with the transactions. Similarly, it would be easier for the new company, which was called Polar Music Invest, to conduct their business if they weren't associated with people with such a high media profile.

The buyers of the company were Stig Engqvist, Lou Talamo and Invest Finans boss Jaan Manitski. Lasse Dahlin and Bertil Karlsson – the head of the financial department – were originally going to be part of the deal, but pulled out at the last minute. Dahlin and Karlsson didn't like the new direction the business had been taking over the past years, and – most importantly – Lasse Dahlin didn't get along with Stig Engqvist. Where the former was a considerate and thoughtful investor whose job had been to conduct safe deals, the latter was occasionally brash and impulsive, thriving on quick transactions with complex details.

Dahlin, who'd been an important part of Polar's relaxed and familial business spirit back at the Baldersgatan offices, had lost out to the clever accountants and immediately handed in his letter of resignation. Stig and Gudrun persuaded Dahlin to stay on as Sweden Music's Chairman of the Board and financial advisor for the Anderson, Ulvaeus and Andersson families. He accepted – a decision made easier by the fact that he wouldn't be required to perform his duties inside the Polar building. But the symbolic significance for the company atmosphere was clear: yet another member of the "family" had abandoned ship.

Contrary to expectations, the foundation of Polar Music Invest didn't put a stop to the troublesome business deals and the attention from the media that followed in their wake. Stig Engqvist, who was appointed President of the company, had previously been used to a low profile in his role as accountant and financial architect of the various schemes. Now he was thrown brutally into the spotlight, simply by being involved in the "Abba investments".

In May 1983, Polar Music Invest proposed to buy the publishing house Saxon & Lindström, publisher of a couple of major weekly magazines. Ironically, one of the magazines was the gossip rag *Svensk Damtidning*, upon which Agnetha had filed a complaint the previous year for writing false and misleading stories about her. The same week that Polar were negotiating for the purchase of Saxon & Lindström, *Svensk Damtidning* had yet another sob story about Agnetha on the cover.

Suspicions were raised that Polar Music Invest was only after the real estate owned by the company, and planned to close down the magazines, leaving hundreds of people unemployed. On May 31, staff from Saxon & Lindström demonstrated outside the Polar offices, resulting in even bigger headlines than usual, as well as television news reports and coverage in the foreign media. The day after the demonstration the whole deal was suddenly cancelled, and the company was sold to another investor.

Chapter 32

"Most of all I'd like to move out of [the Polar building] to underline that we're serious," sighed an annoyed Stig Engqvist. "In the future I only want to be surrounded by black suits." Considering that it was the "light-weight" music that Abba produced that provided the financial basis for Engqvist's "serious" business, it seemed a particularly tactless comment. "Sometimes you get the feeling that the money has created Abba, when the truth is the exact opposite," said Benny. "It's our music that is the foundation of everything. Polar Music Invest, the building we're sitting in: everything is a result of our success."

But the point that Engqvist tried to make was basically correct, and Polar Music Invest soon moved to another building just a couple of blocks away. Both parties heaved a sigh of relief. "We're a company that is under scrutiny from the worldwide media," said Stig Anderson. "People from the financial side moved in with us. They came from a completely different environment and were characterised by the reserve of the business life, where being anonymous is a merit . . . [One of them said:] 'During my 14 years in the regular industry I didn't experience half of what happened during four months at Polar.'"

While Polar Music Invest conducted its business elsewhere, Stig finally admitted defeat in his attempts to become a major business mogul. He retreated to the area he knew best: music and entertainment. His plan was now to use his personal assets as a music man on the international scene to move forward in life.

Together with the major media house Bonnier he founded a home video company. He also declared his intent to give Polar a new start as a major player on the record market. His daughter Marie had been in charge of the pop A&R at Polar for the last few years, and was fairly successful in her endeavours to sign new acts for the domestic market and inject some life into the slumbering company.

Once the Kuben crisis had been sorted out in the autumn of 1983 and he was out of the spotlight brought on by the investments and tax schemes, Stig seemed to regain some of his old spark and brashness. Focusing on what he knew best – the entertainment world – he was in his true element. "I'd love to work abroad a bit more; I want to get out in the world. Sweden is too small for me," he boasted. "My capacity isn't properly used here."

But it wasn't going to be that easy. Over the past few years, while he had mainly been busy with Polar's investments, the musical landscape had changed quite drastically. By his own admission he was now a 52-year-old man who was out of touch with current pop music: indeed, that was why this side of things was handled by other people at Polar. More importantly, as Abba's activities trickled down to a minimum and then ceased completely, the international entertainment business lost interest in Stig. A manager needs to be constantly present on the scene in order to be taken seriously by other major players. Nothing he had offered the world besides Abba had managed to set the world alight, so there was very little to suggest that he would have any other interesting cards up his sleeve.

Things were also changing with the local licensees Stig had dealt with in the past. Many of the record company executives had disappeared from those companies and his own status wasn't as self-evident anymore. When Jerry Greenberg left Atlantic in the mid-Eighties, for instance, the consequences for Stig and John Spalding were quite drastic, as they discovered for themselves when they passed through New York and took the opportunity to pick up some royalty cheques.

"When we visited we used to go straight through to Jerry Greenberg's office on one of the top floors of this skyscraper," Spalding recalls. "But things had changed. Jerry had gone and lots of other people had gone and it was getting to be a very sort of accountants and lawyers type thing. There was nobody still there that we really knew." Instead of being whisked up to the offices for a glass of champagne, Stig and John were obliged to wait in the lobby on the second floor – with a cup of coffee. The two old friends noted how different things had become with a mix of melancholy and wry amusement.

Back in 1984, however, the atmosphere in the Polar building wasn't characterised by much amusement. Despite having sold out most of their interests in the investment business, the schemes and ventures continued to haunt both Stig and Abba. It was only now that it fully dawned on them that some of the deals had been a little too cleverly constructed.

A complex venture involving the purchase of the real estate company Stockholms Badhus back in June 1980 – which was in turn sold back and forth between several different companies within the course of two months – created problems four years later. The tax authorities claimed that the transactions had been purely fictitious, and Abba were now faced with a bill of 8 million kronor (£720,000) in back taxes. They faced the risk of being indicted with tax evasion, and the authorities also raised an eyebrow at several other deals.

The actions taken on Abba's behalf in the early Eighties would continue to haunt them well into the following decade. In the Nineties, the former group members occasionally created headlines as yet another old, unresolved dispute with the tax authorities reached the press. "We had to believe all the experts around us," Stig admitted at the end of this difficult period. "There were some mistakes, but also some people who were out to make money for themselves." For Björn this was the final straw: he wanted out of Polar and everything connected to it. He saw the wisdom of Frida's move to England and decided to follow in her footsteps.

Björn, a confessed Anglophile, shared her need for new perspectives and admitted that the current British tax climate suited him better than in Sweden. "If we'd really wanted to be tax exiles we should have done that while we were still earning money and not five years later," he pointed out. "But more than 80 per cent of the income goes to tax in Sweden. The remaining 20 per cent is more than enough to live on. That's not the problem, rather it's that you're not allowed to take part in the decisions about where those other 80 per cent go."

By November 1984, Björn, Lena and their daughter Emma had settled into a stately mansion in Henley-on-Thames, where other rock luminaries like Beatle George Harrison and Jon Lord of Deep Purple also lived. The move provided Björn with an excellent excuse to finally sever all ties with Polar Music, and Benny took the opportunity to pull out at the same time. The pair sold their 50 per cent of the shares in the company for two million kronor (£180,000).

When the news broke in the press in late October, Stig tried to dampen the heat by stating that there was no rift between them and that Björn was only selling because he was moving to England. Björn, however, was more forthright in his comments. "I would definitely have sold out anyway, even if I hadn't been forced to because of the legislation," he said. He also reflected further on his relationship to Stig. "We are on separate paths professionally. We were different even when we first got together, and it's not like we've grown closer over the years . . . I want to cultivate the artistic side. There's no reason why Benny and I should run a record company." Benny's statements conveyed the same basic message: "I don't want to be a part of this anymore. I want to devote myself to music, not to business."

Stig's more diplomatic comments were intermixed with promises of a new Abba album that "we" were going to make. "That would really be fun. We have some melodies left over from *Chess*. With those and some new material it should be possible to make a new Abba album." That was when Björn and Benny told him that it was extremely unlikely that there would be any more Abba albums. Only with this blunt declaration did Stig fully and finally realise that the *Chess* project and the girls' solo albums were signs of more than a temporary break.

If there had been even the tiniest morsel of a possibility that Stig and Abba would ever collaborate for real again, it perished for all time on

December 28. That was the date when the Abba members individually bought back all their rights from the company New Harlekin, through which all their group income was still distributed up to that point. The company itself had long since been caught up in the web of transactions implemented by Stig Engqvist. As the year of 1984 came to an end, the book closed on the very last chapter of the Abba story. Or so they thought.

Chapter 33

Frida was disappointed and frustrated. The *Something's Going On* album might not have been as successful as Abba, but it sold its million and yielded a sizeable hit in 'I Know There's Something Going On'. It was a promising kick-start to a new career outside the group. Alas, now that her second international solo album, *Shine*, was released, it seemed the world wasn't very interested in her after all.

Shine was originally planned as a reunion with Phil Collins, but he had become a megastar in his own right in the meantime and bowed out as producer, citing time restrictions. However, Frida was determined to continue her reinvention as a finger-on-the-pulse rock singer, and with the help of Thomas Johansson she enlisted the services of producer Steve Lillywhite instead.

Lillywhite was a perfect choice: with production work for acts like Peter Gabriel, U2, Simple Minds and Big Country to his credit, he was the hottest of hot young producers. The bulk of Frida's new album was recorded in February and March, 1984, in Paris, a location chosen in order that Frida could spend time with Bobo Hjert, who lived in the French capital.

Phil Collins had encouraged her to begin writing her own songs, which she had never attempted before, and she accepted this new challenge with gusto. In the spring of 1983 she recorded a few demos of the songs she had completed so far, backed by the band Rendez-Vous, run by her son Hans and Benny's son Peter. However, those titles – 'My Dearest Friend', 'I Don't Wanna Be Alone' and 'Light Of Love' – were never recorded for real by Frida herself.★

Only two of the dozen or so songs Frida had written when sessions for the *Shine* album started were ever recorded properly. The fairly average 'That's Tough', a collaboration with Hans and Kirsty MacColl – Lillywhite's partner and a backing singer on the album – became a single B-side. The ballad 'Don't Do It', however, was included on the album track listing. Like 'I Don't Wanna Be Alone' it had a pleasant enough

★ Frida's son Hans released a version of 'I Don't Wanna Be Alone' during his brief recording career under the pseudonym F/X in 1984.

melody, showing a certain promise had she chosen to continue exploring that side of herself. Björn and Benny also contributed one of their "left-overs" from the *Chess* writing sessions, a mid-tempo ballad called 'Slowly'. To date, it's the last new Andersson/Ulvaeus composition either of Abba's female half has recorded.

When the album was completed, it was felt yet again that the project lacked singles, and only then was the album's lead-off single and title track, 'Shine' recorded. On release in September 1984, these efforts proved fruitless. As a whole the album was professional and well-produced – in Lillywhite's typical bombastic Eighties style – but a bit impersonal. It was hard to see who was going to buy the album or why.

The album and single managed brief Top 10 placings in one or two countries, but sank without trace in most parts of the world – in the UK the album reached number 67, which reflected its fate in most other territories. This was not what Frida had expected. In interviews around the time of release, she raved about how she had been "opened up" creatively by her collaboration with Steve Lillywhite. "I am so much on the go now," she said. "I have already begun writing songs and feel like doing a new album pretty soon."

When *Shine* died a dismal death, it was like a cold shower. Frida's latest re-invention of herself – the modern, international rock woman, the Pat Benatar of Europe, the rich jet-setter commuting between London and Paris – suddenly lost its meaning. She was pushing 40, and as the world's record-buyers turned their backs on her, she was once again forced to re-evaluate her life. As if to further underline the need for changes, around the time of the release of *Shine*, her relationship with Bobo Hjert stumbled to a halt. When they went their separate ways, Frida moved from London, making an apartment in Switzerland her new home base. She also bought a luxurious home on the island of Majorca.

A new man came into her life: Prince Heinrich Ruzzo Reuss von Plauen. Ruzzo was a 35-year-old German prince, with characteristics that were both earthy and refined. A golf course architect by profession, four years Frida's junior, he had young twin daughters from a previous marriage. His mother was Swedish, and as a teenager Ruzzo had gone to the exclusive Lundsberg boarding school in Sweden. Among the friends he made there was Sweden's future King Carl XVI Gustaf.

The blossoming romance with Ruzzo Reuss enabled Frida to perform yet another reinvention. Although she hadn't planned it, this serious new relationship offered her the opportunity to draw a final curtain on her life as "Frida of Abba". Now she could take a step back to reassess her situation and try to catch up with herself. The rock star lifestyle in the showbiz capital of London was phased out, replaced by a more exclusive, discreet, slightly aristocratic ambience. By 1986, the couple were living together in Ruzzo's mansion in Fribourg, Switzerland.

Frida would later reflect on how she had lived her life up until the end of her music career and the meeting with Ruzzo. "I used to put myself and everything that was mine in the first place," she said. "The change didn't happen until I met Ruzzo. Once we had moved in together, I made the decision. For the first time in my life I would give my all to someone other than me. I devoted myself completely to him."

Except for one or two guest appearances on other artist's records over the next few years, Frida withdrew completely from the music business, even requesting her fan club to cease operations. The Eighties experiments with hair styles – everything from bright red and spiky to a blinding white – gave way to her natural brown. Frida and Ruzzo lived a low-key life, socialising with the King and Queen of Sweden and other high society friends. In a rare interview in October 1989 Frida made it clear that she was no longer a public figure, describing herself as "a completely uninteresting person to interview".

Within the same time-frame, Agnetha underwent a similar development. In September 1984 she started recording her second English-language solo album with producer Eric Stewart, formerly of 10cc, who no longer espoused the clever pop at which his old band had excelled during the Seventies. The resulting album, *Eyes Of A Woman*, had slightly more of an edge than Agnetha's previous LP, but was marred by an overblown Eighties-style production, which sounded dated even at the time.

An encouraging sign was the emergence of no less than two Agnetha compositions during recording sessions. One, 'You're There', was relegated to a single B-side, but a song called 'I Won't Let You Go' became the first single from the album. An excellent tune, quite removed from the ballads and mid-tempo material more generally associated with Agnetha, it could have been a worldwide smash had it been produced by, say, the energetic hit factory of Stock/Aitken/Waterman a few years later. Unfortunately, it wasn't. In the spring of 1985, *Eyes Of A Woman* and its attendant singles suffered much the same fate as Frida's *Shine*. Contributions from solid composer talent like Jeff Lynne of Electric Light Orchestra made very little difference: except for the Swedish market, the world just wasn't very interested.

Agnetha's relative lack of promotion didn't help matters. She had decided to withdraw from public life. For several years now she had refused to travel anywhere or attend public functions without her constant bodyguard, Hasse Blomgren, an employee of Thomas Johansson's EMA. Coupled with her wealth and aversion to publicity, Agnetha clearly lacked the motivation to remain in the music business. It was a striking contrast to the situation two decades earlier, when her biggest dream was to become famous and be on television. "Do you really think I will miss this: the stress, the pressure and all this waiting? Not on your life!" she told a reporter while waiting to appear on a television show in Montreux in May 1985.

Songwriting had also become a troublesome struggle, an insurmountable demand on herself. The songs that once poured from her on the piano keys no longer flowed with such ease. At one point it had seemed as if Agnetha would get started with full-scale songwriting again: after a quiet few years immediately following Abba's breakthrough, a couple of tunes appeared in the late Seventies. The first of these new efforts was a song called 'När du tar mig i din famn' ('When You Take Me In Your Arms') for a 1979 compilation album of her greatest solo hits put out by Cupol, her former record company.

"I considered the *Elva kvinnor i ett hus* album as her peak," says Michael Tretow, "but then we recorded 'När du tar mig i din famn' and then *that* became her peak. Abba took time away from her own thing, because I believe she would have continued developing that side of her. As far as I'm concerned, it was Björn and Benny, Agnetha and Ted Gärdestad who represented the music in life at that time. They were all just really solid composers."

Disappointingly, in the late Seventies Agnetha openly declared a distance to the *Elva kvinnor* album. "Many of the lyrics I wouldn't okay today," she said. "I've matured and developed a whole lot since then." The choice of new lyricist was not very inspired, unfortunately. Ingela Forsman, although both experienced and prolific, seldom came up with anything that was more than workmanlike for Agnetha. Forsman may have been more in tune with the new Agnetha but she was never even close to the clever twists of Bosse Carlgren, who had rendered a unique dimension to her music.

Despite Abba's lower profile in the early Eighties, only two further Fältskog songs had seen the light of day before the *Eyes Of A Woman* titles. 'Men natten är vår' ('But The Night Is Ours') was a contribution to the 1981 Swedish selection for the Eurovision Song Contest, performed by Polar recording artist Kicki Moberg. An excellent ballad with a rich melody in the verses, it was let down by the performer and failed to become a hit. 'Man', written for the *Wrap Your Arms Around Me* album, was a pleasant if fairly anonymous number.

Although recent songwriting efforts had been few and far between, Agnetha hadn't lost her tunesmith knack. However, the chances of an ambitious singer/songwriter album in the vein of *Elva kvinnor* were exceptionally slim. "Do you realise how hard it is to compose? It's so boring!" she exclaimed. "It might be easier for those who work in pairs, but I was struggling alone with 'I Won't Let You Go' for the whole of last summer. It's only a matter of hard work, no glamour at all."

Little in her life as an artist felt interesting or challenging anymore. The girl who had burst into tears when her first single charted professed to have become almost indifferent to success after 'Waterloo'. "After that it was different, then you never felt that dizzy feeling of happiness again. We were never blasé with success, but perhaps we were spoiled. It became a habit that every single should reach number one in England. That was just how things should be."

As ever, Agnetha's children were the mainstay of her life. "Time has gone so fast. Christian is seven today and Linda 12, on her next birthday she will be a teenager. It's very hard to be a working woman with a career and raise two children at the same time." It was as if Agnetha was devoting more energy to defining limits in her professional life than finding a way of actually enjoying her work in the music business.

Eyes Of A Woman became Agnetha's last album for Polar. Her own production company, Agnetha Fältskog Produktion AB, was formed just before album sessions commenced, and at the end of 1986 she recorded a one-off single called 'The Way You Are' as a duet with singer Ola Håkansson for Sonet Records. In early 1987 Agnetha released a children's album with Christian, a sort of follow-up to a Christmas album she had made with Linda at the beginning of the Eighties. Unlike the Christmas LP, which hit the Top 10, the album with her son failed to chart.

During the summer of 1987 she spent five weeks in Los Angeles, recording her third international pop album, *I Stand Alone*. The album was produced by Peter Cetera, formerly lead singer with Chicago, whom Agnetha had met in Stockholm in 1986 when they both participated in a televised charity gala. Indeed, it's unlikely the project would have happened at all but for Cetera's enthusiasm. Agnetha professed to regret that everything was decided so quickly that she didn't have the time to write any songs for the album – perhaps there was also some relief at being given an excuse to avoid the long hours at the piano. In the spring of 1987 Cetera started selecting songs, and all Agnetha had to do was to attend the recording sessions. Eventually she was persuaded to board a plane so that the album could be made in Los Angeles, according to the producer's wishes. It was the first time she had recorded a whole album outside of Sweden.

I Stand Alone was a slick product, marked by a relaxed Eighties American west coast sound, released by the Swedish arm of Cetera's record company, WEA, in November 1987. It entered the Swedish charts at number one and went on to sell more than 200,000 copies throughout Scandinavia, but in the rest of the world the results weren't so impressive. Most of the songs on *I Stand Alone* were fairly bland, and the album didn't yield any hits. Moreover, Agnetha was more reluctant than ever to travel to do promotion, preferring to let television crews and reporters come to Stockholm to conduct interviews.

Hans Englund, Benny's old friend from his pre-Hep Stars band, Elverkets Spelmanslag, had since made a career in the record business and was now the Swedish head of WEA. "She did go to London to do a couple of interviews and a television show," he recalls, "but she turned down major shows in West Germany who were really eager to have her on."

According to Englund, what was needed was a proper promotional tour, country by country. "She did a couple of videos and felt that this would be enough, but that's not really how it worked out. We sold just over half a million copies of the album worldwide, but I'm sure we would have done better if she'd been prepared to do more promotion."

Despite her low profile, there was still an aura of magic and mystery surrounding Agnetha, as was evident during the promotional visit to London in early 1988. "We hadn't announced the visit or anything, and there were only a few people at the record company who knew about it," recalls Englund. "Yet there were hordes of young kids – too young to have lived through the Abba years – hanging around outside the hotel."

The London interviews would be Agnetha's last public statements in any shape or form for a long while. WEA had an option for a second album, but it was not to be. Shortly after the release of *I Stand Alone*, Agnetha realised that she had lost all will to remain in the music business, much less continue as a public figure. "There was a time when the music fell silent," she remembered. "Both within me and around me. During a ten-year period I neither played, sang nor listened to music. I didn't even bother to get a decent stereo system. I was tired of composing and tired of singing. I didn't feel that there were any challenges in music for me."

Perhaps part of the reason was that she had elected to hand over much of those challenges to her producers. Three fairly impersonal albums in a row after the highs of Abba and her last Swedish-language recordings would have been enough to extinguish anyone's fire. It could be heard in her vocal performances as well: none of her recent producers had pushed her to excel in the same way that Björn and Benny had done. Her voice was fine, but it lacked the cutting edge achieved by those interminable, patience-testing, ultimately brilliant Abba re-takes.

"Today, when I consider my last three albums after Abba, I'm not especially satisfied with them," she reflected later. "When you're in the middle of working on a new record you think it's just fabulous. Perhaps you feel like that instinctively, just to find the strength to complete it. You give it your all and then you feel that the recordings are incredible. But when I listen to them now I sometimes wonder why on earth we did certain songs. A lot of them don't feel nearly as convincing as they did then."

Thus did Agnetha finally admit defeat in her struggle to balance career and privacy, and stepped out of the limelight for real. She began a period of soul-searching, exploring yoga as well as the spiritual writings of celebrity guru Deepak Chopra, and a long-time interest in astrology was rekindled. A permanent move in 1989 to a secluded farm estate on the island of Ekerö, purchased a few years earlier, further underlined her need to distance herself from the media as well as persistent fans. As the Eighties turned into the Nineties, Agnetha said farewell to life as a public figure.

Around the same time, Björn and Benny were also keeping their profiles fairly low, though the five-year project that was *Chess* – from its original inception to the Broadway flop in 1988 – had involved occasional steps out into the spotlight. In 1985 the pair made use of the pop songs that had fallen by the wayside during the writing of *Chess*. Instead of letting them form the basis of an Abba reunion, as Stig had hoped, Björn and Benny decided to produce an album for brother and sister act Anders and Karin Glenmark.

At the time, the male half of the duo was already a veteran of the Abba circle. The nephew of Glen Studio owner Bruno Glenmark, Anders had appeared as musician and backing vocalist on Agnetha and Frida's mid-Seventies solo LPs, and also played guitar on Abba's 'Money, Money, Money'. Moreover, he was the chorus vocalist on the *Chess* single 'One Night In Bangkok'.★ His sister Karin provided backing vocals on the *Chess* album and also sang the part of Svetlana on the European concert tour that was made to promote the album. In the Seventies, Anders and Karin had both been part of the vocal group Glenmarks together with their uncle and his wife. As a duo act they were now christened Gemini.

When Abba were doing their final bout of promotion at the end of

---

★ Ironically, Murray Head himself doesn't sing a note on this rap number, his biggest-ever hit.

1982, Benny was the only group member to state firmly his opinion that the Abba period had run its full course. Now, when the first Gemini album was released in the autumn of 1985, he made it patently clear that he didn't miss his old group one bit. "This recording has taught me how easy things can be, how smoothly everything can flow," he said. "It has to be fun working together, otherwise it's pointless." The technically proficient Karin Glenmark, who handled most of the lead vocals on the album, was praised profusely. "She can go higher than Agnetha and lower than Frida," Benny enthused, "but otherwise I don't want to make any comparisons. All of them are good – but Karin is a little better." To showcase Karin's vocal prowess, the song 'Another You, Another Me', stretching over two octaves, was especially written for her, but a wide voice range and pitch-perfect singing does not guarantee a successful vocal performance. Karin's voice lacked personality and warmth, which robbed the songs on the album of much of their emotional content. The samey "low-key build-up followed by a crescendo" arrangements on most of the tracks didn't offer her much support.

One of Abba's unreleased 1982 songs, 'Just Like That', was partly re-written and recorded for the first Gemini album. A comparison between the two interpretations lays the problem bare quite clearly: Abba's fully arranged, multi-layered recording bounces along energetically, while the Gemini version is slow and flat, marked by unnecessarily histrionic vocals.

It was clear that this could never have been an Abba album. Although the extraordinary talent for melody remained, Björn and Benny had moved on to completely different arrangement and production aesthetics, their eternal quest for technical perfection pushing them over the edge into an area which had very little to do with the true spirit of pop music. Whereas Abba had come together organically, Gemini was a studio product, shoulder-pad music sorely lacking in soul.

A second, more lively LP by the duo was released in the spring of 1987, but although both albums reached the Top 20 in Sweden, the world at large remained uninterested. With age Karin Glenmark would gain an attractive depth to her voice – it just wasn't there for the Gemini albums. When the Eighties were over, it was clear that none of the former Abba members had any relevance whatsoever in the international pop landscape.

Benny had greater success in the autumn of 1987 when he released his very first solo album, *Klinga mina klockor* (*Ring, My Bells*). It was his long-standing dream to record an album of Swedish folk music, and much of it was created in close collaboration with the fiddlers in the group Orsa Spelmän (Orsa Folk Musicians). Orsa is a town in the district of Dalecarlia in Sweden, where the fiddle-based folk music tradition is especially strong.

Benny's working relationship with Orsa Spelmän has continued since this first album project.

One of the titles on *Klinga mina klockor* was 'Lottis schottis', the folk-style song Björn and Benny had tried to make work as an Abba recording several times.★ Here it became a meeting between Benny's accordion and the Orsa Spelmän fiddles, which the composers concluded was the only suitable arrangement for the song. The album's title track was a fully orchestrated suite featuring an all-star choir of Swedish female singers, including Frida, who made one of her rare late-Eighties recording appearances. The choir aimed at recreating the sound of the girl choir Postflickorna (The Post Girls), an act which had struck a chord with Benny when he heard them on the radio as a child.

Klinga mina klockor was the first album to be released on Benny's own Mono Music record label, and he didn't expect any great sales for an album that by its very nature lacked hits. The initial 12,000 copies proved inadequate, however, as the album reached the Swedish Top 10 and went on to sell an impressive 160,000 copies.

With this album, and the follow-up, *November 1989*, Benny had re-invented himself as a genuinely Swedish composer, working in the tradition of the country's very own music. His image as a national treasure has only increased over the years, and it is within this field that his greatest commercial and artistic success has come since then. In September 2001, he scored his first number one album with *Benny Anderssons Orkester*.

Moving out of the Polar building in 1992, Benny and Görel Hanser, who runs Mono Music and is Benny's representative, set up offices and a recording studio in converted stables on the island of Skeppsholmen in central Stockholm. This has remained Benny's base ever since, and it is there he spends his working days, contentedly composing film themes and other commissioned tunes, as well as planning the odd record release close to his heart. Among those titles was a lavish CD box set of bird songs, an indulgence that reflected his childhood interest in ornithology.

With each year that passes, Benny has become further removed from contemporary popular music. This point was proved in 1993, when he and Björn made a brief attempt to return to pop territory by writing songs for 24-year-old singer Josefin Nilsson. Although the tunes were there, Benny's production on the resulting album, *Shapes*, smelled of Eighties aesthetics. After a brief appearance in the Swedish Top 20, and a limited international release, the album was quickly forgotten.

For his part, Björn kept out of public view for most of the late Eighties,

★ During the *Voulez-Vous* sessions it had been recorded under the title 'Dr. Claus von Hamlet'.

except when *Chess* required his attention. After the second Gemini album in 1987, his interest in record producing diminished quite drastically, and since then no records have carried an Ulvaeus production credit.

Apart from contributing the odd lyric to Benny's songs, he mostly devoted himself to family life in England at this time – a second daughter, Anna, was born to Björn and Lena in April 1986 – and to his new found interest in computers. At one point, he even acted as consultant to companies who needed help in installing computer systems.

Back in Sweden, the once glorious Polar Music record label was limping along. In an attempt to revive interest in the Abba catalogue – and after many years of steady requests from fans – a live album entitled *ABBA Live* was released in August 1986. The tracks were mostly culled from the 1979 Wembley shows, with a few recordings added from the Australian tour in 1977 and the 1981 Dick Cavett television special. A separate agreement regulating the royalty deal between Abba and Polar for this release, giving them a 50/50 split on the profits after costs, was drawn up. As far as Björn and Benny were concerned, the deal confirmed that the revised agreement concerning Abba's recordings was indeed honoured.

The live album, however, failed to beef up the bank accounts of either artist or record company. During the spring and summer of 1986, Michael Tretow had set to work remixing the tapes for release, doing a fairly good job of making the songs sound as if they came from the same concert. Unfortunately, his production was also tainted by a somewhat bombastic mid-Eighties sound which jarred against the original recordings' late Seventies/early Eighties origins.

Rune Söderqvists artwork was similarly uninspired. The cover drawing by one J. Geary, depicting a supposed stage construction being put together, was dull and unattractive. In truth, Abba themselves were fairly indifferent to the release, and it seemed none of those involved had put much into the project. "I hate live albums myself," said Björn. "It's boring to hear 'reproductions' of songs that sound much better in the studio . . . [But] the tapes sounded okay, so we just said, 'Well, go ahead and release it then'. There was nothing to be ashamed of."

The lack of enthusiasm surrounding *ABBA Live* was reciprocated with an embarrassing lack of interest from record-buyers. In Sweden, the album managed two weeks at number 49 in the charts, and many countries, including Great Britain, waited several years before releasing it. Those territories that picked up the album in 1986 experienced even worse chart performances than in Sweden – often complete no-shows. *ABBA Live* became the one major glitch in the official Abba catalogue, proving that half a decade after the group's demise, worldwide interest in their music was at an all-time low.

Meanwhile, Stig's daughter Marie had emerged as Polar Music's true A&R talent. Most of her signings had paid off, but she still found it hard to be taken seriously: many in the business sniggered that she couldn't succeed without her father to back her. Stig's health hadn't improved with the years, and by the late Eighties he was looking pale and run-down. The wild-eyed stare and energetic posture had been replaced by an almost defeated look in his eyes, a more hesitant body language. As he approached his sixties he realised he had to think about the future of his company, but he couldn't muster much energy or enthusiasm for remaining as a full-time player in the music business. He wanted to slow down on his activities considerably, and was also planning to found a music award. Thinking big as ever, his aim was that the prize should attain the status of a Nobel Prize in music.

When Björn and Benny sold their shares in Polar, Stig took the opportunity to reconstruct the entire group of companies. The Sweden Music publishing company, whose more than 50,000 copyrights made it the biggest in Scandinavia, formed the umbrella for the other firms. Stig was hoping that one of his children would take over the company but they didn't. On the contrary, Marie, who married singer Tomas Ledin in 1983, felt that it was time to leave Polar and prove herself by founding her own record company. In September 1986, with her father's melancholy blessing, she and her husband brought with them the major talent she had previously signed to her new label, The Record Station, robbing Polar of much of its *raison d'être* in one fell swoop. In the process the Ledins also acquired the Polar Music Studios.

It was clear that the unique little record label that had built its initial foundation on the success of the Hootenanny Singers and then scored unprecedented triumphs with Abba, was nearing its final collapse as an active company. When no one in the family wanted to take over as he had hoped, Stig had no choice but to look for outside buyers. "Stig offered the Abba members the chance to buy the company, but they didn't have that kind of money at the time," recalled Thomas Johansson. Instead, in May 1989 it was revealed that Sweden Music and all its affiliated companies had been sold to the publishing arm of the multinational record company PolyGram.

The purchase sum was 300 million kronor (£28.5 million) and it has been suggested that it was way too low for the valuable Abba catalogue, not to mention the tens of thousands of copyrights held by Sweden Music. John Spalding, who was part of the negotiations, does not agree. "A year earlier, and after long discussions, an American record company was only going to pay half of what we finally received," he says. Furthermore, at the time no one expected the Abba back catalogue to produce anything other than slow but steady sales in the future. According to the terms of the deal, Sweden Music would continue as an independent operation, with Stig remaining on board as Managing Director for five years. He also donated 42 million kronor (£4 million) of the payment he received towards his current pet project, the founding of a music prize.

The sale of Sweden Music to PolyGram, taking effect in January 1990, brought with it a clear-out of the Polar archives. In the autumn of 1989 much of the paperwork and documents were acquired by Staffan Lindé, the man in charge of Benny and Agnetha's finances. Like Lasse Dahlin, Lindé was a former employee of the bank Skaraborgsbanken. He was recruited as head of the financial department at Polar Music International, but had since set up his own business.

While carefully studying the protocols and contract drafts, and comparing them with royalty statements received by his company on behalf of his clients, Lindé made a distressing discovery. The paperwork seemed to indicate that the Abba members were in fact due a nine per cent royalty on Abba recordings. The royalty statements in his own files showed that they had received only three per cent.

This was the first time Lindé was made aware of the 1984 agreement between Björn, Benny and Stig to raise the royalty. When he confronted Björn and Benny with his evidence, they were shocked and angry. They had trusted Polar to pay out the royalties according to the deal made in the spring of 1984 and hadn't actually studied the statements very closely. With the end of the Abba era they had anticipated a lower income and therefore found the sums to be quite reasonable. Moreover, Björn, who didn't expect any major revenue from Abba recordings in the future, had sold all his mechanical royalty rights to a Dutch company, and was even less aware of the details of the royalty payments. Lindé, meanwhile, claimed that he had tried to acquire copies of documents detailing the basis of the royalty payments from Polar for the past four years, but without success.

Before long lawyers were called in and a correspondence was entered into with Polar Music. Stig claimed that a prerequisite for the higher royalty rate was that Abba made new records. When this failed to happen, according to his point of view, the deal fell through, along with Polar's motivation to give the group a higher back royalty. Subject closed.

All that the Abba members had to refer to as evidence were declarations of intent in the shape of the contract drafts and the signed protocol. The contract did not stipulate that the royalty deal was dependent on the making of any new recordings. The problem was that the last version of the contract – drawn up after Björn, Benny and Stig's meeting in April 1984 – was never signed by all parties.

The matter was unresolved, and on June 5, 1990, a lawsuit was filed against Polar Music International AB at the district court in Stockholm. The plaintiffs were Agnetha Fältskog Produktion AB, Batrax Rotterdam BV (the Dutch company that had acquired Björn's rights), Chaperon (UK) Limited (a British-registered company, owned by Swiss investors, to which Frida had sold her rights) and Benny's MM Mono Music AB.

The plaintiffs demanded that the royalty for all future Abba releases should be adjusted according to the terms of the latest draft of the contract. Furthermore, they demanded a back payment amounting to an estimated 27 million kronor (£2,565,000) as compensation for the difference in royalties from January 1, 1983 to the present date. A month later the news of the lawsuit reached the press, killing, in one instant, whatever vestiges were left of the picture of Stig and Abba as a harmonious success story.

Incredibly, while the drama was unfolding and relationships worsened, Benny remained in the Polar building – which both he and Agnetha still owned a piece of – keeping his studio tower room until 1992. Also still in the building was Görel Hanser, who had gradually eased herself out of the Polar organisation and was now running Mono Music under the umbrella of her own management company.

For close observers, though, it was easy to conclude that the gap between Björn and Benny on the one side and Stig on the other had widened considerably since the former left Polar. In January 1986, Stig was the subject of *Här är ditt liv* (*This Is Your Life*) on Swedish television. From the point of view of the producers, the former Abba members were the most obvious guests for the programme, but Abba themselves were less convinced. They refused to travel down to the television studio in Malmö, referring to "time constraints" and "prior commitments".

A complete non-appearance from Abba would have been decidedly strange, however. The solution was to gather the four members in Benny's attic studio on January 16 – two days before the broadcast – and videotape a light-hearted, impromptu performance of Stig's old hit, 'Tivedshambo'. To date, this remains the very last performance by the former Abba members together that has been seen in public.

At the time of this brief reunion only Björn and Benny were still in regular contact with each other – Frida and Agnetha hadn't even met for two years. One hour after the taping, Frida, who had arrived in Stockholm only a few hours earlier, left for the next plane back to her home in Switzerland. Ever since Abba released their last record, the question of whether they would ever reunite was popping up regularly in interviews with each of the four members. Their answers varied, but usually boiled down to "probably not, but you should never say never", which was obviously as close to a definitive reply as any one of them could give.

Their true feelings were probably summed up quite well by Agnetha in a 1985 interview. "It could never happen," she said. "We have little in common and it's seldom that we meet. The guys have *Chess*, and Frida and I have our own lives. Björn is the one I meet most often because we have children together; sometimes I run into Benny at the office. I never see Frida. I have no longing for Abba again. I'm fine as I am."

Even with the video taping in Benny's studio, the team behind *Här är ditt liv* found it hard to swallow that not one single Abba member would be present in the television studio, and after much persuasion Björn and Benny finally agreed to come down to Malmö. That night, Benny was going to be at a party nearby anyway, and Björn was talked into delaying his return to England. The way their appearance turned out, it would probably have been better if they had stayed away after all. Björn, ever the diplomat, did a fairly good job of not giving the game away. Benny, however, appeared clearly uncomfortable – almost confrontational – throughout their segment of the show. Stig himself looked guarded, as if he wondered why his old protégés had even bothered coming.

Host Lasse Holmqvist, seemingly oblivious to any bad feelings between the three, pushed the obvious angle that Stig had guided Abba to fame and fortune. Holmqvist asked if the difference in musical taste between the two generations had caused any problems. Benny, eternally annoyed at constant exaggerations of Stig's part in their success, grabbed the opportunity to set the historical record straight according to his point of view. "It's never been a matter of taste, really," he replied, visibly restraining his irritation. "We've been doing our thing in our corner, while Stig has been doing his in his corner. You could say that we are each other's prerequisite. If Stig hadn't been there in the beginning things wouldn't have taken off . . ."

Holmqvist, obviously feeling that his question had been satisfactorily answered, interrupted and changed the subject. But Benny would have none of it and was determined to finish his line of argument: ". . . and if it hadn't been for us, Stig wouldn't be sitting here right now." As far as heartfelt tributes to a beloved mentor go, it left much to be desired. A party was held after the live broadcast but Björn and Benny had long since left the premises.

Three years later yet another sign of bad blood became public knowledge. At the end of 1988 the Austrian group Edelweiss released a novelty record called 'Bring Me Edelweiss'. The song became a huge hit all over Europe and by January 1989 was rapidly climbing the charts in Sweden. On his way back from a Hootenanny Singers television reunion, Björn heard the song for the first time on the car radio. He nearly jumped out of his seat when it reached the chorus: the melody was a note-for-note copy of Abba's 'SOS'. "Who the hell gave them the permission to do that?" he spat.

It didn't take long to find out that it wasn't any rip-off: the sleeve properly credited Andersson/Anderson/Ulvaeus. Further investigations revealed that permission had been granted by none other than Stig Anderson. Confronted with his actions, his alleged defence was, "The section of 'SOS' that Edelweiss used is the section that I wrote."

Of course, Stig had no hand whatsoever in the melody part of Abba's songwriting, and even if he did, that didn't give him the right to grant any such permissions without consulting Björn and Benny. At first, the two songwriters decided to let it all pass, not wishing to cause a stir. But when 'Bring Me Edelweiss' became a hit in England later in the spring, forcing Björn to hear the song consistently on the radio, he decided that he'd had enough.

The outcome of the matter was that Stig had to shell out 300,000 kronor (£28,500) in damages to Björn and Benny. The composers donated the money to Amnesty International, but their point had been proven: never again would any samples of their music be approved without their express permission. It was with this incident fresh in everyone's mind that the royalty issue came to court.

The response to the lawsuit from Polar Music International was a point for point denial of all claims made by the four plaintiffs. Beneath the legal talk it was easy to sense Stig Anderson's seething anger. A reference in the suit to Polar's complex business deals and how these had affected Abba's relationship with Stig, contained an acknowledgement that the transactions "may possibly have been pecuniarily rewarding" for the group. The response was: "That the transactions 'may possibly have been pecuniarily rewarding' must be the biggest understatement of the year."

Polar's lawyers also pointed out that the April 1984 protocol, detailing the verbal agreement on the new royalty rate, had been confirmed by Björn and Benny's signatures only when the document was retrieved in 1989. They now alleged that this was a forgery. The plaintiffs replied that the late addition of the signatures was something that was acknowledged, even in the lawsuit. What was important was that Stig himself had signed this declaration of intent *at the time*.

However Polar tried to squirm out of the situation, there was no getting around the fact that there existed paperwork that indicated that Abba were due a higher royalty. Moreover, rock history contained numerous examples of successful renegotiations of unfavourable royalty deals: everything from Allen Klein's actions on behalf of The Rolling Stones and The Beatles in the Sixties, to a fairly recent court case contested by Elton John, an example referred to in the Abba lawsuit. At the end of the day it was hard to escape the conclusion that, morally, Abba were entitled to more than three per cent on their extraordinary sales.

An out-of-court settlement was agreed in July 1991, the exact terms remaining undisclosed, and comments from those involved have been few. Although Agnetha told her biographer Brita Åhman that Abba had "ultimately won", reportedly the group received only 13 million kronor (£1,235,000) in back payments: less than half the sum they had requested. Future royalty levels were said to have been adjusted, if not to the extent demanded in their lawsuit. A Sweden Music insider described the new rate as "still very favourable to us". A decade after the matter had been resolved, there were still grumblings from the group that they were entitled to a better deal.

For Stig, it was a devastating blow to have his private business exposed in this manner. Throughout the course of the lawsuit and beyond, he maintained that he had a clear conscience: if Abba had made new recordings they would have received a better royalty rate, when they didn't, the old deal was still valid – simple as that.

Stig felt he had made it a matter of honour throughout his career to always treat everyone fairly, and to be publicly accused of fraud on this scale made him very bitter. As a coda to the successful journey Stig and Abba had shared together and which had brought them all such fantastic rewards it was – to his way of thinking – nothing less than shameful. "They received every single penny they should have," he said in 1997 when asked to comment on the lawsuit. "There is no gratitude in this world. We resolved things peacefully, but of course the vibes haven't been the best between us since then. We don't have much contact."

Most of those who were close to both Stig and Abba managed to stay out of the conflict. It was not so easy for Görel Hanser: in the late Eighties she was still working part-time for Polar Music and part-time for Benny's Mono Music. Even after she gave up her interests in Polar, when veterans like Berka Bergkvist left the company in the mid-Eighties, she was one of the few who had a full insight into their affairs. It certainly didn't help that the Mono and Polar offices were still located in the same building at the time.

Görel also felt she owed an immense debt of gratitude to Stig for giving her a break in this business in the first place, but with the present conflict it became impossible for her to balance her two loyalties. It was the last remaining shred of the Polar "family" ties shot to pieces. "It took a long time before I had wrangled myself out of it all," Görel admitted later. "Eventually Stig and I became friends again. It took a while, but despite everything we did find our way back to one another."

Even though Björn had sold the rights to his royalties to an outside company, he was in way too deep to be regarded as neutral. Frida's sale made her the only Abba member not to be personally affected by the lawsuit. She was therefore the only one of the four with whom Stig could maintain a good relationship. In a 1993 radio series devoted to Stig's life, taped at the kitchen table in his villa, Frida and Görel appeared together as guests with Marie Ledin in one of the episodes. Naturally, the conversation revolved mostly around Abba and their achievements, and there wasn't the slightest hint of tension between any of the participants.

Björn, Benny and Agnetha were never able to patch things up with Stig: Agnetha later called the affair "a sad and sorry end to a successful collaboration". Björn made some overtures at one point, but his former manager and songwriting partner refused to take any of his calls. The Abba members' failure to fully recognise all the efforts he'd made on their behalf to ensure that at the end of the day they were all very wealthy, was unforgivable to Stig. "Abba have been able to keep their money, which can't be said for many other groups," he established, "and that was because I handled the money." The lawsuit constituted a breach of loyalty of the kind that Stig never allowed to be mended.

The squabbles died down in 1991, but the public breakdown of the relationship between Stig and Abba seemed like the last symbolic nail in the coffin of the Sweden of the Seventies. Like most countries in the Western world, Sweden had gone through the yuppified egoism of the Eighties and the return of a belief in relentless capitalism as the solution to all problems.

Along the way, taxation had been adjusted to better suit high-income earners: although Swedish tax is still regarded as high, ironically, many of the transactions Polar and Abba involved themselves in during the Seventies would probably have been unnecessary had their career happened in the Eighties. As the 10th anniversary of Abba's break-up approached, it was clear that this wasn't the same country anymore.

Shortly before midnight on Friday, February 28, 1986, Prime Minister Olof Palme was assassinated in central Stockholm, a murder that remains unsolved to this day. Palme's death turned into a national trauma, exposing a hitherto unacknowledged crack in the façade of Sweden as an open and safe country. This was supposed to be a place where even the Prime

Minister could stroll home from a movie in the middle of the night, without bodyguards and without fearing for his life.

Seventies sports heroes like Björn Borg and Ingemar Stenmark were caught up in dubious tales of tax exile and disastrous business deals, with ex-wives and ex-lovers attaining celebrity status by proxy. Ted Gärdestad, the blond, long-haired Polar singer whose music had conveyed a message of love, happiness and eternal sunshine, had disappeared from view as he became plagued by psychological problems. In a bizarre, nightmarish mix of the fate of two Seventies icons, at one point there was even a completely unfounded rumour that Gärdestad was Olof Palme's assassin. Ultimately, the singer's torment would end in schizophrenia and suicide in 1997.

At the start of the Nineties the country was on the verge of a severe recession, resulting in the worst levels of unemployment since the Great Depression. As a result, much of the social safety net that Sweden had prided itself in was ripped apart without much hope of ever being fully reconstructed again. No, this new decade certainly wasn't much like the Seventies.

Perhaps as a reaction to the cold chill that swept not just across Sweden but across the entire western world, there appeared on the horizon at the beginning of the Nineties a nostalgic yearning for some of the more colourful and carefree aspects of the Seventies. Who better to spearhead this celebration than the most popular recording artists of that decade, the group whose wild costumes epitomised the fun and the fearlessness of Seventies fashion, and whose music reached out to absolutely everyone, majorities and minorities alike?

Chapter 34

And so they were embraced again, firstly – to Björn and Benny's eternal bewilderment – by gay communities throughout the world. In an interview published in the March 2001 issue of *The Official International Agnetha Benny Björn Frida Fan Club* magazine, Björn was asked whether there was something he had always wanted to ask a fan. His reply was immediate: "Why do gay people like Abba so much?" Even he could not help but recognise how completely Abba had been adopted by large sections of the gay community and how prominent its role had been in the Nineties revival.

It is an undisputed fact that this was where the Abba revival experienced its underground beginning in the late Eighties. Although Abba wouldn't have sold hundreds of millions of records if their fans were exclusively gay, as Abba's original fanbase grew into adulthood a disproportionate number of them turned out to be gay men. Since then, it would seem, this has remained a dominant characteristic among most of the hardcore group of fans.

Hedonistic nightclubbing, kitschy fashion and tragic movie stars like Judy Garland or diva-like singers such as Barbra Streisand were already staples on the clichéd list of gay interests. Now Abba were suddenly absorbed into this culture, a most natural process since the group's attraction contained a little of all these elements.

Abba had several eminently danceable tracks to their credit, from the celebratory 'Dancing Queen' and the tribute to a hectic nightlife that was 'Summer Night City', to the anguished proto-techno of 'Lay All Your Love On Me'. Their imaginative and colourful costumes repelled and attracted in equal doses, and made the group highly recognisable, giving them a more than sufficient air of kitsch while begging for imitation by the discerning drag queen. The torch song tragedies delivered by the seemingly ever-abandoned Agnetha made up the Garland factor, while Frida's dramatic looks and regal postures added a touch of diva to the mix.

The traditional roles of men and women were somehow equalised within Abba by way of the unthreatening, toned-down, almost emasculated images of Björn and Benny. Two married couples presenting themselves to the world in one outrageously spacey outfit after the other functioned like a distorted mirror image of heterosexuality. For a group of people already marginalised by the ideal of society's nuclear family, there was an unquestionable attraction in this neutralised picture of male/ female relationships.

Furthermore, Abba contrasted sharply with rock culture hegemony as defined by the average straight male. Their words and music sympathised with those who struggled with everyday life instead of providing role models for escapism and tribal groupings, and the songs were delivered by female, pitch-perfect voices, far removed from the whisky-shot, male huskiness at the other end of the rock spectrum. Those who'd already been forced to question most other aspects of what is accepted as normal could not fail to take Abba to their hearts, albeit on a subconscious level.

When synth-pop duo Erasure achieved their biggest-ever hit with the *Abba-esque* EP of cover versions in the spring of 1992, for the gay community it simply marked a logical conclusion: Abba were back. "You didn't admit to liking them at school unless you were a bit *femme*, so me and my friends did," remarked Erasure lead singer Andy Bell. A whole generation of closet fans were vindicated when his band brought Abba back to the top of the charts.

For the rest of the world, the success of Erasure and cover bands such as Björn Again helped kick-start a global revival of immense proportions. Australians Björn Again, the first and most popular of the plethora of Abba imitators, filled the gap provided by Abba's refusal to conduct a cash-in reunion tour. The band has since turned into something of an industry, with several incarnations touring the world at the same time. Focusing on exaggerated Swedish accents, a portrayal of the Abba members as both vapid and downright stupid during "in-character" interviews, as well as an overall Euro-kitsch atmosphere, Björn Again have exploited the "pure entertainment" and "good for a laugh" angle of the Abba phenomenon. Their extraordinary success seems to indicate that this is exactly how large sections of the public want it.

In a lucky coincidence PolyGram, who'd been waiting for all of Polar's licensing deals around the world to expire, were planning a compilation album release of Abba's greatest hits at the same time as Erasure hit the charts and Björn Again's ability to draw crowds was recognised. In the UK, for the past few years Abba's presence in record shops had mainly been through budget releases by companies like Pickwick, Castle and Telstar. The release of the first Polygram compilation was now preceded by careful market research as to how such a CD would best be packaged. The result showed that a monochrome image focusing on the Abba logo, with no pictures locking the group into the Seventies, would appeal best to buyers.

This proved to be exactly right. The revival of the kitsch quality of "the decade that taste forgot" proved to be short-lived, but packaging Abba as a classic, timeless act, gave the group's music a new lease of life and a longevity that none of those involved could have imagined. The compilation CD *ABBA Gold*, featuring a simple design of gold lettering against a black background, was released in September 1992 and quickly became one of the huge success stories of the Nineties. Abba were elevated from downmarket hell to the full-price, upmarket area where they belonged: less than a decade after release, worldwide sales figures exceed 20 million copies.

Beyond any ironic longing for flared trousers and platform boots, at the end of the day Abba's true legacy seems to be their music. With rap, techno and grunge as dominating genres at the time of *ABBA Gold*'s original release, there was obviously a void for strong melodies. The album was a huge success in Australia, proving that despite the sudden drop in the group's popularity 15 years earlier, their phenomenal impact was remembered fondly by large sections of the public.

A companion compilation, *More ABBA Gold*, collecting the rest of the groups' hits plus a few album tracks, was issued in 1993. It says something for Abba's extraordinary popularity that this "volume two" release could notch up total sales of over two million copies, more than most acts sell of their premier greatest hits collections. In 1994, Abba received the obligatory box set treatment: *Thank You For The Music* collected all the familiar tracks from the group's back catalogue plus a number of rarities and previously unreleased recordings.

The world media focus on the revival was extended with the release of two Australian movies in 1994. *The Adventures Of Priscilla, Queen Of The Desert*, about two drag queens and a transsexual, had Abba's relevance in the gay world as a running theme. In *Muriel's Wedding*, Abba's status as a self-evident reference in modern Australian culture was explored through the story of an unhappy twenty-something woman who finds solace in the group's music.

The former Abba members themselves were as surprised as anyone by this sudden renewed interest in their music. "When we broke up I thought that Abba was something completely past, behind me," said Björn. "We were going forward, writing *Chess* and so forth and [I assumed] that Abba would vanish. It was stupid and naïve thinking that. The fact that it has survived is immensely flattering." Benny was equally amazed that the music had been able to transcend the group's glittery image and their overall appearance in the Seventies. "We were extremely corny, I think. It's rather fantastic that the music is still around and that they didn't kill us for being so corny at the time."

Abba's influence and inspiration were suddenly being acknowledged on a wider scale than ever before. Endorsement by respected rock stars such as Bono of U2 made it easier for those who felt uncomfortable with Abba's lack of cool to embrace them more openly. When Björn and Benny performed 'Dancing Queen' onstage with U2 during a Stockholm concert in June 1992, it was a pivotal moment for Abba's elevation to the status of "old heroes".

The Abba revival was perfect for the post-everything musical landscape of the Nineties. Rock had lost all its pretensions to being able to change the world, and the arena was open for a band whose significance rested firmly with its music and came attached with a colourful, light-hearted image. It was hardly a coincidence that U2, the world's most popular premier league band-with-a-conscience, used Abba as a tool to reinvent themselves as an ironic and world-weary group.

A fairly diverse cross-section of fans from the annals of modern popular music now crept out of the woodwork to pay tribute. Both Kurt Cobain and Courtney Love professed to be fans – Cobain even insisted that Björn Again should be on the same bill when Nirvana played the Reading Festival in the UK in 1992. R.E.M. did a live cover version of 'Does Your Mother Know', while Evan Dando of The Lemonheads picked up on the dark side of Abba and recorded an acoustic, stripped-down interpretation of 'Knowing Me, Knowing You'.

The Fugees borrowed the bass and synthesizer riff from 'The Name Of The Game' for their 1997 recording 'Rumble In The Jungle' – one of the few times that Björn and Benny would authorise a sampling of Abba's music. "We thought it was amusing that some coloured, ultra-hip people from the USA crossed the Atlantic to Scandinavia to find a riff," said Björn. "That was so cool that we had to okay it."

If Björn was bemused by the attention from younger generations it was almost beyond comprehension to receive an accolade from those magical British Sixties icons who had been his own idols way back when. "One of the most flattering things I've heard in my life was in New York [when] I ran into Pete Townshend [of The Who]," he recalled. "He says, 'Do you know that 'SOS' is the best pop song ever written?' I was *so* proud." Björn and Benny had certainly come a long way since they struggled to put together their first joint "pop song in English" at the paper mill in Västervik back in 1966.

It was hard to pick up any overt Abba influences in the music produced by bands working in the rock field, however. Although many of those in search of strong melodies and catchy hooks have cited Abba as a role model, classical keyboard flourishes and multi-layered female choirs were never going to be the staple of "happening" rock bands. Abba's legacy was more heavily felt in the music of modern hit factories, whose operation rests largely on the Abba-tested base of strong melodies, danceable beats and consistently high energy levels. Pete Waterman of the Eighties chart-ruling team of Stock/Aitken/Waterman, has cited Lennon & McCartney, The Beach Boys, Motown and Abba as the ultimate role models for anyone who wants to make hits.

When Waterman created the boy/girl group Steps in the late Nineties his homage to Abba was even more overt, his vision being to turn them into an "Abba on speed". In spirit, that certainly seemed to be an accurate description of their records: Steps' first UK Top 10 hit, 'Last Thing On My Mind', opened with a 'The Winner Takes It All'-style piano intro before turning into a techno pop stomper, infested with catchy hooks.

In Sweden, hit wizard Max Martin, the man behind many of the smashes by turn of the century teenie acts such as Britney Spears, *N Sync and Backstreet Boys, recognised his place in the Scandinavian pop tradition as spearheaded by Abba. "I'm a sucker for the melancholy," he said. "I guess that's one of the things, coming from this place. If you listen to Abba . . . it's always sort of melancholy."

This reflective, wistful mood also set the tone for the work that was to dominate the greater part of Björn and Benny's Nineties. Björn moved back to Sweden from England in December 1990, and while Abba were going through a revival out of the members' own control, the pair were hard at work with their next stage musical. However, this time they were determined to have a good, solid plot as the basis for their creation and started exploring Sweden's rich literary canon in search of a story.

By the early Nineties they had instigated endeavours to make a musical out of Swedish author Vilhelm Moberg's *Emigrants* suite of novels. The four books – an important part of the nation's literary heritage – dealt with the fate of Swedish emigrants to America in the second half of the 19th century. It was a theme that lent itself perfectly to Benny's continued exploration and development of indigenous folk music traditions. "To take the step of moving to the other side of the world, and to know that you will not be able to return, although that's what you long for all the time and you never rid yourself of that feeling – there's a lot of music in that," said Björn.

Turning this gigantic literary work into a manageable musical turned out to be a hard task. Work started in 1990, but it wasn't until October

1995 that the finished product, *Kristina från Duvemåla* (*Kristina From Duvemåla*), received its première in Malmö. "It took me two years before I realised that there is no way this is going to work unless I dare to say, 'Now this is mine and I do what I want with it!' " recalled Benny. "When you start relying on your own choices you can also start trusting them."

At over three hours, *Kristina från Duvemåla* was a lot to digest, but most audiences didn't seem to mind. The musical turned out to be a long-running mega-hit, playing to more than one million people, alternating between Malmö and Gothenburg before finishing off with a year in Stockholm, closing in June 1999. The show was also a huge critical success, becoming something of a national treasure: the gradual acceptance of Benny and Björn as a major composer team within their realm finally culminating in unanimous, unreserved praise from audiences and reviewers alike. The catalogue of pastiches that had characterised *Chess* had been replaced by a more consistent, epic folk music tone that pulled the work together instead of showing off the composers' versatility.

Part of this success rested on Björn and Benny's decision to clearly divide their roles as creators of music and lyrics. "Björn and I have made the music together through the years," said Benny. "There have been two of us, and through discussions we have decided how we want it to be. You can have such discussions to a certain extent, but with *Kristina* that doesn't work. If this music should have any relevance whatsoever it must spring from one single person's feelings. In this case, my feelings."

Likewise, Björn's lyrics were expertly written, as expected from a veteran of the singable pop lyric, who now combined this talent with an ambition to story-tell in his own language. Even up to the première, the ever-fretful Björn had grave doubts about his own contribution. So sure was he of being panned by the reviewers that he and his wife Lena had booked plane tickets for a holiday abroad the following morning, allowing him to escape any embarrassment. However, Björn received just as much praise for his words as Benny for his music, and the Ulvaeus couple could safely stay at home and bask in the glory.

In Sweden, there was certainly a completely different mood surrounding Abba as a group, and Andersson/Ulvaeus as a team, than two decades earlier. By the end of 1996 both Björn and Benny had turned 50, and were hailed as the elder statesmen of Swedish pop, receiving standing ovations whether they presented a new musical work, or simply showed up at some gala to pick up an award.

The self-sufficient smugness of the Seventies having disappeared completely, it was as if the Swedish population couldn't afford to dismiss what few symbols of national pride were left. Abba's music seemed to have a comforting function, reminding people of the time when a concept like "social security" actually meant something. With problems like severe unemployment and increasing xenophobia to contend with, the question of whether Sweden should participate in the Eurovision Song Contest seemed fairly insignificant.

A preoccupation with the cultural climate of the Seventies has been going on since the mid-Eighties, manifesting itself in movies, books, documentaries and topical newspaper articles. Of course, the pendulum has now swung too far in the other direction – as Benny has opined, the basic intention to make the world a better place was honourable. It certainly beats exasperated cynicism any day as a desirable human quality: if only it hadn't been accompanied by such a judgemental and insulated world-view at the time.

Since the early Nineties, three quarters of the group that was Abba have lived in Sweden, strengthening their status as living legends. Two of those members are even writing and performing music regularly, being available for comment from time to time. Agnetha retained her silence for most of the first half of the decade, but Frida, the only Abba member still living abroad, was slowly re-emerging as a semi-public figure at the beginning of the Nineties.

Five years after her withdrawal from show business, the public became acquainted with yet another reinvented version of Frida. The pastel-coloured bombasto-rock singer had turned into an aristocratic 45-year-old woman, dressed in discreet shades of black, grey, off-white or dark blue, and with a deserving cause on her agenda.

Reading an article about the ongoing acidification of forest soils had awakened an anger in her, she said, along with a will to try to do something about these problems. She became involved in an environmental organisation called Det naturliga steget (The Natural Step). From the basis of this organisation she founded Artister för miljö (Artists For The Environment), whose purpose was to draw attention to environmental issues through concerts and other public appearances.

In July 1992 a group of singers in the organisation released a single. The A-side was an all-star performance of a well-known Swedish song called 'Änglamark' ('Angel's Ground'), but Frida had the B-side all to herself with her cover of Julian Lennon's 1991 hit 'Saltwater'. It was her first solo performance on record in eight years. The following month she organised an Artister för miljö concert at the courtyard of the Royal Palace of Stockholm where, uniquely, the King had given permission for a public event to be held. Frida performed 'Saltwater' and duetted with Marie

Fredriksson of Roxette on the old Louis Armstrong hit 'What A Wonderful World'.

Twelve days after this exclusive concert Frida married Ruzzo Reuss, her companion of some years, in a ceremony at the church of Hørsholm in Denmark. In the tradition of Frida's previous weddings, it was a low-key affair with only family and the couple's closest friends in attendance. Through her union with Ruzzo, Frida now formally acquired the title of Princess, though she would always play down the significance of the title, claiming never to use it in everyday life. It certainly seemed like the symbolic culmination of a fairytale journey that sounded quite unbelievable in condensed form. From her origins as an outcast in post-war Norway, through her poor and lonely upbringing in small-town Torshälla and becoming a teenage mother, she had gone on to achieve worldwide fame in Abba before finally marrying a real-life prince.

Beyond the obvious plot qualities, it was clear that something had gelled for Frida. Circumstances had forced her to tackle adult responsibilities long before she had become a woman in either body or soul. It was as if she was out of synch with herself: as a result, emptiness and insecurity, the fear of being abandoned, had been her constant companions through life. The gap between the responsibilities that life forced upon her and the girl that was abandoned in the process had forced her to cast herself in different roles: the Jazz Broad, the Housewife, the Pop Star, the Rock Chick, the Independent Woman. It seemed it was only when she allowed herself to step back and reassess her life for real that she caught up with her true self. Her physical age had finally become reconciled with her life experience and psychological make-up.

"In my case I was meant to grow up with my grandmother," she reflected. "I had no other choice but to accept this, even when I reached my early teens and saw all the other kids with their families, wishing I was in the same situation . . . I've managed my life in a good way and I'm comfortable with it. When you get older you look back on your childhood as a necessary evil to make you what you are today." In her middle age, Frida had finally found the inner peace and harmony she had longed for all her life.

In December 1993, Frida made another brief return to the stage. In celebration of Queen Silvia's 50th birthday she performed an a cappella version of 'Dancing Queen' together with vocal group The Real Group at The Royal Swedish Opera. Two years later, in November 1995, she turned 50, and the following year she finally stepped back into the recording studio for real again. It was the culmination of a process that had been going on for a couple of years, in which she was trying to decide what kind of album she wanted to make. At one point it looked as if she was going to record ballads in the vein of her first LP, *Frida*, from 1971. At least one recording was made: a slightly modernised version of a Swedish folk song. In the end, however, she went for a commercially safer bet, enlisting the help of Anders Glenmark. Since Björn and Benny's Gemini project Glenmark had emerged as one of Sweden's top producers and a successful recording artist in his own right. A prerequisite for the project was that the producer was willing to collaborate closely with Frida on the songs. She didn't write anything herself except one lyric, but wanted Glenmark, who wrote all of the music and most of the words, to reflect both her past experiences and the woman she was at this stage in her life.

The song 'Hon fick som hon ville' ('She Got What She Wanted'), for instance, referred indirectly to the circumstances surrounding her divorce from Benny. "It deals with a woman who takes another woman's man," she explained, "and I'm not the only person who's experienced that, it has happened to many women." The lead-off single 'Även en blomma' ('Even A Flower') was a tribute to personal growth, containing imagery referring to her interest in nature and environmental issues. Spiritual development was also the subject of 'Kvinnor som springer' ('Women Who Run'), the closing track and the only one to feature a songwriting contribution from Frida. The words were inspired by Clarissa Pinkola Estes' book *Women Who Run With The Wolves*, itself based on the influential writings of psychologist Carl Gustav Jung.

"I believe only a woman could have written those lyrics," said Frida. "It's about dream analysis and going into your 'wild soul' to search for the woman who may be hidden inside of you . . . You could say that it deals with what I've gone through as a human being and as a woman, the development inside. I wanted it to be a tribute to women who've managed to find their wild self, who dare to bring that out of themselves."

Frida also wanted to record a duet with Agnetha for the album, 'Alla mina bästa år' ('All My Best Years'). The idea of the female half of Abba doing an album outside the group had been around since the early Eighties, but had never come to fruition. Alas, the collaboration was destined not to happen this time either as Agnetha declined the invitation to sing on the recording. "When I listen to [Abba's] recordings after all this time, I think our voices sound fantastic together," said Frida. "I've wanted us to do an album for several years and Agnetha is also eager. But not yet. I'll have to give her some time." Marie Fredriksson became Frida's duet partner on 'Alla mina bästa år'.

The resulting CD, *Djupa andetag* (*Deep Breaths*), was issued in September 1996. It was the first release on the brand new Anderson Records label, founded by Stig's daughter, Marie Ledin. She had sold her company The Record Station to the multinational BMG group of labels, initially remaining as Managing Director. When Marie found that she had been sucked into a conglomerate, she jumped ship and started a new label, naming it after her father.

The *Djupa andetag* album was expertly performed, carefully produced, tastefully packaged – with Frida posing in elegant Donna Karan garments – and perhaps a little dull. No one could begrudge Frida her inner harmony, but a whole album's worth of tributes to finding love and inner peace didn't make for an especially engaging listening experience.

The choice of songwriter/producer was also a bit unfortunate. Anders Glenmark's talents are undisputed, but when he's not working with artists with a strong personal identity in their musical expression, he tends to overwhelm as a producer. Much of *Djupa andetag*, therefore, ended up sounding like an Anders Glenmark album with Frida vocals. The ballad album that she originally planned to record would probably have put her vocal talents to more artistically rewarding use. Nevertheless, the CD struck a chord with the Swedish record-buyers, reaching number one and selling 100,000 copies.

Frida's comeback led to a Swedish media blitz, with press, radio and television standing in line to interview her. In a promotion manager's dream of synchronicity, she was the subject of a television special/documentary, broadcast on the day of the album's release. With a mild-mannered interviewer as a guide, the viewers were treated to several exclusive glimpses of Frida's present life. In a sort of toned-down, Swedish version of *Lifestyles Of The Rich And Famous*, several scenes were filmed at her luxurious home in Majorca.

The media coverage reflected the woman that emerged on her album: more beautiful than ever, emotionally fulfilled, in touch with herself and happy in her life together with her husband. However, there were also clear hints that her present circumstances had rendered her slightly out of touch with most people's reality. One interviewer was astonished by her claim to be a socialist. Only when Frida looked up the word in a dictionary afterwards was she able to explain that, no, she wasn't a socialist, but her background was working class. And in the television documentary she was heard to comment that the ability to relax was "a fantastic gift that has nothing to do with money". Meanwhile, viewers were treated to scenes of Frida strolling by the magnificent swimming pool on her Majorca terrace overlooking the Mediterranean. A single parent working 40 hours a week might have a slightly different take on the matter.

A few days after Frida's album hit the shops, Agnetha also made a comeback of sorts. A double-CD compilation of hits was released, along with Brita Åhman's authorised book about her, *Som jag är* (published in English under the title *As I Am* a year later), a project that had finally been completed after its cancellation 13 years earlier.

Despite Agnetha keeping a low profile for nearly a decade, the first few years of the Nineties had seen a great deal of personal turbulence. She had gradually cut herself off from most of her old friends and acquaintances, although she wasn't entirely living the life of the Garbo-like recluse that the press implied. Agnetha often felt uncomfortable being seen in public, but was still spotted shopping and dining in central Stockholm from time to time, just like any other well-to-do woman in her early middle age. Rather, the change was to be found in the contrast between her previous life as a pop star – constantly surrounded by musicians, colleagues and associates – and her present, private existence. It was clear she had no wish to socialise with anyone except her immediate family and closest circle of friends: Agnetha just wasn't available for comment.

In April 1990 she turned 40 and was photographed by fans in her car outside her mansion. Her children were in the back seat, but an unknown man was sitting beside her. Much to Agnetha's annoyance, the pictures ended up in the tabloid *Aftonbladet* the day after. The identity of the man was revealed in December, when Agnetha Fältskog became Mrs Tomas Sonnenfeld at a low-key wedding in her local church. Agnetha's second husband was a prematurely white-haired 44-year-old surgeon, described by Brita Åhman as "skilful and witty". Reportedly, the couple had met at a party. Alas, the marriage lasted less than two years: in November 1992, the pair filed for divorce.

The end of this relationship was followed by further heavy blows. Her mother, Birgit, died in an accident in January 1994, and in December 1995 her father, Ingvar, also passed away. The last years of their lives had been marked by ill health, and their deterioration had been painful to watch for their daughter. When these last remaining symbols of the familial stability of her childhood were snatched away from Agnetha, it affected her deeply. "I think of the last few years and they haven't been kind to me," she said, reflecting on her second divorce and the loss of her parents. "The loneliness weighs heavy upon me."

The decision to make her first extensive public comments for eight years in the shape of an authorised book was triggered by the publication of the 1995 Abba biography *The Name Of The Game* by Andrew Oldham, Tony Calder and Colin Irwin. Oldham and Calder were both music business legends, most famously as managers of The Rolling Stones during the Sixties.

Although Oldham was well known for his maverick personality, his motives for suddenly moving into pop biography writing were unclear: the book was a piece of trash journalism, filled with rambling prose and wild fantasies. Nevertheless, *The Name Of The Game* was snatched up by a Swedish gossip rag which started serialising parts of it in April 1995. Once again Agnetha was confronted with fictional stories constructed from a tiny grain of truth, and sometimes not even that. That was when Brita Åhman's suggestion to revive their old book project was met with a resounding "Yes!"

Unfortunately, *As I Am* was something of a failure. A two-hour read at best, the book was permeated by the feeling that Agnetha's motive was simply to refute the picture that the gossip press painted of her. She didn't want to talk about her marriages, which was fair enough, but nor did she have much to say about the people she had worked with through the years or the creative aspects of her career. Again, more energy seemed to have been poured into defining limits than actually making a positive contribution.

The book was structured between Åhman's sycophantic prose and sections where Agnetha herself was the narrator. Although the reader did gain an insight or two into Agnetha's personality and her memories of certain episodes in her life, the inescapable conclusion was that her actual involvement in the project was minimal. Many of her own comments were taken from Brita Åhman's already published mid-Eighties interviews, several others had clearly been ghostwritten: developed from other books and shoved in as Agnetha's supposed outpourings. How else, one wonders, could Agnetha "remember" Björn and Benny cancelling the sessions for the Abba album *Opus 10* – a project that never existed, but has survived as a myth through an unfortunately worded report in a Swedish newspaper in 1981.

The only bits in the book where Agnetha seemed to be looking back with genuine fondness were when she talked about her children and her own childhood, as well as the very earliest days of her singing career. The Abba years were mainly stress and hardship, the press were evil gossip-mongers and her post-Abba solo career was a long series of bus crashes and unsatisfactory albums. Some of the predominantly negative reviews summed up *As I Am* quite well. "I'm not used to reading books as lousy as this one," wrote a Swedish critic, while Q magazine in the UK opined: "If this is Agnetha as she is, then God help her."

As if to underline the grim tone of her recollections in the book,

Agnetha rejected the original cover picture where she was smiling broadly. Ultimately, a photograph of a serious-looking Agnetha, gazing into the distance, adorned the cover. This book wasn't going to be any laughing matter, the picture seemed to suggest. Meanwhile, the original picture was used for the back of the book and ended up on the front of the English version. Agnetha's beauty had not faded, but she now presented a different kind of visual appeal: gone was the blonde, perky Abba icon, and in its place was a mature, discreetly made-up woman in her mid-forties with her natural hair-colour.

The double-CD compilation *My Love My Life* spanned Agnetha's entire recording career from 1967 to 1987, including a couple of Abba songs. Agnetha was involved in the track selection, and even supplied a previously unheard tape of an early composition from her private collection. This was used for an introductory, short "documentary" track about the events leading to her first record contract which was put together by Michael Tretow, who also taped Agnetha talking about her early days. Again, her voice sounded full of enthusiasm and life as she talked about the beginnings of her career, a striking contrast to the general tone in her book.

None of the projects turned out to be a triumphant return, however. Agnetha herself kept a low profile, refusing to promote either album or book, instead leaving this job to Brita Åhman. Despite a major promotional campaign, the compilation CD only managed to struggle up to number 21 on the Swedish chart, with less than 10,000 copies leaving record shops. The book was also a resounding flop, selling well below expectations for a celebrity autobiography on that level.

"I haven't closed any doors," Agnetha hinted in the book, suggesting that she might be planning a full-scale comeback on the music scene. But nothing like that was on the agenda, and with the failure of the book and record she quickly disappeared from view again, retreating to her life on the farm.

For Stig Anderson the past decade also saw a slow withdrawal from public life. In the mid-Eighties his marriage collapsed when he became involved in an affair with another woman, a friend of the Anderson family. Eventually the inevitable happened, and Gudrun found out about his infidelity. "Maybe I'd known for a time, but there are certain things that you don't want to realise," she reflected later. "I wanted a divorce, but Stig was unsure. Like so many other men he wanted it all."

In the end Gudrun got her way and in January 1985, after nearly 30 years of marriage, the couple separated. Stig moved out of the Djurgården villa, and into an apartment in central Stockholm. The romance with his mistress died shortly after the divorce, and although it was several years before he moved back with Gudrun, they did become a couple again. Stig followed his usual habit of forging ahead to the next stage in life, and once his extra-marital affair was over he wanted to forget what had happened. "He didn't want us to discuss our problems," said Gudrun. "There was nothing else to do but look forward and leave the rest behind." Stig and Gudrun never remarried, however.

With the sale of Sweden Music to PolyGram, Stig formally remained in the company as Managing Director and consultant during the first half of the Nineties, putting together compilation CDs celebrating Polar's former glories. He was also fully occupied with his Polar Music Prize, awarded annually by The Royal Swedish Academy of Music "to persons, groups or institutions in recognition of exceptional achievements in the world of music in its broadest sense", according to the committee's own phrasing. This has mostly meant that the prize is shared each year by a popular music composer and someone working within the classical field.

When the prize was first awarded in 1992 the three Baltic States received 1 million kronor (£100,000) to establish performing rights organisations. The first popular music artist was Paul McCartney, who also received a million. However, the ex-Beatle couldn't be bothered going to Stockholm to pick up the prize, which somehow set the tone for its status throughout the rest of the decade. Although several high-profile recipients, like Elton John, Bob Dylan, Bruce Springsteen, Joni Mitchell, Stevie Wonder and Ray Charles all came to pick up their prizes, it failed to get the international recognition Stig had hoped for.

With his deteriorating health, the awards ceremony each May became about the only time he was seen in public. Worn down by excessively hard work and drink, his body had been damaged beyond repair. He had trouble moving about and was but a shadow of his former self: it was as if the whole point of being Stig Anderson – always on the go, with constant new projects and challenges on the horizon – had been snatched away from him. A few years into the Nineties his speech had become slow and deliberate, his replies in interviews often close to monosyllabic, as if it was too much hard work to give long answers. By the autumn of 1996 his words were severely slurred: the motormouth was suffering an irreparable breakdown.

With all the Anderson children having left home several years earlier, the Djurgården villa had become much too large for two people, and Stig's condition didn't make it any easier to manage. The house had been up for sale for several years, but it wasn't until 1996 that a buyer was found. The following March, Stig and Gudrun moved to an apartment in central Stockholm.

For Gudrun, life with Stig in the mid-Nineties was trying and worrisome. "He didn't want to meet people anymore and he didn't want me to go out," she recalled. "Socialising with friends or having dinner parties was never easy. I would never know for sure if it would happen or not, or how things would turn out . . . Stig would ask me where I was going every time I put on my coat. He didn't even want me to go out shopping."

On the morning of Friday, September 12, 1997, Stig was at home in the apartment as usual. Gudrun was away on a holiday trip abroad, and a friend had come over to visit. At 11.50 a.m., Stig suddenly collapsed with chest pains, suffering a cardiac arrest. Stig's friend called an ambulance and then phoned Marie, telling her to come to the apartment immediately. Marie, whose offices were located just a few blocks away, rushed over. "But although I was there really quickly, I never got the chance to speak to him," she said. Shortly after noon on that early autumn Friday, Stig Anderson, the penniless boy from Hova who became one of the richest men in Sweden, died. He was 66 years old.

Gudrun quickly returned home from her holiday. All their close friends and acquaintances were quickly informed about Stig's death. Görel Hanser called all four Abba members so that they wouldn't have to hear the news on the radio. Benny declined to comment, but Björn issued a short statement. "What has happened is deeply tragic. Stig Anderson meant a lot to me, both as a human being and as a mentor. Today my thoughts go to his wife, Gudrun, and to their children."

Frida was too distressed to come to the phone, said her husband, Ruzzo, when a newspaper called and asked for a comment. Agnetha's reaction went unrecorded. Newspapers, radio and television were filled with artists and other show business people paying tribute to one of the Swedish entertainment world's most successful, influential and controversial figures. "The last few years have been tough," reflected Gudrun a while later. "Stig was so ill and lost the will to live . . . I feel it was good for him that his life ended. He didn't enjoy anything anymore."

Stig's funeral was held on October 10 in Jakobs kyrka (Jacob's Church) in Stockholm. Björn, Benny and Frida all attended the ceremony; Agnetha was ill and sent a wreath together with her children, bearing the simple inscription "Thank you and farewell". The funeral was broadcast live on Swedish television, a very rare tribute granted only to royalty, important politicians and culturally significant personalities.

Singer Lisa Nilsson performed the Swedish version of 'Little Green Apples', the lyric Stig always held up as the best from his own vast catalogue of work. An all-star choir of five artists who'd achieved success with his songs in the Sixties sang Stig's version of 'You Don't Have To Say You Love Me'. The Swedish title was, poignantly, 'Vackra sagor är så korta' ('Beautiful Fairy Tales Are So Short'). An instrumental version of Hoagy Carmichael's 'Stardust', Stig's favourite song, was also performed at the ceremony.

"Stig aimed for the moon and he reached it," said assistant vicar Åke Bonnier in his eulogy. "He got what he wanted, but he ran out of dreams. His body lost its strength and in the end he wanted to die."

Chapter 35

Theatre producer Judy Craymer had an idea. Through previous collaborations with Tim Rice she'd been involved in the *Chess* project from the beginning, and had become a friend of Björn and Benny in the process. Ever since then she'd felt that there must be a way to use the Abba songs in some sort of dramatic context as well.

In 1983 there had been a production called *Abbacadabra*, a fantasy story based on Abba tunes with new lyrics, but that wasn't really what she had in mind. She'd brought her idea up several times with Björn and Benny, who wished her good luck but weren't very interested in the concept. At one point Craymer had her sights set on a television production and several manuscript writers were brought in, but none of them could come up with the right concept. At the time Björn and Benny were almost unaware of these proceedings, having their hands full with *Kristina från Duvemåla*.

The turning point came on a warm summer night, when Björn was strolling in London's West End with his family, waiting to see the show *Grease*. Suddenly he was struck by an almost childish feeling, a pang of longing for the days of *Chess*. "I said to myself: 'Why don't I have a show here; other people have shows here. I should have one, too.'" Watching *Grease* made Björn warm even more to the idea, and he saw the potential for an unpretentious Abba-related musical: a "good night out".

Björn's enthusiasm wasn't shared by Benny, who was observing the Abba revival with a feeling bordering on dismay, especially since it just refused to go away. It went against his whole being to revisit past glories: onwards, forwards to completely new creations was the only reasonable way to conduct your professional life from his point of view. Still, he gave the project his silent approval.

In 1996 Björn and Benny went into partnership with Judy Craymer and her co-producer Richard East to form the company Littlestar Services Ltd, which was to produce the proposed musical. A little while later, Judy Craymer found the right writer, award-winning playwright Catherine Johnson. Her wry sense of humour appealed to Craymer, and Björn eagerly seconded the choice as well.

Johnson was instructed to put together a story which had nothing to do with the Abba saga, but which linked the songs together in a natural way. She came up with a story about a mother and daughter, living on a holiday resort island. The girl had invited three men to her own wedding, and any of the men could be her father. Björn liked the idea: "I realised it was actually possible to use Abba's original lyrics as a basis for a story about relationships. In the beginning of our career the songs were more innocent and naïve, towards the end they were more mature. And it was women who sang them. Therein lay the opening for a story about a mother and a daughter."

Theoretically, the entire Abba catalogue was open for inclusion in the musical, and the dramatic requirements were said to be the main guiding light. However, it was hardly a coincidence that the final version included the entire *ABBA Gold* track listing of familiar hits, with the exception of 'Fernando' and 'Waterloo'.★

Although everybody involved had been careful to point out that the musical had nothing to do with Abba, when news of the project reached the press, some reports still made out that it was going to depict the group's story. Frida read one such article and, unimpressed, fired off an angry fax to Björn, asking what he meant by doing a musical about their career. She calmed down and gave the project her blessing when he explained that the exact opposite was true: the last thing anyone wanted was the Abba saga in dramatic form.

The name of the musical became *Mamma Mia!* and opera director Phyllida Lloyd was brought on board to take charge of the stage presentation. Lloyd recognised the backwards aspect of the show's conception, but decided to view it as "a musical they wrote a few years ago but wanted to release a few singles first".

The lead character, Donna, was played by Siobhán McCarthy, who originated the role of Svetlana in the London stage production of *Chess*. The part of the daughter, Sophie, went to Norwegian Lisa Stokke, while her boyfriend Sky was played by Andrew Langtree. Both were graduates of the Liverpool Institute of Performing Arts, a *Fame*-style school co-founded by Paul McCartney. Ironically, half of McCartney's 1992 Polar Music Prize money had been donated to the institute, which meant that, theoretically, revenues from Abba's success had actually gone into the education of Stokke and Langtree.

On April 6, 1999, the musical finally opened at the Prince Edward Theatre in London. Purely by coincidence, according to Björn, the date

★ 'Waterloo' was eventually added as an encore.

happened to be the 25th anniversary of Abba's Eurovision Song Contest victory with 'Waterloo'. The date had been set to accommodate the schedule of busy director Phyllida Lloyd, he insisted, and had nothing to do with 'Waterloo'.

In the months leading up to the première date Björn involved himself heavily with the production, tweaking some of the lyrics to better fit the plot requirements, overseeing rehearsals and offering advice. Moreover, he conducted innumerable interviews and talk show appearances, both to promote the musical and to reflect on the group's history in conjunction with the 'Waterloo' anniversary.

During the first stages of the Abba revival, Björn had emerged as the spokesman for the group since none of the other members were readily available for comment. Björn was always the Abba member most skilful at playing the public relations game, although there had been an air of guarded reluctance surrounding most of his early Nineties interviews. After all, as he pointed out shortly after the release of *ABBA Gold*, "when Abba broke up, Benny and I wanted to work behind the scenes and not be 'on stage' anymore".

With all the mad rush surrounding *Mamma Mia!* and the anniversary, with people constantly coming up to him in the street to "thank him for the music", he seemed to undergo a transformation. His interviews were more enthusiastic and sincere than in a long while, as if he realised that the Abba revival wouldn't have to constitute a threat to his present creativity but was just something to enjoy and play along with. There was a gleam of a rediscovered young Björn in there, the Hootenanny Singer who'd once got a kick out of that first bout of fame and autograph signings. Benny, more media-shy than ever, quipped that Björn ought to be given an award for all the interviews he had given.

An official television documentary, *The Winner Takes It All – The ABBA Story*, was put together, produced by Littlestar and featuring newly filmed contributions from the former members. Björn was obviously the most comfortable with his status as an ex-Abba member.

Agnetha, maintaining her latter-day tradition of defining limits, claimed to be uncomfortable with speaking English on camera as she appeared on television for the first time in 11 years. Instead, she read relevant passages from *As I Am* aloud, set to silent footage showing her walking in the park of the royal residence, Drottningholm Palace. It was as if she'd made a deal to show who was in charge: you will get my voice and my face, but you won't get them together. Frida, on the other hand, agreed to be interviewed on camera and came over as both reflective and dignified.

Although it was a company part-owned by Benny that had produced the documentary, it was clear he had little involvement or enthusiasm for the end result. "If you're only out to confirm your own preconceptions it won't turn out very well," he said, "then it's only a matter of preserving the myths. I think that's what this programme does."

The reviews after the *Mamma Mia!* première were mostly positive and the show went on to become a truly huge commercial smash, constantly breaking records for attendance and advance ticket sales. One special quirk of the musical was the audience's inclination to second-guess which song was about to follow in the story, leading to laughter as a dialogue cue was followed by an Abba hit.

Phyllida Lloyd tried to find some hidden meaning behind it all. "I don't know how to say this without sounding pretentious," she remarked, "but *Mamma Mia!* is actually quite Brechtian in calling attention to form and the relationship the audience develops with characters onstage. Of course the audience is waiting to hear their favourite songs and wondering what the hell is going to come next, and that's part of it. I'm really not trying to say this is going to change the world. This is just good fun."

Some cruel observers felt that *Mamma Mia!* had more in common with karaoke than Brecht. There were a few surprisingly clumsy segues in the narrative linking the songs together, and there is little question that the musical draws its crowds on the strength of the hits. It panders to Seventies nostalgia and the kitsch aspects of the group's universe, with some numbers even being straightforward performances in flared trousers and glam outfits, their links to any aspects of the plot extremely flimsy. It was as if everyone involved realised that, despite any pretensions of a proper story, the only way to make a show like *Mamma Mia!* a success would be to play along with the audience's expectations of "tongue-in-cheek campness", as Judy Craymer put it – the "good for a laugh" Björn Again philosophy.

Paradoxically, this second wave of Abba's revival within the same decade confirmed that the group's solid popularity went firmly beyond a Seventies nostalgia craze. The *ABBA Gold* compilation enjoyed a new round at number one on the charts the world over, selling an additional 4 million copies to the 15 million already notched up since its 1992 release. In the UK and the US alone, total sales have surpassed the three million mark in each country. In the US, this figure exceeds sales by any of Abba's original albums.

Such extraordinary retrospective success finally and firmly established Abba as a "classic act", which posed a problem for the world's rock historians. Measured purely in sales terms, Abba's international popularity was in the same league as Elvis and The Beatles, yet there still seemed to be no way to fit them into the established history of rock and pop. They hadn't emerged from some American southern state, nor were their roots to be found in a British working-class neighbourhood. By the look of it, Abba just flew in from the land of Europop with a bunch of exceptionally well-made records.

Therefore, the best Abba can ever hope for – assuming they even care about approval from the cognoscenti – is intermittent rehabilitation. The Nineties revival angle has seldom gone far beyond "they were actually quite good", which fixes them to the mast as an act that needs defending rather than one that might take their natural place in the pantheon of rock. When the British classic rock magazine *Mojo* featured a major Abba story in May 1999, some readers even wrote in and complained of the embarrassment at being seen in public carrying a magazine with the group's picture on the cover.

You know the reputation of a group is in trouble when even their own official television documentary has to include an array of supposedly credibility-raising interviewees testifying to their greatness with varying degrees of conviction. Poor Bono looked like he'd been forced at gunpoint to acknowledge that Abba were "one of the best pop groups that there ever was". Tellingly, only Pete Waterman sounded genuinely enthusiastic in his praise: in his universe there was a direct line from Abba to what he was trying to accomplish in his own work.

There is undeniably a strong emotional content in several of Abba's songs that will continue to touch the public for as long as people go on listening to pop music. Pure logic decrees that they couldn't have reached fame on such an unbelievable level – and for so long – if it all had been as superficial and clinical as their detractors claim. But try as anyone might, the majority of music writers will never regard the group as anything but a particularly tasty crème caramel to be enjoyed after the more substantial meat and potato course provided by rock's "true" giants, however minor their international impact in comparison with Abba.

And perhaps that's just how it should be. If Abba's role is to provide some kind of relief, to give the world music that doesn't necessarily come with the heavy baggage of historical significance, then perhaps they are just as important a part of the pop and rock landscape as those that bear their weightiness and credibility on their sleeve.

Parallel with its continued London success *Mamma Mia!* was sweeping relentlessly across the world. Financially, this state of affairs must have been especially pleasing for Björn, who'd found a way for Abba's music to generate income for him after having sold his mechanical royalty rights some 15 years earlier (assuming they haven't reverted back to him in the interim).

In May 2000 the musical opened in Toronto, in Canada, with Melbourne, Australia, following in June 2001. A tour of several key cities in the United States commenced in November 2000, leading up to an October 2001 Broadway première. The tour was primarily geared to building a solid reputation for the show before opening in New York. Björn and Benny wanted to ensure that the Frank Riches of this world wouldn't be able to kill it with their potentially hostile reviews. So well-received was the American tour that – contrary to original plans – it was extended beyond the Broadway opening date.

While Björn and Benny enjoyed the success of their hit musical, the female half of Abba were experiencing more traumatic blows. After her 1996 comeback, Frida found herself in a "will she, won't she" frame of mind as to whether there would be a follow-up album. The encouraging sales suggested a healthy demand, but she hadn't particularly enjoyed being in the focus of the media again. Furthermore, two sad events on a personal level at the tail end of the Nineties rendered any thoughts of recording studio work largely insignificant.

During interviews around the time of her latest album, Frida had spoken warmly of the contact with her children and how close they had grown over time. "It's taken a long time and many talks to sort out our relationships," she said. "Now, afterwards, I can see the price of fame." Those comments acquired a heartbreaking overtone in January 1998 when Frida's 30-year-old daughter Lise-Lotte was killed in a car accident. Lise-Lotte had married an American ten years earlier with whom she had a son, Jonathan, giving Frida her first grandchild. The couple had since divorced, although Lise-Lotte remained in the United States.

As if coping with this loss wasn't enough, a year later Frida's husband, Ruzzo, was diagnosed with cancer. After a tough battle, he finally succumbed to the disease in October 1999 at the age of 49. The funeral was held in the church of Härslöv in the south of Sweden, where Frida and Ruzzo had a home which was their base when they visited the country. The couple retreated to this house during Ruzzo's last days. The last farewell to Frida's husband was attended by Benny and Mona, as well as King Carl XVI Gustaf and Queen Silvia.

Frida subsequently disappeared completely from public life for several months. In May 2000, however, she accompanied Björn and Benny to the North American première of *Mamma Mia!* in Toronto. She had recently taken a greater interest in the show and even become an investor.

Speaking to the press at length for the first time since experiencing her tragedies, she appeared firmly in control of her life. "I've realised that I'm a very strong woman," she said. "I also have a very strong faith in God. I guess that is what's helped me through this." Frida was too hardened by the knocks in life to be reduced to a wreck, even by such devastating ordeals.

As for recording any further albums, however, she said that she had come full circle in that matter. She was in her mid-Fifties and her need to take care of herself on a private level superceded any other thoughts. "I am my own project at the moment," as she phrased it.

If Frida had been struck by real tragedy, Agnetha found herself entangled in a bizarre mix of sadness and the surreal that almost defied belief. In the week leading up to her 50th birthday on April 5, 2000, she again created major headlines when it was revealed that she had sought police assistance in dealing with a stalker, a stocky and balding 34-year-old Dutchman named Gert van der Graaf. He was said to have harassed Agnetha for three years, writing several hundred letters to her in the process.

"He'd call me up to three times a day and he followed me wherever I went," she told the police. "Sometimes he's followed me in his car, other times he's been waiting in places where I take my walks. My life has been extremely restricted because of this and I no longer dare go outside without having my neighbour with me."

After being taken into custody on March 31, van der Graaf revealed that he'd fallen in love with Agnetha as an eight-year-old, after seeing her on the Eurovision Song Contest in 1974. Several visits to Sweden and Ekerö were followed by the purchase of a house without a sewage system near Agnetha's farm. When the police came to arrest him they were met by an unbelievable stench: immediately inside the door there was a bucket filled with excrement and a dead turtle. Gert van der Graaf was issued with a restraining order, forbidding him to get in touch with Agnetha in any way whatsoever.

Although Agnetha had bought her secluded estate specifically to get away from persistent fans, many ardent admirers still made the pilgrimage out to Ekerö to get a glimpse of their idol. Abba fanzines were full of wide-eyed accounts of Agnetha finally driving up in her car, stopping to wind down the window, requesting that no photos be taken, exchanging a few words, signing a CD or two and then driving away; tiresome for Agnetha, no doubt, but basically harmless.

The case of van der Graaf was obviously different: a somewhat over-zealous interest had turned into an obsession. At one point he spotted Agnetha walking her dog on a muddy path near his house, and promptly ordered a truckload of gravel to be spread on the path so that she wouldn't get her boots dirty. Agnetha never walked that way again.

A few days after the story broke in the papers some hitherto unknown angles to the story started to emerge. A letter Agnetha had written to Gert in January was made public. "The reason I'm writing is that I want to be left alone," she wrote. "I stand by my decision – there is no hope for us together." This didn't sound like the way one would address a stranger. Agnetha's phrasing suggested a certain intimacy with van der Graaf: early reports had stated that they were "acquainted" with each other. Agnetha even admitted to the police that there had been "a relationship" between them off and on since 1997.

At the trial in October 2000 the truth was revealed. It wasn't a matter of a mere acquaintance or even a friendship: there had been a full-blown love affair. "His courting of me was very intense and went on for a very long time. In the end I couldn't resist him any more," she told the court. "I wanted to get to know him. We began a relationship."

She realised that he was "mentally unstable", she said, and the relationship was broken off and then taken up again several times. "Sometimes everything was fine. We were never living together, but we saw each other and called each other a lot, like you do in a relationship." Gert van der Graaf told a reporter how they had holidayed together on the Swedish west coast just a few weeks before Agnetha finally ended the affair once and for all in September 1999. "I thought we had a virtually perfect relationship," said Gert. "Of course, we argued sometimes, but it was mostly mere trifles."

From the end of the relationship until he was arrested by the police, Gert wrote Agnetha 86 letters. He started rummaging through her mailbox and phoned her constantly. When he suddenly appeared outside her kitchen window on Christmas Eve she reported him to the police. The case was dismissed because of lack of evidence at the time and it wasn't until he began a countdown to her 50th birthday, making threats in both open and veiled form in the letters, that she went to the police again.

Two weeks after the trial the court ruled that van der Graaf should be expelled from the country and not allowed to return for two years. He was also fined 120,000 kronor (£9,000). "I still love her and that's why I'm moving now," said Gert. "I've realised that it's the best gift of love I could give her."

Agnetha's relationship with Gert van der Graaf was as hard to comprehend as it was heartbreaking. Was Agnetha so starved of love and companionship that she was reduced to seeking solace in the arms of an obsessed fan, someone who had clearly overstepped her private zone by loitering outside her home in the first place? That was her decision to make, naturally, but the inescapable conclusion was that she was an essentially unhappy woman at this point in her life.

The affair with van der Graaf also led to the break-up of Agnetha's friendship with Brita Åhman, her confidante and "official interviewer" since 1982. The failure of the *As I Am* book was the beginning of the end, and when Agnetha got involved with the Dutchman the rift became irreparable. "When she rang me and told me about it I was extremely shocked," Åhman recalled. "I warned her and said it could be dangerous for her and her children. She was furious and continued to encourage him."

Things didn't get better when Agnetha read excerpts from *As I Am* in the Abba documentary, without the author being credited. Ironically, the friendship between Agnetha and Brita had begun when Agnetha needed help putting together an article in protest against the gossip press. Now Brita began publishing critical features about her former friend in exactly the same type of magazine that had once brought them together.

The fascination with Agnetha continues unabated. The end of the Nineties and the beginning of the new century were filled with inconsequential Agnetha spottings that somehow became captivating simply because of her insistence on staying out of the spotlight. Agnetha attending a première, Agnetha at the birthday party of a celebrity friend, Agnetha ordering take-out sushi, Agnetha buying soda at 7–Eleven, Agnetha taking used batteries to the recycling centre – every snapshot or tiny morsel of information seemed worthy of a report in the tabloids. Simply by virtue of doing absolutely nothing of significance, she remained Abba's most popular and intriguing member.

Since the spring of 2000 her business manager, Staffan Lindé, has occasionally confirmed that Agnetha is considering a music comeback and has even been in the studio recording demos. Reportedly, as early as the mid–Nineties she was even composing new songs. Whether any of these activities actually results in an album release remains to be seen at the time of writing.

And what of Abba themselves? Was there still no chance that they would ever get back together again? With the advent of the Abba revival this became one of the most common questions posed by reporters.

Since the mid-Eighties the four members have occasionally sung together for friends at private birthday parties. At the 40th birthday of Claes af Geijerstam in 1986, for instance, they performed the obscure *Chess* number 'Der Kleine Franz' with new lyrics. The latest known "reunion" took place at the 50th birthday party of Görel Hanser in June

1999, when they sang the Swedish birthday song 'Med en enkel tulipan' ('With A Simple Tulip').

If nothing else these casual reunions proved that, contrary to persistent rumours, the members of the group, in whatever combination, are by no means mortal enemies. Although the Abba revival heated up the old stories that Agnetha and Frida hated each other from day one, they were strongly denied by both. They admitted to never having been close friends, acknowledging their different personalities and opposing backgrounds.

"Agnetha was 17 when we first met, I was married and had given birth to two children," Frida explained. "Five years age difference is an enormous timespan at that age – moreover, Agnetha and I are, and will always be, different as people. That doesn't mean that we don't like each other a lot. She's gone through things as well. The much discussed animosity has never existed."

Despite her reluctance to work in the group context again, and although it took a long time to recover from the pressure of the hectic Abba years, Agnetha seems to be fairly reconciled with her history. After her almost decade-long distance from all aspects of music there was a rediscovery in the mid-Nineties. "I needed silence and quiet instead of sounds," she said in the *As I Am* book. "Today I feel that I can enjoy both Abba and some of the things that I've done myself, as well as the music of others. Suddenly I feel the urge to listen again."

When local radio station Radio Stockholm broadcast a six-hour Abba radio special in October 1996, Agnetha phoned in afterwards and thanked the producers, saying that she had listened to the entire broadcast. But no actual reunion in the recording studio or onstage seems to be on the cards. At one point there was talk of releasing a single, and Frida has mentioned that it would perhaps be fun to do something together, but not as Abba. "It's hard to see it happening simply because Agnetha isn't especially willing to consider such a situation," she said. "I'm sure it would be a lot of fun, but then we need to be four."

Money will never be a motivation either: in the spring of 2000 it was revealed that Abba had been offered US$1 billion (£650 million) for an extensive reunion tour. "We get offers every year, and we dismiss them all out of hand," said Björn. "This time, we thought about it. We really thought about it. But then we realised that it wasn't worth taking a whole year out of our lives." All other explanations aside, perhaps it all boils down to one simple reason why they could never reunite. As Björn noted, "Pop music is for the young and we have passed that stage in our lives."

With all four members having turned 50, this was certainly true. By January 2001, when Björn and Agnetha's daughter Linda gave birth to her first child, all four Abba members had become grandparents. Some of their own children had themselves followed in their parents' footsteps with careers in show business. Linda Ulvaeus is an actress who has been featured in movies and on television, as well as taking on a small part in *Kristina från Duvemåla*. Benny's son, Peter, has the band One More Time, which competed in the Eurovision Song Contest in 1996.

As for their own careers, Björn and Benny have announced plans to write another musical at some point, but six years after the première of *Kristina* nothing concrete in that vein has been forthcoming. Not even the creative core of Abba are especially close these days: there is a solid friendship of the kind that is inevitable after working together for 35 years, but beyond their musical collaboration their outlooks on life have become fairly different.

What remains is the music Abba made during their ten year existence, together with the knowledge that it is possible for popular music acts from outside the major rock markets to leave a lasting mark on the international music scene. Eventually, especially in Sweden, the example they set gave an indirect push to several others.

"I think it's a kind of Björn Borg [effect]," said Stig Anderson a few years before his death. "He's a world-famous star. Young people say, 'If he can do it, we can.' It started every young guy playing tennis. Instead of 10 people playing, you get half a million. It's a big chance that some of these are going to be good. That's what I think happened with Abba."

In the mid–Eighties, poodle rock band Europe became the first Swedish act after the demise of Abba to make a significant international impact with their smash hit 'The Final Countdown'. Beginning at the end of the decade, the duo Roxette enjoyed even greater success, including four US number one singles. In 1993, the two girls/two boys group Ace of Base scored worldwide fame, going on to secure the title of the world's best-selling début album with 21 million copies sold of *Happy Nation* (aka *The Sign*).

The producer of Ace of Base's biggest hits was the late Denniz Pop, whose Cheiron production company rapidly developed into one of the world's biggest hit factories. By the start of the 21st century, Pop's disciple, Max Martin, was one of the world's most successful songwriters/ producers. Well-established artists and "manufactured" teen idols alike travelled to Sweden to sample the magic touch of Cheiron and similar production companies that started popping up.

Parallel with this, more traditional acts like The Cardigans and soul singer Robyn also achieved great success with their records. Sweden had suddenly arrived as the third most important producer of popular music after the United States and Great Britain. "I believe the Swedes are doing so well because Sweden is the most Americanised country in Europe," Björn theorised. "Swedish youth have taken the Anglo-Saxon culture to their hearts. Of course, Abba have also paved the way."

Although Abba set an example, none of these successful producers or acts received any concrete help from Stig, the group members or any of the other people working within their organisation. Polar Music's tentacles out to the international music business had been cut off long before the Nineties export wave began.

The only major player with a clear connection to Abba was Thomas Johansson and EMA, which branched out into artist management, adding to their domination as a tour promotion company. Organising Abba's tours and accompanying them on their early promotion trips, plus his own development as Scandinavia's foremost concert arranger and tour promoter, gave Johansson invaluable international connections which have been a help to other acts. Along with legendary American promoter Bill Graham, and his Danish counterpart Knud Thorbjørnsen – who helped arrange Abba's first tour of Europe – Johansson has named Stig as one of his three mentors.

Former pop star and current head of the Universal Music owned Stockholm Records label, Ola Håkansson, also played an important part. Through his time with the group Secret Service, which enjoyed several international hits in the early Eighties, he picked up useful experience of how the various music markets around the world worked. Stockholm Records is the home of several successful Eurodisco acts as well as groups like The Cardigans.

Two decades after Abba opened the door to the world, there were finally industry-based organisations such as Export Music Sweden, formed, in their own words, "with the aim of initiating, assisting and facilitating the promotion and marketing of Swedish popular music worldwide". The government has also opened its eyes, with the Minister of Commerce constantly being seen hobnobbing with pop stars and record producers, or presenting music business-related awards.

But then, nothing is as it used to be in the industry. Most of the old, independent labels have been acquired by the majors, who in themselves were buying up each other on a global level. The Europe-based PolyGram, which had bought Polar, was merged with Universal Music, owned by Canadian whisky manufacturer Seagrams, in 1998. Seagrams themselves have since been acquired by French media titan Vivendi.

What a contrast to the days of complete self-sufficiency, when Stig Anderson almost single-handedly kicked down doors that had previously been firmly closed. In the light of what has happened since then, with the present-day multinational network and the information superhighway revolution, his accomplishments and persistence seem all the more impressive. Poignantly, Stig's daughter Marie has deliberately kept her operation small-scale, and with few exceptions avoiding all attempts to push her artists abroad. "I have seen the price you have to pay," she remarked.

The old Music Movement company MNW still remains as an independent operation, keeping a slightly left-of-centre artist roster. However, in an almost unfathomable turn of events in light of its origins, it was listed on the stock exchange by the end of the Nineties. By that time former label boss and Stig's old nemesis, Roger Wallis, had long since gone on to other assignments in the music industry and affiliated organisations. In an ironic twist, in 1992 he even narrated a Paul McCartney television documentary broadcast in conjunction with Stig's Polar Music Prize.

About the only artist from the old days holding on to his former convictions was Mikael Wiehe. In 1993 Stig wanted him to be a guest in his radio series. Wiehe still hadn't forgiven the former Polar Music director's behaviour two decades earlier, and refused to appear.

Abba fever continues unabated, in various forms. The official fan club holds an 'Abba day' in The Netherlands every year, attracting hundreds of fans. In November 1999, an Abba exhibition was staged at the prestigious Nordiska Museet (The Nordic Museum) in Stockholm. So successful was the exhibition that its original one-year run was extended by a further year.

As a way of cashing in on the publishing catalogue they had acquired, Universal Music company Stockholm Records put together the group Abba Teens. The concept was simple enough: four fresh-faced teenagers – two girls, two boys – brought together to perform techno-pop versions of Abba songs.

When the group was launched in 1999, they became a success beyond all expectations. In Sweden they were one of the biggest sellers of the year with their chart topping single 'Mamma Mia' and the number one album *The Abba Generation*. Incredibly, this fairly anonymous-sounding group went on to make quite an impression in Europe and the United States as well, selling several million copies of their album. The strength of the original material presumably carried all their weaknesses on its shoulders.

According to early reports, Björn and Benny had given their blessing to the group to use the name Abba Teens. However, immediately after their first hit, Benny intervened, ordering that their name should be changed.

"Abba are Abba," he said. "What they're doing is something completely different."

Although this looked like a complete about-turn on his part, it transpired that, in fact, only Björn had okayed the name: someone had forgotten to ask his partner for permission. The name was promptly changed to A★Teens, which ultimately worked in the group's favour. After the success of the first album, they were able to have continued hits with a completely new repertoire, unrelated to Abba. The Abba song catalogue turned out to function merely as an unusually effective launching pad for the A★Teens.

And the success of Mamma Mia! continues unabated. After the successful Broadway opening in 2001, further productions follow in Hamburg, Germany and Tokyo, Japan at the end of 2002. A Spanish-language version is in the pipeline, along with a touring production for continental Europe.

Despite his business interest in the venture, less than a year after the London premiere Benny made clear that he'd had just about enough of the Abba revival in all its forms, particularly the cover bands and the tribute groups. His own credo had always been to move forward, and although the renewed interest in his old songs provided him with a bank account that was even healthier than before, this constant nostalgia for something that was dead and buried was puzzling to him. "Isn't it some kind of sign of poverty, after all?" he mused. "Is there no one who can come up with any new stuff, who can do something corresponding to what we did back then? Of course, I'm proud, happy, flattered and all that – for me it's great. But . . . isn't it kind of empty when the greatest success is generated by something that was made 20 years ago – and in cover versions? Something isn't quite right, that's not how it should be."

There can, of course, never be a new Abba or anything that affects a whole music scene the way they did. Like other acts who defined the decade in which they worked, Abba were dependent on the way the music industry and the media functioned during their period together. At a time when most major acts release an album every third or fourth year, and with a myriad of television channels, radio stations and other media outlets in each country, it's almost impossible for an artist to impress themselves on the world in the way that Abba did.

At the height of their fame Abba were constantly in the media, giving regular interviews even when they didn't have any product to promote, which has become increasingly less common since then. Even their own manager and record company president was a colourful character with a domestic media profile that was almost higher than that of his group. It is doubtful the general public knows the names of any record company presidents in the early 21st century.

Max Martin, probably the nearest Swedish equivalent of Abba today insofar as spreading catchy pop music over the world, is a virtually faceless writer/producer who refuses to give interviews. "Not my job," is his laconic comment. No one can fault him and his colleagues for their expertly executed craft or blame them for wanting to keep out of the spotlight, but it sure ain't very exciting.

By way of contrast, Abba were a group whose creativity and success stemmed from the members themselves: four headstrong, talented individuals moving forwards in an entity so laden with pressure from within and without that it was constantly on the verge of exploding. Most inside observers agree that it's amazing that they lasted as long as they did. The energy rubbed off on everyone in their presence, and it was inevitable that the group would provoke strong reactions from admirers and detractors alike.

Says Berka Bergkvist: "Looking back on it, it was unbelievably great to live through this experience. It's something that will never happen again, not on this level. I'll never forget a classic thing that Michael Tretow once said: 'The day Abba disappears we will know that we were at least a part of it. Then we can all start making speech records or whatever. We were along for the ride.'"

•

•

Selective Discography

Abba's recorded output has been thoroughly documented elsewhere – in my own *ABBA – The Complete Recording Sessions*, for instance, and on numerous websites (consult www.abbaworld.net). However, without going into detail regarding various mixes and edits, I still feel that a basic list of the group's releases merits inclusion here.

Abba released eight proper studio albums between 1973 and 1981. This discography refers to how they were conceived and released by their record company Polar Music for the Swedish and/or Nordic market.

Ring Ring, 1973
A: Ring Ring (Bara du slog en signal) [Swedish version]; Another Town, Another Train; Disillusion; People Need Love; I Saw It In The Mirror; Nina, Pretty Ballerina.
B: Love Isn't Easy (But It Sure Is Hard Enough); Me And Bobby And Bobby's Brother; He Is Your Brother; Ring Ring (English version); I Am Just A Girl; Rock'n Roll Band.

Waterloo, 1974
A: Waterloo [Swedish version]; Sitting In The Palmtree; King Kong Song; Hasta Mañana; My Mama Said; Dance (While The Music Still Goes On).
B: Honey, Honey; Watch Out; What About Livingstone; Gonna Sing You My Lovesong; Suzy-Hang-Around; Waterloo (English Version).

ABBA, 1975
A: Mamma Mia; Hey, Hey Helen; Tropical Loveland; SOS; Man In The Middle; Bang-A-Boomerang.
B: I Do, I Do, I Do, I Do, I Do; Rock Me; Intermezzo no. 1; I've Been Waiting For You; So Long.

Arrival, 1976
A: When I Kissed The Teacher; Dancing Queen; My Love, My Life; Dum Dum Diddle; Knowing Me, Knowing You.
B: Money, Money, Money; That's Me; Why Did It Have To Be Me; Tiger; Arrival.

ABBA – The Album, 1977

A: Eagle; Take A Chance On Me; One Man, One Woman; The Name Of The Game.
B: Move On; Hole In Your Soul; "The Girl With The Golden Hair" – 3 scenes from a mini-musical: Thank You For The Music; I Wonder (Departure); I'm A Marionette.

Voulez-Vous, 1979

A: As Good As New; Voulez-Vous; I Have A Dream; Angeleyes; The King Has Lost His Crown.
B: Does Your Mother Know; If It Wasn't For The Nights; Chiquitita; Lovers (Live A Little Longer); Kisses Of Fire.

Super Trouper, 1980

A: Super Trouper; The Winner Takes It All; On And On And On; Andante, Andante; Me And I.
B: Happy New Year; Our Last Summer; The Piper; Lay All Your Love On Me; The Way Old Friends Do.

The Visitors, 1981

A: The Visitors; Head Over Heels; When All Is Said And Done; Soldiers.
B: I Let The Music Speak; One Of Us; Two For The Price Of One; Slipping Through My Fingers; Like An Angel Passing Through My Room.

ABBA recorded a Spanish-language album primarily aimed at the Latin American market:

Gracias Por La Música, 1980

A: Gracias Por La Música (Thank You For The Music); Reina Danzante (Dancing Queen); Al Andar (Move On); Dame! Dame! Dame! (Gimme! Gimme! Gimme! [A Man After Midnight]); Fernando.
B: Estoy Soñando (I Have A Dream); Mamma Mia; Hasta Mañana; Conociéndome, Conociéndote (Knowing Me, Knowing You); Chiquitita.

Five further Spanish recordings, not included on this album, have also been released: Ring Ring; Andante, Andante; Felicidad (Happy New Year); No hay a quien culpar (When All Is Said And Done); Se me esta escapando (Slipping Through My Fingers).

A live album was released after the group's demise:

ABBA Live, 1986

A: Dancing Queen; Take A Chance On Me; I Have A Dream; Does Your Mother Know; Chiquitita.

B: Thank You For The Music; Two For The Price Of One; Fernando; Gimme! Gimme! Gimme! (A Man After Midnight); Super Trouper; Waterloo.

Extra tracks on CD: Money, Money, Money; The Name Of The Game/ Eagle; On And On And On.

Five further live recordings were released on singles or compilation albums: I Wonder (Departure); Hole In Your Soul; Summer Night City; Me And I; Slipping Through My Fingers.

The following single A- and/or B-sides were not included on the original vinyl versions of the above albums:

Merry-Go-Round; Santa Rosa; Åh, vilka tider; Ring Ring (German version); Wer Im Wartesaal Der Liebe Steht (German version of Another Town, Another Train); Honey, Honey (Swedish version); Waterloo (German version); Waterloo (French version); Ring Ring (partly re-recorded and remixed version); Fernando; Crazy World; Happy Hawaii; I Wonder (Departure) [live version]; Summer Night City; Medley: Pick A Bale Of Cotton – On Top Of Old Smokey – Midnight Special; Lovelight; Gimme! Gimme! Gimme! (A Man After Midnight); Elaine; Should I Laugh Or Cry; The Day Before You Came; Cassandra; Under Attack; You Owe Me One; I Am The City.

The 1994 box set *Thank You For The Music* includes an array of previously unreleased recordings and rarities. In 2001, all eight original studio albums were reissued on CD with bonus tracks. Abba's Spanish recordings have all been collected on the CD *ABBA Oro* (1999). The compilation CD *ABBA Gold* (1992) collects 19 of Abba's greatest hits. The 37-track double-CD *ABBA – The Definitive Collection* (2001) is a compilation of all official ABBA singles.

Sources

Bibliography

PRIMARY BOOK SOURCES (INCLUDING BOOKLETS AND
PRIVATELY PUBLISHED COMPENDIUMS)

Ahlborn, Kenneth, and Nilmander, Urban. *Bengt H. Malmqvist – Stjärnornas fotograf* (Premium, Sweden, 1998)

Ahlén, Tommy, with Lahger, Håkan. *Jag ljuger inte om Rock'n'Roll* (Page One, Sweden, 1997)

Bernstein, Sid, with Aaron, Arthur. *Not Just The Beatles . . .* (Jacques & Flusster, USA, 2000)

Borg, Christer. *Fenomenet ABBA* (Sweden Music, Sweden, 1977)

—— *ABBA By ABBA* (Horwitz, Australia, 1977)

Brolinson, Per-Erik, and Larsen, Holger. *När rocken slog i Sverige* (Arkivet för ljud och bild & Musikvetenskapliga institutionen vid Stockholms universitet, Sweden, 1997)

Coleman, Ray. *Brian Epstein – The Man Who Made The Beatles* (Penguin, UK, 1990)

—— *Phil Collins – The Definitive Biography* (Pocket Books, UK, 1998)

Edgington, Harry. *ABBA* (Magnum, UK, 1978)

Fältskog, Agnetha. *Som jag är. Livsbilder berättade för Brita Åhman* (Norstedts, Sweden, 1996)

—— ; with Åhman, Brita. *As I Am – ABBA Before & Beyond* (Virgin, UK, 1997)

Gaines, Steven. *Heroes And Villains – The True Story Of The Beach Boys* (Grafton, UK, 1987)

Gambaccini, Paul; Rice, Tim; Rice, Jonathan. *British Hit Singles* (Guinness, UK, 1999)

—— *British Hit Albums* (Guinness, UK, 1994)

Guinness rekordbok 2001 (Forum, Sweden, 2000)

Gurell, Lars. *Svensktoppen i våra hjärtan* (Premium, Sweden, 1996)

Hadenius, Stig; Nilsson, Torbjörn; Åselius, Gunnar. *Sveriges historia* (Bonnier Alba, Sweden, 1996)

Hallberg, Eric. *Kvällstoppen i P3* (Drift Musik, Sweden, 1993)

—— ; and Henningsson, Ulf. *Tio i topp* (Premium, Sweden, 1998)

Hartston, William. *Chess: The Making Of A Musical* (Pavilion, UK, 1986)

Hedlund, Oscar. *Da Capo!* (Almqvist & Wiksell, Sweden, 1981)

535

—— *Stikkan – den börsnoterade refrängsångaren* (Sweden Music, Sweden, 1983)

Hedlund, Sven. *I natt jag drömde . . .* (Europa-Produktion, Sweden, 1967)

Johansson, Carl-Owe. *Rock Around The Clock – Saturday Night Fever* (Dominique Muzic-Club, Sweden, 1980)

Kofoed, Rud. *Boken om ABBA* (Askild & Kärnekull, Sweden, 1977)

Lahger, Håkan. *Proggen – musikrörelsens uppgång och fall* (Atlas, Sweden, 1999)

Larkin, Colin (ed.). *The Guinness Encyclopedia Of Popular Music* (Guinness, UK, 1995)

Lexikon 2000 (Bra böcker, Sweden, 1996–1999)

Lindvall, Marianne. *ABBA – The Ultimate Pop Group* (Hurtig, Canada, 1977)

Lundberg, Börje. *Elvis – kung av Sverige* (Premium, Sweden, 1997)

Mamma Mia! programme (UK, 1999)

Matlock, Glen, with Silverton, Pete. *I Was A Teenage Sex Pistol* (Omnibus, UK, 1990)

Olofsson, Hans, and Hallberg, Sture. *Stora popboken* (Premium, Sweden, 1995)

Potiez, Jean-Marie. *ABBA – The Book* (Aurum, UK, 2000)

Rudolfsson, Lars, and Mark, Jan. *Bortom en vid ocean – Kristina från Duvemåla* (LeanderMalmsten, Sweden, 1996)

Schulman, Leif, and Hammarsten, Charles. *ABBA – succé på världs-scenen* (Allerbok, Sweden, 1979)

Svensson, Barbro, with Wahlgren, Anna. *Lill-Babs – hon är jag* (Bra böcker, Sweden, 1996)

Thorsson, Leif. *Melodifestivalen genom tiderna* (Premium, Sweden, 1999)

Tobler, John. *ABBA Gold – The Complete Story* (Century 22, UK, 1993)

Vem är det 1999 (Kunskapsförlaget P.A. Norstedt & Söner, Sweden, 1998)

Waldenström, Björn. *Polars skivproduktion* (Sweden, 1986)

Waller, Johnny. *The Phil Collins Story* (Zomba, UK, 1985)

Waterman, Pete. *I Wish I Was Me* (Virgin, UK, 2000)

Wendt, Wille. *Topplistan – The Official Swedish Single & Album Charts 1975–1993* (Premium, Sweden, 1993)

Whitburn, Joel. *Top Pop Albums 1955–1996* (Record Research, USA, 1996)

—— *Top Pop Singles 1955–1999* (Record Research, USA, 2000)

Williams, Richard. *Out Of His Head: The Sound Of Phil Spector* (Abacus, US, 1974; originally published 1972)

York, Rosemary. *ABBA In Their Own Words* (Omnibus, UK, 1981)

Note: Although some of the Swedish-language titles above were also published in English, I feel that the translations haven't always accurately reflected the original text. Therefore, when I've quoted these volumes I've often taken the liberty of amending the translations or creating entirely new ones to more accurately reflect what I believe to be closer to the meaning of the text.

Sources

NEWSPAPER AND MAGAZINE SOURCES

In Australia: the *Advertiser*, the *Daily Mirror*, the *Daily Telegraph*, *Juke*, *RAM*, the *Sun* (Sydney), the *Sun Herald*, the *Sun News – Pictorial* (Melbourne), the *Sunday Independent*, the *Sunday Observer*, *TV Week*.
In Denmark: *Allers*, *Ekstra Bladet*, *Berlingske Tidene*.
In Germany: *Bravo*, *Joker*, *Pop*.
In Norway: *Aftenposten*, *Det Nye*, *Fremover*, *Hjemmet*, *NÅ*, *Ofotens Tidende*, *Se og Hør*.
In Sweden: *Aftonbladet*, *Alexandra*, *Allas*, *Allers*, *Bildjournalen*, *Citynytt*, *Clic*, *Dagens Industri*, *Dagens Nyheter*, *Damernas Värld*, *Eskilstunakuriren*, *Expressen*, *Folket*, *Goda grannar*, *Göteborgs-Posten*, *Göteborgs-Tidningen*, *Hemmets Journal*, *Hemmets Veckotidning*, *Hennes*, *Hifi & Musik*, *Husmodern*, *Hänt i veckan*, *ICA-kuriren*, *Idolnytt*, *Jönköpingsposten*, *Kommunalarbetaren*, *Kvällsposten*, *Lidingö Tidning*, *Love*, *Mersmak*, *Min värld*, *MånadsJournalen*, *Non Smoking Generation Magazine*, *Novellkontakten*, *Now & Then*, *Nöjesguiden*, *Pop*, *Poster*, *Röster i Radio–TV*, *Saxons*, *Schlager*, *Se*, *Se&Hör*, *Smålands Folkblad*, *Starlet*, *Svensk Damtidning*, *Svenska Dagbladet*, *Svenska Journalen*, *Svenskar i världen*, *Vecko-Revyn*, *Vi*, *Västernorrlands Allehanda*, *Västerviks-Tidningen*, *Z*, *Året Runt*.
In the UK: the *Daily Express*, the *Daily Mail*, the *Daily Mirror*, *Disc*, the *Guardian*, *Melody Maker*, *Mojo*, the *New Musical Express*, *Q*, *Record Collector*, the *Sun*.
In the US: the *Baltimore Sun*, *Billboard*, the *Boston Phoenix*, *Details*, *Goldmine*, the *Los Angeles Times*, *New York News*, the *New York Times*, *Rolling Stone*, *Time*, *Variety*, *Village Voice*.

PRESS RELEASES AND PROMOTIONAL MATERIAL

ABBA News; ABBA – The Interviews, promo CD, 1999; Frida biography in the interactive part of the CD *Djupa andetag* (Anderson, Sweden, 1996); Various Polar Music press releases, 1973–1982.

FAN CLUB MAGAZINES, FANZINES AND OTHER FAN PUBLICATIONS

ABBA Appreciation Club Newsletter, ABBA Australian Tour – 20 Year Celebration, ABBA Magazine/International ABBA Magazine, ABBA News Service, ABBA Report, Agnetha Fältskog Worldwide Fan Club, Hepnickus, Hootenanny-Bladet, Intermezzo, International ABBA Express, The Official International Agnetha Benny Björn Frida Fan Club.

537

SLEEVE NOTES AND AUDIO TRACKS

Anderson, Stig. Track annotations for Sven-Olof Walldoff's Orchestra album *Säj det med en sång* (Polar, Sweden, 1972)

Anderson, Stig. Sleeve notes for the Hootenanny Singers' *Dan Andersson på vårt sätt* (Polar, Sweden, 1973)

Bronson, Fred. Made in Sweden, *Thank You For The Music* (Polydor, UK, 1994)

Fältskog, Agnetha. Track annotations for Agnetha Fältskog album *Tio år med Agnetha* (Cupol, Sweden, 1979)

'Introduktion', track on Agnetha Fältskog album *My Love My Life* (Columbia, Sweden, 1996)

McNamara, Dennis. Pop Video Pioneers, *Thank You For The Music* (Polydor, UK, 1994)

Tobler, John. How It All Began, *Thank You For The Music* (Polydor, UK, 1994)

Tretow, Michael B. Liner notes for Agnetha Fältskog album *My Love My Life* (Columbia, Sweden, 1996)

RADIO PROGRAMMES

The ABBA Story, A för Agnetha, A för Anni-Frid, ABBA i kvadrat, Avsminkat, B för Benny, B för Björn, Det unga gardet, Draget, Efter tre, Hovas vittne, Kristina från Duvemåla, Livet är en fest, Musikjournalen, Möte med grammofonen, Nöjesmagasinet, Pick-up, Plats på scen, På turné, Radio M, Radio Södermanland, Sagan om guldskivan, Solklart, Skivspegeln, The Stikkan Anderson Story, Studio Ett, Svensktoppen, Tonträff, Våra favoriter, various Australian radio reports (1976 and 1977).

TELEVISION PROGRAMMES, MOVIES, HOME VIDEOS AND PRIVATE VIDEOS

A For ABBA, A For Agnetha, ABBA-dabba-dooo!!, ABBA In Concert, ABBA – The Movie, Aktuellt, Benny Andersson, The Best Of ABBA (Australian Bandstand special), Björn and Benny interview: private video tape 1991, Dabrowski, Dick Cavett Meets ABBA, Dokument inifrån: Musikindustrin, Efter min näbb, Frida – mitt i livet, Frida Solo, Gluggen, Gäst hos Hagge, H-trafik rapport: Ikväll, Här är ditt liv, The Late Late Breakfast Show, Magasinet, Mr Trendsetter, MTV News, Måndagsbörsen, Newton, Nöjesmaskinen, O.S.A. Stikkan Anderson, På turné, Rapport, Re-Bjorn ABBA 94, Räkna de lyckliga stunderna . . ., Rätt låt vann, Shelley Benson (née Bamford) interview: private videotape from Australian fan convention 1999, 60 Minutes, The Story Of ABBA, Top Ten, TOTP2, Wiese, The Winner Takes It All – The ABBA Story.

MULTIMEDIA AND INTERNET RESOURCES

Among all its riches, the World Wide Web naturally offers a myriad of Abba sites. Many of them have been useful for various purposes in the writing of this book – along with other sites containing valuable information not directly related to Abba – but are too numerous to mention here in full. Instead, I direct the reader to ABBA World (www.abbaworld.net), which hosts the Internet's largest list of rated and reviewed Abba links.

Nevertheless, I wish to single out a couple of fan sites which proved to be exceptionally useful: ABBA – The Releases (www.visitors.demon.nl/index.htm), ABBA – The Worldwide Chart Lists (www.zip.com.au/~callisto/abba.html) and The ABBA Phenomenon In Australia (www.geocities.com/SunsetStrip/Studio/5073/). A special credit also to the Internet mailing lists ABBAMAIL (www.abbamail.com) and The ABBA Legacy (www.sub.net.au/~winter/), which have given me access to a vast international network of knowledgeable and helpful Abba fans. The Official International Agnetha Benny Björn Frida Fan Club (http://abba. muziek.net/) is Abba's official fan club. ABBA – The Site (www.abbasite.com) is Abba's official website.

The CD-Rom version of Nationalencyklopedin (The Swedish National Encyclopaedia) and the web version of Encyclopedia Britannica (www.britannica.com) have also been useful resources. Pacific – FX Plot Interface (pacific.commerce.ubc.ca) was invaluable in helping me determine the krona/pound ratio at various points in time.

ARCHIVES AND INSTITUTIONS

The following archives and institutions have been helpful and useful in various ways as this book was written: Kungliga biblioteket (The Royal Library: National Library of Sweden), Landsarkivet i Uppsala (The Regional Archive in Uppsala), Press-Text (the research service provided by the Swedish newspapers *Dagens Nyheter* and *Expressen*, and which also holds the cuttings archives for a large number of magazines), Riksarkivet (The National Archives), Riksbanken (Sweden's central bank), Skattemyndigheten (various Swedish tax authority offices), Statens ljud- och bildarkiv (The National Archive of Recorded Sound and Moving Images), Stockholms Tingsrätt (the District Court in Stockholm), Sveriges Författarfond (The Swedish Authors' Fund), various Swedish local registrar's offices.

Acknowledgements

I began researching the Abba story in the early Nineties, shortly before the group's great revival. At the time, I was amazed to discover that despite the group's impact and, above all, the praise they had received for their composing and recording techniques, very little had actually been written about their music. I decided to explore that angle of their career in-depth, and during the course of this I was fortunate enough to receive input from all four Abba members.

Björn and Benny made themselves available to me for repeated interviews, in total amounting to several hours. With Frida I had a one-hour meeting, and she also answered a fair number of follow-up questions in writing. In the summer of 1993, when the interviews took place, Agnetha was at her least communicative with the media and chose to respond to my questions in writing only. I still feel the replies I received from her qualify as something of a scoop: with the exception of the official biography about her, published in 1996, since 1988 I am still the only individual who's been granted anything even resembling an interview with Agnetha.

Those interviews and the research resulted in the book *ABBA – The Complete Recording Sessions* (1994). The book's aim was not only to chronicle the group's recording history, but to outline their career development in general, correcting various errors that had been floating around in previously published books and, indeed, in most newspaper and magazine features about them. On publication I remember thinking, "When someone finally decides to write a definitive biography about the group, perhaps this book will come in handy in the research for the musical side of their career."

For my own part I thought that this was as far as it would go. Project completed: thank you and goodbye. But Abba refused to go away and as assignment after assignment came my way, flashes of a fascinating story began to reveal themselves to me. I kept wondering when someone would finally do the obvious and attempt to tell the whole tale, for real.

I didn't think that I would be the one to do it, until a few years ago when the thought started popping up now and again: perhaps, one day . . . The opportunity finally arrived in early 2000 when I contacted Chris Charlesworth, editor at Omnibus Press, who – independently – also thought a serious Abba book was a worthwhile idea. Because he felt strongly that only a Swedish writer was capable of telling the real Abba story, he'd approached Swedish publishers at the previous year's Frankfurt Book Fair, asking them if they knew of a suitable author. I heard about these approaches and contacted Chris, who then flew to Stockholm and

Acknowledgements

offered me the chance to realise this project.

And here we are, more than a year later. During this time, the writing of the book has dominated my life completely, as projects of this scope and size usually do. Along the way, many people have facilitated my work. I would like to offer my sincere thanks to those who have contributed information. Some may have supplied just a detail or two, while others have done anything from mailing photocopies of magazine articles to writing long, detailed essays via e-mail. Whether the contribution was great or small, it all helped enhance the factual accuracy and level of insight of the book, for which I am eternally grateful. If there is someone I've forgotten, I apologise sincerely – rest assured that your contribution was greatly appreciated:

Thanks, then, to Sören Alverfeldt, Laszlo Arvai, Fredrik Augustsson, Sara Barnes, Monica Bengtsson, Örjan Blix, Håkan Borg, Sture Borgedahl, George Bourdaniotis, Antje Bretschneider, Paul Carter, Jim Cassidy, Colin Collier, Matthew Crocker, Susan Dalloway, Vaughan Davies, Christian Deligny, Cliff Docherty, Kevin Evans, George Friesen, Kaarin Goodburn, Regina Grafunder, Greg Hartney, Jos Heselmans, Steve Jasper, Patrick Jauffret, Anders Johnsson, Alex Jones, Ian Jones, Yvon Jouandon, Kurt König, Jonas Larsson, Carl Lindencrona, Charles Milton Ling, George McManus, Ian Moule, Marc Moulin, Philip Muytjens, Trent Nickson, Sturle Scholz Nærø, Cathy Olds, Helene Palm, Mimmi Palm, Roland Palm, Andrew Parfitt, Jürgen Parys, Rafael Pohlman, Kristina Radford, Mark Raphael, Jason Ressler, Johnny Rogan, Luke Rogers, Aileen Schafer, Patrick Smith, Ralph Hans Steiner, Janet Strayer, John Arild Stubberud, Fredrik Söder, Leif Thorsson, Manuel Tsiatsias, Walter Veldman, Christopher Ward, Campbell Wilson and Yoji Yoshimoto.

The following deserve special thanks. Some put their knowledge and/or large parts of their private collections of cuttings and tapes at my disposal. Others have been just a phone call or an e-mail away from quick return posts with exactly the information I was after. Couldn't have done it without you!: Kari Bye, Claes Davidsson, Jeffrey de Hart, Hjördis Johansen, Gunnar Moe, Thomas Nordin, Peter Palmquist, Graeme Read, Björn Waldenström and Grant Whittingham.

Extra special thanks to my friends Ian Cole in Sydney, Australia and Thomas Winberg here in Stockholm. During the course of my work on this book they have both enthusiastically read through several drafts of my manuscript – and promptly come back with their thoroughly detailed lists of comments – corrected errors and questioned the validity of some of my conclusions, thereby forcing me to tighten up my arguments.

Ian is also a never-ending source of knowledge concerning all things Abba and as such has been an invaluable sounding-board for me for the past three years. It's a relationship I hope and believe will continue for many years to come. Thomas, the knight of the xerox machine, has functioned as an invaluable and tireless research assistant, spending countless hours at various libraries and archives, nailing down crucial queries that have enhanced the factual level of this book immensely.

No less importantly, they have both also offered unwavering support and encouragement, which has been invaluable in carrying me through this project, especially during those occasional, dark moments when I felt like chucking the whole thing in. Words cannot express the deep gratitude I owe you both.

Special thanks also to my agent, Bengt Nordin, who helped me get my career as an author going, and who made an invaluable contribution in getting this project off the ground. Thanks also to Nikki Lloyd at Omnibus Press for her help in sourcing photographs and to Ben Daniel for his comprehensive index. A final special thanks to Chris Charlesworth who provided me with the opportunity to write this book in the first place and also performed an expert editing job on my manuscript. In 1973, as an eight-year-old Beatles addict, I read and re-read a Swedish translation of a John Lennon interview done by Chris for *Melody Maker* – I have kept the interview to this day, but I could never imagine that he would become my editor some 27 years later.

The following were interviewed especially for this book and are warmly thanked for their patience and for giving so freely of their time and, in one case, hospitality: Karl-Gerhard Andrä (formerly Lundkvist), Hans Bergkvist, Sid Bernstein, Evald Ek, Bernt Enghardt, Hans Englund, Jerry Greenberg, Svenne Hedlund, Tony Rooth, Gunnar Sandevärn, Hansi Schwarz, John Spalding and Bo Winberg.

The following were originally interviewed for my previous books, *ABBA – The Complete Recording Sessions* and *From ABBA To Mamma Mia!* Their insights have informed this text as well, and many of the quotes in the present volume are published here for the first time: Kjell-Åke Andersson, Ola Brunkert, Anders Eljas, Rutger Gunnarsson, Lasse Hallström, Anders Hanser, Per Lindvall, Roger Palm, Owe Sandström, Janne Schaffer, Rune Söderqvist, Michael B. Tretow, Mike Watson and Lasse Wellander. Grateful thanks to Görel Hanser for generous assistance through the years.

Last, but certainly not least, my previous interviews with the former Abba members, Agnetha Fältskog, Björn Ulvaeus, Benny Andersson and Anni-Frid Lyngstad, have also left their mark on this text. Although the interviews were originally made for *ABBA – The Complete Recording Sessions*, several comments have been presented in more complete form or appear here for the first time. Extracts from an interview with Björn Ulvaeus for an as yet unfinished book about the Hootenanny Singers have also been used in this book. Additional thanks to Björn for generously giving me access to his personal cuttings collection.

Index

Index

Index

Index

Index

Index

Index